Employment Law

Employment Law

A Guide for Sport, Recreation, and Fitness Industries

written by
Gil Fried
and
Lori Miller

edited by
Herb Appenzeller

CAROLINA ACADEMIC PRESS
Durham, North Carolina

Library of Congress Cataloging-in-Publication

Fried, Gil, 1965–
    Employment law : a guide for sport, recreation, and fitness industries /
written by Gil Fried and Lori Miller ; edited by Herb Appenzeller.
        p.   cm.
    Includes bibliographic references.
    ISBN 0-89089-762-X
    1. Sports administration—United States. 2. Sports personnel—
Legal status, laws, etc.—United States. 3. Sports—Law and
legislation—United States.   I. Miller, Lori K. II. Appenzeller, Herb.
III. Title.
GV713.F75   1998
344.73'099—dc   98-19531
                                                                CIP

Carolina Academic Press
700 Kent Street
Durham, North Carolina 27701
Telephone (919) 489-7486
Fax (919) 493-5668
www.cap-press.com

Printed in the United States of America

Contents

Table of Cases and Statutes

Statutes

Foreword

Employment Law is not limited to the sport industry. It is applicable
to any company, business, organization or governmental agency.

Employment law has become a critical problem for employers who vary
from owners of profession sports teams—with glamorous superstars and
multi-million dollar contracts—and facility owners and operators to small
business owners with a minimal number of employees. Litigation against
employers has dramatically increased in recent years and employers are
confronted with expensive lawsuits on an almost daily basis. Employment-
based disputes such as wrongful discharge represent the leading category
of claims filed against employers with the Equal Employment Opportunities Commission (EEOC). Not only is litigation escalating at a record
pace, but the cost of litigation is increasing in staggering proportions. Damage awards are devastating to employers of organizations, companies,
businesses, and governmental agencies and present a serious dilemma to
employers.

In 1998, the National Collegiate Athletic Association (NCAA) was sued
by a group of assistant coaches for its rule on restricted earnings. A federal
judge held that the NCAA's action to limit earnings of some assistant
coaches to $16,000 per year violated antitrust laws. A federal jury awarded
the coaches $67 million in damages and legal experts predict that the
NCAA will spend an additional $13 million in legal fees if it appeals the
adverse decision. Winning in court is often costly and legal authorities report that, in some cases, the prevailing employer spends over $100,000
in legal fees.

Employers, supervisors and managers who want information regarding employment law that will enable them to understand and interpret
regulations have been searching for a comprehensible and practical guide
to answer their questions. Sexual harassment is a prominent issue addressed in the *Employment Law* which provides helpful information on how
to avoid or deal with this workplace nemesis that can prove costly in terms
of personnel and enormous awards. *Employment Law* effectively interprets mandates by regulatory agencies that are often confusing such as

OSHA, ADA and Title IX. These sections are clear and avoid burdensome legalese and ambiguous regulations.

Carolina Academic Press recognizes the need for such a text and others like it and has initiated a new and exciting sport law series. As editor of the series, I selected *Employment Law: A Guide for Sport, Recreation, and Fitness Industries* as the first sport law text because of the urgent need expressed by so many employers for answers to their questions.

Gil Fried (J.D.) and Lori Miller (Ed.D., M.B.A.) are legal researchers and writers with expertise in sport administration and sport employment practices. They accepted the challenge to provide a text that not only identifies legal issues in employment but also provides valuable solutions for sound and effective employment management for the sport industry. In the *Employment Law*, Fried and Miller describe the similarities between sport and business but alert the employer to significant differences the employer must understand and implement to be successful. Although the *Employment Law* is directed toward the sport industry, it is not limited to sport because of its applicability to any company, business, organization or governmental agency. This fifteen chapter *Employment Law* utilizes 140 court cases and 72 state and federal laws that emphasize the legal principles that are needed to understand and implement efficient employment law. The comprehensive text deals with every possible area of employment including at-will employees, volunteers, interns, hiring practices, interview questions, drugs in the workplace, employee appraisals, negligence (a leading cause of litigation) and discrimination based on gender, race, disability, religion and national origin.

The Appendices are a bonus for the reader with over 100 pages of sample agreements, contracts, letters of termination, list of interview questions, strategies and a model manual.

I congratulate Gil Fried and Lori Miller for recognizing the need for an employment guide in the new sport law series. The authors have written an outstanding text that has set a high standard for future authors in this series. Employers at every level will profit from this guide that furnishes vital information designed to help employers prevent costly problems and meet the challenges of the 21st Century.

Herb Appenzeller
Jefferson-Pilot Professor of Sport Management Emeritus
Guilford College, North Carolina

Introduction

1) Sport as a Business

If you break sport teams and businesses down to their most basic element components, it might be impossible to differentiate the two. The similarities between business and sport are so pervasive that several books have been written about the similarities. One author, Robert Keidel, wrote an entire book (*Sports Strategies for Business*) analyzing the similarities. In his book, Keidel analogizes the designated hitter or pinch hitter in baseball with a "heavy hitting" saleswoman for Mary Kay (Keidel, 1985). Baseball is often analogized to a business with a diverse sales force. Similar to baseball players spread out throughout the field, a diverse sales force could have significant geographical separation between sales territory. Furthermore, while a baseball team is on offense, only one batter is at the plate at any given time. Similarly, a salesperson can rely on her company for support, but when she is trying to finally close a sale, she is normally at the plate by herself (Keidel, 1985).

In football, the coach normally undertakes planning all plays with assistance from observers in the press box who watch the competition. Similarly, businesses need to critically plan for their success and they are not able to undertake any planning without carefully evaluating the competition's every move. If you look at any business periodical, you will normally find at least one article or advertisement relating to coaching, teamwork, or strategic management incorporating a sport theme. Additionally, business people are taught that to defeat their opponents in the same light fighters destroy their opponents. Business is often analogized to war. Sports can also be analogized to war. Football teams fight over several precious yards to help determine the victor.

Businesses and sport organizations need to carry out the primary business tasks: staffing, planning and operating (Davis, 1994). Staffing involves analyzing which players will be playing; planning requires specifying in advance how the game should be played; and operating entails how you can influence the game's flow-such as when to substitute players.

While sport teams and business have very similar characteristics, there are significant differences which separate the two. While most consumers do not care whether or not a cereal shipment was lost, they would be the first person around the water cooler the next day playing armchair quarterback. Some corporations might receive public disapproval for investing in certain countries or employing a child labor force. However, such disapproval is often limited to only concerned consumers. On the flip side, in sport, the fan's whim greatly affects the bottom line. If a fan does not like who is playing or the coaching strategy, then an irate fan can possibly boycott, sue or otherwise affect the sport organization. The Boston Celtics are a perfect example of this concept. The Boston Celtics have 50.5 percent of their team's ownership traded on the New York Stock Exchange. When the team goes through a slump or hires a new coach, the stock price is often affected in terms which are not economically justified. (Cassidy, 1997).

Additionally, some legal concerns differentiate sport from other business sectors. Major League Baseball has a limited anti-trust exemption allowing them to operate their reserve system in a monopolistic manner without any potential legal sanctions (Champion, 1993). No other business has been provided such significant legal deference nor has the United States Supreme Court ever declared any other monopoly the "American Pastime" (*Federal Base Ball Club of Baltimore v. National League of Professional Baseball Clubs*, 1922).

No matter what the circumstance or issue, there are numerous similarities and differences between sport and business entities. To be successful in the sport or business arenas, you have to understand and appreciate the similarities and differences and utilize each to their fullest benefit. One key concern raised in both the sport and business environment relates to personnel matters. As previously mentioned, baseball is a game requiring concentration and focus on the individual players. Having the right team is critical for a business to succeed. Likewise, a sport team, is first and foremost a team. Without the proper personnel it would be impossible for a sport organization to succeed. That is why so many people talk about teamwork in both sport and business. Without the right people, at the right place, at the right time, doing the right thing, you only have one result: chaos.

Similar to human resource departments within large corporations, larger sports businesses such as professional teams have personnel departments dedicated to such matters as personnel management through player scouting. The entire employment process is utilized by both sport teams and business through determining the need for an employee, advertising for the position, identifying potential candidates, interviewing potential candidates and offering the position to the most qualified candidate.

In addition to the hiring process, other similarities between sport and business employment environments include intergroup disputes, rivalries, and turf and ego conflicts that can either be functional or destructive. The sport world is replete with examples of individuals who could not stand one another, but pulled together to win. The 1977 New York Yankees are a good example. Owner George Steinbrenner, Manager Billy Martin, and superstar Reggie Jackson had significant personality conflicts, but were able to put their conflicts aside while they worked to achieve an organizational goal-winning the World Series (Keidel, 1985).

Additionally, "free agency" operates in both the sport and corporate realms where the best employee will be sought out by the competition and will normally land a lucrative contract. Executive recruiters pluck the creme-de-la-creme to help run Fortune 500 companies while professional sport scouts search for top talent to help lead teams to their respective league championships. Employment related issues are so inherent in both sport and other business sectors that Keidel included a complete chapter on how important it is for a business to have the "right team." (Keidel, 1985).

Lastly, employment law represents another striking similarity with sport and business. Businesses have been hit by a tidal wave. The tidal wave involves employment-based disputes, which are flowing at a rapid pace into court. According to the Equal Employment Opportunity Commission (EEOC) the number of employment discrimination claims alone rose 20% from 1992 to 1993 and the EEOC estimated that the rise would continue from 87,942 claims in 1993 to over 93,000 claims in 1994 (Walsh, 1995). The EEOC classifies complaints in 33 different categories. Even with a diverse array of potential employment claims, wrongful discharge claims represent the largest category of claims filled with the EEOC (Frierson, 1994). In the San Francisco EEOC office, 77% of claims received in the early 1990's were Title VII of the Civil Rights Act of 1964 claims. These cases were broken down into the following categories:

Race based discrimination claims	31.0%
Sex based discrimination claims	28.0%
Age based discrimination claims	20.0%
Disability based discrimination claims	20.0%
National origin based discrimination claims	16.0%
Religion based discrimination claims	1.5%
Equal pay based discrimination claims	0.8%

("Update '95",1995)

The numbers demonstrate that few equal pay cases are brought to the EEOC. However, a recent survey conducted with 50,000 working women across the nation highlighted that 99% of the surveyed respondents identified equal pay as "important" ("Equal pay is no. 1 for working women," 1997).

In 1995, 233 sport law cases were appealed to higher courts and produced published court opinions. Even though cases involving professional sports receive the most publicity, they only represented 3.8% of all cases. The highest percentage entailed negligence claims which represented 55% of all sport cases. While the number of federal employment suits has increased, the 1995 cases reveal that the sport industry also faces the same litigation concern. A total of 26 employment law cases (11.2%) were finally resolved through appeal in 1995 (Fried, 1996). These numbers clearly indicate that the sport industry is not immune from the ravages that can accompany an employment suit. Even if employers win at trial, the litigation costs for defending their rightful actions could surpass $100,000 in a simple case while the award fee for wrongful discharge cases averages $1,000,000 (Frierson, 1994). The $100,000 attorney fee figure is misleading. If the employer loses the employment lawsuit, they also might have to pay the plaintiff's attorneys' fees. In one 1992 case, Bethlehem Steel was ordered to pay the winning plaintiff only $60,000 in damages. However, the court also ordered Bethlehem Steel to pay the plaintiffs' attorneys' fees which totaled $512,590 (Frierson, 1994).

Employment law matters can also represent a significant difference between sport and business industries. While a business executive's inappropriate comments or actions might lead to litigation, the same actions by a sport executive would also land on the front page of any given sport newspaper section. The media thirst for inappropriate conduct by athletes and sports executives makes litigating and defending sport employment disputes very difficult.

This guide is designed to provide individuals in the sport, recreation, fitness and leisure industries with the necessary information and tools to handle numerous employment matters that might arise. The business and employment strategies discussed in the following pages are not relegated just to the sport industries. The general legal principles can be applied to any company, business or organization whether or not they are for profit, non-profit or a government agency.

Before addressing specific employment law matters, it is imperative that the reader understands the legal system as it currently exists in the United States. The following paragraphs highlight the legal process and define key terms that will be used throughout this guide. The concepts will then be integrated into a storyline describing the steps that occur when an employee brings a sexual harassment claim. The following section is adapted from the chapter "The Legal System" in Herb Appenzeller's 1998 book, *Risk Management in Sport: Issues and Strategies.*

2) The Legal System

If one asked what the term "law" means, one would probably receive a different answer from each person asked. Law implies a multitude of definitions and concepts. Law is abstract, living, constantly changing and evolving. At the same time, laws provide predictability, accountability, justice, protection and even compassion. Laws comprise the entire conglomeration of rules, values and principles that govern daily conduct and can be enforced by either the government or individual citizens through courts.

Types of Laws

Two primary areas of law will be discussed in this text: *common law* and *statutory law*. Laws that are developed, passed, enacted and enforced by legislative branches at various government levels are called statutory laws (Gifis, 1984). Since laws passed by federal, state, municipal and other government legislative bodies can never cover all potential circumstances or occasions, common law provides specific guidance for interpreting the laws. Common law refers to cases that have been resolved by various courts over several centuries (Gifis, 1984). For example, numerous principles concerning the liability of an individual who failed to live up to a certain standard of conduct has been developed over the past five centuries. These cases comprise common law and provide precedence for future cases involving the same or similar facts. *Precedence* serves to create boundaries to help us decide future cases. Once a case becomes precedence, all future analysis of the same or similar facts in that jurisdiction will rely upon the prior decision (Gifis, 1984). Subsequent courts cannot ignore or overturn the prior decision unless a legislative body changes the underlying law upon which the decision was based or a higher court overturns the decision. Thus, when the United States Supreme Court concluded that Major League Baseball was exempt from antitrust laws, such a conclusion became precedence. Since there is no higher court than the United States Supreme Court, and the Supreme Court does not want to overturn this decision, the only way baseball can lose its antitrust exemption would be if the United States Congress changed the antitrust laws to specifically cover baseball (*Flood v. Kuhn*, 1972). There have been over 70 attempts to repeal baseball's antitrust exemption, but all such efforts have failed (*Toolson v. New York Yankees, Inc.*, 1953). If any of these legislative attempts were ever successful, then the legislature would have developed a new statutory law that modifies the previously existing common law.

Statutory laws are laws originating from and passed by legislative bodies. These laws are only valid for the area governed by the government entity and can cover such topics as anti-discrimination, occupational safety, workers' compensation and related concerns. Statutory laws and constitutional laws are analogous in that both types of laws are adopted or changed by a voting system and help form the framework of laws which guide our everyday actions.

Constitutional law refers to laws embodied in the United States Constitution, but can also refer to laws under individual state constitutions (Gifis, 1984). An example of constitutional law in sports involves prayer in a locker room. While most athletes are familiar with pre-game prayers, the Constitution prohibits states from endorsing any religion. Thus, if a public high school coach required players to pray before a game, the coach would be violating the constitutional required separation of church and state as the Supreme Court currently interprets the law. As the coach is a state employee, the coach would be exposing her high school to a claim that they are violating the Constitution (Fried & Bradley, 1994). Another example involves the constitutional requirement to be free from unreasonable search and seizure which can prohibit an employer from searching employee belongings for drugs or other items (*Hill v. NCAA*, 1993).

Administrative laws refer to laws, rules and regulations that are developed, adopted and enforced by government units responsible for managing specific government agencies (Gifis, 1984). While administrative laws are not as widely applied as statutory or common law, they still affect numerous sport employment issues. Most business related issues are governed by federal administrative agencies. The regulations adopted by national administrative agencies such as the National Labor Relations Board (NLRB) or the Occupational Safety and Health Administration (OSHA) are the law of the land. In 1972, Congress passed the law commonly referred to as Title IX (Title IX, 1972). The law requires equal treatment of men and women in programs receiving federal funds. Colleges receiving federal funds are required to provide similar funding to both men's and women's athletic programs (*Cohen v. Brown University*, 1995). Title IX claims are investigated, monitored and/or resolved by the Office of Civil Rights (OCR).

Administrative law covers all government entities from the local to federal level. For example, local city ordinances or administrative rules may affect employee parking, building zoning and health issues associated with a workplace. Likewise, state administrative agencies have jurisdiction over issues such as workers' compensation, smoking in the workplace and fair employment practices. Federal administrative rules normally apply when a federal issues applies such as actions between individual doing business across state lines. Since union related activity in one state affects other business in other states, the federal government has power under the commerce clause to regulate the unions through the NLRB.

Court System

There are three primary court systems; state, federal and administrative. Legal authority, procedures and the types of disputes heard are different in each court system. While most people are accustomed to seeing full-blown trials on such television shows as Perry Mason or LA Law, most court proceedings are fairly mundane. For example, all pre-trial proceedings such as settlement conferences, summary judgment or a motion to dismiss a suit are all heard only in front of a judge, bailiff and court clerk. The litigation process is most frequently confined to attorney desktops and the mail. Litigation involves significant paperwork wherein most cases sink or swim. If in the discovery process a party determine they have no chance to win, they either settle or dismiss the case. As most cases are resolved before a case proceeds to trial, only 3–5% of all cases filed ever go to trial. (Gross, 1996).

A *state court* has jurisdiction (authority) to hear a case if the case involves an event or activity which occurred within that state. Some major state employment law theories that can be raised by a plaintiff include:

- negligent hiring or retention of employees,
- negligent supervision,
- hiring fraud,
- workplace assault and battery,
- false imprisonment,
- malicious prosecution,
- defamation,
- invasion of privacy,
- breach of contract,
- interference with a contract, and
- a host of specific state employment law claims.

State court systems traditionally consist of general or superior jurisdiction courts which are referred to by various names in different states. They are commonly called circuit courts, district courts, superior courtsvj or courts of common pleas. Some states have other special courts such as probate (to handle the estates of deceased persons), juvenile, family law, municipal, city, and small claims courts (Gifis, 1984).

If a party to a suit does not feel the law was properly applied, he or she could appeal the case to an appellate court. An appeal is the process by which a party to a suit can challenge the legal decision rendered by a court

(Gifis, 1984). The appeals process is designed to guarantee that courts cannot exercise unchecked or abusive power. If the appellate court's decision is also disputed, the litigant can file another appeal to the state's supreme court. State supreme court decisions are final unless the decision involves an issue regarding the federal Constitution, federal laws, or national treaties (Coughlin, 1983). Appellate courts and the state supreme court can only review issues of law. They cannot review the facts or reanalyze evidence (Coughlin, 1983). Thus, an appeal is appropriate if there is an issue as to how the law should be applied or there is a different legal conclusion reached by other courts in the same state. However, if the only issue that a litigant wishes to appeal is the fact that the jury overlooked a key piece of evidence, the appellate court would refuse to hear the case.

Most sport cases are brought in state courts. However, if a dispute involves over $50,000, citizens of different states, a question involving the Constitution or a federal law question, the cases could be brought in federal court (Coughlin, 1983). Employment disputes which need to be filed in federal courts include any claim against an out of state employer, any discrimination case based on federal statutes (such as Title IX, race discrimination, American with Disabilities Act, etc.), and constitutional law disputes. Federal courts also hear patent, tax, copyright, maritime and bankruptcy matters (Couchlin, 1983). If a party determines that the federal court misapplied the law, the party can petition a federal court of appeals. The United States is divided into 12 judicial districts, each with a federal appellate court. The last resort for any party is to request that the United States Supreme Court review a case. The process of applying for review by the Supreme Court involves filing a writ of certiorari (Couchlin, 1983). A writ of certiorari is sent from the Supreme Court to a lower level court when at least four of the nine Supreme Court Justices vote to hear the case. The writ requires the lower court to turn the case over to the Supreme Court.

Picking the proper jurisdiction is critical when a plaintiff brings an employment law case. Some suits which contain both federal law and state law claims can be brought in federal court, but cannot be brought in a state court. Special care has to be made when filing a suit as failure to allege a state law claim in a federal suit bars raising that claim at a later date. Additionally, if a claim is brought in state court, the plaintiff is in essence making a choice not to pursue any federal law claims. Thus, plaintiffs have to make a tactical decision to utilize state laws that might allow greater recovery versus possibly using federal law which might provide a greater likelihood of winning depending on the issues and laws involved. Federal courts can use federal laws for federal disputes and state laws when a nonfederal claim is raised. No matter what claims are raised and in what court, it is imperative that a thorough analysis be taken of the value and merit of each potential claim before choosing in which court the case will be filed.

Administrative courts or agencies are created by Congress or state legislatures and both create and enforce their own rules (Coughlin, 1983). All other courts only enforce or interpret rules made by other courts or legislatures. For example, the NLRB is lawmaker, an executive agency that enforces the law, and a court which interprets and applies the law. If a professional sport league decided to lock its unionized players out of training camp, the players could file a complaint with the NLRB (*Powell v. NFL*, 1989). If a complaint was filed, the NLRB would investigate the allegations and reach a decision concerning the players' complaint. A federal administrator has the power to investigate violations of agency rules and to force individuals to appear before the agency and answer charges against the individuals.

When a dispute arises involving either the application of a statute or an individual's rights, the dispute is traditionally resolved through an appropriate *court* system. A court is a tribunal established by governments to hear certain cases and administer justice (Gifis, 1984). Some matters are not heard by courts, rather, the dispute is refereed to what is traditionally called alternative dispute resolution (Fried, 1996). Alternative dispute resolution techniques include arbitration, mediation and other techniques designed to avoid congested court calendars and save litigants the huge expense associated with full-blown trials. As mentioned previously, a wrongful discharge case could cost over $100,000 in legal fees alone if taken to trial. While there are no concrete figures or studies comparing arbitration costs to trial costs in the sport area, the authors assume that a wrongful discharge case brought to arbitration would only cost about $10,000–$15,000 in legal fees.

Alternative dispute resolution can be similar to the legal system. An arbitrator can act as a judge to determine who should prevail in a given dispute. The arbitrator listens to all the evidence, can make rulings as to what evidence should be allowed and how the arbitration process will proceed and can make a final decisions which are normally upheld by judges if the arbitration decision is subsequently challenged in court. An arbitrator can award any damages allowed by a court in the same jurisdiction, even punitive damages if they are warranted. The arbitration process is very similar to the legal process described below. While an arbitrator or several arbitrators can issue final decisions, a mediator does not make a decision, but rather helps the parties reach their own decision.

Some court automatically refer cases to alternative dispute resolution while other matters are required by contract to only proceed outside the court system. Thus, employees working in the stock or securities industry have an express provision within their employment contract requiring all employees to resolve all disputes through arbitration (NASD introductory training for arbitrators, 1995). If an employee tries to bring a case outside the arbitration process, courts would immediately send the case to arbitration. Normally, if parties resolve a dispute through an alternative dispute resolution technique, most courts uphold the arbitration decision unless the arbitrators acted with wrongful intent or in a clearly unreasonable manner (Fried and Hiller, 1997).

Typically courts are distinguished by the types of cases they can hear. *Criminal courts* only resolve criminals matters in which the people, represented by a public prosecutor, bring charges against individual(s) who violate the law through the commission of a misdemeanor or felony (Gifis, 1984). Cases between individuals, corporations, business entities, organizations and government units involving non-criminal matters are resolved primarily in *civil courts* (Gifis, 1984). The O.J. Simpson murder cases provide an excellent distinction between criminal and civil courts. Simpson was first tried by the State of California for allegedly harming state citizens (Reske, 1995). The criminal case resulted in a not guilty verdict. The double jeopardy rule will prohibit Simpson from ever being tried again on the same charges in a criminal case (Gifis, 1984). However, Simpson was subsequently sued by the victims' families in civil court. The criminal court decision has no bearing on the civil court case because the two courts require a different burden of proof. In order to convict someone in criminal court, the prosecutors must prove the accused committed the crime beyond a reasonable doubt (Gifis, 1984). On the other hand, a person suing in civil court only has to prove by a preponderance of the evidence that the other side is the guilty party. The different legal standards were dramatically highlighted in the Simpson case as the civil jury disregarded the criminal court verdict and found Simpson guilt of various civil offenses including wrongful death. The civil jury awarded the victim's families over $30 million.

Some employment cases can be brought in both civil and criminal courts. An employee who embezzled money could be brought to court by the state under criminal theft charges. The employer can also bring among other claims, a civil claim for embezzlement, breach of contract, breach of fiduciary duties and other similar charges. This represents a critical legal point. While an employee could have engaged in one action — stealing money, there are numerous additional claims that can be raised against the employee based on the facts in the case.

Legal Process

Detailed rules specify the how, when, and where questions associated with bringing a lawsuit. These rules differ in each court and are often very complex. An example provides the best method of discussing the structure and processes involved in a lawsuit. The following is a fictitious example of such a case. Sarah Jones was a secretary for a local high school athletic director in Houston, Texas. While working at her desk, the male athletic director came around the desk and touched her in an inappropriate manner. He also suggested that they engage in certain sexual activities to help "promote" her career. She was forced to resign her position when she rebuffed her supervisor's advances. Additionally, she required over $10,000 in psychological bills and missed seven months of work while she tried to get her life together.

After Jones left the high school, she set up an interview with a lawyer to discuss her legal options. The lawyer was Ruth Smith, a young lawyer recently out of law school. Smith asked numerous questions and discovered that a former secretary had suffered the same treatment and settled her claim with the supervisor out of court. Utilizing her legal prowess, Smith thought she had a great hostile work environment and quid pro quo sexual harassment case and accepted Jones as a client (see generally, Chapter 7).

Smith initially performed research and discovered that the likely parties that should be sued included the school, the school district, Jones' immediate supervisor, the athletic director and the high school principal. Jones, who brought the suit to recover her damages, was called the *plaintiff* while all parties being sued were called *defendants*. Jones and all the defendants lived or operated in Texas. Because Texas has very specific state statutes and favorable case laws concerning sexual harassment claims, Smith brought the suit in a Texas state court.

Smith remembered that special rules applied whenever a governmental entity is sued. Thus, after some initial research, Smith filed a *governmental claim* against the school district. Smith filed the claim specifically to avoid a statute of limitations issue. The *statute of limitation* required the suit to be filed within a certain time period, or Jones would have been forever barred from filling suit. Each state has its own rules concerning filing a claim against the state. These governmental claim rules are designed to provide the state with notice it might be sued. Some states require the filing of a claim while others allow a party just to name the state in a lawsuit. A governmental claim is not a lawsuit. It represents only a preliminary notification process.

Smith prepared a *complaint* that described key facts available to Jones and provided enough information for the opposing side to know why it was being sued. The complaint specifically identified all known defendants, the reason why jurisdiction was proper, and a statement setting forth what remedies Jones demanded. A complaint also indicates the title of the case, identifies all the parties, designates in which court the case is being filed and describes the dispute in a specified legal form. Smith had a specified amount of time within which she had to serve the defendants with a copy of the complaint that she had already filed with the chosen court. Smith was required to personally serve each defendant with the complaint. Some states allow a party to mail a complaint or to serve the complaint through a sheriff.

Within a specified time after receiving the complaint, the defendants filed an *answer* indicating why they were not liable for Jones' alleged damages. Along with their answer, the defendants served Jones (through her attorney) with several discovery requests. *Discovery* was used as a means to find out what Jones knew about the incident and her damages. Discovery is the process used to discover information about the opposing parties in a suit. Answers have to be given under oath or the penalty of perjury. The discovery requests included a request to produce all relevant documents in Jones' possession such as psychological/medical bills, a request to admit certain facts such as admitting she never attempted to find another secretarial job ("Request for Admissions"), specific questions such as her age, her address, or if she has a driver's license (called interrogatories) and a request to take Jones' deposition. Additional discovery tools not specifically addressed above could include: a request to inspect the offices (where the harassment allegedly occurred), an independent medical examination of Jones and possibly an independent psychological evaluation if Jones was claiming severe or extreme emotional distress. Smith responded by serving similar discovery requests on all the defendants. Jones was required to attend a *deposition* where she had to answer numerous questions, under oath, asked by the defendants' attorneys. Smith had the right to request the same types of discovery from the defendants.

After several months of discovery, the defendants filed a *motion for summary judgment.* Summary judgment motions are brought when a party concludes that as a matter of law the undisputed facts are in his/her favor and he/she should win without having to go to trial. These motions are solely based on applicable case law and the facts uncovered through the discovery process. The judge determined that there were still issues of facts that were in dispute and as such, the judge denied the defendants' summary judgment motion.

Summary judgment is one of several possible pre-trial motions. Other such motions include a demurrer, motion to sever, motion to strike, motion to remove for lack of subject matter jurisdiction and other motions that attack the complaint or require the production of requested discovery material. Such motions are brought when, as a matter of law, one party is or should be required to alter its case. For example, Jones might have suffered a serious injury, but due to governmental immunity bestowed to the high school principal, the principal could bring a summary judgment motion to be dismissed from the case as a matter of law.

The parties tried to settle the case, but when they were unable to reach a mutually acceptable settlement, they started preparing for trial. Both sides obtained witnesses on their own behalf. The court chose a trial date that was approximately two years after Jones was first injured.

Smith thought the facts favored her client. Her client also made a good witness. Thus, Jones demands a trial by *jury*. The plaintiff in a civil case always has the choice of whether or not he/she wants a jury. The twelve-member jury was required to decide who was telling the truth and ultimately what were the facts. Each side prepared trial memorandum explaining its case and provided the memorandum to the judge. After resolving some disputes concerning what evidence would be allowed at trial, the judge allowed the parties to pick a jury. Utilizing a process called *voire dire*, each side interviewed prospective jurors and had the right to dismiss all biased jurors or a limited number of jurors that they just did not want. The size and role of a jury vary in different states. Some juries only examine facts or certain components of a case while other juries are responsible for analyzing all facts and determining damages.

Smith provided an eloquent *opening statement* which Perry Mason would have envied. The defendants also had a strong opening statement on their own behalf. The trial proceeded with Smith calling Jones as the first witness. After answering all the questions asked by Smith, Jones was *cross-examined* by defendants' attorneys who were attempting to refute Jones' testimony or highlight any inconsistencies. The former secretary was called as a *fact witness* because she had specific facts concerning the prior incident. Both sides also acquired the services of *expert witnesses* to testify about the trauma associated with sexual harassment, the monetary value of Jones missing work for several months and doctors to testify about Jones' injuries. The trial continued with each side presenting its witnesses and the other side having the opportunity to cross-examine each witness. Each side also introduced documentary evidence. Throughout the trial, each side repeatedly made *objections* to certain questions or the introduction of some evidence. The judge was forced to determine, as a matter of law, which side was correct and which questions or evidence were legally allowable.

Each side concluded its questioning and then made its final *closing statement*. The closing statements provided a factual summary and highlighted the law uncovered by each side during the trial. The jury was given specific instructions by the judge concerning the law and how the jury was to apply the facts to the law. Based on the evidence presented, the jury returned a verdict in Jones' favor. The jury awarded Jones $24,000 for *actual lost damages* (medical expenses and lost wages) and $200,000 for *pain and suffering*. No punitive damages were awarded to punish the defendants. The final award was accessed against her principal, athletic director and school. No damages were accessed against the school district as they had developed and distributed a sexual harassment policy which, unbeknownst to the school district, was not followed by the school or its employees.

The defendants were not happy with the jury's conclusion. The defendants' attorneys knew they could not challenge the jury's evidentiary conclusion, but felt the judge gave the jury an incorrect instruction concerning the school's duty to Jones. The judge could have overturned the jury's decision if the judge felt it was not supported by law or the facts. However, the judge affirmed the jury's decision. Defendants filed a *notice of appeal* which is the first step in the appeals process. Each side was required to submit a "brief" that outlined its legal analysis and then argue its case in front of three appellate judges. The appellate court, after carefully reviewing the lower court's actions, determined that the lower court made a *procedural mistake* in using an incorrect jury instruction. Therefore, the appellate court *remanded* (sent back) the case to the lower court to retry the case using the correct instruction. An appellate court can remand a case, uphold the lower court's decision, or overturn the lower court's decision.

Before the new trial began, the sides reached a *settlement* in which the defendants paid Jones $18,000. By the time Jones finally settled the case, three years had elapsed since she brought the suit. The appellate court's reasoning was published in the state's official case registry and became precedence for any future cases dealing with the appropriate jury instruction to give concerning a school's duty to its employees. However, from reading the published appellate court's decision, a reader would not know that the case was settled once it was remanded to the lower court. The appellate court report only indicated that the court was remanding the case to be retried. Rarely does one discover what happens to remanded cases because lower court decisions are not officially published. Furthermore, many cases are settled and the settlement terms are often confidential. While Jones' fictitious case went to trial, it is estimated that less than five percent of all cases filed ever reach a trial (Gross, 1996; Galanter & Cahill, 1994). Most cases are either dismissed prior to trial, settled, or defeated through summary judgment or other defensive maneuvers (Kritzer, 1986).

Case Reporting

Only state appellate and state Supreme Court cases are officially published. All Federal cases are published. Cases are commonly found in the following reporters: Federal District Court cases can be found in Federal Supplement volumes (cases are cited using the initials "F. Supp."), Federal Appellate cases can be found in the Federal Reporter ("F." or "F.2d" which is the second volume of Federal Reporters), U.S. Supreme Court cases can be found in three different reporters-United States Supreme Court Reports

("U.S."), Supreme Court Reporter ("S. Ct."), and Supreme Court Reports, Lawyer's Edition ("L. Ed.").

Nine different reporters exist for various state courts or regional groupings of courts. These cases are found in the following reporters: Atlantic Reporter ("A." or "A. 2d"), Northeastern Reporter ("N.E." or "N.E. 2d."), Northwestern Reporter ("N.W." or "N.W. 2d."), Pacific Reporter ("P.." or "P. 2d."), Southeastern Reporter ("S.E." or "S.E. 2d."), Southern Reporter ("So." or "So. 2d."), Southwestern Reporter ("S.W." or "S.W. 2d."), New York Supplement ("N.Y.S."), or California Reporter ("Cal.Rptr.").

These initials are important because they provide you with a means by which you can look-up a case. If you see a case site in this guide, or anywhere else, it would read as follows: *Jones v. Valley High School, et al.*, 123 S.W.2d. 456 (3rd Cir. TX, 1997). This citation can be easily translated once you know how to read a case citation. The plaintiff is Jones and the main defendant is Valley High School. The "et al." means there are other defendants who are not listed for brevity purposes. If you wanted to find the case, you could find it in volume 123 of the Southwestern Reporter, 2nd series, at page 456. The information contained within the parenthesis indicates that the appellate decision was handed down by the 3rd Circuit Court in Texas, in 1997. This information is critical because you can determine that if your case is filled in the same jurisdiction, you have an indication of how the law will be interpreted.

3) Employment Law

As you can tell from the legal system section above, the law can be complex. Furthermore, as the law is encroaching more and more into the sport, fitness and recreation industries, understanding the complex web of employment law matters is becoming a necessity for any owner, manager or executive. A complex rubric of laws has emerged over the past seventy years to enhance the current employment law environment. With the ever-changing dynamics of American culture, employment law has been forced to adapt and address these changes. Current employment law trends support this analysis. With the increase of women, seniors and disabled individuals in the workforce, more laws have been passed and courts have interpreted existing laws to extend additional benefits to these individuals. Such laws and court decisions have helped increase the general workforce. At the same time, these laws and decisions have increased the concerns faced by employers.

Legislation has had the greatest impact on general employment law principles developed over several hundred years through the common law system. Initially, employees could only rely upon the individual contracts they had entered into in order to protect themselves. As our society moved into a larger manufacturing based economy, governments had to pass legislation in order to provide additional protection to laborers (Feliu, 1992). Some typical legislative enactments and their passing date are as follows: the National Labor Relations Act gave workers the right to unionize and bargain collectively (1935), the Fair Labor Standards Act established the first minimum wage, child labor laws and overtime work rules (1938), the Equal Pay Act made it unlawful for employers to discriminate between men and women with respect to wages (1963), Title VII of the 1964 Civil Rights Act prohibits all discrimination in employment based on sex, race, color, religion, or national origin (1964), the Age Discrimination in Employment Act prohibits age based discrimination (1967), the Occupational Safety and Health Act established minimum health and safety standards for workplaces (1970), the Rehabilitation Act of 1973 provides protection for disabled individuals (1973), the Employee Retirement Income Security Act protects pension entitlements (1974), and the Americans with Disability Act provides protection for individuals with a multitude of disabilities (1990).

Even with all these laws, no legislation has ever addressed the right of an employee only to be terminated for cause. That is, only to be terminated for doing something wrong as defined by the company, business and/or society. Laws also provide specific exemptions such as family businesses employing less than 10 people, employers who are religious organizations and similar limitations. Thus, there are still significant legal loopholes that provided significant benefits to certain employers. The key to developing and implementing a legally satisfactory employment/labor management program is learning where the loopholes exist and how to avoid the numerous minefields. That is where this guide is designed to assist you.

Numerous sport law books are available to help educate sports, fitness and recreation professionals (Appenzeller, 1975; Appenzeller, 1980; van der Smissen,1990; Champion, 1993). These texts primarily focus on preventing negligence or analyzing issues affecting professional or collegiate sports. While all these texts touch on employment related concerns, no text completely analyzes the sports employment process. Furthermore, this guide is not just a legal guide. Besides providing legal insight, significant space will be dedicated to providing helpful managerial techniques to help with the various employee concerns sports employers face on daily basis.

This guide will analyze currently existing case law and past statutory enactments to provide the reader with the fullest possible body of knowledge to address legal concerns that could affect their hiring, promoting and termination procedures. Throughout this guide, the authors will reference the terms "employer," "manager," "supervisor" and "you" interchangeably to describe the person or organizations that employs or manages employees. Instead of being a strict theoretical work or a basic employment law text, the guide will provide the framework to developing and implementing a comprehensive employment/labor management program. To assist in the implementation process, this guide comes with extensive appendices containing the necessary forms that can be customized and utilized by any business as a template for developing their own forms.

Legal Caveat

As with any legal document, this guidebook would not be complete without a necessary disclaimer. The information contained in this educational guide is designed to provide a basic level of understanding. The guide was not written to cover every legal issue in employment and every law affecting employment issues. Unfortunately, due to the complexity of laws and the existence of over 51 sets of statutes (each state and the federal government) and different case laws, it is impossible to cover employment law issues as they pertain to every individual state and the federal government. Thus, this guide will focus primarily on federal laws and highlight some noteworthy state laws. As with any legal endeavor, the reader should always contact a competent attorney prior to introducing or utilizing new risk management techniques to discover what special quirks might exist in any given state and/or industry.

References

Anderson, R., Fox, I., and Twomey, D. (1984). *Business law*. 12th edition. Cincinnati, OH: South-Western Publishing Co.

Appenzeller, H. (1975). *Athletics and the law*. Charlottesville, VA: The Michie Company.

Appenzeller, H., and Appenzeller, T. (1980). *Sports and the courts*. Charlottesville, VA: The Michie Company.

Appenzeller, H. (1998). *Risk management in sport: issues and strategies*. Durham, NC: Carolina Academic Press.

Gifis, S. (1984). *Barron's law dictionary*. New York: Barron's Educational Service, Inc.

Cassidy, T. (1997). "Putting stock in a basketball coach." *Houston Chronicle* (May 18): 9E.

Champion, W. (1993). *Sports law in a nutshell*. St. Paul, MN: West Publishing Co.

Coughlin, G. (1983). *Your introduction to law*. 4th edition. New York: Barnes & Noble Books.

Davis, K. (1994). *Sport management*. Madison, WI: Brown & Benchmark.

"Equal pay is no. 1 for working women." (1997). *Houston Chronicle* (September 5): 2C.

Feliu, A. (1992). *Primer on individual employee rights*. Washington, DC: BNA Books.

Fried, G. (1996). "Legal trends in the 1990's." *Sports Facility Law Reporter* February, 2(4).

Fried, G. (1996). "Dispute resolution can save you money." *Sports Facility Law Reporter* 2 (June): 9.

Fried, G., and Bradely, L. (1994). "Applying the first amendment to prayer in a public university locker room." *Marquette Sports Law Journal* 4: 2.

Fried, G. and Hiller, M. (1997). "ADR in youth and intercollegiate athletics." *BYU Law Review* 3: 631–652.

Frierson, J. (1994). *Preventing employment lawsuits*. The Bureau of National Affairs, Inc.

Galanter, M. and Cahill, M. (1994). " 'Most cases settle': judicial promotion and regulation of settlements." *Stanford Law Review* 46: 1339.

Gifis, S. (1984). *Barron's legal guide, law dictionary*. New York: Barron's Educational Services, Inc.

Gross, S. and Syverud, K. (1996). "Don't try civil jury verdicts in a system geared to settlement." *UCLA Law Review* 44: 1.

Keidel, R. (1985). *Game plans, sports strategies for business*. New York: E.P. Dutton.

Kritzer, H. (1986). "Adjudication to settlement: shading in the gray." *Judicature* 70: 161.

NASD introductory training for arbitrators. (1995). Chicago, IL: NASD Arbitration Department.

Reske, H. (1995). "Verdict on simpson trial." *ABA Journal* (November): 48.

Update '95, 13th Symposium. (1995). San Francisco, CA: Schachter, Kristoff, Orenstein and Berkowitz.

van der Smissen, B. (1990). *Legal liability and risk management for public and private entities*. Cincinnati, OH: Anderson Publishing Co.

Walsh (1995). *Mastering diversity*. Santa Monica, CA: Merritt.

Cases

Cohen v. Brown University, 879 F. Supp. 185 (D.R.I. 1995).
Federal Base Ball Club of Baltimore v. National League of Professional Baseball Clubs, 259 U.S. 200 (1922).
Flood v. Kuhn, 407 U.S. 258 (1972).
Hill v. NCAA, 7 Cal. 4th 1 (S.C., 1994).
Powell v. NFL, 764 F. Supp. 1351 (D.C. Minn., 1991).
Toolson v. New York Yankees, Inc., 346 U.S. 356 (1953).

Statutes

Americans With Disabilities Act (ADA), 42 U.S.C. Section 12101 et seq.
Age Discrimination in Employment Act (ADEA), 29 U.S.C.A. Section 621 et seq.
Employee Protection Act (EPA), 29 U.S.C.A. Section 206(d).
Employee Retirement Insurance Security Act (ERISA), 29 U.S.C.A. Section 1144 et al.
Fair Labor Standard Act (FLSA), 29 U.S.C.A. Section 201 et seq.
National Labor Relation Act (NLRA), 29 U.S.C.A. Sections 151–169.
Occupational Safety and Health Act (OSHA), 29 U.S.C.A. Section 652 et seq.
Rehabilitation Act of 1973, 29 U.S.C.A. Section 701 et seq.
Title VII of the Civil Rights Act of 1964, 42 U.S.C.A. Section 2000e.
Title IX of the Education Amendment of 1972, 20 U.S.C.A. Section 1681(a).

Employment Law

Chapter 1

The Master-Servant Relationship

Somewhere back in time, individuals became overburdened by their workload or their lack of expertise in a given area and were forced to hire someone. This formed the first employer-employee relationship. Ever since that time, people have worked hard to properly manage the individual(s) who might work on their behalf. Some of the earliest development in personnel management were developed during the Middle Ages (Chruden and Sherman, 1976).

The employment relationship can be referred to as a master-servant or employer-employee relationship. The key component of such a relationship is the control one party manifests over another party. Thus, the employee relationship rests on the premises that the employer can control an employee's work and is liable to pay the employee for the employee's services. Not paying for an employee or worker's service can create significant concerns and represents the first concern when creating the employee and employer relationship.

1) Employee v. Interns or Volunteers

Volunteers and unpaid interns, while they might be performing work that benefits an employer and might be controlled by the employer are not considered employees. Even though they might not be considered employees, if an intern is performing work that directly benefits the employer, the employer might be required to pay the intern at least minimum wage pursuant to the Fair Labor and Standards Act (FLSA) (see Chapter 6). Interns and volunteers pose additional concerns such as scope of control and associated liability for their negligent conduct and the right afforded to unpaid interns or volunteers.

Intern liability issues were raised with an Atlanta based public relations agency which was forced by the U.S. Department of Labor to pay its interns $31,520 in back pay and agree to pay current and future interns the federally mandated minimum wage (O'Connor, 1997). The agency got in trouble when they billed clients for the work which interns performed. This created an "immediate advantage" for the agency over its competitors who had to pay employees to perform similar work. Such an advantage conflicts with the Labor Department's Wage and Hour Field Operations Manual (1990) provision 106.11 (O'Connor, 1997). The same guidelines also prohibit:

- unpaid interns from displacing regular employees,
- using interns who do not receive any benefit from the internship (i.e., they do not develop any skill and only make coffee),
- utilizing interns who are not entitled to a job after their training period ends, and
- whether there is an understanding that the intern will not be paid for their training (O'Connor, 1997).

These factors are critical, but not conclusive. For additional cases, see generally, *Reich v. Parker Fire Protection District* (1993) and *Donovan v. American Airlines, Inc.* (1982).

Internships associated with college programs, such as sports and fitness administration programs, have to follow all labor laws even if the students receive college credit. Thus, an intern who did not receive any training and was used instead of hiring another secretary could sue under the Fair Labor Standards Act to get paid. To avoid potential suits or to throw-off government investigators, some employers are now using internship contracts which specify that the intern accepts a small stipend or college credit in lieu of the minimum wage. These contracts are currently being challenged and a definitive ruling on their validity should be available in the next several years (O'Connor, 1997). Until the legal status of interns is definitively settled, it is best to consider them employees unless they receive significant training opportunities.

In addition, employers should try to follow the follow suggestions which can help you avoid FLSA requirements:

- Training is for the benefit of the trainees or students;
- The trainees do not displace regular employees, but work under close observation;
- The employer that provides the training derives no immediate advantage from the trainee's or student's activities, and on occasion business might be interrupted in order to help teach the trainee or student;
- Trainees are not necessarily entitled to a job after they complete their training period; and
- And the employer and trainee or student understand that they will not be entitled to wages for any time spent in the training process (Dixon, 1994).

An additional concern associated with volunteers and interns relates to the scope of their work and whether the employer can control the work.

If the employer can exercise control over the volunteers or interns then the employer also assumes significant liability similar to liability for employee misconduct. The case law has been well established over the past several years that if a volunteer causes damage to another, the person or entity that utilized the volunteer would be liable for their misconduct (van der Smissen, 1990).

The legal implications associated with volunteer or intern liability helped develop several key risk management concepts discussed in this guide. These concepts include proper screening, training and placement of employees to avoid claims associated with negligent hiring, negligent training or negligent placement/supervision.

An additional difference between employees and volunteers relates to the rights that an employer needs to afford to employees versus volunteers. An employer might have to follow the American with Disabilities Act, equal employment opportunities, affirmative action, sexual harassment, Age Discrimination in Employment Act, federal and state constitutions and a host of other legal concerns when searching for, interviewing, hiring, and terminating an employee. On the other hand, volunteers have no rights. There is no constitutional right to volunteer with a person, entity or organization. There is no constitutional property right to continued participation as a volunteer, nor are there any due process rights that have to be followed if you wish to terminate a volunteer's involvement.

An employer needs to balance the potential concerns associated with possibly having to pay an intern, having to provide full employment rights and assuming liability for an intern's conduct against the purported free labor which can be provided by volunteers who you could terminate at any time. The final analysis is that there is no such concept as free labor. Even if you can get "free" labor, it could end-up costing you in the long run. Interns and volunteers need to be effectively screened, trained and managed to avoid liability concerns. Furthermore, the exact relationship any intern or volunteer has with you should be specified in advance. If need be, an employment contract could be entered into with the intern or volunteer specifically setting forth required duties and obligations to help minimize potential legal concerns such as workers' compensation insurance, wages, benefits and related issues. Appendix R contains sample employment contracts which could be modified for interns or volunteers. (The issues associated with hiring family members as potential "free" labor are discussed at the end of this chapter.)

Based on the potential liability concerns associated with employees, a potential employer has to determine if he wants to or needs to assume the employment law related concerns or if he can get by with possibly family members, volunteers or interns. If family members, volunteers or interns do not help you accomplish your potential employment goals, then you might have to consider outsourcing employment needs in order to reduce employment liability concerns.

2) Employee v. Independent Contractor

Before you can make the determination to hire an employee, you need to determine if you want to assume the various employee liability concerns addressed in this guide, or if you want to hire what are commonly referred to as independent contractors. While independent contractors do not represent a new position within the workforce, they are expanding at a rapid rate as the employment landscape is currently going through a dramatic shift towards greater reliance on independent contractors. Most employees realize they will probably not work for the same employer for thirty years and retire with a gold watch. The shift to independent contractors represents one of the most powerful forces transforming the American workplace today (Jones, 1997). It is estimated that as many as one million individuals who used to be employed with a position that paid a pension and health benefits are now self-employed contractors. This represents about 6–7% of the American workforce (Jones, 1997). Corporations are turning more towards independent contractors as such a move reduces the number of employment lawsuits after downsizing and the independent contractors lose the ability to rely upon age, sex, race discrimination laws, unemployment, minimum wage, overtime, workers' compensation, unionization rights and associated laws (Jones, 1997). An additional attraction associated with independent contractors is that the contractors are liable themselves for any negligent conduct or any criminal activity they initiate. Another attraction associated with independent contractors relates to preserving and maintaining a union free workplace. The rules relating to unionization (see Chapter 14) apply only to individual workers and not to outside contractors. The various concerns and benefits highlighted above are helping to propel the demand for independent contractors and contract laborers. In a 1997 survey of the 428 fastest-growing companies in the United States, 83% indicated they use independent contractors compared with only 64% in 1994 (Jones, 1997).

The temporary worker has become a popular resource used by many businesses. As explained by Jones (1997), using a temporary employee is one of the powerful forces transforming the American workplace today. In fact, according to the Department of Labor, the use of temporary workers has increased 400% since 1982 and more than 90% since 1990 (Neuborne, 1997). It is estimated that approximately 90% of all U.S. businesses use temporary employees ("Valuation of the temporary employment industry," 1996). According to the National Association of Temporary and

Staffing Services, the largest percentage (39%) of temps fill office or clerical positions (Stacey, 1997).

Sport businesses can realize six distinct benefits from using temporary workers. First, temporary workers decrease the expenses of a sport business that are incurred as a result of benefits (e.g., health insurance, vacation, sick days) and taxes. Second, the hiring of skilled temporary workers decrease expenses associated with interrupted operations and upgrading skills. For example, a sport business manager may be very competent, yet lack the financial wisdom of an independent accountant. Utilizing the independent contractor or temporary worker during tax season or other accounting periods enables the sport business manager to meet accounting needs without jeopardizing current operations. Third, temporary workers decrease expenses associated with federal and state legislative compliance. As explained by Jones (1997), temporary workers

> lose the protection of most laws regarding unemployment; minimum wage; overtime; age, sex and race discrimination; the right to unionize; and workers' compensation.

Fourth, temporary workers decrease expenses associated with maintaining a full-time employee during the off-season. The popularity of independent contractors resembles the "just-in-time" management concept adopted by manufacturing companies in the 1980s. Just-in-time management enables a sport park, for example, to contract with a sport marketing firm to handle advertising and promotions during the time of the year only when the park is open versus having to pay a marketing specialist 12 months of the year. Fifth, temporary workers provide immediate expertise that may be otherwise unavailable to a sport business. Sixth, temporary workers eliminate the problems and headaches associated with downsizing and laying off full-time employees.

Benefits accruing to temporary workers include (a) autonomy and (b) varied job experiences which in turn make them more flexible. As a temporary worker or independent contractor, individuals can choose when to work, and choose which jobs to work on, where and when they want. This autonomy provides them with a welcomed benefit not available as an employee operating under someone else's control and in accordance with their agenda. The opportunity to work and learn in a variety of settings is also recognized as a benefit to the temporary worker or independent contractor. As explained by Interim Resources' President Ray Marcy, "They view interim jobs as a way to keep their skills up to date and to maximize career opportunities. They like to be on the cutting edge of their profession" (Verespej, 1996). The various job experiences, in turn, make the temporary worker that much more marketable as they bring accumulated wisdom and insight to each job undertaken.

Although the trend indicates the growing popularity of independent contractors and temporary workers, employers should be cautious regarding the classification of the independent contractor as misclassification can be very costly. The Internal Revenue Service (IRS) requires that monies be paid for taxes, interest and penalties for the past three years (Jones, 1997). A sport business desiring to maintain confidential operations may also find the use of the temporary worker suspect. Further, consideration and evaluation should be given to whether the temporary worker can deliver the same type of customer service as a full-time employee (Jones, 1997).

Professional Employer Organizations

Professional employer organizations (PEOs) represent businesses which lease workers to various employers. Some businesses may use PEOs to employ their entire work force, including both managers and subordinates. Small businesses are finding great benefits in contracting with PEOs. As explained by Jones,

> Small-company owners are tired of being distracted with human resources headaches such as workers' compensation, family and medical leave laws, and discrimination lawsuits. Large companies combat it all with an army of lawyers, accountants and other specialists. Small companies are deciding it's worth turning over their payrolls plus 14% to 30% and relinquishing ultimate control of their workers just to get it all off their backs. (1997)

Jones (1997) describes the PEOs as a way to level the competitive playing field between large and small organizations. For example, according to the Center for the Study of American Business at Washington University, "companies with fewer than 20 employees annually pay about $5,500 per worker to comply with federal regulations, while companies with more than 500 workers pay about $3,000 a head" ("The cost of compliance," 1997). PEOs, in turn, lower their own costs via elaborate in-service training, employee drug testing, and of course a thorough familiarity with labor laws. PEOs are viable options for sport business managers wanting to avoid the time and expense accompanying human resource management and instead, devote time to achieving competitive strategies and maintaining market share.

Similar to independent contractors are "leased workers" who work for a major company that places them with various employers. The employers do not hire the individual leased worker, but enter into a contract with the leasing company to provide leased assistance. In 1995, over 2.5 million employees were leased and an estimated 37 million workers will be leased by 2007 (Jones, 1997). Employers utilizing leased workers derive significant benefits from not having to hassle with such concerns as hiring, training or terminating an employee. Furthermore, leased workers benefit as they can obtain (through economies of scale and the large purchasing power their leasing company might have) significant discounts on benefits such as health, dental, disability and life insurance. As with most convenient services, there is a cost. For one employer with a $1.6 million payroll, the administrative fee paid to lease the workers was approximately $300,000 (Jones, 1997). This cost would cover all the benefits, administrative and other costs incurred by the leasing company as well as the leasing company's profit.

While it might appear there is unfettered opportunity to terminate employees and then hire them back as independent contractors, such an action will draw judicial intervention. In 1997, the United States Supreme Court clearly constrained the latitude employers have to handle employees as independent contractors. The Court ruled on a case where the employers initially utilized employees working for a subsidiary. The employer entered into a new contract with another firm who would perform the same function, using the same employees. The employer then terminated the employees who were then hired by the independent contractor at a lower rate, with a lower pension and with less benefits. The Supreme Court concluded that an employer cannot fire workers and then contract the fired workers' jobs to an independent contractor in an effort to reduce their benefits ("Justices Rule in Workplace Case," 1997).

In the past, employers consistently tried to classify workers as independent contractors to avoid certain tax obligations and other financial inconveniences associated with employees (benefits, maternity leave, vacation time, overtime requirements, etc.). On the other hand, workers strived for coverage as employees to receive tax benefits themselves as well as various protections afforded to employees including various benefits and legal safeguards.

Some of the tax requirements faced by an employer when utilizing employees include:

A) paying the Federal Insurance Contribution Act (FICA) Tax imposed on the employer at the rate of 7.65 % for wages up to $57,600. Additionally, the employer must withhold and pay the same amount for the employee's FICA tax requirement, and

B) paying Federal Unemployment Tax Act (FUTA) taxes imposed at the rate of 6.2 % for the first $7,000 in wages (Husband, Barrett and Miller, 1993).

However, if the worker is considered an independent contractor she will have to pay her own Self Employment Contribution Act Tax (SECA) which is 15.3%. More importantly, employers would not be responsible for any independent contractor's tax obligations or administrative bookkeeping requirements. Many employers who wish to avoid the various employee related taxes and administrative functions try to classify employees as independent contractors. These employers pay the workers a fixed amount, do not withhold taxes, and issue 1099 tax forms at the end of the year. These unintentional or deliberate misclassification of workers as independent contractors rather than employees can result in significant liability concerns. From 1988 to 1994, the IRS audited 11,380 companies and collected $751 million in back taxes and forced companies to reclassify 483,000 independent contractors as employees (Jones, 1997). Currently, if the IRS wins an audit against an employer who misclassifies an employee as an independent contractor, the employer needs to reclassify the employee and pay taxes, interest and penalties going back up to three years (Jones, 1997). The IRS estimates that it has a lot of work to do. The IRS estimates that there are at least 2.5 million independent contractors who are really employees and which costs the IRS over $2 billion in lost taxes (Jones, 1997). The IRS estimates significant losses because if an employer does not withhold taxes, an independent contractor might not pay taxes or will pay significantly lower taxes after deducting all applicable business expenses-which might otherwise not be deductible if the person was really an employee.

Proper Employee Classification

Through the traditional employment courtship, a worker was classified as an independent contractor or employee based on the type of contract struck between the two parties. People assumed that if the contract stated the person was an independent contractor, they in fact were an independent contractor. Some individuals might think they are an employee, but when the tax year arrives, they receive a 1099 tax form (outside revenue). Thus, while the person might have been working under the impression they were an employee receiving all appropriate employee rights (workers' compensation, health, disability, etc.) he/she might not have received these rights. If these rights were denied and if taxes were in fact not withheld, the employee might have a potential fraud claim against the employer. Based on these concerns, no matter what the contract claims, if the government considers an individual an employee rather than an independent contractor, the person is an employee.

Based on the numerous hurdles presented by the IRS if an employee or independent contractor is misclassified, it is essential to properly classify individuals according to the IRS standards. The IRS's analysis is focused on whether or not the employer has the right to control and direct the individual worker in terms of results achieved and the means by which the results are achieved. In Revenue Ruling 87-4, the IRS set forth 20 factors to help determine if the employer controls the worker to such an extent that the worker is considered an employee (Husband, Barrett and Miller, 1993).

The major factors include:

- the degree by which the employer's instructions have to be followed,
- who has the right to hire, fire, supervise, pay and terminate lower level workers,
- whether a continuing relationship exists between the parties,
- who controls the working hours,
- who controls the workplace,
- who pays the business and travel expenses,
- whether full-time work is required,
- whether it is prohibited to work for anyone else,
- whether payment is based on the project or job versus the time worked,
- whether the worker's services are made available to the general public, and
- whether either party has the right to quit without breach of contract liability.

The IRS's factors examine who controls the work and the manner in which the work is performed. If a fitness trainer controls his own hours, the manner in which he works, the place he works, whether he can work for other potential clients, if he has a specific contract and related working conditions, then he would be considered an independent contractor. However, if the same fitness trainer is precluded from working for other gyms, needs to appear at specific hours, has to wear a uniform and reports to a supervisor employed by the health club, then the fitness trainer would probably be considered a health club employee.

To help apply the IRS's 20 key factors, the IRS has established additional guidelines to help apply the factors to specific situations. Other issues the IRS will investigate for independent contractors in the entertainment/sports industries include:

- if they are listed in industry directories and how,
- do they receive compensation between projects,
- who pays for their training and educational expenses,
- do they have to find their next project,
- do they operate under a written contract (the IRS will ask to see it),
- who supervises their work,
- how are they paid, and

- do they provide their own equipment.

These are the primary factors examined to determine if someone should be considered an employee or an independent contractor. No matter how accurate or thorough your analysis, you can make a mistake. What is the penalty for failing to properly classify the worker as an employee rather than an independent contractor? As previously mentioned, besides IRS fines and penalties, an employer can even be liable for possible criminal violations. The most prominent concerns for the unsuspecting employer relate to unpaid employment taxes, failure to include the employee under comprehensive general liability insurance policies and the failure to purchase workers' compensation insurance. The failure to purchase workers' compensation insurance can be both a civil and criminal penalty which can lead to significant fines. For example, California Labor Code Section 3710 et al. provides in pertinent part that:

> Failure of an employer, officer, or anyone having direction, management or control of any place of employment or of employees to observe a stop order issued and served upon him or her pursuant to Section 3710.1 is a misdemeanor punishable by imprisonment in the county jail not exceeding 60 days or by a fine not exceeding ten thousand dollars ($10,000) or both.

In one recent California case, the failure to carry workers' compensation insurance for several months resulted in a fine of over $100,000 (Fried, 1994). Such a penalty can be imposed even if an employer acted in good faith or inadvertently let the insurance coverage lapse because the employer did not think workers were employees.

Contracts represent the surest means to clearly establish that someone is an independent contractor, rather than an employee. Appendix A is a sample independent contractor contract designed to insure an individual understands that they are being retained as an independent contractor. Another means of insuring you are dealing with a legitimate independent contractor is to make sure you retain the services of a legitimate business. This can be accomplished by entering into a contract with that business rather than with an individual. Appendix B provides appropriate contractual language to use when retaining a business entity to perform independent contractor work.

Determining if a worker is an independent contractor or not are made more difficult when federal and state laws are inconsistent. Section 530 of the Revenue Act of 1978 contains safe harbor rules that allow certain workers to be classified as independent contractors even if they are really employees. To be covered by this provision, a company must show that for federal tax purposes (including all filings) the individual was always treated like an independent contractor, all similarly situated workers have been treated as independent contractors and that a "reasonable basis" exists for classifying the individual as an independent contractor. A "reasonable basis' can be proven by showing that the employer relied upon judicial precedent, published IRS rulings, IRS private letter rulings (from past IRS audits) and from long-standing recognized practices followed by a significant industry segment (normally over 25% of similar industries) (Brager, 1997). Thus, through careful planning and structuring, employers can possibly avoid federal tax withholdings. However, it should be remembered that this opinion only affects federal taxes. Therefore, an employee/independent contractor still needs to be covered by the company's pension plan. Furthermore, most states do not have rules similar to Section 530, thus workers might be considered independent contractors for federal withholding purposes, but state law would still classify them as employees for whom workers' compensation insurance would be required (Brager, 1997). As you can tell from the complex rubric of issues presented by the independent contractor versus employee designation, whenever there is any doubt as to an employee's status—consult with an attorney.

Once it is established that an independent contractor is performing your necessary work, this guide becomes somewhat obsolete. If you are dealing with independent contractors, you will not need to apply all the various anti-discrimination laws, unionization, wrongful termination, and the numerous other legal issues which employers typically face with employees. Your primary concern is to conform to your contractual requirements and to make sure the independent contractor does not violate his/her contractual requirements. By keeping the relationship a "strictly business" relationship, you can help solidify your claim that an independent contractor relationship exists.

Independent Contractor Liability Concerns

While numerous legal concerns can be avoided when working with independent contractors, leased workers can provide some unique legal concerns. While these concerns are primarily relegated to leased or contingent workers (who perform payroll, billing and other administrative functions), they can also apply to workers who are possibly independent contractors. The paramount legal concerns include potential joint employer: taxes, liability, wage and hour issues, workers' compensation coverage, and labor relation issues.

Under IRS rules, whoever controls paying wages is the employer for employment tax purposes (Revenue Ruling, 1975). Thus, all leased employees should only be utilized when the leasing company:

- negotiates the conditions for using the worker,
- determines who is assigned,
- retains authority to reassign a worker,

- sets the worker's pay, pays the worker out of the leasing company's own accounts, and
- retains the right to hire and fire all leased workers (California Unemployment Insurance Code Section 606.5).

Similar to contingent or independent, "leased workers" can reduce your liability for various concerns such as taxes, workers' compensation coverage, or discrimination laws. However, numerous courts have held that a leased worker is indeed an employee of both the leasing company and the company that leased the worker. If the leasing company pays the leased worker, but the company that leased the worker controls the hours, tools, method of performing the work and other variables used in evaluating independent contractors, then the worker could be considered a joint or dual employee. Under these circumstances, both employers would be liable for complying with appropriate laws and regulations such as workers' compensation coverage and complying with anti-discrimination laws. An additional concern that you could face is a discrimination claim even if you did not engage in any discriminatory conduct. The EEOC has recently published guidelines indicating that an employer can be liable for violating anti-discrimination laws if the worker leasing company has discriminated in any of their hiring, promoting, compensating and terminating processes (EEOC, 1997). To avoid such a problem, your contract with the leasing company should specifically provide that the leasing company would hold you harmless and indemnify you for any claims that might be raised based on the leasing company's conduct and that the leasing company shall not engage in any conduct which can generate any discrimination claim.

Discrimination

Joint employer liability can be imposed on the employer and leasing (and/or independent contractor) company for liability associated with such issues as discrimination. In the *Magnuson v. Peak Technical Services, Inc.* case, an automobile manufacturer's representative brought a sexual harassment claim against four different defendants. The defendants included the consulting agency which hired and referred her, the auto supplier, the dealer for whom she sold cars and her supervisor. The court ordered a trial to determine which defendant was her employer for purposes of her Title VII suit. The court concluded that the defendants could each be held liable if they knew about the harassment and failed to take any corrective action to remedy the situation (Magnuson, 1992). This case is significant because it demonstrates that employers can be liable for discriminating against workers from a temporary agency.

Overtime Pay

The federal Fair Labor Standards Act (FLSA) (see generally Chapter 6) explicitly imposes co-employment obligations under certain circumstances. If a worker works for two different employers during any given week, the total hours worked and wages paid have to comply with weekly FLSA provisions which requires overtime pay for working over certain set hours. The Department of Labor (DOL) requires the leasing company to keep track of all hours worked and wages paid for any worker they lease-out. However, the employer who retained the leased worker would only be jointly liable with the leasing company for payment of overtime worked exclusively for the employer. Thus, if a temporary worker was utilized for 50 hours with one employer, that employer and the leasing company would be jointly liable for 10 hours of overtime wages (DOL Opinion Letter, 1968).

Workers' Compensation

One of the most litigated issues involving shared or joint employees relates to workers' compensation coverage. Under workers' compensation law, employees can have more than one employer and each employer is entitled to the same immunity from common law suits. Thus, an injured employee would have to file a workers' compensation claim as his/her exclusive remedy against each purported employer. If a temporary day worker's job is strictly controlled, they could be considered an employee for both the placement agency and the entity which requested the worker. Such a worker would be covered by both shared employers' workers' compensation coverage. The employer which retained the leased worker would be liable if they failed to have workers' compensation insurance (see generally Chapter 12). In summary, all employers need to recognize that leasing workers can trigger significant workers' compensation obligations. Therefore, special care should be taken to emphasize utilizing independent contractors through a business, and that business should be responsible for all workers' compensation coverage.

Unionization

While employers traditionally would not think that temporary or leased workers could unionize, under the right condition this concern could become reality. In one National Labor Relation Board (NLRB) case, the Board concluded that workers provided through a temporary agency could vote in a union election along with regular employees. The Board's decision was upheld by a federal court that concluded, that both the temporary agency and the employer exercised substantial control over the workers and helped determine their employment terms and conditions. The temporary agency and employer were considered joint employers because:

- the workers had previously worked for the same employer,
- the employer requested specific employees by name,
- the leased and regular employees worked side-by-side,
- all workers used the same time clock, and
- the employer had an explicit policy that they would consider leased employees for regular positions. Under all these conditions, the court concluded that the leased employees were so close to being regular employees that they could vote in the union election (*NLRB v. Western Temporary Services*, 1987).

To help address the various concerns associated with leased employees, the following steps should be utilized.

1) Thoroughly screen any leasing company to make sure they are in compliance with all applicable employment laws and will enter into a contract expressly assuming responsibility for all employee conduct, including defending against any unioinization attempt.

2) Avoid utilizing the same leased workers for extended periods of time.

3) Utilize leased workers for specific functions such as payroll or accounting, and isolate them as much as possible from work performed by regular employees. Other individuals might disagree with such a practice, however, the more the leased workers are grouped with regular employees, the greater the likelihood that the leased workers could be perceived as employees for tax, liability and insurance purposes.

4) Have all leased workers report to a manager within the leasing company and take directions from that manager. The manager can be specifically required to undertake and be responsible for completing specific assignments as provided for in the engagement contract.

5) Regularly confer with the leasing company to make sure they are providing leased workers with necessary benefits, insurance, tax withholdings and related rights.

6) If at all possible, avoid regularly offering full-time employment to leased workers. If leased workers are hired away, make sure you specifically contract with the leasing company to acquire the rights to that employee. All workers hired in this manner should only be selected from all potential job applicants for the position and not just from leased workers.

7) Vigilantly check with leased workers to determine if they are upset about working conditions which could possibly lead to unionization efforts.

8) Train managers to understand the difference between various workers (employees, independent contractors, leased employees, etc.) and the proper procedures for dealing with each group.

This guide primarily discusses concerns associated with employees. Many of the same issues also affect interns and volunteers. Thus, the primary focus rests on the very personal relationship that exists between an employer and an employee. Significant latitude is given to the very personal relationship except when a pervasive government interest exists, such as eradicating discrimination. Regulations also come into play when other parties are brought into the picture. The primary external, non-government, party who can be brought into the employment relationship, or who wield significant influence to dramatically control the employee relationship are unions.

3) Various Factors Affecting the Employee/Employer Relationship-Unions

Union Development

Unionization represents one of the most dynamic changes this century in employee/employer relations. The balancing of powers and bargaining position enforced by legislative enactment has produced a "level playing field" so both parties can negotiate with somewhat equal power. The union stands in the place of the employees, thus creating a separate entity with which the employer has to negotiate. By requiring the employer to negotiate with a group rather than an individual employee, a balanced negotiating process is created. Historically, the fight for unionization has been a long difficult journey. The impetus for unionization spread from the Pullman Railway strike of 1894 (Rothstein, Knapp and Liebman, 1987). After the strike, President Cleveland appointed the United States Strike Commission to investigate labor trends. The Commission's investigation resulted in the passing of the Erdman Act in 1898 which allowed protection for union members affiliated with the operation of interstate trains. Shortly thereafter though, the Supreme Court struck down the Act as unconstitutional (Rothstein, Knapp and Liebman, 1987).

Six years after the Court's decision (*Adair v. United States*, 1908), Congress passed the Clayton Act which provided that the Sherman Act did not apply to labor unions. The Sherman Act prohibits contracts and conspiracies that constrain trade between the states. Unions inherently represent a conspiracy to not provide labor unless certain factors are met and if those factors are not met, unions can go on strike which inhibits interstate commerce in violation of the Sherman Act. Thus, labor unions could function between and among states without running afoul of the antitrust laws. In 1932, the Norris-LaGuardia Act was enacted which prohibited federal courts from issuing injunctions in labor disputes. The very next year, Congress passed the National Industrial Recovery Act (NIRA) which granted workers the right to organize and bargain collectively. This Act was struck down by the Supreme Court as unconstitutional (*Schechter Poultry Corp. v. United States*, 1935). But, less than two month later Congress passed the National Labor Relations Act (NLRA) which is also called the Wagner Act. The NLRA officially crystallized the government policy of encouraging collective bargaining. The NLRA derived its power from the Federal Constitution's commerce clause which authorizes Congress to make laws regulating business that affect interstate commerce. The same commerce clause provides the legal underpinning for the Sherman Antitrust Act. Specifically excluded from the NLRA's reach are all levels of government employees, agricultural employees, airline and railway employees and supervisory employees. Under the NLRA, a Board (NLRB) was established to regulate union formation, elections and unfair labor practices by employers. Under NLRA Section 8, unfair labor practices include interfering with, restraining or coercing employees from joining unions or participating in union activities. Finally, Congress enacted an act protecting employees and which held up to constitutional scrutiny (*NLRB*, 1937; Rothstein, Knapp and Liebman, 1987).

The playing field suddenly shifted in favor of the employees. In fact, the unions became so powerful, that Congress passed the Taft-Hartley Act in 1947. The Act allowed employees the right to refrain from union activities if they did not want to get involved and prohibited unfair labor practices by unions. After 1947, unions rapidly expanded to become the driving force to protect employee rights to higher wages, better benefits, and safe working conditions (Rothstein, Knapp and Liebman, 1987).

Unions in Sport

Unionization has had a dramatic effect in the sport industry. Particularly in professional sport, the unions have been able to utilize federal laws to force the owners hand and exact significant compromises. The *McNeil v. NFL* and *Powell v. NFL* cases typified the power obtained by the unions to decertify or use other techniques to break the shield protecting team owners from anti-trust scrutiny (*McNeil*, 1991; *Powell*, 1991). As previously stated, the NLRA excludes labor arrangements obtained through the collective bargaining agreement process from antitrust scrutiny. However, such protection only exists when the collective bargaining process is in effect or when the parties are negotiating in good faith to renew the agreement. In the *Powell* case, after several court challenges against the National Football League (NFL) to conclude that the NFL was not negotiating for a new contract in good faith, the players' union voted to decertify as a union. Since the union was decertified, there could not be a collective bargaining agreement as there was no union who could negotiate with the NFL (*Powell*, 1991).

While the examples generated by professional athletes represent a great medium for demonstrating labor law's scope, most traditional employees do not have the same impact as professional athletes. If professional football players go on strike, there are very few replacements that could be marshaled to operate a highly competitive replacement league. Additionally, any activities associated with either the players' union or the professional league will undoubtedly appear in all major newspapers and generate irate politicians. However, if janitors went on strike, there are an ample number of replacements that could fill in for the striking workers. This bargaining power insures professional athlete greater leverage in the collective bargaining process.

Union Trends

Unions represent a significant segment of the workplace population throughout the United States. The AFL-CIO has 12.9 million members (Worsham, 1997). This number is on the rise as the AFL-CIO is taking a significant marketing plan to the workplace in order to create more union shops (Worsham, 1997). It is estimated that the AFL-CIO, the nation's preeminent union umbrella organization with 77 member unions, will spend one-third of its budget, $30 million in 1997 to increase union membership (Worsham, 1997). If all the unions in the United States spend one-third of their budget, over $2 billion dollars would be spent on organizing nonunion workplaces. The push to increase union membership has been sparked by a decline in union membership from 35% of the workforce in the 1950's to only 14.5% of today's workplace (Worsham, 1997). Unions represent only 10.2% of the private-sector workforce, but represented over 37% of the public-sector workforce in 1996. Unions need to replace over 300,000 members each year to replace union members who resign, retire, or their employers relocate. In order to help boost its numbers, the AFL-CIO has organized over 1,500 college students and numerous retired union members to solicit increased union activities in certain parts of the nation and with certain groups such as women (Worsham, 1997). Unions affect diverse groups such as facility janitors, school personnel, athletes, assembly line workers and numerous other employees.

The risk management strategies contained in this book apply to both union and non-union settings. However, as union collective bargaining agreements often provide specific procedures for dealing with disputes, the strategies outlined throughout the guide will apply when the collective bargaining arrangement specifically allows for the enumerated procedures. For example, a collective bargaining agreement could specifically state that a joint employee and employer review team be used to investigate any allegation of sexual harassment. Such a provision would be inconsistent with an employer investigation outlined in Chapter 7. Likewise, safety committees, highlighted in Chapter 11, are a great risk management tool, but could also lead to potential union bargaining unit disputes.

Collective bargaining agreements form the framework for an employment contract involving a third party—the union. They are not necessarily in and of themselves the employment contract. Thus, an individual employee can bargain for better terms. However, any additional agreements have to be consistent with the collective bargaining agreement. Appendix C is a professional baseball player's contract developed through collective bargaining.

The preceding paragraphs were designed to inform the reader about unions and their effect on the personal relationship between an employer and an employee. Whenever an employer looks to creating or continuing the employment relationship, it is essential for the employer to consider third parties who can affect the employer/employee relationship. By knowing how employees have fought for the right to unionize and how our government and courts have worked to insure such rights, an employer can understand how important the union process is for union members and why all union negotiations need to be taken seriously. Chapter 14 provides specific reference to union-related issues and the best techniques to utilize with existing and/or potential unions.

Unionization represents just one of the many issues that impact the employment relationship. The employment relationship is a sensitive, touchy-feely area that often changes based on prevalent attitudes and beliefs. New research or public outcries to change the manner in which employees work are fostering new laws and personnel management strategies. Such topics as pregnant women working around hazardous materials, extended leave for fathers, extended leave for taking care of sick parents, health care coverage for "life" partners, are just some issues which are currently helping to shape and mold the master-servant relationship. These issues will be discussed in the following pages. However, no employment law text would be complete without examining a crystal ball to determine how the master-servant relationship might change in the future. By analyzing these potential societal changes, an employer can adequately prepare for similar changes in the workplace.

4) Future Employment Trends/Legal Implications

Judicial Trends

What rights does an employee have in his/her job? Do they have a property right, contract right, or constitutional right in his/her job? Can the rights to a job be changed through such mechanisms as "post-tenure" reviews? The issues associated with job security and who can interfere with such security was a critical issue for legendary basketball coach Jerry Tarkanian in his approximately ten year battle with the National Collegiate Athletic Association (NCAA). In *Tarkanian v. NCAA*, the NCAA forced a member school, the University of Nevada at Las Vegas, to suspend one of its employee, Jerry Tarkanian (*NCAA*, 1988). Tarkanian claimed that the NCAA could not force the public university to punish him without affording him basic due process rights. Because the university was a state actor (see Chapter 4), the university had to follow all federal constitutional requirements including the Fourteenth Amendment which protects an individual's property rights from being taken by the state without due process. In 1905 the United States Supreme Court concluded that the right to contract for employment and the right to purchase or sell labor are property rights protected by the Fourteenth Amendment of the Federal Constitution (*Lochner v. New York*, 1905). The United States Supreme Court concluded in *NCAA* that while the NCAA is composed of numerous universities that are state actors, that fact did not make the NCAA (which is a private non-profit organization) a state actor. Thus, the NCAA did not need to provide Tarkanian with any due process or other constitutionally protected rights.

The *NCAA* case demonstrates that there are no federal property rights or federal constitutional rights for employees working in wholly private organizations or companies. However, Tarkanian still could have contractual rights and remedies or state constitutional guarantees. If his university employment contract required the university to pay him a certain amount if he was terminated, the university would be forced to pay that penalty if they wanted to terminate his services. Furthermore, if Tarkanian was working in California (ironically, at the time of this writing, Coach Tarkanian was employed by a California-based state supported university), the NCAA would have been forced to provide state constitutionally mandated rights which can be more expansive than certain federal constitutional protections. The NCAA would have been forced to provide these rights because the California state constitution protects basic due process rights to both state entities and private entities. This provision of the California constitution was recently upheld in a drug testing case against the NCAA (*Hill v. NCAA*, 1994). In addition to California, Montana's Constitution also covers private entities (Feliu, 1992).

Federal Versus State Laws

The *NCAA v. Tarkanian* decision highlights the current state of affairs relating to private employers and their ability to avoid federal constitutional mandates. However, as can be seen with the recent *Hill* decision, employers might be able to pass some loopholes and then be confronted with additional hurdles which can impose significant liability concerns. Special attention should be focused in the future on the interaction between federal and state laws, and which law needs to be applied under which circumstances. Conflicting laws such as disability rights and affirmative action laws require employers to understand the mindset in various states and keep abreast of proposed legislation more than ever before.

A good example highlighting the disparity between federal and state laws can be seen in the *Cassista* case (*Cassista v. Community Foods*, 1993). The plaintiff filed her claim in California state court claiming she was not hired because she was obese. The California Supreme Court concluded that there is a difference between being obese based on physiological reasons (low metabolism) and being obese based on psychological reasons (someone likes to eat). While this distinction caused the plaintiff to lose in California court, if she would have filed the same claim under the ADA, she could have had a possible valid claim, no matter why she was obese.

Legislative Changes

An additional trend affecting the sport employment arena centers around Title IX and the rights afforded to women's programs. Now more than ever before, if a female coach or a male coach of a women's team is terminated, the frequent response lies in a Title IX claim against the school. Title IX requires equal opportunity for women and men to participate in federally funded programs. Since women's programs traditionally have not had the same budget as men's program, most universities, colleges and even high schools that receive any federal funding are potentially open for a Title IX claim. Unfortunately, while Title IX is primarily used to defend valid rights, some poor or ineffective coaches threaten suit if they are terminated or if their program is canceled. One such case involved the firing of the University of Missouri-St. Louis women's basketball coach who was terminated after four years as a coach with an overall record of 32–77. The coach claimed he was fired because he challenged the university's treatment of the women's program. The university claimed the coach failed to perform his job assignment which included serving as academic coordinator for athletics. The parties reached a confidential settlement of the dispute which did not change the university's program, but resolved all issues with the coach (Holland, 1997). Similar suits and settlements have been reached with other programs including California State University, Long Beach which canceled women's volleyball and then had to reinstate the team after several lawsuits were filed. The university attempted to save probably $70,000 a year by cutting the team. However, the move cost over $1,000,000 in a settlement to the fired coach, $200,000 in legal fees, national embarrassment, and having to continue funding a team (Fried, 1992).

New Managerial Techniques

Besides legislative, court mandated and societal imposed changes, new managerial approaches can foretell potential liability concerns. One such concern involves the simple matter of providing employee with a nap. Many famous individuals such as Winston Churchill, Thomas Edison, and Bill Clinton all take or took naps (Jackson, 1997). A nap seems like an innocuous activity, but it can lead to future liability concerns. Prior to the light-bulb being invented, the average American slept 10 hours a night. Now, the average American sleeps less than 7.1 hours a night and 33% of Americans sleep less than six hours a night (Jackson, 1997). If an employee losses an hour of sleep a night for a week, their productivity can decline 25% according to one researcher (Jackson, 1997). Thus, some executives are now utilizing napping to help increase employers and employee productivity. In the same breath, some employers are requiring their employees to work harder and longer hours. If someone has been pushed to work excessive hours with little or no rest, they become a productivity hazard. They also can become a liability hazard. A new crop of lawsuits are being brought by injured individuals who claim truck drivers were too tired, were not receiving enough rest, and whose bosses were pushing them to extremes in order to meet deadlines (Moore-ede, 1995). The tired truck drivers are sometimes getting into accidents and injured individuals are suing the drivers and employers claiming the lack of sleep helped contribute to the accident. The same principle could be raised if an accountant or personal trainer was forced to work outrageous hours without adequate sleep and they make an error or injure someone. If the error or injury could have been prevented through providing someone with a half-hour rejuvenating nap, the jury could look upon the employer as someone who failed to act reasonably under the circumstances. This is especially true if the industry standard becomes one where employers encourage employee napping to help reduce accidents and injuries.

5) Family Members as Employees

This chapter has addressed a multitude of potential workers or employees ranging from full-time employees to leased employees and independent contractors. Union members also represent a significant component of the employee pool. Interns and volunteers could also be utilized to help complete necessary jobs. Additional segments also include international laborers and part-time employees who are respectively covered in Chapter 2 and 6. Lastly, family members also represent a significant issue for prospective employers. Smaller sport manufacturing companies, sport apparel boutiques, health clubs, and softball complexes represent typical business which might rely on family laborers. These family laborers represent unique liability issues associated with such issues as employee's age, hours worked, and "no spouse" issues.

Age and Hour Issues

An employer can employ a child under age 14 only when the child is employed by his or her own parent(s) or guardian(s) in a non-hazardous job (Frierson, 1994). Thus, if a father was the head of a local junior league baseball program, he could hire his 13-year-old daughter to be a referee or sell food from the concession stand without running afoul of the minimum working age laws. An employer's own children, or other children between age 14 and 15 can be hired to perform non-hazardous jobs only during non-school hours. Additional rules prohibit the 14- or 15-year-old from working more than 18 hours during a school week, more than three hours on any given school day, nor before 7:00 a.m. or after 7:00 p.m. on school days. However, during vacation, the same employees can work a maximum eight hours a day or 40 hours a week (Frierson, 1994). These provisions in the Federal Fair Labor Standards Act apply to employees, thus, if 14-year-olds are asked to volunteer their services to work for a little league double header after school, which ends at 8:00 p.m. no rules are violated as the volunteers are not employees. No cases were discovered by the authors relating to nonprofit sport organizations hiring 14- or

15-year-olds as employees, and then changing their status to volunteers whenever any FLSA violations occurred. However, such gimmickry, even with your own children, will always raise questions with enforcement agency investigators.

Teenagers (under 16) can work for their parent(s) or others in such positions as:

- office clerical,
- retail work,
- cashiering,
- deliveries,
- clean-up,
- maintenance,
- kitchen work, and
- car cleaning (Frierson, 1994).

Most teenagers can engage in the fundamental jobs associated with sport and recreation programs such as coaching, teaching, cleaning gyms, preparing fields, selling drinks at a concession booth and related activities. At the same time, you have to make sure employees and volunteers under age 16 do not engage in any manufacturing, operating hoisting equipment, operating/repairing motor vehicles, warehousing or construction to name some of the prohibited activities (Frierson, 1994). Based on these prohibited acts, it would seem appropriate that employees under 16-years-old should not operate golf carts nor repair them, not be assigned any building or repairing duties (such as bleacher repairs), nor operate complex electrical equipment such as certain laundering equipment, pitching machines with swing arms or electrical equipment operated in or near water. While the law does not imply teens are incapable of handling such duties, public policy established such rules to protect the youngsters from injury. However, such restrictions are often significantly lifted as soon as the employee reaches 16 or 17 (Frierson, 1994).

Nepotism

Nepotism represents a type of internal recruitment or hiring. Nepotism in the workplace is not prohibited by federal legislation so long as discrimination or bias is not exercised in the traditional employment relationship. If nepotism policies are allowed, they must be allowed in a uniform manner. In other words, if an employee is allowed to apply for positions than both his/her sons and daughters also must be allowed to apply. Policies specifically prohibiting hiring spouses tend to be upheld so long as there is no disparate impact. Similarly, if nepotism is allowed at lower level positions, it must also be allowed in upper level positions (Bennett-Alexander and Pincus, 1995).

Where the line workers in a firm are primarily Hispanic and management is primarily white, an anti-nepotism policy for line workers that does not apply to management would result in disparate impact (Bennett-Alexander 1995).

Similarly, it is legal for an athletic department to hire a coach's husband to work at the same university. However, it would be illegal if this individual was promoted in a discriminatory fashion ahead of better-qualified and more seasoned employees. The following case illustrates the problems presented by nepotism policies. In *Bonilla v. Oakland Scavenger Co.* (1982), the defendant company limited share ownership to family members of Italian ancestry. As explained by the United States Court of Appeals,

> Since the Company ties preferential wages, hours, and job assignments to ownership of its stock, the shareholder preference plan constitutes a condition of employment subject to the mandate of Title VII...The Company points to an allegedly superior interest in protecting and providing for members of the immediate families of the founders of the Company. But Title VII case law has from the beginning made clear that nepotistic concerns cannot supersede the nation's paramount goal of equal opportunity for all (*Bonilla*, 1992).

As explained in the *Bonilla* case (1982), the government does not intend to intrude into the business affairs of small businesses. Title VII, for example, which prohibits discrimination in the employment process based upon race, color, national origin, religion or sex only pertains to those businesses employing more than 15 people (see generally Chapter 4).

Advantages of Anti-Nepotism Policies

Ford and McLaughlin's research in 1986 indicated that 40% of all firms have formal anti-nepotism policies and 17% of firms have informal anti-nepotism policies. Employers often implement anti-nepotism policies for following reasons:

- Anti-nepotism policies attempt to eliminate discrimination or the perception of discrimination in the work place that can occur when employers or supervisors are responsible for supervising and evaluating family members. Employee morale would plummet rapidly if all employment promotions and opportunities were perceived as going to the "boss's wife." Even if the boss's wife had stellar credentials, the perception of favoritism would likely cloud genuine exemplary credentials possessed.

- Anti-nepotism policies can reduce collusive behaviors that related employees can invoke upon a supervisor or other colleagues. The combined efforts of related employees to refute suggestions or needed changes can quickly diminish a business's competitive advantage while simultaneously creating a rather uncomfortable and adversarial work environment.
- Employers often fear that conflicts in the home or family will be carried over to the workplace. This conflict can bring tension, animosity, and divisiveness into the work environment (Werbel and Hames, 1996).

In summary, the primary benefits associated with hiring relatives includes creating an effective recruiting tool, creating a warm family workplace atmosphere and possibly hiring the most qualified person regardless of familial affiliation. While benefits are profound, the detriments associated with hiring family members can be even more profound.

Disadvantages of Anti-Nepotism Policies

Adopting an anti-nepotism policy, however, can be counter productive for the following reasons:

- Anti-nepotism policies may convey distrust for employees. For obvious reasons, employees will rebel against employers who assume that they cannot, for example, exercise judgment in separating personal issues from work issues. Until there is documented evidence indicating the universal, foreseeable problems of nepotism, anti-nepotism policies may best be avoided.
- It is not uncommon for employees to meet in the work place, date, and later get married. Coercing one of those employees to quit or relocate can influence workplace morale as a valued "team member" is forced to quit. Abandoning an otherwise loyal and well performing employee seems illogical. Similarly, an employer may never be able to capitalize on a potentially productive and loyal job candidate who fails to apply as a result of an anti-nepotism policy.

Interfering with dating relationships "in the interest of the sport business" represents a perilous activity that may spur litigation. For example, in *Wilson v. Taylor* (1984), the U.S. Court of Appeals (11th Cir.) held that the termination of a police officer for dating a particular woman violated his liberty right guaranteed by the Fourteenth Amendment as well as his freedom of association right guaranteed by the First Amendment. As stated by the court:

> A state violates the fourteenth amendment when it seeks to interfere with the social relationship of two or more people. We conclude that dating is a type of association which must be protected by the first amendment's freedom of association (*Wilson*, 1984).

It is also foreseeable that additional allegations of intentional infliction of emotional distress and invasion of privacy could be brought against an employer for his or her anti-nepotism policies. Additional detriments can include:

- creating family conflicts,
- nepotism rules being held unlawful based on their discriminatory affect,
- creating security concerns such as the opportunity for joint embezzlement,
- creating potential conflict of interests,
- creating bad feelings when a fellow family member is not hired, disciplined, or terminated, and
- creating workplace disruptions when family disputes enter the workplace (Feliu, 1992).

To avoid legal challenges, many employers adopt limited anti-nepotism policies. For example, employers often consider family members for employment so long as the family member is not supervised directly by an individual to whom he or she is related. This type of limited anti-nepotism policy enables the employer to benefit via a qualified, credentialed worker while eliminating problems associated with real or perceived bias and favoritism.

The flip side is also a concern faced in the workplace. Some employers have specific rules such as "no spouse" rules or "no relatives" rules which prohibit hiring a spouse or relative, or prohibiting a spouse to evaluate their loved one's work performance or compensation awards. The managerial concern associated with "no spouse" rules usually stems from disputes associated with preferential employee performance appraisals and benefits which are not available to other employees. Similar to all other company policies, if the policies is not consistently enforced, it can lead to significant liability (Feliu, 1992). A jury recently awarded a terminated Safeway employee over $800,000 after he was terminated for alleged repeated violation of company policy by allowing his teenage sons to work in stores in an area he managed. According to the company policy, "relatives can work anywhere in the company except where there is either a direct or indirect reporting relationship with an immediate family member, or where the employment creates an actual conflict or appearance of conflict of interest." While the policy is a reasonable policy, Safeway did not follow the policy in a uniform manner which helped lead to the guilty verdict (Jury, 1997).

Wrap Up...

The issues associated with what rights are owed an employee or how to appropriately classify employees represent just some of the numerous concerns affecting employment law and the means by which employers and individual supervisors can be sued. Some other key issues that are arising on regular basis include:

- racketeering charges against those who raid employee pension accounts,
- suits alleging disability-based discrimination,
- violence in the workplace,
- sexual abuse by customers against employees,
- employee theft of everything from office supplies to trade secrets,
- resumes filled with puffery or outright lies,
- unwillingness to give personal references,
- freedom of speech and religion in the workplace, and
- hundreds of additional concerns.

It is beyond the scope of this guide to address every employment law concern. Nonetheless, it is incumbent on all employers to analyze all potential legal issues to determine if they need legal assistance or if a matter is beyond their experience.

An employer can utilize a tried and tested technique to help determine if an issue involves a potential legal problem. The technique is called the "Front Page Headline Test." This test requires someone to examine their conduct in light of how would it look if their mother or father read what they did as the front headline for a major daily newspaper. Before propositioning a subordinate employee at a trade conference, imagine how would your parent or boss view your conduct if it appeared in large print, with a picture on the front page. Of course, the result would lead to lost revenue and a significantly tarnished image if the proposition constituted sexual harassment or a violation of either business or public policy. Therefore, you do not need to know all the laws or be cognizant of all the potential legal issues affecting the master-servant relationship. If any incident arises which you feel might lead to a reporter contacting you for a front-page story, stop what you are doing and talk with a qualified human resource professional or attorney.

The master-servant relationship is where the employment process starts. By properly identifying the relevant parties to the relationship, an employer can determine what steps to take to develop the employment relationship. If a worker is an independent contractor then the relationship has to be properly established and vigorously maintained. If a worker is indeed an employee, you have to determine if you will be forming the employment relationship with an individual or through a third party. No matter how the employment relationship is developed, an employer has to exercise constant vigilance to determine how laws, courts and personnel management trends are changing to properly continue the employment relationship. A master is supposed to be in charge of his/her own destiny. However, the master in the master-servant relationship has a host of external factors that influence his/her ability to control his/her destiny. Only through following a comprehensive employment risk management plan can an employer fully comprehend his/her destiny.

References

Bennett-Alexander, D.D. and Pincus, L.B. (1995). *Employment Law for Business*. Chicago, IL: Irwin.

Brager, D. (1997). "Avoiding payroll taxes, making motions on the pleadings, and defending indigents." *California Lawyer* (May): 31.

Champion, W. (1993). *Sports Law in a Nutshell*. St. Paul, MN: West Publishing Co.

Chruden, H., and Sherman, Jr., A. (1976). *Personnel Management*. 5th edition. Cincinnati, OH: South-Western Publishing Co.

Dixon, R.B. (1994). *The Federal Wage and Hour Laws*. San Francisco, CA: Society for Human Resource Management.

EEOC Notice Number 915.002 (1997). (December 3). www.eeoc.gov/docs/conting.txt.

Feliu, A. (1992). *Primer on Individual Employee Rights*. Washington, DC: BNA Books.

Fried, G. (1992). *Sports Law Reporter* July, 1(1): 2.

Fried, G. (ed.) (1994). "What's the difference between an employee and independent contractor? A lawsuit!" *Sports Facility Law Reporter* July, 1(6).

Frierson, J. (1994). *Preventing Employment Lawsuits: An employer's guide to hiring, discipline, and discharge*. Washington, DC: BNA Books

Holland, E. (1997). "Settlement seems near in UMSL case ex-women's basketball coach sued school." *St. Louis Post-Dispatch* (June 17): 2C.

Husband, P., Barrett, M., and Miller, M.R. (1993). "Independent con-
tractors, employees, the entertainment industry and the IRS-tax ad-
ministration problems head for Hollywood." *The Entertainment
and Sports Lawyer* Fall, 11(3): 3.
Jackson, M. (1997). "Companies waking up to napping." *Houston
Chronicle* (May 20): 1C.
Jones, D. (1997). "Growing gray area where blue- meets white-collar."
USA Today (March 13): B1.
Jones, D. (1997). "Leasing workers eases load for small companies."
USA Today (May 20): 1B.
"Jury Awards Fired Supermarket Manager $800K" (1997). *Los Angeles
Daily Journal* (July 24): 10.
"Justices Rule in Workplace Case" (1997). *Houston Chronicle*, (May
13): 4C.
Moore-ede, M. (1995). "When things go bump in the night." *ABA
Journal* (January): 56.
Neuborne, E. (1997). "Temporary workers getting short shrift." *USA
Today* (April 11): B1–2.
O'Connor, D. (1997). "The price of free labor." *ABA Journal* (Janu-
ary): 78.
Rothstein, M., Knapp, A., and Liebman, L. (1987). *Employment Law,
Cases and Material.* New York: The Foundation Press, Inc.
Stacey, J. (1997). "Where the temps are." *USA Today* (April 11): B1.
"Valuation of the temporary employment industry" (1996). *Corporate
Growth Report* (February 26).
van der Smissen, B. (1990). *Legal Liability and Risk Management for
Public and Private Entities.* Cincinnati, OH: Anderson Publishing
Co.
Verespej, M.A. (1996). "Skills on call." *Industry Week* 245(4): 46–51.
Werbel, J.D. and Hames, D.S. (1996). "Anti-nepotism reconsidered."
Group and Organization Management 21(3): 365–379.
Worsham, J. (1997). "Labor's new assault." *Nation's Business* 16
(June).

Cases

Adair v. United States, 208 U.S. 161 (1908).
Bonilla v. Oakland Scavenger Co., 697 F.2d 1297 (1982).
Cassista v. Community Foods, 5 Cal. 4th 1050 (1993).
Department of Labor Opinion Letter No. 874, October 1, 1968.
Donovan v. American Airlines, Inc., 686 F.2d 267 (5th Cir. 1982).

Donovan v. Sureway Cleaners, 656 F.2d 1368 (9th Cir. 1981).
Hill v. NCAA, 7 Cal. 4th 1 (S.C., 1994).
Lochner v. New York, 198 U.S. 45 (1905).
Magnuson v. Peak Technical Securities, Inc., 808 F. Supp. 500 (Cir. E.D. 1992).
McNeil v. NFL, 764 F. Supp. 1351 (U.S.D.C., MN, 1991).
NCAA v. Tarkanian, 488 U.S. 179 (1988).
NLRB v. Jones & Laughlin Steel Corp., 301 U.S. 1 (1937).
NLRB v. Western Temporary Services, 821 F.2d 1258 (7th Cir. 1987).
Powell v. NFL, 764 F. Supp. 1351 (U.S.D.C., MN, 1991).
Revenue Ruling, 75–41, 1975–1 C.B. 323.
Revenue Ruling, 87–41.
Reich v. Parker Fire Protection District, 992 F.2d 1023 (10th Cir. 1993).
Rutherford Food Corp. v. McComb, 331 U.S. 722 (1947).
Schechter Poultry Corp. v. United States, (295 U.S. 495 (1935).
Wilson v. Taylor, 733 F.2d 1539 (1984).

Statutes

California Labor Code Section 3710, et al.
Clayton Act, 15 U.S.C.A. Sect. 12.
Erdman Act, Chp. 370, 30 Stat. 424 (1898).
FLSA, 29 U.S.C. Section 201 et seq.
NIRA, 48 Stat. 195 (1933).
NLRA, 29 U.S.C.A. Section 151–169.
Norris-LaGuardia, 29 U.S.C.A. Sect. 101–115.
Public Law No. 95-600, 95th Cong. 2nd Session.
Revenue Act of 1978, Section 530, Section 1122 of the Small Business Job Protection.
Act of 1996, Pub. L. No. 104-188, 104th Cong. 2nd Sess. Amended.
Sherman Act, 15 U.S.C.A. Sect. 1.
Taft-Hartley Act, Title 229 U.S.C. Section 151.

Chapter 2

Creating the Job

Most wise business decisions are not made in haste. Hiring an employee should likewise not become an after thought, but rather should entail significant time and energy commitments. You have to determine if you even:

- need to hire a new employee,
- want to assume all the liability concerns associated with employees,
- can afford to pay all employee related expenses such as taxes, benefits, and workers' compensation insurance, and
- have enough work to keep the new employee busy.

If you determine that you do not need to hire a new employee, you can examine contracting for temporary workers or independent contractors. However, if you decide that you indeed need to hire a new employee, you need to create a detailed job analysis and job description to help facilitate finding the right employee. This chapter highlights the process leading up through identifying job components and recruiting to fill the open position.

1) Determining the Need

Vacated positions do not translate automatically into a need to hire. A detailed job analysis provides the employer with a tool to critique the skills, knowledge, and abilities demanded by the employer with the skills, knowledge, and abilities possessed by current employees. A job description benefits both the employer and the employee by defining required job qualifications and responsibilities. Both tools, the job analysis and the job description, provide many benefits including the opportunity to closely scrutinize existing demands with individual capabilities. Often, job responsibilities can be realigned so that a position does not need to be filled and related expenses (e.g., recruiting, interviewing, paperwork, and benefits) can be saved. Appendix D contains a checklist to help you determine the cost associated with hiring a new employee.

On the other hand, if hiring is necessary, it is important that the process be addressed in a prudent fashion. Management literature repetitively states that employees represent the greatest asset of any business (Miller, 1997). However, selecting the "best" employee for a given job represents a time consuming and often-laborious process. Choosing effective employees who "fit" well with a particular sport entity can deliver numerous benefits.

Benefits of Prudent Hiring

Four primary benefits accrue to employers who utilize prudent hiring practices. While these benefits appear simple enough, they represent critical concerns which can also lead to significant liability. If a sports facility hires an untrained facility manager, the owners can be held liable for any injuries which are attributable to the facility manager's inexperience.

1)   Retaining quality employees directly influences an employer's cost. For example, the entire employee recruiting, interviewing, training, and retaining costs can be exorbitant. Mercer (1988) estimated that employee turnover costs amounted to $20,080 for a computer programmer. Mercer's cost of turnover calculations included the following:

- The exit interview (time in salary for both interviewer and departing employee); $60.
- Administrative and record keeping actions; $30.
- Advertising for replacement person; $2,500.
- Pre-employment administrative and record-keeping requirements; $100
- Selection interview; $250.
- Employment tests; $40.
- Meetings to discuss potential candidates (time in salary for committee members); $250.
- Training booklets, manuals, and reports; $50.
- Education (salary and benefits of new employee for 10 days of training courses, workshops, and seminars); $2,400.
- Coaching of new employee (estimated by combining salary of new employee and current employee for 20 day period); $9,600, and
- Salary and benefits of new employee until he or she gets "up to par."

A study conducted by the Employment Management Association, indicates that hiring costs an approximate 15% of an individual's starting annual salary (Messmer, 1996). In other words, an employer could anticipate spending approximately $4,500 when hiring an Aquatic Manager at an annual salary of $30,000. That $4,500 can double if the initial hire quits.

Assume, for example, that an employer hires three individuals and expends 15% of their $30,000 annual salary on hiring costs. According to Messmer (1996), the employer will be paying $13,500 in hiring costs. Assuming all three individuals leave, the hiring costs double to $27,000. Thus, prudent hiring represents a significant investment and should be conducted in a thorough manner.

2)   Employee loyalty directly influences customer retention and related satisfaction. Many patrons view customer service provided by friendly and conscientious employees as an expected component of the provided sport service. For example, the literature states that 68% of all customers switch service providers due to discontentment with the way they were treated (Mariani, 1993). Customers appreciate employees who deliver that "personal touch." For example, assume a patron frequents a health club on a routine basis and enjoys the health club's congenial atmosphere, in part, because of the employees who have worked for the club for a number of years. Employees might address the patron by name and are familiar with a patron's exercise objectives. High employee turnover, in comparison, interrupts this congenial environment and provides an opportunity for patrons to defect to competing clubs. The employee influences the end-comsumer's satisfaction as well as vendor relationships. For example, a particular vendor may be unable to establish the same working relationship he or she had with a previous employee. The intangible costs associated with this broken relationship can include lost accounts and time spent reestablishing vendor relationships. Improving customer retention and satisfaction also influences a sports business' expense structure. As stated by Mariani (1993), it costs a business six times as much money to recruit a new customer than to keep a current customer. More specifically, it costs approximately $118.56 to recruit a new customer whereas it costs only $19.76 to retain a customer (Morgan, 1989). The approximate $100 savings per customer retained provides a sport business with capital for expansion, product improvement or other competitive positioning tactics that necessitate money.

3)   An amiable work environment is more likely to be fostered when individual employees are content and satisfied with their job and the work environment. Positive employee moral is critical to the success of any employer. A positive attitude is also contagious. Employees content with their job and comfortable working in the particular environment exude a positive message. On the other hand, a workplace plagued with internal fighting curtails productivity while sending negative messages to all stakeholders. Prudent hiring practices can mitigate the hiring of a person who is not capable or willing to perform stipulated job description requirements in a positive manner.

4)   Prudent hiring also reduces employer liability. As stated in *Supervision,*

> Of all employment-related lawsuits, 92 percent are related to having hired
> the wrong person, i.e., wrongful discharge, failure to promote, etc. It is
> much more difficult legally and much more stressful emotionally to ter-
> minate a poor employee than to hire the correct people in the first place
> ("When the wrong person gets the job," 1995, p. 11).

As evidenced from the above statement, prudent hiring decreases liability
while simultaneously enhancing productivity and customer satisfaction.

Prudent employment practices can help protect the employer's investment
in any one individual while at the same time defending itself against future legal action. The remainder of this chapter will look at various employee-related issues which can improve the hiring process and reduce the
likelihood that litigation will result from hiring a given job applicant.

2) Developing Precise Job Descriptions

The key to hiring the right employee from the very beginning involves
developing appropriate job descriptions. However, it is impossible to develop job descriptions without first breaking a job down to its most basic
elements which creates a job analysis.

The Job Analysis

A job analysis represents the skills, knowledge, and abilities necessary
to perform a particular job (Clifford, 1994). These terms can be defined
as follows:

> Skill is having performed the work; knowledge is knowing how to per-
> form the work but not having performed it; and ability is having the phys-
> ical, emotional, intellectual, and psychological ability to perform the work
> but neither having done the work nor having been trained to do the work
> (Clifford, 1994).

Many sport business employees, if asked to describe how they perform a
particular job (e.g., soliciting sponsorship dollars, manage a fitness facility) would simply respond with, "I don't know, I just do it." Unfortunately,
this often leaves employers facing a dilemma. Unsure of what intrinsic
tasks are required, it is often easiest to hire another person just like the
last employee who occupied the particular job. In other words, if the sports
information employee, for example, was a male, the employer may eliminate the consideration of any female candidates regardless of qualifications. Unfortunately, this might perpetuate the glass ceiling that exists for
many women and minorities. Employers will find that developing and

using a job analysis can facilitate workplace efficiencies, effectiveness, and help rebut numerous discrimination claims.

Creating the Job Analysis

A job analysis should exist for every job within a business. Creating a job analysis typically begins by gathering all information pertaining to a particular job. Internal documents that might be useful include operation manuals, policy manuals, training materials, organization charts and previous job analyses (Carrell, Kuzmits, and Elbert, 1992). In addition, an interview with incumbent personnel and position supervisors provides valuable information. Direct observation provides additional valuable insight to jobs and their required skills, knowledge and abilities.

Only job specific work behaviors should be analyzed and recorded (Ashe, 1980; "Uniform guidelines," 1993; Webster, 1988). For example, a job analysis for a lifeguard position might reveal that individuals need good eyesight in order to see potential victims, certified and licensed rescue skills, ability to swim and execute rescues for individuals of all sizes and weights, etc. It would be irrelevant to the particular job whether the individual lifeguard was "bronzed and beautiful," for example. As mentioned above, identifying the qualifications, characteristics and attributes of individuals currently engaged in a particular job does not constitute a job analysis.

Benefits of the Job Analysis

There are six primary benefits associated with developing a job analysis:

1)   Undergoing a job analysis is recommended by the EEOC in their 1978 Uniform Guidelines for each position. The EEOC recommends using a job analysis for employee recruitment and selection purposes (Clifford, 1994). The job analysis reduces the likelihood that a job description will be made which includes unessential job functions and unnecessary educational or certification requirements that can result in a discrimination claim. If the EEOC investigates a discrimination claim, one of the first documents they will want to examine is the job analysis and job description.

2)   Job descriptions define a position's required duties and responsibilities. Listing duties and responsibilities is made more exact by reference to the respective job analysis. An accurate job description creates a win-win scenario for both the employer and the prospective employee. The sport business benefits as the costs associated with screening unqualified candidates who do not have required skills is reduced. The prospective employee benefits as he or she is not misled regarding job expectations.

3)   Both managers and employees should be involved in designing or redesigning the job analysis. This process can provide valuable insight for both managers and employees (Clifford, 1994). Managers can learn first hand exactly what, how and why a front line employee does what he or she does. In addition, management is provided with opportunities to educate employees as to why certain functions are integral to the success of the entire business. Similarly, employee's often find management's interest in their position and the opportunity to interact with management rewarding.

4)   It is estimated that adults will change careers approximately six times during his or her working life. As employees depart, it is a natural tendency for employers to automatically commence the hiring process. Routine job analyses, however, enables you to better gage change within the workplace. For example, in some situations, consumer demand, technology, the sport product line, product extensions or the target market may have changed in such a way that a particular position becomes obsolete. In this situation, an employer may save a great deal of time and money by reallocating job responsibilities among existing employees.

5)   New sport businesses and sport businesses pursuing unfamiliar territories (e.g., new programs, target markets) may need to offer employee training programs. A job analysis enables an employer to develop training programs around needed skills, knowledge and abilities (see Chapter 6 for more information on job training).

6)   The abilities, knowledge, and skills contained in one job are often compared to another job when ascertaining pay scales. Logically, an employer can deduce that a particular position requiring extensive abilities, knowledge and skills (e.g., an athletic trainer) requires a higher pay structure than other positions requiring minimal abilities, knowledge and skills (e.g., front desk receptionist). In fact, the Equal Pay Act requires that you defend differential pay scales among employees. A documented job analysis better insulates you from discrimination claims regarding employee compensation differences.

The Job Description

The job description represents one of the most basic and common human relation's tools (Carrell, Kuzmits, and Elbert, 1992). It is often the first impression a potential employee has of an employer. Although a common tool, its importance and relevance has significantly escalated in the last decade as a result of government regulation, litigation, downsizing and increased competition. There is no standardized or required job description format. However, five general tenets of most job descriptions include a job title, essential job duties and responsibilities, job qualifications, starting date and name and address of the contact person.

The essential job qualifications and responsibilities can be derived from the job analysis. Job descriptions representing new jobs should be designed after careful thought and study regarding what a particular job will actually entail. A review of a competitor's job descriptions or prescribed job description forms available through self-study books and computer programs are also useful starting points. Verbs effectively describe to the reader the nature of the job. Common job description terms include:

- supervise,
- train,
- host,
- organize,
- plan,
- schedule,
- lift,
- carry,
- reach,
- diagram,
- maintain,
- clean, etc.

Job duties and responsibilities that are determined to be "nonessential" are suspect to allegations of discrimination (see Chapter 4). Managers should also pay heed to OSHA regulations requiring that job descriptions identify elements of the job "which endanger health, or are considered unsatisfactory or distasteful to the majority of the population" (Carrell, Kuzmits, and Elbert, 1992). One author suggests using a disclaimer at the bottom of the job description to reduce an employer's potential liability. Such a disclaimer could provide that:

> Job descriptions are not intended to be and should not be construed to be a complete list of all the duties and responsibilities performed by incumbents, nor do they constitute an employment contract. Duties, responsibilities, and expectations may be added, deleted, or changed at any time at management's discretion. Further, job descriptions do not represent a complete list of all the performance expectations and characteristics of individuals required to perform a job adequately (Degner, 1995).

The disclaimer above serves as a defense if an employee argues that an employer considered the individual's ability to perform responsibilities not listed in the job description when making employment decisions (e.g., promoting, demoting). Unfortunately, the disclaimer can also create ambiguity for the employee and hardship for the employer. For example, employers evaluating an employee on undefined tasks are less likely to find the job description helpful in preparing a defense to justify adversarial actions (e.g., terminations, demotions). In other words, a demoted employee who failed to perform an unlisted duty or responsibility could successfully argue that he or she was not aware of employer's expectations.

The job qualification section represents another area subject to intense scrutinization. This section emphasizes those minimum qualifications necessary to adequately perform a particular job. Observable skills required, necessary knowledge, abilities and required degrees, certifications and/or licenses should be itemized in this section of the job description. For example, a sports information director might be required to know the rules of the game, strategy, conference tournament schedules, etc. This individual might also be required to possess the skills to operate a fax machine, a computer, e-mail, etc. Further, this individual must have the ability to write media clips detailing sporting events. Required degrees and certifications should be itemized cautiously as the stated requirement must be essential to effective job performance and not serve as a tool to eliminate otherwise qualified candidates (*Griggs v. Duke*, 1971). Thus, do not ask a potential janitor for a college degree if someone with a high school education can perform the job.

A "good" job description can provide various benefits, some of which are also realized when developing and using a job analysis. The primary legal benefit associated with job descriptions is the development of a bonafide occupational qualification (BFOQ). BFOQ are more thoroughly discussed in Chapter 4. However, it is worth noting at this point that an employer can legally discriminate against potential job applicants if the job applicant does not meet the job's BFOQ requirements. Thus, if a sports promoter produces a men's boxing match, being male would be a BFOQ. If a job description includes a provision that the fighters have to be male, a female applicant can be excluded from consideration based on the express BFOQ in the job description. In addition to the BFOQ defense, job descriptions provide ten additional benefits associated with a well-defined job description.

1)   Employee recruitment is a very timely and expensive process. Vague and nebulous job descriptions tend to generate numerous applicant responses as the job itself and related responsibilities and qualifications are not clearly defined. Consequently, an employer may receive numerous applications from marginally qualified individuals. The time and expense required in handling, reviewing and processing these applications can be minimized by the careful crafting of a job description which best represents the actual job, and communicate key job components to prospective applicants.

2)   Carefully crafted job descriptions provide the employer-designated interviewer with a uniform slate of questions which can be asked to every candidate. For example, if one of the job qualifications is "supervise and

train lifeguards" appropriate interview questions might include the following:

- Have you ever been responsible for lifeguard supervision? If so, please elaborate.
- What type of training programs would you design for your lifeguards?
- How often would you have in-service training for your lifeguards?

Standardized questions developed prior to the interview process reduce the chance of bias as all candidates are asked identical questions.

3)   Job descriptions help defines employee expectations. Role clarity reduces employee tension and related stress while simultaneously increasing customer service (Rogers, Clow, and Kash, 1994).

> It is very difficult to serve customers well when employees are unhappy and disgruntled about some aspect of their job. As job tension rises, job satisfaction declines. As job satisfaction declines, employee turnover and absenteeism will rise and customers devaluate the quality of both the product and service experience (Rogers, 1994).

Employees are more motivated toward a prescribed goal and tend to perform better when management expectations are clearly defined (Bell and Zempke, 1992). Job descriptions help define and communicate an employer's expectations to the employee and provide a benchmark for performance appraisals.

4)   Most new employees, and even some seasoned employees, tend to want to do too much. Fearful of saying "no" or appearing to be indifferent, lazy or insubordinate, employees often take on more than they can handle and become "spread too thin." Stellar employees, once able and capable of performing prescribed tasks in an exemplary fashion, can become mediocre. A defined job description serves as a continual reminder to the employee of the primary responsibilities that he or she was hired to perform. Further, a defined job description can mitigate injuries and resultant liability as employees avoid engaging in tasks which they are not trained or competent (e.g., using sophisticated machinery or equipment improperly).

5)   Job descriptions provide information regarding job promotions and what an employee needs to accomplish to reach the next level. Employers should have a notebook containing all employee job descriptions. The particular notebook, in turn, remains accessible to any interested employee. Having job descriptions accessible to all employees benefits those individuals seeking to ascertain the training and skills necessary for promotion. Further, the additional training pursued by employees in hopes

of a possible promotion at a later point in time makes for a more educated work force engaging in more prudent and productive decision making.

6)   The job description is a primary tool in ascertaining what criteria to use when evaluating employees. The job description benefits both the employees and management throughout the evaluation process. Employees receiving unfavorable evaluations due to evaluative criteria unrelated to their job description may have a cause of action against their employer or legitimate grounds to appeal an adverse disciplinary decision. Similarly, employers taking unfavorable actions against employees failing to fulfill job description criteria have a legally defensible tool at their hands should a disgruntled employee legally challenge their actions. Further, job descriptions for individuals performing identical jobs help ensure standardization and fairness when making decisions regarding promotions, demotions, pay and other employment related issues.

7)   Job descriptions enable managers to compare job requirements (e.g., qualifications and responsibilities) and pay, for example, of a particular position with other job requirements of perceived comparable jobs. Comparisons can be made with other jobs within a company as well as with comparable jobs with other similar businesses. As espoused by motivational theories (e.g., the equity theory), employees are motivated when they feel like they are putting in comparable work effort for comparable pay (Gordon, 1991). Job descriptions can be used by employers to ensure that workloads remain equitable and that similar pay is being awarded to individuals performing similar work requiring similar skills, knowledge and abilities.

8)   Job descriptions can help facilitate job outplacement efforts. Employers forced to downsize may enhance public relations and better fulfill ethical responsibilities by helping employees find other work. The job description serves as a valuable tool in the identifying other jobs requiring similar qualifications. Further, the job description is useful in updating or designing a former employee's resume.

9)   Job descriptions can document the distinction between an exempt and nonexempt employee that is integral to compliance with wage and hour laws such as overtime pay. Factors important to the exemption versus non-exemption distinction can include:

- management responsibilities,
- decision making,
- policy making,
- independent judgment and discretion,
- knowledge of an advanced type, and
- creative work (Dixon, 1994).

For example, exempt positions do not receive overtime monies for working overtime hours. On the other hand, non-exempt positions require overtime pay when appropriate. The section of the job description detailing job duties and responsibilities, as well as job qualifications, is likely to convey the employee's status if a Fair Labor Standards Act (FLSA) claim is raised.

10)   In many circumstances, the employer may find that a vacated position does not need to be filled (Messmer, 1996). An analysis of the prior job description, in accordance with an analysis of internal and external changes (e.g., a changing economy, sport product trends, consumer demographics, the sport product line) may convey that the responsibilities associated with the vacated position are: (a) no longer needed, (b) can be reallocated to another position or (c) can be filled by seasonal or part-time workers.

As demonstrated by the points above, significant benefits can be derived from developing job descriptions. Most employers realize the benefits attached to job descriptions, but do not know where to begin. Appendix E has two sample job descriptions demonstrating the depth which can be contained within a comprehensive job description. An employer can also access additional job information from the Dictionary of Occupational Titles (DOT) compiled by the U.S. Employment Services of the Manpower Administration (Chruden and Sherman, 1976). In addition to the sample job descriptions contained within this guide, you can also obtain computer software that can assist you in developing job descriptions. However, as with any "off the self" product, you have to make sure the job description accurately reflects your job and not what is done at a different facility or program.

3) Methods for Finding Employees

You have various avenues available when recruiting employees. Terpstra's survey (1996) of 201 Human Resource executives revealed that the top nine recruitment tools (in order of perceived value) are:

- employee referrals,
- college recruiting,
- executive search firms,
- professional associations,
- want ads,
- direct applications,
- private employment agencies,
- public employment agencies, and
- unions.

As with many issues in managing a sport business, the best recruitment methods will depend on the job itself and the needed competencies. For example, an attractive job with a professional sports team will probably draw numerous unsolicited applications and employment agencies trying to fill the spot. The only qualified person who applied might get lost in the process. Employers cannot rely upon such haphazard options which forces employers to utilize various recruitment alternatives. Primary recruitment alternatives can be bifurcated into external recruitment and internal recruitment options. Each option has specific benefits that might be more appropriate then other options and the appropriate recruitment technique is often based on the job description.

External Recruitment

Two primary advantages of conducting searches through external sources include the opportunity to recruit a more diverse work force and the recruitment of different ideas. First, employers often find solace in hiring individuals like themselves, someone who "thinks like I do." In other words, the person doing the hiring may think that a particular applicant would make the best employee since the individual is a clone of himself or herself. Unfortunately, this mentality is problematic as the employer may be denying employment opportunities to otherwise qualified candidates. Further, there is an adage that says, "If two managers think alike, then one of them is not needed." Businesses flourish via combined wisdom, insights, and experiences; not through hiring "yes" people.

Second, employees who have worked only for one particular employer often are more prone to "operate in a vacuum." In other words, these employees become somewhat immune, complacent and stagnant regarding:

- what the competition is doing,
- new management concepts and ideas taught by university scholars,
- legislation which must be adhered to, and
- challenges presented by a changing economy.

Further, the limitations associated with groupthink may evolve. Many of the limitations listed above can be circumvented via stringent in-service training. However, it is undisputed that hiring someone who has worked in other industries may provide a competitive advantage to employees as existing ideas and thought processes are challenged by the new hire.

External Recruitment Alternatives

Employers often employ one or more of the following external search facilitators in an effort to hire the best candidate for a particular job.

a) Public Employment Agencies

Public employment agencies exist in every state and are funded with federal and state monies. The individuals pursuing employment through such agencies tend to be unskilled and seeking entry-level employment. A public employment agency could provide a good source of applicants when hiring, for example, concession vendors, parking attendants or maintenance workers. The public agency doesn't typically conduct the search (e.g., design the job description, screen applicants, conduct interviews), but rather sends the employer potential candidates for consideration (Stover, 1994). Then it is up to you to screen the applicants for the employee(s) you desire.

b) Private Employment Agencies

Private employment agencies present numerous advantages to employers in the sport industry. Two primary advantages realized by the employer include costs associated with the hiring process itself and the ability to shift liability to the private employment agency. First, using a private employment agency eliminates expenses associated with a nation-wide search. For example, a private employment agency can reduce expenses associated with distributing hundreds of job descriptions, sorting through thousands of incoming applications and resumes, sending follow-up letters, making phone calls, soliciting and interviewing references, etc. Furthermore, the employer can avoid numerous EEOC record keeping requirements. Utilizing the services of a private employment agency allows the employer to carry on routine operations without interruption. Second, sport business managers can often transfer liability associated with the hiring process (e.g., allegations of discrimination) by utilizing an employment agency. As explained by Lord, the editor of *Executive Recruiter News* and other industry newsletters:

> Good search consultants know the law and abide by it. Further, a good search consultant won't simply do whatever you ask, but will let you know if there's something in your request that could raise a legal problem. (Stover, 1994).

Another benefit associated with private employment agencies is the option of trying out employees before hiring an employee on a full-time basis. An employer can contract with an agency to try a temporary worker for several months. If the employer decides to keep the temporary worker, they pay the agency a percentage fee (traditionally based on the prospective salary) and the temporary worker becomes a new employee. This option provides the employer with the option of testing a worker without assuming the liability potential associated with having to terminate an employee who does not work out. Since the temporary worker is under contract, if the employer is dissatisfied with their performance, they are not required to retain that individual and the agency could send a replacement temporary worker.

Disadvantages associated with using a private employment agency include expense and a loss of control. Private employment agencies generally charge the employer 30% of the recruited individual's first year annual salary plus incurred expenses. For many small employers or sport businesses that are operating near or below break-even levels, using a private employment agency is cost prohibitive. Employers also lose some control that they would otherwise retain over an employee. As a quote in Small Business Forum summarizes (Stover, 1994). "Control . . . a legitimate issue if you are looking for someone you have to be able to trust." Many sport business managers choose to engage in the hiring process so that intangible nuances can be detected and mentally registered should two equally qualified candidates top the list of eligible candidates. Most private employment agencies enable the employer to retain as much (or as little) control as desired. For example, sport businesses can contract to write their own job descriptions or be involved in the actual interview process if so desired. An additional clause stipulating that the private employment agency agrees to not recruit your current employees away from you is suggested as a prudent practice (Stover, 1994).

An additional concern associated with working with employment agencies involves being liable for their actions. Under several federal statutes, such as ADA and Title VII, an employer is liable for the discriminatory conduct of an employment agency. Thus, if you engage an employment agency to help satisfy employment needs, you need to make sure the agency is reputable and follows all applicable laws. Compliance can be assisted by including a clause in the engagement contract requiring the agency to comply with all anti-discrimination laws and holding you, the employer, harmless for any liability that might be attached to the agency's failure to comply with discrimination laws. The same indemnity principle applies to the agency covering other requirements such as purchasing workers' compensation coverage.

c) College Career Placement Centers

Most universities and colleges have career placement centers on campuses. The college career placement center benefits employers as you can go to a particular campus and interview numerous potential candidates in an efficient and timely manner. Sport businesses often recruit on only select campuses in which they are intimately familiar with the particular sport administration or related degree curriculum. Sport businesses can bypass the college placement center and directly contact university sport administration, physical education, hotel and restaurant administration or related departments. The employer saves monies associated with travel expenses, lodging and meals for potential candidates as initial interviewing occurs at one central location (i.e., the college campus). Furthermore, individuals employed by the university reduce an employer's expenses associated with interview scheduling, sorting resumes and other related tasks. The National Park Service and Disney World's Magic Kingdom College represent two sport-related businesses that utilize college career placement centers (Culkin and Kirsch, 1986).

d) Newspapers, Trade Magazines and Journals

Many employers find newspaper, trade magazine and journal placements effective in generating qualified candidates. The market niche found by many newspapers, magazines and journals makes this avenue very effective in targeting a special population of potentially qualified applicants. For example, a golf course seeking an Administrative Assistant might find it attractive to place an advertisement in Golf Digest, the Sporting Goods Dealer and/or other golf related publications. Similarly, a sports park (e.g., amusement rides, batting cages, go-karts and arcade) might find it beneficial to place an ad in Athletic Business, Amusement Business and/or Facility Manager. Career Connections, a newsletter published by Franklin Quest, lists 50–75 jobs in the sport industry (e.g., retail, athletics and manufacturing) on a bimonthly basis. Sports Careers and Sports Employment Weekly publish sports industry specific job listings. In addition, several on-line magazines now list sports employment opportunities.

Employers should refer to subsequent chapters (such as Chapter 4) regarding employment legislation to better ensure that advertisements placed in newsletters are legally defensible. For example, you should avoid using terms such as "young," "energetic," "recent College grad" or "good health" which could be construed as trying to exclude older job applicants. In addition, you should avoid sexist terms such as salesman and use instead salesperson. Appendix F highlights various issues associated with placing classified and newspaper advertisements. While placing newspaper advertisements does not appear to be a difficult task, in all actuality, the process should be a complex process analyzing newspaper circulation trends, readership surveys and other data. This data can assist you in defending your hiring practice through demonstrating that you are actively recruiting minority candidates through placing advertisements in newspapers which are read or received by minorities.

e) Professional Associations

Membership in professional associations provides numerous benefits. Many professional associations such as the North American Society for

Sport Management (NASSM), Society for the Study of Legal Aspects of Sports and Physical Activity (SSLASPA), Sports Turf Managers Association and the American Alliance of Physical Education, Recreation and Dance (AAHPERD) provide members with all or some of the following:

- networking opportunities,
- receipt of a journal(s) and/or newsletters,
- opportunities to present and listen to current research, and
- leadership opportunities to serve the profession and constituency.

In addition, most professional associations provide members with a job exchange networking opportunity. For example, at AAHPERD's conventions, members are allowed to both solicit and interview potential candidates while other members are able to market their skills, knowledge, and abilities. Associations' communications (e.g., journals, newsletters and home pages) also often include a job opportunities listing and/or classified employment section.

f) Internet

The Internet represents a communication medium that has permeated schools, homes and businesses. Internet information is vast, including information on current events, news, shopping, sports, recreation, politics, religion, etc. Similarly, networks exist for the exchange of job information. For example, employers could consider posting jobs on the following sites:

- Online Sports Career Center
  http://www.onlinesports.com/pages/CareerCenter.html
- SportWerk Consulting, Inc.
  http://www.onlinesports.com/sportwerk/
- Sports Business Center at Online Sports
  http://www.onlinesports.com/pages/BusinessCenter.html

Employers can realize two primary benefits when advertising jobs on the Internet. First, cost reductions associated with postage, paper and staff can be reduced. When undertaking a nationwide search, these savings can be significant. Second, time delays associated the dissemination of information through the U.S. Postal mail are eliminated. In other words, people all over the nation can instantaneously receive a job announcement whereas announcements traveling through the traditional postal mail may take as long as five days. Furthermore, using e-mail can help reduce phone and postage expense while speeding-up the entire application process.

An additional benefit that can be accessed by using the Internet involves attracting international candidates. Sometimes, it is impossible to find the right candidate in your region, or even throughout the United States. For example, if you are searching for a cricket or badminton coach, the prospect of landing a highly qualified candidate is greatly increased when candidates in other countries can access your Internet advertisements. Special care should be taken with international employees to ensure they can work in your state or region. Special concerns can range from visa status to taxing concerns. Chapter 3 addresses some of these issues, but a competent immigration attorney should be contacted to assist in the hiring process.

One disadvantage employers encounter when distributing announcements solely through the Internet is the potential for a disparate impact cause of action. One could argue, for example, that an employer intentionally recruited from the affluent white upper class population while negating other qualified candidates in a protected class who are unable to afford access to the Internet and its related services.

g) Internships

The internship represents a "win-win" situation for both the employer and the potential employee. Most, but not all interns, are students completing degree requirements. Sport employers are able to use the internship as a way to gain competent employees at an affordable price. Further, as indicated by Patrick Scheetz's research, an author and director of the Collegiate Employment Research Institute at Michigan State University, 50% of new hires completed career-related internships (Taylor, 1997). As the internship progresses, the employer can assess whether the intern has the traits and characteristics desirable in full-time employees. Similarly, the intern can ascertain if the sport business represents the career choice they wish to pursue and whether the particular employer provides a work environment conducive to growth and success. Internships can be researched on the web at www.tripod.com/work/internships.

While internships represent for many the chance to obtain free labor, as discussed in Chapter 1, you can be liable for FLSA violations if interns do not in fact obtain meaningful experience. You can also be liable for any negligent conduct that the intern caused.

h) Walk-in Applicants

Walk-in applicants represent candidates who either by word-of-mouth, or simply from being in the right place at the right time, discover a job opening. Monies saved in the recruiting process itself represent a primary advantage associated with the walk-in applicant. Similar to employers recruiting via college career placement centers, employers having access to walk-in applicants avoid expenses associated with transporting, housing and dining potential employees. However, such expenses are normally minimal for walk-in applicants as such applicants normally fill low-level positions where little money is dedicated to the hiring process.

Walk-in applicants, however, also present two primary disadvantages. First, the walk-in candidate may not be genuinely interested in, or qualified for, the particular job. Rather, the individual candidate desperate for a job (any job) may be applying for every and any job available, regardless of his or her qualifications. This can lead to potential negligent hiring concerns and increased hiring costs.

Second, walk-in applicants may apply because they hear of the opening via word-of-mouth and/or live in proximity to the place of business. In this situation, disparate impact allegations could ensue while advantages associated with a diverse work environment are forfeited. For example, assume a health club is located in a very affluent, elite part of town. Walk-in applicants will most likely represent the same demographic make-up of the surrounding community. Regardless of an individual's actual interest in a particular job, allegations of disparate impact could come from a protected class that was not made aware of the job opening.

i) Unions

While unions are only sometimes seen in the sport industry (primarily with professional sport, some sport facilities, and government employees such as public high school teachers/coaches), you should still be aware of various union-related concerns. While Chapter 14 covers union related issues, you should keep in mind that if you need special assistance such as laborers, electricians, construction personnel and related trade professionals, you could try to access hiring halls. Union hiring halls provides you with the comfort of knowing that all individuals associated with the hall have reached a certain status within the union such as apprentice or master craftsperson status.

Internal Recruitment

As noted by the above survey, employee referrals represent the number one recruiting mode for many businesses, including sport businesses. Many employers prefer to hire from among their current employees or to hire based upon a referral from a trusted employee (Terpstra, 1996).

Five primary benefits are gained by adopting and adhering to a policy of filling vacated or new jobs with internal candidates (i.e., candidates currently working for the employer).

1)   Many argue that internal hiring boosts the morale of current employees as clear and distinct opportunities for advancement and promo-

tion are recognized. Even if individual employees do not pursue the particular opening, there is a feeling that employers respect employees enough to recognize their own strengths and weaknesses.

2)   Employers typically have a better understanding of current employee's characteristics and capabilities. Employers hiring current employees have seen these individuals working on a daily basis; they have witnessed the individual's strengths and weaknesses while observing performance under pressure and tension. In comparison, hiring a new employee always represents some risk. Employers never know for sure a new employee's work ethic, mood swings, ability to work under strict deadlines, respect for colleagues, administrators, and the customer and an employee's future plans and aspirations.

3)   Costs associated with recruiting and training are significantly reduced when hiring or promoting internal candidates. As mentioned earlier, the entire hiring process represents a significant expense for an employer. Internal recruitment and hiring reduces expenses associated with recruiting, entertaining and orientating an otherwise new employee.

4)   The time spent learning the tasks of a particular job is reduced when hiring internally. As indicated by Mellen's research (1995) on insurance agents, productivity was 25% greater for individuals hired internally versus externally. Current employees familiar with the sport business structure, the sport product mix and product line and the responsibilities of various employees and departments are able to access needed information and make necessary decisions more efficiently and expeditiously when compared with new employees.

5)   Research indicates that internal candidates are more likely to remain loyal to a particular organization for a greater duration of time (Mellen, 1995). The internal candidate's greater understanding of what a particular job entails, management expectations and the work required is suggested as a contributing factor to this enhanced longevity.

Internal Hiring Disadvantages

Internal hiring practices risk promoting individuals comfortable with current sport products and related operations. Employees too comfortable with the status quo and the current work environment often become reluctant to change, viewing sport product extensions or new sport product introductions as an attempt by a "rookie" to create chaos in the work environment. Individuals and their comments such as, "They just don't understand the way we do things around here," can become insurmountable obstacles.

In addition, internal hiring tends to perpetuate a more homogeneous environment as employers and supervisors tend to promote those with similar traits, characteristics, knowledge, skills and abilities. Internal hiring may sacrifice the competitive advantages associated with a diverse work force and can lead to discrimination claims.

Wrap Up ...

A great deal of work is involved, and a great deal of liability exists, when hiring new employees or ascertaining the need to replace individuals who held current positions in a sport business. The job analysis serves as a tool to facilitate the development of the job description. The job description forces employers to identify specific job qualifications and responsibilities. The qualifications prove essential in defending many employment-based claims such as discrimination or wrongful termination. Both tools provide many benefits to the work force. Employers have a wide variety of resources to use in the employee selection process. Both external and internal recruitment sources provide employers with viable candidates. Combining recruitment sources enables employers to capitalize on benefits offered through the various alternatives. Regardless, it is imperative that employers exercise prudence during the job creation process as choosing the right employee involves both short- and long-term financial and legal implications.

References

Ashe, R.L., and McRae, G.S. (1985). "Performance evaluations go to court in the 1980s." *Mercer Law Review* 36(3): 887–905.

Bell, C.R., and Zempke, R. (1992). *Managing Knock Your Socks Off Service*. New York: American Management Association.

Carrell, M.R., Kuzmits, F.E., and Elbert, N.F. (1992). *Personnel/human Resource Management*. 4th edition. New York: Macmillan.

Chruden, H., and Sherman, Jr., A. (1976). *Personnel Management*. 5th edition. Cincinnati, OH: South-Western Publishing Co.

Clifford, J.P. (1994). "Job analysis: Why do it, and how should it be done?" *Public Personnel Management* 32(2): 321–340.

Culkin, D.F., and Kirsch, S.L. (1986). *Managing Human Resources in Recreation, Parks, and Leisure Services*. New York: Macmillan Publishing Company.

Degner, J. (1995). "Writing job descriptions that work." *Executive* 35(6): 13–17.

Dixon, R.B. (1994). *The Federal Wage and Hour Laws*. San Francisco, CA: Society for Human Resource Management.

Ford, R., and McLaughlin, F. (1986). "Nepotism: Boon or bane." *Personnel Administrator* 31: 79–89.

Gordon, J.R. (1991). *Organizational Behavior*. Boston, MA: Allyn and Bacon.

Mariani, B. (1993). "The importance of customer service." *The Professional Skier* (Fall): 51–52.

Mellen, N.A. (1995). "Which are better? Personal v. impersonal recruiting services." *Manager's Magazine* 70(1): 30–32.

Mercer, M.W. (1988). "Turnover: Reducing the costs." *Personnel* (December): 36–42.

Messmer, M. (1996). "The politics of hiring." *Journal of Accountancy*, 181(4): 59–61.

Miller, L.K. (1997). *Sport Business Management*. Gaithersburg, MD: Aspen Publications.

Morgan, R.L. (1989). *Calming upset customers*. Los Altos, CA: Crisp Publications, Inc.

Rogers, J.D., Clow, K.E. and Kash, T.J. (1994). "Increasing job satisfaction of service personnel." *Journal of Services Marketing* 8(1): 14–26.

Stover, C. (1994). "I want to hire a top-level employee. How do I go about it?" *Small Business Forum* 12(2): 6–26.

Taylor, E.J. (1997). "The new rung on the corporate ladder." *Tools for Life from Tripod* 1(2): 12–19.

Terpstra, D.E. (1996). "Recruitment and selection: the search for effective methods." *HR Focus* 73(5): 16+.

Uniform guidelines on employee selection procedures. (1993 edition). 29 CFR Ch. XIV-7.

Webster, G.D. (1988). "The law of employee evaluations." *Association Management* 38(9): 118–119.

"When the wrong person gets the job..." (1995). *Supervision* (May): p. 11.

Case

Griggs v. Duke, 401 U.S. 424 (1971).

Chapter 3

Employee Information Gathering

The first step undertaken in determining what information will be required for evaluating a job applicant is a thorough understanding of the potential employer's goals and objectives. Will the person you need to hire further in some significant manner your goals? The next step involves analyzing what duties and responsibilities the individual worker will have to undertake. This information will provide the potential applicant with the knowledge of what he or she can expect if hired. The third step in the process requires establishing rational and measurable criterion for success. Individual employees will need to know what minimum effort will be required in order to help avoid termination. The fourth step in the evaluation process requires determining specific traits, skills, abilities and qualities required by any applicant. While it might be advantageous to specify certain skills, if at all possible, this step should focus on the results to be obtained rather than requiring a specific skill. Thus, the job specification analysis can determine that a secretary needs to be able to *process* 100 words a minute rather than *typing* 100 words per minute. An individual with arthritis might not be able to type 100 words a minutes, but might be able to use a voice synthesizer to process 100 words a minute. This constitutes reasonable accommodations required by the Americans with Disabilities Act. The last component of the evaluation process is the development of specific devises to evaluate a potential employee. These instruments should measure an applicant's ability to perform the specified job requirements set forth in the job description. Instruments can include forms such as an application form or could entail physical fitness tests that do not violate the law. This chapter will focus on the information that is needed to properly evaluate an applicant and the various steps needed or allowed for acquiring such information. There are no short cuts in this process. There are no miracle pills that expedite the process nor should one ever be invented. Any shortcuts in the process can lead to disaster. This is especially accurate in the sports and fitness industries where individuals can be called upon to engage in various activities ranging from cleaning and sales work to supervising athletic facilities and performing life saving exercises. While it is very difficult to find the one applicant who can perform all the defined job functions, all applicants have to be thoroughly screened to ensure the top candidates can competently perform the job's essential functions. The process outlined below provides a framework for properly screening both job applicants and prospective volunteers. Gathering information on employees is a dynamic process which can range from pre-application materials through employee performance evaluations.

1) Application Process

Many employers require potential job applicants to complete an application form. Other potential employees start the application process by seeing an advertisement in the paper and send a cover letter and resume for consideration. Other potential employees send unsolicited resumes to potential employers. This is especially true in the sports industry. So many individuals are infatuated with the sports industry that they send countless resumes to professional teams and collegiate programs in search of part-time, full-time, volunteer or intern positions. These unsolicited resumes represent a significant liability concern. When any unsolicited resumes are received, you should respond to them with a letter specifically stating that that you are not currently accepting resumes to fill any position. You should not mention that you have reviewed, read, circulated or considered the resume or the applicant's qualifications (Adler and Coleman, 1995). Likewise, you should not mention that the resume was processed or will be put in a file for future consideration. The primary reason why you should take the above mentioned steps is based on the Equal Employment Opportunity Commission's rules which require all accepted applications to be kept on file for two years after their receipt (Adler and Coleman, 1995). Therefore, if you accept unsolicited resumes, you will have a major record keeping concern for several years. Furthermore, unless a potential job opening has an express expiration time period, you will have an obligation to review each resume received whenever a position becomes available (Adler and Coleman, 1995).

Application Form

Application forms represent the best opportunity to target the information you want rather than having an applicant provide only the information they think you might want to see. Thus, careful consideration has to be given to design a simple, but informative application form. Furthermore, an application should provide useful information in a convenient format. The application represents the first chance an employer might have to educate applicants about the company and any specific rules that will be followed during the employment process. As mentioned above, the EEOC specifies significant documentation requirements and application re-review if no application termination date is specifically stated. Thus, the application form should specifically mention in bold print that the application is only valid for a certain time and a certain specific position. The application should further indicate that if the applicant want to apply at a later date or for a different position, they would be required to complete an additional application.

The following sample language is useful to appear at or near the beginning of the application form:

> This application will be kept current and valid only for two weeks from the date the application is submitted. After the two week period, if you are still interested in employment, you will need to reapply by completing a new application (Adler and Coleman, 1995).

All the information requested in the application needs to comply with the law. The wide range of questions that can and cannot be asked can fill a complete book. Every question has to be examined to determine if there is either a direct or indirect potential that the question might screen out a disproportionate number of otherwise qualified candidates. Thus, requiring an applicant to have a college degree to perform janitorial duties would have a disproportionate impact on non-college educated applicants who otherwise would be exceptional candidates. To help determine if there could be discriminatory impact from various questions, it is imperative that you analyze what information is being requested in each question. By analyzing the key information requested in each question, a comprehensive library of acceptable questions can be developed for future applications.

a) Name

It is acceptable to ask for an applicant's first, last or middle name. It is also lawful to ask for any other names under which they might have been previously employed. However, an applicant cannot be asked for their prefix (Mr., Mrs., Ms., etc.), marital status, or a previous name changed by court order. Marital status can become a discriminatory impact issue when an employer does not hire young women thinking they might get pregnant and leave. As young women who are married are more likely to have children then unmarried women, by asking for a title such as Ms. or Mrs., the employer could possibly utilize the information to discriminate against potential applicants.

b) Work History

It is legally permissible to ask about an applicant's prior work history including their specific job title(s), a description of their duties, their immediate supervisor's name, their salary, their former employer's (s') address and phone number, whether or not they were bonded and their reason for leaving (Adler and Coleman, 1995).

c) Discriminatory Questions

It is unlawful to ask about an applicant's sex under Title VII. Furthermore, under several state laws, it is also illegal to ask about an applicant's sexual orientation. It is permissible to inform an applicant that you have a company policy regarding work assignments involving employees who are related by birth or marriage. An applicant cannot be asked about their race, religion, national origin, color, height, weight, or similar categories of information which can be used to discriminate against potential applicants (see Chapter 4). The exception to these questions occurs when such information forms the basis of bona fide job requirements. Thus, if you are searching for female fighters for a boxing exhibition, you can legitimately ask an applicant if they are female. As will be discussed in Chapter 4, courts closely examine any race, sex or age job requirements to make sure they are in fact a necessary and bona fide job requirement. If someone can perform the job, but is excluded by the limited job requirements, a court can conclude that a prima facie (first blush analysis) discrimination case exists. It is unlawful to ask an applicant's religion, creed, church, parish, temple, level of observance, whether a school listed under an application's education section is a religious school or the dates they observe religious holidays.

d) Residence

It is lawful to inquire about an applicant's place of residence and length of residence at that address. However, it is not lawful to ask if an applicant is from a foreign country or lived at a foreign address. Furthermore, it is unacceptable to ask if the applicant owns or rents their residence.

e) Age

You may ask if an applicant is over the legal age to work without parental consent. However, prior to employment you cannot ask an applicant for their birth date. You cannot ask an applicant when they graduated from high school nor can you ask any questions which might identify an applicant as being over age 40. Some acceptable questions concerning an applicant's age include: "If hired, can you prove your age?" "Are you over 18?" and "If you are under 18, can you, after employment, submit documentation proving the applicant's age through documents such as a work permit?" (Rothstein, Knapp and Liebman, 1987).

f) Dependents

It is impermissible to ask the applicant for the number of his or her dependents. It is permissible to ask for the number of dependents, after hiring, if such information is utilized for a legitimate means such as calculating tax withholdings or health insurance premiums (Rothstein, Knapp and Liebman, 1987).

g) Photograph

Applicants cannot be asked to provide their photograph until after they have been hired and only for legitimate reasons such as security clearance (Rothstein, Knapp and Liebman, 1987).

h) Citizenship

It is impermissible to ask about an applicant's citizenship or birthplace. You cannot ask an applicant what is their "mother tongue" nor can you ask an applicant how they learned to speak, write or read a foreign language. You can ask an applicant if they read, write or speak a foreign language. An employer can require as a condition of continued employment that the applicant, upon being hired, prove citizenship, require a work permit or evidence of alien status (Rothstein, Knapp and Liebman, 1987).

i) Arrests

It is unlawful to ask about prior arrests. This information has proven to have a disparate effect on racial minorities. However, as distinguished from arrests, it is permissible to ask about criminal convictions if such information is job related. Inquiries regarding criminal convictions should not act as a complete bar to employment. The EEOC has held that employers must be able to demonstrate that the nature of the conviction would prevent the applicant from performing the job in an acceptable, business-like, manner (Adler and Coleman, 1995).

j) Relatives

It is impermissible to inquire into a relative's place(s) of business or if a relative has or had ever been employed by the employer. However, employment can be limited based on a validly applied and lawful nepotism policy, as discussed in Chapter 1. After hiring an applicant, it is lawful to asks for the name and address of a relative in case of emergency (Rothstein, Knapp and Liebman, 1987).

k) Military Service

An employer can inquire into an applicant's experience, position and duties in the United States Armed Forces. It is not permissible to require discharge papers or an applicant's discharge number (Rothstein, 1987). Another military related issue, which applies to both hiring decisions and promotions, involves leaves of absence to serve in the armed forces for active duty. If an employee needs to go on active military leave, they can miss up to four years from their workplace and still be considered as if they were on a leave of absence. Thus, securing their position while they are away. These times need to be considered in the application process as someone could have listed seven years of active employment with a given employer, but only actually have worked for the employer three years. To avoid any confusion, veterans should be specifically asked about skills obtained from their employer(s) and from the military with more emphasis than time they worked for any given employer.

l) Association

It is permissible to inquire about organizational membership as long as these organizations do not refer to an applicant's race, religion, sex, national origin, ancestry, color or union membership.

m) Medical

Medical conditions represent a significant concern. The ADA prohibits certain questions which were at one time common to job applications. For example, the following 13 questions have been identified by the Equal Employment Opportunity Commission (EEOC) as questions that cannot be asked on application forms or in job interviews.

1) Have you ever had or been treated for any of the following conditions or diseases? (Followed by a checklist identifying various conditions or diseases.)
2) Please list all conditions or diseases for which you have been treated in the past 3 years.
3) Have you ever been hospitalized, and if so, for what?
4) Have you ever been treated by a psychiatrist or psychologist and if so, for what condition(s)?
5) Have you ever been treated for any mental condition?
6) Is there any health-related reason why you may not be able to perform the job for which you are applying?
7) Have you had a major illness in the last five years?
8) How many days were you absent from work last year due to illness?

9) Do you have any physical defects which preclude you from performing certain kinds of work, and if so, please specify the defect and the specific work limitations?

10) Do you have any disabilities or impairments that may affect your performance in the position for which you are applying?

11) Are you taking any prescription drugs?

12) Have you ever been treated for drug addition or alcoholism?

13) Have you ever filed for workers' compensation insurance coverage? (Miller and Fielding, 1996).

The potential questions that can be asked or which cannot be asked are immense. As noted in Chapter 1, volunteers do not have any constitutional rights. The discrimination laws specifically refer to employees, job applicants, employers and related terms, but do not apply to volunteers. Thus, the array of questions that could be asked to volunteers is much broader than regular employees. Even though volunteers can be asked more questions than potential employees, if inappropriate, sexists, discriminatory or offensive questions are utilized, the potential backlash is immense. The backlash could include negative publicity, boycotts and facing an impossible task for recruiting future volunteers.

Typical Application Forms

After ensuring all questions are legally appropriate, and will provide information to answers the critical questions you have about a candidate, it is imperative that you organize the application form in a meaningful manner. Critical background material should be lumped together. Appropriate educational and work experience should also be grouped together. Several sample application forms can be found in Appendix G.

The general rule of thumb provides for an application form that is roughly one page for entry-level positions. However, there are numerous applications that are several pages. Multi-page application forms are being used more frequently by conciencous employers wishing to acquire as much information as possibly to ensure hiring qualified employees and to develop a strong defense to a potential negligent hiring claim. Universities and government employers often have several page long forms. The federal government requires job applicant to complete a Standard Form 171 which is usually at least five pages long. While these applications will generate a significant amount of information, they can often turn away potential, qualified, applicants. A high level executive that is asked to complete a five page application when they already have a resume or curriculum vitae covering the same material could possibly avoid completing the application.

In addition to asking the legally correct questions, an application form needs to provide additional required language to meet Equal Employment Opportunity Commission requirements. Such requirements can be met by simple notation that the employer is an "AA/EOE" or similar notation as discussed in Chapter 2. However, some applications contain an even more detailed paragraph such as the example below.

> Bob's Gym is dedicated to equal employment opportunities for all job applicants and employees. Bob's does not consider a person's race, age, gender, color, religion, ancestry, marital status, national origin, medical condition or physical handicap in reaching any employment decision. Every person is judged on the basis of personal skills and ability. Both the spirit and intent of all anti-discrimination laws and regulations are fully implemented in all our employee dealings.

Distributing the Application Form

Besides developing appropriate application forms, you have to provide the greatest opportunity for distributing and receiving completed applications in the most efficient manner possible. Often, a receptionist or human resource office employee can have several sealed envelopes with all necessary information (including the job description, application form and possibly some information about the employer or the surrounding community) available for distribution. Whenever anyone calls about the position, the employee just has to write the name on the envelope and mail the package. This saves times and possible delays which might occur when someone waits until a more convenient time to put the application package together. Application material can now be distributed in numerous unique methods such as mall kiosk information stations, facsimile distribution, job or employment fairs, high school and college guidance counselors or career centers and through the Internet. There is no limit to the manner in which applications are distributed. However, any distribution plan should be carefully prepared to avoid any discrimination claim.

Applicant Screening

In order for application forms to be effective, all applicants have to neatly complete the entire application. Completion instructions for difficult questions can help ensure receiving more complete answers and works as a psudo test to help determine an applicant's reading comprehension level. Any incomplete or illegible applications (including names, dates, addresses, etc.) should result in automatic ejection. The application should clearly state that "[t]he application will not be reviewed, processed or considered unless all application instructions are followed." In addition to providing complete answers, applicants need to be reminded that only truthful answers will be accepted and the consequences for providing false information. The following represent text that can help ensure truthful responses and provides a strong weapon when someone lies.

> Falsifying or omitting any material information requested in this application will be automatic grounds for immediate refusal to hire, or for termination if the falsity or omission is not discovered until after the applicant is hired. The employer specifically reserves its rights to impose harsher penalties including pursuing civil redress against anyone who knowingly, unknowingly or intentionally provides false or fraudulent information on this application.

The above statement is a very powerful statement. Job candidates should use caution when completing applications to ensure that all information provided is factual. For example, it is best to list the exact title of degrees earned. Based on the above text, individuals listing they have a masters degree, for example, in sport administration maybe stretching the truth (or lying) and can subject themselves to an abrupt termination if they actually only earned a degree in physical education.

All completed applications should be sent to the appropriate individual screening the applications. That person is responsible for reviewing the application and determining whether or not the applicant meets the job's minimum qualifications as set forth by the job description. All individuals who do not meet the minimum job qualifications should be sent a nice note indicating that they did not meet the minimum job qualifications for the position they applied for or state the non-discriminatory reason for refusal (i.e., the application was not received in time). While some companies do not feel it is important to respond to all applicants, the simple step of sending a form letter can generate significant goodwill with potential future applicants for other positions or generate or maintain customer goodwill. If an applicant never hears back from a possible employer, they will probably never reapply to that company even if they are eminently qualified or become qualified at a latter date. Furthermore, ill will can be generated with an applicant who spent possibly an hour applying for a position, and then they never hear back from the employer. Such inactivity on the part of an employer can also foster charges of resentment or discrimination by individuals claiming that the only reason why they did not hear back from the employer is because they are a minority. While there might not have been an attempt to alienate, the end result of not following-up with an applicant makes the small investment of a simple note or letter very worthwhile. Appendix H is a sample rejection letter that can be utilized when individuals do not make the first round cuts in the application review process. The person responsible for processing applications and response letters should be cognizant and follow all proper documentation rules discussed later in this chapter.

2) Review of Qualifications

The individuals who have passed the first screening round are regularly moved along to next phase in the process which often entails a review by several others in the department or division in which that employee might work. If the position is a sales position, members of the marketing department might be asked to rank the applicants based on their education or work experience. It is very important to develop specific, objective measures for ranking applicants. For example, a job might require a bachelors degree in sport administration. All applicants who have this minimum qualification would probably be in the advanced pool which passed the first review hurdle. However, individuals will always have their prejudice against institutions and their perceived educational value. While it might be appropriate to give a Stanford or Harvard graduate a higher ranking on the interview list, applicants that graduated from traditionally black colleges or Gallaudet University (a university serving the hearing impaired) should not be penalized or discriminated against solely based on the university they attended.

One of the best means to avoid a discrimination claim is to develop five or six variables that are essential for the job and each applicant that has those qualities, skills or experience can receive a point. Every resume or application form should go through this process and all applicants that have the highest numerical score move on to the next phase, the interview phases. Appendix I is an example of a review matrix which can help evaluate multiple applicants. The form can be modified depending on what criteria the employer wants to evaluate.

One concern that needs to be addressed when reviewing application forms and resumes is a trend called resume boosting (Miller, Pitts and Fielding, 1997). A recent article indicated that 15% of top executives lie on their resume about the degree they earned or their graduation date (Jones, 1996). Some recruiters estimate that about one-third of all resumes include lies. Most lies are put in resumes early in an applicant's career to get a foot into the door. However, many people lie later on to cover embarrassing episodes in their lives such as dropping out of school or going to prison. Keys to examine when looking for resume problems include exaggeration of job titles, compensation or responsibilities, hiding the true length of employment to cover-up periods of unemployment, listing down time or prison time as self employment and listing friends as references. One key to examine is whether or not work dates are listed by year or by year and month (Miller, Pitts and Fielding, 1997). For example a person can work at a business from December 1990 through January 1992. While this period represents only a 14-month period, someone can correctly indicate that they worked from 1990 through 1992. This statement provides an additional 10 months of employment cushioning for a resume. Any such boosts to a resume could result in potential legal problems for the employer. If an applicant is required to have met a certain government or industry standard for experience, such as for physical trainers, and the applicant in fact did not meet these requirement, the employer could be potentially liable for negligent hiring (see also Section 8, below).

Due to the concerns associated with negligent hiring threats and resume boosting, all employers have to thoroughly screen each applicant for various concerns including being an eligible employee, proper education or certification and other related concerns (criminal background check, passing drug test and other concerns addressed throughout this chapter). Being an eligible employee has two components. First the employee has to meet all the necessary job prerequisites such as education or experience. Secondly, the employee needs to be able to work in the United States.

United States Citizenship

The Immigration Reform and Control Act of 1986 (IRCA) imposes an obligation on all employers to verify each employees eligibility on a Form I-9 (Kaplan, 1996). IRCA contains severe penalties for those who fail to comply with IRCA's requirements. IRCA is violated when and employer:

- hires an unauthorized foreign-born worker,
- continues to employ an unauthorized worker,
- uses, accepts or receives any false documentation to satisfy IRCA's requirements,
- violates any IRCA anti-discrimination provisions, or
- when an employer fails to properly complete the Form I-9 (Kaplan, 1996).

Failure to complete Form I-9 for each new employee can lead to fines from $100 to $1,000 for each violation. Each mistake on a Form I-9, whether a simple error or omission can result in significant and separate penalties. In 1993, a California entertainment company received a $260,000 fines solely for 1,156 paperwork violations unrelated to anything having to do with undocumented workers (Kaplan, 1996). Stricter penalties apply for hiring unauthorized workers.

The Form I-9 has to be completed within three business days after an employee commences their employment (Kaplan, 1996). The form must be completed immediately upon hiring if the worker will work less than three days. Never backdate Form I-9 or use correction fluid as these actions can prompt the Immigration and Naturalization Service (INS) to send the Form to a forensic lab for further analysis. The employee chooses which documentation they will use to complete Form I-9, from the choices listed on the Form's back. The documents which can be used to help satisfy the I-9 reporting requirements include a United States passport, certificate of U.S. citizenship, certificate of naturalization, foreign passport endorsed by the Attorney General, or a resident alien card (Adler and Coleman, 1995). After the Form is completed, an employer needs to keep the Form in their records for three years or at least one year after an employee was terminated (Kaplan, 1996).

The INS can conduct a raid without prior notice. While an employer has three days to produce all Form I-9, it is recommended that if an INS raid occurs you should immediately produce all Form I-9s, but only Form I-9s. Thus, all original Form I-9s should be kept in a separate file and photocopies kept in the employee's file. This will prevent disclosing personal information with requested Form I-9. If the INS wants the Form I-9s, give them photocopies. If the INS produces a subpoena, you should immediately contact your legal counsel for guidance. While the INS has recently increased enforcement efforts, by undertaking proper qualification review of applicants and informing them prior to being hired that certain documentation will be needed, you can help facilitate proper record collection to comply with IRCA.

Arranging Interviews

Oftentimes, there might be numerous qualified individuals for a position. No attempt should be made to interview all top applicants if there are more than five highly qualified candidates. While five is an arbitrary number, any number higher would result in the opportunity costs of lost money from people spending too much time in the hiring process rather than generating revenue. Applicants that do not make the last round prior to the interview process should be sent tactful rejection letters. Often called "ding" letters, these letters normally provide significant praise of the applicant's ability, but also indicate that they would not be asked to attend an interview. A sample "ding" letter can be found at Appendix J.

Individuals who you wish to interview should be formally contacted over the phone to schedule an interview date. Special attention should be made for interviewees coming from out of town to make sure their arrangements are made in advance by the interviewing company. While it might save some time for the employer to ask the interviewee to make the travel arrangements, such a procedure can result in hefty bills. An interviewee who just want a practice interview and really isn't serious about the position might make airline reservations the day they travel, thus resulting in an exorbitant bill for someone that will probably not be a future employee. Appropriate accommodation for a traveling interviewee includes coach or business class transportation, above average housing and above average meals. It should be stated that the reception and accommodations experienced by the interviewee helps shape the interviewee's opinions about the employer. If the employer looks cheap, the interviewee will probably be more reluctant to accept an offer from the employer. On the other hand, while an extravagant trip and accommodations look impressive, the wrong message could also be sent to the interviewee and to current employees who rarely if ever are treated in the same manner. Thus, the best tool for gauging appropriate expenditure is to take a middle road of not being too cheap, nor, too extravagant. By handling arrangements, you can possibly rebut any inference that certain applicants received favorable treatment or accommodations which can lead to a discrimination claim.

All interviewees should receive a follow-up letter providing the street address where the interview will be held and the exact interview time. The letter should also specify that the interviewee should call if they need any reasonable accommodation to make the interview process easier. Easier accommodations could include such actions as hiring an interpreter, providing transportation assistance from the airport, and picking an accessible restaurant. A sample interview confirmation letter can be found at Appendix K.

3) Job Interview

Job interviews are not utilized for the sake of meeting people. There are specific goals which need to be achieved through the interview process. The first goal is to determine if interviews will help further the hiring process in a substantive manner. The key to interview effectiveness relates to interview reliability. There are two types of interview reliability, intrarater reliability and interrater reliability. Interrater reliability occurs when the interviewer interviews the job applicants or listens to a recording of the interview to determine if their original impressions are reconfirmed. Interrater reliability occurs when two or more individuals evaluate the same applicant either together or separately using the same interview questions (Chruden and Sherman, 1976). The same interview questions can be found on structured interviews.

Types of Interviews

There are three types of interviews: structured, semistructured and unstructured (Rothstein, Knapp and Liebman, 1987). Structured interviews normally are conducted from a set form which does not allow deviation from a script and provides the greatest protection from asking potentially unlawful questions. A weakness with structured interviews is the lack of flexibility to ask certain follow-up questions. On the flip side, structured interviews have been found to generate the greatest reliability of all interview techniques (Chruden and Sherman, 1976). Semistructured interviews provide the opportunity to ask necessary follow-up questions that deviate from the script. In unstructured interviews, the interviewer has the opportunity to ask any question. The problem with this technique is the enhanced opportunity to ask a legally impermissible question.

No matter which interview technique is utilized, and even if you feel very comfortable with an applicant and you might informally chat for a good portion of the interview, you cannot forget to ask the critical questions or to look for the clues that might pinpoint a potential problem. In order to help pinpoint potential problems, the interviewer needs to be adequately prepared for the interview. Preparation typically includes examining the interview's purpose, the proposed job description, and review application forms, references, writing samples, test scores and any additional documentation received prior to the interview. Standardized interview forms and rules helps keep interviews on track and more reliable. The following interview rules, suggestions or cues for further investigation represent a partial list of issues that all interviewers should follow.

Interview Rules

1)   Interviewing is only effective when all applicants are thoroughly screened.

2)   If at all possible, try to have at least two people at each interview so if a discrimination claim is raised, you could possibly have two witnesses who can testify as to what happened. Furthermore, you can base decisions to hire someone based on the opinions of two people rather than one individual.

3)   All interviewers should be intimately familiar with and follow the employer's sexual abuse policy.

4)   If possible, receive permission from the interviewee to videotape or audiotape the interview. Otherwise, you can make taping mandatory. Mandatory or permissive taping are not illegal as long as the interviewee knows in advance that the interview is being taped and expressly consents to proceeding under such conditions. If an interview is being taped, you

should mention from the very beginning that the interviewee was informed of the taping. The interviewee should be asked officially on the record if they agree to the taping or if they understand that the interview is being taped.

5)   Utilize all available resources such as police for investigation or fingerprinting, school districts for educational records and any other potential source of information concerning position applicants to help prepare for an interview (See criminal records below). Some records such as transcripts can be requested in advance.

6)   Prior to starting all interviews, check at least two pieces of identification-at least one with a picture to make sure the persons being interviewed are in fact the individuals who are applying for the job. This process also helps collect data that can be used for additional background checks-such as reviewing an applicant's driving record from seeing their driver's license. You should try not to overly examine any identification cards, especially the address or age without the interviewee's consent to prevent a discrimination claim. If you allow the interviewee to choose which ID card they produce at the interview, you can often uncover significant information you otherwise might not be able to obtain without violating the law.

7)   Ask more intense questions regarding an applicant's background when there exists frequent, unexplained, moves.

8)   Ask more intense questions regarding an applicant's background when there exists gaps in employment or education dates. These gaps can represent potential incarceration or other potential concerns.

9)   Ask more intense questions regarding an applicants background when there exists any criminal convictions or serious motor vehicle violations (i.e. drunk driving, vehicular homicide, gross vehicular misconduct, etc.). Determine the specifics concerning the convictions or violations including specific dates, jurisdictions, exact charges, exact adjudication and the exact resolution of the conviction. Specifically ask the person being interviewed if they feel the criminal conviction and associated crime impairs or affects their ability to perform the job's necessary requirements (Miller, Pitts and Fielding, 1993; Fried 1996; Patterson, 1994).

10)   To assist in your Affirmative Action evaluation, you should ask interviewees how they heard about the position.

Special Questions for Youth Employees

Besides typical concerns associated with new employees, employers have to be very cautious with any individuals who might work with or around children. Caution should be extended to both potential employees and volunteers who frequently work as coaches and administrators with youth leagues and/or teams (Fried, 1997). Some specific issues that should be addressed with an applicant who might work with children, as recommended in *Sexual Abuse Prevention Manual* (Fried, 1997) include:

1) Follow-up with what hobbies are listed and if they are appropriate for someone of similar age and background. This can be a concern when dealing with potential child sexual abuser.
2) Follow-up with what the applicant's attitudes are towards children.
3) Be cognizant of appropriate and inappropriate nonverbal queues given by the interviewee.
4) Be cognizant of potential problems if the applicant is single with no "age-appropriate" romantic relationships. You cannot ask if an applicant is single, but if he/she provides information, you are free to utilize such information in helping to make appropriate hiring decisions.
5) Be cognizant of potential problems if all activities and interests center on children.
6) Be sensitive, but also cautious, when an applicant was sexually abused as a child. An interviewee should not be asked about such matters, but the interviewee might offer such information. If the information is offered, and the interviewee has received or continues to receive treatment for the mental anguish, then they could be protected by the ADA.
7) Be cognizant of potential problems if the applicant is fearful of adult world.
8) Be cognizant of potential problems if the applicant sees children as "pure," "innocent," and/or "clean."
9) Be wary if the applicant is overanxious to get the position.
10) Deny any applicant who is willing to bend the rules to allow overnights or other actions that might violate the employer's policies or rules (Patterson, 1994).
11) Deny any applicant who abuses alcohol or drugs (Fried, 1997). Such actions are not discriminatory based on the critical need to properly supervise children which cannot be effectively accomplished when an applicant is under the influence.

Once an interviewer has a feel for what information is needed from the interview process, the interviewer needs to ask the specific questions. The application form provides a good template for interview questions. Any questions that solicit information which could lead to discrimination against a candidate are probably illegal. Any information relating to age, sex, sexual preference, race, religion, nationality, national origin or related topics represent a significant concern. While it is probably likely that the applicant's name or appearance will give the interviewer significant clues concerning an individual's background, the interviewer should never assume anything from a person's appearance. It is hard to avoid interjecting personal prejudice into the interview process. However, the interviewer should be specifically trained to focus on soliciting the right answers regardless of any personal prejudices. Only the most qualified and trained individuals should be assigned responsibility to conduct interviews. This is especially accurate when utilizing unstructured interviewing techniques.

While the forgoing techniques apply to most interviews, some employers have found the computer to be an effective tool in the interview process (Armour, 1997). Cyberinterviews, as well as teleconferencing, can significantly reduce costs associated with on-site and in-person interviews.

Interview Questions

Besides developing some general guidelines for interviews, all interviewers should understand what questions they can ask and what questions will solicit the requisite information sought from the applicant. The following represent some acceptable questions that will provide useful information in analyzing a candidate's qualification. It should be remembered that you should not ask leading questions, yes or no questions nor questions that are too general. Provide the applicant with questions that allows them to elaborate on responses and provide information voluntarily that could not have been requested through traditional questioning. Additionally, all questions should be relevant and further the informational needs required to make a final decision concerning the applicant. The following questions represent some specific questions appropriate for an individual who is being interviewed for a position working with children.

1) Why are you interested in the position?
2) How would you describe yourself?
3) Have you ever had to discipline a child, and how did you do it?
4) Why do you like to work with children?
5) What traits do you think you have that qualifies you to supervise children?
6) What about the position/job appeals to you the most/least?
7) Are you familiar with the issues associated with child sexual abuse?
8) Have you read our policy statement concerning sexual abuse?
9) What do you think about the policy?
10) Have you ever been convicted of a criminal offense including criminal driving violations?
11) Have you ever worked in a position for which you were bonded?

12) How do you relate with children?

13) Are you aware of any problems or conditions that could interfere with your ability to care for children or in any way endanger any child under your care?

Questions can be adapted for each position to stress critical issues associated with that specific position. The specific questions should be drawn from the job description. Thus, someone who is applying to work in the accounting department should be asked numerous questions regarding handling money, being bonded, employee theft and related questions which might address their trustworthiness. Appendix L lists various questions which could be asked during an interview.

All responses given by the interviewee should be recorded in a response form to provide evidence concerning what questions were asked and relevant responses. This step should always be taken even if the interview is video taped. If an interview is not videotaped or audiotaped, these written responses will form the basis for defending potential claims alleging negligent hiring (failing to ask certain questions), and discrimination-through asking inappropriate questions. Appendix M is an interview response form to be completed during each interview. Special care should be taken to make sure only objective, not subjective, information is reported on the form.

Interviewer's Role

The interviewer represents a gatekeeper to protect and advance a company. By failing to ask the proper questions and obtain relevant information, an interviewer can unwittingly allow someone with criminal intentions into a company. Furthermore, based on answers, body language and attitude, an interviewer can determine if the proposed candidate will benefit the company as a productive employee interested in pursuing the company's goals and willing to be a team player.

The interview should be examined as a decision making process. A Canadian study highlighted the decision process which interviewers utilize to arrive at their conclusions (Chruden and Sherman, 1976). Key components within this process include:

1) interviewers develop a stereotype of an ideal candidate and then seek to match the applicant with the stereotype,

2) a bias is established early in the interview and that bias is normally confirmed with the final analysis,

3) interviewers are normally more influenced by negative information rather than positive information,

4) interviewers often reach a decision during the interview and then try to find information which supports their hypothesis and, when satisfied, they then turn their attention elsewhere,

5) some interviewers place themselves in the applicant's shoes to try and understand the applicant's motives,

6) when information is fed slowly to the decision maker, such a slow trickle affects the final decision in comparison to the better decision reached when all information is received at once,

7) experienced interviewers tend to make the same decision about prospective applicants and tend to be more selective than less experienced interviewers (Chruden and Sherman, 1976).

Once an interviewer can appreciate how they reach a decision, they can work to avoid infusing any bias or prejudice. Furthermore, interviewers can learn how to solicit the information they will need in order to develop the most accurate portrait of each job applicant.

While there is no perfect interviewer, there are specific skills and traits that make an individual better suited to interview job applicants. One highly regarded trait is humility because it motivates interviewers to avoid hasty judgments, encourages skill development and encourages the use of alternative selection or screening devises (Chruden and Sherman, 1976). Other critical skills or traits include:

- poise,
- maturity,
- free from extreme opinions,
- free from biases,
- the ability to listen well,
- the ability to think objectively, critically and systematically,
- experience with various backgrounds,
- experience with people similar to the applicant in age, gender and related attributes,
- extensive experience with various people in a particular occupational group (Chruden and Sherman, 1976).
- training in effective and legally appropriate interview techniques, and
- knowledge of individual job descriptions and job analysis.

Interviewers should be cognizant that their decisions can be affected by various concerns. Even the best-trained interviewer can let their opinions or ambitions interfere with the hiring processes. Interviewers are often faced with a dilemma that if they hire someone who is too qualified, then that person could one day be their boss. This often leads to hiring mediocrity to help protect current employees. Other concerns include personal prejudices, the halo effect (judging someone favorably in various areas based on one strong point), physiognomy influence (interviewers like individual who look and act like themselves) and separating fact from inference (Chruden and Sherman, 1976).

The interview process is serious. It should not represent just a free meal or opportunity to socialize. The interview should represent a test to determine whether or not someone can be a team player and help reach business goal while being able to accomplish duties prescribed in the job description. Talented interviewers, who can separate their prejudices from the process, serve as the gatekeeper to let only the right people into the company. However, since even well trained people can be fooled by a slick resume and polished interview skills, applicants would be hard pressed to pull the wool over someone's eyes, especially their prior employer's eyes. That is where reference checks become essential.

4) References

After the interview process has been completed, the employer needs to follow-up with all the listed references. Some employers prefer to contact references before the interview process begins to reduce travel and entertainment expenses which might be wasted on an applicant with poor references. Either option is acceptable. Many interviewees (especially for lower level positions) will come from the local community, thus, reducing travel expense related concerns. Business references, as well as personal references (if provided), should be meticulously checked with all responses carefully documented. The following example highlights how important it is to investigate references.

A young man applied to work as a volunteer with an in-home care agency that placed volunteer helpers into the homes of older individuals. The young volunteer filled out an application and was called in for an interview. During the interview, the man indicated that he indeed had a criminal history which was just an arrest for disturbing the peace. He indicated that he was in a fraternity during his college days and they sometimes had parties that went out of hand. All the fraternity brothers were arrested. The interviewer did not follow-up concerning the incident and did not check the references because the man appeared to be a nice young man. Furthermore, the agency was in need of as many volunteers as they could find. The young man was placed in an elderly Hispanic woman's home. Two weeks later she was dead. The volunteer was the key suspect. In fact, the young man was found guilty of the crime. In the civil trial against the agency for negligently placing the volunteer, it was disclosed that the young man was indeed a fraternity member. The fraternity is popularly called the Ku Klux Klan. The references he listed also became an issue. It was discovered that the young man listed his mother, sister and a KKK Grand Dragon as references. If the agency had undertaken just a minimal effort to contact references and check criminal records, the murder could have been prevented (Fried, 1997).

While reference checking is a tested technique to uncover critical information, the ability to acquire truthful and accurate information is often hampered by fear. The fear is present in former employers, business associates and even friends who provide inaccurate information or refuse to provide information. A reference who provides false information could possibly be sued for fraud if there was an intent to deceive. While a fraud claim is very remote, a defamation claim is not as remote. Likewise, references can also face a legal assault on the other side, based on their failure to provide information or failure to provide enough information. Thus, references can be sued whether or not they give any information or refuse to disclose any information. By understanding the fine line on which references walk, a reference checker can hopefully solicit the right information while still protecting the reference from potential suit.

As highlighted above, employee references provide great value to a potential employer. The recent sexual assaults upon young individuals participating in sport and physical activity has intensified this issue for sport business managers ("Association ponders," 1997). In addition, the proliferation of internal crime represents another reason employers should be concerned about an applicant's integrity. Calling an employee's references serve three significant purposes (Miller, Pitts, and Fielding, 1993; Paetzold and Wilburn, 1992; Von der Embse and Wyse, 1985). First, references verify application information provided by the prospective candidate. The solicited reference helps ensure that the itemized degree(s), certifications and experiences are accurate. Second, the pre-employment reference can inform a prospective employer about dysfunctional or dangerous behavior. For example, an employer might view a prospective employee with exemplary skills, certifications and experiences differently after learning that the individual had been reprimanded by his/her prior employer for physically striking a patron-invitee or that the individual was discharged and convicted for embezzling inventory and money. Third, thorough reference screening procedures facilitate the hiring of competent, qualified individuals. Proper hiring reduces business expenses associated with employee turnover, absenteeism, recruiting and training.

However, if a former employer is unwilling to give information over the phone or through the mail, you should explore other options. One such option is to avoid the human resource person who hides behind the company's "no comment" policy and talk to the applicant's direct supervisor or lower level co-workers who might be familiar with the applicant's work record (Adler and Coleman, 1995). No matter who is interviewed, you need to understand the changing dynamics associated with defamation.

Defamation

Defamation is a critical concern with references because an applicant who is denied a position might sue a former employer claiming that the former employer gave false information which prevented the applicant from being hired. Even if a former employer gives accurate information, that will not prevent a defamation suit. Truth is an absolute defense to a defamation claim. However, many employers are unwilling to provide any information, even if it is truthful, because they do not want to pay to fight a frivolous defamation claim. Even if a party can prevail against a defamation claim by proving all statements were truthful, the litigation costs to reach such point could easily cost over $10,000. Defamation is covered in more detail in Chapter 12, as most defamation issues arise when an employee is terminated. However, defamation is raised at this point in the guide to highlight why so many former employers refuse to provide references when asked. The fear of being sued for defamation can become a significant hindrance in the reference collection process.

Qualified Employer Immunity

Historically, common law granted employers a qualified or conditional privilege to comment about employees that are, or were at one time, employed by a particular business. As explained by the Supreme Court of Minnesota in *Lewis v. Equitable Life Assur. Soc.* (1986),

> The doctrine of privileged communication rests upon public policy considerations....the existence of a privilege results from the court's determination that statements made in particular contexts or on certain occasions should be encouraged despite the risk that the statements might be defamatory...
> In the context of employment recommendations, the law generally recognizes a qualified privilege between former and prospective employers as long as the statements are made in good faith and for a legitimate purpose.

The qualified privilege is designed to benefit society at large by keeping problematic employees out of the workplace. Aberrant behaviors and related consequences could be reduced while simultaneously reducing expenses associated with the orientation and training of newly hired employees who later cause havoc in the workplace.

As noted by the *Lewis* court (1986), the qualified privilege is not absolute. Courts recognize the privilege only when employers make statements in "good faith" and for a legitimate purpose. Recommendations made as an attempt to blackmail an ex-employee, or made maliciously with a disregard for the facts are subject to liability (Daniloff, 1989; Martucci and Boatright, 1995; *Robinson v. Shell*, 1997).

The following case represents a typical defamation claim concerning references. The plaintiff was discharged for the stated reason of "gross insubordination" (*Lewis*, 1986). Lewis claimed she was discharged in violation of an employment contract and that she was defamed because the company knew that she would have to repeat the reason for her discharge to prospective employers. The company never published nor stated the reason for Lewis' termination. The company's policy was to only disclose the terminated employee's dates of employment and job title upon termination. In order to prove a case of defamation, the defamed party must show that the accused communicated to someone else a false statement which harmed the defamed party. However, in this case, the company did not communicate with any prospective employers. Rather, Lewis herself told prospective employers why she was terminated. The court sided with Lewis concluding that when a defamed party is forced in some manner to communicate the defamatory statement to a third party, and it was foreseeable that they would be compelled to make such statements, then the defendant could be held liable for defamation (*Lewis*, 1986).

Nonetheless, even though the court felt Lewis could bring a defamation claim, the company had a privilege that it could communicate the reason for a termination without being held liable for defamation. The court extended such a privilege to former employers in order to keep open lines of communications so that employees and potential employers will know the reason for an individual's discharge. Since the company's statements were not made with actual malice, they were entitled to be considered privileged communications, not subject to defamation analysis.

Unfortunately, the threat of liability has curtailed employer willingness to provide job references. Defamation is the most frequent allegation associated with a contested employee reference, although a plaintiff's causes of action could also include "intentional infliction of emotional distress, public disclosure of private facts, and interference with contractual relations or with prospective business" (Eikleberry, 1995). The only sure defense for combating a defamation claim is the truth. As long as you tell the truth, and can prove the truth, you will not prevent defamation suits, but will have the evidence necessary to prevail.

Middleton (1987) estimates that 33% of all defamation claims involve former employees suing employers alleging defamation. A study conducted by the University of Nebraska in 1992 revealed that the average, successful employee defamation award was $57,000. However, more extreme awards are not uncommon. To defend against potential liability, employers have adopted "no comment" policies or simply provide "skeletal" information including the dates during which the individual was employed, job title, and job responsibilities. As explained by Martucci and Boatright (1995), "The rationale is that, if nothing is communicated, an employee may not claim defamation." Unfortunately, this no-comment policy adopted by businesses has influenced the importance that prospective employers place on employee references. More specifically, it is estimated that 75% of prospective employers forego the practice of reference checking as they find former employers uncooperative (Middleton, 1987).

However, a newly recognized tort, that of negligent referral, is likely to alter current "no-comment" and "neutral" reference policies (*Tarassoff v. Regents of the University System of California*, 1991). Negligent referral is a tort recognizing an employer's responsibility to warn a prospective future employer about a past employee's abusive or violent behaviors. Both torts, negligent hiring and negligent referral, have left employers in a quandary. On one hand, an employer could face invasion of privacy and/or defamation charges if they state or misrepresent information about an employee. On the other hand, an employer could face liability if they fail to mention some facet of information deemed essential to a prospective employer or a victim who is later harmed by the particular employee.

Failure to Disclose Misconduct

The *Lewis* case highlight the fear employers can face when giving a reference. The fear associated with a perceived lawsuit has created an atmosphere where employers try to avoid giving information. However, this strategy can also backfire as employers are now being sued for failing to provide appropriate information that is necessary to protect future employers or the customers/employees associated with a future employer. In 1997, the California Supreme Court concluded that a former employer is required to provide prospective employers with any warnings if they believe the employee represents a danger ("Court rules job references need warning," 1997). The decision was handed down in a case where a middle school girl was molested by her vice principal. The plaintiff sued the vice-principal's former supervisor and three school districts where the molester had previously worked. The suit claimed that the letters of recommendations should have included warnings about his prior sexual misconduct. The court concluded that the defendants owed the plaintiff a duty not to misrepresent the vice-principal's background in the letters of recommendations. The decision imposes a duty on all employers who write letters of recommendations that they include any negative information they know about the former employee ("Court rules job references need warning," 1997). The same conclusion was reached by a Texas court after the former employers failed to inform a subsequent school district of the employee's past sexual misconduct (*Doe v. Bridgeport ISD*, 1997).

The failure to disclose past egregious conduct is especially acute when sexual harassment and/or molestation is involved. Sexual harassment experts call this scenario "passing the harasser," which is especially prevalent in schools and colleges (Leatherman, 1996). Under such scenario, an employer runs someone out of town to avoid any further problems, but do not provide any positive or negative references. This allows the harasser to move to the next town and engage in the same conduct. However, the headache now belongs to the subsequent employer rather than the first employer.

The case law associated with defamation in references does not just highlight failure to disclose information on reference letters. In a Florida case, the court concluded that the family could recover from a former employer when the former employer failed altogether to provide any warning about the person's violent tendencies (McCall, 1996). Thus, an employer can be sued for failing to disclose potential harmful facts, even if they did not provide a reference letter.

These cases demonstrate that former employers asked for a reference are caught in a catch 22 position. If they give a reference—they can be sued for defamation; and if they do not provide a reference—they can be sued for failing to disclose a person's dangerous propensity. Based on this difficult quandary, some states are considering immunity laws to protect employers who provide references (McCall, 1996). The following list identifies states with statutory protections for employers:

1. Alaska
2. Arizona
3. California
4. Colorado
5. Florida
6. Georgia
7. Idaho
8. Illinois
9. Indiana
10. Kansas
11. Louisiana
12. Maine
13. Maryland
14. Michigan
15. Minnesota
16. New Mexico
17. Ohio
18. Oklahoma

19. Oregon
20. South Carolina
21. South Dakota
22. Texas
23. Utah
24. Wisconsin
25. Wyoming

States with legislation introduced or pending:

1. Missouri
2. Nebraska
3. Virginia (Price, 1997)

In an attempt to remedy this dilemma, states have enacted legislation insulating employers from defamation liability for providing honest, good faith and truthful employee references. Georgia enacted the first reference-checking statute in 1991 to legislate the privilege concept (Leonard, 1996). As of May, 1996, 14 additional states have enacted legislation limiting the liability of those providing employee references (Leonard, 1996). In addition, independent, private businesses that perform background checks are "beginning to appear in many parts of the country" (Harvey, 1997). Human Resource Review Service in Middletown, Kentucky, for example, can perform a cross-country, cross-state investigation on a potential employee for a cost ranging between $10-$100 depending on the desired thoroughness of the background check itself.

Employer Reference Checkers

Reference immunity laws might not come quickly enough as a company founded in 1992 has performed over 500 defamation checks on behalf of employees; not employers. Documented Reference Checks (DRC), a California based company, uses affiliates to contacts former employers and pose a s a potential employer to get the information on a former employee who allegedly has applied for a new position. The information DRC uncovers is recorded in a transcript and can be used by plaintiff's in a defamation claim. The information DRC uncovered in one investigation (that the former employee was often absent, did not get along with management, and would not hire her again) was used to help a plaintiff receive a $1.6 million defamation verdict (Lublin, 1996).

Literature identifies a number of suggestions which can assist the employer in his or her efforts to act as a reasonable prudent professional (Clay and Stephens, 1996; Eickleberry, 1995; Fried, 1996; Miller, Pitts, and Fielding, 1993).

Suggestions When Soliciting References

- Many employers insert a waiver on the bottom of the job application granting permission to the employer to check references. This waiver serves to protect the employer against future defamation or invasion of privacy claims as the job applicant has authorized obtaining such information.
- To deflect discrimination allegations, you should call all references listed by the finalist for the position. Let's assume, for example, that a sport franchise has narrowed its applicants list down to three individuals consisting of one Asian woman, a Hispanic male and a white male. It would be in error to call the references listed by the Asian woman and the Hispanic male and not to call the white male's reference. Rather, the references for all three potential candidates should be called and responses documented. Documentation is essential in defending a claim of negligent hiring. Standardized forms containing the questions asked of each reference with space provided for responses present one way of preserving needed information.
- Discrimination allegations can be refuted if each reference is asked the same (or very similar) set of questions about the particular individual. Using the above illustration of a sport business that has narrowed the pool of candidates down to include an Asian female, Hispanic male and a white male, it would be problematic to interrogate the references listed by the minorities for an hour while the conversation with the reference listed by the white male was limited to three minutes. Regardless of the intent to discriminate, the laborious questioning might appear as if the employer was searching for reasons to deny employment to the Asian female and Hispanic male.
- References called should be limited to those that possess knowledge about a candidate's abilities or potential to perform essential job responsibilities. You should avoid calling family members, friends, or social affiliates.
- Legislation such as the ADA and the EEOC clearly dictate that sport business employers cannot ask other individuals questions they themselves are prohibited from asking. For example, an employer cannot ask a past employer questions about a candidate's disabilities, age, marital status, workers' compensation claims, etc.

- Employers who delegate reference checking responsibilities should ensure that individuals have the appropriate training and knowledge regarding what questions to ask and to whom. Further, the courts could view reference checker's training itself as a "good faith" effort by employers to remain in compliance with existing legislation.
- It seems obvious that individuals looking for a job would select those individuals as references who would provide prospective employers with positive information. Consequently, an employer may consider contacting other colleagues or professionals not listed to gather as accurate of information as possible.

While defamation-related concerns addressed above refer to obtaining a reference from another source, such as a former employer, defamation-related concerns also apply to any references you might provide. The following section provides some hints to avoid liability when providing references.

Suggestions When Providing References

- A written request aids a defendant attempting to prove that the plaintiff/ex-employee was cognizant of the anticipated reference contents and consented to disseminate the information. Insertion of a clause such as, "In response to your request,..." can provide further evidence that the letter was not written maliciously or for revenge or retaliation.
- It should be noted, however, that providing a written reference is somewhat controversial. Written references provide documented evidence of what was actually communicated. You are always protected the most when you provide truthful information which can be supported with documented facts. On the other hand, some lawyers dissuade the use of written references as they provide a paper trail that can lead to more extensive litigation. If written references are provided, those providing the reference should retain a copy in the former employee's personnel file for use in defending any potential defamation claim. Competent counsel or properly trained human resource professionals should review any reference letter prior to the letter being sent. Furthermore, the written reference should not be circulated to other employees and only key managers with a vested interest should be involved in the reference process.
- Addressing a letter with the salutation, "To Whom It May Concern," provides an inference that the letter was written

for multiple readers. Unfavorable comments, if disseminated to individuals who do not have reason to read the letter, could invite a lawsuit for invasion of privacy and defamation. This concern represents a key point in relation to defamation claims. If you defame someone by telling one other worker, then you could be liable for one defamation claim. However, if that employee tells five others, and they each tell five other people, you would be liable for each subsequent publication. Thus, one bad statement could lead to countless defamation claims if the defamatory statement was publicized.

- Do not speculate about the causes for poor performance or a high rate of absenteeism. Thus, all statements should remain objective and only verifiable facts should be reported. Comments should respond only to information that is requested. Wandering thoughts and statements often provide opportunities to say more than intended or to have what is said misinterpreted.
- Keep an employee's medical records separate from employment records. A prior employer should not answer medical inquiries that a prospective employer is not allowed to ask due to the ADA.
- It is important that all employees know how to respond to reference checks. It is best that all written and oral references be provided through a designated body such as the Human Resources Department. References provided by individuals who have not been in a supervisory capacity should be avoided. This policy is important because corporate immunity for internal communication can apply to supervisors, but rarely extends to lower level employees. You should include a policy within the employee manual or handbook a rule specifically disallowing any comments by personnel about former personnel to any and all outside sources unless accompanied by a company attorney or when pursuant to a government investigation.
- Besides providing truthful references, employers should avoid responses that are misleading or incomplete.

Reference Questionnaire

Based on the potential concerns associated with asking the wrong questions, not obtaining the right information or a former employer's litigation concerns, it is imperative to create a pre-set reference questionnaire. Such a questionnaire establishes legally appropriate questions to ask and specially indicates what the information will be utilized for—i.e., specific position applied for and if there is access to specific dangers. For example, if the job candidate is going to be working with children, then the reference provider should be informed what duties the person might assume and what dangers might be present. Such dangers can include one on one contact with children (i.e., having to supervise restrooms, supervising changing into swimsuits, etc.). To avoid a potential negligent hiring claim you have to specifically ask if they have had any past disruptive, dangerous or other questionable contact. By documenting that the question was asked, how it was answered and by whom, you can establish a strong defense that you did everything a reasonably prudent employer could have done. Similar to specific concerns associated with youth, critical questioning is required for anyone working with seniors, who might not have daily supervision and individuals working with money such as payroll, accounting, cashiers, etc. Normally an employer has a greater obligation to investigate individuals working with children and the elderly than to investigate a grounds keeper's background.

In addition to asking the right questions, it is imperative that you properly record the answers. Thus, Appendix N contains a list of sample questions to ask a former employer or someone listed as a reference on the job application. Appendix O is a response form unto which answers should be recorded for the questions you might ask. It is recommended that a different questionnaire and response form be utilized for each position and to properly tailor all the questions.

Release Records Form

An additional concern associated with references involves requiring signed and written authorization to release records. A signed request is typically required by any school, college or university to release any academic records. Additionally, some employers require a signed release before providing a reference. If such an employer is encountered, the applicant can be asked to specifically write or call the former employer to provide the necessary reference. If at all possible, the burden of securing the reference should be the applicant's responsibility. If the applicant fails to obtain a written reference, such a failure can constitute reasonable grounds for not hiring an applicant.

Credit Reports

Another pseudo-reference tool that represent specific legal concerns are consumer credit reports. These reports can be used to establish an applicant's eligibility for employment or if they might be under so much debt that they represent a fiscal risk to the employer. Under the Fair Credit Reporting Act (FCRA), the employer needs to let the applicant know that such records are being requested. An employer can request either a consumer report or an investigative consumer report (Frierson, 1994). No notice needs to be given that a standard consumer report is being obtained. However, since investigative reports also contain information on an applicant's reputation, lifestyle and characteristics, an applicant needs to be given a three day notice before obtaining an investigative consumer report (Frierson, 1994). No matter which report is requested, the employer is required to tell credit reporting agency the exact purpose behind the report (Frierson, 1994). If the report is used to help solidify a negative hiring decision, the FCRA requires the employer to let the applicant know that the report was used and the specific name and address of the reporting agency (Chruden and Sherman, 1976). Furthermore, the FCRA might be replaced by stricter state regulations. Under the FCRA, credit reports cannot be obtained for positions paying less than $20,000 per year. However, under California state laws, credit reports cannot be obtained unless the position pays more than $30,000 per year (Frierson, 1994).

A typical credit report costs an employer about $27.00 while investigative consumer reports cost a little more. Reports can be obtained from the three primary credit-reporting companies in the United States. However, similar information is also making its way onto the Internet, and should present a quicker, less expensive option in the near future. To help prove that the applicant knew their credit history was being researched, you should make sure the applicant has signed a background information release which allows the productions of various background information which might otherwise raise a privacy concern without the signed authorization. To avoid any discrimination claim, you should only utilize credit checks if all applicants are beings checked. Furthermore, credit checks should only be utilized for sensitive positions such as cash handlers, accounting personnel, ticket takers/managers, research and development personnel and related positions.

5) Character Review/Investigation

In addition to reference checks, background checks can take additional forms. Reference checks provide only a limited picture of a potential job applicant. The applicant normally lists who they want you to contact. Thus, they might list family members or friends. Some job candidates only list certain jobs which might exclude employers who fired them. Thus, it is often important to utilize other information to ensure you are getting the applicant's complete picture. Other sources of information can be obtained from an independent investigator. Such investigators charge from $45 to several hundred dollars depending on what information they examine (Fried, 1997). Private investigators utilize various databases from driver license records, to court records, through criminal databases. Often investigators can gain access to state materials such as disability claim records, unemployment records and other such records that can be useful. While many employers can also research some of these databases, especially with more and more information available on the Internet, it is often easier to leave the digging to trained professionals who know the system and know how to legally access pertinent files without violating any anti-discrimination laws.

Criminal Background Checks

While various records can be accessed to uncover additional background information. No such background material is more controversial—and at the same time as necessary—as criminal background material. This is especially so when someone has a past criminal conviction for assaults against people, sexual assaults, indecency with a minor, fraud, embezzlement and related criminal convictions. However, as discussed previously, it is illegal to have a wholesale exclusion of anyone with a past criminal history unless there is a relevant connection with what duties he or she will be assuming. Therefore, if someone will not be working with money, any money-related criminal convictions would probably be inappropriate. Thus, criminal convictions information should only be pursued when someone is working in an environment requiring confidence or the highest moral character.

Special Concern-Children

In sports and recreation programming, criminal background checks are a major concern due to the numerous volunteers and employees who regularly work with children in unsupervised settings. While some employers prohibit hiring anyone with a record of past abuse, other employers only prohibit such a person's involvement when they are actively involved with children or are in some manner engaged in a custodial or supervisorial capacity. Some employers utilize a scale of allowability based on the proximity to, or vulnerability of, the participants. Some additional concerns include how much solitary time the applicant might spend with children, the dependency inherent in the relationship between the applicant and the participants, the frequency of contact and the length of time the program lasts. As a general rule, stricter screening rules are required when the frequency and intimacy of the contact increases.

The key to any criminal background checking procedure is an authorization signed by the job applicant or volunteer. Criminal records are highly protected documents with access typically limited to law enforcement officials, government officials, and the convicted person. In some jurisdictions such as the state of Washington, law enforcement officials will provide free criminal background checks for nonprofit agencies employing someone on a paid or voluntary basis. However, even if you wish to utilize such a service, the nonprofit agency needs an authorization to release records. Appendix G includes a sample criminal record release form which an applicant can complete when applying for a position. The benefit associated with such a form is that individuals who do not want their criminal history disclosed might not apply for the position. This represents a double-edged sword. You might scare away potential "bad apples" from even applying. Some individuals claim that certain minority groups have a greater likelihood of having a criminal record. Thus, some minority groups might face extensive discrimination as the application can possible dissuade a significant number of individuals from that minority group who might otherwise be qualified. While this concern is very remote, it could possibly lead to a discrimination claim. Additionally if all applicants sign such a release, there might be a financial hardship required to check each applicant. Various private firms, when equipped with a signed release can perform the background checks using various databases for $45 to $100 per name, depending on how many databases are checked (Fried, 1997). To perform a thorough job, the private firm should be requested to check the federal, state and any previous state the applicant has lived in over the past five to ten years.

Various databases exist to research criminal records. The Federal Bureau of Investigation (FBI) maintains the Interstate Identification Index (Triple I system) and the National Crime Information Center (NCIC). The Triple I system tracks all criminals (both state and federal criminals) and indicates the individual's name, sex, race, date of birth and in which states individuals live. A potential employer can then contact a state criminal records repository to uncover additional information. The NCIC database contains information on missing persons, wanted persons, stolen vehicles and related issues. At least 11 states require certain employers, such as schools, to access these databases to examine the criminal background of each new job applicant (Fried, 1997). Based on the increased need to check applicants, access to such information is currently being liberalized by various state and federal laws (Fried, 1997). California residents can, for a small fee, check any resident's sexual crime conviction record over the phone (Fried, 1997). Additionally, the Victims of Child Abuse Act (1990) requires all federal agencies involved in child care services to perform a criminal background check on all existing and potential employees. Childcare services include educational and recreational programs. The Act requires all applicants for such positions to sign an investigation consent form and are to be provided with a copy of the complete investigation results. Another federal statute, the Indian Child Protection and Family Violence Prevention Act of 1990 is designed to prohibit certain applicants with criminal records from working with Indian children.

Another approach which can save significant money and possibly prevent any privacy rights violations involves a post review criminal background check. Under this approach, an applicant who has passed all pre-employment phases such as interviews, references, etc. can be asked as a final condition of being offered the job that he/she go to their local law enforcement agency and request his/her own criminal background record. If the applicant does not have any criminal background, the law enforcement agency can complete a letter as follows:

On _____, 199 ___, _____ (applicant) requested that I perform a criminal background check. I accessed the following databases _____ _____ and was unable to find any prior criminal convictions.

Name _____
Title _____
Badge Number _____
Agency Name _____
Agency Address _____
Agency Phone Number _____

If an applicant does not produce the completed form, you can offer to perform the background check for him/her after he/she signs a release, but the background check would be a thorough check of both state and federal databases. If the applicant refuses to sign the release then the application should be denied. The job application should specifically indicate that failure to authorize a background records request automatically voids the application. A caveat applies to this general rule. If the position does not involve any trust or special duties such as working with children, then any criminal background check might not be appropriate. If a criminal background check is inappropriate for the position (such a janitor or field maintenance person) then you cannot void the application for failing to sign the criminal records release form.

As can be expected, whenever anyone produces criminal records, you are being entrusted with very private information. As with any valuable information, you have to develop safe keeping procedures to ensure the materials are not lost, stolen, or left around for other people to see. Similarly, a key concern with evaluating any potential applicant is the preservation of her/his application material. Special precautions need to be taken if you are holding any documents for further review such as items required to comply with the IRCA's I-9 form, any medical records that were produced without your request, and an individuals past salary history or letters of recommendation. Keep any and all materials received in a background check in separate file from the individual's personnel file. Personnel files are more accessible during the discovery process as compared with other files. If background check materials are kept in a separate file with limited access and designated solely for security or litigation purposes, then a court will be less willing to allow another party to see those documents or would only allow certain documents to be disclosed. The courts allow a process called "in camera" review where a judge can examine any documents before producing them to the other side. If a judge does not feel the information is relevant or is too intrusive, then the judge can prevent access, allow limited access, or require the documents to be photocopied in a manner which hides sensitive data. If there is no expected privacy, then the courts normally allow the background information to be released. That is why the background material needs to be kept separately from all other personnel materials, and under lock and key.

An employer has to walk a careful line between protecting clients and co-workers versus punishing exonerated felons. The purpose of our penal system is to rehabilitate a criminal. If a felon has completed her/his time, she/he should not be forever punished for her/his crime. However, because some crimes have a high recidivism rate (such as child molestation), it is not fair to expose your clients to such a risk (Fried, 1997). The typical rule of thumb adopted by prudent employers is to exclude those convicted of crimes against people (assault, battery, rape, molestation, etc.) for anyone who will be responsible for working intimately with the public such as cashiers, personal trainers, coaches and referees.

6) Job Tests

With the increase security and sensitivity associated with certain positions such as counselors, accountants, money handlers and related positions, more and more employers are utilizing various testing devises to ensure an applicant is honest, trustworthy or not criminally disposed. Tests are also utilized to obtain information about an applicant's abilities, aptitudes and personality which can help predict probable success (Chruden and Sherman, 1976). While similar information might be obtained through an application form, reference checks or interviews, tests can be both objective and unbiased. A variety of different electronic, written and oral examination techniques are available for a prospective employer. However, a legal thicket exists concerning which tests the law allows an employer to use, under which circumstances such tests can be used and who can be tested. Tests represent a significant concern based on the perceived fairness or unfairness and affect on minority applicants which has led to numerous court challenges and legislation. Therefore, if you have current pre-screening exams or if you are considering instituting such exams, it is critical that you do not proceed any further without obtaining legal counsel. The law is so complex in this area that including one wrong question or using the wrong standardized examination can lead to litigation.

Based on the numerous legal concerns associated with pre-employment screening tests, the first consideration is the determination of whether such test are even necessary. You can often obtain the same information from contacting references or past employers. Through interviewing candidates, you can examine veracity and how they would handle a given situation. You can examine truthfulness by examining their resume to see if there is any fluff, exaggeration or outright lies. To help you understand the various testing options available, the most popular testing methods will be briefly described in the following pages. Not covered are questionable approaches which are nonetheless utilized by some employers. These questionable techniques include astrology, handwriting analysis (graphology), facial characteristics (physiognomy) and other quasi-scientific techniques.

Test Validity

Validity is a key issue often addressed in discrimination litigation. If a test was not valid, and resulted in a large percentage of a given group being denied employment, a prima facie case of discrimination could be raised. Thus, it is essential that if a test's validity is not known, the test should not be used. Additionally, the EEOC's Guidelines on Employee Selection requires any test which adversely affects groups protected by Title VII of the Civil Rights Act of 1964 to be professionally validated as an effective and significant predictor of effective job performance (Chruden and Sherman, 1976). Discrimination can be present in both the testing material and the testing procedures. An individual who did not perform well on the examination could claim that they suffered from test anxiety, the test content was unfair (minorities might not have been exposed to certain concepts discussed in the test) or the test was not valid for the minority group from which the applicant came from (Chruden and Sherman, 1976).

Need for Test

Before utilizing any personality tests it has to be determined if the tests are necessary. Has the test been scientifically or clinically proven to be accurate as a pre-employment test? Does the test address some relevant, legitimate or necessary job-related requirement? Does the test tend to result in the hiring of a homogeneous and passive work force? Has the test been proven to be accurate as a pre-employment test? Are they relevant to legitimate job-related concerns? Are the tests overly intrusive and ask too many personal questions which will eventually lead to personnel files containing highly sensitive, personal information? Are tests being utilized as a high-tech shortcut to thoroughly interview employees including appropriate background and reference checks (Rothstein, Knapp and Liebman, 1987)? These questions need to be answered before moving forward with testing procedures. These answers also help identify which tests will provide the appropriate information sought by the employer.

Testing Options

Some tests that have been used with mixed results in the employee screening process include vocational interest inventories (Rothstein, Knapp and Liebman, 1987). One such test is the Kuder Preference Record Vocational Test which has been criticized because respondents can give the answer they think the employer might want to hear/read. Furthermore, the Kuder Tests only analyze an applicant's interests rather than real work experience. The Minnesota Multiphasic Personality Inventory (MMPI) asks questions concerning such issues as attitudes towards sex, love, family, morals, honesty and religion. Responses are used to formulate a diagnostic scale which can lead to misleading psychiatric labels. Several honesty questionnaires exists such as the Reid Report, the Stanton Survey or the Personnel Security Inventory (Rothstein, Knapp and Liebman, 1987).

Rorschach ink blot tests contain ten cards with five all black ink blots and five ink blots incorporating several colors. These tests are famous for their wide use by psychologists in movies. The subject is asked to describe what they see in the blots and their observations are recorded. Subjects are then given a chance to review all their responses and indicate why they gave that response (Rothstein, Knapp and Liebman, 1987).

Numerous tests exist to measure various personal issues or traits. The following chart adapted from Chruden and Sherman's *Personnel Management* text highlights various tests and the jobs for which the tests are used as an evaluation tool. This is not an exhaustive list as new tests are being created, adapted or manipulated on a regular basis.

Intelligence Tests

The Wonderlic Personnel Test, Adaptability Test and Wesman Personnel Classification Test are all utilized for general clerical, maintenance and sales jobs. The Concept Mastery Test is primarily used for managerial and executive applicants. The United States Employment Service programs use the General Aptitude Test Battery. The Employee Aptitude Survey and Flanagan Industrial Kit are utilized for all types of jobs.

Dexterity Tests

The Stromberg Dexterity Test is utilized for individuals who will be using punch presses, assemblers and related positions. Purdue Pegboard and O'Connor Finger and Tweezer Dexterity Test are both tests used for individuals employed in the assembly or production industries.

Clerical Aptitude Tests

The Minnesota Clerical Test, SRA Typing Skills and The Short Employment Test all test individuals interested in clerical or office jobs.

Mechanical Aptitude Tests

The Test of Mechanical Comprehension and the Revised Minnesota Paper Form Board Tests are designed to test engineering, mechanical and drafting skills.

Personality Tests

The Gordon Personal Profile and Inventory and Edwards Personal Preference Schedule are frequently utilized for office workers and computer programmers. The Guilford-Zimmerman Preference Schedule was designed to test salespersons and supervisors. Both the Thematic Appreciation Test and the California Personality Inventory are designed to test executives and managers.

Creativity and Judgment Tests

There are three basic tests identified by Chruden to test creativity, AC Test of Creative Ability, Owens Creativity Test for Machine Design and Watson-Glaser Critical Thinking Appraisal. All three tests apply to either engineers or executives.

Supervisory and Managerial Abilities Tests

The following four tests can be given to managers and supervisors: How Supervise?, Supervisory Practices Test, Management Aptitude Inventory and Leadership Opinion Questionnaire.

Interest Tests

The two main tests for examining an applicant's interest are the Strong Vocational Interest Bank and the Minnesota Vocational Interest Inventory.

Besides the various tests and procedures outlined above, employers can utilize other significant tests designed to provide extensive information about a job applicant. These tests range from polygraph and personality tests to drug and medical tests.

Polygraph Tests

Historically, polygraph tests were often utilized to assist in hiring decisions made by federal security agencies, state and local police, banks, security guard companies and other sensitive positions. While polygraph testing was widely used, the Congressional Office of Technology Assessment studied polygraphs in 1983 and concluded that while polygraph testing can assist criminal investigation, there was no evidence that polygraph screening held any validity. Yet, while polygraph tests were and still are inadmissible in criminal cases, the test results were utilized in making thousands of employment decisions (Rothstein, Knapp and Liebman, 1987).

The federal government passed the Employee Polygraph Protection Act of 1988 prohibiting the use of polygraph testing in the pre-employment process. The Act also covers examination for current employees. The Act applies to all non-government employees with exception for only specific job categories such as security guards or employees with access to drugs. Employers can test current employee for drug use when you are investigating dishonest or theft, but you cannot use the test to help defeat a workers' compensation claim. While you can investigate a current employee suspected of theft or dishonest, you have to have independent evidence that the employee has engaged in dishonest conduct before giving the test. Such independent evidence could include an eyewitness seeing the dishonest behavior. The Act has very specific requirements that need to be met before a polygraph test can be applied. These requirements include:

- the employee has to be provided with notice about the proposed test,

- the employee has to be given the written questions before the test is administered,
- the employee has to be given a statement of her/his rights before the test,
- the employee has the right to stop the test at anytime without suffering any retaliation,
- only licensed testers can perform the test, and
- all results have to be kept confidential.

In addition to the Federal Act, some states specifically prohibit polygraph testing for employment decision making. For example, Connecticut General Statute Annotated Section 31–51g(b)(1) specifically prohibits any person, firm, corporation, association or the state from requesting or requiring any current or prospective employee to submit to or take a polygraph examination as a condition of obtaining or continuing employment, or to dismiss or discipline any employee for failing to or refusing to submit to such testing. Similar laws exist in most states and the District of Columbia (Rothstein, Knapp and Liebman, 1987).

Personality Testing

Since polygraphs tests cannot be used, some employers use personality tests. Personality tests are also referred to as psychological tests. These tests are designed to test an applicant's veracity or character. The tests measure an individual's human characteristics such as abilities, aptitudes, interest and personality in quantitative terms (Chruden and Sherman, 1976). The hallmark of personality tests centers on test reliability and validity. Additional concerns include:

- costs (most test are well constructed, even the inexpensive ones),
- time (short tests are preferred),
- face validity (test takers are more inclined to complete a test if the test is directly related to the issues they might face on the job), and
- ease of administration and scoring (test which have to be graded by an expert are normally too expensive and time consuming) (Chruden and Sherman, 1976).

Of critical concern when administering any personality tests is privacy rights and the contents of certain questions. Questions revolving around family values, sex, religion and personal habits might be too intrusive. Furthermore, the same questions might be prohibited as they tend to solicit responses that will help determine an applicants, age, sexual orientation,

marital status, etc. which can lead to an inference of discrimination. Therefore, any test which inquires into such personal matters, should only be
utilized if they relate to a bona fide occupational requirement, or are given
after an applicant has been hired and is used for placement within the company.

Most tests can be purchased already prepared and tested for validity
and reliability. Such tests can be purchased at office supply or stationary
stores. In addition, specialty tests such as the Wonderlic Personnel Test
can be purchased directly from the company in either a written form or personal computer version. Individuals can purchase 25 paper and pencil versions of the test for approximately $85.00. Likewise, 25 tests adminis-
tered through a computer cost an employer approximately $85.00.
Wonderlick can be contacted at (800) 963-7542 or on the Web at
http://www.wonderlic.com.

Drug Tests

Several jobs in the sports, fitness and recreation industries require employees to be at their peak mental and physical condition. A lifeguard for
example needs to be constantly vigilant to prevent any drowning. Any impairment from alcohol or drugs can lead to disastrous effects. Therefore,
under some conditions, drug testing as a pre-employment screening mechanism might be appropriate.

Drug testing was once rarely utilized by major corporations in the 1960's,
but has rapidly advanced in the 1990's. In the past five years the number
of Fortune 500 companies conducting drug testing on job applicants has
risen from 3% to 30% (Adler and Coleman, 1995). In the past five years,
the advocates of pre-employment drug testing point to higher quality applicants, and after hiring, individuals that pass such tests show reduced
absenteeism, higher productivity and fewer accidents (McEwen, Manili
and Connors, 1986). Thus, drug testing can help employers find the right
employees. Furthermore, it should be noted that drug testing is not considered a medical exam under the ADA.

Drug Testing Options

Technology associated with drug testing has improved marketably from
the 1970's and 1980's. Most employers utilize urine sample tests such as
an initial EMIT (Enzyme Multiplied Immunoassay Technique) test which
is fairly inexpensive and has a reputation for accuracy (95% to 98% accurate). However, especially when someone such as a current employee
has a positive test result, a confirmatory test is critical to avoid a false pos-

itive. The most popular confirmatory tests are the gas chromatography and gas chromatography/mass spectrometry tests which are considered the most accurate as well as the most expensive (McEwen, Manili and Connors, 1986). One drawback from these tests is that they do not specifically indicate when the drugs were taken, where were the drugs from, or how much drugs were taken. These potential inaccuracies could effect individuals who are not drug users, but consume the wrong product. Numerous stories exist about individuals who have positive drug tests from eating poppy seed bagels in the hours or days before a test. Therefore, even when both tests are utilized, it is still possible to receive a false positive result. That is when further investigation needs to be conducted to confirm that the individual is not being incorrectly labeled a drug user, which can lead to a defamation or discrimination charge. (See Chapter 15 for a thorough discussion of on the job drug testing and drugs in the workplace issues.)

Another testing format is blood specimen testing which can more accurately detect the level of impairment. However, blood tests are considered more intrusive as they require drawing blood from the applicant. Other potential tests include breathalyzer, saliva, brain waves, eye (pupillometer) and even hair sample tests which can detect drug and alcohol usage (Adler and Coleman, 1995).

Privacy Concerns

Drug testing presents various legal concerns. While various tests can be very effective measuring potential drug usage, the tests can also detect pregnancy or AIDS which can possibly lead to discrimination. Furthermore, tests can identify drug usage associated with prescription drugs which can lead to potential ADA concerns. Applicants might be forced to reveal what medical condition(s) they suffer from which require certain medication-an ADA violation. Privacy issues also arise from urine specimen collection and whether someone needs to be in the same cubicle as the person giving the sample. If close supervision is not provided, the potential exists for doctored samples being provided (Adler and Coleman, 1995).

Discrimination Concerns

An additional concern associated with drug testing is the potential discriminatory impact the test might have on certain minority groups being eliminated from consideration. This could be based on some individual's perception about illegal drug usage. To help avoid this problem, some employers are allowing individuals who fail a test to undergo company-sponsored rehabilitation prior to hiring applicants as employees (Adler and Coleman, 1995). While such employer sponsored rehabilitation is not required, such a program might attract some otherwise qualified candidates who might have been turned away by other potential employers.

Drug Testing Notice

Job applicant drug testing, in both the public and private sector, has been upheld as long as reasonable prior notice is given that a test will be administered. In a key case, *Wilkinson v. Times Mirror Corp.*, a California appellate court concluded that a pre-employment test which all applicants knew about in advance was reasonable. The fact that the test were performed on job applicants was very important because job applicants knew from the very beginning they would be required to disclose certain personal information to the employer. The court also highlighted the safeguards undertaken by the potential employer including advance noticed, utilizing an independent medical screening laboratory, all results were kept confidential, and the tests were not used to identify any other conditions such as pregnancy. Samples were given in private, positive results were confirmed by a second test and applicants were given a chance to challenge the test results (*Wilkinson*, 1989). While the *Wilkinson* case appears to provide employers with the right to perform an informed drug tests on job applicants, the ADA has changed the law and now employers still need to provide notice of drug testing, but the testing results cannot be reviewed until the job applicant has been conditionally offered the job.

Union-Related Drug Testing Issues

Drug testing (as well as all other testing techniques) is not just a concern for individual job applicants, but also for unions. Certain unions have a drug-testing requirement built into the collective bargaining agreement between the union and the employer. This is especially true in regards to professional sports unions such as the National Football League Players' Association (NFLPA) and the National Basketball Players' Association (NBPA). Pursuant to the National Basketball Association's (NBA) collective bargaining agreement with the NBPA, players are subject to various forms of drug testing prior to being drafted and after accepting a contract by virtue of the collective bargaining agreement specifically providing for such tests (Weiler and Roberts, 1993). If a player is not interested in being subject to the random drug tests, than he/she can play in another league which might not require such tests. Additional information on drug testing for employees, rather than applicants, can be found in Chapter 15.

Genetic Testing

Currently no federal laws directly address genetic testing in the workplace. Seven states have enacted various restrictions on genetic testing in the workplace (Bielski, 1996). Some employers screen applicants for traits that may increase the risk of illness when workers come in contact with certain chemicals. These employers sometimes utilize genetic tests. With rising health costs, an employer, able to catch potential health risks, might try to exclude such individuals even though such actions amount to outright discrimination. Based on the great potential for discrimination, the EEOC has opined that when a genetic test uncovers a health concern and that health concern is used in any manner during the employment process then the Americans with Disabilities Act applies (Bielski, 1996).

Genetic screening, blood exams, urinalysis and related matters are often components within a comprehensive medical examination. Medical screening represents a significant liability issue based on various discriminatory actions that can be taken against a potential job applicant.

7) Medical Screening

Pre-employment medical examinations were commonly used during the early 1900s when the first workers' compensation laws were passed (Rothstein, Knapp and Liebman, 1987). Job applicant medical screening became more important over the last several decades with the increased cost of group health care plans, increased workers' compensation claims and insurance costs and the loss of productivity associated with numerous sick days taken by certain regularly sick employees.

Discrimination Concerns

Medical screening is often justified on the basis that the prospective employee might pose a serious hazard to co-employees, the public or property. Under the ADA, individuals can be excluded from employment opportunities if they represent a serious risk to themselves or others (see generally Chapter 4). To help alleviate discrimination concerns, the law specifically prohibits an employer from asking for a medical examination prior to employment. However, an employer can offer a job applicant a tentative position based on the applicant passing a medical examination. If the applicant fails the exam, then he or she is denied the job. Thus, passing the medical exam becomes a condition precedent to the job applicant actually starting their work (Feliu, 1992). An applicant can be denied employment if the applicant has a medical concern, the concern affects a job-related business necessity they represent a direct threat to themselves or to others and no reasonable accommodation is available to help the applicant perform the necessary essential job requirements. For example, a youth coach might pass all the employment screening steps and is tentatively offered the job. However, during the mandatory medical exam, it is discovered that the applicant had a vision problem that could not be rectified. As seeing children and supervising their conduct is a necessary component of the job description, and no reasonable accommodation is viable, the applicant would not need to be hired.

The potential discrimination that can occur in medical testing was highlighted in a famous case. The *Wroblewski v. Lexington Gardens* case involved an employer who claimed bonafide occupation qualification or requirement (BFOQ) as the basis for demanding more medical information and independent verification of a female applicant's health record. The applicant proved a prima facie case of discrimination. Thereafter, the store claimed that women were more susceptible to incurring health problems and that pregnant women could be exposed to potentially dangerous insecticides. However, the store failed to prove they utilized those dangerous insecticides. The court concluded that the store's claims were insufficient to justify the store's discriminatory practices. The court further concluded that even if a generalization (possible health problems from being exposed to insecticides) applied to many within a protected class, that classification would be discriminatory to an individual for whom the generalization does not apply (*Wroblewski*, 1982). In the sports context, you cannot force a fitness trainer to take a weight lifting test to evaluate strength if the job description does not require any lifting. Furthermore, you cannot force all concessionaires to take a screening test for hernias as some concessionaires might work hawking beer in the stands and need to carry significant weight, but others might work behind a counter.

A close cousin to medical screening involves asking potential applicants about any legally prescribed medication they might be taking. A 1996 case involving a Colorado resort struck down the resort's insistence that employees needed to disclose all drugs present within their bodies. Applicants also needed to notify their supervisor of any prescription drug they took. The prescription drug disclosure policy was part of the resort's comprehensive drug and alcohol testing program administered to both employees and potential employees. The court concluded that absent significant job-related requirements or business necessity, the resort violated the ADA by requesting the prescription drug disclosure (Cusick, 1996).

Medical Tests and Results

Medical screening can be as unobtrusive as a single question concerning whether or not you can physically perform the job's necessary components to full physical examinations. Other tests include blood, urine, genetic and pulmonary function tests, chest x-rays, audiometric examinations or ophthalmologic examinations (Rothstein, Knapp and Liebman, 1987).

Similar to other confidential records, medical records should not be kept with an employee's personnel file. In fact, in California, employers are required to keep any medical information confidential. These restrictions could include instructing employees about the confidentiality of files and restricting access to files (California Civil Code Ann. Section 56–56.37). All medical-testing results should be kept under lock and key. An especially critical concern involves any documentation of false positive results which, if released or misplaced, could lead to a defamation claim. Thus, in addition to properly securing medical test results in separate files, all such records should be shred three to five years after an employee is terminated/resigns or after the hiring process for the specific position closes.

Physical Performance Screening

Medical screening can often include a component emphasizing physical ability to perform a certain task. Such tests can involve lifting certain weights or demonstrating the ability to stand in a given manner. All such tests or inquiries can raise potential ADA violations or sexual discrimination claims. As with most ADA analysis, the focal point for performing required job components is not the specific manner in which the task is completed, rather the analysis is on being able to achieve the results. However, if the job requirement includes the carrying of fifty pound equipment bags as the team's equipment manager, it is permissible to test applicants to determine if they indeed can move the equipment in the requisite manner or with reasonable accommodations. However, if the team is not particular on how the equipment is moved (golf carts, hand carts) and what size the bags might be, then a physical test would be inappropriate because it is not necessary to complete the job and the test would tend to discriminate against disabled individuals.

Additionally, physical requirements can indirectly result in sexual discrimination. In one case, a 113 pound female truck driver was given a test to see if she could handle a 18-wheeler (*EEOC v. Ryder*, 1986). The applicant was not hired after she failed the road test. She was unable to connect the cab with the trailer. The applicant sued claiming sex discrimination. However, the court concluded that no sex discrimination occurred even if most women would not be able to successfully pass the test (*EEOC v. Ryder*, 1986). Since the test related to an essential job function, the inability to perform that function was sufficient non-discriminatory grounds to deny the position.

After all tests are performed, all references checked, and after carefully scrutinizing a resume, it would seem that an applicant would have a hard time getting away with even a small lie. However, it occurs all the time. Employees often pass the entire hiring gauntlet without being detected. This is especially true with slick talking candidates who can quickly provide excuses for missing information or to justify prior misconduct. However, what happens when an employee who has passed the hiring gauntlet, but at a later date the lie is uncovered. Can the employer terminate him/her for a lie or misstatement that was not uncovered until several years after someone was hired?

8) Fraudulent Background Information

An employer has a duty to investigate an applicant's background to uncover any obvious disqualifications. For more sensitive positions such as working with children, the duty to properly investigate an applicant's background is that much more paramount. Failing to identify a noticeable dangerous trait or work history can lead to a negligent hiring charge discussed in Chapter 5. Additionally, if you later discover that someone has lied or doctored his or her background, you could be liable for negligent retention. Therefore, if you discover that someone has lied or falsified information during the application process, such person should be immediately terminated. Off course, you should conduct a thorough investigation and document the process according to the procedure set forth in Chapter 12 before termination. Retaining them any longer can expose you to significant potential liability.

To help avoid the potential liability concern associated with fraudulent background information, the employment contract and employee manual should specifically indicate that any fraudulent statements identified before, during or after employment constitute a significant breach of the employment contract. Such breach should be fully prosecuted to the full extent of the law and the contract can specifically provide for liquidated damages if a person has lied or made even innocent misstatements during the entire employment process.

The scenario above differs from firing an employee and then checking each statement he/she made on his/her resume to find an error which can help justify the termination. Employers are now using the after acquired evidence approach to help defend wrongful termination cases. However, this approach requires extensive investigation that is often prompted by a lawsuit. In these suits, the employer could still be held liable for wrongful termination if they cannot prove the termination was instituted after discovering the lie. Thus, an effective technique to utilize prior to terminating employees involves re-scrutinizing their resumes and all application materials to detect any inaccuracies. These inaccuracies could then be highlighted in the termination letter-thus providing basis for the termination. An example of such an inaccuracy might be indicating that an individual is computer capable, but they require more computer training then anyone else within the organization to reach an acceptable competency level, which is never met.

Chapter 12 provides more thorough information concerning after acquired evidence and terminating an employee for misstatements that might have managed to get by screening process.

9) Confidentiality

This chapter previously mentioned the confidentiality concerns associated with criminal background information and medical information. An ancillary confidentiality concern involves state and federal organizations engaged in hiring employees. Most states have open meeting law and "sunshine laws" which requires the disclosure of sometimes sensitive information when demanded by the general public. Organizations have to check with their counsel to determine the scope of these rules and regulations concerning their organization. If open meetings are required or if the public has the right to access certain public records, it is imperative that no personal or confidential information be written outside the applicant's file or discussed outside the closed interview process. Otherwise, the potential exists for the public disclosure of sensitive or personal information that could jeopardize the employment process.

The Toledo Blade (an Ohio newspaper) filed a lawsuit against the University of Toledo to stop the hiring process for a new athletic director until the court had a chance to determine if the University violated Ohio's public records and open meetings laws. The newspaper claimed they were barred from an employee search committee meeting set up to help find a new athletic director. A judge granted a temporary restraining order that prohibited the University from conducting any business relating to hiring a new athletic director. Before the newspaper filed the lawsuit, two prior search committee meetings were held in closed sessions. Thus, if the paper succeeded, the court could have invalidated the meetings from which the reporters had been barred ("Judge stalls hiring at University of Toledo," 1996).

Sunshine laws present a unique challenge in the hiring process. Prospective applicants can face significant retaliation or termination if their current employer discovers that they are looking at other job opportunities. The authors have yet to find a suit relating to this concern, but it is conceivable that a job applicant could claim that you should have protected their confidential application or, at least post a warning in the advertisement specifically indicating that all submitted material was conceivably open for public disclosure. Keeping application records confidential might be difficult or impossible for a government entity. However, by providing proper documentation throughout the process and informing individuals that the media is attempting to obtain the list can provide applicants the opportunity to withdraw their name from consideration.

Invasion of Privacy

A final concern associated with confidentiality involves invasion of privacy. While invasion of privacy is really a separate issue, the sensitive and highly personal information requested on some personality tests represent a significant confidentiality concern. As previously indicated, only questions directly relevant to job success should be requested on any testing instrument. However, once answers are provided, only minimal access should be allowed to personality tests results and only for official business reasons. This confidentiality concern is the same concern affecting criminal and medical information. The only means with which to handle such information is to intentionally limit access to such information and comply with the entire document handling guidelines set forth below.

10) Proper Documentation

As with all facets of business, you need proper documentation to survive. No business would survive if it did not properly record sales and account payables. Similarly, the failure to properly document all facets of the employment process can lead to disastrous results. Losing a key document reprimanding an employee or failing to maintain questions and responses from interviews can be disastrous. Furthermore, failure to keep applications, I-9 forms and related statutorily required documentation is against the law and can lead to significant fines.

If you do everything you are supposed to do to document the employment process, the record will speak for itself. A perfect example involves a 1990 case revolving around a payroll clerk who worked for Coca-Cola for approximately 22 years before being terminated (*Beard v. Coca-Cola Bottling Co.*, 1990). She sued for age discrimination and was able to show that over her extended work history she had received several merit pay increases in the 1980's and her boss in the 1970's rated her as good. However, the employer was able to defeat the claim based on the record presented from documents in her personnel file. A 1981 memo highlighted that she had difficulty getting things done and she was not that cooperative with co-workers. The memo further warned that if she did not change her outspoken behavior, she would be transferred. Shortly thereafter she was transferred, but was later reassigned to her prior position. Her supervisor wrote a letter to the general manager claiming she was foul mouthed and did not complete work on time-yet still had time to make personal phone calls. She received several subsequent poor evaluations and in 1986 was placed on 90 days probation. She was given a detailed letter outlining the terms of her probation and the need to substantially improve her performance. Each concern was identified with specific measures provided to help remedy the problem. The termination letter highlighted all these problems and her inability to accomplish her required improvements. Thus, all the documents contained in her personnel file helped serve to defeat her discrimination claim (*Beard*, 1990). If the employer had not kept all these documents over a 20-year period, he or she might have lost the case.

To help insure proper document acquisition and protection, you should implement the following documentation tips. These tips are useful not just in the hiring process, but apply throughout the entire employment relationship. Documenting is especially critical for preserving facts concerning the hiring process, sexual harassment claims, promotions/demotions, and terminations.

1) Everyone should understand that documentation is designed to create a record for trial. Thus, abbreviations or jargon should not be used as the person who prepared the notes might no longer be with the company when a matter heads to court and it might be impossible to interpret the notes. You should try to type notes while they are still fresh in your head.

2) Always avoid any subjective statements about an applicant. For example, if an African-American woman who does not perform well during an interview should not be described as "uppity" or "pushy," but can be described as not having the requisite communication skills required by the job description. The key is to provide accurate information, but as it relates solely to the job and not the interviewer's personal prejudices.

3) Always avoid any conclusory statements about an applicant. Similar to concern #2 above, you should always avoid claiming that the applicant is "dumb" or "poor white trash."

4) Always document any incident or important matter as quickly as possible. However, if you are overly excited or upset, you should wait several minutes before documenting what occurred.

5) Be factual and do not embellish or exaggerate. Avoid statements such as "she was the best candidate to date and should be the top pick."

6) Specify dates, times, locations, names, etc., for each incident, interview, evaluation or related activities.

7) Thoroughly interview and investigate all appropriate details before documenting any facts. It is recommended that unofficial notes be taken until you are ready to prepare the final document. Then you can transfer the information to a final version. You should always remember to destroy the preliminary notes after you have written a final version. If any preliminary notes are contained on a computer, these "working files" should be erased after the final document is prepared.

8) Stamp "DRAFT" on all preliminary documents or notes. After the document is finalized, destroy all drafts copies (shred) and delete all computer data files.

9) Use exact quotes from witnesses, references, etc.

10) Never backdate a document.

11) Always use spell check, proofread, and re-read all documents as every word matters.

12) Do not include any proprietary, confidential, medical or criminal history background material in the personnel file. All such documents should be put in a locked cabinet where only the Human Resources Manager or similar person in authority has access to the documents. A file cabinet that is never locked and contains forms used for various occasions does not qualify as a file designed to hold confidential documents. Counsel should be utilized to determine appropriate state and federal laws concerning who can have access to personal records/files and when access is allowed.

13) Do not include any attachments unless they meet numbers 1–12, from above.

14) On a regular basis follow-up with your employment law attorney to determine the required record keeping requirements to comply with the various federal and state reporting requirements (see below).

15) Attorney-client privilege protects most documents covered by this protective cloak as long as the document was specifically written in order to communicate with a company's attorney. You cannot protect all communications, but you protect all bona-fide communication to counsel related to sensitive subjects involving potential liability. To help ensure you can garner this protection, you should try to take the following steps:

a) address documents to your company attorney,
b) the first sentence should specifically indicate that the letter is

being written to ensure the hiring is legally proper and that the document is being prepared at the attorney's request,

c) limit document distribution to only key management personnel and kept in confidential "legal" files,

d) stamp "Attorney-Client Privilege Communication" on top of the document, and

e) only use privilege when absolutely necessary.

16) An employer should develop an extensive library containing all appropriate employment forms that might ever be needed for day-to-day employment matters. The following represent some key forms and records highlighted by a national employment law firms. These represent typical forms or issues that should be recorded each business is different and has unique concerns. By having pre-developed forms, you would not be sent scurrying to develop a form at the last minute or writing something on a slip of paper which can easily get lost or misplaced.

- Requisition for Employees
- Application for Employment
- Interview Guide
- Reference Inquiry Form
- Physical examination Form
- Reporting for Work Form
- Introduction Form
- Security Badge/Pass Form
- Work Pass
- Change of Status Form which can highlight the following changes:
  - Pay Rate
  - Employment Status
  - Change of Department
  - Clock Number Change
  - Reinstatement After Leave or Probation
  - Employee Resignation
  - Employee Layoff
  - Employee Discharges
  - Employee Leave of Absence
  - Job and Worker Specification
  - Request for Transfer
  - Notice of Discipline
  - Probation Notice
  - Performance Evaluation
  - Individual Progress Report
  - Accident Report
  - Absence Report

- Investigator's Report
- Tardiness Reprimand
- Incident Report
- Exit Interview
- Termination Report
- Clearance Card
- Military Service
- Workers' Compensation Injury Report ("Update '92," 1992).

State and Federal Laws

While state and federal laws change on a regular basis, the following represent the currently applicable reporting requirements and regulations affecting personnel documents.

The Department of Labor, pursuant to the Fair Labor Standards Act, requires all employers to make and keep certain payroll records for three years. The information that needs to be kept includes:

- name of each employee,
- employee number,
- age,
- sex,
- address,
- occupation,
- when (time/day) their work week begins,
- regular hourly rate,
- hours worked each day and each week,
- total straight and overtime payments,
- deductions or additions to wages,
- wages paid in each pay period,
- when payment was made, and
- what period was covered by the payment.

The same law requires basic employment and earning records (including wage rate tables and work-time schedules) need to be kept for two years.

Under the Equal Pay Act, wage payments, wage rates, job evaluations, job descriptions, merit plans, seniority plans and collective bargaining agreements all need to be kept for two years. Especially critical are any documents explaining why certain positions have a disparity between male and female employees at the same level.

Title VII of the Civil rights Act of 1964 requires employers to retain all employment and personnel records (everything from application forms, promotion documents, and termination documents) for one year from when the record was made or one year after the incident occurred, whichever is longer. Records also need to be kept concerning any alleged Title VII violation until the matter is finally resolved. These same record keeping provisions also apply for Americans with Disabilities Act claims and associated documentation.

Employers, pursuant to the Age Discrimination in Employment Act (ADEA), are required to keep each employee's name, address, birth date, pay rate, occupation and compensation earned on a weekly basis. These documents need to be kept for three years. In addition, some documents need to be kept for one year after someone covered by ADEA is terminated. These documents include records pertaining to:

- the refusal to hire anyone,
- promotion,
- demotion,
- transfer,
- training decisions,
- layoffs, recall or discharge documentation for any employee,
- any job orders to an employment agency for any job openings,
- any test results pertaining to personnel decisions, and
- any advertisements relating to job openings, promotions, training programs or opportunities for overtime work.

After a termination concerning an ADEA covered individual (over 40), the employer is required to keep all records for temporary work/assignments for at least 90 days. All documents covered by the ADEA need to be kept in a safe location and must be made available during regular business hours for inspection by an authorized EEOC representative.

The Employee Retirement Income Security Act requires all welfare and pension plans to be kept for six years after the plans are filed.

As discussed previously in this chapter, the Immigration Reform and Control Act requires each employer to retain I-9 forms for three years after the person was hired or one year after they were terminated, whichever comes later. If a job applicant completed an I-9 form, but was not hired, the I-9 form still must be kept three years after they were recruited.

Even though polygraphs are no longer permitted for hiring purposes, they still can be utilized during a worker's employment term under specific conditions. Under the Federal Employee Polygraph Protection Act, all polygraph testers are required to maintain all opinions, charts, reports, notes, written questions, and any other documents relating to the test for at least three years after the test. The examiner is also required to record how many exams were conducted each day as well as the length of each examination.

Several federal acts (such as the Rehabilitation Act of 1973 and the Vietnam-Era Veterans Readjustment Assistance Act) require employers to keep all federally filed reports for various periods that conform to the general rules discussed above.

The Occupational Safety and Health Act requires covered employers to keep medical and health risk exposure records for 30 years after an employee terminates their involvement with the employer. This is in addition to various more specific reporting requirements discussed in greater detail in Chapter 11.

In addition to the above federal record retention periods, each state might also have similar or longer record keeping requirements. In California, the California Fair Employment and Housing Act requires all applications and related employment records to be kept for at least two years. Similarly all records relating to a termination must be kept for two years after the date of termination (Kristoff and Blackburn, 1994). California also has numerous requirements for handling medical records, which sometimes parallels the ADA's requirements. Because there is a diversity of dates involved in the federal and state record keeping requirements, it is essential that no documents are disposed of without the authorization of competent counsel or a fully trained HR professional.

It is imperative that proper documentation form the primary emphasis relating to all your employment policies, rules and regulations. Proper documentation also refers to allowing individuals the opportunity to review their personnel file. Under California Labor Code Section 1198.5, an employee has the right, during reasonable hours, to review all documents setting forth the employee's qualifications, promotion, compensation, termination and/or any other disciplinary actions. The statute specifically excludes access to reference letters and investigation of criminal matters. The statute does not require the employer to provide the employee with a copy of the file. However, other Labor Code sections do require the employer to give the employee copies of any documents signed by the employee such as application and tax documents. The laws in California are replicated throughout the United States. The general rule for disclosure is to provide reasonable disclosure of only that employee's record, to that specific employee or their authorized representative (signed authorization should be requested and copied) in a timely manner during regular business hours.

Various state laws regulate employee access to personnel files, medical information and hazardous chemical exposure. By state law, employees in Alaska, California, Connecticut, Delaware, Illinois, Iowa, Maine, Massachusetts, Michigan, Minnesota, Nevada, New Hampshire, Ohio, Oregon, Pennsylvania, Rhode Island, Washington and Wisconsin can review and copy their records on a periodic basis and at reasonable times (Feliu, 1992). Employees have access to most records except internal investigations, management planning documents, reference letters and some confidential information. Some state laws are so pro-employee, they allow employees the right to make corrections to any mistakes contained in their personnel file (Feliu, 1992). Even if employees are not afforded a legal right to correct mistakes, it is a sound management approach to allow for employee review and error correction to ensure employment decisions are based on appropriate, correct information.

In at least six states (Connecticut, Delaware, Massachusetts, Michigan, Rhode Island and Wisconsin), employees are allowed to access their medical records (Feliu, 1992). Some states put limits on medical information disclosure. North Carolina permits an employer to exempt from disclosure information that "a prudent physician would not divulge to a patient" (Feliu, 1992). In other states such as Arkansas, Massachusetts and Wyoming, an employer is obligated to release results of an employment-related physical examination (Feliu, 1992).

Still other state laws require joint disclosure of OSHA violations. Employers can be required to disclose hazardous chemical exposures to both OSHA and employees (Feliu, 1992).

Postings

Additional required documentation can include mandatory posters and notices which need to be posted around the workplace. This documentation concern is addressed in more detail in Chapter 6. However, it should be noted that posting requirements represent one of the final documentation requirements which both state and federal laws can cover.

Wrap Up...

This chapter has presented some of the many concerns that can be faced when trying to hire an employee. There are no short cuts in the process. While you can possibly delegate responsibility to others, you will ultimately be held accountable for any discrimination perpetrated by the procedures your employees use or the manner in which they ultimately make the hiring decision. The only means to help prevent litigation associated with the hiring process entails developing pre-approved forms for all phases of the hiring process. All individuals involved within the hiring process need to be properly trained in following the prescribed procedure without deviation. While it is impossible to prevent any deviation, especially in the interview process, it is imperative that deviations be limited as much as possible. Testing and/or screening might be critical for a prospective employee, however, such steps need to be taken into context based on how much weight such tests represent in the hiring process. If they only form a minor component in the final hiring decision, then their value has to be weighted against potential prejudice or legal challenges that such tests or screening might raise.

Additionally, all phases of the hiring process should be appropriately documented with litigation in mind. Vigilant documentation will become your most important weapon and shield if you face a lawsuit alleging improprieties in the hiring process. Lastly, whenever a question arises, do not act on instinct or intuition. Contact a qualified attorney or human resource professional.

The following represents a handy checklist to determine if you are covering all your bases during the employee hiring process

- Have you reviewed the application form to insure you are requesting appropriate, necessary and non-discriminatory information?
- Have you reviewed the procedures for recruiting and interviewing employees?
- Have you carefully reviewed all forms that will be used during the hiring process?
- Have you determined where employee information will be kept and develop appropriate storage location for confidential files?
- Have you inserted a copy of the job description into the employees or applicants file?
- Do you allow former workers to re-apply for open position and if so establish under what conditions someone can be re-hired?
- Have interviewers been trained in all legal minefields?
- Have you documented when any interviewer training was provided, by whom and who attended?
- Have you developed a policy for disposing or storing applications if they are not immediately needed?
- Do all interviewers utilize a structured, form oriented approach and if not, what safeguards are in place to appropriately document the interview?
- Have you determined if you want private interviews or panel interviews?
- Have you developed a policy for handling unsatisfactory job references?
- Are there any other criteria not expressly mentioned in the job description or application form which form a critical component within the hiring process-such as communication skills?
- If you utilize a placement agency to help hire and or locate future employees do you ensure they comply with all federal

and state laws and supply you with appropriate written report concerning each applicant's background?

References

Adler, R., and Coleman, F. (1995). *Employment-Labor law audit.* Washington, DC: BNA, Inc.

Armour, S. (1997). "Firms key up PCs for job screening." *USA Today* (October 20): 6B.

"Association ponders background checks." (1997). *USA Today* (January 13): 12C.

Bielski, V. (1996). "Your boss wants more than your blood." *California Lawyer* (November): 18.

Bordwin, M. (1994/1995). "Firing 101: before, during and after." *Small Business Forum* 12(3): 44–57.

Chruden, H., and Sherman, Jr., A. (1976). *Personnel management.* 5th edition. Cincinnati, OH: South-Western Publishing Co.

Clay, J.M., and Stephens, E.C. (1996). "The defamation trap in employee references." *Cornell Hotel and Restaurant Administration Quarterly*, pp. 18–24.

"Court rules job references need warning." (1997). *Houston Chronicle* (January 20): 3C.

Cusick, D. (1996). "Employee not required to disclose prescription drugs." *Daily Court Review* (February 2): 1.

Daniloff, D. (1989). "Employer defamation: Reasons and remedies for declining references and chilled communications in the workplace." *The Hastings Law Journal* 40(3): 687–722.

Eikleberry, J.L. (1995). "Job references: a legal and management paradox." *Arizona Attorney* 32(2): 20–23, 41–42.

Feliu, A. (1992). *Primer on individual employee rights.* Washington, DC: BNA, Inc.

Fried, G. (1996). "Unsportsman like conduct." *American Humanics* 5(2): 3–6.

Fried, G. (1997). *Sexual Abuse Prevention Manual.* Houston, TX: University of Houston.

Frierson, J. (1994). *Preventing employment lawsuits, an employer's guide to hiring, discipline, and discharge.* Washington, DC: BNA, Inc.

Gifis, S. (1984). *Barron's legal guide, law dictionary.* New York: Barron's Educational Services, Inc.

Harvey, J. (1997). "Background checks vital even for small businesses." *Wichita Business Journal* (September 19): 14, 18.

Jones, D. (1996). "Resume boosting can bust careers." *USA Today* (September 13): 2B.

"Judge stalls hiring at University of Toledo" (1996). *The Columbus Dispatch* (March 24): 2C.

Kaplan, L. (1996). "Verifying employees' eligibility." *California Bar Journal* (August): 24.

Kristoff, R., and Blackburn, S. (1994). *Managing within the law-update.* San Francisco, CA.: AST Research, Shachther, Kristoff, Orenstein & Berkowitz.

Leatherman, C. (1996). "To get rid of a difficult employee, a college may hush up problems in a professor's past." *The Chronicle of Higher Education* (December 6): A14.

Leonard, B. (1996). "Five more states enact reference-checking laws." *HRMagazine* (May): 8.

Lublin, J. (1996). "Company checks references for workers feeling wronged." *Houston Chronicle* (November 17): 9E.

McCall, B. (1996). "Does Texas need a law shielding employers from liability for negative job references?" *Texas Lawyer* (October 28): 26.

McEwen, J., Manili, B., and Connors, E. (1986, October). "Employee drug testing policies in police departments." *National Institute of Justice-Research in Brief* (October).

Martucci, W.C., and Boatright, D.B. (1995). "Immunity for employment references." *Employment Relations Today* 22(2): 119–123.

Middleton, M. (1995). "A changing landscapte." *ABA Journal* (August): 56–61.

Miller, L.K., Pitts, B.G., and Fielding, L.W. (1993). "Legal concerns in writing job recommendations." *The Physical Educator* 50(1): 47–51.

Paetzold, R.L., and Wilburn, S.L. (1992). "Employer (ir)rationality and the demise of employment references." *American Business Law Journal* 30(1): 123–142.

Patterson, J. (1994). *Staff screening tool kit.* Washington, DC: Nonprofit Risk Management Center.

Price, D. (1997). "Good references pave road to court." *USA Today* (February 13): 11A.

Rothstein, M., Knapp, A., and Liebman, L. (1987). *Employment law, cases and materials.* New York: The Foundation Press, Inc.

Uniform guidelines on employee selection procedures. (1993 edition). 29 CFR Ch. XIV-7.

Update '92, In-house counsel colloquium. (1992). San Francisco, CA: Schachter, Kristoff, Orenstein & Berkowitz.

Von der Embse, T.J., and Wyse, R.E. (1985). "Those reference letters: How useful are they?" *Personnel* (January): 42–46.

Weiler, P., and Roberts, G. (1993). *Sports and the law, cases, materials and problems*. St. Paul, MN: West Publishing.

Cases

Beard v. Coca-Cola Bottling Co., 60 Empl. Prac. Dec. (CCH) Paragraph 42,012 (S.D. Ohio, 1990).
Doe et al. v. Bridgeport ISD, et al., Texas Lawyer, Case Summaries, January 20, 1997, 25.
EEOC v. Ryder, 649 F. Supp. 1282 (W.D.N.C. 1986).
Lewis v. Equitable Life Assurance Society, 389 N.W. 2d 876 (Minn. 1986).
Robinson v. Shell Oil Co., 70 F.3d 325 (4th Cir. 1997).
Tarassoff v. Regents of the University System of California, 17 Cal.3d 425 (1991).
Wilkinson v. Times Mirror Corp., 264 Cal.Rptr. 194 (Ct. App. 1989).
Wroblewski v. Lexington Gardens, Inc., 448 A.2d 801 (Con. 1982).

Statutes

ADA, 42 U.S.C. A. Section 12101 et seq.
ADEA, 29 U.S.C.A. Section 621 et seq.
California Civil Code Ann. Section 56–56.37.
California Fair Employment and Housing Act, Cal Gov. Code Section 12900 et seq.
California Labor Code, Section 1198.5.
Connecticut General Statute Annotated, Section 31–51g(b)(1).
Employee Polygraph Protection Act of 1988, 29 U.S.C.A. 2001 et seq.
ERISA, 29 U.S.C.A. Section 1144 et seq.
Environmental Protection Act (EPA), 42 U.S.C.A. Section 4321.
FLSA, 29 U.S.C.A. Section 201 et seq.
Immigration Reform and Control Act of 1986, Pub Law 99-603, Section 1 et seq., 100 Stat. 3359.
Indian Child Protection & Family Violence Prevention Act, 25 U.S.C.A. Section 3201.
OSHA, 29 U.S.C.A. Section 652 et seq.
Rehabilitation Act of 1973, 29 U.S.C.A. Section 701 et seq.
The Victims of Child Abuse Act of 1990, 42 U.S.C.A. Section 13001.
Title VII of the Civil Rights Act of 1964, 42 U.S.C.A. Section 2000e.
Veterans' Reemployment Rights Act, 38 U.S.C.A. Section 4301.
Veterans' Readjustment Benefits Act, 38 U.S.C.A. Section 3471.

Chapter 4

Discrimination in Hiring

Prior to the 1960s, employers had great leeway in how they recruited, hired, compensated, promoted, treated and terminated employees. Today, interaction with employees and employment-related decisions are closely scrutinized. The 1990s represent an era heavily fraught with employment litigation. In fact, employment litigation currently represents "the fastest growing area of civil litigation in the federal system" and is viewed by some as being in a "state of crisis" ("Developments," 1996). Equal opportunity legislation and litigation have greatly altered employment practices and there is no sign that this trend will abate. The following legislation, described very briefly below, greatly influences management's interactions with job applicants and existing employees. The remainder of this chapter reviews various pieces of legislation influencing personnel management and operations in general. This chapter strives to only introduce the student to legislation influencing the sport business employer. Employers are encouraged to delve further into each piece of legislation to obtain a better and more thorough understanding.

1) Title VII of the Civil Rights Act of 1964

Many legal scholars and academicians refer to Title VII as "the single most important piece of legislation that has helped to shape and define employment law rights in this country" (Bennett-Alexander and Pincus, 1995). Indeed, the legislation is encompassing and far reaching. The Civil Rights Act of 1964 prohibits discrimination in employment as well as in housing, education, public accommodations and federally assisted programs. Employment litigation quickly became the most common form of Title VII litigation since access to hotels and public accommodations became a moot point if members of the protected class could not earn the income to frequent these places.

Title VII prohibits discrimination in the entire employment process (e.g., hiring, promotions, compensation, terminations, opportunities for training, the work environment) based upon race, sex, national origin, religion or color. Sex discrimination does not include affinity orientation or transsexuals although individual state laws may provide protective legislation. For example, eight states and over 125 municipalities have legislation ex-

115

tending employment protection and benefits to gays and lesbians (Bennett-Alexander and Pincus, 1995). "Color" refers to one's skin pigmentation (e.g., dark or light). Research shows that the income of light complexion blacks is significantly higher than the income of dark complexion blacks. More specifically, Title VII provides that (42 USC 2000e-2(a)),

> (a) It shall be an unlawful employment practice for an employer —
> (1) to fail or refuse to hire or to discharge any individual, or otherwise to discriminate against any individual with respect to his compensation, terms, conditions, or privileges of employment, because of such individual's race, color, religion, sex, or national origin.

The Equal Employment Opportunity Commission (EEOC), created in 1978, is responsible for enforcing and interpreting Title VII. The legislation pertains to only those businesses affecting commerce and which employ 15 or more employees for each working day in each of 20 or more weeks in the current or preceding calendar year. Bona fide private clubs (e.g., country clubs) are not required to comply with Title VII (Sawyer, 1993). As of 1991(through the 1991 Civil Rights Reform Act), Title VII also covers individuals employed by American firms outside the United States. Filing a Title VII claim is not the same as filing any other tort action. Plaintiffs must first file a claim with the EEOC within 180 days of the last discriminatory act (e.g., harassment). This statute of limitations is significantly shorter than the traditional one to three year limitation adopted by most states. The EEOC can choose to actively litigate the claim itself. In the alternative, the EEOC can issue a "right-to-sue" letter to the plaintiff. The plaintiff then has 90 days to file a suit with the federal district court upon receiving the "right-to-sue" letter.

2) Types of Discrimination

Before analyzing the various pieces of legislation covering discrimination, it is important to distinguish between two types of discrimination. Disparate treatment and disparate impact represent the two types of discrimination that can take place in violation of Title VII.

Disparate Treatment

Disparate treatment refers to the intentional, differential treatment of employees based upon race, color, religion, national origin or sex. Disparate treatment represents overt discrimination. For example, a sport business adopting a policy prohibiting the employment of women as sports information directors illustrates disparate treatment. If direct evidence of intentional discrimination is unavailable, an inference of discrimination can be deduced by the following four-prong analysis defined by the U. S. Supreme Court in *McDonnell Douglas Corp. v. Green* (1973). According to the Court, the plaintiff may successfully prove a prima facie (first blush) case of discrimination by showing,

a) membership in a protected class (i.e., African-American, Women, etc.),
b) plaintiff applied and was qualified for a job for which defendant was seeking applicants,
c) despite qualifications, plaintiff was rejected, and
d) after the rejection, the position remained open and the employer continued to seek applicants with similar qualifications.

Upon proving the above by the plaintiff, the burden of proof then shifts to the defendant. The defendant-employer must then come up with some reason other than discrimination to justify the contested employment-related action. A valid reason can include a bona-fide occupational qualification (BFOQ). The burden of proof then shifts back to the plaintiff where the plaintiff must prove the defendant's justification represents "pretext" only. "Pretext" means that the justification provided is not "good" or sufficient, but represents a nonmeritorious and inadequate attempt to disguise discriminatory employment practices. As explained by the U. S. Supreme Court *in Texas Dept. of Community Affairs v. Burdine* (1981),

> The plaintiff retains the burden of persuasion. She now must have the opportunity to demonstrate that the (defendant's) proffered reason was not the true reason for the employment decision.... She may succeed in this either directly, by persuading the court that a discriminatory reason more likely motivated the employer or indirectly by showing that the employer's proffered explanation is unworthy of credence.

Unfortunately, the uniformity among the courts regarding the significance of pretext material or the degree of weight given to pretext material differs among circuits ("Developments," 1996).

A closely watched case, *Postema v. National League* (1992), can be used to illustrate the application of the *McDonnell Douglas* (1973) analysis. Postema, a female professional baseball umpire, sued a number of defendants alleging discrimination in violation of Title VII. Postema argued,

> She was fully qualified to be a major league umpire, and she had repeatedly made known to Defendants her desire for employment in the major

leagues. While she was not promoted to or hired by the National League or American League, male umpires having inferior experience, qualifications, and abilities were repeatedly and frequently promoted and hired by the National and American Leagues (*Postema*, 1992).

In accordance with the above *McDonnell Douglas* criteria, Postema, a female, met the first requirement of belonging to a protected class. The second prong of the McDonnell analysis required Postema to prove that she was qualified to umpire in the major leagues yet was rejected based upon her sex. Lastly, Postema was required to show that after her denial, the defendant baseball leagues continued to seek employment from males with similar qualifications. Unfortunately for Postema, she was not able to prove that the defendant League had a position that hired or promoted an individual (male or female) to the position she sought.

Disparate Impact

Disparate impact deals with the consequences of a particular employment policy. Policies, for example, that appear to be neutral may in fact might have a disparate or adverse impact on an otherwise protected group (*Griggs v. Duke Power Co.*, 1971). As explained by the U. S. Supreme Court in *Griggs*,

> What is required by Congress (under Title VII) is the removal of artificial, arbitrary, and unnecessary barriers to employment when the barriers operate invidiously to discriminate on the basis of racial or other impermissible classifications.

Courts have held that educational requirements, arrest records, credit status and height and weight requirements represent screening devices with a disparate impact on certain protected individuals. Height and weight requirements, for example, are not discriminatory at face value. However, the consequences of a height and weight requirement may serve to eliminate women or people of Asian descent who are smaller than male, Caucasian counterparts. For example, baseball league policies requiring umpires to be a certain height and weight were argued as necessary to ensure that umpires would be able to endure the physical aspects of the game and generate the player's respect. Unfortunately, these requirements are discriminatory as they tend to unjustly discriminate against women and other minorities. Similarly, imposing height and weight standards for lifeguards due to a misperception that "strong, large men" make better lifeguards represents a policy with a disparate impact on a protected class.

However, all testing and measuring procedures are not prohibitive. Employers making employment-related decisions based upon testing or measuring procedures must ensure that the particular skill or trait tested or measured represents the ability to perform an essential, required job function and does not influence a "term, condition, or privilege of employment." In 1978 the EEOC provided quantifiable guidelines to help clarify what constitutes a disparate impact. The 1993 edition of the Uniform Guidelines on Employee Selection Procedures ("Uniform Guidelines," 1993) provides that disparate impact is "statistically demonstrated when the selection rate for groups protected by Title VII is less than 80 percent or four-fifths that of the highest scoring majority group member." This test is commonly referred to as the four-fifths rule. The burden of proof is on the employer to show how the particular criterion is job related. Bennett-Alexander and Pincus (1995) explained the dynamics of the four-fifths rule as follows,

> 100 women and 100 men take a promotion examination. One hundred percent of the women and 50 percent of the men pass the exam. The men have only performed 50 percent as well as the women. Since the men did not pass at a rate of at least 80 percent of the women's passage rate, the exam has a disparate impact on the men. The employer would now be required to show that the exam is job related. If this can be shown to the satisfaction of the court, then the job requirement, though it has a disparate impact, will be permitted.

To summarize, any test or measuring device administered should never have greater than a 20% discrepancy among the protected classes identified in Title VII. Even if you are sued for discrimination, there are several significant defenses available to help rebut the plaintiff's claims.

3) Defenses to Discrimination

Proof that a particular business policy or practice was exercised out of a business necessity or as a bona fide occupational qualification (BFOQ) can serve as a major defense for an employer.

Business Necessity

A defense against a claim of disparate impact is that the alleged employment decision or workplace policy/test is "necessary" to ensure effective business operations. For example, a credit history performed on all individuals applying for the position of Ticket Manager at Professional Team, Inc. could be defensible even though female or minority job candidates could challenge this policy as discriminatory since statistics validate that women and minorities have less stable credit histories. The employer, however, could be justified in collecting credit history information since the employer would want to hire an individual who could effectively manage money generated from ticket sales.

English Only Rules

Employers have argued that English-only laws, although alleged to have a disparate impact on employees of a particular national origin, represent a business necessity. For example, an individual managing a sports park may adopt an English-only policy to ensure the safety of employees and patrons as employees encountering accidents or hazards need to communicate in a language others can understand. Due to the nature of the emergency and the probability of injury, time is of essence and English-only communication may represent a business necessity. While English only rules (which further a legitimate business necessity) could be valid during work hours, especially for employees with direct public contact, the rules however are not valid when the require employees to speak only English during their work breaks (Moreno, 1997).

Uniforms

Employers have also defended questionable dress requirements imposed on female employees as a required business necessity. Denouncing employers' contentions, the courts tend to rule in favor of the female plaintiff(s) in such cases. For example, in *Carroll v. Talman Federal S.& L. Ass'n of Chicago* (1979), the female plaintiffs were required to wear uniforms while the men were permitted to wear business-type apparel. In denying the defendant's motion for summary judgment the U.S. Court of Appeals (7th Cir.) concluded,

> While there is nothing offensive about uniforms per se, when some employees are uniformed and others not there is a natural tendency to assume that the uniformed women have a lesser professional status than their male colleagues attired in normal business clothes.

The *EEOC v. Sage Rlty. Corp.* case (1981) is instructive regarding employer mandates about women's required attire. In the *Sage* case, female employees were required to wear revealing Bicentennial uniforms. The plaintiff and the EEOC alleged that the employers violated Title VII and engaged in sex discrimination when requiring the female plaintiff to wear such a scant uniform. As expressed by the *Sage* court,

> While wearing the Bicentennial uniform and as a result of wearing it, Hasselman was subjected to repeated harassment. She received a number of sexual propositions and endured lewd comments and gestures. Humiliated by what occurred, Hasselman was unable to perform her duties prop-

erly.... The wearing of the uniform was made a condition of Hasselman's employment, and her employment was terminated when she refused to continue wearing the garment (*Sage*, 1981).

The plaintiff complained numerous times to her supervisors and others regarding the harassment she encountered when wearing the uniform of the uncomfortable environment the uniform requirement imposed. The supervisors took no step to remedy the situation. Similar cases could arise in the sport industry if sport business managers requiring women working in a health club or golf shop lounge, for example, to wear revealing clothing as their business attire in order to attract customers (*Slayton v. Michigan Host*, 1985).

Hair

Grooming standards, such as hair length requirements imposed upon men, have also been contested as a Title VII violation. Case precedent, however, supports the employer's enforcement of grooming standards (specifically hair length requirements). Thus, requiring males to maintain the length of their hair above the collar when female employees can wear long hair is not discriminatory in violation of Title VII. As explained by the court in *Dodge v. Giant Food, Inc.* (1973),

> Neither sex is elevated by these regulations to an appreciably higher occupational level than the other. We conclude that Title VII never was intended to encompass sexual classifications having only an insignificant effect on employment opportunities.

Title VII was designed to address immutable characteristics (e.g., sex, race, national origin) versus characteristics which can be controlled (e.g., hair length). On the other hand, state actors (e.g., park and recreation departments and public schools) may have a more difficult time enforcing grooming and attire standards as plaintiffs, in addition to alleging Title VII violations, may argue that such standards are also in violation of liberty rights guaranteed by the federal constitution. The United States Court of Appeals (7th Cir.) gave good advice for employers in *Carrol v. Talman Federal S. & L. Ass'n of Chicago* (1979). The court concluded that,

> So long as they find some justification in commonly accepted social norms and are reasonably related to the employer's business needs, such regulations are not necessarily violations of Title VII even though the standards prescribed differ some-what for men and women (*Carrol*, 1979).

Employers contemplating a policy that requires different standards among employees should ensure that the adopted policy addresses a genuine business necessity.

Bona Fide Occupation Qualification (BFOQ)

A BFOQ legalizes discrimination against an individual based upon sex, religion and national origin only when such ascribed characteristics can be considered essential for job success. For example, Southwest Airlines argued that its female-only hiring policy was a BFOQ (*Wilson v. Southwest Airlines Company*, 1981). The court concluded differently and held that Southwest's female-only hiring policy did not qualify as a BFOQ. Central to the court's decision was the fact that business operation and resultant revenues would not be reduced if male flight attendants were hired because the primary customer concern was safely reaching his or her destination at an affordable price. In a sport-related case, *US EEOC v. Audrey Sedita* (1991), the defendants argued that their policy of hiring only female, assistant managers and instructors in the health club for female patrons was a BFOQ. The court held in favor of the plaintiff as the defendant manager of Women's Workout World failed to prove that hiring male managers would result in member attrition. Thus, business harm has to be proven to prevail under a BFOQ claim. A sex-based BFOQ may exist, for example, in hiring locker room attendants for female locker rooms if the attendant is present when student-athletes are showering and dressing. Religion also may constitute a BFOQ. For example, educational institutions may employ those of a particular religion "if they are owned in whole or in substantial part by a particular religion" (*Pime v. Louola University of Chicago*, 1986; *EEOC v. Kamehameha Schools/Bishop Estate*, 1993). National origin has been used as a BFOQ when the employer deems it necessary to preserve the authenticity or ambiance of a particular business (e.g., hiring only Chinese employees for a Chinese restaurant). Today's sport managers will find BFOQs very narrowly construed and rarely applicable in defending Title VII cases.

If one person can break the BFOQ rule, then it is an invalid rule. Thus, stadium security companies might try to hire strong assertive men who weigh over 250 pounds to help manage crowd-related security concerns. However, if one woman meets the above criteria or can demonstrate competence to accomplish job duties, and is not considered as a potential candidate, then she has been discriminated against. Furthermore, the BFOQ defense is invalid as it can be disproved by someone in the protected class. This example helps demonstrate why it is so important to develop comprehensive job descriptions. To ensure you can hire the qualified individuals you need, you can make a legitimate job requirement that an individual can lift a certain amount of weight in order to handle crowd surges. This can help ensure hiring individuals (regardless of their gender) who can effectively accomplish all the required job components.

Harassment

Sport business managers should be cognizant that "discrimination" in employment encompasses harassment. The manager's best defense against harassment claims is a good offense. In other words, sport managers should make it clear that all forms of harassment will not be tolerated or condoned. In addition to prohibiting harassment as defined by federal legislation (e.g., harassment based upon sex, race, religion, national origin, age or disability), sport business managers should also pay heed to harassment based upon other classifications (e.g., sexual orientation) that may be prohibited by a state's human rights law. Further, all allegations of harassment should be taken seriously, quickly investigated and corrective action implemented when necessary.

Sexual Harassment

Sexual harassment is a growing area of litigation and of great importance to sport managers. In fact, a 1993 poll revealed that sexual harassment is "now the primary concern of human resource managers in the United States" (Kirk and Clapham, 1996). Sport business employees, vendors, and customers subjected to sexual harassment have access to recourse under Title VII. The number of sexual harassment complaints increased by 53% between 1991 and 1992 (Bennett-Alexander and Pincus, 1995). The costs associated with sexual harassment are alarming.

> Sexual harassment cost the federal government $267 million from May 1985 to May 1987 for losses in productivity, sick leave costs, and employee replacement costs (Bennett-Alexander and Pincus, 1995).

These costs do not include litigation costs. More important, however, are the costs incurred by victims including emotional stress, trauma, humiliation, embarrassment, anxiety and guilt. Sexual harassment is discussed in more detail in Chapter 7.

Same-sex Harassment

Same-sex harassment allegations are no longer rare in today's litigious society. According to a 1995 survey, 14% of all sexual harassment cases dealt with same-sex harassment (Kirk and Clapham, 1996). The appellate courts are divided about the law's intent to protect harassing treatment among homosexuals and heterosexuals of the same sex. Many argue that extending liability to victims of same-sex harassment would expand the intended scope of Title VII. As explained by the court in *Goluszek v. H.P. Smith* (1988),

> The discrimination Congress was concerned about when it enacted Title VII is one stemming from an imbalance of power and an abuse of that imbalance by the powerful which results in discrimination against a discrete and vulnerable group.

In *Quick v. Donaldson Co., Inc.* (1995) the court summarized holding for the defendant by reasoning that Title VII serves to rid environments of discrimination, not to regulate juvenile behaviors. According to Kirk and Clapham (1996), "goosing" (poking a person in a sensitive spot) and "bagging" (grabbing one in his groin area) have become common gestures of "horse play" in some work environments. This same behavior, albeit immature and unprofessional, forms the basis of sexual harassment claims among heterosexual men.

On the other hand, others (e.g., the Justice Department and the EEOC) argue that Title VII should be broadly interpreted.

> The Justice Department urged the high court to resolve a split among the federal appeals courts and hold that civil-rights law protects all employees from sexual harassment by all co-workers—regardless of gender or sexual orientation (Davis, 1997).

As explained by the court in *Prescott v. Independent Life and Accident Ins. Co.* (1995), the statute prohibits "discrimination based upon sex." Congress's failure to stipulate "discrimination based upon sex by members of the opposite sex" negates the exclusion of same-sex harassment as an recognizable cause of action protected by Title VII. The U.S. Supreme Court decided this issue in 1998 in the case of *Oncale vs. Sundowner* (Felsenthal, 1997). The Court finally resolved the dispute between the lower courts by concluding that the civil rights laws protect men and women who have been harassed by someone of their own gender (Sixel, 1998).

5) Discrimination Based Upon Religion

Sport managers are becoming increasingly familiar with the constitutional problems associated with prayer or other religious activities in public institutions or on public school playing fields. However, sport managers also need to use caution when conducting prayer before business meetings or on company property. Discrimination based upon religion is predicted to be an increasingly common cause of action facing employers. In 1993, 5% of all claims filed with the EEOC alleged discrimination based upon religious beliefs (Schaner and Erlemeier, 1995). The EEOC also reported a 30% increase in religious discrimination claims filed against employers since 1990 (Kurtz, Davis, and Asquith, 1996). As society continues to diversify and the workplace becomes more and more occupied with people of various religions, the potentials for conflicts are likely to accelerate. Since 1991, religious discrimination claims have increased 43% (Armour, 1997). As explained by Schaner and Erlemeier (1995),

> If an employer sponsors or creates religious-based activities in the workplace, whether it be a required prayer meeting, Bible study, or reading of the Torah, the employer risks Title VII liability.

In addition to responsibility for his or her own potentially religion-based harassing behaviors, employers are also responsible for the potentially harassing behaviors of other stakeholders (e.g., patrons, employees and vendors). The following activities may constitute religious harassment (Zachary, 1996),

1) Employer's refusal to allow employees to wear religious insignia or dress at work;
2) Threats or religious slurs directed at an employee;
3) Refusal to allow employees to read religious materials at work;
4) Denying of employment benefits based on an employee's religious beliefs;
5) Discipline or discharge resulting from an employee's religious beliefs;
6) Varying treatment of an employee based on the employee's perceived religious beliefs;
7) Retaliation against employees for protesting religious harassment;
8) Requiring employee attendance at religious services or meetings conducted at the workplace during work hours;
9) "Preaching," workplace prayer meetings, attempts to convert employees, religious items in the office of a supervisor, and frequent discussions and distributing of religious literature by a supervisor at work (religious expression may be viewed as threatening and controlling due to position of power or authority);
10) Retaliation against employees who protested religious discrimination by an activist employer or supervisor.

The most common allegation made by plaintiffs in religious harassment cases is that they are the target of derogatory comments based on individual religious preferences. As noted above in *Compston v. Borden, Inc.* (1976), the court found the defendant supervisor's continued arsenal of verbal abuse constituted religious discrimination in violation of Title VII. Another format of harassment includes the continued proselytizing to employee(s) who are not interested or receptive to the "message" being delivered. For example, in *Ground Transport Corp. v. Pennsylvania* (1990), the court held that the printing of Bible verses on employee paychecks and printing religious articles in the company newspaper constituted harassment for non-Christian employees.

Schaner and Erlemeier (1995) suggest that religious harassment be judged according to the factors defining a hostile work environment adopted in the 1993 *Harris v. Forklift* sexual harassment case (see Chapter 7). Factors guiding a court's analysis regarding the alleged religious harassment and its contribution to a hostile work environment include:

- the conduct's frequency,
- the conduct's severity,
- whether the conduct is physically threatening or humiliating,
- whether the conduct is merely an offensive utterance, and
- whether the conduct unreasonably interferes with work performance.

Quid pro quo religious discrimination, similar to *quid pro quo* sexual harassment cases, would prohibit employers from providing or denying employment or employment-related benefits to certain individuals based upon religious beliefs. Plaintiffs alleging a prima facie case of religious discrimination must prove the following:

1) The plaintiff has a bona fide religious belief that conflicts with an employment requirement;
2) The plaintiff informed the employer of this belief and the resultant employment conflict;
3) The plaintiff was disciplined for failure to comply with the conflicting employment requirement.

Employers must attempt to reasonably accommodate an employee's religious requests unless the accommodation would impose an undue hardship. As explained by the EEOC (1994), reasonable accommodations include "flexible scheduling, voluntary substitutions or swaps, job reassignments and lateral transfers." In *Wilson v. US West Communications, Inc.* (1994), the plaintiff was terminated for her refusal to remove or cover an antiabortion button depicting a color photograph of a 18–20 week fetus. The plaintiff argued that she could not remove the button for religious purposes. However, coworkers found the button offensive, disturbing and stressful. As a result of the tension, the workplace environment became very uncomfortable. The court in this case ruled in favor of the employer-defendant who had attempted to reasonably accommodate the plaintiff by providing her with alternatives, such as wearing the button with the fetus covered up.

Further, it is not necessary that a plaintiff-employee's religious belief replicate an established religious faith (e.g., Protestant, Catholic and Jewish). Court precedent indicates that employers will be required to accommodate an employee who expresses a sincere religious conviction (*EEOC v. JC Penney Co. Inc.*, 1990). As explained by Kurtz, Davis, and Asquith (1996),

> The definition of religion includes the well-recognized faiths, but also goes much further to encompass sincerely held, unorthodox beliefs as well. Even atheism is considered a religion....In addition, a religious practice, observance or belief does not have to be mandated by a religion to receive protection.

The above quote was reinforced in *Wilson v. US West Communications, Inc.* (1994) where the plaintiff insistent on wearing the abortion button felt compelled to wear the button as a devout Roman Catholic even though the Roman Catholic religion does not mandate that all believers wear similar buttons. Further, it *is not* necessary that a plaintiff-employee prove religious association. For example, in *Compston v. Borden, Inc.* (1976) the plaintiff sued under Title VII alleging religious discrimination because his supervisor routinely referred to him as "the Jew-boy," "the kike," "the Christ-killer," "the damn Jew," and "the goddamn Jew." At trial, the defendants attempted to prove that the plaintiff-employee was dismissed for reasons related to poor performance, not for discriminatory reasons based upon religion. In support of their argument, the defendants' argued that the plaintiff,

> Testified that he is not now, nor has he ever been, a practicing member of the Jewish faith. His grasp of the fundamental tenets of Judaism is a rather poor one (*Compston*, 1976).

The U.S. District Court, in holding for the plaintiff, provided in part,

> When a person vested with managerial responsibilities embarks upon a course of conduct calculated to demean an employee before his fellows because of the employee's professed religious views, such activity will necessarily have the effect of altering the conditions of his employment.

As illustrated above, inflammatory statements made in the heat of an argument can be daunting. The key is for all supervisors and employees to exercise religious tolerance and to learn from new experiences. An employer can foster such education through sponsoring different ethnic food days where a kosher meal is served, or different ethnic food is served. Such an action shows genuine interests and helps employees explain themselves so others feel more comfortable.

6) Discrimination Based Upon Race and/or Color

Title VII prohibits discrimination based upon race and/or color. Stereotypes and assumptions about abilities, traits and performance are illegal when they influence employment or a term, condition or benefit of employment. Geographic assignments, for example, may foster a discrimination claim. For example, a health club franchisor could not limit people of one race from acquiring a franchise in a particular area. In other words, it would be illegal to grant Asians a franchise only in a geographic area heavily populated by Asians. Employers also should avoid policies that specifically exclude or impact persons of a particular race or color. As explained by the EEOC (1994),

> Since sickle cell anemia predominantly occurs in African-Americans, a policy which excludes individuals with sickle cell anemia must be job related and consistent with business necessity. Similarly, a "no-beard" employment policy may discriminate against African-American men who have a predisposition to pseudofolliculitis barbae (severe shaving bumps) unless the policy is job related and consistent with business necessity.

As with other prohibitions defined by Title VII, harassment based upon race (e.g., racial slurs, jokes, offensive or derogatory comments) is illegal.

7) Discrimination Based Upon National Origin

Discrimination based upon one's national origin is unlawful. The EEOC provides a comprehensive explanation of prohibited discrimination based on one's national origin. As explained by the EEOC (1994),

> No one can be denied equal employment opportunity because of birthplace, ancestry, culture, or linguistic characteristics common to a specific ethnic group. Equal employment opportunity cannot be denied because of marriage or association with persons of a national origin group; membership or association with specific ethnic promotion groups; attendance or participation in schools, churches, temples or mosques generally associated with a national origin group; or a surname associated with a national origin group.

Employees should not be chastised or ostracized for unique accents or speech mannerisms. Employment ramifications based upon poor fluency in the English language are justified only if the language requirement represents an essential job characteristic directly influencing performance. Such BFOQs exists only when all communications need to be in English. The BFOQ will fail if a European soccer coach can communicate to players with a combination of rough English and sign language. Detailed job descriptions and job analysis can serve as useful tools for employers contemplating employment-related decisions that influence or exclude individuals from a particular national origin.

More recently, English-only laws have come under scrutiny as having a disparate impact on employees of a national origin. According to a 1997 article in *USA Today* (Mauro, 1997), 23 states have English-only laws while 10 states have similar laws pending. Although recognized by the EEOC as a possible Title VII violation, the U.S. Court of Appeals (9th Cir.) in *Garcia v. Spun Steak Co.* (1993) upheld the employers right to have an English-only policy and held that the policy did not have a disparate impact on the employee's terms, conditions or privileges of employment (see also *Cota v. Tucson Police Dept.*, 1992). In the *Garcia* case, the plaintiffs argued that the work place policy represented a disparate impact on those employees of a Spanish descent for the following reasons:

- It denied employees an opportunity to express their cultural heritage on the job;
- It denied employees a privilege of employment that is enjoyed by monolingual speakers of English; and
- It created an atmosphere of inferiority, isolation, and intimidation.

In deciding for the defendants, the U. S. Court of Appeals held that Title VII "does not protect the ability of workers to express their cultural heritage at the workplace." Furthermore, the denied privileges must have a "significant impact" on a term, condition or benefit of employment to represent disparate impact. The plaintiffs failed to present evidence documenting the policy's contribution to a hostile work environment. Similar to other Title VII concerns (e.g., sex and religion), a person harassed about his or her national origin by employees or administrators also have cause of action.

8) The Civil Rights Act of 1991

Title VII was not intended to be punitive in nature. Rather, the law intended to restore plaintiffs to pre-injury position or the position likely to be occupied had the discrimination never occurred. Back pay was commonly awarded to successful Title VII plaintiffs. The Civil Rights Act of 1991 revolutionized the way Title VII is interpreted by all stakeholders in two dominant ways. First, plaintiffs alleging intentional employment discrimination can now sue for both compensatory and punitive damages. Employers with more than 14 and fewer than 101 employees can be subject to liability not greater than $50,000. Employers with more than 100 and fewer than 201 can be subject to liability not greater than $100,000. Employers with more than 200 and fewer than 501 employees can be subject to liability not greater than $200,000. Employers with more than 500 employees can be subject to liability not greater than $300,000. Second, plaintiffs alleging intentional discrimination now have the right to a trial by jury.

The employer's window of liability was further expanded as a result of the U.S. Supreme Court's decision in *Robinson v. Shell* (1997). In *Robinson*, the Supreme Court held that the term "employees" used in the language of Title VII includes former employees as well as current employees. In other words, employers need to recognize that lawsuits alleging discrimination can be brought against them by individuals no longer employed by the sport organization. Please refer to the section on references and defamation in Chapter 3 for ways in which employers can protect from defamation related claims.

9) The Age Discrimination in Employment Act (ADEA), 1967, 1978, 1986

The ADEA was passed in 1967. Later amendments were made in 1978 and 1986. The 1986 amendment prohibits any mandatory retirement previously allowed in the earlier law. The 1986 ADEA amendment prohibits employers from discriminating against individuals over 40 years of age. ADEA claims are unique in that they normally generate significantly higher damages due to the earning level of employees over 40. As the population ages, ADEA claims are likely to increase in number. Employers have a variety of reasons discouraging them from hiring older workers. Some of these reasons include:

- Smaller employers typically pay twice as much in health-care premiums for a worker age 55 to 64 in comparison with a worker 35 to 39.
- Older workers are three times as likely to die from falls.
- Older workers are more than twice as likely to die in transportation or equipment-related accidents.
- Older workers often require more time and more money to train.

- Older workers are often less able to handle new technology (Armour, 1997).

Similar to the Title VII analysis set forth in the *McDonnell Douglas* case, employers have a *prima facie* case of age discrimination if the following apply:

1) The individual is a member of the protected class;
2) The individual was terminated or demoted;
3) The individual was doing the job well enough to meet his or her employer's legitimate expectations;
4) Others were treated more fairly.

A 1996 decision by the U. S. Supreme Court in *O'Connor v. Consolidated Coin Caterers* held that the plaintiff need not prove he or she was replaced by someone younger (i.e., outside the protected age group). As explained by Justice Scalia, "The fact that one person in the protected class lost out to another person in the protected class is thus irrelevant, so long as he has lost out because of his age." However, the most common example of ADEA violations involves an older employee being replaced by a younger, less expensive employee.

As illustrated by the U.S. Court of Appeals (8th Cir.), one of the most perilous facets of the ADEA exists for liability based upon superfluous comments made without malice or intent to discriminate. Employers need to be cautious of comments that could be construed as discriminatory. For example, Westinghouse encountered discriminatory age allegations resulting from a memo which quoted an employee as saying, "We...need to get younger individuals who think well and who think differently involved in the process as well." Another person was quoted as saying, in reference to the older employees, "We need to get the blockers out of the way." (Thomas, 1996). Similarly, comments such as "seeking recent college graduates" and "we need to promote a younger image" can prove problematic for employers when attempting to defend an age discrimination law suit (Coleman, 1985). For example, in *Hodgson v. Approved Personnel Serv.* (1975) the United States Court of Appeals (4th Cir.) granted an injunction against an employment agency that routinely used terms including, "sharp recent grads," "recent college grads," "recent high school grads," "recent math grads" (*Hodgson*, 1975). Quoting from the district court decision, the appellate court concluded that,

> Most "recent graduates" are composed of young people. When the term is used with a specific job, it violates the Act since it is not merely information to the job seeker but operates to discourage the older job hunter from seeking that particular job and denies them an actual job opportunity (*Hodgson*, 1975).

In a different case, the plaintiff used comments including, "It's about time we started to get some young blood in this company" and "You're too damn old for this kind of work" as evidence of a discriminatory work environment permeated with age bias (Sullivan, Kaikati, Virgo and Carr, 1996).

The employer may use the BFOQ as a defense if substantially all of the individuals in a particular age category are unable to perform the job adequately. For example, a sport business manager may discriminate against an older individual when seeking an employee to transport children to and from campgrounds since statistics exist to document the diminished driving ability of elderly individuals. A careful consideration of the job relatedness of selection requirements mitigates the likelihood that a sport manager will unlawfully discriminate based upon age (see Chapter 12, Section 3 and Chapter 13 for further application of the ADEA).

10) Title IX, 1972

Title IX was passed in 1972 although the impact of the law was not felt for nearly a quarter of a century later. Title IX provides in pertinent part that,

> No person in the United States shall, on the basis of sex, be excluded from participation in, be denied the befits of, or be subjected to discrimination under any education program or activity receiving Federal financial assistance.

Individuals employed in a for-profit sport industry receiving no federal monies have no recourse under Title IX. Title IX has great influence, however, on interscholastic and intercollegiate physical education, athletics, intramural programs, and park and recreation departments. Common Title IX allegations include pay disparities among coaches, sport program inequities for student-athletes, sexual harassment and even sexual assault. There is abundant legal research and case law analyzing the history, practices, trends and allegations against universities failing to comply with Title IX. However, case precedent regarding Title IX's application to the employment sector remains limited.

Title IX allegations contesting pay disparities between men and women coaches, as explained by Claussen (1995), are often more plausible than Equal Pay Act or Title VII violations (see Chapter 7 for application of pay disparity issues among coaches and recourse available via the Equal Pay Act). EPA and Title VII focus on discrimination based upon the employee's gender. Since both men and women employed to coach girl's and women's team receive lower pay than the men coaching men's team, sex discrimination allegations are difficult to prove. Claussen (1995) argues that Title IX remains the best recourse against employment discrimination in coaching intercollegiate athletics.

The NCAA provides good advice for institutions striving for Title IX compliance in their publication, *A Basic Guide to Title IX and Gender Equity in Athletics for Colleges and Universities* (1997). According to the NCAA Guide, institutions should ensure that the number of coaches employed to coach the women's team equals the number of coaches employed to coach the men's teams, including assistant coaches. The Guide provides that,

> For example, if men's basketball has a head coach, two assistants and a restricted-earnings coach, then women's basketball should have the same. For dissimilar sports, coaches should be available to the same extent appropriate for the sports. (Guide, 1997).

The length of contracts awarded to employees represents another area investigated by the Office of Civil Rights (OCR). Common compliance problems can arise when coaches of men's sports are on 12-month contracts and the coaches of women's sports are only on nine-month contracts. Another area that can generate compliance problems exists when coaches of men's sports are given multi-year contracts and the coaches of women's sports, on the other hand, are given annual contracts. As explained in the Guide,

> For example, the men's program may have 25 coaches while the women's program has 13 coaches. If three of the 25, or 12 percent, of the men's coaches have multi-year contracts, then two of 13, or 15 percent of the women's coaches should have multi-year contracts. If 17 of 25, or 68 percent, of men's coaches have 12-month contracts, then nine of 13, or 69 percent, of women's coaches should have 12-month contracts. (Guide, 1997).

Disparities may also exist in the employment conditions assigned to the coaches of women's sports versus men's sports. For example, problems can emanate when coaches employed to coach women sports are given additional duties including teaching, administration, student advising or committee work whereas male coaches are responsible solely for coaching.

OCR suggests that experience among coaches of women's versus men's sports be compared by averaging the years of experience among all coaches. More specifically, the Guide provides,

> For example, if the 25 men's coaches have a total of 513 years of coaching, of which 347 years are at the college level, then men's coaches aver-

age 21 years of coaching experience with 14 years at the college level. If the 13 women's coaches have a total of 208 years of coaching experience, of which 147 years are at the college level, then women's coaches average 16 years of coaching experience with 11 years at the college level (Guide, 1997).

However, as elaborated on by the Guide, an outstanding record can justify hiring individuals with little coaching experience to coach women's sports. As stated by the Guide (1997), "A coach with five years of coaching experience may be a much better coach than someone with 20 years of experience..." Employers should heed caution, however, when employing individuals with little or no experience to coach the women's sports while individuals employed to coach the men's teams have stellar records.

11) The Americans with Disabilities Act (ADA); Title I: Discrimination in Employment

The Americans with Disabilities Act (ADA) of 1990 mandates that employers eliminate policies, procedures, and practices which discriminate against the estimated 49 million disabled individuals living in America. Title I was phased in slowly to mitigate employer compliance costs. As of July 26, 1994, the ADA applies to all sport businesses with 15 or more employees. Title I seeks to better employ the 13 million unemployed, disabled people between the ages of 21 and 64 (Epstein, 1995). As reported by a Lou Harris poll conducted in 1989, 82% of the disabled constituency said they would exchange their benefits for a full time job. Employing the disabled enhances the self-esteem and self-worth of the disabled individual. In addition, society would benefit as tax monies needed to support this constituency would be reduced and the disabled individual's earned discretionary income could increase sales.

A principal element in understanding ADA legislation is to understand how the ADA defines a "disabled individual."

The ADA defines a disabled individual as one whom:

1) Has a physical or mental impairment that substantially limits one or more of his/her major life activities;
2) Has a record of such impairment; or
3) Is regarded as having such an impairment (ADA, 1990).

The first category prohibits discrimination against qualified individuals with a particular disease or condition (e.g., cancer, AIDS, epilepsy, depression, and mental retardation). The question regarding the validity of a plaintiff's alleged physical disability raises little debate. Mental injuries, on the other hand, present a more perplexing dilemma for the employer. The ADA includes in the definition of "mental impairments" the following:

- major depression,
- bipolar disorder,
- anxiety disorders (which include panic disorder, obsessive compulsive disorder and post-traumatic stress disorder),
- schizophrenia, and
- personality disorders.

Mental injuries represent the second most common complaint filed with the EEOC between July, 1992 and September 1995. Between July 1992 and September 1996, the EEOC reported that 17% of all claims were based on emotional or psychological impairments (EEOC, 1997). Unfortunately, emotional problems present complicated issues for both employers and the courts because mental diseases often entail symptoms that are difficult to measure. The EEOC clearly states, however, that traits like "irritability, chronic lateness and poor judgment are not in themselves, mental impairments, although they may be linked to mental impairments" (EEOC, 1997). In other words, employers cannot automatically discount an employee's chronic lateness if it is linked to a mental impairment which substantially limits one or more major life activities. Remedies for mental impairments are not as clear as remedies for physical impairments. Installing a wheel chair ramp, for example, is an obvious and reasonable accommodation for the mobility disabled. Further, psychiatric impairments present sport business employers with perilous dilemmas as they attempt to balance ADA compliance with the maintenance of a safe, violence-free work environment.

The second category, having a "record of such impairment," prohibits discrimination against qualified individuals who, for example, have a history of cancer or mental illness. Medical records and related documentation facilitate a plaintiff's ability to prove he or she is a "disabled individual" subject to coverage under the ADA. Coverage also extends to those who suffered from a prior medical malady such as cancer, but currently do not suffer any symptoms.

The third category of defined disability, "regarded as having such an impairment," prohibits discrimination based on preconceived, subjective stereotypes. Facial burns and other physical deformities qualify as discrimination under this third category and are covered by the ADA legislation. For example, a health club could not deny a person employment opportunities on the basis of a feared negative reaction from paying members.

The law also identifies conditions, behaviors, and impairments which do not qualify as disabilities. For example, left handedness, blond hair, baldness, blue eyes, compulsive gambling, kleptomania, pyromania, pedophilia, homosexuality, bisexuality, transsexualism, voyeurism and transvestitism are not disabilities covered by the ADA ("Nondiscrimination," 1994). In addition, temporary impairments such as a broken leg or the common cold are not qualified as disabilities impairing a major life activity ("Nondiscrimination," 1994).

Possessing a physical or mental disability as defined in any one of the above three categories, however, does not automatically qualify someone as disabled under the ADA. The particular disability must "substantially limits one or more major life activities." The ADA does not cover a disabled individual unless the disability limits a major life activity (*Jasany v. United States Postal Service*, 1985; *Taylor v. US Postal Service*, 1991). "Major life activities" are defined as "caring for one's self, performing manual tasks, walking, seeing, hearing, speaking, breathing, learning and working" (EEOC and the DOJ, 1991). However, employers are often in a quandary in defining a qualified disability since according to the 1997 EEOC Guidelines, "there is no exhaustive list of major life activities." Sleeping and interacting with others, for example, have also been identified as constituting major life activities. The vaguarities of the ADA require employers to pay heed to most all ADA based requests for reasonable accommodation or ADA claims. For example, someone might complain that the air conditioning is causing them breathing trouble. Such a notification cannot be lightly disregarded. Asthma and allergies are considered disabilities if they substantially limit an employee's ability to work.

Whether an impairment "substantially" limits a major life activity is determined on a contingency basis. Considerable attention is given to (a) the severity of the limitation (e.g., disrupts sleep a little versus a lot) and (b) the length of time the limitation has persisted (e.g., one month versus twelve months). An employee who becomes depressed for two to three months following the demise of a romance, for example, does not qualify as an individual possessing a substantially limiting impairment.

Physical disabilities tend to present less vaguarities. For example, the determination of whether the plaintiff's disability in *Anderson v. Little League Baseball, Inc.* (1992) limited one or more major life activities is less subjective. In the Anderson case, the plaintiff-coach sought to enjoin the defendants from enforcing a rule that would prohibit him from coaching from the on-field coach's box in a wheelchair. The coach who needs to use a wheelchair was disabled and could not stand or walk. As defined by the Federal Regulations, walking represents a "major life activity." Consequently, the plaintiff had little trouble qualifying as a disabled individual as defined by the ADA. In this particular case, the court upheld the coach's request for a temporary restraining order. Even though it was not mentioned in the court's opinion, Little League administrators could have provided reasonable accommodations by moving the coach several feet behind the coach's box, asking the coach to provide padding for protruding parts of the wheelchair, or other steps to protect him and/or potential players from injury.

> The ADA defines a "qualified individual with a disability" as one whom: Satisfies the requisite skill, experience, education and other job-related requirements of the employment position such individual holds or desires, and who, with or without reasonable accommodation, can perform the essential functions of such positions (ADA, 1990).

The ADA does not require employers to hire disabled individuals who are not qualified for the particular job. The BFOQ defense is a valid defense to an ADA claim.

Essential v. Non-Essential Job Functions

The ADA prohibits employers from excluding the disabled from job opportunities because a disabled individual who meets job prerequisites (e.g., education, work experience, training, licenses) cannot perform non-essential (i.e., marginal) job functions. For example, assume Hypothetical University's (HU) Athletic Department is housed in a two-story building. Also assume HU is hiring a person to work at the first floor ticket window on campus. HU's Athletic Department would not be able to eliminate a candidate who was unable to deliver mail to the upstairs office, as it is unlikely that this task represents an essential job function. The Equal Employment Opportunity Commission suggests that the employer handle non-essential job functions by either:

a)   providing an accommodation that will enable the individual
       to perform the function,
b)   transferring the function to another position, or
c)   exchanging the function for one the applicant is able to perform.

The EEOC classifies job functions as essential or non-essential on a case-by-case basis. The EEOC guidelines (1992) identify various factors which can facilitate an employer when classifying task as either "essential" versus "non-essential." This list includes the employer's judgment, job descriptions, time spent performing particular functions, the impact or consequences of not performing a function, a collective bargaining agreement, the work experience of people who have either in the past or are presently performing the job and the organizational structure. Completed job analyses are critical to an employer attempting to defend why a particular task was deemed "essential" (see Chapter 2 for more information on the job analysis).

Regardless of the assistance provided by the EEOC, debate continues over what constitutes an "essential" job function. Job attendance, for example, has been viewed as an essential job function when work cannot be performed at home (*Tyndall v. National Educ. Ctrs*, 1994; *Wimbley v. Bolger*, 1986). In the *Tyndall* case the employee-plaintiff was a teacher who had lupus and frequently needed to remain at home on account of her own illness or to care for her disabled son. The Fourth Circuit Court concluded that attendance was an essential job requirement. Further entrenchment of the virtual office on employment practices could foreseeably alter this "essential" nature of attendance. To illustrate, the continued interest in telecourses, course lectures provided by technology and communication and service commitments being fulfilled via e-mail and teleconferencing may alter the ability of a defendant school to successfully argue that job faculty attendance constitutes an essential job function. This case raises a critical point. The ADA also covers those with a relationship with a disabled individual. A relationship is defined as a parental or close familial relationship to a roommate. Thus, you have to provide reasonable accommodations to a secretary who has to take several small breaks several times during the day to take care of a dying spouse as long as such breaks do not interfere with an essential job function. Furthermore, this requirement has been raised on several occasions in sports facilities where individuals have brought claims alleging that a facility violated the ADA by not providing seating for able bodied patrons next to their disabled companions.

Selection Criteria

Employers can establish job selection criteria based upon a variety of physical and mental qualifications. Job selection criteria can reflect both essential and non-essential job functions, as noted by the *EEOC Technical Assistance Manual* (1992). Selection criteria may relate to:

a) education,
b) skills,
c) work experience,
d) licenses or certification,
e) physical and mental abilities,
f) health and safety,
g) other job-related requirements, such as judgment, ability to work under pressure or interpersonal skills, and
h) physical agility tests.

Only when the criteria has a disproportionate impact on the disabled individual(s) does the ADA require employers to show how selection criteria is both job-related and consistent with a business necessity. Again, reference to the job analysis facilitates ambiguity by providing the employer with specific information regarding selection criteria directly related to adequate job performance.

Application Accessibility

Employment opportunities for the disabled exists only if the disabled have access to employment related information. The ADA requires employers to make application procedures accessible to disabled individuals (EEOC, 1992). For example, facilities posting job information must provide access to the mobility impaired. Wheelchair ramps and first floor postings illustrate two simple ways employers can better assist the disabled population. Job applications listing telephone numbers also must list a telecommunication device or text telephone for deaf persons when no established telephone relay service exists. Further, the ADA requires employers to help disabled applicants who need assistance in completing the application form (e.g., writing assistance, reading assistance). Posting job descriptions in trade magazines, at conferences and at training facilities targeting the disabled constituency represent additional ways employers can comply with the ADA's spirit and legal requirements.

Interview and Application Inquiries

The ADA greatly alters the manner in which sport employers design job applications and conduct employment interviews. The issue regarding medical exams and inquiries is best categorized into three different stages: (a) pre-offer, pre-employment, (b) post-offer, pre-employment, and (c) post-employment. The following paragraphs address the distinctions and privileges associated with each phase of the employment process.

Pre-offer, Pre-employment Questioning Practices

Prior employment practices allowed employers to extensively question a candidate about his or her medical history and require a medical exam in the pre-employment stage. Disability-related questions and medical exams revealing "hidden" disabilities (e.g., epilepsy and diabetes) often posed a barrier to employment. For example, employers harboring biases about epilepsy or fearful of escalating insurance costs associated with cancer victims could previously refuse to hire an otherwise qualified individual.

Employers are no longer able to ask "disability-related questions" or require medical examinations during the pre-offer, pre-employment stage. The EEOC provides assistance in ascertaining what constitutes "disability-related questions" and a "medical exam." As defined by the EEOC (EEOC, 1995), a "disability-related question" means a "question that is likely to elicit information about a disability." The questions below represent disability-related questions identified by the EEOC (1992) that cannot be asked on application forms or in job interviews.

1) Have you ever had or been treated for any of the following conditions or diseases? (Followed by a checklist of various conditions and diseases.)
2) Please list any conditions or diseases for which you have been treated in the past 3 years.
3) Have you ever been hospitalized? If so, for what condition?
4) Have you ever been treated by a psychiatrist or psychologist? If so, for what condition?
5) Have you ever been treated for any mental condition?
6) Is there any health-related reason why you may not be able to perform the job for which you are applying?
7) Have you had a major illness in the last five years?
8) How many days were you absent from work because of illness last year?
9) Do you have any physical defects which preclude you from performing certain kinds of work? If yes, describe such defects and specific work limitations.
10) Do you have any disabilities or impairments which may affect your performance in the position for which you are applying?
11) Are you taking any prescribed drugs?
12) Have you ever been treated for drug addiction or alcoholism?
13) Have you ever filed for workers' compensation insurance?

Employers interviewing job candidates can ask numerous questions about the individual's ability to carry out various job responsibilities. Employers can freely inquire about the applicant's ability to perform specific job functions. For example, an employer hiring a Fitness Program Director can ask about a candidate's ability to demonstrate how to use the fitness equipment and knowledge of related benefits. Further, sport employers are free to inquire about non-medical qualifications and skills including the applicant's education, work history, and certifications and licenses (EEOC, 1995). The employer also can ask the applicant to "describe or demonstrate how he or she will perform specific job functions" provided the employer makes this same request of every applicant regardless of disability (EEOC, 1992).

The law defines two situations in which an employer may discriminate among candidates during a job interview. First, employers may divert from a uniform list of questions asked of all candidates when an applicant's disability is overt (e.g., a missing limb). For example, a health club manager could ask a potential candidate having only one leg to demonstrate how he or she would teach swimming lessons. In this situation, the law does not require the employer to ask every applicant to make the same demonstration. In a rather "gray" area, the EEOC (1995) states that it is legal to ask about temporary physical impairments that do not limit a major life activity. In other words, an employer may ask an applicant with a leg in a cast how the leg was broken. However, further questioning such as, "Do you expect the leg to heal normally?" or "Have you had many broken bones?" would constitute illegal disability-related questions (EEOC, 1995). Second, an employer may ask additional questions of a particular applicant, such as the need for a reasonable accommodation, that are not asked of other applicants when a particular candidate has volunteered information about a disability or has requested reasonable accommodations.

Past drug and/or alcohol addictions qualify as disabilities under the ADA. Questions regarding past drug or alcohol addictions are illegal. Questions regarding current legal drug use are also illegal as use of certain drugs could provide information about a qualified disability that could result in the refusal to hire an otherwise qualified individual.

Employers can ask applicants about their attendance record at their prior job during the pre-offer, pre-employment phase. As explained by the EEOC (1995),

> There may be many reasons unrelated to disability why someone cannot meet attendance requirements or was frequently absent from a previous job (for example, an applicant may have had day-care problems).

However, a sport business employer could not ask the candidate the number of sick days taken with their prior employer as this represents a prohibited disability-related question.

During the pre-offer, pre-employment stage, unfounded questions regarding the applicant's need for a reasonable accommodation are also prohibited. For example, an employer could not ask whether the applicant, "Can operate ticket sales software on either an IBM or a Macintosh computer with _____ or without _____ a reasonable accommodation? (Check one)." Sport business employers can legally inquire about the candidate's need for a reasonable accommodation only when the candidate displays an obvious disability, the candidate voluntarily disclosed a disability or the candidate voluntarily disclosed the need for a reasonable accommodation. Two examples provided by the EEOC illustrate legal queries (1995).

> (a) An individual with diabetes applying for a receptionist position voluntarily discloses that she will need periodic breaks to take medication. The employer may ask the applicant questions about the reasonable accommodation such as how often she will need breaks, and how long the breaks must be. Of course, the employer may not ask any questions about the underlying physical condition.
>
> (b) An applicant with a severe visual impairment applies for a job involving computer work. The employer may ask whether he will need reasonable accommodation to perform the functions of the job. If the applicant answers "no," the employer may not ask additional questions about reasonable accommodation (although, of course, the employer could ask the applicant to describe or demonstrate performance). If the applicant says that he will need accommodation, the employer may ask questions about the type of required accommodation such as, "What will you need?" If the applicant says he needs software that increases the size of text on the computer screen, the employer may ask questions such as, "Who makes the software?" "Do you need a particular brand?" or "Is that software compatible with our computers?" However, the employer may not ask questions about the applicant's underlying condition. In addition, the employer may not ask reasonable accommodation questions that are unrelated to job functions such as, "Will you need reasonable accommodation to get to the cafeteria?

Reasonable accommodations needed now or in the immediate future are legal whereas inquiries regarding reasonable accommodations in the distant future are prohibited. A disabled plaintiff who failed to get a particular job may view employers' inquiries regarding a reasonable accommodation as discriminatory. Documentation regarding individual job deficiencies should be clearly documented and maintained for all candidates to best defend against potential discrimination claims.

The ADA prohibits employers from administering or requiring medical exams at the pre-employment, pre-offer stage. The EEOC also provides an employer with assistance regarding the definition of a "medical exam." As explained by the EEOC, the following factors tend to infer that a particular exam represents a "medical exam."

1) Test is administered by a health care professional or someone trained by a health care professional;
2) Tests results are interpreted by a health care professional or someone trained by a health care professional;
3) Test is designed to reveal a physical or mental impairment;
4) The employer is attempting to determine the applicant's physical or mental health or impairments;
5) The test is invasive (e.g., blood test, urinalysis);

6) Test measures the applicant's physiological responses to performing the task;

7) Test is normally given in a medical setting (e.g., a health care professional's office); and

8) Test administration involves the use of medical equipment.

The above eight factors may be viewed individually or collectively based upon the particular situation.

Employers often question whether using physical agility tests, physical fitness tests, or psychological exams constitute a medical exams in violation of the ADA. Again, the EEOC provides employers with interpretive assistance. According to the EEOC, such tests can be legally administered. Although not required, physical agility and fitness tests should simulate actual job requirements. Employers denying employment to a disabled candidate based upon the applicant's performance on a physical agility or fitness tests must be prepared to show how the test results are job-related and consistent with business necessity.

However, physical agility or fitness tasks can turn into medical exams, if the tests measure or monitor physiological or biological responses. As explained by the EEOC (1995),

A messenger service tests applicants' ability to run one mile in 15 minutes. At the end of the run, the employer takes the applicants' blood pressure and heart rate. Measuring the applicant's physiological responses makes this a medical examination.

Similarly, employers may give psychological exams which measure traits including "honesty, tastes, and habits" (EEOC, 1995). Psychological exams disclosing mental disorders or impairments, however, represent medical exams. Further, personality tests asking questions about sexual practices or religious beliefs are often discouraged as information revealed may later be used by a plaintiff in an invasion of privacy claim against the employer (Schuster, 1996). The EEOC supports the use of waivers, obtaining the candidate's prior written consent to the exam and requiring the applicant to provide medical approval regarding the individual's ability to safely perform an agility or physical exam. Additional information can be found in Chapter 6.

Post-offer, Pre-employment Questioning Practices

This second phase of the employment process represents a situation when an employer, for example, has offered the job to a candidate conditional on the passing of a medical exam and related inquiries. This situation might transpire, for example, when hiring an exercise prescriptionist to work with elderly clientele. An employer might want to ensure that the individual did not have any disabilities that would pose a direct threat to other employees or patrons. Questions regarding "workers' compensation history, prior sick leave usage, illnesses/diseases/impairments, and general physical and mental health" are appropriate at this time (EEOC, 1995). An employer, however, cannot arbitrarily require only certain "suspect" candidates to take a medical exam or answer medical inquiries. If an employer requires one candidate to take a medical exam or answer medical inquiries, the employer must require all other candidates applying for that same job to do the same.

During the post-offer, pre-employment stage, medical exams and inquiries regarding medical conditions do not have to be job-related or consistent with business necessity. However, employers who revoke a job offer based on the outcome of the medical exam or inquiry must show that the disclosed medical information precluded the candidate from meeting existing, essential job criteria. Further, the employer must show that no reasonable accommodation was possible without subjecting the employer to an undue burden (ADA, 1990).

Post-offer, Post-employment Questioning Practices

The post-offer, post-employment stage refers to established employees. Employers can only require current employees to take medical exams or answer medical inquiries when an individual's mental or physical condition detrimentally impacts job performance (ADA, 1990). For example, an employer could require an employee who is continually falling asleep on the job to take a medical exam (EEOC, 1992).

The ADA recognizes two exceptions to the above general rule that permit an employer to subject a current employee to medical exams or inquiries that are not job-related and consistent with business necessity. First, current employees can volunteer to take a test or answer inquiries as "part of an employee health program (such as medical screening for high blood pressure, weight control, and cancer detection)" (EEOC, 1992). Second, federal legislation mandates medical testing for employees working in certain occupations. For example, the U.S. Department of Transportation requires medical examinations of personnel employed as air controllers, airline pilots and interstate truck and bus drivers (EEOC, 1992). The only testing which could possibly apply in the sports areas relates to athletic trainers, but any such rules would be state based rather than federal.

Drug testing is not a medical examination as defined by the ADA. Consequently, employers can drug test job applicants and current employees at any stage in the hiring or employment relationship (ADA, 1990). However, employers who require a drug test at the initial pre-employment, pre-offer stage, cannot demand follow-up medical exams or inquiries. Consequently, employers should wait until after the job offer has been made before requiring a drug test (EEOC, 1992).

Reasonable Accommodations and the Undue Hardship Exception

The issue of what constitutes a "reasonable accommodation," as well as who may request a reasonable accommodation, has generated extensive debate. Current employees do not need to say to the employer, "I need a reasonable accommodation." Rather, employers are expected to infer the need for reasonable accommodation based on an employee's use of "plain English" (EEOC, 1997). The EEOC Guidelines (1997) provides the following illustration for clarification.

> An employee asks for time off because he is "depressed and stressed." The employee has communicated a request for a change at work (time off) for a reason related to a medical condition (being "depressed and stressed" may be "plain English" for a medical condition). The statement is sufficient to put the employer on notice that the employee is requesting reasonable accommodation.

The EEOC does add, however, that the employer can request reasonable documentation regarding the "employee's disability and functional limitation" if the employee's disability is not obvious.

Someone can request a reasonable accommodation other than the employee. As stated by the EEOC (1997), a "family member, friend, health professional, or other representative may request a reasonable accommodation on behalf of an individual with a disability." Again, clear definition of who qualifies as an "other representative" is not provided. Further, requests for reasonable accommodations do not have to be in writing.

The ADA requires employers to make reasonable accommodations for disabled individuals who are otherwise capable of performing essential job functions. Approximately 26% of the employable disabled population require some reasonable accommodation (Epstein, 1995). The ADA requires employers to make reasonable accommodations only at the request of the disabled job candidate or current employee. The ADA does require the employer to look at each case independently to ascertain whether a reasonable accommodation can be made (*Anderson v. Little League*, 1992; *Bombrys v. City of Toledo*, 1993). The EEOC Technical Assistance

Manual (1992) provides the following examples of reasonable accommodations.

- making facilities accessible;
- job restructuring;
- modifying existing work schedules;
- acquiring or modifying equipment;
- providing qualified readers or interpreters;
- reassignment to a vacant position;
- permitting use of accrued paid leave or unpaid leave for necessary treatment;
- providing reserved parking for a person with a mobility impairment.

Additional reasonable accommodations described by the EEOC in the 1997 Guidelines include adjusting supervisory methods (e.g., providing more supervision) and the providing temporary job coach who assists with severe disabilities, job placement, and job training. Reasonable accommodations resulting in "undue" hardships are not required. The EEOC (1992) classifies an undue hardship as any accommodation that is (a) financially excessive, (b) disruptive, or (c) fundamentally alters the nature of the business. Complying with the ADA can be an inexpensive proposition. Studies have shown that 15% of all ADA accommodations cost no money, while 50% of all accommodations cost less than $500 (Walsh, 1995).

The ADA does not mandate that employers make accommodations that are financially excessive although large, profitable businesses are expected to incur more expensive accommodations than the small, meager businesses. However, even wealthy employers will not be required to accommodate the every whim of a disabled individual. As explained by the U.S. Court of Appeals (7th Cir.) in *Vande Zande v. State of Wis. Dept. of Admin.* (1995),

> Even if an employer is so large or wealthy...that it may not be able to plead "undue hardship," it would not be required to expend enormous sums in order to bring about a trivial improvement in the life of a disabled employee. If the nation's employers have potentially unlimited financial obligations to 43 million disabled persons, the Americans with Disabilities Act will have imposed an indirect tax potentially greater than the national debt.

Four states (e.g., Delaware, Louisiana, North Carolina, and Virginia) have quantitatively defined "financially excessive." Delaware and North Carolina, for example, cap the amount an employer must spend to reasonably accommodate a disabled employee to 5% of the individual's annual salary. Virginia takes a more conservative approach and limits the amount required by the employer to $500. Louisiana, however, states that employers are not required to spend any money on accommodations.

An accommodation's costs becomes irrelevant when the disabled is willing to pay for and provide the needed accommodation. As an employer, you are not responsible for purchasing personal assistance items such as hearing aids or glasses. Disabled individuals may also mitigate otherwise financially excessive accommodations by splitting the cost of the accommodation with the employer. State vocational rehabilitation agencies also provide money for the funding of reasonable accommodations. Tax benefits are included in the legislation for those employers spending monies to provide reasonable accommodations. As reported by Epstein (1995), tax benefits include:

- a tax deduction of up to $15,000 a year for removal of qualified architectural or transportation barriers,
- a tax credit of up to $5,125 a year for the provision of reasonable accommodations by small businesses, and
- a tax credit of up to $2,400 a year for the employment of individuals with "targeted" disabilities.

The ADA does not require employers to make accommodations that disrupt the work environment. For example, the law would not expect a health club to accommodate an aerobic dance instructor who was hard of hearing by maintaining the intercom system at an excessively high decibel level that would be disruptive to the surrounding health club activities.

Furthermore, the ADA does not require employers to make accommodations that would fundamentally alter the nature of a business. For example, the law would not require a dance club, operating with dim lights, to increase lighting for an employee who had difficulty seeing in dim lighting ("Equal Employment Opportunity," 1991). Further, the law would not require a country club hosting a swim party to have a dance instead due to a disabled person's inability to partake in swimming.

Confidentiality

Employers have a legal obligation to keep medical examination information (including drug test results and exams taken on a voluntary basis) and inquiries in confidential files that are separate from personnel files. Personal medical information should only be made available to the following individuals, if they have a legitimate reason to review such information:

- appropriate supervisors and managers,
- first aid and safety personnel,

- government officials,
- insurance companies, and
- state workers' compensation offices or second injury funds (ADA, 1990).

Thus, employers must ensure that medical information is shared only with those individuals who need to know the related information. Employers violate the ADA (as well as subjecting themselves to possible defamation and invasion of privacy claims) by carelessly disclosing either an employee's disability or any information regarding the employee's need for, or use of, a reasonable accommodation. Careless disclosure includes unauthorized disclosure to police, media, family members and co-workers.

The Direct Threat Defense

The direct threat defense is available to employers when the hiring or continued employment of a disabled individual would pose a significant risk or a direct threat to other employees and/or patrons. However, before barring employment, employers must search for reasonable accommodations that would eliminate or reduce the associated risk. An employer can legally refuse to hire the individual only if a reasonable accommodation which lowers the severity of risk would impose an undue hardship (ADA, 1990).

As mentioned above, the employee with a mental disorder or psychiatric impairment presents a sport manager with a perplexing problem. Psychological and mental disorders are often difficult to detect and document. As explained in the 1996 HRFocus article, "Caught between violence,"

> Employers cannot discriminate against such employees unless they pose a "direct threat" to someone's health and safety that cannot be solved with a reasonable accommodation. But if the company does not dismiss the worker because the actual or threatened misconduct does not amount to a direct threat, coworkers or other injured parties may charge the employer with negligence.

Professional evaluations provide protection for employers deciding to dismiss employees opined as a direct threat to the individual and surrounding others. You may find solace by imitating the policy taken by Wells-Fargo Bank which immediately dismisses employees engaging in "bodily harm, physical intimidation or threats of violence" ("Caught between violence," 1996). As mentioned before, policies uniformly enforced among all employees are not problematic.

Conduct and Policy Enforcement

Employers may impose the same disciplinary measures on the disabled as it does on the non-disabled employee for those policies that pertain to the workplace and are consistent with business necessity. For example, assume an employer has a policy prohibiting guns in the workplace. Also assume that the employer's policy states that employees can be immediately terminated for violating the above policy. So long as the policy is enforced on a non-discriminatory basis, employers have the right to discipline any employee, regardless of disability, for violating the policy. On the other hand, policies that are not directly job-related and consistent with business necessity cannot be rigidly enforced against a disabled employee. The EEOC Guidelines provide the following example of when a policy could not be rigidly enforced (the site of employment has been changed for purposes of illustration).

> An employee with a psychiatric disability works [for an athletic department lining the fields.] He has no customer contact and does not come into regular contact with other employees. Over the course of several weeks, he has come to work appearing increasingly disheveled. His clothes are ill-fitting and often have tears in them. He also has become increasingly ant-social. Coworkers have complained that when they try to engage him in casual conversation, he walks away or gives a curt reply. When he has to talk to a coworker, he is abrupt and rude. His work, however, has not suffered. The employer's company handbook states that employees should have a neat appearance at all times. The handbook also states that employees should be courteous to each other. When told that he is being disciplined for his appearance and treatment of coworkers, the employee explains that his appearance and demeanor have deteriorated because of his disability which was exacerbated during this time (EEOC, 1997).

As illustrated above, the employer would be prohibited from enforcing the policy since the policy is not job-related and consistent with business necessity.

Wrap Up...

Compliance with the various anti-discrimination laws is becoming both easier and more difficult every year. With the increased knowledge and information available, it is much easier for an employer to understand what they need to do in order to avoid liability. At the same time, prospective employees have their own weapons. Various civil rights groups are using "tester" who apply for jobs solely for the purpose of testing the employer to determine which candidate would be hired (Frierson, 1994).

"Testers" involve a process where a minority job-applicant and another applicant (primarily a Caucasian male) have very similar resumes developed and are taught to say the same basic facts during an interview. Testers go through the motions of applying for a job and the interview process. The testers then wait to hear which tester, if any, was hired. If the minority candidates was not offered the position, the organization that utilized the testers can approach the employer for an explanation concerning the employer's conduct. If the organization is not satisfied with the purported rationale behind the employment decision, they can help file a discrimination claim. Thus, vigilance always needs to be maintained throughout the workplace.

In Walsh's book *Managing Diversity*, the author emphasizes one main point when examining how to avoid discrimination. Communication. Through employing proper communications and teaching people how to listen and what to say—as well as what not to say—you can develop the greatest protection level. You need to educate all employees, all managers, and even customers to their rights, duties and obligations. Failure to properly communicate expected conduct can lead to disaster.

References

Armour, S. (1997). "Firms key up PCs for job screening." *USA Today* (October 20): 6B.

Bennett-Alexander, D.D. and Pincus, L.B. (1995). *Employment Law for Business*. Chicago, IL: Irwin.

Black, H.C. (1990). *Black's Law Dictionary*. 6th edition. St. Paul, MN: West Publishing Company.

"Caught between violence and ADA compliance." (1996). *HRFocus* (March): 19.

Claussen, C.L. (1995). "Title IX and employment discrimination in coaching intercollegiate athletics." *Entertainment & Sports Law Review* 12(1, 2): 149–168.

Coleman, J.J., III (1985). "Age-conscious remarks: What you say can be used against you." *Personnel* 62(9): 22–29.

Davis, A. (1997). "When ribaldry among men is sexual harassment." *The Wall Street Journal* (June 5): B1, B6.

"Developments in the law: Employment discrimination." (1996). *Harvard Law Review* 109(7): 1568–1692.

EEOC and the U.S. Department of Justice (1991). *Americans with Disabilities Act Handbook*. Washington, DC: U.S. Government Printing Offices.

EEOC (1992). *Title I of the ADA: EEOC Technical Assistance Manual.* Chicago, IL: Commerce Clearing House, Inc.

EEOC (1995). *ADA enforcement guidance: Preemployment disability-related questions and medical examinations.* Washington, DC: U.S. EEOC.

EEOC (1997). *EEOC enforcement guidance on the ADA and psychiatric disabilities.* Washington, DC: U.S. EEOC.

Epstein, S.B. (1995). "In search of a bright line: Determining when an employer's financial hardship becomes 'undue' under the Americans with Disabilities Act." *Vanderbilt Law Review* 48(2): 391–478.

"Equal Employment Opportunity for Individuals with Disabilities" (1991). 29 C.F.R. 1630.

Felsenthal, E. (1996). "High-Court highlight is an 'English Only' law." *The Wall Street Journal* (September 24): B1, B15.

Frierson, J. (1994). *Preventing employment lawsuits.* The Bureau of National Affairs, Inc.

Kirk, D.J., and Clapham, M.M. (1996). " 'Bagging' or 'goosing': How the courts are ruling in same-sex harassment claims." *Labor Law Journal* (July): 403–417.

Kurtz, J., Davis, E., and Asquith, J.A. (1996). "Religious beliefs get new attention." *HRFocus* (July): 12–13.

Mauro, T. (1997). "Court skirts the 'official English' issue." *USA Today* (March 4): 3A.

Moreno, J. (1997). "Spanish ban on job draws fire." *Houston Chronicle* (October 10): 1C.

NCAA (1997). *A Basic Guide to Title IX and Gender Equity in Athletics for Colleges and Universities.*

Nondiscrimination on the Basis of Disability by Public Accommodations and in Commercial Facilities (1991; 1994).

Sawyer, T.H. (1993). "Private golf clubs: Freedom of expression and the right to privacy." *Marquette Sports Law Journal*, 3(2): 187–212.

Schaner, D.J. and Erlemeier, M.M. (1995). "When faith and work collide: Defining standards for religious harassment in the workplace." *Employee Relations Law Journal* 21(1): 1995.

Schuster, R. (1996). "Personality tests and privacy rights." *HRFocus* (March): 22.

Sixel, L. (1998). "Harassment cases likely to rise at job." *Houston Chronicle* (March 5): 1C.

Sullivan, G., Kaikati, J., Virgo, J., Carr, T.R., and Virgo, K.S. (1996). "Supreme Court expands age discrimination protections." *Labor Law Journal* (May): 310–314.

Thomas, P. (1996). "Restructurings generate rash of age-bias suits." *The Wall Street Journal* (August 29): B1, B14.

Uniform guidelines on employee selection procedures (1993 edition). 29 CFR Ch. XIV-7.
Walsh (1995). *Mastering diversity.* Santa Monica, CA: Merritt.
Zachary, M.K. (1996). "Handling religious expression in the workplace." *Supervision* 57(12): 5–7.

Cases

Anderson v. Little League Baseball, Inc., 794 F.Supp. 342 (D.Ariz. 1992).
Bombrys v. City of Toledo, 849 F.Supp. 1210 (N.D. Ohio 1993).
Carroll v. Talman Federal S.& L. Ass'n of Chicago, 604 F.2d 1028 (7th Cir. 1979).
Compston v. Borden, Inc., 424 F. Supp. 157 (S.D. Ohio 1976).
Cota v. Tucson Police Dept., 783 F.Supp. 458 (D.Ariz. 1992).
Dodge v. Giant Food, Inc., 488 F.2d 1333 (9th Cir. 1973).
EEOC v. JC Penney Co., Inc., 753 F.Supp. 192 (N.D.Miss. 1990).
EEOC v. Sage Rlty. Corp., 507 F. Supp. 599 (S.D. N.Y. 1981).
Garcia v. Spun Steak Co., 998 F.2d 1480 (9th Cir. 1993).
Goluszek v. H. P. Smith, 697 F. Supp. 1452 (N.D. Ill. 1988).
Griggs v. Duke Power Company, 401 US 424 (1971).
Ground Transport Corp. v. Pennsylvania, 578 A.2d 555 (Pa. 1990).
Harris v. Forklift Systems, Inc., 114 S.Ct. 367 (1993).
Hodgson v. Approved Personnel Serv., 529 F.2d 760 (4th Cir. 1975).
Jasany v. U.S. Postal Service, 755 F.2d 1244 (6th Cir. 1985).
McDonnell Douglas v. Green, 411 US 792 (1973).
O'Connor v. Consolidated Coin Caterers Corp., 116 S. Ct. 1307 (1996).
Postema v. National League of Pro. Baseball Clubs, 799 F. Supp. 1475 (S.D.N.Y. 1992).
Prescott v. Independent Life and Accident Ins. Co., 878 F. Supp. 1545 (M.D. Ala. 1995).
Quick v. Donaldson Co., Inc., 895 F. Supp. 1288 (S.D. Iowa 1995).
Robinson v. Shell Oil Co. 70 F.3d 325 (4th Cir. 1997).
Slayton v. Michigan Host, 144 Mich. App. 535, 376 N.W. 2d 664 (Ct. App. Mich. 1985).
Taylor v. US Postal Service, 946 F.2d 1214 (6th Cir. 1991).
Texas Dep't of Community Affairs v. Burdine, 450 U.S. 248 (1981).
Tyndall v. National Educ. Ctrs., 31 F.3d 209 (4th Cir. 1994).
US EEOC v. Sedita, 755 F. Supp. 808 (N.D.Ill. 1991).
Vande Zande v. State of Wis. Dept. of Admin., 44 F.3d 538 (7th Cir. 1995).

Wilson v. Southwest Airlines, 880 F.2d 807 (5th Cir. 1981).
Wilson v. US West Communications, Inc., 860 F. Supp. 665 (D. Neb. 1994).
Wimbley v. Bolger, 642 F. Supp. 481 (W.D. Tenn. 1986).
Wright v. Columbia University, 520 F.Supp. 789 (E.D. P.A. 1981).

Statutes

Age Discrimination in Employment Act (ADEA), 29 U.S.C.A. Section 621 et seq.
Americans with Disabilities Act of 1990, 42 USC 12101.
Title VII of the Civil Rights Act, 42 U.S.C. Section 2000(e).
Title IX of the Education Amendments of 1972, 86 Stat. 235 (codified at 20 U.S.C. §§ 1681–1688 (1990)).
Veteran's Reemployment Rights Act, 43 U.S.C.A. Section 2021–2026.

Chapter 5

Negligence in the Employment Setting

Negligence is a form of a legal wrong called a *tort*. A tort is defined as a "private or civil wrong or injury resulting from a breach of a legal duty that exists by virtue of society's expectations regarding interpersonal conduct" (Gifis, 1984). Society expects people to behave in such a way that when a Mr. X puts his health and well-being into Mrs. Y's hands, Mrs. Y has to act in a manner that respects and protects Mr. X's rights. Thus, a tort is an act or omission that breaches a duty owed and causes an injury to another person. Negligence is just one of the numerous types of acts categorized as a tort. Other well known torts include assault, battery, nuisance, trespass, invasion of privacy and intentional infliction of emotional distress (Fried, 1997).

Negligence has been defined as the failure to act in a manner of a similarly situated "reasonable" individual (Gifis, 1984). Negligence has also been defined as the failure to observe and exercise that degree of care, precaution, and vigilance that the circumstances justly demand, to protect another person from injury. The key to negligence analysis is whether or not you acted as a reasonable person *and* exercised care to individuals you owe a duty to protect.

Negligence is comprised of four elements which, when proven, will lead to liability and paying a damage award. Each of the four negligence elements have to be present for a person to recover under a negligence claim. The four elements are:

- owing someone a duty,
- breaching that duty,
- the breach of that duty was the proximate cause of the person's injury, and
- the person was actually injured (Gifis, 1984).

Injury

An injury is defined as a legal wrong that causes damage to someone (Gifis, 1984). An injury does not have to be physically visible. Thus, injuries can include psychological injuries, emotional distress, pain and suffering and future medical or financial requirements. Injury represents the easiest element to understand. The other three elements comprising a negligence theory are more difficult to define in one simple paragraph.

Duty

A duty is a legally sanctioned or societally imposed obligation which, if breached, creates a potential negligent atmosphere. Every employer owes his/her employees a duty to provide a safe work environment based on the relationship. For example, an employer is responsible for exercising reasonable care in providing work equipment. As an employer, you also owe your customers a duty to provide properly trained employees and a safe business premise. Thus, you owe both employees and customers a duty to avoid exposing them to potential hazards that are either known or likely to occur. Injury foreseeability is the central factor for determining negligence. By knowing what potential injuries are foreseeable, employers can determine what duty they are required to exercise in order to avoid liability. As numerous injuries are foreseeable in the workplace, an employer owes numerous duties to provide a safe work environment. Examples of the types of duties that you might be held accountable for include:

- the duty to provide adequate ventilation for employees working with certain chemicals,
- the duty to make sure employees are properly trained,
- the duty to make sure all OSHA requirements are met,
- the duty to pay employees in a timely manner and provide all legally mandated benefits,
- the duty to provide employees with safe access to their vehicles when the business is located in a high crime area, and
- the duty to protect customers from the foreseeable acts of an employee which can range from battery to sexual harassment (Fried, 1997).

If you do not uphold these duties in a manner that is "adequate," "proper," or "reasonable," then you would have breached your duty.

Most duties associated with running a safe work environment are classified as affirmative duties which are positive duties. A positive duty requires you to take at least a certain minimum amount of precautionary steps to protect the safety of other people. If you personally discover or are informed that an employee is sexually molesting some children in your program, you have an affirmative duty to correct the problem. That is, you have to thoroughly investigate the allegations, possibly contact the police, notify parents, remove the employee from all contacts with minors and related actions (Fried, 1997).

Actually finding a defect or problem with employees is not required to trigger your duty. You could owe a duty to warn against unknown risks or defects that you "should" have or "could have" discovered through reasonable inspection. Simply stated, you have to make sure that you take the minimum steps required to know basic information about each employee, each volunteer, the workplace environment and the interactions between personnel and customers. If a facility is too dangerous for employees to work there or if some equipment cannot be repaired, then you have a duty to avoid using the dangerous area or equipment. If the facility or equipment has to be used, and repairs cannot be completed, then you have to warn everyone about the potentially harmful condition. The term "reasonably safe" is often used because you have a duty to provide "reasonably safe" premises, not "perfectly safe" premises. You are not an insurer of safety. You are only required to provide a reasonably safe facility and reasonably selected, trained and supervised employees. If you fail to provide a reasonably safe facility or fail to properly screen an employee, then you might have breached your duty. Even if you breach a duty, you still might not be held liable if breaching the duty was not the proximate cause of the injury (Fried, 1997).

Proximate Cause

Proximate cause refers to direct cause. You can only be held liable for negligence if your breached duty proximately caused the injury. A good example would be operating an ice skate blade sharpener without a faceguard to protect the machine user's hands. You breached your duty to provide safe equipment for your employees. However, the injury really occurred because two employees were horsing around and one pushed another into the machine. Thus, while you breached a duty, the breached duty was not the proximate cause of the injury. The proximate cause of the injury can be attributed to the employees horsing around.

Defenses

An intervening condition such as two employees horsing around represents one key defense that can be utilized to block a negligence claim. Additional defenses include assumption of risk, contributory negligence and comparative negligence. These defenses examine the injured party's actions to determine if they were reasonable and/or if they voluntarily assumed a risk. If you have provided all reasonable safeguards, comply with all OSHA requirements and provide appropriate warnings, employees will still get injured. If an employee knows about a risk, but voluntarily assumes the risk and proceeds with whatever he was doing and is injured, he has assumed the risk. However, unlike assumption of risk involving an athlete assuming the risk in running in a road race, the workplace is covered by different rules. More specifically, the employer could not raise an assumption of risk defense to block a potential suit from an injured employee. Furthermore, the injured employee would also be barred from suing because the worker's exclusive remedy involves a workers' compensation claim. Workers' compensation claims represent an exclusive remedy for employee injuries on the job and employers are prevented from raising a traditional defenses allowed in traditional negligence claims. Workers' compensation related issues are covered in Chapter 12.

Additional defenses can also be raised based on various laws such as immunity protections for government entities or laws which require lawsuits to be filed in a certain time frame-such as statute of limitations (van der Smissen, 1990). While the entire spectrum of issues associated with a negligence claim are beyond the scope of this manual, there are several key negligence issues which pose significant liability concerns to employers. The major negligence concern include the primary aspects involved in the hiring process including hiring, training, supervision, retention and negligent referral, which are discussed below. Furthermore, an employer can face negligence claims under the above mentioned theories for injuries that employees cause to customers or other employees. However, an employee injured by other employees might only have access to the workers' compensation system, rather than a traditional negligence claim.

1) Negligent Hiring

The 1990s has witnessed an explosion in work environment criminal activity. Workplace violence is at an all-time high. As reported by Schaner (1996),

1) In 1993, for example, homicide was the third leading cause of death in the workplace and the leading cause of occupational death for women.
2) The National Institute for Occupational Safety and Health reports that on average 15 workers are victims of work-related homicides every week.
3) The Northwestern National Life Insurance study found that more than 2 million people were physically attacked in the workplace from July 1992 to July 1993.

Besides potential harm that can confront other employees, a dangerous employee also presents significant risks to customers or patrons. Individuals injured by an employee's criminal act(s) are now challenging traditional tort law and arguing that employers should be liable for hiring people known to have dangerous propensities or likely to present perilous situations which is also fostering numerous suits claiming negligent hiring or other negligent-related claims.

For example, in *D.T. by M.T. v. Independent School Dist. No. 16* (1990), the plaintiff sued the Oklahoma School District alleging the negligent hiring of a 30-year-old male teacher-coach who sexually molested three elementary school students. Similarly, the plaintiffs in *Doe v. British Universities* (1992) argued that the defendant should be liable for negligently hiring a camp counselor who sexually assaulted a camper. Hence, the negligent hiring tort. As explained by Levin,

> Negligent hiring occurs when the employer knows, or should have known, of an applicant's dangerous or violent propensities, hires the individual, and gives the employee the opportunity to repeat such violent behavior (1995).

While it is impossible to identify all potentially violent or dangerous employees, a survey conducted by the Society for Human Resource Management, for example, revealed that, "Two out of three respondents believed that they could have identified the aggressors in advance as possible perpetrators of violence acts" (Schaner, 1996).

Negligent hiring involves breaching a duty to properly and reasonably hire appropriate personnel. A good example of breaching such a duty entails hiring a lifeguard. In most, if not all states, lifeguards are required to have at least Red Cross certification or some other life safety training. If the state law requires you to hire only certified lifeguards, and you hire someone who is not certified, you can be held liable for negligent hiring. Such liability arises if the lifeguard is unable to perform his or her job which leads to someone drowning. Even if there is no state law requiring lifeguard certification, you could still breach your duty to reasonably hire appropriate employees if the industry standard requires hiring certified lifeguards. Additional unfitness for the job can include a criminal record, complaints from past employers and/or customers, witnessing employee misconduct and poor job performances (Feliu, 1992).

In addition to making sure a prospective employee has the proper certification, you have to thoroughly examine his/her background for job specific concerns. Examples of job specific concerns include proper knowledge of the sport or activity, appropriate degree providing requisite experience, appropriate training in using required equipment or chemicals and related concerns. As previously discussed in Chapter 3, applicants often lie on their applications or resume. Based on this fact, a reasonable employer would take the time to verify certain information. You can demand that an applicant provide transcripts as proof that they indeed complete a certain degree plan or they took a certain number of courses in a given area. Thus, if an applicant indicates that they have significant classroom experience in exercise and nutrition, have them prove this assertion. Otherwise, they could give some inaccurate information which might injure someone. That injured person could claim that if you had properly screened the candidate, which is a reasonable task, they would not have been injured.

Utility

The example above addresses a very important legal point which is "utility." Utility refers to value and worth. If it would have cost the employer five minutes and $10 dollars to conduct a reasonably thorough background check, then that number would have to be weighted against the potential damage that could be caused if the time and money was not spent. If it would have taken little time and very little money to prevent a major hazard such as hiring someone who could engage in conduct that might kill someone, then the law would punish the employer for failing to take reasonable steps that would have reduced a serious hazard. A good example of the utility theory can be seen in sexual abuse cases involving minors. Suppose someone completes an application leaving numerous blanks, failing to disclose certain time periods, and does not list references. It would not take a significant amount of time to require that these areas be completed and then agree to release criminal background records, if any exists. If the job requires significant child contact, it is reasonable to assume that assigning the child with the wrong supervisor can possibly lead to sexual abuse or even death. If you are not willing to invest the time and money necessary to act as a reasonable employer, then you might be held liable for negligent hiring and subject to hefty jury awards.

2) Negligent Training

Negligent training refers to providing employees with the necessary skills to successfully accomplish their job description. Nearly three-fourths of the nonagricultural businesses in the United States utilize some form of employee training. In, 1995, 49.6 million employees were formally trained by their employers at a cost of over $52 billion (Millman and Peery, 1996).

This does not include the roughly $20 billion the government spent in 1995 alone for various job training programs (Millman and Peery, 1996). Significant time and money is spent trying to make employees more productive and teach them the proper techniques necessary to complete their jobs.

If specialized equipment is utilized or if specific safety policies and procedures are in place, then all new employees or people transferring into a new position should be properly trained. For example, if a sport day camp hires a counselor to also function as a camp nurse, then the person has to be properly trained to effectively execute her assigned duties. If the nurse is not trained in dispensing drugs, then she could possibly kill a child through providing the wrong medication, the wrong dosage, or not understanding how some drugs interact. While no one would confuse the nurse with a pharmacist, a reasonable nurse would have been trained to know how to ask parents or a physician about a given child's medication and potential concerns that might need to be addressed.

Specific issues that should be addressed to help prevent a negligent training claim include:

- understanding rules, policies and procedures,
- knowing where safety equipment is located,
- knowing basic first aid concerns,
- knowing how to identify and remedy specific risks faced by employees,
- knowing how to properly report an incident
- knowing where first aid equipment is located and how to use the equipment,
- ensuring constant retraining and skill testing, and
- evaluating training methods to ensure they are consistent with industry standards.

Negligent training provides a natural transition to negligent supervision claims. Failing to properly supervise employees can hinder your ability to identify employee deficiencies. Many of these deficiencies could be resolved through employee retraining.

3) Negligent Supervision

Negligent supervision is frequently seen in the sport liability arena. Teachers, coaches and administrators often lose negligence cases because they failed to provide reasonable supervision. The primary concern with these cases normally relates to failing to properly watch or spot an athlete while the athlete is engaged in certain activities. Similarly, employers can also be held liable for negligent suspension if they fail to properly supervise an employee. Vicarious liability is the term used to describe an employer's liability for the negligent acts of an employee. Various names exist to describe the legal relationship and resulting liability that can be attached to the employer/employee relationship. Vicarious liability, *respondeat superior* and master-servant relationships are all terms that refer to the employer's liability for the negligent conduct of an employee.

Scope of Work

Negligence is only imparted to the employer if the employee is engaging in acts that benefit the employer. Running an errand for the employer is considered an act that benefits the employer even if it is not listed in the employee's job description nor does it occur on the employment premises. However, if after completing the errand the employee decides to drive the car to visit a friend's house, then the employee is no longer engaged in an activity that benefits the employer. If on the way to the errand the employee crashes the car, the employer would be vicariously liable for any resulting damages. If the crash occurs when the employee is visiting his/her friend, the employer would not be liable because the crash was not work related. Activities or tasks performed outside the scope of duty or beyond the job description refer to *ultra vires* acts for which the employer does not retain liability.

Illegal Acts

In addition to being outside the employee's scope of work, an employer will not be liable for an employee's conduct if the conduct is illegal or demonstrates complete disregard for another's safety. This exemption to the general vicarious liability rule only applies if an employer is unaware of the employee's violent or criminal propensity. Not knowing that an employee has the propensity to engage in certain conduct can be both a blessing and a curse. Under certain circumstances, you cannot be held liable if you did not know that an employee could engage in certain conduct. Just like an ostrich that sticks its head into the sand, the less you know has some benefits. On the other hand, if you failed to properly supervise an employee, you could be held liable for failing to act in a reasonable manner that would have uncovered suspicious conduct. It is considered standard industry conduct for employers to properly supervise their employees and to know their mannerism, what can trigger emotional outburst, what are their hot buttons, etc. While it is impossible to know every situation in which an employee might become violent, proper supervision often provides useful indicators about an employee's conduct. Furthermore, comments from co-workers, complaints filed by co-workers and complaints filed by customers all serve as queues that additional supervision is required to make sure certain activities are not repeated. A good example demonstrating the need for vigilant supervision can be seen in sexual harassment claims. A female employee might complain about a certain individual's unwelcomed conduct. If the employer fails to take necessary corrective action, and the harasser reengages in the conduct, the employer could be held liable for failing to properly supervise the work environment to prevent a foreseeable sexual harassment.

The key to help prevent a negligent supervision claim involves developing, distributing, communicating and enforcing specific workplace rules and regulations. These rules serve the dual purpose of controlling the workplace and establishing review criterion for performance evaluation. Immediately after employees are hired, they should be given a copy of the rules and regulations which they have to follow (see Chapter 6). These rules become the first defensive line when combating a negligent supervision claim. For example, you can point to your sexual harassment policy (see Chapter 7) and prove that the policy was not followed, then there is a very good chance that the employer engaged in negligent supervision. The employer could be found innocent based on the fact that a reasonable employer develops rules and implements them in a consistent manner. An employer is not an insurer of safety and can never be expected to stop all communications or inappropriate behavior no matter how many rules or policies are developed. Thus, you have to make sure all employees know what conduct is acceptable and the penalties associated with failing to follow the rules. Besides knowing rules and penalties, a vigilant employer needs to constantly review and evaluate employee compliance and ensure continued compliance.

A relatively similar example to sexual harassment involves an employer's failure to properly supervise employees who engage in abusive conduct. Such abusive conduct can include child abuse (i.e., spanking or yelling), elder abuse, abuse of individuals with disabilities and child sexual abuse. These concerns need to be addressed with specific rules designed to prevent conduct which might encourage or allow such behavior to continue. It is imperative that rules are developed addressing not just employee conduct, but also how the business or organization operates. An employer can develop a sexual abuse prevention policy for employees working with children. Once such policies are developed, they have to be consistently updated and communicated to all parties including employees, volunteers, customers and parents.

Negligent Supervision Leading to Sexual Harassment

In addition to child sexual abuse and employee on employee sexual harassment, employers have to be concerned about sexual harassment against all other patrons or customers. While sexual harassment represents a significant public relation problem, legal ramification can also arise from such conduct. Traditional sexual harassment claims are raised between employees and others within the workforce. Title VII, which provides the primary basis for sexual harassment claims only applies to employers when employees are sexually harassed. California is the first state that has passed a law which now creates a cause of action for sexual harassment when an employment relationship does not exist. Under the law, a sexual harassment claim could be brought by someone who is sexually abused as a result of being involved in a business, service or professional relationship with designated individuals including doctors, lawyers, landlords, teachers or any similar individual. Liability is imposed if the sexual advances, solicitations, sexual requests or demands for sexual compliance, that were unwelcomed and persistent, continue after a request has been made to stop the conduct (California Civil Code Section 51.9). As an additional penalty under the California law, victims who prevail at trial are allowed to recover trebled (tripling their damages) damages as a punishment to prevent future similar conduct.

Sexual harassment and abuse represents just one concern associated with negligent supervision. Negligent supervision can also apply to a supervisor abusing subordinates, employees mistreating one another, employees misusing equipment and employees engaged in fiscal abuses such as embezzlement. The inappropriate conduct demonstrated by an employee is often dismissed as a once in a life time event or that the employee was under significant stress. An employee might be going through a midlife crisis, going through a divorce or might have lost a relative. Whatever the reason, employers are accustomed to giving an employee another chance. The issue becomes when should an employer not provide another chance? If continued misconduct is reasonably foreseeable, then you should not provide another opportunity. Termination or reassignment might be the only options.

4) Negligent Retention

Negligent retention refers to the liability which can befall an employer when an employee is kept too long. If an employee has engaged in some egregious conduct, in violation of the company's express rules or policies, then the employer has to immediately take action to prevent any further reoccurrence. If the employee has been disciplined in the past for the same violation, possibly using drugs during work hours, and then injures someone while in an impaired condition, the injured person can sue under the negligent retention theory. Based on the prior violations, and possible prior discipline, the employer is on notice that the employee represents a potential risk to others. By allowing the employee to return to his or her position, the employer is in essence allowing the unreasonable behavior to continue. A reasonable employer would have eliminated the environment (i.e., possibly bringing the police and drug dogs to the work environment to check for drugs) or eliminated the employee from the environment through termination, temporary suspension or extended leave to receive treatment. Whatever the approach used, the employer is responsible for making sure only fit employees are retained and any employee who engages in dangerous or criminal conduct is eliminated from the work environment.

One caveat has to be mentioned when dealing with a drug or alcohol user in the workplace. An employer can terminate an employee who appears at work on drugs or under the influence. However, if the same employee is currently enrolled in a drug or alcohol abuse clinic or treatment center, you are prevented from terminating the employee based on the Americans with Disability Act (see Chapter 4). Therefore, before terminating an employee, you should specifically ask them if they are currently enrolled in any drug or alcohol abuse treatment program. If they indicate they are engaged in such a program, you should seek guidance from the treatment program to determine the best approach to handle a relapse. If they indicate that they are not enrolled in any program, then you can utilize any disciplinary tool consistent with the employer's disciplinary rules. Termination might not be available if the violating employee is a union member, or has a contract limiting the available discipline.

An unfortunately perfect example of negligent retention in the sports industry could be seen with the University of Nebraska allowing former Cornhusker, Lawrence Philips, to stay on the team despite his violent tendencies. Philip's coach, Tom Osborne, was quoted s saying: " It's not as though Lawrence [Philips] is an angry young man all the time and a threat to society. But there are some occasions every four to five months where he become[s] a little bit explosive" (Fried, 1997). Under the negligent retention theory, when Philips put the football program on notice that he engaged in "explosive" conduct, the university could have a duty to protect other students, administrators, fans, etc., from any harm which Philips could cause. By not taking any steps to appropriately challenge Philips' explosive nature or to terminate his involvement with the program, the university could have breached its duty. Eventually, Philips once again exploded and attacked his former girlfriend crushing her head into a wall (Fried, 1997). While Philips was suspended from the team, his coach later allowed him back onto the team (Fried, 1997). If it was not for Philips' spectacular athletic skills, he probably would have been expelled for violating university regulations concerning assaulting other students. This preferential treatment is often seen in sports and represents a major liability threat. If you allow an athlete to violate the rules, but do not punish them you can possibly face:

- negligence charges,
- discrimination charges (for benefiting some individual, but not all—i.e., a female athlete or employee would not be treated in the same manner),
- charges that the disciplinary action violated union rules and/or the collective bargaining agreement, and/or
- possible breach of contract for not uniformly enforcing or applying the contract.

In another case involving the University of Nebraska, the University agreed to a $50,000 settlement to a former student who claimed that former Cornhusker football player Christian Peter raped her twice in 1991. Both incidents occurred inside a university residence hall on campus. A lawsuit filed in the U.S. District Court claimed that "school officials failed to provide the student with a safe environment to learn" (*From the Gym to the Jury*, 1997).

The question often raised by negligent retention claims involves what constitutes enough evidence that someone should be terminated or he/she could pose a negligent retention risk. In an Illinois case, a store manager drove by the store and saw loiterers in front of the store. The store manager eventually assaulted one of the loiterers who was a child. A jury returned a verdict of $150,000 under a negligent retention claim. The store manager had two prior incidents including throwing a milk crate at a coworker seven years earlier and allegedly assaulting his son at home. The court felt these two incidents were enough to put the employer on notice that hostile activity was reasonably foreseeable from the manager and the employer should not have retained the employee in a managerial capacity (*Bryant*, 1993).

5) Negligent Referral

Chapter 3 addressed the concern associated with providing references and the potential liability. The discussion in Chapter 3 also highlighted the issue associated with failing to provide an appropriate reference to a former employee. An inappropriate reference can include failing to report criminal activities, embezzlement or unusual activities that warrant further review such as bringing a loaded gun to work. Another inappropriate reference can include providing a positive reference which is wholly inaccurate. Thus, the tort of negligent referral related to the failure to provide appropriate reference information or providing inaccurate references when an employer owes others a duty to provide appropriate references.

Chapter 12 discusses termination and the process which will be utilized when a future prospective employer asks for a reference. The terminated employee needs to specifically understand what future prospective employers will be told. This can create a significant bargaining tool. A terminated employee might wave his/her right to sue for discrimination or other potential claims in return for receiving a positive or neutral referral. However, you should never agree to withhold critical, true, information such as criminal wrongdoing. Such non-disclosure can lead to a negligent referral claim from the subsequent employer and any other injured individuals who would not have faced injuries if a correct referral was provided.

6) Liability for Employee Negligence

As previously discussed in the introduction to this chapter, employers are normally liable for their employees negligent conduct. Numerous cases abound highlighting an employer's liability for an employee's negligent conduct. In one case, a school district was held liable when a teacher decided to play "blanket tossing" which involves children using a blanket to catapult a fellow student into the air and then catch them again similar to a trampoline. A child was injured when the blanket ripped. The school district claimed they hired competent teachers and supervisors, but the jury still held the school district liable (*Rook v. State*, 1938). Numerous other cases have been well documented analyzing a school's responsibility to avoid negligent instruction, matching, training, supervision and equipment (van der Smissen, 1990).

Notice forms a critical element when analyzing employer liability. If an employer has notice or is put on notice that an employee is engaging in some unacceptable behavior, then even if such behavior is outside the scope of employment, the employer can still be liable. By knowing about the conduct, the employer is deemed to have condoned or given approval to the conduct. Thus, in one case a lifeguard was throwing a horseshoe around while working. The horseshoe hit a child who later sued for her injuries. The employer claimed that throwing horseshoes was not part of the lifeguard's duties. However, since the employer knew the lifeguard had been playing with horseshoes for two weeks prior to the accident, the employer was held liable for his conduct (*Rafsky v. New York City*, 1939).

Liability for Employee Injuries

In addition to traditional negligence claims, an employer also has to avoid negligence claims associated with negligent misrepresentation. Such claims normally center around economic losses suffered by an employee in reliance to statements made by the employer. In one case, a business owner recruited a new manager who left his prior job and moved to assume his new managerial responsibilities. During the interview process, the prospective employee specifically asked about the company's financial condition. The owner knew the business was going under, but indicated that the company was doing very good, was part of a larger business, and was recently written-up in a very favorable magazine article. A jury awarded the defrauded employee $90,000 in actual damages and $360,000 in punitive damages under a negligent misrepresentation theory (*Berger v. Security Pacific Information System*, 1990). If the jury determined that the owner's misstatements were intentional, then the jury could have possibly concluded that the owner engaged in fraud, rather than just negligent misrepresentation.

Liability can fall onto an employer in other ways including such claims as host liquor liability concerns. Under this theory, the employer can be liable if she/he hosts a Christmas party where alcohol is served. If an employee is served too much alcohol and is allowed to continue drinking and then to drive shortly thereafter, the employer could be liable for any resulting injuries. Thus, even though the party was not officially part of the employee's job description, the employer's liability does not just stop at your facility entrance, but can continue into social engagement, team softball games, company picnics and other associated activities.

Wrap Up...

With employees as with children, there is no guarantee they will work out they way you imagined they would. Putting away thousands of dollars for college does not mean that your child will go to college. Similarly, screening an employee does not provide you with blanket protection for an employee's negligent acts. Background screening just represents one step in the process aimed at reducing the likelihood of a negligence claim.

The key to defray as much liability as possible is to act in a reasonably prudent manner. One of the surest means to help act in a reasonable prudent manner is to envision that your children are involved in the sport program. If your child was going to your camp would you take every reasonable action possible to make their camp experience safe? The answer is yes. Similarly, when individuals entrust you with their own or a loved one's safety, they assume you will treat them like they were your own flesh and blood. Clients and customers entrust you every day and not just in sport camps. Even if someone walks into a sporting goods store, they expect a safe environment where they can shop, not be attacked, or can change in a dressing room without being observed by hidden cameras.

Once you have developed the proper negligence prevention mindset, you will be able to evaluate your program by trying to identify any situation or circumstance which might pose a potential concern. Once a dangerous practice is identified (such as using poorly trained employees or not terminating dangerous employees) than you have to take specific action. Once you are on notice, you are required to act—and act in an appropriate manner. This is the step in the process where good intentions can come back to haunt you. In one case that one of the authors heard about, a parking attendant was finally terminated after many years. The attendant had worked at the garage for over 30 years. However, the garage was purchased by a new company which required every employee to submit his/her driver's license. The older attendant did not submit a license and when approached he indicated that he did not have one nor did he ever have one. Imagine if the attendant had been in a car accident and the matter went to a jury. What would a jury say. They would not look at the fact that you did a nice thing by giving the older man some work, they would say you were negligent for failing to properly screen and negligent for retaining a non-qualified employee.

References

Fried, G. (1997). "Illegal moves off-the-field: university liability for illegal acts of student athletes." *Seton Hall Journal of Sports Law* 7(1): 1.

Fried, G. (1997). *Safe at first, an event administrators guide to reducing liability*. Houston, TX: University of Houston.

From the gym to the jury. (1997). 8(4).

Gifis, S. (1984). *Barron's legal guides, law dictionary*. New York: Barron's Educational Services, Inc.

Levin, R.L. (1995). "Workplace violence: Sources of liability, warning signs, and ways to mitigate damages." *Labor Law Journal* 46(7): 418–428.

Millman, R.F., and Peery, Jr., G.F. (1996). "Basic Training, Labor and Employment Law." *Los Angeles Daily Journal* (July 25): 14.

Schaner, D.J. (1996). "Have gun, will carry: Concealed handgun laws, workplace violence and employer liability." *Employee Relations Law Journal* 22(1): 83–100.

Silver, M. (1987). "Negligent hiring claims take off." *ABA Journal* (May): 72–78.

Update '95. (1995). San Francisco, CA: Schachter, Kristoff, Orenstein & Berkowitz.

van der Smissen, B. (1990). *Legal liability and risk management for public and private entities.* Cincinnati, OH: Anderson Publishing Co.

Cases

Berger v. Security Pacific Information System, 795 P.2d 1380 (Colo. App. 1990).

Bryant v. Livigni, 619 N.E. 2d 550 (5th Dist., IL. 1993).

Doe v. British Universities North American Club, 788 F.Supp. 1286 (D. Conn. 1992).

D.T. by M.T. v. Independent School Dist. No. 16, 894 F.2d 1176 (10th Cir. 1990).

Rafsky v. New York City, 12 N.Y.S. 2d. 560 (1939).

Rook v. State, 4 N.Y.S. 2d. 116 (1938).

Statutes

California Civil Code Section 51.9.
Title VII of the Civil Rights Act of 1964, 42 U.S.C.A. Section 2000e.

Chapter 6

Terms and Conditions of Employment

After reviewing an applicant's qualifications, insuring that no discrimination has taken place in the interviewing process and making sure no duty was violated in the hiring process, it is time to narrow the potential list of candidates and to talk to various applicants about job terms and conditions. Picking the first applicant to be offered the job is sometimes like Russian roulette. Every otherwise qualified individual regardless of his or her sex, race, religion, national origin or physical condition has to be grouped in the final pool. One means of weeding out potential applicants involves preliminary negotiations to determine what their final position will be regarding salary and related employment benefits. While numerous terms and conditions are identified in the job announcement or advertisement, additional terms and conditions are always the subject of potential negotiation. Individuals demanding too much or unwilling to compromise can either be rejected or might in fact demonstrate strong negotiation skills which justify additional compensation.

The major concern involved with preliminary negotiations is the prospect of the negotiator going too far and offering too much. California case law provides a perfect example of such a problem. Under traditional California case law, an employee cannot bring a wrongful termination case under a fraud theory, rather the terminated employee would have to bring a breach of contract claim (*Foley v. Interactive Data Corp.*, 1988). However, in the *Lazar v. Superior Court* case the plaintiff/employee received a glowing employment proposal. He was told there would be continued employment as long as he performed well. He also would continue job advancement and receive increased salary raises if he performed well. Relying on the glowing promises, the employee accepted the offer and moved across country to work for his new employer. Two years later, and despite exemplary performance, he was told his position was being eliminated. The fraud claim was successful because it was not based on fraud in his termination, rather the fraud claim was based on fraudulent conduct in the employer's attempt to induce him to accept the employment offer (*Lazar*, 1996). This case (coupled with the negligent misrepresentation case in Chapter 5) clearly shows the potential problems that occur when a recruiter promises the moon, and does not even deliver some stars. A primary concern during the negotiation process involves not overselling the position. If you intentionally misrepresent a material term you will be charged with fraud. If you just negligently or carelessly make a misrepresentation you will be possibly liable for negligent misrepresentation. The actual components of a negligent misrepresentation claim include:

- making a misrepresentation,
- you should have known the truth,
- the employee reasonably relied upon your misrepresentation, and
- the employee was injured by the misrepresentation.

If the misrepresentation causes serious emotional distress, and if the employee can show that the distress is the result of some extreme or outrageous behavior, then the employee can also raise a negligent infliction of emotional distress claim. Examples of conduct that can produce a negligent infliction of emotional distress claim include:

- racial harassment,
- promising employees continued employment if they do not bring a discrimination claim, and then terminating them after they do not raise the claim,
- promise employment contingent on performing some preliminary work, but then never giving the person a job, and
- telling someone during an interview that they are too old to work with your company.

This is why it is so important to put all the job terms, conditions and expectations in writing. Additional steps that should be considered in the negotiation process include:

- not letting recruiters promise anything not dedicated to the job position,
- not hiding critical, known, issues from the recruit,
- reviewing all recruiting information for any statements that might indicate a term of employment other than at-will (unless specifically part of the job position),
- review the policies and procedures of any outside recruiting or placement service to make sure they are not making any misrepresentations, and
- be especially vigilant when dealing with prospective employees who would be forced to relocate.

These negotiation factors all help lead to the final offer being accepted by the best applicant. This process culminates with the employer making the job offer and obtaining some form of acceptance from the job applicant. Not every employee needs an employment contract. However, a written contract (discussed below) provides specific proof as to what were the contract's exact terms and conditions. Such documentation reduces the cost required to prove contractual terms in court. Thus, it is always advisable to provide an employee contract for even minimum wage employees to help prevent future misunderstandings. Besides providing written contractual terms, the final hiring process also involves notifying all other candidates that they are no longer being considered. Such notification should be completed as soon as possible to prevent any ill will associated with long delays, and then a denial. Appendix H or J provide sample rejection letters which can form the foundation for the final rejection letter.

A final employment agreement cannot be considered until all job specific terms and conditions are developed and presented to the final candidates. This chapter highlights numerous concerns which need to be addressed when finalizing the employment relationship and to ensure the new employee can properly adjust into their new work environment. This chapter first analyzes specific position attributes such as wages, work hours, benefits and work environment. The chapter then analyzes contractual concerns including what constitutes contractual components such as employee manuals, posting requirements and specific contractual clauses. The last section of this chapter focuses on integrating the new employee into the workplace and monitoring their progress. Emphasis will be made throughout the text on the importance of documenting all pertinent employment terms in a final document which incorporates all prior discussion. However, it should be specifically noted that while many suggest including as much information as possible in a final employment contract, some colleges and universities are being advised by their attorneys not to issue contracts. Instead, the colleges and universities are just sending a letter indicating that a coach is being employed at will and sets forth rudimentary terms such as salary and position title.

1) Wage Issues

The Fair Labor Standards Act (FLSA) has great influence over terms and conditions of employment in three primary areas: minimum wages, overtime pay, and child labor laws.

Private employers are subject to the FLSA if they are engaged in interstate commerce and either exceed specified dollar volumes of business or are engaged in certain industries.... Effective April 1, 1990, enterprises are subject to the Act if their annual dollar volume of business exceeds $500,000 per year, exclusive of excise taxes (Dixon, 1994).

Many employers exceed the $500,000 sales volume and almost every employer engages in interstate commerce. Small employers doing business on a local basis only with sales less than $500,000 are exempt from the FLSA's regulations. Thus, almost all sport businesses are affected by the FLSA regulations that significantly impact the terms and conditions of employment.

Minimum Wage Laws

The FLSA originally sought to protect women and children who were often forced to work 60 plus hours per week. More specifically, the law sought to prohibit big businesses from exploiting the powerless labor force. Further, FLSA intended to assist those in low paying jobs to achieve an adequate standard of living. Minimum wage laws, although frequently abused and circumvented, remain a contentious issue. The penalty for non-compliance is minimal. For example, violators of the FLSA's minimum wage requirements are only required to pay owed back wages. Consequently, many adopt the philosophy that they will pay below minimum wage until they are caught. This gives employers more working capital for today and again, little problems unless investigated. As stated by Zachary (1996a), "Indeed, minimum-wage laws at both the federal and state levels are among the country's most frequently flouted statutes, making the congressional battle irrelevant for many intended beneficiaries."

In 1938 the minimum wage was 25 cents per hour. President Clinton signed legislation in August, 1996 which increased the minimum wage to $5.15 in 1997 (effective Sept. 1, 1997). Various states, however, advocate much more stringent minimum wage laws. For example, Montana voters are considering an increase in minimum wage to $6.25. Oregon is considering an increase in minimum wage to $6.50. Missouri is considering an initiative that will increase the minimum wage to $6.75 by 1999. Denver has advocated increasing the minimum wage to $7.15 by 1999 ("Minimum wage battles," 1996).

FLSA regulations enable you to pay lower wages for apprentices, learners or disabled workers. Employees exempt from both overtime pay and minimum wage laws include:

1) Outside salespeople, executive, administrative, and professional employees, including teachers and academic administrative employees in elementary and secondary schools (Bennett-Alexander and Pincus, 1995).
2) Any physically separate business establishment which only employs the parents, spouse, children or other immediate family of the owner (Dixon, 1994).

3) Employees of certain seasonal amusement or recreational establishments and organized camps which: (a) do not operate more than 7 months in any calendar year and (b) during the preceding calendar year, "average receipts for any six months of the year were not more than one-third of its receipts for the other six months of the year." (Dixon, 1994)

4) Employees of interstate, state and local public agencies who volunteer to perform services without any compensation, or in exchange for the receipt of an expense reimbursement, reasonable benefits or a nominal fee, are considered to be volunteers and not employees while performing such services (e.g., park and recreation volunteers) (Dixon, 1994, emphasis added).

5) Volunteers who provide services to private employers are not considered to be employees (Dixon, 1994).

Numerous sport businesses fall into the above exempt categories. For example, batboys working for the Detroit Tigers sued in federal court ("Tiger Batboys," 1997). Allegations included being paid below minimum wage levels between 1992 and 1995. The judge classified the batboys as exempt due to their seasonal employment and dismissed the lawsuit (pursuant to exception number 3 above). Sport businesses exempt from FLSA benefit from a reduced cost structure via lower wages and unnecessary overtime pay compliance requirements.

Employers subject to the FLSA's coverage need to follow the points outlined below.

1) Compensable work time includes all ancillary activities associated with a particular job (e.g., equipment maintenance, loading or fueling a vehicle, etc.).

2) Travel time to and from work is generally non compensable.

3) Travel which is compensable by contract, custom or practice must be counted as work time.

4) Meal periods are non compensable if they are 30 minutes or longer, if the employee is relieved of all duties, and if the employee is free to leave his or her work station.

5) Sleep time can be excluded from work time only if an employee is on duty for 24 hours, the employee can usually enjoy an uninterrupted night's sleep, the employee has reasonable sleeping facilities, not more than 8 hours of sleep are excluded from any 24-hour period and the employee has agreed to exclude sleep time from compensable hours of work.

6) On-time call is not compensable if the employee can use the time spent on call primarily for his or her own benefit.

7) Brief breaks up to 15 minutes are considered to be work-time.

8) An employee's attendance at training programs will not be considered to be work time where attendance is outside of regular work hours, attendance is in fact voluntary, no productive work is performed during the training and the training is not directed toward making the employee more proficient in the individual's present job.

9) Time spent in a meeting pertaining to an employee's job is compensable (Dixon, 1994).

The minimum wage laws are important to employers, in part, because long hours are often the standard faire in the sport service industry. Employer's decisions on what time to compensate and how much to compensate should be guided by the FLSA requirements as well as other state-related laws.

Besides the specific legal requirements, concerning proper wage payments, you should also examine additional wage related concerns such as:

- Is the compensation policy in writing?
- Are specific procedures established for determining when salaries increase and by how much (i.e., across the board raises versus merit increases)?
- Is there a permanent, communicated compensation program which all employees understand?
- Have you anticipated all the various day-to-day wage management concerns such as:
  - how often are employees reviewed for raises?
  - how large are the raises?
  - how would you respond if someone needs an immediate raise?
  - how should you go about hiring new employees will cost more than current employees?
  - should raises follow cost of living increases?
  - who makes the final decision concerning raises?
  - are salary and wage related issues kept confidential?
  - where will you get the additional funds to pay for wages? (Jensen, 1997).

These questions help reflect on the numerous managerial concerns which need to be considered when determining wages and potential raises. These questions do not address the specific managerial concern associated with not giving any raises. Such action could lead to significant employee unrest, dissatisfaction, and resignation. However, in some segments of the sports employment market, such as professional sports teams front office personnel, the supply available to help fill lower level positions is so great that teams often pay low salaries without raises as lower level employees can always be quickly replaced.

2) Hour Issues

As highlighted in Introduction, individuals are starting to sue employers when employees engage in negligent conduct attributable to working extensive schedules. While employees in the sports, fitness and recreation industries traditionally do not work the same hours as truck drivers, fatigue can be a factor if an employee is forced to both open and close a gym while serving as a lifeguard or related position. Thus, besides making sure overtime issues and hour compliance issues (such as youth work hours), you should vigilantly monitor employees to ensure they are competently performing their job from the minute they walk into the workplace until they go home.

Overtime Pay

In general, the FLSA requires "that an employee be paid an additional one-half of the individual's regular rate for all hours of work in excess of forty in a week" (Dixon, 1994). Overtime refers to pay at 1.5 the base pay. For example, an employee paid $6.00 hour would make $9.00 during overtime. Employers are not allowed to "average" the hours worked from two different workweeks. In 1996, Republicans in Congress supported a bill providing the employee with the option of either receiving overtime pay or paid time off that could be redeemed at a later time. Congress adjourned without passing the bill ("Time off for workers," 1996).

Employees in the sport industry have historically worked long hours. It is important that managers be cognizant of legislation regulating overtime pay. Many employees working in the sport industry represent nonexempt (v. exempt) employees as defined by the FLSA. Exempt employees tend to occupy white-collar positions (e.g., executives, administrators, professionals and those with specialized computer skills) and are paid on a salary basis. The law also requires an exempt status for people employed in sales positions. However, to qualify for exempt status the salesperson must perform 80% of the total workweek in the area of sales and conducts sales business away from the employer's business establishment itself. As explained by Dixon (1994), "An individual who is engaged in sales work at a fixed location, such as a residence or branch office, will not be considered to be engaged in exempt outside sales work." What constitutes an "exempt" sales person is of legal significance to the employer as many sport businesses employ individuals in sales-related positions (e.g., bowling alleys, professional and collegiate sports, health club membership sales and sporting goods sellers). The consequence of error or failure to adhere to the FLSA is exemplified by a 1996 litigation against the Seattle Supersonics. As explained by Dean and Smith (1996), "a federal jury in Seattle...awarded more than $13 million to five former Seattle Supersonics—commissioned salespeople who alleged they were fired in retaliation for complaining about overtime pay violations. The verdict included $12 million in punitive damages." The Supersonics were liable for the following acts in violation of FLSA,

- designating a fixed sum of $2,000 as compensation for all required overtime;
- requiring employees to take compensatory time off in lieu of payment for overtime hours; and
- carrying compensatory time forward beyond the pay period in which overtime hours were worked.

Although unintentional, the Supersonics were in violation of the FLSA. As explained by Dean and Smith (1996), "Most FLSA violations are the result of ignorance, negligence, or inadvertence and can be fixed through self-auditing, careful planning, and smart drafting."

Complying with Overtime Pay Laws

The following guidelines and suggestions can facilitate an employer's FLSA compliance efforts in the area of overtime pay (Dean and Smith, 1996).

Applying Both Federal and State Laws Regarding Overtime Pay

In addition to the FLSA, most states have legislation regulating wage and hour laws, including overtime pay. In situations where the federal and state legislation differs, employers will be required to comply with legislation that is the most beneficial to the employee. In states that do have laws, the FLSA is the more lenient of the two. For example, a recently proposed bill in Massachusetts would limit individuals 17 and under to a maximum of four hours of work each school day and 28 hours during the school week (White, 1997). Currently, those 17 and under can work as many as nine hours a day and 48 hours during a school week. New York, Wisconsin, and Washington are other states with more stringent laws than what is demanded by the federal FLSA (White, 1997). Employers in these states would be required to comply with the more stringent state labor laws. The Department of Labor (1997) provides free literature to assist businesses in their knowledge of the law. The DOL publishes guides such as the Employer's Guide to Compliance with Federal Wage-Hour Laws and the Handy Reference Guide to the Fair Labor Standards Act. Similar literature should be also available from state governmental agencies and local libraries.

Record Keeping

As previously discussed in Chapter 3, records conveying employee's work hours, pay rate and wages earned should be retained for a period of 2 years while basic earning records should be retained for 3 years. In addition, Dixon (1996) identifies additional information that must be documented and available for review.

- Name;
- Home address;
- Occupation in which employed and sex;
- Time of day and day of week in which each workweek begins;
- Hours worked each day and total hours worked each week;
- All inclusions and exclusions from the regular rate;
- Total straight-time and overtime earnings;... and
- Date of payment, amount of payment, and period included in payment.

A review of the above records, specifically records relating to overtime pay, facilitates compliance with the law while simultaneously benefit an employer's efforts to budget and plan for future labor expenses.

Monitor Employee's Time Cards

Employees sometimes inaccurately record their working hours. It is also not uncommon for employees working in the sport industry to voluntarily "work through lunch hours, not take breaks, and not write down overtime hours, without realizing that they are exposing the company to unwanted overtime liability" (Dean and Smith, 1996). Such incorrect record keeping can lead to significant liability. Four instances can alert an employer to problems.

- employees who record eight hours of work for every day, regardless of the amount of time they actually spend;
- nonexempt employees who arrive at work early on their own initiative and begin working before their scheduled starting times without prior approval;

- nonexempt employees who determine for themselves whether to work overtime; and
- nonexempt employees who take work home in the evenings without prior approval just to catch up (Dean and Smith, 1996).

Employers who know, or should have known, about FLSA violations are liable for all related penalties.

Examine Formal Policies

Formal policies can help mitigate violating FLSA requirements. Communicating via an employee handbook can effectively convey to employees how to "correctly" record hours. For example, management could consider using the following policy manual clauses.

> If you are a nonexempt employee, you must personally record the number of regular and overtime hours that you work each workweek and certify with your signature that you have accounted for all hours you worked during the week.
>
> Misrepresenting information on your time card, working overtime without recording your time (working "off the clock"), and working overtime without prior supervisory approval are strictly prohibited and will result in corrective action, up to and including termination (Dean and Smith, 1996).

The above language shifts responsibility to the employee while simultaneously imposing stiff penalties for error or omission.

Time Sheet Certification

Time sheets could contain a similar clause to be read and signed by the employee and another clause to be read and signed by their supervisor. The employee-related clause could provide as follows:

> My signature below certifies that I have accurately and honestly recorded all of the hours that I have worked for the company's benefit—whether at work or at home—and that I have sought and obtained approval in advance for all overtime hours worked. I understand that I am subject to corrective action, up to and including immediate termination, if I have misrepresented any information on my time card or have failed to record all of my hours worked (Dean and Smith, 1996).

Policy language that could be used for the supervisor's clause is as follows:

> My signature below certifies that this time card is accurate to the best of my knowledge, that I authorized in advance all of the overtime hours identifies on this time card, and that I am unaware of and have no reason to believe

that the employee has worked any hours not reflected on this time card—whether at work or at home. I understand that I am subject to corrective action, up to and including immediate termination, if I have misrepresented any information regarding this time card (Dean and Smith, 1996).

Although the above clauses may be viewed as some as "lawsuit paranoia," they can provide protection for the employer when defending claims alleging overtime pay violations.

Employee Volunteer Activities

Many sport businesses encourage employees to engage in uncompensated volunteer capacities. For example, sport franchises may require employees to visit local public schools and promote the upcoming season and related promotions to young people in the community. This time is compensable.

Time spent on volunteer activities must be considered time worked if the work is done at the employer's request, under the employer's direction and control, or while the employee is required to be on the employer's premises. Time spent voluntarily in civic and charitable activities outside of normal working hours is not generally compensable (so long as there is no employer compulsion). In examining employer policies and informal practices, the auditor should examine whether there is overt or covert pressure on employees to participate in after-hours charitable activities to determine whether participation was truly voluntary (Dean and Smith, 1996).

Compensating indirect job responsibilities increases a business's cost structure. However, the increased cost structure is far less onerous than potential penalties for FLSA noncompliance.

On-call Activities for Exempt Employees

The maintenance of an employee's exempt status (for overtime compensation) is jeopardized if the employer pays the employee "extra" (e.g., an hourly wage) for being "on call." For example, a franchise may pay its risk management manager an hourly wage above and beyond his or her salary if he or she is willing to be on call during all events (sport and nonsport related) hosted at the stadium or arena. Unfortunately, the hourly wage may jeopardize the employee's otherwise exempt status.

Proper Training

The FLSA is a very encompassing piece of legislation. Employers can demonstrate good faith compliance efforts by hosting in-service training sessions for all employees (both supervisory and staff). Employers needing more thorough training and education should consider using outside contractors or consultants specializing in FLSA compliance.

Breaks

Employer are required by statutes to provide workers with breaks. However, there are several disputes that have arisen concerning how these laws are applied when workers are given multiple breaks at different times during the day. Statutes require that "[r]est periods of short duration running from 5 minutes to about 20 minutes are common in industry. They promote the efficiency of the employee and are customarily paid for as working time. They must be counted as hours worked (29 C.F.R. 785.18 (1990))." While employers are required to give employees paid breaks during the day, there is not set standard that an employer is required to provide five minutes every hour or any other standard. However, while an employer might consider the employees on break, the law does not qualify time off as a "break" if the time is spent primarily for the employer's benefit. Thus, you should always make sure that when employees are taking breaks, they should not be engaging in any activity that primarily benefits you.

Employees are elegible for taking lunch breaks of at least 30 minutes in any given day (29 C.F.R. 385.19 (1990)). This bonafide meal period is a non-compensable time where the employer does not need to pay the employee as long as the employee is completely relieved of all duties. Thus, if a receptionist eats her lunch at the front desk and answers periodic phone call then they need to be compensated as she was not completely relieved of all her duties.

3) Benefits

Numerous employees choose a job because there are specific benefits which might be provided. Some benefits can range from an employer paid car and extensive vacation time to completely covering all medical and life insurance premiums. Employees with more responsibilities and accountability tend to receive more benefits. There is no one set formula for what benefits should be provided to each employee and "benefits" law represents one of the most difficult subjects to cover in detail. Based on the numerous federal and state laws which apply and the complexities associated with calculating benefits, it is beyond the scope of this guide to closely examine all benefit. However, some key issues associated with benefits will be addressed in the following pages.

Many benefits are required by law. By statute, an employer must pay FICA taxes (Social Security), pay unemployment compensation, pay workers' compensation insurance coverage and cannot terminate an employee for exercising their right to vote (in most states) or for serving on a jury (in most states). Veterans, pursuant to the Veteran's Reemployment Rights Act receive a benefit which allows them to return to work up to five years after leaving for service and to return to their positions as if they were on unpaid leave.

Family Medical Leave Act (FMLA)

One federal law that directly impacts the benefits employees receive is the Family Medical Leave Act which establishes certain rights for employees facing medical emergencies. While the FMLA establishes minimum rights, many employers utilize the FMLA as the base for additional benefits and provide additional benefits over and beyond the FMLA. For example, while a male employee might receive 12 weeks to help care for their new child, an employer can provide an employee with additional time or allow them to telecommute for an additional month.

The FMLA (1993) represents one of the most recent legislative pieces influencing benefits in the work environment. The FMLA was passed by the Clinton administration in 1993. The FMLA pertains to employers with 50 or more employees working within a 75-mile radius. Subsequent legislation was introduced in June 1996 by Rep. Patricia Schroeder (D. Colorado) to expand the coverage to employers with 25 or more employees. President Clinton proposed an extension of the FMLA to make the workplace more "family friendly" in June 1996. As reported in The Wall Street Journal, President Clinton advocates legislation requiring employers to provide all employees with 24 unpaid hours per year to "handle such obligations as taking an elderly parent to a doctor's appointment or meeting with a child's teacher" (Stout, 1996). Critics of the legislation argue that President Clinton's proposal is for political reasons only as most companies already agree to let employees off work to tend to family emergencies or responsibilities.

The FMLA applies to any employer who employs 50 or more employees for at least 20 workweeks in a given year. Unpaid leave is allowed for an employee upon the birth of a child, placement of an adopted child, care for an employee's spouse, children or parents who are in serious condition, and for an employee's own health concern which lasts more than three days. The Act does not provide benefits for taking care of in-laws. The

Act allows employees to take up to 12 workweeks off in a 12-month period. Employees can combine this 12 week period with any accrued vacation, sick leave or personnel leave offered by the employer (Frierson, 1994).

During the employee's leave, an employer is required to keep the employee's health insurance intact. Upon the employee's return, they should be returned to the same or similar position with equivalent pay and benefits. An employee who has been on leave is not entitled to receive seniority or wage increases while on leave. If the employer has had to incur department-wide layoffs, then the employee on leave does not have to be rehired (Frierson, 1994).

The employee's benefits can be terminated if employee fails to return to work or if the employee is otherwise terminated at a later date due to, for example, downsizing or breaking company policies (Pranschke and Laderman, 1995)

The law does not just impose burdens on the employer. The employee is required to provide the employer with 30-day advance notice. If the advance notice is not provided, the leave period is delayed until the 30 day period has expired. Interim days could be missed through applying accrued vacation, sick or personnel days (Frierson, 1994).

The FMLA can be violated by:

- failing to post the FMLA poster explaining the law,
- refusing to grant a leave,
- failing to continue fringe benefits,
- failing to reinstate the employee to their former position, and
- retaliating against an employee for exercising their rights under the law.

An employer who violates the FMLA can be fined $100 for each violation. An employee who's rights were violated can recover double the amount of lost wages, any expenses for alternate care required for the sick person, and attorney fees and legal costs (Frierson, 1994).

The FMLA can create significant economic hardships. Employers must incur the costs (recruiting, hiring, training or job reallocation expenses) of finding a replacement during the employee's absence. Employers incur additional costs in reorienting and updating the employee to current operations upon his or her return. These costs have to be weighed against the fact that the FMLA is used by only 5% of all eligible employees ("The FMLA: Benefit or Burden?", 1996). In a 1996 survey, 75% of all survey respondents indicated that "the FMLA caused daily administrative headaches." "About 64 percent also said the FMLA created little or no benefit" ("The FMLA: Benefit or Burden?" 1996). The FMLA has a two-year statute of limitations beginning from the date of the last violation.

Suggestions for FMLA Compliance

James J. Carabetta, Director of Human Resources for a Connecticut company, provides good suggestions for sport business managers (Sunoo, 1996).

- Post the FMLA poster in a visible location and in employee handbooks.
- Encourage each employee to develop his or her own replacement.
- Encourage multi-functional employees employee cross-training which reduces expenses associated with the hiring and training of new employees.
- Assign one employee as the FMLA coordinator.
- Maintain regular contact with employees on leave.
- Keep FMLA records separate from personnel records and medical files to prevent inappropriate disclosure or discrimination based on an employee taking leave.

Regular contact is critical, but such contact needs to be effectively documented. As explained by Carabetta (1996),

> Document each contact. Track expenses incurred for each leave in time, training, accommodation or replacement labor. The procedure will become valuable in forecasting financial impact on a monthly, quarterly or annual basis.

Federal and State Laws

One key federal protection afforded employees is the Employee Retirement Income Security Act (ERISA). ERISA is discussed in greater detail in Chapter 13. ERISA covers more than just retirement and pension benefits, but also covers medical, surgical, or hospital care or benefits in the event of sickness, disability, unemployment, or vacation benefits (Rothstein, Knapp and Liebman, 1987).

Various state laws can affect benefits. For example while states require some type of employee health insurance coverage or option, such benefits could be affected by state nondiscrimination statutes. Additionally, federal laws can also be modified by state laws that are more expansive than the federal laws. The FMLA is expanded in California by a specific pregnancy disability statute which allows up to four months more leave and requires a state specific leave poster (*Update, 1995*). Some states have statutes specifically forbidding an employer from offering insurance to men and women at different costs or other minorities having to pay higher rates (Rothstein, Knapp and Liebman, 1987). A major battle is being fought throughout the United

States concerning extending employee benefits to non-spouse, or more appropriately considered-life partners. Such life partners often involve the "significant other" partners of homosexual men and women who are barred in most states from getting married. As rights normally only apply to spouses, "significant others" would not be considered a spouse for benefit's qualification or registration. Some businesses are now offering extended coverage for "significant others." Surveys show that 10%- 15% of larger companies with more than 200 employees are now offering benefits to homosexual and/or non-married partners (Jones, 1997). Approximately 23% of employers with more than 5,000 employees offer similar benefits (Jones, 1997). In April 1997, The San Francisco 49ers became the first NFL team to "provide domestic partner benefits for team employees and players (Jones, 1997).

Besides specific federal and state laws which might mandate specific benefits, benefits traditionally entail significant managerial discretion based on the bargaining position held by each party. Thus, while the law might mandate numerous employee rights, no law dictates whether or not an employee should be given a corporate car. The list of potential benefits offered to current or potential employees is almost limitless. Benefits can include: special insurance coverage, salary incentives, performance bonuses, company perks, and a host of other items which provide a limitless selection of items which might help motivate employees.

A major concern associated with benefits involving vesting and when does an employee become entitled to benefits so that an employer cannot revoke or change the benefits to be received. Typically, benefits vest as the labor is rendered. Thus, unless benefits are specifically tied to future service, benefits vest when services are renders. Therefore, if an employee earns one week of vacation time after working for six months, the employee is entitled to the one-week or the monetary equivalent after working for six months. If the employee works for less than six months, no benefits are vested and the employee is not entitled to any vacation time/pay (Adler and Coleman, 1995).

In addition to specific terms and conditions, prospective employees will need to comply with legal or work place rules designed to prevent injuries. Two such concerns include child labor issues and workplace safety concerns.

4) Child Labor Laws

The FLSA regulates all working individuals under 18 years of age. Federal and state laws typically categorize children and related restrictions in three categories: (a) 16 and 17 year olds, (b) 14 and 15 year olds, and (c) those under 14 years. As mentioned above, the law strives to protect children, often viewed as "cheap" labor, from working long hours and exposure to unsafe conditions. Employing children remains a genuine concern to society as teen employment climbs to its highest levels (Smith, 1995). The Department of Labor reports that annually, "70 teens are killed on the job, about one every five days and that 210,000 working teens are injured." (Department of Labor, 1997).

Labor activists and the media continue to scrutinize U.S. manufacturing companies employing children in foreign countries to manufacture various products (Jones, 1996). As explained by Joel Joseph, Chairman of the Made in the USA Foundation (Joseph, 1996),

> Fully half of the soccer balls sold in the United States are made in Pakistan, and every one of those soccer balls had an assist from a child under 14 who toils 10 hours a day in subhuman sweatshops, stitching the ball or cutting material used to make it.... Nike similarly bases its operations on finding the lowest-cost labor to make its athletic shoes. Twelve-year-old girls work in Indonesian sweatshops 70 hours a week making Nikes in unhealthy plants that reek of glue.

A school board member in Portland, Oregon, was so disturbed by Nike's alleged exploitation of children that he actually advocated rejecting a large donation from Nike as a symbol of protest regardless of the plight of decreasing federal funds (Zachary, G.P., 1996b). The problem, as explained by Joseph, not only evolves around the inhumane treatment and exploitation of children, but on loosing American jobs as well. India, Pakistan, Nepal, Bangladesh, Malaysia and Indonesia allegedly employ children at a young age to work for minimal, if any, pay in dismal conditions (Joseph, 1996). Those living and working in foreign countries are filling jobs that could be filled by Americans. In April 1997 President Clinton sanctioned an apparel-industry code. Provisions of the Code include the following ("Anti-sweatshop proposal," 1997),

> Guarantees a minimum wage pegged to existing standards in individual countries, a maximum 60-hour work week with at least one day off, and an independent monitor of conditions in overseas factories used by U.S. companies. Manufacturers that adhere to the voluntary code of conduct would be rewarded with a "no sweatshop" label for their products.

Both Nike and Reebok, in addition to eight other manufacturers, voluntarily agreed to abide by the above code of conduct ("Code," 1997).

As reported by the Department of Labor (1997), the retail industry employs 51% of all teens and the service industry (e.g., YMCAs, swimming pools, parks and recreation, ball parks and amusement parks) employs 34% of all teens. The FLSA directly influences operations in the above service sectors as well as in manufacturing. In 1993, for example, the U.S. Labor Department prohibited a 14-year-old bat boy from working during the summer with the South Atlantic League ball club due to the teenage work rules. As explained by *The Atlanta Journal* in a 1993 article (Bennett-Alexander and Pincus, 1995),

> It's hard to imagine how the time-honored tradition of being a bat boy — or bat girl, for that matter — could adversely affect a youngster's health or education. Baseball is a summer game with minimal conflicts with school nights, and there's hardly a more wholesome environment left in our jaded society than the old ballpark.

As noted above, similar allegations were also brought against the Detroit Tigers ("Tiger Batboys," 1997).

Many states have modified state labor laws that exempt sport businesses employing minors. For example, in Montana, minors "employed as officials or referees for nonprofit athletic organizations were...exempted from the child labor law." Similarly, Illinois law exempts children working in the entertainment industry so long as waivers were obtained, completed, and approved. Arkansas amended their state labor law "to allow children under age 16 to work in bowling alleys" (Nelson, 1996).

Failure to comply with the FLSA exposes an employer to fines of up to $10,000 per violation, possible imprisonment for second convictions, and product boycotts. During a 12 month time period (October 1995 - September 1996), the Department of Labor "assessed $6.8 million in civil money penalties for violations involving 1,341 establishments," or $5,071 per establishment. As evident, the cost of compliance can be far less than the penalty for infractions.

Complying with Child Labor Laws

The sport industry employees a large number of teenage workers. For example, it is common to find teen workers employed as sporting goods retail clerks, health club exercise prescriptionists, lifeguards and amusement park attendants. The following Department of Labor suggestions can facilitate teen safety and better ensure FLSA compliance.

Properly Train Teens

Teenagers working for sport businesses often have little, if any, job experience. Consequently, the teen worker has minimal knowledge to apply to any given job. Unfortunately, the sport industry mandates that teens working in amusement parks or at water parks, for example, be adequately trained as their actions directly influence patron and employee safety. As stated by the Department of Labor guidelines, "What may be obvious to an adult or simple common sense to an experienced employee may not be so clear to a teen tackling a task for the first time." A comprehensive amount of time should be spent in showing the employee exactly what to do and what can happen if jobs are performed improperly. Time spent showing a teen the best way to handle a job will be paid back threefold through work done right and without harm to products, patrons or injury to the teen. The DOL suggests the following components within a multi-faceted training program.

- Give them clear instructions and tell them what safety precautions to take.
- Ask them to repeat your instructions and give them an opportunity to ask questions.
- Show them how to perform the task.
- Watch teens while they perform task, correcting any mistakes.
- Finally, ask if they have any additional questions.

Educate Teens on Risk Management Plan

Risk management plans should be adopted and used by every sport business. A risk management plan is useless if it is not properly communicated. Teen employees should be taught those risk management steps to take to prevent injury and in case of an emergency. Emergency situations often breed panic and unclear thinking. An employee who has learned and implemented the risk management plan will be able to execute the plan efficiently and effectively versus having to rely on instincts which may or may not represent prudent thinking.

Know the Law

Ignorance of the law is the most frequent reason for failure to comply with the FLSA (Smith, S.L., 1995b). As explained by Darlene Atkins, co-coordinator of the Child Labor Coalition, "Many employers feel like they are doing these kids a favor by giving them a job and keeping them off the street" (Smith, I., 1995a). Many employers post the required FLSA poster, but fail to read the information. In addition to prescribing hours that the teen employee can work, the FLSA prohibits teenagers from working in any of 18 jobs listed by the law. Managers should check with the experts before placing teen employees on lawn mowers or having them build or mend fences, work late at night, or operate mechanical amusement rides. Knowing the law and compliance with its requirement benefits an employer via increased employee morale, improved public relations, decreased insurance expenses, and a safer work environment.

There are a variety of resources provided by the Department of Labor and others, which facilitate compliance. For example, during the summer of 1997, the Department of Labor included information about the following on its web page (Department of Labor, 1997):

- A Work Safe This Summer Poster
- Fact Sheet: Protecting Working Teens
- Employer's Guide to Teen Worker Safety
- The Teen Worker's Bill of Rights

Also available are charts conveying where teens work during the summer:

- Where teens work during summer
- Where teens are injured at work
- How teens are injured at work
- How teens are killed at work

Underage Workers

Age discrimination laws prohibit asking workers their age if they are 18 years or over. However, age cannot be dismissed so easily when hiring teen workers. Employers must identify those workers which are 17 years or younger. Applications which ask the teen employee to identify whether he or she is 17 years or younger are legal. Proof of age is also a prudent measure that can facilitate better compliance with the FLSA mandates.

5) Work Environment

Chapter 11 provides a thorough analysis concerning workplace injuries and injury prevention strategies. However, it is critical for the employer at this point in the employment process to thoroughly acquaint a new employee with safety concerns, policies and procedures. The two key elements within safety education include work environment safety and occupation safety. Work environment safety refers to general safety issues associated with the work environment. Such concerns can range from helping prevent employee assaults in the company parking lot to teaching employees how to contact security personnel if a violent person enters the workplace. There are numerous safety issues that are not directly relevant to the exact employee job description, but should be covered in the initial employee orientation. Some major concerns that should be addressed in the orientation can include:

- Crime prevention techniques and strategies as they relate to facilities, co-employee, and customers.
- First-aid techniques, procedures, and equipment location.
- Security protocol and who is responsible for what activities (such as facility evacuation, etc.).
- Safety protocol for fires, earthquakes, tornadoes and other disasters.
- Workers' compensation system overview.

All the concerns addressed above help develop a comprehensive occupational safety curriculum for new employees.

Occupational Safety

Occupational safety concerns involve teaching people how to properly and safely perform their required job duties. While numerous positions require little physical exertion or occur in relatively safe environments, other positions can raise significant dangers. Such dangers can include electrocution, stress related safety, repetitive stress syndrome, equipment malfunctions, job specific safety equipment (i.e., for lifeguards who might need special hooks, floats and other safety devises) and related concerns. All applicants should be thoroughly briefed on security concerns. However, in addition to being properly briefed, all applicants and employees should proceed in the employment process only if they agree to follow all safety rules or policies. The employment contract can contain a specific provision requiring the employee to comply with all safety rules or policies and failure to comply can result in termination.

Safety concerns extend past the initial hiring process. The key to occupational safety is to properly inform new employees about known safety concerns. Failure to notify new employees about known safety concerns will produce a significant negligence claim. The following case highlights this point. A machine operator slipped on machine coolant that had accumulated on the floor by her workstation. The employee injured her back in the fall. The employer was aware that there was a leakage problem from the plaintiff's machine. The employer provided wooden pallets for the workers to stand on as well as clean up rags and absorbent material to throw on the ground. However, the employer did not hold safety meetings or give specific safety instructions to the employees. The court concluded that the employer failed to instruct its employees on how to properly perform their job while avoiding known safety dangers. The fact that the employer provided some safety measures was not enough to defeat their failure to more adequately control safety concerns and properly train employees. The jury awarded the injured employee $291,000 in damages. Traditionally, such a suit would be precluded by workers' compensation coverage. However, the employer in this case failed to purchase workers' compensation insurance which allowed the case to proceed and precluded the employer from claiming any contributory negligence or assumption of risk defense (*Woodlawn Mfg. v. Robinson*, 1996).

Once an employee or prospective employee has been properly briefed as to what workplace concerns they might face and if the applicant is still interested in the position, the employer is then free to explore additional contractual concerns which will hopefully form the basis for the employer-employee relationship. While many employers provide safety education after an employee has been hired, such timing might be inappropriate. If an employee is unwilling or unable to comply with specific safety rules, it is imperative that you uncover such information before someone is hired. Furthermore, some applicants might not accept some job related safety risks and if they are not aware of any such risks, they might be able to bring a negligent misrepresentation or fraud claim for failure to disclose the safety concerns. Thus, it is recommended that safety rules and policies be reviewed with an applicant before they are hired and after they are hired, to ensure more intensive training can be provided if necessary.

6) At-will Employees

The employee at-will doctrine was introduced into law in the 1880s (Feliu, 1992). The doctrine has only undergone slight changes in the past 100 years. At-will employees can be simply defined as employees that can be terminated at any time for any reason or for no reason whatsoever. At-will employment is a critical managerial concern as it provides the employer the opportunity to manage the workplace without fear that you might not be able to terminate someone. At-will refers to very specific situation and specific employees. Most executives have established contracts that might guarantee employment for a certain set period or might specifically indicate that the executive cannot be fired except if he or she engages in certain specified conduct (see generally section 10, below). Government workers normally can only be terminated for cause-which means engaging in some egregious conduct such as stealing, assaulting someone or multiple negative reviews. Similarly, based on union collective bargaining agreements (CBAs), most union members cannot be summarily dismissed without violating the CBA. This leaves lower level employees or employees without specific contractual protections as the individuals most likely to be covered by the at-will doctrine. At-will is not available in all states as at least one state, Montana, has abolished the doctrine (Frierson, 1994).

The basis for at-will employment rests on the principle that an employer or employee should be able to fire someone or quit whenever they wish without any repercussions, unless the contract specifies otherwise. Many employees who work at lower level jobs want to be able to leave if they get a better offer and thus do not want to be locked into a written contract requiring them to work for a certain number of years. Employers prefer at-will employees as they can terminate them at anytime without having to prove the employee did anything wrong. While an employer can terminate an at-will employee without any cause (reason) an employer is not advised to take such action. The primary reason why employers should only terminate even at-will employees for cause is that while you might consider an employee an at-will employee, the court might not consider the employee an at will-employee. For example, if you promised an employee additional rights outside of the contract through oral statements or in an employee manual then the employee could lose his or her at-will status. If they do not have the at-will status and they are terminated without just cause, the terminated employee has a very good potential wrongful termination case. However, if you terminate an at-will employee for cause and the court considers the employee not at-will, you still have the defense that you terminated the employee for cause.

While it appears that at-will employment contracts are a cure-all, there are some exceptions. At-will employment contracts are not upheld if they violate public policy, if an implied contract supercedes the at-will contract and if an implied covenant of good faith and fair dealings dictates to the court that a different should be upheld rather than the at-will contract based on equity principals.

The At-will Principle in Coaching Cases

There are numerous sport coaching cases involving terminated coaches who claim they were terminated without just cause and sue for violation of their alleged constitutional right to be free from losing their continued right to employment without adequate due process. What follows are several sample cases which highlight this struggle.

Charles Babb was a high school basketball coach and physical education instructor (*Babb v. Harnett County Board of Education*, 1995). He signed a contract that stated in pertinent part that "separation or resignation from either duty is tantamount to complete separation and resignation from employment as both teacher and coach notwithstanding that fact that the employee may have gained career status." After several years of coaching and being assigned different coaching responsibilities, Babb was

notified that he would no longer be a coach. Babb brought suit for violation of his due process rights under the North Carolina constitution.

The court initially dismissed the contract breach claim by concluding
that the contract only required the mutual consent of the parties for a
change in the coaching duties, but such consent was not needed when he
was not assigned any duties. The court also analyzed the North Carolina
constitution, which protects teachers from being deprived of their property interest in teaching. However, this provision considers coaching to be
wholly distinct from teaching, which means there is no property right in
continued coaching. This means that a coach could be terminated at any
time-"at will" without raising a constitutional issue in North Carolina.
Based on the fact that both the contract and the constitution did not provide any property right in continued coaching, Babb could be deprived of
his interest with or without due process (*Babb*, 1995).

One key concern associated with employment-at-will clauses involves
employee manuals. While almost all employees start as at-will employee,
their status normally changes if they enter into a contract that specifically
provides otherwise or if an employee manual clearly provides additional
rights.

7) Employee Manuals

The following represents a comical view concerning employee manuals and
regulations, and how strictly matters can be addressed in the workplace.

Dear Employees,

It has been brought to management's attention that many employees
have been dying while on duty for no good reason. Furthermore, it also
appears that some employees are refusing to fall over after they have died.
This, in some cases, has resulted in unearned overtime payments, which
are not provided for under our employee benefit program.

Effective immediately, this practice must be discontinued!

On and after today, any employee found sitting up after he/she has died will
be dropped from the payroll at once, without further investigation. This action is covered by Company Regulation #20 (non-productive labor). When it
can be proven that the employee is being held up by a desk, typewriter, drawing board, telephone, or any other means of support which is the property of
the company, a one (1) day period of grace will be granted. In the event of apparent death, the following procedures will be strictly adhered to:

1. If, after several hours, it is noted that any employee has not
moved or opened at least one eye, the department head will investigate. Because of the highly sensitive nature and/or origin of some
employees and because of the close resemblance between death and

their normal working attitude, the investigation will be made quietly so as to avoid waking the employee if he/she is asleep (which, of course, is permitted under present union contracts).

2. If some doubt still exists as to the employee's true condition, a pay check will be used as the final test. If the employee fails to reach for the check, it is reasonable to assume that death has occurred. Note that in some cases the instinct is so strongly developed that a spastic clutching may occur even after death; do not be misled by this manifestation.

3. In the event that an employee fails to abandon whatever he/she is doing at Coffee Break time, no investigation is necessary as this is conclusive proof that rigor mortis has already set in.

Best Regards,
The Management (Source unknown)

This comical example clearly shows the disdain some employees have with employment manuals and the rules contained therein. No matter how much employees complain, rant and rave about employee manuals and related rules, it is imperative that you develop a comprehensive manual which forms the blueprint for the employment relationship.

Employee manuals or handbooks:

- serve to communicate rules and policies;
- are an essential component of a new employee's orientation process;
- are a critical employee relation tool for educating current and prospective employees;
- contribute to uniform understanding and following of company rules; and
- can serve as a strong defense for claims alleging improper employee conduct (Adler and Coleman, 1995).

If any government agency investigates the employer for discrimination, sexual harassment and/or safety related issue, the first document they will normally request include copies of any employee handbooks/manuals, EEOC statements, and sexual harassment policies. The failure to produce these documents represents a negative inference which can taint the entire investigation (Adler and Coleman, 1995).

Employee manuals can also serve to help maintain a union-free workplace. The manual should specifically state that the employer prefers a direct, personal employment relationship, which would be hampered in a union environment. By including a dispute resolution provision within the manual, employees will know they have a voice and a mechanism to resolve disputes. This is especially true if peer mediation is offered and management is willing to accept the decisions reached through the peer mediation process (Adler and Coleman, 1995).

Puffery in Manuals

Using "puffery" or comments representing inflated promises made in an attempt to lure new employees from the competition, enhance employee motivation or generate community goodwill can cause significant problems for the employer. For example, comments inferring "lifetime employment" or "this sport business takes care of its people forever" can hinder termination efforts for the employer-at-will. The following quote from *Woolley v. Huffman-La Roche* (1985) illustrates the court precedent. As stated by the court:

> If such a commitment is indeed made, obviously an employer should be required to honor it. When such a document purporting to give job security, is distributed by the employer to a work force, substantial injustice may result if that promise is broken.

Make Handbooks User-friendly

Management benefits from handbooks that are user-friendly. User-friendly suggestions include the following:

- reader-friendly print (e.g., not too small; no large blocks of text)
- use of graphics (e.g., charts, tables)
- understandable language
- concise yet comprehensive language
- a table of contents
- color coding
- an index
- question-and-answer sections.

Reader-friendly handbooks improve the likelihood that employees will read the handbook as well as use it for later reference. Employers should also remember that reader-friendly handbooks must also be available for those needing special accommodations (e.g., audiotapes for those visually impaired) (Waterman, 1992).

Content

Employee manuals can contain countless clauses and conditions based on the specific work environment, business or regional concerns. A sample employee manual can be found in Appendix Q. Employee manuals can contain sections covering the following issues:

- company history,
- company philosophy,
- company mission,
- employee welcome statement,
- company overview with possibly organizational chart,
- customer relations,
- investor relations,
- employee relations,
- EEO/Affirmative Action statement,
- immigration law compliance,
- employment reference checks,
- process for reasonably accommodating employees/customers,
- working hours,
- work days,
- time management systems (i.e., time clocks),
- break times and duration,
- overtime and how to receive overtime authorization,
- pay,
- raises,
- merit increases,
- administrative pay corrections,
- travel expenses,
- pay deductions and set-offs such as wage garnishment,
- job promotions,
- vacation time,
- holiday time,
- religious holiday time,
- sick leave,
- AIDS in the workplace,
- personnel leave,
- time off to vote,
- jury duty,
- witness duty,
- bereavement leave,
- relocation benefits,
- insurance,
- benefits continuation (COBRA),
- educational assistance,
- child care benefits
- fringe benefits,
- retirement,
- pension plans,
- 401K plans,

- profit sharing plans,
- company required physical,
- health benefits and reporting guidelines,
- off-the-job political activities,
- outside employment,
- non-disclosure agreement or policy,
- workplace smoking policy,
- sexual harassment policy,
- anti-discrimination policy,
- anti-retaliation policy,
- anti-solicitation or distribution rules on company premises,
- dress codes,
- facial hair policy,
- using company property,
- using company vehicles for personnel reasons,
- using company phones for private calls,
- using company Internet access for personal reasons,
- search policy,
- recycling policy,
- conflicts of interest,
- safety rules,
- visitors in the workplace,
- nepotism rules,
- employment of relatives,
- right to access personnel records,
- workplace confidentiality rules,
- maintenance of confidential health records,
- performance appraisals,
- attendance policy,
- tardiness,
- workplace drug and alcohol policy,
- drug and alcohol testing policy,
- resume and job application fraud,
- AIDS and HIV policy,
- discipline policy,
- discipline for criminal activity,
- arbitration policy,
- employee termination rules,
- severance pay,
- an employee's right to appeal adverse employment decisions, and
- an employee at-will statement (Frierson, 1994; *Policies Now*, 1993).

Some more specific concerns that should be included within an employee manual are highlighted below.

1) Your employee manual has to clearly establish company rules and policies and the punishment for violating such rules. For example, the manual can provide that any employee who lied or engaged in any other deceptive or fraudulent conduct during the application process is subject to possible immediate termination (*Wideberg v. Tiffany & Co.*, 1992). When listing punishments which can be imposed for violating company rules, it is imperative that the manual provide, as follows, "Potential penalties include, but are not limited to...." Such a phrase would not limit the types of punishment that you can utilize. This will give you the option to provide stronger punishment or weaker penalties based on each case's facts.

2) To help prevent potential claims alleging that you had a contract through the employee manual which cannot be changed, you should make sure that a phrase is added specifically indicating that,

> the employer has the right to change the terms and conditions of the employee manual at will, without notice, and that the manual is not an employee contract nor part of the employee contract, but rather just a policy guide (Adler and Coleman, 1995).

As succinctly explained by Waterman (1992),

> Handbooks should not be prepared and forgotten. They are intended as "living" documents, with changes made along the way as state and federal laws change and the company itself undergoes variations in structure or commitments.

Employers retain the power to amend the original employee manual (*Kulkay v. Allied*, 1986). This right needs to be specifically addressed in the manual itself. Employers must, however, inform all personnel of any changes or amendments in order for the revised policy manual to be binding (*Lee v. Sperry*, 1987; *Helle v. Landmark*, 1984). Producing manuals in a loose-leaf format enables a sport business to insert amendments while removing old language without copying and distributing the entire manual every time a change is made ("The Handbook," 1993). Others suggest that policy amendments be provided online ("Employee handbooks," 1997). Dating the document insert enhances the orchestration and efficiency of disseminating amendments and keeping manuals current (Smith, 1995a). Disclaimers can be used to inform employees of possible alterations and changes to manuals.

3) The manual should specifically indicate that unless otherwise specified in the employee's employment contract, employment at-will should be specifically indicated. The following statement helps ensure such an understanding. The statement was upheld in a major case where

the court affirmed the policy statement developed by Sears, Roebuck and Co.

> In consideration of my employment, I agree to conform to the rules and regulations of Sears, Roebuck and Co., and my employment and compensation can be terminated, with or without cause, and with or without notice, at any time, at the option of either the company or myself. I understand that no store manager or representative of Sears, Roebuck and Co., other than the president or vice-president of the Company, has any authority to enter into any agreement for employment for any specific period of time, or to make any agreement contrary to the foregoing (*Reid v. Sears, Roebuck and Co.*, 1986)

An additionally valid sample at-will statement provides as follows:

> Your employment with ACME is voluntarily entered into and you are free at any time to resign for any reasons including with or without cause. We are likewise free to conclude your employment at any time, with or without cause, when we feel it is either necessary or appropriate. While we hope our relationship will be both long and mutually beneficial, it should be recognized that neither you, nor we, have entered into any type of contract, whether express or implied, with terms contrary to the above. Thus, our relationship is strictly, and will always be, a voluntary "at-will" relationship ("Update '92," 1992).

Either statement should provide all employees with sufficient knowledge that they do not have a permanent employment relationship, but rather have an at-will relationship, which cannot be changed except under very limited circumstances.

4) All rules and benefits listed in the employee manual should be regularly reviewed to make sure they comply with existing state and federal laws. An additional concern is associated with changing benefits from one manual to a subsequent addition. If changes occur, the prior changes become obsolete. Even if an at-will employee is hired under the terms in one employee manual, they will lose those terms if they are subsequently changed in future manuals (*Gamble v. Gregg County*, 1996). It should be specifically stated that employees need to be notified of all subsequent changes in subsequent employee manuals. Employees who have long term or for-cause contracts normally have specific benefits built into their contracts and these benefits cannot be changed without raising a potential breach of contract claim. To help prevent confusion and suits concerning which terms and which manual takes precedence, the employee manual should specifically state that,

> the employer reserves the right to unilaterally modify the manual at any time, and all prior terms, conditions, or benefits are modified by subsequent manuals unless their employment contract provides otherwise.

5)   A dispute resolution clause serves two major functions. It reduces an employee's ability to utilize the court system and can possibly help resolve the dispute in an informal manner. Additionally, a proper dispute resolution program can also help maintain a union-free workplace, as the employees will know that their grievance will be heard. Thus, an open door dispute resolution policy is critical. Such a policy can be incorporated in an employee manual as follows:

> It is our company's policy to foster, welcome and encourage employee suggestions or concerns. Management strives to hear each suggestion brought forward by any and all employees. The best means to provide a suggestion is to write the suggestion on an official suggestion form and process the suggestion through your supervisor. You will be given a carbon copy or photocopy for your own records which is signed by your supervisor. An additional copy will be included in your personnel file.

In addition to suggestions, employees are also encouraged to submit any concern on the same suggestion form. Upon receiving a suggestion form containing a concern, your supervisor will ask you how you wish to address the concern. If you are just interested in notifying management about the concern then no further action would be required. However, if the employee wishes to pursue the concern, the employee will be required to follow the company's official dispute resolution procedure set forth below.

The dispute resolution or appeal process should be meticulously followed with employees being afforded standard due process rights such as the right to know the charges against them, the right to face their accuser, the right to be represented and/or the right to an impartial hearing. Full legal due process is not required and the manual should specifically indicate that full due process rights are not afforded. Rather, all employees will receive due process rights, without due process rights being specifically defined. As much due process rights as possible should be provided to employees as such actions can help prevent suits claiming rights violations or an unfair system. Furthermore, due process rights also provide for greater evidentiary exploration opportunities as more individuals are willing to fully disclose pertinent facts. This can help prevent false positives such as an employee being incorrectly blamed for criminal wrongdoing. If all the facts are analyzed through due process, you are less likely to incorrectly terminate or discipline an innocent party, thus reducing wrongful termination claims.

6)   While the "suggestion policy" language above might encourage individuals *not* to pursue unionization, a more specific statement can directly work to limit unionization efforts. However, limiting unionization practices can result in an unfair labor practices charge (see Chapter 14). Thus,

a "no solicitation rule" which limits the time and manner of selling or providing materials during the working time and on company property can help accomplish the same results, but not violate the unfair labor rules. The same policy also prevents employees from selling Girl Scout cookies or other products during company time. The key to any "no solicitation rule" is consistent enforcement. If you let someone sell Girl Scout cookies during work time, but prohibit someone from distributing union related material then you can face an unfair labor practices charge. Such a policy statement has significant managerial benefits as employee will be able to concentrate on their work requirements and not feel obligated to get involved in disruptive activity during their work time. A "no solicitation rule" can be worded as follows:

> To prevent disruption in the operation of the company, and in order to protect employees from harassment and interference with their work, the following rules regarding solicitation and distribution of literature on company property must be observed. Violation of these rules will result in appropriate discipline.
>
> During working time, no employee may solicit or distribute literature to another employee for any purpose. "Working time" refers to that portion of any working day in which the employee is supposed to be performing actual job duties; it does not include such time as lunch, break time, or time before or after a shift. No employee who is on "non-working time' will solicit or distribute literature to an employee who is on "working time.
>
> No employee will distribute literature to another employee for any purpose in working areas of the company.
> No employee will solicit or distribute literature to any visitors at any time for any purpose.
>
> Persons who are not employed with the company will not distribute literature or solicit employees or visitors at any time for any purpose on company grounds or inside the company's plant or offices (Adler and Coleman, 1995).

While these rules can possibly help deter unionization or the atmosphere that fosters unionization, employers have to be careful not to force employees into giving up their right to unionize. The National Labor Relations Board (NLRB) has concluded that union-free statements establishing a strong opposition to unions, when coupled with an employee signed statement acquiescing to comply with all rules and policies within the employee manual, represents a possible unfair labor practice (Adler and Coleman, 1995). To avoid this concern, you should make sure you advise all employees that they have the right to unionize. The statement should be paraphrased with a statement indicating that you feel that a direct, personal employment relationship is highly desirable (Adler and Coleman, 1995). The following represents potential language addressing the unionization threat,

> While employees in any industry have the right to unionize, we pride ourselves in the personal attention we currently provide to all employees. Such atmosphere would change if the company employees voted to unionize. No longer would employees communicate directly through management. Rather someone would traditionally speak on your behalf. We feel that such an atmosphere is counter-productive to everything we hope to accomplish together. If you are interested in unionizing, you are entitled by law to various protections. However, before taking any such step, we encourage you to explore all options and learn as much as possible about the benefits and detriments inherent in unionization. Only through open communications can we assure ourselves that we understand all issues and have the opportunity to address all issues.

7)   Care should be taken in developing policies designed to limit employment or advancement opportunities to family members or prohibiting dating between co-employees. These policies can discourage qualified individuals from applying while at the same time, they can be seen as over-intrusive regulations designed to control non-workplace related concerns. However, there are very specific legal and managerial reasons why properly tailored clauses can be very effective.

Legally, an employer is entitled to have a "no spouse" policy prohibiting a spouse from working in the same department or workplace unit. However, such policies are only legally sound if they are applied equally to both men and women.

If different components within the policy statement allow or authorize the company's dispute resolution process as the exclusive means for handling employee disputes, wrongful discipline matters, wrongful termination reviews and related concerns, then the policy manual need a section devoted to describing the dispute resolution process. While the discipline process should be utilized in a thorough manner, including all due process rights described above, sometimes the processes need to be curtailed during emergency conditions. The dispute resolution statement should specifically indicate that "less formal reviews are available under limited circumstances involving significant financial or personal injury risks to the company, employees, or customers."

The manual could also specifically indicate that the discipline process does not always need to be followed completely if egregious conduct occurs and the employee can face "progressive discipline and/or discharge may result." Based on such a statement a United States Circuit Court concluded that the employee handbook did not create a requirement for the employer to follow the progressive discipline procedures prior to firing an employee (Wharton, 1996). Such modified disciplinary processes should be utilized infrequently and only under critical conditions to help prevent wrongful termination suits claiming a denial of due process or failing to follow the company's discipline process.

Hiring family members or preventing dating between coworkers represents a significant legal and managerial concern. Any clause limiting employment opportunities can exclude potential job applicants from the very beginning, which can lead to lost valuable employees, but at the same time, such a policy prevents potential family disputes from spilling into the workplace. As a management concern, "no spouses" policies or no dating policies can present specific problems including:

- difficulty in defining prohibited relationships,
- difficulty in enforcing the policy,
- difficulty in ensuring consistent application and punishments,
- difficulty limiting the policy to "on-the-job" activities rather than off-the job relations.

Such managerial concerns can also prompt legal concerns. No spouse or no dating policies can develop various claims including sex discrimination, sexual harassment, violation of marital status laws, implied covenants of good faith and fair dealing and potential claims of negligent infliction of emotional distress. Thus, the key consideration for any such policy focuses on the legality of such a policy.

Any "no spouse" policies limiting the ability of spouses to work in the same department is lawful if it is equally applied to both men and women (Feliu, 1992). Thus, any policy statement should specifically mention that the rule applies to both men and women and be consistently applied. Furthermore, the policy statement will gain further judicial strength if the policy specifically mentions that the reason the rule is in place is to prevent situations where a spouse or significant other is in direct supervisorial position and/or is required to evaluate their lover or spouse, which can lead to biased opinions. Such a policy statement should also specifically allow one spouse or lover to transfer from one department to another in order to avoid the direct supervision or evaluation conflict.

In addition to policies affecting workplace relationship, policies can also address off-the-job relationships, but these policies present significant legal concerns associated with employee privacy rights. Thus, some courts allow such policies to pass judicial scrutiny while other prohibit off-the-job romance policies (Feliu, 1992). Other off-the-job policies can also represent potential concerns in the employee manual. Besides relationship, off-the-job policies can cover such issues as activities during business trips, representing the employer outside the workplace, and unacceptable forms of client entertaining. In the sports context, especially collegiate and professional sports, coaches often develop specific off-the job policies prohibiting hazardous activities, requiring eating certain foods or undergoing specific off-season therapy or training.

8)   With the politically correct age, a sexual harassment policy statement in an employee manual (see Chapter 7) can be supplemented with a "no-ogling" policy. Such a policy would be designed to prohibit employees from leering at women which can cause women to feel uneasy or embarrassed. Such a policy was adopted for work crews in Minneapolis. Workers who violated the policy could first face a verbal reprimand and later could face termination for subsequent violations (Karnowski, 1995). While some people might feel such a policy is taking political correctness too far, some customers and co-employees might feels such a policy is highly warranted. This is especially true with regards to the sports and fitness industry where numerous individuals wearing very little clothing around aerobic classes or swimming pools.

9)   A buyout clause either in a contract or employee manual is critical when employing an individual with significant employer appeal who could easily jump ship and move to another program. Such clauses are often found in coaching contracts involving highly regarded college coaches who have a propensity to negotiate contracts with significant benefits, but attempt to minimize liability on the tail end. Buyout clauses are designed to provide a penalty for pulling out of the contract prior to the contract expiring. Coaches typically contract their right to future contractual payments or agree to pay a lump sum if the leave their position before the contract is completed. Such clauses have to be worded correctly as some states such as Tennessee consider penalty provisions in a contract unlawful. Penalties incorporated into a contract are often referred to as liquidated damages clauses (Gifis, 1984). If the contract requires significant penalties, most courts would not uphold such a clause.

10)   The following represent additional policies, opportunities and/or concerns which could be appropriate for different employers:

- A multilingual workforce may require utilizing an "English only" policy which prohibits speaking other languages on the job, but allows other languages to be spoken during breaks and off the job. Such policies and other policies should be specifically translated to make sure all employees understand all workplace policies.
- Multistate employers need to ensure each manual complies with the specific laws in each state.
- An introduction section should be personalized for each employee. Such a step provides the employee with a sense of importance from their first day on the job.

- The employee manual should establish specific evaluation processes, time periods and expected outcomes.
- As pensions and benefits change on a regular basis, the manual should list broad provisions and then refer employees to a plan or benefits administrator or human resource professional for further assistance.
- Policies should be written in clear to understand, simple language so employees with average reading abilities could read and understand the basic issues inherent in each policy statement.
- Manuals should be formatted for loose leaf binders rather than bound manuals which are harder to update and employees often loose new inserted or revised provisions.
- While professional consultants can help develop employee manuals, and several companies sell computer programs designed to help produce employee manuals, all manuals should be reviewed by human resource professionals and legal counsel prior to distributing the manuals to employees.

A manual maintenance program should entail analyzing all policies on a regular basis and updating inaccurate policies or possibly eliminating policies that are no longer appropriate. Any changes should be circulated to all employees with a sign-off form for the employee to indicate that they read the new changes and accept them as new terms and conditions of their employment relationship with the employer. Failure to complete such a sign-off form should subject the employee to immediate disciplinary action including possible termination. As previously discussed, the initial manual should specifically allow for future revisions, thus any revisions do not represent a new contract requiring additional consideration, but are considered a modification specifically allowed by the initial contract (*Policies Now*, 1993).

Document Acknowledgment and Receipt of Manual

The employee manual is of little benefit to sport business employers unless employees receive the manual, read, and understand the contents. Problems associated with "lost manuals" or an employee's allegation that the manual was never received can be omitted by having all employees sign a form acknowledging receipt of the manual and an understanding of the manual's contents. Inserting a clause such as, "I have read and understand the manual. I have been provided with an opportunity to ask questions and have had all my questions answered" provides additional support for the employer.

Utilize Disclaimers Appropriately

The use of clear and conspicuous disclaimers in an employee manual provides many benefits (*Dell v. Montgomery Ward*, 1987; Miller, Fielding and Pitts, 1991). Disclaimers, for example, can aid a sport business in disputing a plaintiff's claim that the manual's contents are binding. For example, Montgomery Ward used disclaimers in both their Progressive Discipline Reference Guide (PDRG) and the human resource policy manual that prevented a plaintiff's claim in 1987 (*Dell*, 1987). The plaintiff claimed that Montgomery Ward did not follow the discipline procedure as stated in the company literature. However, qualifying language in the discipline guide protected Montgomery Ward. The guide stated that the "procedure does not form an employment contract" (*Dell*, 1987). Consequently, the plaintiff's claim was not recognized. Montgomery Ward also used a disclaimer in its policy manual. The disclaimer stated that the manual's "procedures should not be interpreted as constituting an employment contract" (*Dell*, 1987).

The above policies and clauses within an employee manual represent typical issues which can be encountered when trying to formalize a comprehensive manual. There are no perfect manuals which cover all conceivable issues. That is why manuals need to be written with enough flexibility that when issues do arise, a formal mechanism is in place to help develop appropriate interpretation and application of existing policies to handle new concerns as they arise.

8) Job Descriptions

Job descriptions were discussed in Chapter 2. Job descriptions should be revisited during the final hiring and employee orientation/educational process because each candidate brings specific skills to the table. Based on who is hired, the job description might need to be revised to cover specific tasks identified in the hiring process, which are more commensurate with the employee's skills. By changing one job description, other job description might also need changes to ensure their accuracy.

Failing to modify an employee's job description after the employee is hired can lead to significant problems when an employee is subsequently disciplined or terminated. An employee who was hired to perform certain task, but ended-up completing different task, would have a very valid complaint if they were terminated for failing to meet required job duties. While an employer can claim that the employee was hired to perform certain tasks and legitimately failed to accomplish the tasks, the employee could claim that when the started working they were asked to work on different topics or their job was enriched or modified to include subsequent tasks which were not added to the original job description. To avoid this potential confusion, employees should be required to reevaluate their job description and any revisions should be specifically accepted by both parties in writing signed by the employee and their immediate supervisor.

After reviewing and making any necessary revisions to a new employee's job description, a new employee should be shown the office layout. Besides showing where the copy room, fax room, locker room or any other functional areas are located, all new employees have to be shown the key employee gathering areas such as a kitchen, employee lounge, water cooler or similar areas. The reason these areas also should be highlighted is two fold. First, new employees should feel as comfortable as possible, which includes identifying the areas where employees can relax and unwind. The second major factor involves a legal requirement for employers to post specific legally mandated posters in areas where employees have the greatest access to read and review the mandatory posters.

9) "Posting" Requirements

Both federal and state laws require certain posting in the workplace. These laws require employers to disseminate various information to employees and dissemination can be accomplished through posting the law, employee bulletin boards, videos, letters to employees, special employee meetings, payroll stuffers included with an employee's paycheck and in employee handbooks.

Numerous state and federal statutes require posting various educational materials including:

- consolidated EEO poster,
- Polygraph Protection Act Notice poster,
- Family Medical Leave Act poster,
- Fair Labor Standards Act poster,
- any state wage/hour orders,
- Age Discrimination notice,
- Equal Pay Act notice,
- OSHA notices,
- California Proposition 65 (Toxic Hazards) notice,
- Workers' Compensation notice,
- Unemployment Compensation notice,
- State Fair Employment Practices notice,
- Industrial Injury Prevention Plan notice,
- Americans with Disabilities Act poster, and

- California State Disability Compensation notice ("Update '92," 1992).

The numerous posters or notice an employer needs to make available to all employees, coupled with injury reporting requirements highlighted in Chapter 12 can create significant administrative hassles if employers do not know where to find all the various posters and notices. Luckily, most employment law experts have access to such forms. Office supply stores also sell some posters and notices. Lastly, state and federal governments are a great source for obtaining various forms and notices that meet the legal requirements. Posters or forms can be obtained from the EEOC, 1801 L St., N.W., Washington, DC 20507 and the U.S. Department of Labor, Employment Standards Administration, Wage and Hour Division, Washington, DC 20210.

10) Arbitration Agreements

A recent survey of the top 1,000 corporations in America shows that the vast majority of these corporations utilize alternative means of dispute resolution ("Nationwide Survey: Top Companies Favor ADR Use," 1997). The American Arbitration Association has handled over 14,500 labor cases each year since 1994 ("AAA reports jump in case filings last year," 1997). Arbitration is increasingly becoming the most sought alternative for resolving employment-related disputes. The Department of Labor, fostered with the 1996 Administrative Dispute Resolution Act has started screening all cases to send a significant number of cases to mediation or arbitration. The DOL's proposed referral program will cover environmental "whistleblower," discrimination, OSHA discrimination, FLSA violation, and Vietnam Era Veterans' Readjustment Assistance Act cases ("Labor Dept. plans to expand role of ADR," 1997).

Arbitration has gained significant attention in the employment law field as arbitration presents specific advantages over traditional courtrooms including:

- being less expensive as arbitrations can average around $5,000 and court trials could cost over $100,000,
- being faster as an arbitrator can develop specific timelines versus courts that have to follow established laws governing how fast litigation can proceed,
- providing an informal environment to resolve disputes,
- providing privacy for the parties versus open court records,
- being held in front of an arbitrator with specific industry experience,

- avoids the crap shoot often presented by biased jurors,
- arbitrators have more flexibility in making an award,
- arbitration results can be final, but may not set precedence for future cases as only courts can establish precedence for their jurisdiction, and
- arbitration can cover a broad array of potential cases which otherwise might be brought in several different courts (Frierson, 1994).

It is becoming more common for employment contracts to contain an arbitration agreement. An arbitration agreement requires the employee to pursue arbitration rather than file a claim in any other forum for any dispute expressly set fourth in the employment contract. Often times, employment contracts require all discrimination, wrongful termination, sexual harassment, workplace controversies and related disputes to be brought to arbitration. Arbitration normally results in less legal expenses, quicker decisions and greater participant satisfaction with the dispute resolution process (Fried, 1997). Employees prefer to utilize the trial process because they often are proceeding on a contingency basis, which means no money up front. Employees also like to have their case heard by a jury which might be more sympathetic and more inclined to award larger verdicts to punish an employer.

The United States Supreme Court specifically endorses these arbitration clauses. In *Gilmer v. Interstate/Johnson Lane Corp.*, the United States Supreme Court concluded that Gilmer was required to pursue arbitration of his age discrimination claim because he had signed an agreement as part of his employment application that he would arbitrate all employment disputes (*Gilmer*, 1991). The key to an effective arbitration clause is to specially indicate what rights or remedies are being affected. If the remedies are not specified the courts could strike down the clause for being overly vague. For example, if you do not specify that certain claims such as discrimination claims can only be brought through arbitration, then an employee can argue that because the discrimination claim is specifically excluded from the contract language, the employee does not need to follow the arbitration clause.

While arbitration clauses are legal, it does not mean there are not any distracters. Many individuals challenge arbitration clauses including the EEOC as some employee rights can be lost in the process. However, the *Gilmer* case is still the law of the land as long as the arbitration clauses are very specific. Arbitration clauses have to be specifically written to cover issues arising under the contract and any other documents that might form the basis of the employment relationship. Additional documentation can include employee manuals, sexual harassment policies, safety plans and specific compensation documents. In a 1996 decision, a Texas court concluded that an arbitration clause applied: "as to all or any part of the agreement." However, the dispute centered around not the employment agreement, but a yearly sales plan and commission schedule. Because the employment agreement did not mention sales plan and commission schedules, the court concluded that any dispute concerning the sales plan and commission schedule could be brought in court without violating the arbitration agreement (*Weber v. Hall*, 1996). To avoid such a mistake, the employment contract should specifically state that all contract disputes, employment disputes, evaluation disputes, salary and bonuses disputes and any other disputes affecting the employment environment have to be resolved through arbitration.

An arbitration clause should contain a provision that a party needs to file for arbitration within 180 days after a claim arises. This forces the allegedly injured party to file for arbitration within a certain time period. If the injured party fails to file within that time frame, the contract could be used to possibly preclude the claim. Additionally, if the injured party pursues litigation in the court system after the 180-day period, the non-injured party could always assert that they did not waive their right to arbitrate. Since courts have a strong presumption to uphold valid arbitration agreements, the court would require the parties to pursue arbitration, even after the 180 day window has expired (*EZ Pawn Corp. v. Mancias*, 1996).

11) Non-compete Clause

A non-compete clause serves to inform an employee from the very beginning that they will be acquiring valuable skills and contacts from their position. If the employee wishes to terminate their employment or if they get fired, they have contractually agreed not to steal employees or lure them away; not to steal existing clients; and not to open a competing business in a certain limited time frame or location. Non-compete clauses also can specify that any products, concepts or ideas which were generated while the employee was working for the employer are the employer's sole property. The concepts behind such a clause is to properly and adequately compensate the employer who paid the salary and related costs to help develop the product and it is unfair for an employee to reap such remuneration and then run away with the product. The key to a non-compete clause is not writing the clause in such a restrictive manner that it prevents a person from earning a reasonable livelihood. Thus, a non-compete clause would be valid if it required someone to wait a year before opening a competing business or not to open the business within ten miles of the current business. However, a clause would not pass judicial scrutiny if it indicated that once an employee worked for an employer, they would be forever barred from opening a competing business or they could never open a competing business in the same state. Additional examples where courts have struck down non-compete clauses include a restriction prohibiting starting a competing business within 400 miles, anywhere in the nation, and within 50 miles of any city where the employer operates a franchise (Feliu, 1992).

While it appears that a non-compete clause represents a great defensive strategy to prohibit employees from stealing concepts or idea, they are not legal in every state. California, for example, has a law that specifically voids any non-compete clauses. For years, companies have tried to circumvent the state law to no avail. Some companies have tried using choice-of-law clauses in contracts to allow using the law of a state that allows covenants not to compete. Under such a theory, a contract in California can provide that while the parties are located in California, the contract will be interpreted according to the laws of Nevada, or some other state. However, this maneuver has been struck down by several courts (Feliu, 1992). The only means to avoid the statutory prohibition on non-compete clauses are the two allowed statutory exceptions. One exceptions allows non-compete clauses in contracts for the sale of a business where the person selling the business and accompanying good will is prohibited from starting a new business in the same area. Similarly, the second statutory exceptions also allow non-compete clauses in partnership dissolution contracts where a partner agrees not to compete in a similar business. For non-compete clauses to be successful under these exemptions, the clauses have to be narrowly tailored (Frank and Tenhoff, 1996) Besides the statutory exceptions, California courts allow non-compete clauses where an employee misappropriates trade secrets or when employee breaches his loyalty duty to the company. The trade secret exemption is the most dynamic because anything which a company has developed for many years such as key industry contacts and means of doing business with these contacts could arguably be a trade secret if it is closely guarded and never released outside the company (Frank and Tenhoff, 1996).

Even if there is a law against non-compete clauses, it is still worthwhile including a clause specifically referring to a narrowly tailored prohibition designed to protect trade secrets and reasonable company goodwill, clients, employees and customers in a certain geographic area, product area or time frame. As with any contract term, courts analyze the clause's reasonableness and any terms that are held unreasonable will be judged void, illegal and unenforceable as contrary to public policy (Segal, 1997). Even if a court would subsequently disallow such a clause, many employees might think they have given-up valuable rights and might not wish to pursue a threatened court battle.

Employers often include a liquidated damages clause within a non-compete clause. Liquidated damages are designed to prevent misconduct by letting a party know in advance how much damages they would have to pay if they violate the contract (Gifis, 1984). Such contractual provisions are held valid by the courts if the actual damages are extremely difficult to determine and if the liquidated damages are reasonably related to the ultimate losses the company could suffer if the non-compete clause was violated (Segal, 1997). A liquidated damages clause could read as follows:

> The employee understands that valuable skills and information will be obtained during the course of their employment. In order to protect the employer's investment in their personnel and continued educational opportunities provided to all employees, it is expressly agreed that all employees will refrain from engaging in any conduct detrimental to the employer's interest, business plan, business objective, or shareholders' value. In case an employee violates this clause, such employee shall be liable for liquidated damages equal to one-third of the employee's salary or $10,000, whichever is greater.

The foregoing contractual clauses represent typical contractual clauses, which need to be thoroughly integrated into a comprehensive employment contract. In addition to liquidated damages clauses, employers can also include a buy-out clause. Such a clause was highlighted in a coaching dispute case. The head women's basketball coach at Florida State left that school to coach at the University of Southern California ("Gobrecht, Florida State Settle," 1997). The coach's employment contract required her to be responsible for her base salary ($95,000 per year) if she left early. Based on the coach leaving before the contract terminated, she was responsible for paying her buy-out provision, which was eventually settled for a $108,000 payment from the coach to Florida State ("Gobrecht, Florida State Settle," 1997). While most minimum wage employees have basic contracts or possibly no contract, most executive have comprehensive contracts highlighting such issues as executive bonuses, golden parachutes, stock options, and related benefits. The trick with either complex or simple contracts is to make sure they meet the minimum requirements for a valid contract as discussed below.

12) The Employment Contract

For a contract to be valid, it needs the four following elements: offer, acceptance, consideration and legality. An offer to enter into a contract is legal whether it is written or oral. In addition a third party such as a manager or an employment agency can bind another party (such as an employer) when the manager has authority to enter into such a contract. There are no specifics that all offers are required to contain. However, to be valid, an offer has to have enough specificity that all parties understand the essential terms and conditions *(Jevic v. Coca-Cola Bottling Co.,* 1990).

Once an offer is made, the person to whom the offer has been made has to accept the exact terms offered. If the exact terms are not accepted, but the potential employee desires to change the offer, then a counter-offer has been made and the initial offer is terminated (Feliu, 1992). This principle forms the basis for contingent or conditional job offers where an employer offers to hire someone based on passing a physical examination. If the job applicant fails the physical examination, then the original offer has been terminated because the applicant never fulfilled the condition. To help protect potential employment decisions, lower level managers who are involved in the hiring process should only offer employment opportunities contingent on approval from their supervisor or board of directors. If such approval is not obtained, the applicant does not have a job.

If the offer meets the applicant's approval, they can accept the offer and the primary components for a valid contract are in place. However, a valid contract also requires adequate consideration between the parties. Consideration is defined as something of value exchanged between the parties (Gifis, 1984). The consideration present in an employment contract involve the employer agreeing to employ and compensate the employee and the employee agreeing to work or start working and/or continue to work (Feliu, 1992).

The last essential element need for a valid employment contract is legality. A contract is invalid if it calls for someone to perform illegal activities. Thus, an employment contract requiring a trainer to help distribute and administer steroids is an illegal contract and the courts would refuse to enforce the contract if any dispute arose between the parties. Another closely related contractual concern involves the capacity to enter into a contract. An individual who is visibly intoxicated, mentally handicapped or under 18 is considered without capacity to enter into any contract and any contract they enter into is voidable. Voidable does not mean the contract is illegal, but it means the individual without capacity can withdraw from the contract at any time, without repercussions. Thus, any contract with an employee under 18 can be terminated by that youth at any time. However, once the youth turns 18 and continues working under the previously existing contractual terms, then the youth accepts the contract and would be legally bound by the contractual terms. The lack of a legally binding contract is the most definitive defense to attack an employee's claim that contract existed between the parties. Other contractual defenses are discussed below.

Contract Defenses

Adhesion contracts refer to contracts that are entered into without equal bargaining power. For example, assume a health club enters into a contract with an individual employee. Also assume that the terms of the contract include a restrictive covenant, drug testing and routine employee monitoring. At this particular health club, testing positive for drugs results in immediate employment termination. The employee tests positive for drugs during her third year of employment and is immediately terminated in accordance with her contract. The employee, in an attempt to challenge her termination, could come back and argue that the contract represented an imbalance of power and that he or she was coerced into signing the contract because bills had to be paid and food had to be provided for children. In these situations, however, courts tend to rule in favor of the employer as courts recognize that if the individual did not agree to the terms of the contract than employment could have been sought elsewhere.

Fraud is another defense that is not uncommon to the sport industry. A fraud claim includes the following allegations:

- A misrepresentation of a material fact;
- Offeror was cognizant of misrepresentation;
- Misrepresentation was made with intent to induce action;
- Action resulted in injury (Gifis, 1984).

For example, assume a sport business promises a very marketable and sought after employee that he or she should not seek employment elsewhere. As part of the inducement to keep this valued employee, assurances are made that the employee will receive a raise and a promotion in the near future. Within a year, the employee is fired. This individual employee could sue for breach of contract, fraud in the inducement, as well as promissory estoppel. It is also foreseeable that a similar suit could arise if during the recruiting process an athletic director promises a candidate for a position as Assistant Coach that he or she undoubtedly will be promoted to the Head Coach ranks within five or six years. Subsequent failure to promote the assistant coach could result in liability. If the misstatements were not intentional, a party can raise a negligent misrepresentation claim.

A major concern associated with sports contracts involves the often inflated claims made by sports promoters. Such unsubstantiated claims often lead individuals to follow the wrong path. When an individual has relied on someone's promise, which is untrue, then that person might have a potential claim referred to as promissory estoppel. Under this theory, while there might not be a specific contract, but a court imposes a contract to prevent injustice to an individual whom, in good faith, relied upon an employer's action to their detriment. To prevail under a promissory estoppel claim, the injured party has to prove:

- they received a clear and definite promise,
- reliance on that promise was reasonable expected by the employer,
- the employee in fact relied upon the promise, and
- the action taken by the employee were induced by the employer's promise (Feliu, 1992).

Promissory estoppel cases are traditionally seen when an employer promises a job applicant a position and the applicant relies upon the offer to move across country, or quit their current job (Feliu, 1992). To help avoid such claims, all applicants should be told that no actions should be taken by the prospective job applicant until they receive a final (not a draft) written signed contract.

The best-laid plans of mice and men is the best way to describe the need for written contracts. A contract normally does not need to be in writing to be valid. The only exception to this rule involves the statute of frauds which requires employment contracts which cannot be performed in one year to be in writing (Gifis, 1984; Feliu, 1992).

The primary reason you need written contracts is to provide specific evidence as to what the contracting parties intended to cover. Otherwise, parties would be always engaged in a "he said...she said" argument as to the true terms and conditions of the contract. An all but too familiar example of this type of dispute revolved around the contract of a former assistant coach with the Winnipeg Jets of the National Hockey League. The former coach filed a $200,000 claim after being terminated. The coach claimed that the team's general manager *orally* agreed that the coach would assume more significant responsibility and an additional one- year contract extension. When asked to put the agreement in writing, the general manager claimed that one was not needed and that he, "had his word on it." ("Sport," 1996) A sympathetic jury awarded the former coach $160,000, when the team's trusting general manager terminated the coach the following year.

No two contracts are alike. The work relationship and responsibilities associated with each employee requires a unique and distinct contract with each employee. Each contract will have a unique employee start date, compensation rate, job duties, benefits and other terms that can differ from one employee to another. In additional to the various contractual issues addressed above, one contractual concern, which is becoming an increasingly larger program in sports, involves contractual interference by a third party.

Contractual Interference

One key contractual provision that needs to appear in any sports employment contract is a clause dealing with who will evaluate the employee's performance. Such a clause is different that an "at-will" clause that indicates that an employee can be terminated for cause or no cause whatsoever. A performance evaluation clause emphasizes who and how an employee will be evaluated for promotion, bonuses, suspension or termination. One key concern faced by sports and recreation employees is the specter of contractual intervention by individuals such as the parents of a player being coached by the employee. While a coach is hired by a school to train a child, it might be the parent that files a complaint against the coach. The school might not have any problem with the coach, but would have to respond to the complaints. The athletes might love the coach who is teaching them well and putting together a winning team. However, an irate father or mother might file an official complaint because their child is not playing enough or is not playing in a position that will maximize the athlete's exposure which could hurt the athlete's chances of obtaining a college scholarship.

A recent example highlighting this concern was reported in Los Angeles, A girl's basketball coach was terminated after a player's father complained to the archdiocese when his daughter was not given a spot on the team. The coach's contract was not renewed at season's end (Sondheimer, 1997). The same scenario has occurred on many occasions with school boards overruling coaches' decisions and forcing coaches to change their programs to comply with a parent's demands. This can lead to a wrongful termination claim based on the fact that the coach was hired to coach a sports and the board's actions usurped the coach's authority and made the job impossible to perform. This is often referred to as a constructive discharge case as the coach's work conditions are altered to such an extent that it is impossible for the coach to function under such circumstances. Constructive discharge is an independent action that can be brought after someone leaves their employment based on the changed workplace circumstances.

Such official complaints could be part of a file, but should not be considered in the final analysis of the employee's performance. Legitimate claims by a parent concerning child abuse, profanity or other forms of misconduct can be considered, but coaching related decisions should never be considered unless such complaints are filed by a party to the relationship such as other coaches, school officials or players. Employee evaluation should also not be contingent on the playing time, placement or other criterion associated with the children of prominent individuals such as school board members, faculty members or local business leaders. This issue highlights how important contracts are in the employment arena. If the evaluation criteria is graduating children or having a winning season, then that should be the criteria used, not whether or not a prominent politician or businessperson's child receives enough playing time to qualify for a scholarship. If you utilize the wrong evaluation tool, you can face both legal challenges for breach of contract and you can face significant public backlash.

Besides third parties interfering with a contract, other individuals in the workforce also can present a liability risk for the employer by changing contractual terms. To avoid this threat, the contract should specifically provide that the contract can only be modified, by a writing signed by the employee and a senior manager. In addition, the contract should contain a clause specifying that all negotiations are concluded and all matters discussed in the contractual process are finally resolved and memorialized in the final written contract. This clause is often referred to as the parole evidence clause which provides that no additional contractual terms are present outside the final written contract. Courts do not allow any prior drafts, or contractual terms to be applied to the final contract if a parole evidence clause is contained in the final contract (Feliu, 1992).

As can be inferred in the past several pages, contracts can be very complex and specific. That is their beauty. As the employer you have an opportunity to provide yourself with the greatest level of protection by drafting appropriate, thorough contracts. Besides being thorough, the contract should be crystal clear without significant legalese. The contracts should be written that average employees can read and understand all contractual provisions. As you draft the contracts, any confusion or ambiguity in the contract will be resolved by the court against you as you had the opportunity to write a clearer contract. Thus, all contracts should be reviewed both by human resource personnel and an attorney to make sure there are no trouble spots. To help you appreciate the various concerns associated with a comprehensive employment contract, Appendix R contains several sample employment contracts. While you might be tempted to utilize a form contract for all employees, this practice is not recommended as each contract, similar to each employee, is unique and needs to be developed on a case by case basis. The following contractual clauses represent typical clauses contained in contract, but they might not be appropriate for all settings. For example, the liquidated damages clause might appear to be a worthwhile tool to protect you from investing in an employee and then having that employee leave you after completing their training. However, courts might consider such a clause an adhesion clause and can either strike that clause or the entire contract. None the less, having a poorly chosen or written clause can lead to significant liability claims.

To avoid having an employee claim the contractual terms were discussed, but not added to the final contract, you should include an integrity clause. As defined by Black (1996), an integration clause is:

> A contract which contains within its four corners the entire agreement of the parties and parole evidence tending to contradict, amend, etc., is inadmissible...

Integration clauses benefit sport business managers as employees are unable to enter parole evidence (e.g., prior discussions, documents used in arriving at final agreement) in an attempt to alter or change contractual conditions.

Besides integrating all issues discussed in the negotiation process, the contract should clearly define key contractual terms. The former head coach, "Pepper" Rodgers, at Georgia Tech sued his former institution for breach of contract in *Rodgers v. Georgia Tech Athletic Ass'n* (1983). According to Rodger's contract, he was to receive a salary, health insurance, pension benefits and perquisites. The contractual dispute focused primarily on what constituted a "perq" owed to Rodgers. For example, some of the perquisites which Rodgers sought damages for included country club initiation fees, monthly dues, and bills; parking privileges at all Georgia Tech home sporting events; meals at the Georgia Tech training table; game tickets; general expense money; the use of a new Cadillac; financial gifts from alumni and supporters of Georgia Tech; the cost of housing; and profits from Rodgers' television football show. The entire case could have been averted had the employment contract specifically quantified the value of "perquisites" to be received upon contract termination.

Lastly, an indemnification clause represent a contractual agreement in which one party agrees to reimburse another party for monies paid out as a result of litigation. For example, an employer may be able to recruit an employee in high demand by agreeing to indemnify the employee for damages he or she has to pay if the employee becomes involved in a lawsuit. Due to the nature of sport itself and the likelihood of injury, this clause can serve as a competitive advantage when recruiting high demand employees. Although rare, a sport business employer may insert an indemnification clause requiring the employee to reimburse the employer for damages paid out as a result of the employee's negligence.

As can be seen by the three clauses highlighted above, a wealth of different issues can be included in any given contract. The examples in Appendix R should provide you with the foundation to develop a draft contract. However, no employer should ever just utilize a sample contract without first obtaining approval from a local attorney trained in contract law. As can be seen by the sample contracts, some clauses are fairly standard and most attorneys can quickly customize an employment contract by cutting and pasting various valid clauses which comply with local laws, and which are available on some computer software systems.

Finalizing the contract does not eliminate your duties as an employer. Once an employee has finalized the hiring process and the ink is dry, the hard work begins. You are responsible for making sure the employee fits into the workplace. This entails significant efforts to properly place the employee, train or retrain the employee, and to properly supervise the employee. These issues are covered in the following three sections.

13) Placement

Once an employee has completed the entire hiring process, the contract has been negotiated and the ink dried, the employer needs to stay involved in the process in order to avoid post hiring negligence claims. The first critical concern that can be faced after hiring someone involves proper employee placement. While this concern might not seem that significant, it could create a significant concern overlooked by most employers. Often, an employee has distinct skills, which differs from the exact job description. If they are over-talented, their skills might go to waste. More importantly, if an employee lacks the proper skills to perform certain job components, placing them in an unfamiliar position without the necessary skills can lead to negligent hiring, training or retention claims.

After an employee is hired they should follow specific steps during their first day, and during their first several weeks on the job. To help orientate new employees to their workplace, during the first day, the employee should be:

- welcomed by their direct supervisor,
- shown locker rooms, restrooms, coat racks and closet spaces,
- shown any cafeteria or lunch facilities,
- acquainted with all safety and security regulations and procedures,
- acquainted with personal work space,
- acquainted with any time recording system such as time clocks,
- acquainted with co-workers, secretaries, and receptionists,
- started on their job (it is very important to try normalizing the employee with the expected job routine as soon as possible),
- acquainted with whom to talk to regarding personnel and supervisorial concerns,
- acquainted with pay, parking, benefits, recreation and other components of the employee's compensation package,
- acquainted with the organizational chart and reporting requirements, and

- monitored to insure they are progressing well.

During the first several weeks, the employer needs to follow-up with the employee to ensure they are completing their work assignments, not having any problems, understand all their job requirements and to ensure they are following all safety and security rules and regulations (Chruden and Sherman, 1976).

After a new employee is hired, it is incumbent on the employer to ask the employee if they can perform all the job components and procedures set forth in the post hiring training process. It is not unusual for someone to claim they can perform certain tasks on his/her resume and in the interview process, but once they start working you determine his/her skills are not what you expected. If an employee specifically indicates they can perform all the job components, they still should be closely monitored to make sure they in fact are performing all the job's necessary components correctly. If an employee cannot perform the job's necessary components, then you have to consider retraining, additional education, or possibly replacement within the organization. Another option entails termination. If a job applicant has lied throughout the entire hiring process, they will normally be caught in the first several weeks after being employed. You should be especially attentive for excuses with a new employee blaming everyone except himself or herself for the inability to properly complete their job.

Terminating a problem employee before they have received any significant benefits or rights can help reduce the threat of possible litigation if the employee was terminated at a future date. For this very reason, the authors recommend that the employee's first three months should always be set forth in the employment contract as a probationary period. If the employee fails to meet expectations within that time frame, you are entitled to dismiss them without the need to provide the necessary steps in the disciplinary process. It should be noted that a probationary period might not be allowed under certain union collective bargaining agreements.

In addition to legal concerns during an employee's placement period, employers need to recognize the stresses involved with changing employment. Such stresses can be reduced through providing a comprehensive placement program designed to orientate the employee with the workplace and then to follow the orientation with job specific training.

14) Training

Training courses need to be developed with the desired outcome specifically set forth in pre-established training objectives. These objectives traditionally set forth desired outcomes in terms of skill or knowledge acquisition. A training program's performance centered objectives can include being able to type over 60 word per minutes for 10 minutes with only a 1% error rate. If this is the objective, then the training program will focus on developing the typing skills, which will help the trainee accomplish the desired objective.

Various training methods exist for providing the greatest results. Employer can choose from such training methods as on-the-job training, conferences, discussions, lectures, continuing education programs, computer assisted learning, simulators and related training techniques (Chruden and Sherman, 1976). A key component for successful training programs involves conducting in-service training on a regular basis.

Negligent training was highlighted as a significant concern in Chapter 5. Furthermore, this chapter has already touched on the issue of safety training and new employee assimilation to help them understand and more effectively acclimate to their new work environment. Employee training does not end after an employee's first month on the job. Employers are responsible for helping to maintain employee skills.

Discrimination

An additional concern associated with training involves preventing discrimination during training. Training opportunities have to be offered to all qualified employees. Furthermore, if certain training is required for advancement, all employees should be on the same track to undergo the same training. If significant numbers of minorities are excluded from further advancement due to being excluded from the required training program, those excluded individuals would probably have a viable discrimination claim (Millman and Peery, 1996). The training program also has to make sure there is reasonable accommodation for any disabled employees. Thus, the training program cannot be held in an areas that is not accessible to wheelchair access or lacks sign language interpreters for those requiring such a service.

Employers and trainers should be careful if they record notes from the training sessions. Such notes which might indicate that a certain employee lacked certain skills or had discriminatory views could always comeback to haunt the employer (Millman and Peery, 1996). Furthermore, the training sessions should be free of discriminatory language. Several cases have succeed where a trainer called trainees offensive terms, ignored insensitive comments from others trainees and/or refused to provide assistance to certain trainees (Millman and Peery, 1996). Lastly, you have to be concerned about trainees injuring each other. Such occurrences can occur in such unusual circumstances as a ropes training course designed to foster and promote teamwork. If the employer forces employees to attend such a training session and the employee is injured, then the employee would be covered by the employer's workers' compensation coverage.

Some key concerns which need to be analyzed with any employee training program include:

- identify training goals and objectives,
- scrutinize the skills and training of all trainers,
- instructors should be educated in the laws associated with discrimination and sexual harassment,
- make sure the training program does not directly or indirectly discriminate against any employees,
- design the training program with a mindset of accommodation for anyone who might attend,
- make sure the training program follows all federal and state training guidelines such as OSHA guidelines,
- provide adequate notice to all potential trainees concerning what issues will be covered and what supplies or preparation are required to be ready for the training,
- spot check the training sessions to determine if the training session complies with the law,
- develop a specific policy forbidding note taking about individuals undergoing the training-which can produce damaging evidence if someone is not promoted after successfully completing the training program,
- document who was given notice of the training sessions and who attended,
- require all trainees to complete a written evaluation after the training session to evaluate both the session and the trainers,
- test the trainees to determine if they learned what was required from the training session, and
- follow-up with your legal counsel to determine how long test scores need to be retained for OSHA and related training compliance (Millman and Peery, 1996).

Numerous issues associated with training new employees also represent significant supervision concerns. Thus, employee supervision represents a natural topic to be considered when evaluating any training program and when monitoring an employee throughout their employment term.

15) Supervision

After hiring an employee, the employers duties continue throughout the employment term for each employee. The primary concern, in addition to proper placement and training, relates to proper supervision. The primary goal associated with proper supervision includes making sure employees follow all workplace rules (i.e., sick days, taking company property home, completing time sheets, etc.), that employees do not violate specific workplace policies (i.e., sexual harassment and related anti-discrimination rules) and making sure employees function well together (i.e., helping to resolve disputes between co-employees).

The key to proper supervision entails consistent education and enforcement. Employees should be provided with friendly reminders whenever they stray from their required tasks, if the infraction is minor. Besides serving as a re-educational tool, friendly reminders can help reinforce your discipline process while letting employees know that you will vigilantly monitor their progress. Whenever you are enforcing workplace rules or employee duties, you have to consistently enforce violations across the board and punish managers with the same severity in which employees are punished. Such consistent enforcement helps convey to the employees that you will treat management and employees well when they accomplish their tasks and will punish them equally when they fail to meet expected outcomes. Besides education and enforcement, an additional critical tool is employee monitoring.

Employee Surveillance

One concern associated with supervision involves potential over-supervision. It is not uncommon for an employer or manager to supervise employees through monitoring their work product, monitor business/personal phone calls, monitor the number of photocopies made and monitor time sheets. However, with the advent of new technologies, employer monitoring can extend to employee changing rooms being monitored through hidden cameras or monitoring e-mail messages and Internet use. One key to any investigatory or supervisorial activities designed to monitor employees involves providing them with advance knowledge that they will be watched or that certain activities will be monitored. Another key to a valid monitoring policy involves having a rational basis for the procedure depending on the severity of the conduct trying to be prohibited. Thus, cameras in an employee dressing room would be inappropriate if you are trying to prevent personal use of the company phones. Employees are entitled to a certain degree of privacy which needs to be balanced against the employers need to protect their assets (Paley, 1997). Three states (Connecticut, Georgia and Michigan) prohibit surveillance in restrooms, locker rooms or employee lounges and in Massachusetts employees are prohibited from utilizing 2-way mirrors for surveillance (Feliu, 1992).

To properly address privacy issues, an employer has to carefully balance rights according to a test established by the United States Supreme Court. The test requires "a search of an employee's office by a supervisor will be 'justified at its inception' when there are reasonable grounds for suspecting that the search will turn up evidence that the employee is guilty of work-related misconduct" (*O'Connor v. Ortega*, 1987). The best means to apply this test is on a case-by-case basis. A perfect example of how to weight an employee's expectancy of privacy and an employer's right to investigate can be demonstrated through the following example. An employer receives a complaint that an employee is sending sexist e-mail messages to other employees. Even though the employees were told that e-mail communications would remain confidential, could not be intercepted and would not be used as the basis for making any disciplinary decisions. The e-mail messages in fact were intercepted and were used to discipline the employee. However, the court found that there was no reasonable expectancy of privacy when the e-mails were sent voluntarily to his supervisor. The court also concluded that even if prior statements indicated a certain level of privacy, the employer's interest in preventing inappropriate and unprofessional comments—and possibly illegal conduct—outweighs any privacy interest the employee might have had (*Smyth v. Pillsbury Co.*, 1996).

To help prevent such claims, it is imperative that you specifically indicate that there should be no expectancy of privacy involving company e-mail and Internet usage. These mediums are strictly for business purposes, not personal entertainment. Such a message has to be clearly articulated to each employee and through the employee manual. Even with a statement indicating that you can inspect employee's e-mail, such a statement does not prevent an employee from sending trade secrets to other companies through e-mail. To help prevent this occurrence, you can purchase software that searches e-mails for key word or terms and pulls anything that might contain specified words or terms. This replaces a manual search of all e-mails which would be impossible with larger employers (Paley, 1997). To reduce personal Internet use, you can limit access to those that really need access, or block-out inappropriate Internet cites.

Voice Monitoring

The federal Omnibus Crime Control and Safe Street Act of 1968 make it unlawful to intentionally intercept wire, oral or electronic communications such as electronic bugs or wiretaps. All violators can face imprisonment and fines including $100 a day for each day or $10,000 whichever is greater. Laws and punishments can vary as state laws often provide more extensive penalties. Even though the law prohibits an employer from monitoring traditional employee phone calls, there are several exceptions. You can still monitor employee communications in the ordinary course of business if employees and customers/callers are informed in advance that the communications will be monitored to help improve service provided by employees. An additional exception is available for employers who have multiple phone extensions or phone companies that are required to monitor various lines for mechanical or other service checks (Feliu, 1992).

The Omnibus Crime Act of 1968, was expanded in 1986 with the Electronic Communication Privacy Act of 1986. Under the updated law, wire communication was expanded to include digital voice transmissions, radio, fiber optic cable, electronic mail, digitized transmissions and video teleconferencing.

Polygraphs

Employee supervision can also be enhanced through truth detection devices, but such efforts have been curtailed through significant federal and state legislation discussed earlier in this chapter. Thus, any employee surveillance technique utilized in the employee supervision process needs to be specifically developed to comply with all applicable law and should only be utilized when serious supervision concerns exists which cannot be corrected through other, less aggressive, techniques. However, employee surveillance should implemented when no other alternatives exist to help correct improper employee conduct.

Wrap Up...

Hiring an employee requires significant dedication, devotion and money. From finalizing the contractual terms, entering into a contractual relationship and assimilating an employee into the workplace, you will face numerous potential concerns that if appreciated from the beginning can help prevent most litigation disputes. As described throughout this guidebook, the key to finalizing the employment process and merging new employees into the workplace involves effective communications. You are required to accurately communicate contractual terms, conditions, policies, rules and other important facts from the very beginning to avoid any confusion or misunderstanding. Most lawsuits involving personal injuries involve someone failing to properly clean, maintain or supervise an event. Such failure can often be attributable to communication problems. Similarly, communication problems are also the primary cause of employment litigation. A supervisor or manager might say the wrong thing, might fail to properly document events or might not understand what an employee or applicant is really asking for. The hiring process provides the greatest opportunity to reduce the potential for future litigation associated with miscommunication. Thus, throughout the entire hiring process, guard you tongue and your pen to prevent any inaccuracies, overstatements, misstatements and exaggerations as such actions will always lead to trouble. Furthermore, all employees should receive a complete package including an employee manual and all other policy statements, which compromise the entire employment relationship.

References

"AAA reports jump in case filings last year" (1997). *Dispute Resolution Times* (Summer): 5.

Adler, R. and Coleman, F. (1995). *Employment-labor Law Audit*. Washington, DC: BNA, Inc.

"Anti-sweatshop proposal getting mixed reviews." (1997). *The Wichita Eagle* (April 13): 5A.

Bennett, P.M. (1996). "Courts attack studies used for set-asides." *The Wall Street Journal* (September 26): B1, B7.

"Biggest threats to associations." (1996). *Association Management* (March): 30.

Black, H.C. (1990). *Black's Law Dictionary*. St. Paul, MN: West Publishing Co.

Chruden, H., and Sherman, Jr., A. (1976). *Personnel Management*. 5th edition. Cincinnati, OH: South-Western Publishing Co.

"Code: Effort to combat sweatshop labor is an important step, despite flaws." (1997). *The Wichita Eagle* (April 21): 6A.

Dean, R., and Smith, M. (1996). "Fix it now — Before your employees fix it for you: How to conduct a wage and hour self-audit." *Employee Relations Law Journal* 22(2): 31–56.

Department of Labor (1997). "Protecting working teens (Online)." Available: http://www.dol.gov. Summer, 1997.

Dixon, R.B. (1994). *The Federal Wage and Hour Laws*. San Francisco, CA: Society for Human Resource Management.

"Employee handbooks: Good protection or binding contract?" (1997). *You and the Law* 27(8): 6–7.

Feliu, A. (1992). *Primer on Individual Employee Rights*. Washington, DC: The Bureau of National Affairs.

Frank, R., and Tenhoff, G. (1996). "The upstart, labor and employment law." *Los Angeles Daily Journal* (July 25): 8.

Fried, G. (1997). "ADR in youth and intercollegiate sports." *Brigham Young Law Review* (3): 631.

Frierson, J. (1994). *Preventing Employment Law Suits: An Employer's Guide to Hiring, Discipline and Discharge*. Washington, DC: The Bureau of National Affairs.

Gifis, S. (1984). *Barron's Legal Guide, Law Dictionary*. New York: Barron's Educational Services, Inc.

"Gobrecht, Florida State Settle" (1997). *Seattle Post-Intelligencer* (September 4): D3.

Jensen, J. (1997). "Salary management for nonprofits." *The Grantsmanship Center Magazine* Fall (33).

Jones, D. (1996). "Critics tie sweatshop sneakers to 'Air' Jordan." *USA Today* (June 6): 1B.

Joseph, J.D. (1996). "Abetting child slavery." *The Wichita Eagle* (May 31): 8A.

Karnowski, S. (1995). "Minneapolis won't wink at 'visual harassment.'" *San Jose Mercury News* (July 21): 2A.

"Labor dept. plans to expand role of ADR" (1997). *Dispute Resolution Times* (Summer): 2.

McGuire, C.R. (1989). "The Legal Environment of Business." Columbus, OH: Merrill Publishing Company.

Miller, L.K., Fielding, L.W., and Pitts, B.G. (1991). "The policy manual as a binding contract." *The Journal of Fitness Risk Management* 1(9): 3–4.

Millman, R., and Peery, Jr., G. (1996). "Basic training. Labor and Employment Laws." *Los Angeles Daily Journal* (July 25): 14.

"Minimum-wage battles continue as drivers for local ballot initiatives escalate." (1996). *The Wall Street Journal* (August 27): A1.

"Nationwide survey: top companies favor ADR use." (1997). *Dispute Resolution Times* (Summer): 1.

Nelson, R.R. (1996). "State labor laws, 1995." *Monthly Labor Review*, 119(1–2): 47–59.

Nobile, R.J. (1996). *Guide to Employee Handbooks*. Warren Gorham Lamont.

Paley, A. (1997). "Monitor conduct. Employment Law." *Los Angeles Daily Journal* (July 24): 30.

Policies Now (1993). Petaluna, CA: Knowledge Point.

Pranschke, S.C. and Laderman, L.G. (1995). "The FMLA of 1993: Final regulations change rules on employee benefits." *Benefits Quarterly* 11(4): 48–56.

Rothstein, M., Knapp, A., and Liebman, L. (1987). *Employment law, cases and materials*. New York: The Foundation Press, Inc.

Segal, M. (1997). "Equalizing the competition." *ABA Journal* (April): 80.

Smith, I. (1995a). "Going by the book to extend the contract of employment." *People Management* (October): 5.

Smith, S.L. (1995b). "In harm's way: Child labor in the 90s." *Occupational Hazards* 57(11): 23–26.

Sondheimer, E. (1997). "Conflict on rise at prep level: Parent-coach relationship becomes more confrontational." *Los Angeles Daily News* (June 7): 53.

"Sport" (1996) *Tulsa World, Sports* (March 27): 8C.

Stout, H. (1996). "Clinton to seek wider family-leave law." *The Wall Street Journal* (June 25): A2.

Sunoo, B.P. (1996). "Managing the FMLA: A big or little challenge?" *Personnel Journal* 75(9): 149–150.

"The FMLA: Benefit or Burden?" (1996). *HRFocus* (February): 11.

"The Handbook." (1993). *INC.* (November): 57–64.

"Tiger batboys seek overtime pay and minimum wages—but strike out." (1997). *The Wall Street Journal* (September 23): A1.

"Time off for workers" (1996). *Nation's Business* (December): 60.

Update '95, 13th Symposium (1995). San Francisco, CA: Schachter, Kristoff, Orenstein & Berkowitz.

Waterman, C. A. (1992). "Update handbooks to avoid risk." *HRMagazine* (November): 97–99.

Wharton, J. (1996). "Guide doesn't create employee contract." *ABA Journal* (December): 39.

White, K.A. (1997). "Mass. proposal seeks to reduce hours teenagers can work." *Education Week* (June 11): 18.

Zachary, G.P. (1996a). "Nike comes under increasing attack over Asian wages." *The Wall Street Journal* (June 28): B4.

Zachary, G.P. (1996b). "While Congress jousts over minimum wage, some people ignore it." *The Wall Street Journal* (May 20): A1.

Cases

Babb v. Harnett County Board of Education, 454 S.E. 2d 833 (Ct. App. N.C. 1995).

Dell v. Montgomery Ward and Company, Inc., 811 F.2d 970 (6th Cir. 1987).

EZ Pawn Corp. v. Mancias, Texas Lawyer Case Summaries, November 25, 1996, 7.

Foley v. Interactive Data Corp., 47 C.3d 654 (1988 en banc).

Gamble v. Gregg County, Texas lawyer, Case Summaries, October 14, 1996, 6.

Gilmer v. Interstate/Johnson Lane Corp., 500 U.S. 20 (1991).

Jevic v. Coca Cola Bottling Co., 1990 U.S. Dist. Lexis 8821 (D. N.J. 1990).

Kulkay v. Allied Central Stores, Inc., 398 N.W.2d 573 (Minn. Ct. App. 1986).

Lazar v. Superior Court, 12 C. 4th 631 (1996).

Lee v. Sperry Corporation, 678 F.Supp. 1415 (D. Minn. 1987).

O'Connor v. Ortega, 480 U.S. 709 (1987).

Pine River State Bank v. Mettille, 333 N.W.2d 622 (Minn. 1983).

Reid v. Sears, Roebuck and Co., 790 F.2d 456 (6th Cir., 1986).

Rodgers v. Georgia Tech Athletic Ass'n, 303 S.E.2d 467 (Ga. App. 1983).

Smyth v. Pillsbury Co., 914 F.Supp. 97 (E.D. Pa. 1996).

Weber v. Hall, Texas Lawyer Case Summaries, September 23, 1996, 12.

Widenberg v. Tiffany & Co., 60 Empl. Practice Doc. (CCH) Paragraph 41,961 (N.Y. Sup. Ct. 1992).

Woodlawn Mfg. Inc. v. Robinson, Texas Lawyer Case Summaries, November 11, 1996, 9.

Woolley v. Hoffmann-LaRoche, Inc., 491 A.2d 1257 (1985), modified 499 A. 2d 515 (1985).

Statutes

29 C.F.R. Section 385.19.

29 C.F.R. Section 785.18.

Electronic Communication Privacy Act of 1986, 100 Stat. 1871, Section 3127.

Employee Retirement Income Security Act (ERISA), 42 U.S.C. Section 994 et seq.

Fair Labor Standards Act of 1938, 52 Stat. 1060, 29 U.S.C. Section 201.

Family Medical Leave Act of 1993, Pub. L. No. 103-3, 107 Stat. 6 (1993).

OSHA, 29 U.S.C.A. Section 652 et seq.

Omnibus Crime Control and Safe Street Act of 1968, Pub. L. 90-351, 82 Stat. 197.

Veteran's Reemployment Rights Act, 38 U.S.C. Section 4301 et seq.

Veterans' Readjustment Benefits Act, 38 U.S.C.A. Section 3471.

Chapter 7

Sexual Harassment

As discussed in Chapter 4 a discrimination and harassment free workplace is the goal behind Title VII of the Civil Rights Act of 1964. Subsequent legislation such as Title IX also strived to achieve the same goals. Unfortunately while these laws, subsequent court decisions and administrative rulings have provided additional insight, they have yet to significantly change the public perception of women in the workplace, especially in the sport industry. If anything, legislation designed to benefit women has generated significant disdain from some in the "old boys" network who wish to continue promoting men's sport. While some individuals in the sport industry are often being forced into providing women with their lawful rights, they are none the less providing some of these rights and starting to combat some prior inequities.

Sexual harassment cases have reaped significant rewards for harassed employees. In 1995, Chevron settled a sexual harassment case for $2.2 million (Chiang, 1995). The settlement was inspired, in part, from a 1994 jury award of $7.1 million dollars to a legal secretary. While the California verdict was later reduced to $3.5 million, it still represented a wake-up call to most employers that one sexual harassment case can put them out of business (Chiang, 1995). The average sexual harassment award from 1988 through 1995 was $38,500 (Neuborne, 1996). While the awards in sexual harassment cases appear on the rise, so are the number of cases being filed. The EEOC has seen the number of sexual harassment claims from 1990 to 1995 more than double to over 15,700 claims a year (Neuborne, 1996). The greatest number of complaints traditionally emanate from blue-collar occupations such as mining or construction, and then followed by such occupations as public administration, communications, wholesale/retail, insurance, manufacturing and service industry jobs (Neuborne, 1996). Sport and fitness are industry segments that are not immune from sexual harassment litigation. Various cases will be highlighted in the following pages where coaches, administrators, and supervisors have engaged in various activities raising sexual harassment claims.

The hallmark for handling sexual harassment entails understanding what really constitutes sexual harassment versus horsing around, joking, or flirting which does not interfere with the work environment. There is no simple answer to sexual harassment and how an employer has to combat such activities to preserve a harassment free workplace. The only known

solution to sexual harassment problems is through developing a comprehensive sexual harassment prevention program to effectively reduce sexual harassment in the workplace. The first step in developing an effective
program is to understand what is sexual harassment.

1) *Quid Pro Quo* Harassment

Quid pro quo sexual harassment represents the most obvious and disturbing form of sexual harassment still practiced in the allegedly politically correct 1990s. *Quid pro quo* refers to am employer (supervisor, boss
or anyone with a position of authority over the employee) requiring sexual activity as a condition of employment, future employment, future job
advancement or future salary increases (*Sex Harassment: Innovative Approaches for Minimizing Liability*, 1994). There are fewer examples of
quid pro quo harassment as many employees, mangers and employers understand that it is inappropriate to directly utilize sex as a vehicle for job
advancement. However, examples still occur of secretaries through senior
managers being forced to choose between their body or their career. This
difficult choice is the reason why sexual harassment is such an important
issue. Individuals should not have to choose between their dignity and
their job and a jury can punish anyone who forces someone to make such
a decision.

2) Hostile Work Environment

The United States Supreme Court held in (*Meritor Savings Bank v. Vinson*, 1986) that Title VII is violated by harassing conduct that creates a
hostile or offensive working environment. The case involved a bank teller
who was subject to four years of sexual harassment by her boss. The bank
argued that it was not aware of the harassment and the harassment was conducted without the bank's consent or approval. The Supreme Court concluded that not all conduct amounts to sexual harassment, but the conduct has to be "sufficiently severe or pervasive to alter the condition of
the victim's employment and create an abusive working environment."
The Supreme Court did not decide if the bank was absolutely liable for
it's employee's conduct. However, the Court did conclude that the bank's
general non-discriminatory policy was not specific for sexual harassment
and the bank did not have a viable grievance procedure because she would
have only been able to bring the grievance to the exact person who was

harassing her. Additionally, no contingency existed to handle the situation if the abuser was in fact her supervisor (*Meritor*, 1986).

The hallmark for analyzing sex discrimination cases is the existence of a hostile work environment. Some courts have held that a hostile work environment has not been established where an employer, upon learning of harassing conduct against an employee, takes prompt remedial action against the offending employee (*Sex Harassment*, 1994).

The criteria required to prove a hostile work environment claim under Title VII are as follows:

1) the employee belonged to a protected group (women),
2) she was subject to unwelcomed sexual harassment,
3) the harassment was based on sex,
4) the harassment affected a term, condition or privilege of employment, and
5) the employer knew or should have known of the harassment and failed to take prompt remedial action (*Scribner v. Waffle House, Inc.*, 1997).

Some bosses and employers might claim that a woman or a man should have to suffer psychological harm in order to recover under a hostile work environment claim. Thus, if the plaintiff was not able to prove mental anguish or emotional trauma, he/she would be barred from raising a sexual harassment claim. These thoughts have been dismissed by the United States Supreme Court in *Harris v. Forklift Systems, Inc.*. Thus, a victim of hostile work environment sexual harassment now does not need to suffer psychological harm. The mere act of sexual harassment is actionable even if the employee does not suffer psychological harm (Harris, 1993). However, an employee is entitled to recover mental anguish damages where the severe humiliation, disgust and despair she endured went far beyond just being hurt or angry, but resulted in stress and humiliation (*Scribner v. Waffle House, Inc.*, 1997).

Examples of sexual harassment or potential sexual harassment due to a hostile work environment abound in the sport arena. In 1996, the Rose Bowl General Manager was accused of sexual harassment by a former executive secretary. The suit claims that the GM told vulgar jokes, made sexual remarks about women, constantly hugged her, once pulled her onto his lap and another time patted her on her buttock ("Rose Bowl chief accused of sexual harassment," 1996). Two years later, and after spending $500,000 on defense costs, the General Manager was acquitted of sexual harassment ("Rose bowl chief is acquitted of sexual harassment," 1998). Another example involved the settlement of a case involving 25 women who allegedly were forced by their cleaning supervisor to endure such actions as grabbing, trying to take off their clothes, attempting sex with them and threatening them with termination if they did not have sex with him. The women filed a claim with EEOC against their employer/contract assignment, Astrodome USA. The EEOC and Astrodome USA worked out a settlement of over $500,000 to settle the claims (Hanson, 1997).

While blatant sexual harassment cases pose the easiest examples, less blatant incidents pose significant managerial concerns. In a recent case highlighted in the national press, an employee with a past history of alleged sexual harassment was terminated after he told a female co-worker about a television show episode ("Fired brewery exec gets last laugh in Seinfeld suit," 1997). The executive was referring to an episode in the Seinfeld show where the main character could not remember his girlfriend's name. He could only remember that her name rhymed with a female body part. After trying unsuccessfully to guess her name she leaves him. He then remembered that her name was "Dolores." The case went to a jury who concluded that the executive was wrongfully terminated. The jury awarded the former executive $26.6 million dollars even though the executive had a past history of alleged sexual harassment, with the Seinfeld show representing the employer's "last straw" ("Fired brewery exec gets last laugh in Seinfeld suit," 1997). This case demonstrates that if you go too far to make your workplace harassment free you can go overboard and possibly draw a wrongful termination case from someone who has engaged in conduct deemed by the court to be non-discriminatory.

Same Sex Harassment

One question often raised is whether or not there can be same sex, sexual harassment. This type of harassment involves two men or two or more women. Typically, sexual harassment involves a man or men and a woman or women. However, what would happen if other men harassed a male employee because he is still a virgin or gay? As highlighted in Chapter 4, the United States Supreme Court has now concluded that same sex harassment represents a valid federal claim affecting the workplace. Employees should be specifically trained not to harass or intimidate any other employee or customer for any expression of their sexuality or any other sex based criteria. If an employee feels he or she is being approached by co-worker(s) or customer(s) in an inappropriate manner, they should not take the matter into their own hands, but should immediately report such conduct to their supervisor. If appropriate, the harassed employee can be relocated to a different department, different shift or the offenders should be limited in their association with the victim. No matter which decision is made, that decision should be made in consultation with the harassed employee.

3) Violation of State or Federal Statutes

Issues associated with federal and state discrimination laws are discussed in detail in Chapter 4. However, specific EEOC rules and state laws provide additional insight into sexual harassment prevention and legal compliance which deserves additional detail. For example, the California Department of Fair Employment and Housing's (DFEH) sexual harassment poster is required to be posted by all California employers. Similar posting requirements exist in other states. Thus, all employers need to determine if they need to post the federal requirements, state requirements, and possibly local posting requirements. While numerous laws apply to the potentially harassed, other regulations apply to those reporting or intervening in sexual harassment that has occurred to someone else.

One federal statute with significant impact on sexual harassment, and other types of discrimination, stems from Title VII. Section 704(a) of the Title VII of the Civil Rights Act of 1964 makes it unlawful "for an employer to discriminate against any of [its] employees or applicants for employment... because [the employee] has made a charge, testified, assisted, or participated in any manner in an investigation, proceeding, or hearing." This statute is designed to prevent retaliation against employees who complain about discrimination. Retaliation represents one of the subtle, and sometimes not so subtle, techniques used to punish someone who files a sexual harassment claim.

The various federal and state laws help form the foundation for developing a company's sexual harassment program. While there is no program that can prevent all harassment, the following suggestions form the basis of a program that can demonstrate to the court that you have done everything possible to reduce sexual harassment. As with negligence claims, you are not an insurer of employee safety. It is impossible to eliminate all sexual harassment. However, it is possible to develop strategies that will significantly reduce harassment claims, deflect liability to others and hopefully insulate the company from significant liability.

4) Preventive Strategies

The multitude of federal and state regulations form the framework for developing the sexual harassment policy statement. All companies should have a comprehensive sexual harassment policy statement given to all employees. The following statement represents a comprehensive document that can be given to employees, signed by employees and kept with an employee's personnel records. The hallmark for any policy statement is providing a vehicle for educating all employees about sexual harassment, the company's stance against it, and the punishment which would be applied to anyone who violated the policy. Any policy statement that includes these elements will be effective and adhere to the law. Every state might have different specific rules concerning what needs to be included in a sexual harassment policy statement. Like all other legal documents produced by an employer, a competent attorney should be hired to review the policy statement (see Appendix S).

After providing a sexual harassment policy a company's efforts are just beginning. While courts look positively on a sexual harassment policy, the more important step is implementing and following the policy. All talk and no action does not go far with a jury or a state investigation agency. A company that closely follows its policy and procedures will traditionally receive favorable support from a jury. The key question is how can you effectively implement sexual harassment policies and procedures? The following represent some key steps that need to be taken to ensure proper implementation of a sexual harassment policy and prevention program.

a) Environment

Create an environment involving constant education and vigilance. This can be accomplished through effectively drafting, distributing and educating employees about the policy and program.

b) Listen

Make time to listen to complaints. You have to make sure you obtain all necessary facts required for an investigation. This includes the names, dates, times and associated information from the alleged victim. Try to be as personable and caring as possible, but make sure you reaffirm the company's sexual harassment policy and procedures.

c) Investigate

Conduct a thorough, confidential, investigation immediately after the complaint is filed. the investigation should be conducted in a manner that will thoroughly support any disciplinary decisions or sanctions which might be imposed. Thus, someone who has engaged in prior misconduct and has been warned that subsequent conduct could lead to termination should be investigated more thoroughly with the intent to develop solid-documented support for the termination decision (*Sex Harassment: Innovative Approaches for Minimizing Liability*, 1994).

A California case highlights how important it is for an employer to follow-up with any, and every complaint alleging sexual harassment. An employer is required to take necessary steps reasonably calculated to end sexual harassment, which normally means more than just providing counseling on one occasion. In *Intlekofer v. Veterans Administration* (9th Dist. 1992), Intlekofer was a Veterans Administration (VA) employee who was involved in a consensual intimate relationship with Mr. Cortez. After the relationship ended, Intlekofer started filing complaints against Cortez who was engaged in such conduct as unwelcomed touching and sexual comments to calling her at home, verbal abuse and following her to her car while threatening her. Within approximately a one-year period, Intlekofer filed 16 complaints against Cortez. The VA responded by attempting to separate the two and counseled Cortez on several occasions that further harassment would result in disciplinary action.

The VA could not provide any evidence that they reprimanded Cortex, issued him any warnings or disciplined him in any manner. Based on this evidence, the court concluded that the VA was liable for sexual harassment because an employer is liable for violating Title VII when it knows or should have known of co-workers harassment, but fails to promptly and effectively intervene to end the conduct (*Intlekofer v. Veterans Administration*, 1992).

d) Personal Rights

The accused harasser should be given his or her full rights. While investigating an alleged sexual harassment, it is imperative that the employer not create an additional potential litigation scenario from abusing the rights of the accused. The following represent some key issues relating to the rights of the accused.

1)   The accused harasser is entitled to full "due process' rights which include notice that a claim has been filed, an opportunity to respond to the complaint, the right to full, impartial investigation, and the right to reasonable discipline appropriate with the severity of the alleged misconduct.

2)   The accused harasser has a right to privacy which includes the right not to have non-work related activities controlled by the employer and the accused should not be questioned on private matters unless there is a legitimate necessity for such information. Past affairs and relationships represents a significant investigation concern. The law protects a victim from intrusion into his or her past sexual relationships. In fact, most states'

evidentiary laws (such as California Evidence Code) specifically prohibit any reference to past relationship. However, the same protection does not apply to the alleged perpetrators. Thus, the accused can be asked about past relationships and it is appropriate to ask the accused if they have had any prior relationships with other employees.

3)   The accused has a right not to be defamed. The only way to protect this valuable right is to disseminate only correct information that is necessary to be released to appropriate personnel (including government entities), only release information after a thorough investigation has been completed, only release key provable facts to third party and only release information after receiving written permission from the accused.

e) Discipline

Take prompt, decisive and appropriate remedial/disciplinary action on a consistent basis. Failure to apply the same discipline to similar factual situations can help develop a wrongful termination claim. Besides providing appropriate discipline against an individual who through diligent research you discovered has in fact sexually harassed another employee, you have to make sure that all remedial action should avoid harming the victim. Disciplining a harasser seems like an easy process, but numerous questions need to be addressed before discipline can be imposed.

The question is often raised concerning what to do with a person who has committed sexual harassment? Should the punishment be more severe if they initially denied the complaint? Should you fire the employee and then investigate the claim? Should the harasser be put on administrative leave? Should the leave be paid or unpaid? These are just some of the questions that arise when trying to decide what type of discipline should be utilized. No matter what final discipline tool is used, the key is consistency. Furthermore, it is imperative to show that steps were taken to correct an employee's misconduct prior to imposing serious disciplinary action. However, it is also imperative to examine the seriousness of the alleged misconduct, any past record of prior harassment and the length of service the employee had within the company. Additional contractual concerns which should be considered include whether or not physical contact was part of the accused's job description, did they sign the sexual harassment policy statement, did the employment contract provide for the accused being financially responsible for their own conduct outside the scope of their employment and is their a collective bargaining agreement which might provide specific disciplinary steps. Employers also have to examine mitigating circumstances such as provocation or a consensual relationship. While all these issues have to be analyzed, the hallmark of analysis centers on developing a comprehensive, documented warning system utilizing both verbal and written warnings to help prepare the required benchmark for either eliminating harassing behavior or forming the factual basis for terminating the harasser.

Warnings

Verbal warnings are normally informal, private communications between an accused harasser and one or more supervisors. Such warnings are normally the first step in any progressive disciplinary program. Verbal warnings are not designed to provide punishment, but rather to inform and correct inappropriate behavior. Verbal warnings should be used to reiterate how serious an offense it is to violate the company's sexual harassment policy. Verbal warnings are an effective first step in dealing with hostile work environment, but are rarely used in *quid pro quo* cases due to the seriousness of such harassing behavior.

Verbal warnings are best utilized if the alleged harasser has read and signed the company's sexual harassment policy. Thereafter the employee knows what is expected of him/her to comply with the sexual harassment policy. Verbal warnings are often most effective after there has been a chance to informally discuss the matter with the individual employee.

Verbal warnings should be given privately, should not be given in the presence of the alleged victim, should identify specific conduct that is problematic, should provide the employee a chance to respond/defend him/herself, should specify what conduct change is required and should clearly indicate that management feels the harasser has the skills to correct the conduct (*Sex Harassment: Innovative Approaches for Minimizing Liability*, 1994).

The warning itself is not the end of the warning process. The warning has to be documented and included in the employee's file to establish the exact time and substance of any given warning(s). Any documentation should contain the exact date, time, location and individuals involved in the meeting in which the warning was given. The documentation should also thoroughly describe the complaint against the employee, the expected modified behavior from the employee and any mitigating circumstances that should be remembered.

The following represents a potential verbal warning notice that could be included in an employee's personnel file.

On May 17, 1997, I gave Jerry Johnson a verbal warning for posting some inappropriate, sexually explicit cartoons on the employee bulletin board which offended Janet Doe. Ms. Doe indicated this was not the first time

Jerry has done this, and that she had asked him on a previous occasion not to post the cartoons anymore.

Jerry claimed he was unaware that Ms. Doe found these cartoon so offensive. Jerry specifically stated that he knows about ACME Co.'s sexual harassment policy and knows what disciplinary actions are allowable pursuant to the policy statement. Jerry specifically stated that he will refrain from doing any similar acts in the future. This is the first time any such claim has been filed or raised against Jerry. Therefore, I felt it was appropriate to give him just a verbal warning.

Signed: *Sally Sue*
Dated: May 17, 1997

Written Warnings

When a verbal warning is insufficient (after receiving prior warning(s) or engaging in egregious conduct), a written warning might be the appropriate solution. However, if the activity was so outrageous, immediate termination might be appropriate depending on the circumstances and the applicable discipline process. A written warning represents a formal communication, embodying both a verbal communication and a follow-up memorandum, summarizing the verbal communication and being provided to the employee and inserted into his or her personnel file. The written warning should contain the same basic information contained in the verbal warning documentation. Additionally, the memorandum should specify that the manager or supervisor has confidence that the accused harasser can rectify his/her behavior and will not take any retaliatory actions. If the manager does not think that the accused harasser can rectify his/her conduct, then more serious disciplinary, termination or job rotation issues need to be considered. A sample written warning is set forth in Appendix T.

Terminating the Harasser

If the accused harasser has been found to egregiously violate the company's sexual harassment policy or has not rectified his/her behavior after being warned verbally or in writing, then termination might be the appropriate disciplinary step. Whenever any employee is terminated, it is critical to make sure all documentation is preserved and that the employee has been provided with significant personal rights. If termination is the decided course of conduct, a termination letter should be prepared and given to the former employee. Appendix U is a sample termination letter relating to sexual harassment discipline. In addition to a termination letter and the associated tax, benefits, and termination procedures, a company has to be cautious of possible post termination violence. Chapter 12 provides a thorough analysis of the termination process and steps to take to insure proper safety for the company and all employees.

A note should be added on the standard of proof required before terminating an employee. The California Supreme Court is now struggling with the issue of when you can terminate an employee. The Court will be reviewing a case where the employer claimed they had a "good-faith" belief that the employee had committed the sexual harassment, but not an absolute determination. The employer had talked with several witnesses and two women who had experienced sexual harassment. The victims had indicated that the employee (who was *not* an at-will employee) exposed himself to them, masturbated in their presence and made obscene phone calls to them both at work and at home. Relying on this information, and the denial from the accused, the employer terminated the accused. The fired employee sued and a jury awarded him $1.78 million for wrongful termination. The company appealed claiming that the jury should not have decided whether in fact the accused sexually harassed the women, but rather, whether or not the company had a good-faith belief that he had sexually harassed the women. The appellate court agreed and overturned the jury award. However, the case is now in the California Supreme Court to determine the final legal outcome (Micheletti, 1997). This represents a major concern for employers as they might have a good-faith belief that someone is a harasser, but no solid proof. If the employee is kept, and another employee gets harassed, he/she could point to the employer and say, you knew he/she was a harasser and did nothing to make the workplace harassment free. Thus, the employer fostered a hostile work environment. This controversy puts the employer in a no-win situation.

f) Documentation

Document all activities from the complaint, investigation and remedial action. If you undertake proper listening and investigating, you will have the necessary backdrop to effectively document all the necessary material that might be required to defend a wrongful termination claim.

1)   The following facts should be documented:
   • a description of the conduct which forms the basis of the complaint,
   • the date(s) and time(s) the incident(s) occurred,
   • the relative position of each party within the company,
   • a description of the investigative steps taken,
   • whether any outside individual(s), company(ies) or organization(s) were involved in the investigation and what was their role,
   • a description of all remedial steps considered and imposed,

- copies of any correspondence sent to the victim, accused and witnesses,
- copies of any documents sent to government agencies or commissions,
- notations concerning the date on which the company's sexual harassment policy was re-emphasized to all employees
- signed sexual harassment policy statement, and
- all documented warnings or disciplinary notices.

2)   It is critical to document all activities extemporaneously. You can ask the victim or accused if they would be willing to give a recorded statement (audio or preferably video) to ensure prompt and accurate recording of all facts. It is also preferable to have two people present when interviewing the alleged harasser so a witness can help verify the accuracy of any notes from the investigation. This step is especially important when disciplining a union member. When interviewing a union member in the presence of a union representative, you can tape the meeting and also have the union representative review the facts you wrote and sign the notes indicating they are true and correct.

3)   A key concern when documenting any facts is ensuring that only objective facts are written. More often than not, individuals preparing written reports often include opinions, analysis or subjective analysis which can create a significant liability concern. Anyone required to complete any documentation should be instructed on how to write only the objective facts and to avoid any subjective analysis or opinions in the documentation. Furthermore, there should not be any conclusion of law or moral judgments inserted into the documentation. It should be stated that by filing a lawsuit, a plaintiff is normally entitled to all internal company documents except correspondence with the company's attorney or documents prepared in response or anticipation to litigation. Thus, nothing should be included in writing that you would not want the victim to see and to produce at trial. This does not mean or even infer that you should ever destroy or conceal relevant documents. Most attempts at trickery or deceit are often uncovered and result in harsher penalties than if the document was provided in the very beginning.

4)   If there are any doubts as to how to proceed in documenting a complaint, immediately contact an employment law specialist with experience handling sexual harassment claims.

Do not throw away the documentation after the issue has been resolved and any remedial action taken. Some suggest that documents should be retained for at least ten years in case the same employee engages in similar conduct at a future date (*Sex Harassment: Innovative Approaches for Minimizing Liability*, 1994). Similarly, documents should be retained when a youth is injured, if a harassed victim brings a subsequent claim of negligent referral or similar negligence-based claim. However, when youths are involved, all documents should be retained for ten years after the youth reaches majority. Thus, documentation concerning a 10-year-old who was injured should be kept 18 years after the injury.

g) Retaliation

Take any and all necessary steps to prevent retaliation. This is a key step that is often ignored, and which usually leads to juries imposing even steeper financial penalties.

A key concern when faced with a sexual harassment claim is retaliation against the victim. Unfortunately, co-workers often see employees who report sexual harassment as the enemy. Thus, employees should know that if they are harassed, they can report the harassment without fear they might face retaliation by the perpetrator, co-workers or management. Preventing retaliation is not just a good strategy to keep employees happy, it is required by law.

A 1996 dispute highlighted the need to prevent retaliation. The University of Kentucky was being sued for sex discrimination by a former athletic trainer. After one employee gave damaging testimony at a deposition, the University's basketball coach, Rick Pitino, was highlighted in newspaper articles as strongly admonishing the employee for disclosing potentially damaging information. Pitino's letter to the testifying employee was characterized by the newspapers as basically claiming she lied under oath. The letter made the employee fear for her job, until the athletic director intervened ("Pitino has strong words during suit," 1996). Ultimately the matter was settled for $220,000 ("Ex-UK trainer settles sex discrimination suit," 1997). Such acts of retaliation have to be prevented from the very beginning. During an investigation of an alleged act of sexual harassment, the perpetrator has to be informed in writing that any direct or indirect act of retaliation by him/her will result in immediate suspension and possible termination for cause (see below).

The Pitino case is not an isolated incident and is being repeated in athletic programs throughout the United States. A federal jury awarded a teacher and former girl's basketball coach $107,000 after Shelby County school officials retaliated against her after she complained that another coach raped her. The teacher/coach was harassed, stalked and eventually raped by another coach. She filed a sexual harassment complaint with the school. The board responded by giving her poor work assignments, delaying her tenure and hampering her career ladder progress. The school board prevailed on the hostile work environment claim because it took immediate steps to prevent future harassment. However, the retaliation issue associated with putting her on paid leave after reporting the rape was a perfect example of punishing the wrong party (Semien, 1997).

Furthermore, in a 1997 case, an employee was forced to resign based on continued retaliation. The employee reported sexual harassment and several days later resigned. The court concluded that an employer is required to conduct a prompt investigation and immediately implement remedial and disciplinary measures when facing a hostile work environment claim. Because the employer took these actions, the former employee's claim was dismissed. However, the court accepted the employee's claim that she was retaliated against when she was yelled at, cursed and had her sales quotas doubled. The court concluded that such action could lead to constructive discharge if the work environment was made so intolerable that a reasonable employee would feel compelled to resign (*Hopkins v. Nationwide Recovery Systems, Inc.*, 1997). Under a constructive discharge claim, an employee would be able to receive back pay and other damages including emotional distress (*Hopkins*, 1997).

The following represent specific steps to take to prevent or reduce the likelihood of retaliation.

1)   At the initial receipt of the complaint, notify the victim that the company does not tolerate retaliation and provide a convenient means for the victim to inform someone about any retaliatory acts. An appropriate sample letter can be seen in Appendix V.

2)   Immediately contact the accused harasser and inform him/her that any retaliation will result in immediate disciplinary action and that other employees cannot be enlisted to engage in any retaliatory conduct. An appropriate sample letter to the accused harasser can be seen in Appendix W. Be vigilant for subtle retaliation including ostracism, avoidance, and/or negative comments.

3)   All managers and supervisors should be warned about potential retaliatory conduct and immediately report any such conduct to the Human Resources Department.

4)   Periodically contact the victim to make sure there has not been any retaliatory acts (*Sex Harassment: Innovative Approaches for Minimizing Liability*, 1994).

h) Victim Follow-up

On a regular basis check with the victim to see if there are any lingering problems. The victim should be treated like a regular employee and should not be shunned because you might not have finished your investigation and owe him/her an answer. Be honest. Indicate what is holding up the investigation process.

i) Government Claims

A company has to be prepared to handle a claim raised by a government agency. While employees often bring a sexual harassment claim to their supervisor's or employer's attention, a significant number of victims do not feel they will receive adequate support or response from their employer. These individuals might immediately file suit, go on disability, "rough it out" or file a claim with an appropriate state agency.

If at all possible, upon receiving an inquiry or investigative letter from a government agency, immediately contact a competent attorney. Even if an attorney is retained, it is imperative that you provide only accurate information. All responses to government inquiries are subject to public disclosure. Thus, only disclose information you are certain is both correct and appropriate. If the government agency asks questions which the company does not have an answer for, just say that no answer has been uncovered. Resist the disclosure of private information, such as medical records. Disclosing a victim's, accused's, or other employee's records should be resisted at all cost, even under the threat of a subpoena. However, if a court upholds a challenged subpoena, then only the records specifically approved by the court should be produced.

Sometimes government agencies request statistical information. Such information should not be provided. Only raw data used in the computation of the requested statistical formulas should be produced. If the government (or the plaintiff in a sexual harassment suit) requests the average number of complaints, there is a possibility that the government is requesting the statistical mode, mean, or median which might be different numbers. By producing the raw data, a company can ensure they will not incorrectly guess what the government is requesting.

If the government agency requests an on-site investigation, resist such an attempt as much as possible to narrow the focus. The best way to avoid an on-site investigation is to provide as much truthful/honest information you have in a timely manner. Also limit the government's investigation to the charge at hand and do not open your company to investigation into unrelated matters such as OSHA violations or workers' compensation coverage. If an interview is requested, and you cannot avoid the interview, only provide information about the involved parties and witnesses. Do not release any information about other past instances, alleged perpetrators or victims as such actions might violate other's privacy rights or can lead to possible defamation claim if the information was released.

Lastly, do not provide the government with any signed affidavits unless a corporate counsel has been involved from the very beginning in drafting the affidavits. All employees should be informed that they should feel free to talk with government investigators in the presence of a company representative, but to never sign any document without the company's attorney being present.

j) Insurance Coverage

Similar to all other discrimination claims, sexual harassment claims are normally not covered by insurance policies. Thus, a history of blatant sexual harassment can result in a finding of "intentional and willful conduct" which *would not* entitle the employer to reimbursement from its insurance carrier for either defense costs or any judgment amount (*Coit Drapery Cleaners, Inc. v. Sequoia Insurance Co.*, 1993). It is critical for you to examine the precise coverage language to determine who is actually covered by the insurance policy. Some policies provide protection to "the insured," which would only cover the company, if the company itself purchased the insurance. Coverage would not be provided under such language for the defense or claim payment associated with the conduct of an individual employee. However, if the policy applies to "an" or "any" insured, than coverage might be available for the acts of an employee who allegedly committed sexual harassment. Additionally, the policy should be carefully examined to make sure it covers not just "accidents', but also "events" as sexual harassment is not defined as an accident, but is a component of an "event." Furthermore, policies should cover emotional distress within the definition of "bodily injury" or "personal injury." Lastly, umbrella insurance policies and/or Employment Practices Liability (EPLI) policies often provide additional protection for such claims as harassment and discrimination which are not found in traditional comprehensive general liability policies or primary coverage policies (*Sex Harassment: Innovative Approaches for Minimizing Liability*, 1994). Chapter 15 provides additional information on insurance related concerns.

5) Equal Pay Act Claims

The EPA is an extension of the FLSA discussed in Chapter 6. Passed in 1963, the EPA sought to remedy pay differentials based upon antiquated beliefs. For example, in prior years many employers justified pay differentials between men and women by arguing that men, serving as the household breadwinners, should be paid more than women. The EPA prohibits pay discrimination based upon sex when jobs require substantially equal work. The law provides recourse for both men and women alike. Factors used to decipher what constitutes substantially equal work include:

- skills,
- effort,
- responsibilities, and
- working environments (Weinstein, 1996).

Cases must be examined on a case-by-case basis due to the intricate differences existing in different jobs and different settings. The plaintiff must prove inequality in only one of the above factors to prove an EPA violation (Weinstein, 1996). These four factors are discussed below in greater detail. Additional information is contained in Chapter 4.

Skill

Black's Law Dictionary (p. 1387) defines a skill in the following manner.

> Practical and familiar knowledge of the principles and processes of an art, science, or trade, combined with the ability to apply them in practice in a proper and approved manner and with readiness and dexterity.

An employee who is able to make a brochure or design a newsletter, for example, displays skill in desktop publishing. Employers need to remember, however, that an employee with more credentials (e.g., licenses, degrees, certificates) is not necessarily more skilled. These factors become important only if they are necessary for job performance or a critical component within the legitimate minimum qualifications for the job.

Effort

Quoting from the Code of Federal Register, Weinstein concludes that,

> Effort is concerned with the measurement of the physical or mental exertion needed for the performance of a job. Job factors which cause mental fatigue and stress, as well as those which alleviate fatigue, are to be considered in determining the effort required by the job. (Weinstein, 1996),

The inquiry on effort will focus on the totality of the effort (physical and mental) required by a particular position versus a task-by-task effort analysis (Weinstein, 1996). In other words, a position as head coach commands more effort than the assistant coach when considering the physical and mental exertion needed to please administrators, fans, the business community, student-athletes and other stakeholders.

Responsibility

Again, quoting from the CFR, Weinstein (1996) defines responsibility as the, "Degree of accountability required in the performance of the job, with emphasis on the importance of the job obligation." Again, there is no standard formula dictating the degree of difference in responsibilities that will trigger an EPA award for the plaintiff. Additional responsibilities, for example, that a male coach may be accountable for that a female coach may not include speaking engagements, publicity exposures, radio shows, TV shows, etc. Employers wishing to ward off future EPA violations should be sure to distinctly itemize the responsibilities of respective jobs through a detailed job description.

Similar Working Conditions

Similar working conditions pertain to, among other components, "surroundings" and "hazards" (Weinstein, 1996). Noise, interference, space, and other environmental factors may differentiate the working conditions between two otherwise similar jobs. As explained by Weinstein (1996), "if two jobs require equal skill, effort, and responsibility, then they are most likely performed under similar working conditions."

Proving Unequal Pay

Similar to other discriminatory laws, a *prima facie* analysis requires the plaintiff to prove (Weinstein, 1996):

a) that he or she performed substantially equal work in a position requiring equal skill, effort, and responsibility under similar working conditions; and

b) that she received lower wages than the employee(s) of the opposite sex providing the basis of comparison.

The EPA does not require the plaintiff to prove an intent to discriminate. If the plaintiff proves the above two elements, the burden of proof then shifts to the defendant to show that the pay differential was based on some reason other than sex. The law permits pay differentials if based on one or more of the following: (a) seniority, (b) merit, (c) quality or quantity of work produced and/or (d) a differential based on any other factor besides gender. The most popular defense is the "any factor other than sex" defense. Willful EPA violators may be assessed damages for three years prior to the suit being filed. If the EPA violation was not willful, the plaintiff's recovery is limited to a period of two years prior to filing suit. (*EEOC v. Shelby County Government*, 1988).

The EPA has been an avenue of litigation used by females employed in athletics departments. For example, plaintiffs in *Tyler v. Howard University* (1993), *Pitts v. Oklahoma* (1994), and *Stanley v. USC* (1994) alleged EPA violations when they were paid less than the men basketball coaches. However, using the EPA by a female plaintiff coaching a woman's basketball team is limited for two primary reasons. First, the fourth prong of EPA's affirmative defenses overlooks discrimination in pay if based on other factors beside gender. Other factors recognized by the courts include the maintenance of media relations, revenue generating pressures, market forces and background experiences (Fitzgerald, 1995). Accepting the "market forces" defense is, at face value, contrary to the purpose of the EPA as it seemingly allows pay differentials based upon antiquated assumptions and biases. However, the law recognizes this defense only if the "market forces accord different values because of other factor(s) other than sex" (Weinstein, 1996). Second, both men and women coaching women's teams tend to receive less money than men coaching men's team. As explained by Claussen (1995),

> If both men and women are performing the same job (coaching women's sports) for the same low pay, it is difficult to argue that women are being discriminated against simply because of their sex. The EPA serves as only one avenue of recourse for pay disparities existing in the work place. Other avenues remain available to plaintiffs including Title IX and Title VII (see Chapter 4).

Wrap Up...

In the sport, fitness and recreation industries, there is ample opportunity for sexual harassment to fester and rear its ugly head. However, sexual harassment claims often exist which can be either outright or subtle in their manifestation and impact.

Liability is almost certain when a jury hears a harasser blaming the victim or accusing the victim of not being a team player. Employers are not the only ones who are being hit with jury's wrath in such cases. Individual employees and managers can also be held liable under various theories. In one case, an employee dated her supervisor, but later broke-off the relationship. The supervisor swore at her, threw things at the employee and harassed her for six months. The employee finally quit. The employee was able to successfully bring a tortuous interference with contract claim against her former supervisor for his harassing behavior which forced her to quit (*Lewis v. Oregon Beauty Supply Co.*, 1987).

Communication once again represents your greatest tool for reducing sexual harassment. You should always be realistic that it is impossible to prevent sexual harassment. Employees will always experiment with dating even if you have a no-dating policy. Thus, while you attempt to eliminate sexual harassment, you should simultaneously educate all employees about your sexual harassment policies and procedures. A thorough communication program coupled with a stringent documentation process represents the key to reducing sexual harassment in the workplace.

References

Black, H.C. (1990). *Black's Law Dictionary*. 6th edition. St. Paul, MN: West Publishing Company.

Chiang, H. (1995). "Companies wise up to harassment." *San Francisco Chronicle* (February 27): 1A.

Claussen, D.L. (1995). "Title IX and employment discrimination in coaching intercollegiate athletics." *The University of Miami Entertainment & Sports Law Review* 12(2): 149–168.

"Ex-UK trainer settles sex discrimination suit for $220,000." (1997). *The Courier-Journal* (November 13): 1A.

"Fired brewery exec gets last laugh in Seinfeld suit." (1997) *Houston Chronicle* (July 16): 9A.

Fitzgerald, M.P. (1995). "Pay equity: Two case studies in intercollegiate athletics." *Journal of Legal Aspects of Sport* 5(2): 104–116.

Hanson, E. (1997). "Sex harassment lawsuit settled for $500,000." *Houston Chronicle* (June 12): 33A.

"Justices won't tackle same-sex harassment." (1996). *Houston Chronicle* (October 8): 4C.

Micheletti, M. (1997). "Faith or fiction." *Employment Law, Los Angeles Daily Journal* (July 24): 18.

Neuborne, E. (1996). "Complaints high from women in blue-collar jobs." *USA Today* (May 3–6): 1A

"Pitino has strong words during suit/coach lashes out at an Assistant AD." (1996). *The Cincinnati Inquirer* (June 6).

"Rose Bowl chief accused of sexual harassment." (1996). *Los Angeles Times* (May 10): 1B.

"Rose Bowl chief is acquitted of sexual harassment." (1998). *Los Angeles Times* (May 30): 8B.

Semien, J. (1997). "Jury backs teacher who said she was punished for reporting rape." *The Commercial Appeal* (August 1): B1.

Sex harassment: innovative approaches for minimizing liability. (1994). San Francisco, CA: Schachter, Kristoff, Orenstein & Berkowitz.
Weinstein, S.M. (1996). "The modern equal pay act: Liability in 'white collar' jobs." *Labor Law Journal,* pp. 356–375.

Cases

Coit Drapery Cleaners, Inc. v. Sequoia Insurance Co., 14 Cal. App. 4th 1595, 18 Cal.Rptr.2d 692 (CA, 1993).
E.E.O.C. v. Shelby County Government, 707 F.Supp. 969 (W.D.Tenn. 1988).
Harris v. Forklift Systems, 114 S. Ct. 367 (1993).
Hopkins v. Nationwide Recovery Systems, Ltd., Texas Lawyer, Case Summaries, February 24, 1997, 22.
Intlekofer v. Veterans Administration, 973 F. 2d 773 (9th Dist. 1992).
Jackson v. Arthur Anderson & Co., Texas Lawyer, Case Summaries, March 17, 1997, 16.
Lewis v. Oregon Beauty Supply Co., 302 OR 616 (1987).
Meritor Savings Bank v. Vinson, 477 U.S. 57 (1986).
Mogilefsky v. Superior Court (Silver Pictures), 20 Cal. App. 4th 1409 (1993).
Pitts v. Oklahoma, No. CIV-93-1341-A (W.D. Okla. 1994).
Scribner v. Waffle House, Inc., Texas Lawyer, Case Summaries, March 17, 1997, 15.
Stanley v. U.S.C., 13 F.3d. 1313 (9th Cir. 1994).*Tyler v. Howard University,* No. 91-CA 11239 (D.C. Super. Ct. 1993).

Chapter 8

Other Forms of Harassment

Employee harassment can take many forms. Harassment can be something as minimal as having other people park in a given employee's assigned parking space on a regular basis to outright violating a person's constitutional rights. As with any potential rights violation, legal issues are dependent on what rights are being violated and who is violating such rights. Some rights—such as to unionize—are protected by specific laws such as the NLRA. The federal constitution, state constitutions, Title IX, Title VII, ADA and other state and federal legislation provide broad protection to protect employees from various harassing acts ranging from being harassed for filing a claim against the employer to wistleblowing protection.

No matter what laws are being examined, every employee expects to have certain rights in the workplace. Failure to provide such rights will create a disgruntled and paranoid workforce. Thus, strictly from a management perspective, it is imperative that you critically weigh the purpose behind any workplace policy which limits employees' rights with the expected resulting benefits. Under this analysis, an employer might wish to punish a given employee for drawing derogatory cartoons about company executives, but there could be repercussions for such a punishment. In fact, ABC experienced such balancing issue in their 1997 broadcast of a major golf championship when the broadcasting employee's union staged a one day walk-out in response to a union member being disciplined for drawing and posting an allegedly degrading cartoon (Barron, 1997).

1) Free Speech

Free speech involves the right to engage in political debate. Free speech under the federal constitution does not allow someone to have an unfettered right to talk when his/her words represent commercial speech, fighting words or words that can be limited by reasonable place and time restrictions. Thus, if a school specifically prohibits protest marches by any group between 10:00 am and 2:00 p.m. as a means to keep the school quiet and not disturb classes, such a restriction would typically not be held a constitutional violation when someone is not allowed to protest. Protest can occur at other times and at other locations. Thus, the political voice is not being silenced. Instead, political speech is being redirected for a limited time. The key to such a rule being validated is consistent enforcement. If one protest march is allowed, then all other marches need to be allowed. That is the hallmark of constitutional protection. Government cannot selectively screen communications and only allow messages which it wants the public to hear (*Resort Development International, Inc. v. City of Panama City Beach*, 1986).

In the sport context, free speech often arises when an employee attempts to comment about a coach or athletic director and is terminated for making such comments. In 1968 the United States Supreme Court concluded that employees do not relinquish their First Amendment rights to comments on matters of public interest by virtue of government employment (*Pickering v. Board of Education*, 1968). The *Pickering* court set forth the test for analyzing free speech claims. The test includes:

- whether the communication would interfere with close working relationships,
- whether the communications would provoke conflict or otherwise undermine the employer's authority,
- whether the communication concerned a matter of public interest or concern,
- whether the employer had an opportunity to rebut or refute any errors in the communication,
- whether the communication showed the employee's incompetence at their job, and
- whether the communication was intentionally false (*Pickering*, 1968).

In a subsequent case, a district attorney in New Orleans was asked to transfer to a different section (*Connick v. Myers*, 1983). She refused and started a mini-insurrection by distributing a questionnaire to co-workers asking their opinions, among other issues-their opinion about her supervisor. The district attorney was terminated based on her refusal to accept the transfer and her act of insubordination. The plaintiff filed suit under 42 U.S.C.S. 1983 contending wrongful termination based on exercising her free speech rights. The trial judge required her to be reinstated and awarded back pay, damages and attorney fees. The case was appealed to the United States Supreme Court.

The *Connick* court was forced to analyze the balance between the interest of the employee's right to comment on matters of public concern and the state's (employer's) interest in promoting the efficiency of the public service the state performs through its employees. The district attorney's boss claimed that the communication did not involve issues of public concern as the questionnaire related to issues which solely concerned internal office matters. The court supported this contention as the questionnaire represented her commenting on matters of personal interest. There was no effort to inform the public that the district attorney's office was neither discharging its governmental responsibilities nor was there was any wrongdoing or breach of public trust. The questionnaire was designed to solicit information for her own purpose to challenge her transfer. Therefore, the court concluded that the questionnaire represented primarily personal speech and not protected speech concerning a matter of public concern. The court also concluded that when close working relationships exist, the courts are normally more willing to defer to a supervisor's conclusion and that the timing, location and content of the communication have to be examined in totality to determine if free speech rights are violated (*Connick*, 1983).

Thus, in the sport context, if an assistant coach complains about a head coach's conduct, the communication would be considered public communication if:

- the assistant coach reported the coach's inappropriate hitting of students to the school board and parents,
- informed the school paper that the head coach was discriminating against black players, and/or
- told the players that the head coach was caught using drugs and therefore should no longer supervise the players.

Of course, such communication is only protected if it is the truth. Furthermore, if the assistant coach complained that the coach did not give the assistant enough responsibility or did not allow the assistant to run plays the assistant designed, such communication is not considered a matter of public concern.

Matters of public concern can be limited by reasonable time, place and manner restrictions which are clearly communicated and enforced. However, such regulations often lead to litigation. In the *Knapp* case, a school teacher/coach petitioned school board members about some concerns associated with the grievance process available to teachers under the Collective Bargaining Agreement (*Knapp v. Whitaker*, 1983). Approximately one year later the coach filed a grievance regarding unequal mileage reimbursement for coaches and the lack of liability insurance for coaches who drove students to athletic competition. The grievance was denied and Knapp asked a board member to raise the issue with the school board. Shortly thereafter, the school superintendent pointed to a provision in the superintendent's contract requiring all communications to the board to go through him. Based on this rule being violated, Knapp was reprimanded, which later led to losing his coaching position and being transferred to a grade school from the high school. Knapp sued for violations of his first amendment rights and was awarded $500,000 by a jury. The court concluded that the rule requiring all teachers to report to the board through the superintendent was unconstitutional. The court also held that the policy was never communicated to Knapp and Knapp was speaking on public concern (not just related to him) and such communication was protected speech which could not be prevented by arbitrary or capricious rules (*Knapp*, 1983).

Private Sector

Almost all free speech cases involve public employees as the federal constitution only applies to federal and state actors. However, free speech can also apply in the public sector. If an employee reports a health club dumping toxic pool chemicals down a storm drain rather than following specific state environmental regulations, such communication can be protected. Instead of being protected by the constitution, such communication would be protected by the public policy promoting wistleblowing and protecting wistleblowers. The legal protection afforded wistleblowers is more thoroughly discussed in Chapter 12.

Freedom of Religion

An ancillary claim involves freedom to discuss religious issues. Discussing religious issues is allowed. Discussion represents an unobtrusive and possibly educational tool to teach individuals about religious tolerance, different customs, and different attitudes. Persuasion on the other hand is not geared at educating, but is designed to foster action. A state employee can discuss religion, but cannot use his/her position and the authority vested in him/her by the state to persuade someone to follow a specific religious ideology. As the law currently stands, a state employee cannot encourage or foster religious activity without violating the strict wall separating church and state (Fried, 1994). Federal courts have upheld this principle over the past several years in the high school sport arena. In one case a coach was terminated after trying to coax a student into attending his church, pressuring students into joining the Fellowship of Christian Athletes, forcing students to listen to Christian music and forcing students to read scriptures from the Bible (Buchanan, 1996). Similarly, no pray-no play policies have been struck down by courts, but student, self-initiated prayers or moments of silence are currently legal in some states (Fried, 1994).

Chapter 4 has highlighted several concerns associated with discrimination and religious activity in the workplace. The same concerns apply in non-hiring situations. Thus, besides providing deference in the hiring process to different religious beliefs, you are required to foster tolerance in the workplace and to make sure all employees and managers respect each other's rights.

As mentioned in this chapter's opening paragraphs, failure to properly accommodate employee needs for personal expression helps create a closed environment. This environment is not conducive to running an effective cooperative workplace with dedicated employees. Even if you are not a government employer-and thus, not liable for violating constitutional mandates, you still need to foster an accommodating workplace to prevent losing talented workers and scaring away future potential employees.

2) Political Affiliation

Sport and politics have made strange bedfellows for many years. President Clinton recently appointed Jake Steinfeld, from the fitness show "Body by Jake," to the President's Council on Physical Fitness and Sports. The appointment came after Jake donated $100,000 to the Democratic National Committee (Newsmakers, 1997). Now more than ever, politics is becoming a bigger issue with sport employers. Public support for several hundred million-dollar stadiums represents a perfect example of the politics that often underlies decisions made by sport organizations. Professional team, sport facility architects, facility management companies and numerous affiliated businesses need to play political hardball to help secure winning bids and long term public financial commitments. The same concern applies to colleges and high schools. Oftentimes, political leaders have to be entertained, educated and given financial donations to help secure success. The question raised by such conduct is whether or not employees can be terminated because they vocally speak out against a politician or political issues which runs contrary to the company's goals and objectives.

In a Tennessee case (*Springer v. Williamson County Board of Education*, 1995), the issue of political affiliation and job demotion was addressed. In the *Springer* case, a school administrator who was also a former state senator had some major clashes with a school supervisor who ran on the Republican ticket. Springer ran on the Democrat party ticket for a political position. The school supervisor developed an extensive five-year plan which called for eliminating two supervisory positions, and one position was Springer's position. The plan was adopted by the school board and Springer was accordingly transferred to teach physical education at a middle school. While other positions were available and Springer applied for each position, he was denied each position. Springer sued claiming his transfer was politically motivated (*Springer*, 1995).

Under Tennessee law, a tenured school teacher cannot be transferred for arbitrary, capricious or politically motivated reasons. Tennessee courts had interpreted this law to mean that as long as the people instituting the move had sufficient demonstrable grounds upon which to base their transfer, a partially politically motivated decision was still acceptable. The court concluded in *Springer* that there were some valid non-political issues associated with the transfer as his former position was not filled by someone else, that another person was also transferred and that the decision was supported by the school board (*Springer*, 1995).

Partisan Activity

It is important to distinguish between partisan and nonpartisan activities for public employees. While nonpartisan political activities are almost always protected by the first amendment, partisan activity can be more closely regulated (Rothstein Knapp and Liebman, 1987). The Hatch Act, 5 U.S.C.S. 7324(a) prohibits federal employees from taking active part in a political campaign. Similar laws exist at the state level and they are specifically designed to prevent an employee from being forced to support a particular candidate or for a public official to use his/her position of authority to benefit a candidate (Rothstein Knapp and Liebman, 1987).

Loyalty Oaths

An additional concern often seen in the 1950's and 1960's were loyalty oaths signed by public employees. These oaths were struck down by the United States Supreme Court in *Baggett v. Bullitt* (1964). Loyalty oaths can be valid if they specify that employees will refrain from engaging in any illegal activities (Rothstein Knapp and Liebman, 1987).

Private Sector

Political affiliation rights can also apply to private sector employees. In a Louisiana case, an employee was fired because he became a candidate for political office. The employee sued under a state statute and was awarded $24,000 that was upheld on appeal. The employer received a significant amount of his/her business from the local government unit without having to bid for the work. Needless to say, the employer did not want to aggravate the hand that fed him/her, and there would be real losses if the employee kept running for office. In essence, the employee running for office was a direct threat to his employer. But the state statute was clear in its intended coverage: "the employer may not control political candidacy of his employees." (*Davis v. Louisiana Computing Corp.*, 1981). Thus, if there is a statute that specifically allows an employee to run for office or engage in other protected activity, the employer cannot terminate the employee even if the employee's actions are detrimental to the employer.

Wrap up...

It should be remembered that freedom of association and other privacy rights are protected not just in the workplace, but also might cover extra-employment activities for public employees. However, such rights are also potentially limited if they interfere with a significant employer interest. Thus, in one case, a court upheld a teacher's demotion when the teacher was engaged in a lesbian relationship with a student (*Naragon v. Wharton*, 1984). While a teacher would normally be able to have a lesbian affair, the employer had a right to interfere with such activity when students are involved and the school was responsible for protecting.

The key term to remember when dealing with employee rights and associated concerns is reasonableness. Showing flexibility and willingness to allow employees some flexibility within broader rules will help facilitate employee growth and expression while at the same time maintaining workplace harmony and the growth of other employees. In addition to reasonableness, you have to make sure any rule is consistently applied to all employees and any rule or policy violation receives the same punishment. This will prevent a claim that you are discriminating against one group to benefit another group.

References

Barron, D. (1997). "Teed-off TV crew pulls plug on PGA." *Houston Chronicle* (Nov. 2): 1A.

Buchanan, O. (1996). "Elgin ISD doesn't renew assistant coach's contract." *Austin American-Statesman* (April 6): 2B.

Fried, G., and Bradley, L. (1994). "Applying the first amendment to prayer in a public university locker room." *Marquette Sports Law Journal* 2 (4).

"Newsmakers: New U.S. fitness leader." (1997). *Houston Chronicle* (June 22): 2A.

Rothstein, M., Knapp, A., and Liebman, L. (1987). *Employment law.* New York: The Foundation Press, Inc.

Cases

Baggett v. Bullitt, 377 U.S. 360 (1964).

Connick v. Myers, 461 U.S. 138 (1983).

Davis v. Louisiana Computing Corp., 394 So.2d 678 (La. App. 1981).

Knapp v. Whitaker, 577 F. Supp. 1265 ((C.D. Ill. 1983).

Naragon v. Wharton, 572 F.Supp. 117 (M.D.La. 1983) affirmed 737 F.2d 1403 (5th Cir. 1984).

Pickering v. Board of Education, 391 U.S. 563 (1968).

Resort Development International, Inc. v. City of Panama City Beach, 636 F. Supp. 1078 (N.D. FL 1986).

Springer v. Williamson County Board of Education, 906 S.W.2d 924 (Tenn. Ct. App. 1995).

Statutes

42 U.S.C. Section 1983.

ADA, 42 U.S.C.S. Section 12101 et seq.

Hatch Act, 5 U.S.C. Section 7324(a).

NLRA, 29 U.S.C.A. Section 151–169.

Title VII of the Civil Rights Act of 1964, 42 U.S.C.A. Section 2000e.

Title IX of the Education Amendment of 1972, 20 U.S.C.A. Section 1681(a).

Chapter 9

Promotion

1) Performance Appraisals

In a 1992 survey, the Journal of Management concluded that the average employee evaluation systems utilized by businesses are 11 years old. These systems contain little or no input from management or employees (Bretz, Milkovich and Reed, 1992). The average time spent on evaluating low level employees only amounted to three hours a year. Upper level executive, on average, were evaluated for only seven hours per year (Bretz, Milkovich and Reed, 1992). Lastly, the survey highlighted that most businesses conducted their employee training when the employee training system was initially adopted, but few companies utilized training programs throughout the year (Bretz, Milkovich and Reed, 1992). Thus, the survey results highlight that employers are less likely to spend a significant amount of time evaluating employee performance. However, when time is spent, employers often utilize an antiquated evaluation system and employees often have not been exposed on a continuous basis to appropriate employee training.

Decisions regarding employee promotions, raises, bonuses and so on are best defended by adopting and implementing a good performance appraisal process. The performance appraisal process has been discussed in the management literature since the early twentieth century. The topic continues to prompt a critical discussion in management literature, common law, and legislation. Smith, Hornsby and Shirmeyer's research (1996) reveals that approximately 89% of all surveyed firms (n=250) use performance appraisals. The remaining 11% should be using a performance appraisal to receive the benefits identified below.

Performance Appraisal Benefits

The performance appraisal process provides significant benefits to both employers and employees working in the sport industry. One benefit demonstrated by a detailed performance appraisal system is enhanced communication between employers and employees. Approximately 92% of surveyed firms in the Midwest required that performance appraisals be accompanied by a review and feedback session between manager and subordinate. Performance appraisals provide a time for an employer and the employee to discuss performance obstacles, needed resources, limited resources, objectives, competitive constraints, etc. This open communication facilitates the understanding between both parties regarding related objectives and needs. An employee who feels that an employer is a genuine advocate for his or her success is more likely to strive for optimal performance. Further, communication and the agreed upon outcome regarding employee objectives and expectations can enhance employee commitment versus the traditional top-down dictation of work performance standards.

Occasionally, employees perform at sub-par levels. It is illogical for sub-par performers to be immediately terminated or demoted as the employer has likely made quite an investment in recruiting each employee. Further, courts look unfavorably on employers taking punitive action on employers without providing training and skill improvement opportunities. Sub-par performance, once identified, often can be improved via training or assistance. Although poor performers should not be retained indefinitely, training and assistance can better protect your investment in a particular employee while helping to prove good faith efforts for the court.

Employees are increasingly contesting managerial decisions about hiring, firing, promoting and training. However, performance appraisals can be an effective defense to such claims. This is especially true when, "memories fade or perceptions differ, the best evidence of what occurred, and why, is performance appraisal records" (Eyres, 1989). Performance appraisals serve to document poor performance (as well as good performance) and opportunities provided for improvement prior to an employee's termination.

The Performance Appraisal Process

The benefits of a well-implemented performance appraisal process are vast. However, attention to a variety of related issues can best provide an employer with a legally defensible performance appraisal process (Miller, Fielding, and Pitts, 1993). The remainder of this chapter addresses eleven suggestions for employers engaged in the employee appraisal process.

a) Use Frequent Reviews

Annual reviews, although common, require an employer to remember the employee's past performance for an entire 12 months. Engaging in the evaluation process on such a rare occasion can diminish or marginalize the magnitude of earlier accomplishments. Rather, an employee's more recent performance (good or bad) tends to take precedence. In fact, annual evaluations tempt managers to simply "pull out last year's review, update it and do it quickly" (Schellhardt, 1996). An employer's limited attention given to the performance appraisals has an economic impact of the business, as well as other ramifications. As explained by Schellhardt (1996),

> One recent study may persuade companies to try frequent reviews. Using data from Boston Consulting Group of New York, Hewitt Associates, a Lincolnshire, Ill., a benefits-consulting concern, found that from 1990 to 1992, companies with year-round systems significantly outperformed competitors lacking such systems in financial measures such as return on equity, total shareholder return, sales growth and cash flow. The study also indicated that a company's financial results strengthened considerably within two years of adopting a year-round system.

Using a more frequent performance evaluation process provides three significant benefits. First, employers evaluating on a monthly basis, for example, can quickly and efficiently enhance employee productivity and net revenues by identifying an employees performance weakness or related concerns in January versus having an employee operate at sub-par levels for 11 months prior to an annual December evaluation. Second, the intangible benefits (e.g., improved morale, decreased absenteeism, decreased turnover) associated with a more content employee represent significant benefits justifying a more regular review process. Lastly, the extra documentation generated by a frequent review process facilitates the legal defense for combating wrongful termination. If reviews are conducted on a monthly basis, you can determine that an employee is not performing up to expectations in a short time period. However, if reviews are only conducted on a yearly basis, it can take up to one and one-half years (one year for the evaluation and an additional six months to reevaluate and monitor the employee's conduct) to perform evaluations and specifically inform employees that corrective steps need to be taken to avoid termination.

b) Enforce Existing Policies

Policy manuals frequently elaborate on a performance appraisal process used by a particular sport business. For example, a policy manual may promise annual performance appraisals, due process and/or a grievance procedure. Literature (Chagares, 1989; Harris, 1986) notes that provisions within a policy manual may be binding regardless of a state's adherence to employment-at-will practices. A health club manager, for example, may be liable for breach of a unilateral contract (e.g., the policy manual) by failing to adhere to the manual's contents (Eyres, 1989; Nobile, 1991). Consider the following statement, "Each employee will be evaluated in December." The employee who was not evaluated in December may raise a breach of contract claim. The following statement exemplifies how an employer can better transfer the responsibility back to the individual employee.

> Management will attempt to evaluate the performance of each employee at least once, on an annual basis. Notify your immediate supervisor if you are not evaluated at least once in the prior fiscal year.

The statement undoubtedly provides the employer with more latitude than a statement that promises the employee an evaluation every December.

c) Maintain a Written Evaluation System

Surprisingly, archaic performance evaluation processes based upon memory and perceptions are still used by some older managers. In a somewhat alarming case (*EEOC v. Shelby County Government*, 1988), the defendant-supervisor responsible for 54 employees did not use a written evaluation system, failed to communicate evaluation results to employees, and failed to maintain records. As expected, he presented a very weak case when sued under the Equal Pay Act by discontent plaintiffs. Some attorneys recommend not writing anything relating to employee evaluations to help avoid any conflict where an employee receives a positive evaluation and then is terminated. The problem with such a strategy is that while a paper trail is not established, the lack of a paper trail can also stir significant suspicion. If an employer documents all other facets within the workplace, it would appear suspicious to a jury that such a critical component is not documented. Furthermore, the plaintiff's lawyer could ask a manager why evaluations are not documented and it would appear to be a cover-up when the manager responds that they did not want to create a paper trail.

d) Use Proper Evaluation Criteria

The Equal Employment Opportunity Commission refers to the Uniform Guidelines on Employee Selection Procedures (Uniform Guidelines, 1993) when evaluating the legality of a performance appraisal process. The Guidelines encourage using validity studies to identify non-discriminatory evaluation criteria. Three validity studies specifically addressed by the EEOC include:

- criterion-related studies which predict performance based upon job related criterion,

- content validity studies which measure actual performance, and
- construct validity studies which evaluate whether one has the psychological profile required to perform a particular job (e.g., ability to work as a team member).

A criterion with no adverse impact does not need to be validated. Literature encourages the use of a job analysis when selecting performance appraisal criteria (Barrett and Kernan, 1987; Uniform Guidelines, 1993; Huber, 1983) (see generally Chapter 2).

When deciding the legality of selection criteria courts continue to refer to the United States Supreme Court's landmark decision in *Griggs v. Duke Power Co.* (1971). The plaintiff Griggs challenged the criteria for employment and job transfers. Justice Burger concluded that,

> Under the Act, practices, procedures, or tests neutral on their face, and even neutral in terms of intent, cannot be maintained if they operate to "freeze" the status quo of prior discriminatory employment practices (*Griggs*, 1971).

Antiquated job descriptions or job analysis should not be used to document evaluative criteria. To summarize, employers should structure performance evaluations exclusively around objective evaluative criteria directly related to tasks necessary to accomplish specifically assigned tasks.

Modern management tactics will likely foster new legal territory regarding the legality of unique or non-traditional performance appraisal processes. For example, should different evaluation techniques be employed when individuals perform as a member of a larger "task team?" Some businesses have employed a 360-degree review system in order to better assess individuals involved in both individual and team-oriented projects. In a 360-degree review or evaluation system, employees are evaluated by immediate supervisors as well as colleagues, customers, and/or stakeholders. Special precautions need to be taken with such review systems to prevent creating an unintentional union (See Chapter 12). In addition to evaluating team performance as perceived by other team members, the 360-degree evaluation provides additional documentation for management regarding the unsatisfactory performance of a particular employee. A sports analogy helps portray the evaluation process.

> An analogy can be drawn to diving, ... There's one dive and a group of judges who all see the dive and rate it differently. Ideally, when you bring everybody's perspective together you get a clearer picture (Hein, 1996).

Multi-reviewer systems are beneficial as they reduce the "one-perception" evaluation given only by the employee's immediate supervisor. On the other hand, multi-rater evaluation ratings reflect a number of potential problems.

- Evaluations by colleagues and other stakeholders can turn into a popularity contest and the valid evaluation criteria can become hidden behind personal influences.
- Potential litigation based upon improper evaluation criteria used, coupled with workplace morale problems, can be problematic.
- Employment decisions may be difficult when the evaluators differ on the merit of the individual employee's work. For example, whose evaluation takes precedence — the supervisors or the individual's colleagues?
- It is likely that others who are not familiar with an employee's particular job description are evaluating people. This unfamiliarity with job descriptions and related skills, knowledge, effort, and responsibilities can foster litigation.
- Disagreements among performance evaluators (e.g., a supervisor's evaluation versus the evaluation of colleagues) can breed litigation when employment is negatively influenced as a result of the performance evaluation process.
- Using evaluation information in making employment decisions enhances liability due to evaluating inappropriate criteria.
- Multi-rater training is time consuming and many sport business managers would rather have employees selling sponsorships, for example, than sitting in a room studying job descriptions and employee credentials.

While significant concerns can be attached to multi-reviewer systems, the solution to overcome most concerns involves establishing objective criteria. If objective job results are communicated through the employee's job description and the employee's performance then most evaluation-related concerns could be avoided.

Objectives, however, need to be quantifiable, measurable, reasonable and understandable (Miller, 1997). For example, an objective that merely states, "Increase sponsors" is of little use for evaluative purposes. Generating $100,000 in sponsorship sales may not be satisfactory if the annual average sponsorship sales generated over the past 10 years amounts to $1 million. Berating an employee for not increasing sponsor dollars enough will be problematic if the employee failed to understand exactly what the employer expected. A better objective would state, "Generate $1 million worth of sponsorship dollars by May, 2001."

A health club may curtail rater bias via a second or multi-review process. However, you are cautioned about providing second raters with the first rater's evaluation. As noted by the Oregon District Court, the likelihood of an objective rating is diminished when the prior rating results are known (*Louiseau v. Dept. of HR*, 1983).

e) Communicate Specific Strengths and Weaknesses

It is important that an employer convey the performance evaluation results, both positive and negative, to the evaluated employee (Ashe, 1980; Burchette and De Meusse, 1985). It is just as important, however, that employers communicate definitive ways the employee can improve negative ratings. Communicating negative ratings alone is not sufficient (Barrett and Kernan, 1987). As stated by Lewis (1996) when discussing liability for wrongful discharges, it is not enough to terminate an employee based upon an employee's inability to perform adequately. "It is the employer's responsibility to train the employee to do the job correctly..."

Many employers find it difficult to communicate negative information to employees for a variety of reasons. For example, employers may fear that employees will retaliate against their manager. Researchers at Temple University and Rennselaer Polytechnic Institute found, "that 98% of 151 Philadelphia-area managers encountered some type of aggression after giving employees negative appraisals." (Schellhardt, 1996).

Other employers find it difficult to give negative ratings knowing an employee's particular financial constraints. For example, an employer, realizing that a negative evaluation will influence merit pay, may find it difficult to provide a negative evaluation realizing that the financial constraints of a particular individual (e.g., kids in college, spouse with cancer). Often, employers fail to communicate negative ratings to preserve exiting friendships and amiable work place relations. Unfortunately, failing to address deficiencies to protect the feelings of an employee can prove to be legally devastating (Ashe and McRae, 1985; Eyres, 1989; Nobile, 1991).

After discussing the performance appraisal with the perspective employee, you can solidify the evaluation process by asking the employee to sign a completed evaluation (Ashe, 1980; Metz, 1988). A recent court decision (*Woolery v. Brady*, 1990) supports the employer who had employees read and sign their performance evaluation. Management's liability is more difficult to prove when an employee, who has read and signed a completed appraisal, fails to pursue a grievance within a reasonable time span. Failure to express dissatisfaction about the performance appraisal tends to infer that the employee agreed with the appraisal's accuracy.

f) Non-performing Employees

Many sport managers procrastinate in terminating employees who have poor performance appraisals or who have contributed to an adversarial, unhealthy and/or uncomfortable work environment. Negligent employee retention creates a great concern for all employers. Consumers suffer as service or product quality may deteriorate, co-employees suffer if the non-performing employee is given all the benefits of comparable colleagues and managers fail to manage departments as effectively or efficiently. But just as important, negligent retention can result in traumatic and fatally injurious consequences. Employers can avoid negligent retention allegations by carefully documenting and dating concerns and issues in an employee's personnel file and quickly terminating a poor employee.

An employer also should be concerned about continually providing positive evaluations, job promotions, title "up-grades," etc. If you regularly offer such positive evaluations and rewards without carefully evaluating employees you will have a difficult time defending against a wrongful termination claim based on the prior positive evaluations and rewards.

g) Defamation Concerns

The performance appraisal process can possibly lead to a defamation claim from disgruntled employees. "Defamation by self-publication" defies the traditional interpretation of communication to a third party, a required element that a plaintiff must prove. Defamation claims can occur, for example, even though the communication occurred between the employer and the employee in a remote and secluded location. The courts consider the "communication to a third party" requirement fulfilled if the allegedly disparaged individual feels compelled to communicate the conversation (in part) to a future employer.

Communication among mangers regarding a particular employee's performance has traditionally been given qualified immunity as the benefits derived from the flow of information outweighs any resultant harm (Duffy, 1983/1984). For example, communication among colleagues about employee performance may be justified when making decisions about promotions, bonuses or disciplinary actions. However, employers should restrain sharing performance information only to that extent as necessary to achieve business objectives as the courts very clearly agree that the qualified privilege is fairly narrow. For example, a manager at General Motors elaborated on a plaintiff's "resignation" (alleged theft) to other non-supervisory personnel to curtail the occurrence of similar behavior (*Gaines v. Cuna*, 1982). The Fifth Circuit Court of Appeals held in that case that the manager's comments had extended beyond those who had a reason to know. (*Gaines v. Cuna*, 1982). Similar defamation claims can be avoided through thoroughly investigating performance problems. For example, a sport park day manager should not merely presume that the night manager's oral description and interpretation of an incident is accurate. Employers should investigate the validity of all allegations, which may, or may not, be truthful prior to taking punitive action or sharing information with others.

h) Properly Train Raters

It is not always possible, or even desirable, for one employer to perform all employee performance evaluations in large businesses. However, it is also not prudent to have inexperienced individuals evaluating employee performance. Rating errors include:

- the halo effect (i.e., the individual's most salient characteristic(s) dominate the evaluation),
- the horn effect (i.e., low ratings in one area contaminate other areas where performance is average or above average),
- stereotyping (actual performance tainted by cultural bias), and/or
- the recency effect (i.e., most recent behavior overshadows overall performance) (Gordon, 1991).

These rating errors, in addition to others, have long been recognized as problems within a performance appraisal process. Prudent employers should educate others involved in the evaluation process on ways to avoid these errors. Research indicates that courts look more favorably on plaintiffs when a defendant company lacks rater-training procedures (Barret and Kernan, 1987).

Longnecker (1989), on the other hand, acknowledges that a comprehensive rater-training program will not eliminate all bias. Longnecker (1989) stated, "Occasionally managers feel the need to manipulate ratings in the perceived best interest of their employees, their departments and perhaps even themselves." For example, a manager that shies away from confrontation, is sensitive to personal influences (e.g., divorce, illness), or who fears resultant attitude problems may intentionally bias performance appraisals. This "intentional inaccuracy" and related perils should also be discussed with prospective raters (Longnecker and Ludwig, 1990). Barret and Kernan (1987) suggest that novice raters thoroughly study employee job descriptions and engage in practice rating exercises prior to evaluating individual employees. However, these concerns can be almost entirely eliminated by objective evaluation which focus on such information as the number of days the employee missed through analyzing time cards.

i) Minority Raters

In *Rowe v. General Motors* (1972) the Fifth Circuit Court of Appeals stated that minorities may have "been hindered in obtaining recommendations from their foremen since there is no familial or social association" between the all-white supervisory work force evaluating minority employees. Stacey (1976) addresses the need for minority raters which reflect the employee constituency. Similar allegations continue to be made 25 years later. For example, a *Wall Street Journal* article details a lawsuit against S.C. Johnson & Son Inc. (known as Johnson Wax) (Schellhardt, 1997). Johnson Wax, like many other businesses including sport businesses, adopted self-directed teams that led meetings, determined pay raises, and resolved product-quality problems. However, several African-American employees argued that all white team members placed blacks at a disadvantage when it came time to employee evaluations. Employers can work to prevent the above occurrence via affirmative efforts to employ and promote a diverse work force, including using diverse raters.

j) Periodically Review the Performance Appraisal Process

Employers should periodically review the performance appraisal process. Appraisal processes should be reviewed on an ongoing basis to ensure that all appraisal documents reflect current job description criteria and job analysis data. Implementing and using a grievance system (discussed below) also can effectively identify strengths and weaknesses within the performance appraisal processes.

k) Implement a Grievance Procedure

In *Rowe v. General Motors Co.* (1972) the court's opinion stated that the lack of "safeguards in the procedure" insulated discriminatory effects. Employers implementing a formal grievance system or dispute resolution system (see Chapter 12) are viewed favorably by the courts and can provide evidence that the performance appraisal process is monitored for bias, discrimination and other improprieties (Ashe, 1980; Barrett and Kernan, 1987; Burchett and De Meuse, 1985; Eyres, 1988). Employers should provide employees with an opportunity to file a written grievance when there is disagreement about a particular performance appraisal evaluation. The grievance system employed should be clearly outlined in the employment manual and communicated to employees. Several grievances can serve as an alarm that the performance appraisal may contain flaws or rater errors.

l) Avoid Language Inferring Life-time Employment

While communication can provide your best defense in employment related disputes, inappropriate communications can destroy a case. Comments during an evaluation such as:

- keep up this type of work and you'll be here for a lifetime,

- you are definitely irreplaceable,
- I'm looking forward to working with you as we move into the next millennium,
- I will never get rid of you, or
- any other references to permanent employee status could contradict employment-at-will clauses or status.

All such references should be avoided. This contradictory language could provide a question of fact as to whether an implied or oral contract was made or if an injunction should be granted based upon the doctrine of promissory estoppel. As explained by Bordwin (1994/1995),

> Don't "blow hot and cold" in stating the negatives in your evaluation. A recent cartoon illustrates the point: The boss, standing at the employee's-desk, is saying, "Harrison, as of 5 o'clock today your services will no longer be required. Till then, keep up the good work."

However, the same author cautions that evaluations themselves may convey to an employee that they can be terminated only after receiving a poor performance evaluation. (Bordwin, 1994/1995). Thus Bordwin suggests that a disclaimer printed in an employee handbook can help curtail this misperception. The language Bordwin suggests is as follows:

> This position is one of at-will employment. This means that you are free at any time to leave for any reason or no reason and likewise, the company is free at any time to discharge you for any reason or no reason. The fact that the company conducts periodic performance evaluations will not change this arrangement (Bordwin, 1994/1995).

m) Maintain Confidentiality

Sport business managers need to ensure that personnel files containing performance evaluations and other employee-related information remain strictly confidential. Files should be kept in a locked file cabinet in a location where other employees do not have access. Unlocked and easily accessed files more easily generate lawsuits alleging defamation and invasion of privacy.

After an employee evaluation or performance appraisal has been completed and the results reported to the employee, you often have issues such as whether or not an employee deserves a raise or possibly a reduced salary. Many appraisals occur immediately prior to or in conjunction with an annual salary review. However, such a practice should not be utilized. Rather, a constant, ongoing salary review process should be used. Several concerns exist with conducting annual salary reviews. The primary concern relates to creating an employment relationship other than an employee "at-will" relationship. Any salary review should state employment compensation in terms of weekly or monthly salary to avoid any confusion that the employee has a guaranteed one-year contract. To help prevent any such confusion, the salary review should specifically provide that:

> The statement of an annual salary is not intended to imply that the company agrees to employ any employee for a one year period. The parties specifically intend to create an at-will employment relationship which is in no way abrogated by any statements or terms contained within this salary review and/or promotional evaluation letter.

2) Seniority

Numerous studies have shown that job security ranks as the highest concern for most employees (Rothstein, Knapp and Liebman, 1987). It is very unusual for someone to work for the same employer for 40 years. In fact, the average employee switches jobs on average six times during their work career. Two types of security exist for employees. Benefits seniority refers to the ability to receive benefits based on the length of service provided to the employer. On the other hand, competitive seniority refers to a priority system for allocating employment conditions, such as job transfers, protection from layoffs and other related benefits (Rothstein, Knapp and Liebman, 1987).

Title VII, Section 703(h) provides an employer with statutory protection for a *bona fide* seniority system which provides different employees with different benefits and compensation levels as long as the differences are not the result of an intention to discriminate.

An additional concern associated with seniority involves union members. Under most CBAs, the employer is required to follow specific formulas for promoting or demoting union members. Such rules need to be analyzed prior to making any promotion decisions.

3) Goal Attainment

As previously mentioned, an employee needs to know on what basis he/she will be judged in order for the employee to be effectively evaluated. As part of the contractual agreement under which the employee was hired, the employee was hopefully given specific and reasonable goals and objectives as set forth in the job description. A major concern arises if the employee was willing and eager to comply with their assigned job responsibilities, but was prohibited from completing the tasks by no fault of his/her own. An example could be a ticket sales person who was only given two months rather than half-a year to sell 5,000 tickets because the ticket pricing and printing was not completed until two months before the purchase deadline. If the ticket salesperson was not involved in the delay, it would be unfair to penalize him/her and give them a bad appraisal. A bad appraisal could also lead to litigation. The ticket salesperson could claim fraud, deceit, impossibility, frustration of purpose, intentional interference with prospective economic advantage and other contract based claims relating to his/her inability to complete the contract. Under these theories, a judge could order payment of all foreseeable damages which could include salary, potential future salary, and moving expenses if the ticket salesperson was induced to move across the country to sell tickets-and then was not given a meaningful opportunity to sell.

Setting Appropriate Standards

The concern associated with inappropriate goals can be corrected by setting appropriate standards. One means to ensure that appropriate standards are in place is to regularly review an employee's work product and determine what progress he/she making towards his/her required goals and objectives.

4) Discrimination in Promotion

A key concern to help avoid discrimination claims entails utilizing objective evaluation criteria rather than subjective criteria. Thus, if an athletic trainer performed poorly, the performance appraisal should not indicate that the employee had poor skills. Rather, the performance appraisal should mention objective standards and indicate that the employee failed to achieve an enumerated goal.

JoAnn Hauser was asked to switch from being the athletic trainer for the University of Kentucky men's basketball team to the women's basketball team. Hauser had satisfactory performance evaluations and claimed the proposed new trainer for the men's team was a less qualified male. The dispute resulted in a sexual discrimination suit against the University, athletic director and basketball coach (Sports, 1996).

Sometimes, the promotion or performance appraisal process is affected by an employee's medical conditions. Let us assume that an office worker receives a negative evaluation and does not receive an anticipated promotion. The negative evaluation was based on a physical condition that prohibits the employee from completing certain tasks. The employee might have told the human resources department about the problem, but not her immediate supervisor. Under such circumstances, the human resource department is entitled to disclose the medical condition to her immediate supervisor in order to reassess the evaluation and denied promotion. Since the medical information is serving a legitimate business purpose, such disclosure does not violate any ADA restrictions. However, a special caveat exists for AIDS as several state laws forbid disclosing AIDS status to others in the workplace. If the employee did have AIDS, the human resources department should only indicate that she has a medical condition that might require modifying her work routine to reasonably accommodate her needs.

Wrap Up...

If an employer fails to properly promote competent employees, the employer could be liable for an injured party under a negligent promotion theory. Thus, if an athletic trainer was promoted to work in a position without supervision, and he/she does not have the requisite skill, any individual who is injured due to the trainer's inexperience could claim that you negligently promoted the trainer.

The following represent some key concerns and questions that should be examined when reviewing a company's promotions program.

- Do you always promote from within, and if so why?
- What would be the impact if you promoted from outside the ranks?
- How do you promote employees?
- When do you know that an employee is ready to be promoted?
- How do you inform employees that they are being promoted?
- How do you inform employees that they are not being promoted?
- What mechanism is in place to help employees in the promotion process?
- How are employees informed about upcoming promotion opportunities?
- What factors are used to help make the promotion decision?
- Does lost time, illness, vacation, etc., affect promotional possibilities?
- Are salaries always increased when an employee is promoted?
- Who has the authority to make promotional decisions?
- Is seniority affected by promotions?
- How do you monitor an employee's progress after he/she has been promoted?

- What happens if the promoted employee does not perform satisfactorily? (Update '92, 1992)
- Are employees properly trained?
- Do you consistently follow specified promotion guidelines?
- Are evaluators afraid to rate certain employees?
- Do evaluators overrate employees they like?
- Are all evaluations thoroughly explained to an evaluated employee?
- Is there an appeal process available for arbitrary evaluation decisions?
- Is there a systematic review process to constantly evaluate the promotional policies and procedures?

References

Ashe, R.L. (1980). "How do your performance appraisals perform?" *EEO Today* 7(3): 216–222.

Ashe, R.L., and McRae, G.S. (1985). "Performance evaluations go to court in the 1980s." *Mercer Law Review* 36(3): 887–905.

Barrett, G.V., and Kernan, M.C. (1987). "Performance appraisal and terminations: A review of court decisions since *Brito v. Zia* with implications for personnel practices." *Personnel Psychology* 40(3): 489–503.

Bordwin, M. (1994/1995). "Firing 101: Before, during and after." *Small Business Forum* 12(3): 44–57.

Bretz, R., Milkovich, G., and Reed, W. (1992). "The current state of performance appraisal research and practice: concerns, directions, implications." *Journal of Management* 16(2): 330–333.

Burchett, S.R., and DeMeuse, K.P. (1985). "Performance and the law." *Personnel* 62(7): 29–37.

Chagares, M.A. (1989). "Utilization of the disclaimer as an effective means to define the employment relationship." *Hofstra Law Review* 17(2): 365–405.

Duffy, D.J. (1983/1984). "Defamation and employer privilege." *Employee Relations Law Journal* 9(3): 444–454.

Eyres, P.S. (1989). "Legally defensible performance appraisal systems." *Personnel Journal* 68(7): 58–62.

Gordon, J.R. (1991). *Organizational Behavior*. Boston, MA: Allyn and Bacon.

Harris, G. (1986). "Labor law—employment at will doctrine." *Rutgers Law Journal* 17(3, 4): 715–736.

Hein, K. (1996). "Searching 360 degrees for employee evaluation." *Incentive* 170(10): 40–42.

Huber, V.L. (1983). "An analysis of performance appraisal practices in the public sector: A review and recommendations." *Public Personnel Management Journal* 12(3): 258–267.

Lewis, V.V. (1996). "Hirings, firings can make or break an agency". *Property & Casualty/Risk & Benefits Management* 100(43): 13, 45, 56.

Longnecker, C.O. (1989). "Truth or consequences: Politics and performance appraisals." *Business Horizons* 32(6): 76–82.

Longnecker, C.O., and Ludwig, D. (1990). "Ethical dilemmas in performance appraisal revisited." *Journal of Business Ethics* 9: 961–969.

Metz, E.J. (1988). "Designing legally defensible performance appraisal systems." *Training and Development Journal* 42(7): 47–51.

Miller, L.K. (1997). *Sport Business Management.* Gaithersburg, MD: Aspen Publishers.

Miller, L.K., Fielding, L.W., and Pitts, B.G. (1993). "Implementation of the performance appraisal process: Concerns for the health club manager." *Journal of Legal Aspects of Sport* 3(1): 44–50.

Nobile, R. J. (1991). "The law of performance appraisals." *Personnel* 68(7): 7.

Rothstein, M., Knapp, A., and Liebman, L. (1987). *Employment Law, Cases and Material.* New York: The Foundation Press, Inc.

Schellhardt, T.D. (1996). "It's time to evaluate your work and all involved are groaning." *The Wall Street Journal* (November 19): A1.

Schellhardt, T.D. (1997). "Race-bias suit centers on worker teams." *The Wall Street Journal* (February 13): B2.

Smith, B.N., Hornsby, J.S., and Shirmeyer, R. (1996). "Current trends in performance appraisal: An examination of managerial practice." *SAM Advanced Management Journal* (July): 10–15.

"Sports" (1996). *The Courier-Journal* (April 5): 6c.

Stacey, D.R. (1976). "Subjective criteria in employment decisions under Title VII." *Georgia Law Review* 10(3): 737–752.

Uniform Guidelines on Employee Selection Procedures. Fed. Reg., 29, 1607.1–16.17 (1991).

Update '92, In-house counsel colloquium. (1992). San Francisco, CA: Schachter, Kristoff, Orenstein & Berkowitz.

Cases

EEOC v. Shelby County Government, 707 F.Supp. 969 (W.D. Tenn. 1988).

Gaines v. Cuna Mutual Insurance Society, 681 F.2d 982 (5th Cir. 1982).
Griggs v. Duke Power Co., 401 U.S. 424 (1971).
Loiseau v. Dept. of Human Resources of State of Or., 567 F.Supp 1211 (D. Or. 1983).
Rowe v. General Motors Corporation, 457 F.2d 348 (5th Cir. 1972).
Woolery v. Brady, 741 F. Supp. 667 (E.D. Mich., S.D. 1990).

Statute

Title VII of the Civil Rights Act of 1964, 42 U.S.C.A. Section 703(h).

Chapter 10

Discipline

Just as kids often learn from strict discipline, employees often reform their inappropriate actions only after being properly disciplined. While some employees can reform their behavior after receiving positive reinforcement, other employees need strict discipline. Disciplinary activities can range from simple verbal warnings to termination proceedings. However, no matter what discipline tool is utilized, the key point for analysis will always center on what disciplinary process was offered through the employment contract process and what disciplinary process was ultimately delivered. A recent survey of 222 employers found that 79% of nonunion employers and 85% of union employers have written employment rules and disciplinary policies (Frierson, 1994). All these policies are rendered useless if the written policies are not followed.

If the employment contract or union CBA does not contain any reference to the disciplinary process, the employer still does not have an unfettered right to arbitrarily discipline an employee. While arbitrary or capricious discipline might not constitute a contractual breach under the above facts, an employee could still possibly claim a 14th Amendment constitutional claim that the disciplinary acts violated the employee's right to due process or equal protection. As discussed previously in this text, such a claim might be valid for public high school coaches or physical education instructors, but is not available for private employees (except in California and Montana). Thus, private employees traditionally only have a contractual basis to bring a claim that their employer failed to follow previously enumerated disciplinary policies.

1) Informing Employee of Penalties Prior to Undertaking

The primary tool for informing employees about potential penalties and the disciplinary process is through the employment contract and employee handbook. The following case highlights what can happen when an employer provides specific disciplinary policies, and then fails to follow the policies.

281

A bank employee was hired without any formal employment contract (*Pine River State Bank v. Mettille*, 1983). However, an employee handbook had a specific disciplinary policy highlighted below.

> *Disciplinary Policy.* In the interest of fairness to all employees, the Company establishes reasonable standards of conduct for all employees to follow in their employment at Pine River State Bank. These standards are not intended to place unreasonable restrictions on you, but are considered necessary for us to conduct our business in an orderly and efficient manner.
>
> If an employee has violated a company policy, the following procedure will apply:
>
> 1) An oral reprimand by the immediate supervisor for the first offense, with a written notice sent to the executive Vice President.
> 2) A written reprimand for a second offense.
> 3) A written reprimand and a meeting with the Executive Vice President and possible suspension from work without pay for five days.
> 4) Discharge from employment for an employee whose conduct does not improve as a result of the previous action taken. In no instance will a person be discharged from employment without a review of the facts by the executive officer (*Pine River*, 1983).

The bank employee appeared to have a good employment history with favorable evaluations and raises. Approximately one year after he was hired, a state bank examiner uncovered serious technical errors for which the loan officer appeared to be responsible. The loan officer was immediately terminated and provided with two months severance pay. Even though the employee engaged in egregious conduct, he had a contractual right, through the employee handbook's terms, to a comprehensive disciplinary process. When he was not afforded such a process, he had a valid breach of contract claim (Frierson, 1994).

In order to avoid similar contractual disputes, it is imperative that you write any contracts or handbooks with specific clarity that employees understand what rights they are afforded, but broadly enough that unusual circumstances can also be handled without incurring liability. Thus, the disciplinary policy in *Pine River* specifically informed employees that they had several stages in the disciplinary process prior to being terminated. Such a provision informs the employees that they can have several strikes before they are out. If an employee knows they have had several strikes, then they should not be surprised that after another strike they are terminated. To ensure you can terminate an employee under these facts, you have to specifically develop a thorough paper trail documenting what disciplinary steps have been taken so you can show to the court that you, in fact, have complied with your contractual requirements.

Besides developing proper documentation to help you in court, proper documentation can also help develop a more consistent warning program that can inform employees where they are in the process so they cannot claim at a later date that they only thought they had received an oral warning. To help prevent such claims, all reprimands and disciplinary punishments should be signed by the employee acknowledging that they have received the indicated discipline and that they understand where they lie on the disciplinary tracks if they violate any additional rules.

In addition to having employees sign all disciplinary documents such as oral or written warnings, you should specifically write disciplinary rules to maximize flexibility. If a coach engages in minor violations such as making some unauthorized personal phone calls, then the disciplinary policy utilized in *Pine River* might be effective. However, such policy is not effective if the same coach is accused of raping a student. Therefore, any disciplinary policy statement should be written in broad enough terms to allow for additional penalties, fewer steps in the process, and more flexible procedures. Such flexibility can be developed through utilizing flexible terms such as:

- "possible violations include,"
- "penalties or discipline can include, but is not limited to," and
- "possible penalties include."

2) Investigation

Similar to investigating sexual harassment claims, investigating disciplinary-related matters requires the utmost in care and thoroughness. Sexual harassment represents a significant concern within the company and associated company liability, discipline cases are sometimes more sensitive as they can involve criminal misconduct at and/or outside the workplace. Criminal misconduct raises a critical issue, which is whether to turn the matter over to the police or to first conduct an internal investigation before referring the matter to the police.

The best advice for any employer is to contact the police whenever any criminal misconduct is suspected within your company or affecting your clients or employees. By failing to immediately report any suspicious activity to the police, an employer can be responsible for obstructing justice. While this concern is not paramount in the sports industry, it has occurred on several occasions. Recently, Tom Osborne, the former Nebraska football coach, was highlighted in the press for possibly obstructing justice by keeping a gun utilized by one of his player's in an alleged shooting (Fried, 1997). Even if such action did not bring criminal penalties against the coach, it did generate significant negative publicity across the country.

The investigation process would not be complete without properly identifying all relevant facts and recording all such observation for use in the disciplinary process.

3) Documentation

Appropriate documentation is critical for the disciplinary process to serve it's intended purpose to modify behavior. However, documentation also serves the purpose of focusing someone toward your intended final disposition, if you are intent on terminating an employee. As discussed in Chapter 3, Documentation serves the purposes of providing you, a supervisor or manager, an employee and a jury with brief snapshots highlighting why a given employee was treated in a given manner. If an employee goes through the disciplinary process and is exonerated, then the documentation should properly reflect that the employee was not guilty of the alleged misdeeds. All negative inferences or implications should be removed from the record to prevent any future charges which form their impetus from prior alleged misdeeds which proved to be incorrect or unsubstantiated.

However, if an employee is found to have violated company policies or rules, the documentation should reflect all facts, witnesses, evidence, personnel and associated information in a tangible form to be utilized in future actions-such as litigation brought after an employee was terminated. Signed affidavits, made under the penalty of perjury, should be obtained from each witness or party involved. Such a step will help prevent you from losing important information from people subsequently quitting, moving or changing their story.

Documentation maintains an important role prior to and throughout the disciplinary process. In addition to the disciplinary process, employees might also wish to utilize a grievance process when they might not have violated any rules, but wish to challenge sanctions or penalties against them. The following section discusses the grievance process which forms a critical sounding board to help resolve employee disputes and allow employees the opportunity to challenge injustices in the workplace.

4) Grievance Process

While conflict is a positive force as a catalyst for creativity in some businesses, that is not always the case. While security precautions can help prohibit guns, or remove a disgruntled employee from the premises, such actions do not address the underlying issue or conflict. This has led to significant managerial training in "emotion management" and conflict resolution. (Lancaster, 1997). While implementing employee searches or adding extra security personnel can be accomplished fairly quickly, effective conflict resolution takes significant time. Time needs to be taken to listen to all the appropriate issues and to siphon out the superfluous from the key facts and issues. After you have heard the issue, you should reiterate the issue to the disputing parties. While managers might think they understand the issue, they might in fact only touch on a tangential issue. One of this book's authors once mediated a landlord tenant dispute in Ohio. The matter was very heated and it appeared there would be no way to avoid a trial. However, the real dispute was uncovered only after separating the parties and talking with each person individually (called "caucusing" in mediation). It turned out that a rental unit dispute was not the real dispute, just a spill over from a prior dispute. The landlord and tenant had been lovers and the landlord did not want his wife finding out about the relationship. Once the underlying issue was resolved, the rest of the case was easy to resolve and the parties were able to reach a negotiated settlement.

Identifying the dispute is especially critical when the manager is involved in the dispute. Employees might not like a manager's personality or style. Employees should also be encouraged to freely express themselves without the specter of retaliation hanging over their head. Thus, frank and continuous communications are key to the dispute resolution process and violence avoidance (Lancaster, 1997).

Many employees will not want to open-up their true feelings or concerns for fear that someone else might feel the issue or dispute is petty or not important. This concern helps demonstrate why listening and knowing the right questions to ask are two of the most important steps needed to help defuse workplace violence.

In addition to listening and identifying the issues, it is critical for managers to keep their emotions in check (Lancaster, 1997). By taking disputes among or between other parties to heart, a manager can lose his/her neutrality and objectivity, which will further inflame a dispute.

The dispute resolution process is not perfect. No manager should expect to be able to solve all problems. Sometimes individuals do not want assistance. They do not want anyone "helping" them solve their problems. If an employee does not want to participate in dispute resolution and does not appear to want or embrace needed change, a manager has to know when to cut his/her losses. Similarly, if the dispute has been going on unabated for too long, then the problem employee(s) need to be eliminated from the dispute. If this means relocating an employee, demoting an employee or terminating an employee, all necessary termination steps, especially appropriate documentation should be followed.

Chapter 12 provides additional insight into the disciplinary process and how to avoid a wrongful termination suit alleging failure to comply with the company grievance or disciplinary program.

The following represents key concerns that need to be addressed in any dispute resolution process:

- Is there a formal or informal complaint process and if so, what is that process?
- How is the complaint process communicated to all employees?
- How often do employees utilize the process and does it need to be revised?
- Are all supervisors or managers trained in dealing with employee complaints and instructing employees on how to access the process?
- Who will hear the dispute?
- Will the individuals that hear the dispute, judge the dispute as well?
- Are complaints monitored for frequency and claim types?
- Are employees required to file specific forms to initiate the complaint process?
- What follow-up procedures are in place once complaints are filed?

Wrap Up . . .

This chapter has primarily addressed issues associated with preliminary disciplinary issues such as proper contractual clauses, incident investigation and documentation and grievance procedures to hopefully avoid disciplinary disputes. However, the critical issue that needs to be analyzed refers to the actual discipline that is applied to the employee. The following questions and progressive disciplinary guidelines should provide significant insight into the issues that arise and how to handle actual employee disciplining.

The following questions should be considered in analyzing the disciplinary process and policies to determine if they are appropriate or legally defensible.

- Does the company have a published disciplinary policy communicated to all employees and made a part of all employee contracts?
- Are disciplinary rules and penalties posted in a visible location?
- Do employees receive their own copy of the disciplinary rules and are these rules written in clear, easy to understand language?

- What penalties are provided for violating company rules and do all employees know these penalties?
- Are direct supervisors responsible for discipline problems?
- What are the most common rules violations and what are the penalties for such violations?
- Who monitors the disciplinary process?
- What appeal process, if any, is available for employees who feel they have not received due process rights?
- Was the incident that triggered the disciplinary process thoroughly investigated prior to undertaking any serious discipline?
- Has the employee been given an opportunity to explain his/her side of the story?
- If other individuals had committed the same offense in the past, were they punished to the same degree and if not, what justifies the different treatment?
- Has the employer done anything to support a reasonable belief that such action was condoned?
- Are all employee rules violations documented in personnel files?
- Has the employee been punished in the past for similar misconduct?
- Has the employee been warned in the past not to engage in such misconduct?
- Has the employee ever received a final warning expressly indicating the penalty for future misconduct?
- Is the rule that was violated in place to ensure the orderly, efficient and safe operating of the business?
- How soon after the act was the discipline imposed (Update '92, 1992)?

After analyzing the above questions, you can determine what might be an appropriate disciplinary process if you wish to discharge an employee for engaging in egregious conduct. Most employers utilize a progressive discipline process utilizing warnings or escalating penalties before an employee is discharged. Such procedures would be appropriate for any minor violations, but more egregious conduct often requires immediate action. One author, James Frierson, recommends immediate discharge when an employee engages in:

- falsifying job applications or resumes,
- willfully damaging employer property,
- divulging company trade secrets and/or other confidential information,
- stealing employer's property,
- physically assaulting customers or employees at the workplace,

- possessing or selling illegal drugs or alcohol at work,
- possessing or discharging a weapon at work, and
- discharge for falsifying work records such as time sheets (Frierson, 1994).

While Frierson recommended discharge for egregious misconduct, less egregious conduct was ranked according to what most employers are the most egregious to less egregious conduct for which a progressive disciplinary process should apply. Such misconduct is ranked below.

1) Absences without permission, leaving work early and excessive break times.
2) Insubordination and disloyalty.
3) Gambling, substance abuse or a criminal conviction.
4) Conducting personal business on company time or using company equipment for personal gain.
5) Sexual harassment and other discriminatory conduct.
6) Negligent work performance and incompetency.
7) Low productivity and/or disturbing other employees or customers.
8) Violating employer dress codes, soliciting co-workers for charitable contributions and distributing political material in the workplace (Frierson, 1994).

While Frierson proposed a worthwhile progressive disciplinary process based on the employee's offense, his conclusion concerning immediate discharge might be an extreme measure, especially when an employer is forced to act quickly without all the facts. Thus, an athletic director might try to immediately discharge a coach accused of sexually inappropriate behavior. While such conduct would be grounds for discharge under Frierson's enumerated discharge plan, such a discharge might not be the appropriate response. Discharge should only be considered in place of the progressive disciplinary policy when the misconduct has been thoroughly investigated. Until the misconduct has been thoroughly investigated, the employee should not be discharged, but rather should be placed on paid leave pending a formal investigation.

There is no one best way to discipline an employee. All employees should be given a chance to prove their innocence to prevent a wrongful termination claim based on your failure to properly discipline the right party. To assist you in this endeavor, you are required to separate the issues and controversy from the person charged with the misconduct. If you or the employee's direct supervisor has a personality clash with the charged employee, then someone else should supervise the disciplinary process to ensure equality. Any final disciplinary report or warning should indicate what specific changes need to be made in order for the employee to right his/her wrong. Such changes should not be broad and subjective such as "John needs to improve his attitude." Rather, the changes should entail specific objective recommendations such as, "no co-worker complaints concerning productivity for a two month period."

Frierson explained the discipline process succinctly when he indicated that policies:

- need to be written in enough detail,
- need to be consistent evenhandedly applied to all employees,
- need to specifically spell-out wrongful conduct,
- need to provide for quick reviews, but allow for appeals, and
- need to utilize a progressive discipline process whenever possible (Frierson, 1994).

References

Fried, G. (1997). "Illegal moves off-the-field, university liability for illegal acts of student athletes." *Seton Hall University, Journal of Sports Law* 7(1): 69–101.

Frierson, J. (1994). *Preventing Employment Lawsuits*. The Bureau of National Affairs, Inc.

Lancaster, H. (1997). "Managing your career." *The Wall Street Journal* (May 27): B1.

Update '92, In-house counsel colloquium. (1992). San Francsico, CA: Schachter, Kristoff, Orenstein & Berkowitz.

Case

Pine River State Bank v. Mettille, 333 N.W. 2d 622 (Minn. 1983).

Chapter 11

Job Related Injuries

Some work environments are prone to significant and sometimes serious injuries. Construction, hazardous chemicals, fire fighting, security, punch press machine operation and related areas produce either frequent or possibly life threatening injuries on a consistent basis. These employment areas might generate the greatest publicity associated with employee injuries, yet they do not represent the biggest proportion of the injuries regularly claimed in the workplace. In 1992, approximately 6,500 individuals died in the workplace and another 13.2 million were hurt in work-related accidents (Coleman, 1997). That translates to 18 deaths and 36,000 injuries every day. Furthermore, occupation-related injuries such as lung diseases and lead poisoning caused 165 deaths daily and 2,300 new ailments daily (Coleman, 1997). The direct costs associated with these injuries totaled $65 billion in 1992 while the indirect costs, such as lost wages, totaled $171 billion (Coleman, 1997).

Worker injuries represent a serious risk affecting more than just the bottom line. The repercussions associated with employee injuries include:

- lost productive time,
- lost time associated with employees and supervisors assisting the injured employee,
- down time in the production process,
- time required to retrain employees until the injured employee returned,
- time and costs associated with damaged equipment,
- costs associated with having to pay the injured employee's wages and benefits,
- reduced morale among other employees,
- increased workers' compensation premiums, and
- costs associated with investigation, attorneys, lawsuits, depositions, and related costs (Thierman, 1995).

These problems help demonstrate why preventing injuries and workplace safety is such a critical concern.

Employers have various options to help address workplace safety concerns. Numerous industry consultants offer various safety audits designed to help businesses optimize their safety record and reduce payouts for workers' compensation and general comprehensive insurance policies. Employers can also attempt to comply with the various workplace safety laws without external assistance. However, because the laws are so specific and detailed, it is always recommended that an external consultant should be hired when developing a safety program and for regular reviews. One concern that can be reviewed by an employer is the insurance protection afforded injured workers.

1) Workers' Compensation Insurance

The purpose behind workers' compensation insurance is to have a no fault safety net under every employer. If an employee is injured, the courts are not required to apportion liability while an injured person is unable to afford or receive required treatment. Coverage begins immediately after the employee is injured and provides complete coverage. In exchange for prompt and complete claims payment, the injured employee waives his/her right to sue the employer unless the employer engaged in wrongful conduct such as failing to eliminate a known hazard. While the employer is insulated from further claims, the employee might be able to bring a claim against a negligent third party who is not his or her employer. Thus, if an independent vendor supplied a defective weight bench which injured the fitness trainer, the fitness trainer would be covered by his or her employer's workers' compensation insurance coverage and then could sue the vendor under a product liability theory (Thierman, 1995).

Based on the above example, it is quite evident that workers' compensation insurance is just like any other type of insurance; it is designed to protect your assets. The major difference being that the law requires you to have workers' compensation insurance (similar to automotive liability insurance) and the law specifically limits the recovery allowed an injured employee. An injured employee can normally bring a negligence claim against an employer for injuries that occur in the workplace. However, under the workers' compensation laws, if an employer has proper coverage, the employee is forbidden from filing any claim against an employer other than the workers' compensation claim. This is referred to as the exclusive remedy rule. The exclusive remedy rule applies strictly to the employer and does not insulate third parties from potential negligence claims.

Premiums

Workers' compensation insurance charges the employer indirectly based on the cost of any workplace injury award. The lower the number of injuries, the more the insurance premiums declines. Most policies utilize a retrospective rating for calculating insurance policy premiums. Under this method, the state sets the premium rate on a set factor such as the number of employment hours worked or on a percentage of the company's payroll. If the employer has no claims, they can earn a discount on their next year's premiums or a rebate on the already paid premiums. This benefit is often referred to as the "mod rate." If an employer has a relatively injury free year (more appropriately "claim free" year as some injuries might not result in any claim payment) then they might receive a mod rate of 90% which means next year's premiums would be 10% lower. The industry average safety record results in a mod rate of 1.0. A company which has a mod rate of 1.2 means the firm's accident rate is above the industry average and the employer will be accessed a 20% penalty. If the injuries do not result in additional claims, the employer can request a refund of any excessive reserve (Blakely, 1997). Savings under these mod rates could be in thousands to several hundred thousand dollars for larger companies.

Purchasing and Maintaining Insurance

Most states allow an employer to purchase workers' compensation insurance from private insurers. State or private insurers can be utilized in 13 states and state run monopolies exists in six other states. While there are numerous states and private companies that offer insurance coverage, not all policies are the same. Some policies provide enhanced medical and rehabilitation benefits while others provide significant savings for having safe work histories. Some policies require the injured person to use a Preferred Provider Program which reduces the medical options available to the injured employee (Glick, 1997). Based on the various policy options available to employers and the changes that can befall any insurance company, even state sponsored programs, you have a duty to critically investigate all insurance options. If you fail to properly track an insurance provider who is facing bankruptcy or related concerns, you could possibly be sued by an injured employee for negligent investigating and purchasing workers' compensation insurance. Thus, if an insurance company offers a premium that sounds too good to be true, you should thoroughly investigate the company prior to purchasing the insurance.

While some states allow employers to choose from various workers' compensation policies, an employer has to vigilantly review and administer his/her program to make sure he/she controls his/her costs. For example, employers need to take the time to analyze how they classify workers for coverage. Most job classifications are determined by the National Council on Compensation Insurance (NCCI) in Boca Raton, Florida (Blakely,

1997). This service is utilized in at least 37 states. NCCI publishes a classification bible called the "Scopes Manual." The Manual helps establish premiums rates for various classified positions based on the dangers inherent in the position (Blakely, 1997). Thus, a dangerous job such as a roofer might entail a workers' compensation premium of $17.97 for every one hundred dollars of pay. A truck driver generates $7.61 in premiums per $100 in wages. A clerical worker on the other hand is a very safe position and insurance premiums only amount to 29 cents per $100 in wages. Thus, a secretary earning $20,000 a year would generate approximately $58 a year in workers' compensation insurance premium obligations. A truck driver, using the above reference figures, and earning $35,000 would cost the employer $2,663.50 a year in premiums (Blakely, 1997).

The job-classification process usually is started by the insurance agent who bases his or her decision on employer payroll, job descriptions, business operations and past safety/injury experience. This information is further reviewed by the insurance underwriter (private or state) who then sets the premium calculations and job-classifications. Each state sets its own premium rates. However, if the employer disputes the job-classifications the process normally involves contacting the agent, who contacts the underwriter, who then send out an investigator to examine the office or workplace. If the underwriter refuses to change her initial determination, an employer can petition the final arbiter, a state-level workers' compensation appeals board (Blakely, 1997).

The concern associated with proper classification is a critical concern that can save an employer thousands of dollars while costing the same amount. Job-classifications can be erroneous either on your behalf or against your interest. Thus, if you are unsure if you have received a favorable job-classification, and still challenge the classification, you could be assessed significant back pay requirements. To insure you are paying the appropriate premium, regularly check your job-classifications either through your agent or through the Scopes Manuals that are available in many public libraries. You should also regularly check job descriptions to ensure they are appropriate and adequately describe the risks a given employee might face.

Federal Workers' Compensation

Similar to the state workers' compensation system, a similar system was created for federal employees through the Federal Employees' Compensation Act (FECA), 5 U.S.C.S. 8101–8193 et seq. The system mirrors the state based system, but provides more generous awards. Additional federal regulations include:

- the Federal Employers' Liability Act (FELA) 45 U.S.C.S. 51–60 covers railroad workers,
- the Jones Act 46 U.S.C.S. 688 extends significant injury illness and injury remedies to "seamen"who are defined as a "master or member of a crew of any vessel;" and
- the Longshoremen's and Harbor Workers' Compensation Act (LHWCA), 33 U.S.C.S. 901–950 which provides injury remedies for employees working in maritime employment upon the navigable waters of the United States.

These various laws can come into play when a shipment of sporting goods is transported by rail and someone is injured unloading the cargo or if a crew member is injured during a sailing competition occurring off U.S. soil. Federal laws are required to deal with such disputes as the injury could occur between states or in an area without state law and federal workers' compensation coverage is in the best position to resolve such disputes.

Social Security Disability

An ancillary right afforded by federal law applies to any injury "off the job" which prevents an employee from returning to work. This additional fringe benefit works as a safety net for all employees and is referred to as Social Security Disability coverage. 42 U.S.C.S. 423 et seq. The program has paid out over $20 billion per year to approximately 4 million people who have been permanently and totally disabled (Rothstein, Knapp and Liebman, 1987). In addition, Section 223 of the Social Security Act provides disability benefits to individuals between the ages of 50 and 65 in the event they are unable to engage in any substantial gainful employment by reason of any medically determinable physical or mental impairment which can be expected to result in death or long term disability (Rothstein, Knapp and Liebman, 1987).

A patchwork of federal and state laws are designed to compensate injured employees, make such employees whole and expedite an employee's return to work. Besides analyzing injury compensation, the various federal and state laws also examine injury prevention and make a workplace safe for employees and customers.

2) Work Related Injuries

The largest percentage of workplace injuries normally relate to overexertion, which represents 27% of all OSHA claims (Warner, 1997). The other top categories reported to OSHA in descending order of occurrence and percentages of cases in parenthesis are listed below:

- Struck by an object (13%)
- Fall on the same level (11%)
- Bodily reaction-slip or twist (10%)
- Struck against an object (7%)
- Caught in or compressed by equipment or object (5%)
- Falls to lower levels (5%)
- Exposure to harmful substances or environments (5%) (Warner, 1997).

Rounding-out the list of most frequent injuries are transportation, repetitive motion and assault and violent acts in the workplace (Warner, 1997). Back injuries represent 18.8 percent of all ADA claims filed with the EEOC through 1994 (Walsh, 1995).

Repetitive Stress Injuries

Numerous injuries need to be combated to make the work environment safe. One injury coming into vogue and representing a significant concern to any organization that utilizes data entry is Repetitive Stress Injury (RSI) which has become the workplace curse of the 1990's. RSI can produce tendentious through lower back pain, but is primarily associated with carpal tunnel syndrome and 99 other types of job-induced injuries. Carpal tunnel syndrome occurs during manual tasks when the wrist is repeatedly flexed and extended which causes the wrist tendon to compress around a wrist nerve resulting in numbness, tingling or pain (Neuborne, 1997). The current cost estimate for RSI related injuries is estimated at $20 billion a year in workers' compensation claims and another $80 billion of lost costs such as absenteeism and lost productivity (Neuborne, 1997). The Bureau of Labor Statistics estimates that 25% of all injuries that result in lost work time are due to RSI problems (Neuborne, 1997). The Bureau also concluded that 62% of all workplace injuries in 1995 were disorders caused by repetitive motion on muscles or tendons (Swoboda, 1997). Two reasons why RSI has expanded into such a major problem is the number of baby boomers in their 40s and 50s who are utilizing computers at work and whose bodies are more prone to injuries. Secondly, a significant number of Generation X'ers utilize keyboards at work and then surf the net and utilize e-mail during their free time, which means additional time engaging in repetitive activities (Neuborne, 1997).

RSI has resulted in more than just lost work. RSI has spawned lawsuits and new laws. In 1996 a New York jury awarded $6 million to three office workers who claimed they were injured using keyboards manufactured by Digital Equipment Corp. (Neuborne, 1997). These and similar jury verdicts have traditionally been thrown out on appeal. However, the numerous lawsuits filed against keyboard manufacturers has resulted in the development and sale of new keyboards more appropriately designed to prevent injuries caused by excessive use.

RSI represents just one type of injury that has fostered a national concern in the workplace. Similarly, AIDS and other infectious diseases also represent a serious national concern, especially in the sports and fitness industries where individuals are frequently expelling bodily fluids. All these injury concerns have fostered the development and implementation of the federal and state OSHA standards.

OSHA and State Occupational Safety Hazard Administration

OSHA is a term often thrown around discussing workplace injuries. Rightly so. OSHA is the acronym used to refer to the Williams-Steiger Occupational Safety and Health Act of 1970, 29 U.S.C.S. 651 et seq. OSHA sets *national* minimum standards for workplace safety. OSHA applies to basically all employers as it covers any business with one or more employees. States can implement higher standards if they desire. Currently, 23 states the U.S. Virgin islands and the Commonwealth of Puerto Rico have separate OSHA standards. The states with separate OSHA rules or their own enforcement agencies include Alaska, Arizona, California, Connecticut, Hawaii, Indiana, Iowa, Kentucky, Maryland, Michigan, Minnesota, Nevada, New Mexico, New York, North Carolina, Oregon, South Carolina, Tennessee, Utah, Vermont, Virginia, Washington and Wyoming. In six states, Alaska, California, Hawaii, Michigan, Oregon and Washington, the states have enacted different safety standards than the federal OSHA. Also, numerous states regulate local industries that are not covered by the federal OSHA regulations (Thierman, 1995). For example the crabbing industry might have special regulations in Maine, but no similar regulations are required in Nebraska.

It should be reiterated that OSHA sets a minimum standard while some states require higher standards. While meeting the minimum standards will likely get you past a federal inspection, they might not be enough to get you past a suit if your workplace does not meet possibly tougher local or industry standards.

Reporting and Record Keeping Requirements

One factor addressed by OSHA regulations focuses on record keeping and reporting requirements, which like all other OSHA requirement, apply to all employers with one or more employees. Such requirements apply to all employers with 11 or more employees who are required to report all injuries resulting in:

- medical treatment,
- loss of consciousness,
- loss of motion injuries, or
- transferring to a different position.

Additionally any fatalities or injuries, which require hospitalization for five or more employees, requires OSHA notification within 48 hours after the accident. While OSHA reporting requirements are very specific for some industries utilizing hazardous equipment or utilizing hazardous techniques, the sports industry has not been immune from its coverage. Various entities such as health clubs have to follow OSHA rules related to blood borne pathogens from injured patrons or employees. Rules also cover such matters as pool chemical storage, handling and disposal. However, while numerous rules are currently in place, these rules change on a frequent basis.

OSHA is currently revamping its rules and regulations concerning reporting requirements. All specified employers with more than 10 employees are now required to keep injury records and post on an employee bulletin board previous year's statistics of on-the-job injuries or illnesses (Bates, 1997). Some new "specified" employers who need to report such injury information include restaurants, job-training services and boat dealers. However, some "specified" employers will now not have to report injuries in the ever-changing legislative minefield that constitutes OSHA regulations. The primary sports employer who will now be exempt from the reporting requirements are bowling centers (Bates, 1997). Even if bowling centers do not need to report prior year's injuries, all employers still need to report all workplace fatalities to OSHA (Bates, 1997). "Specified" employers change when industries go through changes and/or when they become less dangerous through technological innovations.

OSHA Inspection

One key provision which helps mark OSHA's effectiveness in reducing injuries is the OSHA inspector program designed to operate as "safety police officers." Under OSHA regulation Section 8(e), the owner or operator of a business has to provide an OSHA inspector with the opportunity to,

> inspect and investigate during reasonable times, and within reasonable limits and in a reasonable manner, such places of employment and all pertinent conditions, structures, machines, apparatus, devices, equipment, and materials therein and to question privately any such employer, owner, operator, agent or employee.

In essence, OSHA inspectors have carte blanche authority to inspect anything they want within broad limits. This power raises some concerns such as Fourth Amendment unconstitutional searches, and whether or not the inspector(s) has probable cause to inspect (Thierman, 1995). Several cases have specifically limited OSHA's power and required probable cause to inspect an employer. Among these cases are *Marshall v. Barlows, Inc.*, 434 U.S. 307 (1978), *Textron v. Marshall*, 625 F.2d 1313 (7th Cir. 1980), and *Marshall v. North American Car Co.*, 626 F.2d 320 (3rd Cir. 1980).

While employers have a right to demand a warrant, attorneys are split on whether or not to demand a warrant. If an employer prohibits an inspection and demands a warrant, the OSHA inspection might be even more rigorous exposing hazards which the inspector might have previously only provided a verbal warning. However, due to the inconvenience the employer caused the inspector, the simple warning could be replaced with a full-blown complaint. On the flip side of the coin, if you allow a warrantless search, you cannot complain at a later time that they should have had a warrant to search your business. Thus, as is often the case, if you ask inspectors to wait a minute while you contact your lawyer, they probably will be sitting in the lobby drafting a declaration for the court to obtain a search warrant. (Thierman, 1995).

The inspection process begins with an opening conference where the employer and an employee representative meet with the OSHA inspector. The inspector gives his/her reason for the visit and might indicate that a complaint was filed. Employees, former employees, customers or anyone else who might know about workplace safety concerns can file a complaint. Typically, the inspector will ask to see:

- written safety plans,
- accident logs,
- safety committee meeting minutes (if available),
- accident reports,
- proof of workers' compensation coverage, and
- related documentation discussed below (Thierman, 1995).

The inspector would then conduct a walk-about, which is a visual inspection of the workplace. During the walk-about, an inspector might take pictures, test equipment and/or interview employees. After the tour, the inspector normally conducts an exit conference where the results will be reviewed, violations, if any, will be identified and any warnings or citations will be issued (Thierman, 1995). If violations are serious, the inspector might reschedule another inspection during a set period. If the violations are minor, the inspector might request a written abatement plan discussing how the violations will be corrected. The inspection typically ends with the inspector giving the employer an explicit warning that any retaliation against an employee for filing a complaint or mentioning problems during the visit is illegal (Thierman, 1995).

Investigation Hints

To protect you during an investigation, it is critical to have a management representative going through the walk-about as well as a maintenance person who can fix things on the spot. A video recorder should capture the entire investigation. Taking pictures and extensive notes will also provide good evidence as to how the investigation proceeded. A useful hint is to ask for the inspectors credentials for your secretary to make copies (so there is no confusion in the future as to who did the inspection) and to verify the inspector's credentials with OSHA. During this lag time, you can go to your office and contact your attorney to help determine the scope or breath of the proposed investigation (Thierman, 1995). You should also ask to get a copy of any complaint that might have been filed, copies of any photographs taken, and portions of any samples taken. In order to secure evidence for an OSHA or civil trial, you should have your own representative or scientist involved in any testing procedures to guarantee accuracy.

While an OSHA inspector has the right to interview employees, you can require that all such communications occur after hours or away from work to prevent downtime. As supervisors are considered management, you can require a company lawyer to be present when a supervisor is being interviewed (Thierman, 1995).

OSHA Violations and Penalties

OSHA regulation, Section 9(a) requires any OSHA citation to:

- describe the violation with "particularity,"
- reference which standards were violated,
- establish a reasonable time within which to fix the problem, and
- impose any monetary sanctions which might have been levied (Thierman, 1995).

Citations that can be given to an employer are classified in the following categories:

- willful,
- non-willful,
- serious,
- non-serious,
- repeat,
- first-time violation, and
- a failure to abate a previously identified hazard (Thierman, 1995).

Sanctions are based on several factors such as the company size, the gravity of the violation and whether the employer has demonstrated good faith in past matters. In case of serious violations, the beginning rate for penalties starts at $7,000 per violation. Willful violations typically require multiplying the starting penalty by a five, resulting in penalties starting at $35,000. Serious willful violations are multiplied by ten. Each exposure to harm can be a separate violation. Thus, if 30 people were exposed to a serious toxic gas leak, OSHA fines could start at $2.1 million (30 time $70,000). This penalty is designed to punish so the employer would be more inclined never again to break the rules and face even more punishment at a later date (Thierman, 1995).

OSHA utilizes a formula to develop an "adjusted penalty" which can be reduced by an "abatement credit," for quick compliance with any abatement requests. This penalty is designed to help make safety repairs quickly. Otherwise, employers would often delay making necessary repairs until they had excess money to pay for the repairs. In an extreme case, under Section 13(a), a court can issue a restraining order shutting down a business. Criminal penalties can also be imposed for serious violations such as providing advance warning that an OSHA inspection will take place, filing false information with OSHA, assaulting an inspector or willfully violating an OSHA standard when such violations results in an employee's death (Thierman, 1995).

OSHA penalties can also be supplemented with state penalties as states can also fine employers for workplace injuries. One example can be seen from a $8,000 fine levied against Arizona Boring Co. and another contractor working on constructing the Bank One Ballpark in Arizona. State investigators claimed the company violated state law by operating a crane within 10 feet of a power line. The crane came in contact with the power lines sending 7,200 volts through a pipe in which a man was working. The man died as a result of the accident (McCloy, 1997).

In addition to fines, state laws can also impose criminal penalties. Criminal penalties are *not* accessed against corporations or business who can be only fined. Criminal penalties apply to individuals who might face both fines and jail time for violating work safety laws. In California, Penal Code

Section 387 provides for criminal penalties against managers who hide or refuse to report serious concealed dangers to employees (Theirman, 1995). In some state, district attorneys or public prosecutors are being encouraged to bring criminal charges against mid-level managers who create or do not correct unsafe workplace conditions. In Virginia, for example, the State Attorney General has announced plans to bring manslaughter charges against any employer or supervisor who allows unsafe conditions to exist and which eventually cause fatal injuries (Theirman, 1995).

OSHA Defenses

Before dipping into your pocketbook to pay a fine or repair a potential hazard, you should analyze potential affirmative defenses that might get you out of OSHA's wrath. Employers can claim various defenses such as the hazard did not exist, an OSHA standard was not violated, or the hazard was not a workplace hazard. An employer can also claim that the incident was a "isolated instance" in that there were already specific rules covering the hazard, employees were specifically trained to deal with the hazard, and the incident had never occurred in the past. A second affirmative defense is impossibility of compliance where the hazard cannot be avoided as it would be impossible to work without the hazard. Under this defense, an employer can petition OSHA for a variance. A variance allows the employer to continue operating with the hazard without incurring any OSHA violations.

If fixing the hazard would expose the employees to an even greater risk, the employer can use the hazard as an affirmative defense to an OSHA citation. In order to prevail under this theory, the employer must prove that the hazard of compliance is greater than the hazard of noncompliance, alternative compliance means are unavailable, and that a permanent variance would be appropriate. Another affirmative defense can be raised if the OSHA regulations were vague and there is a contradiction between specific regulations and general regulations. Lastly, an employer can claim that OSHA does not have appropriate jurisdiction and that another Federal agency has regulatory control over the employer (Thierman, 1995).

All the defenses can be raised with the Occupational Safety and Health Review Commission within 15 days after the citation is issued. Any decision reached by the appellate law judge can be appealed within 20 days after the judge has made his/her decision. All citations need to be posted for three days. However, during the appeal process, the citation does not need to be publicly posted until all appeals are exhausted. Procedurally, in addition to specific time lines, OSHA regulations specify that the case should be heard before a stenographer or tape recorded. The proceedings are public records. Thus, plaintiffs can use all information discussed at the hearing to benefit any civil case they might pursue. Lastly, the appellate law judge is required to forward his/her decision to the OSHA review board which can either adopt or reject the judge's decision (Thierman, 1995).

While the comprehensive rules outlined above cannot guarantee a safe workplace, the rules set forth minimum government standards for a safe workplace. However, employee safety also extends to dangerous conditions or accidents that occur outside the workplace. An employer is liable for safety outside the workplace when the employee activity involves actions within the employee's scope of employment. Thus, an athletic director is liable for safety-related concerns when participants are transported in a chartered bus and attend a game in a different city's sports facilities.

Scope of Employment

A key component for any alleged workers' compensation claim is the identification of the claim as a type that occurred during the scope of employment. As with the liability for the negligent conduct of an employee (Chapter 5, Section 6), any workers' compensation claim can only be valid if the injury occurred during the scope of performing work to benefit the employer. If an employee is running an errand for his or her boss and is injured in an automotive accident, the employee would be covered under the workers' compensation coverage. However, if the employee ran an errand for the employer, but then went on to do his/her own thing and got injured, workers' compensation coverage would not apply. Thus, the key point of analysis will always focus on what the employee was doing and whether or not such activity was expressly authorized by the employer and whether or not the employee violated any express rules or regulations which might negate coverage.

Scope of employment can sometimes transcend the workplace and affect external activities. One significant concern involves employer mandated or approved sports activities. Claims have been brought for injuries during sports events if:

- the injury occurred on company property and/or during job hours;
- the employer provides uniforms, equipment and encourages participation; and
- if the employer receives some benefit from the activity such as public relation or free advertising (Champion, 1993).

For such activity to fall within workers' compensation coverage, the employee has to show that the injury in fact, occurred within the course of employment. Factors to be considered include:

- was the team registered by the employer and organized in a corporate league;
- is the championship trophy displayed by the employer;
- did the employer pay any entry fees, uniform fees, travel expenses or other costs;
- whether the equipment was stored at the company's premises;
- if the employer's name appears on the uniform or other locations;
- the employer paid for umpires or other officials;
- the employer distributed game schedules and results throughout the office; and
- that if the employer withdrew support for the team, the team would disband (Champion, 1993).

If an injury occurred during the course of employment, the injured individual's injury has to be analyzed to determine the extent to which he/she is possibly disabled. Such injury severity analysis will help determine the individual's disability level and what benefits he/she might receive.

3) Disability Level

Each injury can produce various repercussions. Some injuries heal quickly and produce no long-term residual effects on the employee or his/her work. Other injuries can produce lifelong complications, the inability to work, the need for physical rehabilitation, the need for career changes, counseling or retraining and other long term costs. For example, an employee who loses his/her arm in an industry-related accident would receive workers' compensation coverage for the medical costs associated with the amputation. Thereafter all physical therapy would be covered. Such physical therapy could include retraining the remaining hand (especially if the lost arm was the dominant arm) to write or perform other functions such as dressing through psychiatric counseling to resolve phantom pain issues. If the employee worked in an industry that required two good hands and a prosthesis would not be an effective substitute, then the employee would receive career retraining and placement assistance. All these costs are still covered by workers' compensation insurance. Workers' compensation insurance also covers future medical expenses. Thus, if additional surgeries might be required to lengthen the stump or to cosmetically disguise the stump, such costs would be covered. Additionally, some costs might extend for over 20 or more years for such matters as future prosthesises which can cost over $50,000 each. Often such future expenses are discounted to current dollar value and paid in a lump sum. Thus, a prosthesis user might anticipate purchasing a new devise every 10 year for $40,000 and his/her life expectancy is an additional 30 years, the cost for future prosthesis would be $120,000. The workers' compensation carrier might pay the individual $50,000 now and then be released from any future monetary obligations.

When dealing with large monetary sums, you often have individuals who are interested in abusing the system. Significant abuse has occurred in the soft tissue related injuries. These injuries, such as sore back, strains, sore joints and related conditions are often difficult or impossible to locate using various x-ray techniques. These injuries for years have been the bane of the auto injury litigation arena with people claiming years of therapy and rehabilitation for pain, which might not be provable. While such injuries are not false, they present the opportunity for injured individuals to collaborate with doctors and lawyers to abuse the system. This problem has been a driving force behind "no-fault" auto injury insurance and streamlined workers' compensation laws.

Workers' compensation fraud is a serious issue and should not be overlooked when a relatively small injury languishes for a significant period. Various techniques exist to flush-out potential workers' compensation fraud. Significant media play has been given to various fraud cases where an employee claims they are too sick to work or have back problems, but are then videotaped dancing, putting a roof on a building, or water skiing. Of course, once someone has been caught under these circumstances, his/her workers' compensation coverage is terminated and they are typically referred to law enforcement authorities for insurance fraud prosecution, which could be a felony. Furthermore, an employer or insurance company can sue the individual to recover all moneys paid to the purportedly injured individual.

While most workers' compensation claims are legitimate, there are specific signs that can help uncover potential problem cases. Some signs that can hint to possible workers compensation fraud include:

1) The alleged injury occurred on a Friday afternoon but was not reported until the following Monday. Likewise, if the injury occurred right before or after a planned vacation or federal holiday.
2) The accident occurred immediately after or prior to someone being terminated, a strike, layoff or company bankruptcy.
3) There are no witnesses to the claimed injury.
4) The employee has a pattern of claiming injuries every several months.
5) There was a substantial delay between when the injury occurred and when the claim was filed.
6) The injured employee visited several doctors before finding a doctor who provides significant treatment without a concrete or identifiable diagnosis.

7) There are various versions or descriptions of the injury which differ between the medical reports, insurance claims and/or the injury report.
8) An employer has difficulty reaching the injured individual at his/her home.
9) The injured person refuses to undergo any diagnostic testing designed to confirm the claim.
10) The claimant has recently acquired or increased the value of any disability insurance, which he/she purchased for him/herself.
11) The lawyers or doctors involved in the claim have a history of working with controversial claims.
12) The injured individual often changes his/her doctor or physical therapy provider.
13) The injured person often changes his/her doctor the week or day before he/she is supposed to return to work. These changes often occur without the first treating physician's knowledge.
14) The injured person changes his/her physician after receiving a release to return to work.
15) The injured person consistently misses scheduled doctor appointment(s) without any valid reasons. (Glick, 1997).

While these concerns might not prove fraud, they do represent suspect activity which should be monitored. Workers' compensation fraud could be monitored by requiring copies of all injury-related paper work and analyzing such paperwork to determine if there is a change in doctor(s), insurance carrier or when appointments are scheduled and changed. Lastly, you should closely read any voluntarily produced medical records which can indicate progress or proposed dates to return to work.

Permanent Disabilities

Permanent disabilities involve any condition that is not temporary. Permanent conditions can range from paraplegia to a broken bone which prevents the employee from once again assuming the position they occupied prior to being injured. While paraplegia and quadriplegia represent the most visible and highly publicized permanent injuries, numerous employees have suffered other less obvious permanent injuries. Such injuries include cancer, black lung disease, AIDS and other diseases contracted in the workplace. AIDS represents a critical permanent disability concern in the workplace. In the non-medical environment, the primary AIDS concern arises in industrial accident cases where co-employees are required to render first-aid (Adler and Coleman, 1995). Employees with first-aid experience should be designated as the official first-aid provider for co-employee and customer- related injuries. These employees should be specifically trained in bloodborne disease care and proper disposal of bodily fluids. Furthermore, you should provide each first-aid station with respiratory equipment designed to help prevent the transmission of the AIDS virus.

You also have to focus efforts on informing and educating individuals about AIDS and how the virus is transmitted. This is especially acute in the sports industry where bodily fluid are often dripping on equipment or other people. Employees and customers both need education and reassurance that the facility is safe and the risks associated with bodily fluid contact are minimal.

The EEOC has clarified conflicting questions arising as employers try to comply with both the ADA and workers' compensation laws. The *EEOC Enforcement Guidance* provides the following assistance to help employers understand their obligations.

1) An occupational injury is not synonymous with a disability within the meaning of the ADA. In order to be classified as a disability, as noted in Chapter 4, the employee must have a physical or mental impairment that substantially limits a major life activity, a record of such an impairment or being regarded as having such an impairment. An occupational injury does not qualify as an ADA disability if it is not severe enough to limit a major life activity, or if only temporary, non-chronic, injuries exists without any long term impact.

2) The filing of a workers' compensation claim does not mean that the individual has a "record of" a disability unless he or she has a history of such a disability or has been classified as having a mental or physical impairment that substantially limits one or more major life activities.

3) Disability related questions or medical examinations can be required at the time the employee experiences an occupational injury or when the employee seeks to return to the job following such an injury. However, the questions asked must not exceed the scope of the specific occupational injury and its effect on the employee's ability-with or without reasonable accommodation-to perform essential job functions or to work without posing a direct threat to himself/herself or others.

4) Information relating to occupational injuries must be kept confidential. Similar to the ADA requirements, disclosure of occupational injury information should only be provided to:
   • Direct supervisors and manager,
   • First aid and safety personnel,

- Government officials investigating ADA compliance, and
- State workers' compensation offices, state second injury funds and workers' compensation insurance carriers in accordance with state workers' compensation laws.

5) Decisions to return to work cannot be made based upon presumptions that an employee presents a likely risk for reinjury resulting in increased workers' compensation costs.

6) Employers do not have a responsibility to provide reasonable accommodations for occupational injuries unless they represent a disability as defined by the ADA.

7) An employee with a disability-related occupational injury is entitled to return to the same position unless the employer demonstrates that holding open the position would impose an undue hardship.

8) An employer is not responsible for creating a new position to reassign an employee who can no longer perform essential functions of his or her original position, with or without a reasonable accommodation.

9) An employer cannot substitute vocational rehabilitation services in place of a reasonable accommodation required by the ADA for an employee with a disability-related injury. The ADA requires that a reasonable accommodation be made unless it presents an undue hardship (EEOC, 1997).

Partial Injuries

Partial injuries represent a major concern as they relate to injury management. While an employee might have a minor injury, if the employer does not allow time, equipment or accommodation for the injury to heal or to prevent further damage the injury could lead to significant additional costs. The same concern applies to an employee who suffered a serious injury and is in the recovery period. An employer can pay for the employee to attend an independent medical evaluation to ensure the employee is fit to return to work. Special concerns can be raised by such examinations if a disability affects the employee's return to the workplace in violation of the ADA. Thus, an employee should be allowed to return to work if the examining physician indicates that the employee is fit to perform the necessary job duties which he/she previously performed prior to an injury. An evaluating physician should also specify to the employer whether any special accommodations or retraining are necessary. The ADA might require job accommodations if the person received a serious enough injury that he/she is considered disabled under the ADA's definition.

4) Injury Prevention

Injury prevention is a serious business. Significant dollars are spent on lost work days, medical costs, lost productivity and related concerns which could be significantly reduced through simple risk management steps. Often the same steps that are utilized to make the workplace safe for customers can be utilized to help protect employees. Thus, if security escorts are used to walk customers to their cars, the same individuals should also walk employees to their cars. If an employee is injured while walking to his/her car, such an injury might be considered within his/her scope of employment and would invoke workers' compensation coverage. Furthermore, the injured employee could also sue the employer under potential negligence theories and premises liability theories if the employee's injuries are considered outside the scope of employment.

Ergonomics

The science of workplace design and it's effect on workers is called ergonomics (Neuborne, 1997). A good example of ergonomics in action involved a garment manufacturing company in New York. The business employs 400 workers and had 18 RSI claims in 1994 and paid out approximately $97,000 for these claims. The factory, employing ergonomic theories, installed 400 adjustable chairs and redesigned machines used by most employees. Injuries dropped from 18 to five and workers' compensation costs dropped to only $4,500 in 1996 (Neuborne, 1997).

OSHA is currently pursuing implementing new ergonomic rules for the workplace. OSHA estimated that if their proposed standards are adopted, it could cost business about $4.5 billion annually. The cornerstone of the ergonomic rules relate to a set of risk factors and corresponding limits that employers would have to identify. These risk factors include:

- performing the same motion(s) for more than two hours at a time,
- using vibrating tools or machines for more than two hours a day,
- handling 25 or more pound objects more than once in a work shift,
- working in fixed or awkward positions for more than two hours at a time, and
- performing mechanically or electronically-paced work for more than four hours at a time.

Based on the complexities associated with these rules and associated compliance costs, the rules brought stiff congressional opposition in 1995, but will probably be reconsidered as the number of repetitive stress injuries increase (Warner, 1997).

OSHA is also considering a proposed minimum federal standard for employer safety and health programs. A 1995 draft of the regulations included a provision that the employer would have to inspect his/her work site as "often as is necessary" or when "appropriate" to identify potential hazards. Such terms are argued as being too vague for enforcement purposes. While no one argues that safety-and-health programs reduce/prevent injuries and reduce workers' compensation claims, many employers feel that the federal government should not be mandating or penalizing employers for not implementing such programs. Another concern involves potential implementation wherein an employer might pay significant amounts for a program, which might not meet federal standards even though the employer's program reduces injuries (Warner, 1997).

While federal regulations are on hold, California became the first state to enforce repetitive motion injury (RMI) standards in the workplace. The regulations require employers to conduct site evaluations, educate employees and redesign the work environment whenever a physician identifies and diagnosis two or more RMI cases within a 12 month period as being predominantly work related. An employer is required to make changes to prevent further injuries unless the changes incur unreasonable costs. Since there is no exact definition of unreasonable costs, employers are left to determine if they should pay a consultant thousands of dollars or pay a Cal-OSHA fine which typically run about $7,000 (Edson, 1997).

Crime Prevention Through Environmental Design (CPTED)

A distant relative to ergonomics is CPTED-crime prevention through environmental design, which focuses on making the workplace and facilities or program safer for employees and customers. (Smith, 1996). CPTED can be implemented through designing work areas so crimes become more difficult to perpetrate. Thus, a cashier's booth could be designed so that see-through glass is placed at waist level so managers can see if a cashier is trying to pocket any money. You can also help reduce the potential for assaults on the cashier as witnesses can see all activities going on inside the booth and if posters or letters were posted on the walls, witnesses might not have an opportunity to see any assault. Environmental design can be utilized for more than just crime prevention. CPTED and related environmental risk reduction techniques are also designed to help employers create a safe work environment before any employees start their work. Thus, if a workplace requires wet parts to be moved from one location to a another, that space should be minimized and appropriate drainage and non-skid surfaces can be installed. CEPTED is just one technique to promote workplace safety.

Management Support

Good management is another technique that can help reduce workplace injuries. A critical concern for effectively managing workers' compensation entails acquiring "buy-in" from top managers. An incentive compensation plan can be implemented to reward managers who reduce the number of claims generated by individuals on their shift or under their command. An appropriate adage states, "control their pocketbook and their hearts and minds will follow," should form the basis of rewarding managers and employees who help reduce workers' compensation claim numbers and costs (Glick, 1997). In addition to receiving management support, safety and injury prevention normally requires "buy-in" from all employees.

Safety Committees

Management should organize a safety committee comprised of managers and various lower level employees who consistently work in environments with hazardous surroundings such as pools, food service, maintenance, weight room, and related program areas. The safety committee can be empowered to:

- analyze safety concerns,
- suggest potential safety precautions,
- help develop a safety manual,
- help update the safety manual,
- help train other employees and
- assume overall responsibility associated with safety matters.

Committee members can be motivated through financial incentives and/or job enrichment. One inexpensive incentive is to split any workers' compensation insurance rebate or dividend with committee members. Thus, if the committee helps implement a significant risk management plan that reduces claims and results in a "mod rate" that saves an employer $10,000 in a given year, the committee could receive $5,000 of this savings to be split evenly between the committee members.

Besides being an effective risk management tool, a safety committee also might be required by state law. Nevada, Oregon and Washington all require employers with eleven or more employees to establish safety committees (Thierman, 1995). You are required to do more than just establish safety committees (if you utilize them), you are also required to act upon their recommendations. The safety committees should:

- meet at least once a month to discuss current issues,
- prepare minutes from all meetings,
- make periodic site inspections,
- review all incident/injury reports,
- review any safety complaints, and
- process any safety suggestions/recommendations (Thierman, 1995).

While safety committees appear to be a win-win proposition, several major problems arise from utilizing such committees. The primary concern associated with safety committees relates to potentially inadvertent unionization, which is discussed below.

Unions and Safety Committees

A major concern with safety committees involves unions and safety committees. Under the National Labor Relations Act (NLRA) if the safety committees have certain characteristics they can be defined as labor organizations or unions and therefore fall under the NLRA regulations (Zaccardi, 1995). Labor organizations are defined as entities that are based on employee participation, exist in part to help "deal with" the employer, and address critical issues relating to the working environment including wage, hours and safety issues (See Chapter 14). If the safety committee meets the definition of a labor organization and the committee is dominated by management, then the employer has committed an unfair labor practice (Zaccardi, 1995). An employer who has committed an unfair labor practice through the safety committee could have the committee dissolved, all the actions undertaken by the committee reversed, and the employer could be fined. To help avoid this concern, the safety committee should be comprised primarily by workers and have very few managers. Furthermore, the committee could be used as a brainstorming group, rather than a policy group. Through just brainstorming, the element of "dealing with" the employer is eliminated and the suggestions serve as a resource for the employer. Similarly, the committee is not dealing with management when it works to acquire, synthesize and share information or conduct educational programs (Zaccardi, 1995). The key question that will be raised if an unfair labor practices allegation is raised is whether or not the employer is merely cooperating with he committee or controlling and influencing the committee.

Injury Reporting

While incident reporting is not a prevention issue, it does represent a financial consequences issue. Besides potential fines for inaccurate or non-reporting (See also Chapter 6, Section 5), statistics show that the later a claim is filed, the larger the final payment is to resolve the claim (Glick, 1997). A recent study by Kemper National Insurance Co. concluded that claims filed 30 days after the injury date typically resulted in payments 50 percent greater than claims filed immediately after an injury (Glick, 1997). Promptness is critical for filing claims and for processing all applicable paperwork. Doctor bills and hospital charges should be processed immediately to ensure that fees do not exceed the amounts agreed to by the state compensation board (Glick, 1997). Thus, it is imperative to encourage employees to immediately report any illness or injury and a reward or punishment system can be included within the employee manual to help encourage immediate reporting (See Chapter 6). Appendix X contains a copy of an incident reporting policy and necessary forms that will be useful for evaluating and tracking workplace injuries.

Each employer, company and facility present different risk factors and degrees which requires a commitment from management to:

- obtain employee involvement and commitment,
- produce a thorough and complete documentation and record keeping program,
- identify, assess, control and prevent hazardous situations.
- assign responsibility, authority and accountability for safety compliance,
- commit appropriate resources and authority for proper accident investigation.
- commit appropriate resource, both internal and external for accident and injury prevention,
- provide appropriate and thorough safety training, and
- annually review all safety concern, workers' compensation coverage and injury reports,

After developing a company wide commitment to reducing injuries and providing a safer work environment, management is responsible for providing proper safety training. OSHA has developed specific voluntary training guidelines to help properly train employees. The first step in any training process is determining whether or not training is needed. If the employees collectively work to create a safe environment and have their own process in place that works, do not tinker with such a system. Training should not be developed and implemented just for the sake of having training. That is why training is voluntary under OSHA.

Safety Training

If safety training is adopted, specific goals and objectives need to be established and approved by all the affected parties. Next, specific educational activities need to be adopted. Various companies offer safety training. Safety training can be as simple as requiring employees to take a Red Cross CPR class to intensive training program on high pressure press machinery. Training does not need to be provided to address every safety concern. The most serious concerns that can result in fatalities or serious injuries should receive the highest consideration when developing a training hierarchy. A training timetable should also be established delineating when training should occur for all employees and what training courses (and in what order) need to be taken by new employees. Training scheduling also should consider employees who are changing their position within the company and possibly using different equipment.

As with any educational program, the training has to be informative and interesting for those receiving the training. Interest can be maintained by regularly introducing new training programs and requiring participation for employees to keep their jobs. New training programs are often created for all employees when new hazards are identified, new government regulations are promulgated, new equipment is purchased and when new industry standards are created. To maximize interest training programs are often modified based on such factors as the trainees' age, experience, culture, gender, length of seniority with the company, the company size (will training sessions be split to address only 20 employees at a time?), whether numerous hazards exist and whether the training offered by existing training providers might not need to be modified (thus, saving the employer significant time and money).

To assist the effectiveness of the training process, it is critical to supplement the training with written handouts that the employees can refer to at later times. The Safety Manual (discussed below) should be contained in a three ring binder with enough space that allows training materials to be added for different employees or workstations. Postings should be hung in prominent areas such as water cooler, time clock, employee kitchen, and any other areas where employees congregate. Such postings should highlight training issues and provide safety information in an understandable manner. OSHA produces specific posters that help fulfill safety-posting requirements (see also Chapter 6).

Evaluation

As with any new program, the program has to be measured at a certain point to determine its effectiveness. Benchmarks should be established prior to launching the safety-training program. Typical benchmarks analyze how many injuries and injury types were reported in the previous year. If a new venture establishes a training program, information on industry trends can be obtained from insurance companies, industry trade association or from similar businesses in other communities. These benchmarks can be evaluated with data obtained after the proscribed analysis period, which is typically one year. If the number of injuries has not gone down, there might be other factors which should be analyzed before determining whether the training program was successful. The number of serious injuries should be analyzed. Likewise, the type of injuries that occurred, the number of absent days, the total amount of compensation paid out and related critical insurance concerns issues should be analyzed to determine if the training program was effective.

In addition to looking at the straight numbers, it is imperative to get feedback from the people undergoing training to determine if they perceive any intangible benefits. Do the trainees feel the employer is investing in their future? Is the employer helping the employees expand their skills and train for higher level positions? Is the employer looking-out for employee safety? After thoroughly analyzing the program benefits and drawbacks, management has to determine if the program is effective enough to warrant continuation, whether the program should be terminated, or whether changes are needed. Besides the managerial benefits associated with this analysis, such actions can reduce liability concerns by demonstrating that you are doing everything within you power to create a safer environment and the data will hopefully support your assertions.

Record Keeping

A critical and legally required component, in any safety plan revolves around proper record keeping. Under OSHA regulations, accident information needs to be reported on an OSHA 200 Log. OSHA regulations set forth specific reporting requirements including:

- reporting on every injury or illness which requires hospitalization,
- recording the illness or injury on the OSHA 200 Log,
- reporting the injury on an Employer's Report of Injury or Illness such as Supplemental Record, Form 101.
- synthesizing all the previous year's injuries and illnesses from OSHA 200 Logs and posting the summary in a visible location no later than February 1(it cannot be removed before March 1) and have copies available on request, and
- maintaining all injury and illness records for at least five years (for employees under age eighteen). While OSHA does not require it, you should keep injury records for at least eight years, which would generally mean that they have reached majority age and the statute of limitations has passed-barring any suit. If the records are disposed while the individual could still bring a suit, the employer could be sued under the theory of "spoliation of evidence" the destruction of evidence.

Copies of all necessary OSHA forms can be obtained at OSHA offices listed in appendix Y.

5) Investigation

When an accident has occurred, it is management's top priority to thoroughly investigate the injury or illness. Investigation serves several very important purposes. Investigation could hopefully pinpoint any hazard to prevent the same or similar injuries from occurring to other employees. Investigation also provides the employer with notice that a hazardous condition exists. Once on notice, the employer is required to eliminate, reduce and warn employees about the potential hazard or the employer would have breached his/her duty to employees and customers. Investigation also helps expose potential problems such as miscommunication, using improper technique or utilizing incorrect equipment. These issues can be addressed through re-training or modifying the training procedures.

Third Party Liability

Investigation also serves the benefit of placing the blame. Workers' compensation is a no fault system. Thus, if an employee is completely at fault, you cannot raise an assumption of risk or contributory negligence claim against him/her to reduce damages. While an employer might not be able to place blame at the injured employee's feet, blame can be placed on other employees or unrelated individuals. Other employees can be sued if they engaged in willful, reckless misconduct or if they acted outside their job scope or job description (See Chapter 5). For example, if an employee decides he wants to try archery in the gymnasium during his lunch break, most people would consider such action outside the scope of their employment. If an arrow is shot and hit a custodian who is cleaning the floor then the workers' compensation coverage changes. While the custodian can file a workers' compensation claim, he/she also could file a civil suit against the shooter. Even if the custodian does not want to file suit against the shooter, the employer or insurance carrier can sue the shooter. The employer can sue for all expenses incurred such as replacement workers, lost benefits and related costs. The workers' compensation carrier would sue for all losses incurred and will continue to incur.

Joinder by Insurer

As the workers' compensation carrier has paid out money to cover medical costs and associated expenses, if the employee bring a suit against a third-party who contributed or directly caused the injury then the workers' compensation carrier can assess a lien on the suit to recover expenses. For example, if the custodian in the example above decides to sue the negligent employee, the suit would probably proceed as follows. The workers' compensation carrier would regularly ask the custodian if a suit had been filed (if the custodian lies trying to keep the insurance company out of the loop, then he could be liable for insurance fraud). If the custodian does file suit, the insurance company could either join or put a lien on the case. If the case is very difficult or if there is a chance the custodian might lose, joinder allows the insurance company to become a party to the suit and be involved in all pre-trial discovery and the actual trial. If the insurance carrier just has a lien, the lien becomes effective only when the case is settled or the jury returns a verdict for the custodian. In either a joinder or lien, if the custodian loses, the insurance carrier receives nothing. However, if the custodian wins, any recovery first goes to the insurance company and then to the custodian. Thus, if the custodian recovers $500,000 at trial, and if medical bills paid by the carrier total $200,000 then the workers' compensation carrier receives their share first. The remaining amount ($300,000) has to be split between the custodian and his/her attorney. If the employer is also involved in the suit, he/she could possibly split his/her share proportionately with the insurance company. Thus, if the jury only returns a verdict of $150,000 and the medical bills are $200,000 and the employer spent $50,000 the two could receive and possibly split the entire $150,000 verdict with the carrier receiving $112,500 and the employer receiving $37,500. It should be noted that the final payments and percentage retained by each party is always negotiable between the parties.

External Investigators and Techniques

As these numbers demonstrate, there is often a significant dollar amount at stake. That is why it is so important to properly investigate all injuries or illness. In addition to internal investigations, other entities might also conduct an investigation. Sometimes the workers' compensation carrier will send out investigators. This investigator might try to discover whether or not to shift blame to others and/or to reduce their ultimate costs. Additionally, in serious injury cases or fatality cases, OSHA often sends investigators. Police and fire department personnel might also undertake some investigation. If any parties undertake any investigation, it is critical that you receive copies of all reports and conclusions reached by these investigators. As part of your monitoring process, you have to determine what any investigator took from the scene, what potential tests were performed on the evidence and by whom.

Proper investigation involves utilizing tact and ingenuity. It never makes sense to attack the injured parties or place blame at their feet if the employer has not thoroughly investigated the matter. In fact, pointing an accusatory finger could be the proverbial straw that breaks the camel back, which motivates the employee to sue. Further, if the employer's accusations are incorrect the injured employee might now be armed with a potential libel or slander claim.

When investigating the incident, managers should visit the injury site as soon as possible. If a serious accident or death occurred, the area should be shut-off or roped-off to prevent any tampering. While this might be an inconvenience, it is the required course of conduct. After any investigation is completed by any outside government agencies, it is often worthwhile for employers to conduct their own investigation. Any samples (such as chemical) from the accident should be preserved. This is especially important when there is a defective product that possibly caused the injury and it is critical that you preserve the potential product liability claim.

All witnesses should be questioned thoroughly. No witnesses should ever be intimidated or forced not to disclose relevant facts. Such actions can result in insurance forfeiture from the workers' compensation carrier. Special attention should be focused on what witnesses saw, heard, smelled or felt. If a controversy exists, the employer should try and obtained signed statements as soon as possible form witnesses. This would prevent witness coaching which can be performed to plant new observations or opinions into a witness. If a witness did not hear, see, smell or otherwise know what occurred, they should be asked to sign a statement to this effect. Appendix Z contains a witness statement form that can be used to document observations or indicate that a bystander did not witness anything.

6) Safety Manuals

Knowledge provides the greatest weapon in reducing work place injuries. As with all educational tools, oral warnings and instructions only go so far. That is why written safety manuals represent a necessary risk management tool. Additionally, it is the law. OSHA requires all covered employers to develop an effective occupational safety plan that must address: management commitment, employee involvement, work site analysis, hazard prevention, and employee training (Thierman, 1995). While The federal regulations do not require the plan to be in writing, the best evidence that a plan is in place can only come from a distributed safety manual.

OSHA regulations require two basic sections within a developed safety plan or policy. OSHA first requires a "process" section discussing how OSHA works and employee rights. OSHA then requires several "safety" sections which presents specific rules appropriate for that employer or industry (Thierman, 1995).

In addition to OSHA requirements, states also might require written safety plans. In California, a 1990 law requires employers to maintain a written illness and injury prevention policy. California is not alone, seven other states also require written safety plans including, Alaska, Hawaii, Minnesota, Nevada, Oregon and Washington (Thierman, 1995). These states require among other elements, a written plan, designating a safety representative, establishing a compliance system, ensuring effective plan communication, a risk management plan for identifying workplace hazards including inspection schedules, a method for reporting unsafe condition and employee training practices (Thierman, 1995).

Safety Audit

The first step necessary to develop a comprehensive safety manual involves conducting a thorough safety and health audit. Items that should be reviewed during this audit include:

Equipment — List all tools and equipment and any safety concerns which they might pose (i.e. power tools could cut or puncture a user) and then provide specific suggestions as to how the threat of injury could be reduced (i.e. saw or drill guards), when the equipment needs to be inspected or maintained and how the equipment should be maintained.

Facility—Examine the facility layout to determine safe exit routes and where emergency equipment such as eye wash stations, fire extinguishers, phones and first-aid kits can be located. Additional concerns include monitoring ventilation quality, smoking within the facility and opportunities to utilize restrooms.

Chemicals—A list should be prepared for all chemicals used in the facility. If any chemicals are listed as more than standard household cleaners, such as chlorine, an OSHA Material Safety Data Sheet on the chemicals or materials should be used. All chemicals should be properly stored and appropriately labeled. MSDS sheets need to identify the chemical, indicate physical and chemical characteristics, identify physical hazards (i.e., the potential for fire or explosion), known potential health effects, precautions for safe handling, first aid procedures and related issues. The MSDS needs to be completed in its entirety. MSDS are often not a major concern as the chemical's manufacturer, distributor or seller often provides complete sheets. The MSDS needs to be posted in a reasonably visible area.

Working Conditions—Special attention should be given to observe the work environment to determine if employees have to engage in certain repetitive motions, or follow safety rules, utilize appropriate tools and properly store hazardous equipment.

Safety Rules—Does the employer currently follow all applicable state and federal safety rules? The safety survey should analyze whether OSHA and state rules are sometimes followed, always followed, or never followed and the reasons why an employee fail to properly conform his or her conduct.

Prior Incident—The audit should critically analyze prior incidents to help determine what safety techniques are working and where improvements can be made. Issues that should be critically analyzed include:

- What days do accidents normally occur (i.e. are Mondays the most common day when accidents occur, or Fridays when people are anxious to leave the office)?
- During what time of the day do most injuries occur (i.e. are they most often occurring first thing in the morning or at the end of the day when more people are tired or rushing to leave)?
- What is the absenteeism and turnover rate?
- Has there been any prior safety committee, meetings, policies or manuals?
- What training has been provided to workers?
- Have the employer ever received any prior OSHA citations?

- Are all required notices and posters hanging in appropriate areas?
- Have you reviewed current workers compensation policies?
- Have you analyzed current workers' compensation policy premiums?

Safety Manual

Once an audit has been completed, a comprehensive safety manual can be developed from the various concerns identified through the audit process. Most safety manuals have several components including prevention, resources, safe practices, safe procedures, special applications and industry specific concerns (Thierman, 1995). No one safety manual is absolutely correct. Each manual is and should be different. Thus, you should never photocopy another employer's safety manual and utilize that manual without first adapting the manual to specifically address unique concerns in your workplace. You should also make sure that any safety manual that you might implement reflects any specific safety bias you might have. Thus, if hazardous chemicals are your most important concern, then more emphasis needs to be placed on covering that topic.

The prevention and safe work practices section focuses on the reason the manual was produced...to reduce injuries, comply with the law and operate a smooth and efficient organization. This section should describe the employer's dedication to risk management as it applies to a safe work environment. The safety committee, if any, should be described as well as discussing how training will be implemented, what goals are expected and what benefit can be obtained by the employees if they reduce injuries and illnesses.

A code of general safe work practices set forth basic safety concerns which apply to all employees. Such basic rules could relate to noise hazards, electrical hazards, material handling concerns, employee transportation concerns, kitchen safety, ventilation hazards, ergonomic principals, infection control, general fire safety, how to handle power tools and related concerns (Thierman, 1995).

Handling Blood-Based Concerns

Special attention should be paid to specific industry work practices that might be unique to the sports, recreation and fitness industries. One such concern involves individuals (patrons and employees) who suffer cuts, bruises or other injuries that result in bleeding. OSHA has established clear standards for medical and non-medical employees who come in contact with blood borne pathogens. The standards address various concerns such as human immunodeficiency (HIV) virus, hepatitis B (HBV) virus, hepatitis C, malaria, syphilis, babesiosis, brucellosis, leptrospirosis, arboviral, relapsing fever, Creutzfeld-Jakob disease, Human T-lymphotrophic Virus Type 1 and viral hermorrhagic fever (Thierman, 1995). The OSHA standards address these concerns and require the employer to report even simple accidents such as needle pricks and routine cuts. The safety manual should specifically address all the issues associated with handling blood related injuries. Everything from blood stained garment disposal to appropriate cleaning procedures after someone drips blood should be addressed.

Blood-borne pathogens are a special concern for sport employees. Extensive OSHA regulations cover handling blood-borne pathogens and some of these regulations are reprinted below.

1) Hand washing facilities or appropriate alternatives need to be assessable to all employees.
2) Container for handling potentially infectious materials must be appropriately labeled or color- coded prior to being stored, shipped, transported or appropriately disposed by an appropriate waste management company.
3) The employer must document each and every time employees fail to use required safety equipment.
4) Garments with blood on them must be immediately removed and properly disposed.
5) Contaminated surfaces must be decontaminated with appropriate disinfectants, especially when blood is spilled as hepatitis cells can survive several days on an uncleaned surface.
6) Contaminated laundry (e.g. blood stained shirt) must be handled with gloves and when sent out for cleaning, the laundry should be appropriately labeled identifying the hazard.
7) All employers must make the hepatitis B vaccine and vaccination series available to all employees who have occupational exposure (e.g. personal trainers, masseuses, lifeguards, etc.). Employees who refuse to receive vaccinations are required to sign an OSHA prepared statement that they refused the vaccination.
8) All employers must provide employees with post-exposure examinations, evaluation and follow- up after any exposure incident.
9) Employers must provide employee training for every employee who is regularly exposed to occupational exposures.
10) Develop, adopt and implement a hazard communication plan to handle all facets of a hazard incident from media relations to contacting EMTs.

Such rules are not designed for show. Especially in the sport area, these rules need to be closely followed. In a recent survey, 73% of student trainers surveyed had direct contact with blood/body fluid at least once a year. In addition, 61% of the trainers had contact with blood or bodily fluid between two to five times a year. These students who had contact with OSHA covered hazards only utilized gloves 42.5% of the time and 79% indicated they would perform CPR on an athlete who was bleeding from the mouth (Claussen, 1995). The National Collegiate Athletic Association conducted a recent study wherein 40% of the surveyed head athletic trainers at NCAA member universities regularly followed universal precautions for dealing with blood and bodily fluids. As would be expected, student and assistant trainers used such precautions less frequently (Claussen, 1995).

Tracking Hazardous Chemicals

Additional attention needs to be documented for dealing with hazardous chemicals. The safety manual should set forth a specific person as the chemical safety officer who should be responsible for the hazardous chemical inventory list, Material Safety Data Sheet, all labels and warnings, employee training and program evaluation.

To assist in the preparation of safety manuals, the authors recommend contacting your Regional OSHA office for specific forms that could be included in the three-ring safety manual binder or summarized with the information incorporated within the manual. The following forms are the most applicable to the sports, fitness and recreation industries. Other forms are also available through OSHA, which has an extensive collection of prepared forms in both English and Spanish.

2001 Occupational Safety & Health Act of 1970 (English or Spanish)
2098 OSHA Inspection
2203 Job Safety and Health Protection-Poster
2221 How OSHA Monitors State Plans
3021 OSHA: Employee Workplace Rights
3029 OSHA: Your Workplace Rights in Action
3046 Office of the Occupational Safety & Health Administration-Poster
3047 Consultation Services for the Employer
3118 You Have a Right to Job Safety & Health...It's the Law-Poster
3127 Occupational Exposure to Bloodborne Pathogens
3128 Bloodborne Pathogens and Acute Care Facilities

3132 Process Safety Management
3133 Process Safety Management Guidelines for Compliance
1904 Recordkeeping Req. for Occ. Injuries & Illnesses
1904 A Brief Guide to Recordkeeping Req. for Occ. Injuries
& Illnesses
Report 814 Evaluating Your Firm's Injury and Illness Record:
Service Industries
Form 200 Log & Summary of Occ. Injuries & Illnesses
Form 174 Material Safety Data Sheet (MSDS)
Safety & Health Pro. Mgmt. Guidelines; Issuance of Voluntary
Guidelines

OSHA INSTRUCTIONS
CPL 2-2.44C Enforcement Procedures for Occupational
Exposure to Bloodborne Pathogens Standard, 29 CFR
1910.1030 (3/6/92)

FACT SHEETS
89-09 Back Injuries-Nation's Number One Workplace Safety
Problem
91-35 OSHA: Employee Workplace Rights & Responsibilities
91-37 Voluntary Safety & Health Program Management Guidelines
91-41 Workplace Fire Safety
91-43 OSHA Help for New Businesses
91-44 OSHA Emergency Hot Line
92-01 Job Safety & Health
92-02 Inspecting for Job Safety & Health Hazard
92-03 Eye Protection in the Workplace
92-04 The OSHA Consultation Service
92-05 General OSHA Recordkeeping Requirements
92-07 Improving Workplace Protection for New Workers
92-10 Voluntary Protection Programs
92-12 Variances Under OSHA
92-14 Setting Occupational Safety & Health Standards
92-15 State Job Safety & Health Programs
92-16 Protecting Workers in Hot Environments
92-19 Responding to Workplace Emergencies
92-22 Where to Apply for Variances from OSHA Standards
92-36 New OSHA Penalties Policy
Bloodborne Facts-Holding the Line on Contamination
Bloodborne Facts- Personal Protective Equipment Cuts Risk
Bloodborne Facts-Reporting Exposure Incidents
Bloodborne Facts-Hepatitis B Vaccination-Protection For You
Bloodborne Facts-Protect Yourself When Handling Sharps

Wrap Up...

We all assume that we can go to work, and be safe in that environment. As demonstrated throughout this chapter, that is not always the case. While it is impossible to avoid all workplace accidents and injuries, a conscientious employer can help reduce the likelihood that injuries might occur. The first key to injury avoidance in the workplace entails properly ensuring yourself from various risks-especially injuries that can prevent an employee from ever returning back to work. Insurance compliance, including appropriate workers' compensation coverage requires a thorough understanding of the various federal and state laws which impose themselves on all employers.

OSHA compliance is one critical federal law that is frequently violated due to inadequate knowledge of the law. Communication once again plays a key role in avoiding litigation and unnecessary fines. As an employer, you have an obligation to effectively provide an environment wherein all safety-related concerns are communicated to all employees. An effective means for communicating safety concerns and risk management strategies entails developing, writing, distributing and effectively communicating concerns through a safety manual. A safety manual should clearly communicate concerns in a language all employees can understand and should be updated whenever a workplace changes. In the every changing sport field, new risks are frequently arising. In the 1960s, several key cases involving electrocution in locker rooms graced legal clippings. In the 1970s, trampolines represented a significant liability concern. The 1980s brought significant additional and continued litigation associated with football helmets. In the 1990s, significant litigation is being brought alleging unsafe sports facilities. If facilities are unsafe for patrons, they are likely unsafe for employees as well. Thus, significant attention has to be given to making the workplace as safe as possible. Specific techniques that can help make the workplace safer includes:

- educating employees about bloodborne pathogen related issues,
- how to clean-up spilled bodily fluids,
- how to identify tripping, slipping and falling risks,
- how to report hazardous conditions,
- how to follow-up when hazardous conditions are not repaired, and
- developing specific hazardous condition reporting forms.

References

Adler, R., and Coleman, F. (1995). *Employment-Labor Law Audit.* Washington, DC: BNA, Inc.

Bates, S. (1997). "OSHA revised rules on injury records." *Nation's Business* (May): 9.

Blakely, S. (1997). "Costly numbers in workers' comp." *Nation's Business* (September): 40.

Champion, Jr., Walter T. (1993). *Sports Law in a Nutshell.* St. Paul, MN: West Publishing Co.

Claussen, C.L. (1995). "Title IX and employment discrimination in coaching intercollegiate athletics." *Entertainment & Sports Law Review* 12 (1, 2): 149–168.

Coleman, B. (1997). "Job-related injuries, illness take heavy toll." *Houston Chronicle* (July 28): 1A.

Edson, J. (1997). "Through the motions, employment law." *Los Angeles Daily Journal* (July 24): 14.

EEOC (1997). *EEOC enforcement guidance on the ADA and psychiatric disabilities.* Washington, DC: U.S. EEOC.

Glick, P. (1997). "Workers' compensation fraud." *Parking Today* March, 2(2): 26.

McCloy, M. (1997). "$8,000 in fines urged in ballpark death." *The Arizona Republic* (February 14): B1.

Neuborne, E. (1997). "Workers in pain, employers up in arms." *USA Today* (January 9): B1.

Rothstein, M., Knapp, A., and Liebman, L. (1987). *Employment Law, Cases and Material.* New York: The Foundation Press, Inc.

Smith, M. (1996). "Crime prevention through environmental design in parking facilities." *National Institute of Justice, Research in Brief* (April).

Swoboda, F. (1997). "Report connects work, motion injuries." *Houston Chronicle* (July 2): 2C.

Thierman, M. (1995). *SafetyPlan builder.* Mountain View, CA: JIAN Tools For Sales, Inc.

Walsh, J. (1995). *Mastering diversity.* Santa Monica, CA: Merritt Publishing.

Warner, D. (1997). "OSHA is moving on ergonomics rule." *Nation's Business* (August): 29.

Warner, D. (1997). "A rule mandating safety and health?" *Nation's Business* (September): 28.

Zaccardi, H., and McDonald, S. (1995). "Worker safety committees and the law." *Occupational Health and Safety* (November): 48.

Cases

Marshall v. Barlows, Inc., 434 U.S. 307 (1978).
Marshall v. North American Car Co., 626 F.2d 320 (3rd Cir. 1980).
Textron v. Marshall, 625 F.2d 1313 (7th Cir. 1980).

Statutes

29 CFR 1900.
California Penal Code.
Federal Employees' Compensation Act (FECA), 5 U.S.C.S. 8101–8193
    et seq.
Federal Employers' Liability Act (FELA), 45 U.S.C.S. 51–60.
Jones Act, 46 U.S.C.S. 688.
Longshoremen's and Harbor Workers' Compensation Act (LHWCA),
    33 U.S.C.S. 901–950.
OSHA, 29 U.S.C.A. Section 651–678.
OSHA Regulation, Section 8(e).
OSHA Regulation, Section 9(a).
OSHA Regulation, Section 13(a).
Social Security Act, 42 U.S.C.A. Section 404.1901 et seq.
Social Security Disability Act, 42 U.S.C.S. 423 et seq.

Chapter 12

Termination of the Employee

A critical, but extremely difficult decision faced by all managers involves terminating an employee. Many issues are raised when deciding whether or not to terminate an employee.

- Will the termination effect any existing friendship with the employee?
- How will co-workers react to the termination?
- Will co-workers demonstrate hostility towards management?
- Will the terminated employee become violent?
- Will the terminated employee retaliate against the business or other employees?
- Has management done everything within its power to give the employee a chance to redeem him or herself?
- Did the employee perform such an egregious act that he/she did not deserve a "second chance"?
- Has the entire termination process been adequately documented?

These represent some key questions that have to be addressed prior to terminating any employee. Wrong answers can be costly as wrongful termination suits have very large potential awards as demonstrated by the following survey results of various jury verdicts from 1988 through 1994:

- Age bias claims averaged $219,000
- Race bias claims averaged $147,799
- Gender bias claims averaged $106,728
- Disability bias claims averaged $100,345
- Pregnancy bias claims averaged $87,500
- Sexual harassment claims averaged $38,500 (USA Snapshots, 1996)

Age bias awards are traditionally the largest wrongful termination awards as employees fitting within the Age Discrimination in Employment Act (ADEA) protection normally have higher salaries and are therefore awarded greater amounts for lost current and future wages.

Industry experts agree that termination is the only recourse in certain circumstances. Thus, while under performance can be coached or corrected, once an employee engages in stealing, most people would not expect that person would stop their stealing (Quintanilla, 1997). Even if the termination was justified, this does not prevent a former employee from suing for wrongful termination. Most people do not want to admit they were wrong or performed poorly. That is one reason why the Equal Employment Opportunity Commission estimates that nearly half the cases it receives involve wrongful termination charges (Quintanilla, 1997). One concern associated with wrongful termination claims is that the back-pay meter, which can be awarded to a successful litigant, begins to run when the employee is terminated. As a terminated employee can utilize the legal process for several years and exhaust several appeals, a successful litigant could generate several hundred thousand dollars in back-pay over several years.

How to Terminate an Employee

Before analyzing the reasons for termination, contractual concerns and discriminatory concerns, it is imperative to at least provide some examples showing how terminations are accomplished.

Every employer utilizes different techniques to determine if an employee should be retained or terminated. Some techniques are simple such as determining if an employee is accomplishing his/her assigned duties. For example, a former cleaning person's boss hid trash around a facility to see if the employee found it (Quintanilla, 1997). Such measures are not uncommon to test an employee's performance or commitment. One of this guide's authors had a friend who was offered $2,000 to copy a trademark protected computer diskette. He refused. It turned out the offer was just a test by the employer to determine his commitment. If he accepted the money, he would have been paid and then terminated. By refusing to do the illegal act, he was promoted and received a $4,000 pay raise.

The examples above demonstrate that there is no one best method to terminate an employee. Some employers like to wait until the end of the day or pay period before terminating an employee. Others do not like to avoid the inevitable and terminate immediately after an incident occurs. Others, suspend employees and when the employee is at home, terminate him/her to avoid a scene or at-work confrontation. Other employers utilize the one-on-one execution technique which has several variations such as the bait and switch wherein the employer offers a position for the doomed employee that is too good to pass-up. Once the employee takes that position, the old position is filled and then the employer cuts back and eliminates the new position. Other employers try to make the employee feel so bad or worthless that the employee quits. Still other employers start withholding resources or assistance which make it impossible for an employee to perform well and helps produce negative employee evaluations. Yet other employers promote an unqualified individual to a higher position with the expectation that they will flounder and eventually quit from the pressure (Sixel, 1995).

While such techniques can be successful in running off an employee, they can also lead to litigation under the constructive discharge theory. The constructive discharge theory alleges that the employer or other employees made the work environment so impossible that an employee can no longer function. Thus, an assistant coach who is prohibited from having any interaction with players, not allowed to travel with the team and is shunned by all other coaches and administrators could claim that such conduct forced the coach to quit.

Some consultant recommends wearing open clothes when terminating an employee. Open clothes include avoiding turtlenecks, pin-stripe suits, sharp lines, black, and geometric ties (Quintanilla, 1997). This approach is designed to make you appear less domineering or authoritative, which can reduce potential negativism. In addition to appearing the proper way, the consultant recommended taking pre-planned steps to reduce confusion and spur-of-the-moment decisions or statements that might imply discriminatory intent. For example, if an employee is terminated at the end of the day, make sure a policy is in place delineating who will empty-out the employee's desk. If the company will empty the desk and send everything to the terminated employee, the individual should be assured that proper care will be taken to prevent any property breakage. Additional steps could include:

- changing computer passwords,
- securing company property (credit cards, cars, keys, permits, computers, etc.),
- having security guards, doctors and counselors available if necessary,
- practicing pre-approved dismissal speeches,
- returning any employee identification cards, badges or business cards,
- returning company property such as purchase order forms, checks, stationery and envelopes, and
- refraining from identifying themselves as company employees or representatives (Jones, 1996; Frierson, 1994).

Protective Measures During Termination

Changing security passwords represents one technique utilized to prevent terminated employees from extracting significant and potentially disastrous revenge against his or her former employer. While employee sabotage or theft is not relegated to just terminations, any employee who is being terminated, thinks he/she might be terminated, or is interested in leaving can possibly utilize his/her remaining time to steal as much value as possible. While revenge or sabotage is not common in the sport industry, cases have been reported in the sporting goods, broadcasting and sponsorship industries. Specific concerns that could be considered include:

- planting bugs in conference rooms,
- stealing computer diskettes containing programs, customer lists or other sensitive data,
- stealing company property such as office supplies,
- limiting sensitive conversations to internal, closed offices,
- assigning shadow employees to overlook a person's work,
- shredding all documents before throwing out the trash,
- utilizing a virus check software system to detect any planted virus,
- separate the account receivable and account payable functions so accounts cannot be tampered,
- be cautious of any employee who refuses or rebuffs your attempts to examine their work-especially if he/she is in charge of accounting/bookkeeping,
- monitor employees to determine if they are suddenly having a significant change of life style (they drove a VW Bug for ten years then all of a sudden appear with a $60,000 Porsche),
- conduct exit interviews as departing employees with nothing to lose might let you know what is really going on in your company,
- make sure all employees understand your employee honesty policy and that all violations will be strictly prosecuted, and
- lock-up computers including laptops so the hardware would not be stolen (Weinstein, 1996).

An employer often does not know when an employee might leave or conduct activity which might lead to termination. Furthermore, an employee can steal company secrets at any time, even while on the company clock. With the rapid increase in home computers, potential theft of company secrets from an employee's home now represents a new major concern for employers. One strategy to help reduce lost data is to closely guard all computers. Limited access to computer modems should be coupled with a tracking system that monitors everyone who enters the systems, limits access to specific programs, and monitors every data file accessed through a modem. Such a system is most effective if employees are *unaware* of the system. If employees know that modem access is being monitored they would probably try to brazenly steal data from their workplace terminal instead. However, unsuspecting employees normally feel more comfortable downloading data from home where the employee does not face the prospect of someone walking-in and catching him/her with inappropriate data. Additionally, employees traveling with laptops should be given specifically programmed laptops with only the bare necessities (Weinstein, 1996).

You are responsible for more than just determining how to terminate an employee and what strategies need to be taken to protect yourself in the process. You can provide additional benefits to the terminated employee such as counseling, the opportunity to take early retirement, the opportunity to work part-time rather than full-time are all approaches that can be used to help eliminate negative impressions and hopefully reduce the prospect of litigation from disgruntled employees who have just been terminated or laid off for any number of reasons. Thus, post-employment counseling or retraining should be a considered option.

Being fired has been called many things over the years. One term which is gaining popularity is "redirecting careers" (Quintanilla, 1997). No matter what technique is used, if proper steps had been taken, the termination decision would not be a surprise for the terminated employee. Nonetheless, even if the employee knew he/she was going to be terminated, it can be a significant shock. Employees might go through denial, might attempt to retaliate, might attempt to sabotage a business or other similar activities. While an employer is not legally required to provide counseling, any constructive efforts to help the terminated employee can help soften the blow and help reduce potential liability concerns.

Counseling should be integrated with "exit interviews." Exit interviews provide you with an opportunity to determine what is wrong, if anything with your company. A disgruntled coach might claim that he/she was not provided the tools necessary to be successful or he/she might feel they were discriminated against by others. The exit interview often provides the first expression from a terminated employee about any potential claim or suit that might be filed. Any individual responsible for conducting exit interviews should be trained in evaluating communication signs such as body language and non-verbal queues. If a terminated coach is irate, unwilling to talk or vindictive in his/her comments, such signs can indicate future legal claims. The interviewer has to carefully itemize any facts raised by the terminated employee during the interview process as such facts will be critical for refuting future claims or uncovering critical problems within your business. While it is permissible to video or audio tape exit interviews (after providing notice to the terminated individual that the interview will be recorded), such taping might stifle the individual's interest in communicating any concerns based on a possible perception that the employers would only tape the interviews if they wanted information to protect themselves from future litigation.

After the decision has been made to terminate an employee and they have been provided with any appropriate counseling and post termination interviews, employers might think they are home free. However, the liability clock starts ticking way before the decision was made to terminate an employee. Liability analysis for terminating employees begins the moment an employee is hired. The employee needs to be monitored prior to being hired through the time he/she might fail to meet expectations or engage in other conduct which merits termination. The following sections address specific concerns that need to be addressed when deciding if an employee should be terminated through how to properly word the termination agreement or release to best protect the sports business employer.

1) Reason For Termination

Traditionally, terminations occur after an employee has engaged in unacceptable behavior. While many terminations are affiliated with wrongful conduct, numerous other terminations are affiliated with poor economic conditions or a company going through downsizing. As long as the termination is justified by some legitimate reason, which is nondiscriminatory and not illegal, then the terminated individual would have a hard time prevailing unless the termination violated a specific contractual term. For example, a competent, 56-year-old employee with 24 years experience, was terminated along with 21 other employees (*Wilson v. Samsonite Furniture Co.*, 1990). The terminations were associated with a reduction-in-force move by the employer. The court concluded that sometimes you have to terminate an individual even if he/she is a good employee for conditions that you could not control. Such terminates do not support an age discrimination claim (*Wilson*, 1990).

Terminations can occur for good reasons, but can an employee be terminated for engaging in actions, which are not acceptable to his/her employer, but highly regarded by society? In one highly publicized case, an armored-car driver exited his truck to rescue a bank manager who was running from a knife-wielding robber (Simon, 1997). His employer fired him for failing to follow company policies forbidding employees from abandoning trucks with money. The armored-car service claimed the driver should have stayed in his truck and radioed the police for assistance. The lower court held for the employer. On appeal, the Washington State Supreme Court reversed holding that the driver knew the bank manager and thus, could concluded that the attack was real and not a ploy to lure the driver out of the truck (Simon, 1997).

There are no specific laws on the books which protect a Good Samaritan employee who violates company policies (Simon, 1997). Thus, a gas station employee was terminated after she foiled a 1991 gas station attempted robbery. Company policies prohibited employees from resisting robberies. Rather than turn over the money, the employee switched on an automatic lock that trapped both the suspect and the employee in the station. The company adopted the no resistance policy to protect both employees and customers. The fired employee sued claiming she was promoting the public goal of assisting the police in bringing criminals to justice. The judge disallowed the suit claiming that the police never requested her assistance and taking the law into her own hands was not part of her rights as an employee (Simon, 1997).

These cases highlight the need to educate employees on what conduct will result in termination, no matter what the circumstances. Such a policy will help prevent public relation nightmares because you can point to the specific policy and the rationale supporting the policy. If the policy is reasonable, then the public and the courts will normally be supportive or accepting.

Discriminatory Reason

While it might not be the easiest task to tell someone why he or she is being terminated, the failure to let someone know why he or she are being terminated can often lead to a suit. This is especially the case when the termination produces some potential discriminatory effects. Thus, even if there were no discriminatory intent, the disgruntled terminated employee can claim that discrimination was the underlying or real, reason for the termination. The following case represents an example demonstrating an inappropriate reason for terminating an employee. It should be specifically mentioned that while termination is the key term utilized throughout this chapter, not rehiring an individual is tantamount to termination if the employee was not rehired due to a discriminatory reason

Cornell University owns a golf course that hired several rangers to make sure golfers proceeded at a reasonable pace (*Austin v. Cornell University*, 1995). Two such rangers were Edward Austin, age 73, and Henry McPeak, age 67. The course management decided not to rehire the two elder rangers. Management wanted to have less employees and for employees to work longer hours. At no time did management ever ask Austin or McPeak if they would work longer hours. The two were just told that the course was going through some reorganization. Management concluded that the two course elders were not qualified for the job. Management stated they received many complaints about the two, that bottlenecks occurred on their shifts, and the two were socializing and looking for balls rather than doing their job. Based on these complaints and the fact that the two would be required to work even longer hours, management felt the two were not qualified. However, the two were never told why they were not rehired. However, four new rangers were hired, one in his 50s, three in their 20s. Austin and McPeak brought an Age Discrimination in Employment Act (ADEA) claim against Cornell and the course management.

An AEDA claim has three steps. The plaintiffs had to prove a *prima facie* case, the defendants must then show that there is a legitimate, nondiscriminatory reason for the termination. Lastly, if the defendant can show a legitimate, nondiscriminatory reason, the plaintiff has to show that the reason given was just pretext to cover-up the discrimination (see Chapter 4). Austin and McPeak were able to show that they belonged to the protected group (individuals over age 40), they were qualified to be golf course rangers, they were not retained despite their qualifications, and younger workers filled the ranger positions. Cornell's primary claim was that the two were not qualified for the position. The court did not accept Cornell's claims because the two were never criticized for their work any time prior to the decision not to rehire them. Furthermore, the two both claimed they could implement and work under the new reorganization plan.

Cornell responded by asserting the legitimate nondiscriminatory rationale that the two could not perform satisfactorily in the new ranger positions. Austin and McPeak had to show that Cornell's asserted claim was merely pretext. The two had to prove that Cornell's claim was false, and that the actual reason for the failure to rehire was age discrimination. Several facts supported their claims. First, one supervisor claimed the course needed "fresh help." Furthermore, one former golf professional stated that the course could not be run using " part time senior citizens." Lastly, another supervisor claimed that Austin was too timid to be an effective ranger. Based on the failure to provide any past complaints or to even ask the two if they could work increased hours, Cornell's summary judgment motion was denied by the court (*Austin*, 1995). Thus, the two were allowed to continue with their case.

As evidenced by this case, when a termination is based in whole or in part on discriminatory grounds, a terminated employee can sue his or her employer for wrongful discharge. Wrongful discharge cases represent one of the fastest growing liability areas for employers. In addition, the median jury award for wrongful termination cases has increased 38% in less than a year with a $149,385 average in 1995 and rose to $205,794 in 1996 ("Stat sheet," 1997).

Suits Against Employer for Wrongful Discharge

Traditionally, most employees in the sport, recreation, and fitness industry are at-will employees. As discussed in Chapter 6, employees who do not have a written contract specifying their employment term (i.e., five years, one season, etc.) are considered at-will employees who can be terminated or quit at anytime, for any reason, or for no reason. However, there are specific exceptions that can lead to a wrongful discharge-related claim even for at-will employees. Even employees who traditionally are considered "at-will" cannot be terminated for:

- an employer retaliating against an employee who raised a federal or state statutory claim,
- engaging in union-related activities protected by the National Labor Relations Act,
- filing an appropriate workers' compensation claim,
- refusing to mislabel unsafe or defective products,
- refusing to fix prices contrary to the Sherman Antitrust Act,
- refusing to falsify documents,
- refusing to practice medicine or engage in any other regulated profession without proper licensure,
- refusing to serve alcohol to minors or intoxicated individuals,
- filing a safety-related concern with a federal or state agency, and
- refusing to violate any law, statute or regulation.

Terminating an employee for any of the forgoing actions could lead to wrongful discharge claims based on:

- violation of public policy,
- breach of the employment contract, and/or
- breach of the covenant of good faith and fair dealing.

Wrongful discharge in violation of public policy is rapidly becoming one of the largest litigation areas being faced by former employers. Public policy represents a broad category of issues which primarily relate to the violation of a state or federal law designed to protect employees. Such policy claims can include:

- activities which promote the public good,
- issues which represent a public concern rather than a private concern,
- performing acts required by the law,
- refusing to violate a law, and/or
- exercising a right entitled to the employee (Feliu, 1992).

While public policy rights are protected, private issues are not protected activities and an employee can be terminated when his/her private concerns conflict with the employer's concerns. Private concerns include an employee differing with management on how to run a fitness facility, consulting an attorney concerning a potential claim against an employer and/or having a workplace romantic relationship that is disruptive. The cases primarily point to public policy concerns and as such, the primary focus for any employer should be public rather than private concerns. Activities that constitute public policy violations include any discriminatory actions which violates Title VII, ADEA, ADA, FLSA, ERISA, CCRA, NLRA, OSHA, Veterans' Employment Act, Clear Air Act and/or the Federal Water Pollution Control Act.

The FLSA contains an anti-retaliation provision that protects employees who file a complaint alleging violation of the minimum wage law. If you are violating minimum wage laws, you cannot terminate the individual who brought the issue to your attention and to the attention of any public governing authority. There is no prohibition against terminating someone who files an internal complaint. However such actions might violate an employment contract, collective bargaining agreement, employee handbook or other policies.

You are prohibited from terminating employees because their wages are being garnished. Different rules potentially apply to subsequent wage garnishment, but the laws are so complex it is recommended that a competent employment law attorney be used for terminating or disciplining individuals because their wages were repeatedly garnished.

OSHA provides specific protection for an employee who complains about unsafe work conditions and/or refuses to work under such conditions. This rule applies when the employee reasonably believes the work conditions are dangerous to his or her health and safety. The Federal Hazardous Communications Act protects employees from termination when they ask for information concerning toxic substances or other workplace hazards. Additionally, the NLRA protects unionized workers who remove themselves from an unsafe work environment.

It is against the law in many states to terminate employees because they take time off to vote. Even if it is not against the law to terminate someone for exercising his or her right to vote, such a termination seems so "Un-American" that there still could be a violation of public policy (encouraging people to vote).

An additional concern relates to terminating individuals for expressing their political views. The general consensus provides that under the first amendment an individual has significant rights to express his/her political views, but such expression could be limited by reasonable and content neutral, time, place and manner restrictions.

Many states have laws prohibiting an employee from being fired for taking time off for jury duty. As jury duty is a civic responsibility similar to voting, even if there are no laws preventing terminating an employee for serving on a jury, the employer's actions would still probably violate public policy (Adler and Coleman, 1995). Furthermore, public policy concerns arise with terminating an employee for refusing to commit perjury in connection with an official government investigation (Adler and Coleman, 1995).

Workers' compensation laws generally prohibit employers from terminating an employee who files a workers' compensation claim. This does not mean you cannot terminate an employee after they have been injured as long as you can prove that the basis for termination related to some other actions other than filing the workers' compensation claim. A good example of this point can occur when someone is injured at work and their injury was caused by his/her blatant disregard for company rules. The termination could be linked to violating company rules rather than filing the workers' compensation claim. An additional concern associated with employee injuries relates to missing work and terminating someone for violating company attendance rules. Attendance rules can possibly run afoul of the ADA and/or the FMLA and have to be carefully crafted with the opportunity to raise disputes through the disciplinary process (Adler and Coleman, 1995).

An employer can violate the NLRA by terminating an employee for engaging in concerted union activities including supporting a union. The NLRA also protects two or more employees who join together to protest wage, hour and working conditions (Adler and Coleman, 1995).

Most employers have heard about "whistleblowers." A whistleblower is an individual who reports illegal workplace actions to proper authorities. Since reporting criminal activity is a civic duty, any termination arising from such reporting is usually considered a violation of either a court established or legislative public policy protection. The public policy protection applies to more than just reporting criminal activity. The protection is also afforded to reporting health concerns, safety issues, environmental contamination, unfair labor practices and other additional violations of federal or state laws (Adler and Coleman, 1995).

Terminating an employee because they have a disease such as cancer, AIDS or related illnesses is clearly a violation of the ADA, unless the employee poses a real risk to themselves or to others. Similarly, it is against public policy and statutes to terminate a woman because she is pregnant (Adler and Coleman, 1995).

The concerns addressed above are just some examples of the breadth of issues covered by the public policy protection afforded employees. The best course of action for an employer to undertake is to never terminate an employee for asserting a critical right (such as a constitutional right) or for trying to do what the general public would consider right under the circumstances-such as helping the bank manager in the first case in Section 1. A reasonable risk management step utilized by one of the authors is called the "front page headline test." Under this test, an employer would examine their conduct, actions and speech to determine how would someone (especially your mother or a jury) respond if the real reason someone was terminated was because he/she was the wrong race and this news story with your picture made the front page of a newspaper.

Even though you cannot terminate any employee for exercising their lawful rights or for violation of any established public policy, there are specific reasons upon which you can terminate someone without facing liability. As previously mentioned, you can terminate an employee for exercising a private right contrary to express or implied workplace rules. You can also terminate an employee for violating contractual terms. There are other legitimate reasons for terminating an employee and such reasons are discussed in more detail below.

Specific Layoff

At times during the life of a business, there will be slow times. During these times, half-day work scheduling or reduced staffing techniques can be utilized. One technique that can be utilized when facing such concerns involves asking for volunteers to quit. Someone who voluntarily resigns cannot bring a wrongful discharge case. Some employees are always contemplating career changes and such an offer for early retirement or voluntary resignation could be very beneficial. Often, you might have to pay an employee an early retirement bonus or some other incentive to leave, which is not illegal and a smart approach to help reduce the labor pool. However, any such action should comply with the ADEA and other applicable anti-discrimination laws.

Employers asking for volunteers to cutback their work hours or resign might face significant problems. Problems can include logistic problems such as who should take vacation time and when, who should do the messy work assignments, who should receive early or late lunch breaks and who should evaluate remaining employees and related issues (Graham, 1995). Another concern involves unproductive employees who stay while the qualified employees voluntarily leave. This leaves an employer with a quality vacuum. Thus, if times get tough, you should carefully consider whether or not you want to ask for volunteers. Normally the best technique is to terminate or reduce the work hours of the employees who contribute the least to producing revenue.

Even with the various legal threats posed by terminated employees, employees who do not perform to expectations or engage in continued unreasonable conduct or egregious misconduct need to be terminated. Employees who are considered at-will employees can be terminated at any time for any reason. All other employees, especially employees with specific contractual provisions that provide for continued employment unless they engage in some unreasonable conduct, can often only be terminated for breaching their contracts. Otherwise, you can breach the contract and pay any resulting damages. Specific unreasonable conduct can include any activity from assaulting a co-worker to losing a major client. The lists of possible reasons for a specific layoff are infinite. However, all such reasons for termination are typically lumped together and defined as "just cause terminations."

Termination for Cause

Just cause is hard to define, but it basically refers to whether a reasonable person, taking into account all relevant circumstances, would find sufficient justification in the employee's conduct to warrant termination (Rothstein, Knapp and Liebman, 1987). Similarly, a company can have just cause for terminating an employee for violating workplace rules and regulations. However, the rules upon which the termination was based must be directly related to the employer's legitimate business needs and interest and such an interest must be balanced against the employee's freedom to conduct his/her own affairs. This is especially true when the alleged offending actions took place away from the workplace or during non-working hours (Rothstein, Knapp and Liebman, 1987).

If the employment contract does not specify how long the employee's contractual period might last (i.e., one year), the courts will define the contract as an at-will employment relationship, even if there is a contract clause requiring termination only for cause (Rothstein, Knapp and Liebman, 1987). Thus, if a potential employee wants a contractual clause that they will not be terminated with justification, you might be able (depending on the law in your jurisdiction) to offer them such a clause, but leave the contractual term open to help maintain the employment-at-will relationship.

Even if you can terminate an at-will employee for no reason, the best practice is to have a reason. The primary benefit for such a policy is that it helps prevent and/or provides a defense against unemployment insurance claims filed by terminated employees. If an employee is terminated for cause they are normally precluded from recoevering any unemployment insurance. Thus, the employer can help prevent any payouts from the unemployment insurance pool, which will save the employer future premiums by specifying that an employee was terminated for cause. In addition to unemployment insurance savings, some states require the employer to provide a discharged employee with a specific cause for the discharge, in writing. These laws are often called service letter laws (see generally

Mo.Rev.Stat. Section 290.140; *Stark v. American Bakeries Co.*, 1983). Based on such laws and cases, it is imperative that you check with qualified counsel in your jurisdiction concerning appropriate or required documentation.

The following conditions represent specific instances where the employer will probably be held liable for terminating someone without just cause. This liability could be based on the fact that the employer's decision was premised upon possible arbitrary, capricious or unreasonable grounds which can possibly used to show an abuse of managerial discretion.

1) The employer did not provide any forewarning concerning possible disciplinary consequences of the employee's conduct.
2) The employee was never given clear definitions of what was expected from him or her to succeed.
3) The employer put too much emphasis on the employee violating minor rules and not concerns associated with the safe, orderly or efficient business operations.
4) The employer did not fully investigate the alleged incident which form the basis for his or her termination.
5) The employer did not conduct an unbiased or fair investigation-such as interviewing all parties or not documenting positive evidence on behalf of a terminated employee.
6) The employer did not have enough evidence or the evidence was not conclusive-yet the employee was terminated.
7) The employer did not administer and apply its rules across the board to everyone in the same manner.
8) The employer did not apportion the penalty with the seriousness of the infraction or the employee's past record. Thus, terminating someone with a previously clean record for being ten minutes late one slow morning would be considered too sever for the "crime" and would be perceived as termination without just cause.

The following examples represent "just cause" for termination:

1) decisions to reorganize your business,
2) reduction in force due to slow economic conditions,
3) an employee falsifying expense records,
4) cost-cutting based on lower consumer demands, and
5) cutting back after overstaffing your business.

As highlighted above, just cause can be proven by carefully documenting what employees have done or failed to accomplish. At the same time, you should not terminate an employee for minor infractions or if you do not have sufficient information to justify a final disposition of the matter. The failure to properly investigate and follow disciplinary policies can often lead to the greatest challenges to an employee's termination.

Proper Timing

Even though you may be justified in terminating an employee, the timing of the particular termination is important. As explained by Bordwin (1994/1995),

> Although you can terminate at-will employees at any time for any reason, you cannot fire them for a "bad" reason. You cannot violate their rights under laws such as the Employee Retirement Income Security Act (ERISA), Civil Rights Act, Americans with Disabilities Act (ADA) or Family Medical Leave Act. So if a termination appears to coincide with an employee's attaining legal status or engaging in "protected activities" under such laws, you create the suspicion of improper or unlawful behavior. And that, in turn, can tempt your ex-employee's lawyer to say, "You've got a great case! Let's sue!"

Let's assume you fire a ticket manager after returning from a 12 week leave protected under the Family Medical Leave Act. Let's also assume that this person has received two negative evaluations (documented and signed by employee), has missed several training sessions and supervisor concerns have been documented as well. Also assume that ticket sales actually increase during the employee's leave of absence. Upon return from the disability leave, you decide it is time to fire the employee. Unfortunately, the termination's timing may appear as retaliation against the employee for exercising a legal right (Bordwin, 1994/1995).

Due Process

Due process concerns often raise either a constitutional law issue or a discrimination claim (see Chapter 4). The most effective means to help prevent a due process violation is to explicitly follow all disciplinary steps and provide the employee(s) an opportunity to explain their action(s) or inaction. A sample disciplinary policy is attached as Appendix AA. As defined in the *Tarkanian* case, Chapter 1, due process under the 14th Amendment and Fifth Amendment (for federal matters) relates to having the opportunity to face your accusers, to know what charges are being raised against you and the right to know what evidence will be raised against you.

Due process issues often involve a constitutional claim. In order for an employee to bring such a claim, he/she have to be working for the state or work for a private employer in a state such as California where the state constitution specifically covers private employers. In the sports context, due process claims have been raised on numerous occasions where a coach and teacher resigns or is terminated from one position which results in a significant change in their employment status.

In *White v. Banks*, Larry White was a secondary school teacher and two-sport coach. After five years in both positions, the school board relieved him of his coaching duties even though he was retained as a teacher (*White*, 1981). The Supreme Court of Tennessee concluded that a teacher who coaches has two basic rights, "(1) [H]is position as a teacher is protected by tenure, assuming that he has acquired tenure status, and, (2) his position as a coach is protected by whatever contract he has with the board to perform coaching duties, but not by tenure" (Appenzeller, 1985). Therefore, the court upheld White's lost coaching position. If a coaching position is not covered by state tenure rights, then the coaching position can be removed at anytime without due process, so long as contract terms are not violated or the school is willing to risk a breach of contract claim. However, tenure represents a teacher's property right as there is expected continuation pursuant to the tenure achieved by the teacher. If a tenured position is removed from a teacher, the teacher needs to be afforded all pertinent due process rights such as a hearing, knowing what charges are being raised against the teacher, and the right to face the teacher's accusers.

In a 1984–85 survey by Dr. Herb Appenzeller, 35 states specifically indicated that coaches cannot be granted tenure while eight states indicated that coaches could receive tenure. The survey also showed that 13 states allow coaches to have a formal hearing when relieved of their coaching duties while 22 states did not allow any such formal hearings (Appenzeller, 1985).

Besides constitutional due process, due process rights can also attach themselves to state statutes providing teachers/coaches with specific rights. The Lancaster case raised this very issue (Brown, 1996). Ron Lancaster was a football coach who was terminated by the Jenks School District. Lancaster sued claiming his due process rights were denied. The school district contended that coaches and others serving "special-duty" jobs may be terminated without due process. Lancaster contended that football is part of the high school curriculum as defined by the school's own planning guide and therefore, Lancaster was owed due process rights under the Oklahoma Teachers Due Process Act. Under the Teacher Due Process Act, a tenured teacher could not be fired except under extreme circumstances such as criminal activity or moral turpitude (*Brown*, 1996).

Due process can also be a contract claim, especially if due process is a right provided for in an employee contract or a union's collective bargaining agreement. Under such circumstance, you have to be extremely vigilant to follow the letter of the contract to avoid automatically creating a cause of action for violating contractually-mandated conditions.

Intentional Infliction of Emotional Distress

A close cousin of due process claims involves claims alleging intentional infliction of emotional distress. While workplace policies specifically provide for disciplinary procedures, policies often do not specify what conduct should not occur during the termination process. Most employers anticipate that their managers will act in a professional manner. However, at times individuals are not conscientious of their actions and will possibly fail to provide appropriate due process rights and also might injury an employee psychologically. Examples of distress which can be raised, during the termination process includes:

- publicly terminating an employee,
- falsely accusing an employee of egregious acts involving moral turpitude,
- failing to act professionally, and
- trying to make an example of the employee.

These various acts can often be avoided by proper education. All employees are entitled some modicum of decency, even if they have engaged in egregious conduct. Numerous wrongful discharge cases have raised emotional distress claims based in part on company officials hovering over employees while they cleaned-out their desk in front of other co-employees.

Group Layoff

Another justified reason for terminating employees involves closing a given manufacturing plant, fitness facility or sporting goods store. The safest method for terminating individuals when you are required to undergo a reduction-in-force is a seniority-based system where junior employees are laid off prior to other employees with greater seniority. Such a system helps prevent age discrimination claims (Frierson, 1994). However, you should specifically avoid asking for and/or making any determination based on employee's ages. You should focus exclusively on service period or employee rank. Furthermore, you should carefully follow layoff provisions, if any, from the employee handbook.

Plant closings represent a significant concern due to both federal and state law providing specific requirements for the employer. The Federal Worker Adjustment and Retraining Notification Act (WARN) requires certain employers to provide advance warning of plant closures, relocation or mass layoffs to all pertinent entities. Employers covered by WARN employ over 100 employees who work in aggregate at least 4,000 hours a week. Notice need to be provided if 50 or more employees will be laid off. Layoffs must be permanent or exceed six months in duration. Under the act, employers would be required to notify the employees, any unions, and any potentially affected government entities such as job training programs at least 60 days before anyone is affected by the layoff. Failure to comply with WARN can subject an employer to penalties owed to both employees and affected government agencies (Adler and Coleman, 1995).

State laws also can affect plant closing. At least five state already have specific laws requiring employers to provide advance notice, severance pay and/or continued health care coverage with more states and local governments passing new laws (Adler and Coleman, 1995).

Bankruptcy

While no employer wants to think that they might have to file for bankruptcy, it is a very real option for employers to take when the creditors are pounding down the front door. Bankruptcies also represent a significant concern for employees. The primary questions employees will ask when an employer indicates that bankruptcy is the only way out include:

- Will I get paid?
- Will bankruptcy terminate my written employment contract?
- Will I lose my benefits?
- Do I still have a job?
- Will the employer have to pay the creditors first before paying employees?
- Can bankruptcy allow an employer to escape from a CBA?

These questions will be answered in the following paragraphs.

Bankruptcy in fact provides significant protection for employees. While employees can be terminated if the business has to reduce expenses, those employees who are retained are given significant priority in the bankruptcy distribution process. Two statutory provisions provide protection for employee salaries. Section 507(a)(3) of the federal Bankruptcy Act gives preference to paying employee previously earned wages over paying general creditors (11 U.S.C.S. 507). However, this preference is limited to $2,000 in wages per employee earned within 90 days before the employer filed for bankruptcy. Any amount owed over and beyond this $2,000 cap is folded into other general creditor obligations.

Another important statutory protection requires priority payment to those individuals or entities who provide goods and services to the employer in bankruptcy. These "administrative fees" are designed to keep the business running so it can hopefully get back on its feet and become financially viable again. Wages for employees who work after a business has filed for bankruptcy are considered administrative expenses. However, the law is unclear as to how to handle severance pay and pension obligations which blend past and future obligations (Rothstein, Knapp and Liebman, 1987).

In a major 1984 case, the U.S. Supreme Court concluded that a collective bargaining agreement is only an "executory contract" and thus can be rejected by the employer after bankruptcy if the CBA burdens the company and through balancing equitable principles, the court feels that the scales weighs in favor of rejecting the CBA. (*NLRB v. Bildisco & Bildisco*, 1984). The Court also concluded that an employer in bankruptcy does not commit an unfair labor practice by unilaterally changing the terms of an existing CBA even prior to the bankruptcy petition being reviewed by a bankruptcy court (Rothstein, Knapp and Liebman, 1987).

Employers are often pulled in multiple directions when undergoing bankruptcy proceedings. Creditors, attorneys, customers and employees all want either money or information. Employees need to be provided with appropriate information in a timely manner to avoid any confusion or an abandoning of the ship. Employees need to be told that payroll checks will be covered and that the business will continue as usual. The same information should be given to employees when you sell a business.

Sale of Business/Consolidation

Layoffs after a business is sold also represent unique concerns. At-will employees can be terminated by either the former employer or the new employer without any reason. However, as discussed above, it is not wise to terminate someone without a reason as such action often stirs the emotions within an employee, which could lead to litigation. However, if the new business owner wants to start with a clean slate, there is no law prohibiting such actions as long as no contracts are breached, no federal or state laws are breached, no CBA is violated and/or no acts involving discrimination were utilized or resulted from the terminations.

A key concern any new business owner faces involves inheriting the contracts of the previous owner. Just because there is an ownership change does not mean the previously signed contracts are void or voidable. In fact, employees in a company that is purchased are similar to an apartment tenant. If a new landlord buys the apartment complex, the tenant can remain in the unit until their contract expires. Thus, when evaluating whether or not to buy a new business, you should ask for copies of all employment contracts, if any. If there are no contracts, you should not take the business seller's word that all employees are employees-at-will. You should specifically include a provision in the business sales contract that the sellers make assurances that all employees are at-will and that no representations were made orally, in writing or by actions that can create a different employment relationship. The same contract should also provide an indemnity clause that the seller will pay all litigation costs and awards if an employee claims the business seller gave them permanent employment. Additional concerns that should be analyzed when buying an established business include, but are not limited to:

- determining if any union-related activities have ever occurred,
- determining if a CBA was ever in place,
- determining if there ever existed an employee manual or handbook,
- acquiring a copy of any employee handbooks or manuals,
- determining if there existed any safety, sexual harassment or other policies, rules or procedures,
- analyzing pension accounts to transfer control and insure proper accounting,
- analyzing insurance coverage to determine when the contract comes-up for renewal,
- determining is there are any federal or state agencies currently conducting or concluding any investigations or if any complaints have been filed with such agencies,
- analyzing retirement accounts and stock/employee ownership issues,
- whether any safety risks exist within the business, and
- analyzing unemployment insurance and workers' compensation records and concerns.

An additional issue associated with purchasing a business involves employee buyouts. In the 1980s several major businesses were purchased in part or wholly by employees through outright purchases or employee stock ownership plans (ESOP). These businesses include Chrysler Corporation (25% ownership stake), Pan American World Airways and Eastern Airlines (Rothstein, Knapp and Liebman, 1987). ESOPs represent a unique quandary as both the managers and the employees are both owners. Such an arrangement only works if open communications exists among all parties. ESOPs provide some significant benefits such as easier salary negotiations and benefits as the employees understand the economic impact higher wages will have on shared profits. However, ESOPs also present significant challenges such as how to terminate an employee who is also an owner. Furthermore, what happens to an employee who is sexually harassed because she in essence is suing herself or himself when a suit is filed against the employee owned business. It is recommended that a competent counsel be consulted regarding such legal issues.

Wrongful discharge cases involve more than just a claim that employees were terminated when there was no good reason for termination. An employer also should be cognizant that terminating an employee without just cause can result in claims such as intentional infliction of emotional distress, negligent infliction of emotional distress, invasion of privacy, fraud and misrepresentation, negligence and tortuous interference with contractual relations (Rothstein, Knapp and Liebman, 1987). Wrongful discharge cases can also involve such claims as breach of contract, discrimination, violation of statutory obligations, defamation and related causes which will be discussed below.

Termination and After-acquired Evidence

After-acquired evidence refers to evidence of an employee's wrongdoing that is acquired after the negative employment action has already transpired. In other words, employers often use after-acquired evidence to justify employment decisions that later are challenged by disgruntled employees. After-acquired evidence can include:

- lying on a resume and/or job application (e.g., stating false degrees or dates of prior employment),
- divulging confidential information with competitors,
- embezzlement, or
- harassment.

Discovering after-acquired evidence allows an employer to argue, for example, that "the employee would have been fired anyway," regardless of any discriminatory or otherwise illegal employment acts.

The U. S. Supreme Court addressed the issue of whether after acquired evidence barred allegations of illegal employment activities if the discharge or demotion or other adverse affect would have resulted had the employer been aware of the after acquired evidence in a 1995 case. In *McKennon v. Nashville Banner Publishing Co.* the discharged 62-year-old plaintiff alleged that the employer's dismissal violated the ADEA. The employer later discovered that the plaintiff had copied and removed confidential documents from the office in violation of company policy and argued that this activity provided cause for termination and that this cause should supersede the ADEA allegations. The court held that after-acquired evidence cannot serve as a *complete bar* to recovery since it would negate the intent of legislation such as the ADEA or ADA. More specifically, the court concluded,

> The Act's remedial provisions are designed both to compensate employees for injuries caused by prohibited discrimination and to deter employers from engaging in such discrimination. The private litigant who seeks redress for his or her injuries vindicates both of these objectives, and it would not accord with this scheme if after-acquired evidence of wrongdoing barred all relief (*McKennon*, 1995).

The Supreme Court, however, was not willing to dismiss the after-acquired evidence as inconsequential or irrelevant and stated that the after-acquired evidence,

> Must be taken into account...addressed on a case-by-case basis. However, as a general rule, neither reinstatement nor front pay is an appropriate remedy. It would be both inequitable and pointless to order the reinstatement of someone the employer would have terminated, and will terminate, in any event and upon lawful grounds (*McKennon*, 1995),

Thus, prior to terminating an employee, take the time during a paid-leave or suspension to review all job applications, resumes, interview forms and other documents to identify matches and lies. With this proof in your hands, you can present such information to the employee when you hold the termination meeting or exit interview.

2) Contractual Concerns

The first contractually-related issue which should be analyzed when terminating an employee is whether or not the employee changed his/her career, moved a significant geographic distance or engaged in other conduct (based on your assertions) which could cause him/her significant harm or loss. Under these circumstances, employees could claim that they relied on your promises and changed their position accordingly. This represents a classic case of promissory estoppel where courts might go outside the four corners of the employment contract to find fraud (whether intentional or negligent) or misrepresentations (either negligent or intentional). If no misrepresentations, illegal activities (such as discrimination) or fraudulent conduct were utilized to hire or keep the employee working for you, then the next point of analysis would be the employment contract.

The initial contractual concern relates to whether or not the initial employment contract provided a specified employment term. If there was no specified employment term (i.e., one year or five years), the contract needs to be examined to determine if there is any security provided through the contract that an employee will not be terminated except for certain specified reasons. The contract also need to be scrutinized to determine if the employee agreed to specific disciplinary process which included termination as an appropriate remedy for egregious or unwanted conduct or actions. It is assumed that if you followed the contractual steps set forth in Chapter 6 your contract would not have been for a specified period, did not contain language implying termination only for cause and specifically provided termination as a disciplinary measure. The disciplinary measures component within the contract should specifically refer to the employee handbook and any and all additional rules or regulations which the employee was required to follow. The employee handbook acknowledgment form should be examined before an employee is terminated to make sure he/she has signed the form indicating he/she read the handbook and agreed to abide by all the company's rules and regulations (Adler and Coleman, 1995). It is often a good idea to have the form witnessed by at least two people who can indicate they saw the employee read and sign the form. These witnesses could also verify that the employee was allowed to ask any questions concerning company rules and regulations before signing the form.

The disciplinary process represents a critical concern. As a component of the company's disciplinary process, employees should never be summarily terminated, even if they have engaged in egregious conduct. The employee should first be put on administrative leave or unpaid suspension. This step will allow you time to properly investigate the employee's actions and significantly reduces the likelihood of a breach of contract claim for failing to follow the required disciplinary steps.

During the suspension, the employee should specifically know that he/she is suspended subject to discharge pending a complete investigation. The employee should not report to work nor should the employee have any contact with any current employee or management unless initiated by company representatives. During this suspension:

- the parties are given an opportunity to "cool down,"
- allows the parties to make objective decisions,
- allows for a full investigation including obtaining written statements,
- allows you the time to obtain evidence including stolen property, drugs, alcohol, etc.,
- allows you to determine what the final disciplinary actions should be,
- allows you to review past performance appraisals and disciplinary actions,
- allows you the time to contact an attorney for any final thoughts, and

- it allows you time to announce the decision to others in a fair, non-defamatory, manner (Adler and Coleman, 1995).

The disciplinary process also gives you a chance to see what the terminated individual might claim as a defense, which should be carefully documented. Such a defense can include statements that someone else actually engaged in the wrongful conduct or the employee was forced to engage in the specified conduct by a manager. Such information can influence the investigation process and can help prevent a suit alleging intentional infliction of emotional distress or defamation.

A further contractual concern that needs to be considered is terminating a union member. The employee would be covered by the CBA and would be entitled to all the rights set forth in the CBA. Such rights could include the right to be represented at any disciplinary session by counsel or a union representative. It often occurs that unions regularly challenge all terminations through the disciplinary process and also through arbitration.

An additional concern that needs to be addressed is what benefits are owed the terminated employee. Such benefits or contractual obligations can include:

- statutory benefits such as COBRA coverage (see Generally Chapter 6),
- unused vacation,
- unused sick days,
- unused personal days,
- pension and retirement benefits,
- wage's through the employee's final work days, and
- other entitlement (Adler and Coleman, 1995).

Oftimes, these rights are combined with additional benefits to form the final severance agreement. Severance agreements are often called releases as they are designed to provide a terminated employee his/her required benefits and an additional sum to "buy" any potential claim the employee might want to bring after being terminated.

Employers may find using a release beneficial in an era of litigation that commonly includes allegations of wrongful discharge and discrimination. A release represents (Black, 1990),

> The relinquishment, concession, or giving up of a right, claim, or privilege, by the person in whom it exists or to whom it accrues, to the person against whom it might have been demanded or enforced.

In other words, a release is an employee's waiver of liability against a particular employer. To be effective, the release must meet all the requirements of a valid contract, including consideration. As explained by Bordwin,

(1994/1995), "[B]e prepared to pay something for the release, some bene-fit or sum of money that you are not otherwise obligated to provide or pay." The consideration must exceed that which the employee is legally entitled to receive (e.g., unused sick pay, earned vacation time and health benefits under Cobra) (Bordwin, 1994/1995). Although it may be distasteful to pay someone when terminating the person for cause, it often becomes a case of "pay me now or pay me later" (Bordwin, 1994/1995). You should always remember that while most individuals can enter into any contract they feel is appropriate, legislation has been passed to provide specific rights that cannot be waved by any contract language. For example, if a 60-year-old coach is terminated, The coach might be willing to sign a con-tract to pay her a total lump sum today. However, under the ADEA, the coach will have 21 days to reconsider the pay-off and to cancel the termi-nation contract even if the contract expressly provided for immediate pay-ment and immediate relinquishment of rights to sue (see Chapter 13 for more information on ADEA requirements).

You can pay a departing employee greater benefits, provide better pen-sion benefits, provide outplacement services or provide a neutral reference. In exchange, the employee is often asked to make a decision on the spot that they will accept these benefits in exchange for releasing the employer from all future liability. While some employers might try to utilize strong arm tactics to obtain a release, any release or severance agreement needs to be obtained voluntarily, comply with all federal and state statutes such as the ADEA and an employee can only release known claims (i.e. specific amounts of money owed or releasing a possible discriminatrion claim). Un-known claims normally cannot be released (Frierson, 1994). Sample sev-erance agreements and releases are contained in Appendix BB. One caveat that needs to be stressed is that you should avoid having a standard sever-ance policy or program. Each termination should be handled individually to avoid raising any ERISA related claims or discrimination claims.

Specific contractual issues are addressed below. However, two major con-cerns need to be addressed prior to analyzing specific contractual clauses. The first issues related to good faith dealings by the employer. The second issue relates to contractual liability, which the employee might owe the employer.

Good Faith and Fair Dealing

An employer can also be liable for violating the implied covenant of good faith and fair dealing for contractual disputes relating to both the initial employment contract and any severance agreement. Normally con-tracts are construed against the author. Most employers prepare the em-ployment contract and present the contract as a take-it-or-leave-it proposition. Sometimes, an employer might change a specific amount or time period. Under such circumstances, the employer has to make sure he/she does not act unreasonably in breaching the contract. Unreasonable conduct such as promising a full disciplinary hearing and then not giving such a hearing form the basis of the bad faith breach claim. Furthermore, indicating that an employee only has one week of vacation time owed when actually he/she has double that amount can raise a breach claim. If any changes are made to a contract or if a new contract is ever created, new consideration needs to be provided by both parties. An additional contractual tip includes writing contracts for less than a yearly period (i.e., renewable monthly) to minimize potential benefits which might have to be paid. In one case, a security guard was informed by his school/employer that he would be continuing his employment under a new one-year contract. Four months later the guard was terminated. The guard was able to recover eight months worth of additional wages and benefits (*Hurst v. Clairborne County No. 45*, 1988).

Employee Contractual Obligations

While most contract-related issues center around the employer breaching or terminating the contract, employees can also breach a contract. This situation normally occurs when an employee on a yearly contract is asked to continue the following year. The employee agrees, but later accepts a different position. Such an occurrence can often be remedied by finding another employee. However, what happens when the initial employee was highly skilled and it is difficult or more expensive to hire a replacement? The employer thought he/she had an employee for the following year, and instead, they have to pay more money for a replacement. The employer can sue the former employee for all additional money the employer has to pay out. These damages are called expectancy damages because the person breaching the contract should expect that that other side would incur reasonable expenses to remedy the contractual breach. Expectancy damages can be contained within a buyout clause or a liquidated damages clause. To assist you in the negotiation process, if an employee threatens or asks to be let out of the contract, you should specifically indicate what the costs might be which you would incur if the contract is not completed. You should also make sure the departing employee understands that you intend to vigorously enforce the contract and will take all pertinent actions to recover any additional expenses.

Chapter 6 highlighted employment contracts and the same critical elements for a valid employment contract are present in any severance agreement. If all the proper contractual elements are in place, you next have to craft the contract to appropriately meet your termination requirements or goals. As addressed above, there are very specific contract clauses to help protect against a breach of contract claim or to prevent an employee from injuring you or your business/organization.

Non-compete Agreement

As discussed in Chapter 6 Section 11, non-compete clauses are sometimes utilized in the initial hiring contract to ensure an employee knows from the very beginning that he/she will be forced to curtail his/her activities upon leaving the company. Additionally, key personnel and individuals with access to critical company information should be reminded about the non-compete agreements. This will establish your position when you are bargaining for a terminated employee's severance package. The employee severance package is a critical location to include a new non-compete agreement or to reference a prior non-compete clause remphasize the importance of this clause. If the employee wants to receive a certain walk-away sum representing his/her severance pay (in non-union employment conditions), you can condition receipt of such moneys on entering a contract wherein he/she agrees to accept the money in exchange for signing the termination agreement, which contains the non-compete clause. The same contract should also contain a covenant not to sue and that all claims are extinguished.

If a terminated employee subsequently starts competing or in any other manner violates the termination agreement, the employer could provide a liquidated damages, injunction or other penalty clauses within the termination agreement which can be used to punish the former employee.

A 1981 case involving a famous sportscaster helps highlight the specificity associated with non-compete clauses and why they have to be crafted meticulously to avoid any loopholes (*American Broadcasting Company, Inc. v. Wolf*, 1981). Warner Wolf was a well-known sportscaster in the late 1970s and early 1980s. He entered into a contract with ABC wherein he was obliged to negotiate with the network in good faith for 90 days before his contract expired. The contract also required Wolf to wait 45 days into the negotiation process before entering into negotiations with any other networks. Lastly, the contract required Wolf to avoid working as a sportscaster, sports news reporter, commentator, program hosts or broadcasting analyst for three months after he left ABC. Wolf entered into an oral agreement with CBS after the exclusive negotiation period ended. In fact there were two contracts. One contract referred to sportscasting services, the other contract required Wolf to produce several sports specials for CBS. The contracts were later formalized in writing. ABC sued

Wolf and CBS for breach of contract and requested equitable relief to force Wolf to return to ABC. The court refused ABC's request for equitable relief. The Court concluded that Wolf failed to comply with the 90-day good faith dealing provision because he started negotiating with CBS within the 90-day window. However, this is only a minor breach for which money damages could have been sought from Wolf and/or CBS. The court was unwilling to enforce the non-compete covenant or to force someone to complete a personal services contract when Wolf specifically wished to avoid such a contract and other adequate remedies existed. Other remedies could have included paying monetary damages to relieve himself of the contractual obligations (*American Broadcasting Companies, Inc. v Wolf*, 1981). Two key points can be gleamed from this case. One, CBS worked to carefully craft a contract that would allow Wolf to switch stations, produce shows and then become an on-air personality which would not violate the three month non-compete clause. Secondly, ABC should have written the contract to cover a wider range or non-compete concerns including producing, directing, consulting and related sports media positions.

Another concern associated with non-compete clauses relates to limiting the employment opportunities of a given employee when that employee did not have access to critical customer information, sales contacts or other key employer assets which could significantly injure the employer. If the sales director was leaving an employer, a non-compete clause relating to soliciting past clients for several months would seem reasonable. However, the same provision would not pass judicial scrutiny if the janitor was requested to sign the same agreement. This general principal is fairly well established and requires application of the rule of reason. Pursuant to the Restatement of Contracts 2d, Section 188 (1981):

> (1) A promise to refrain from competition that imposes a restraint that is ancillary to an otherwise valid transaction or relationship is unreasonably in restraint of trade if
>> (a) the restrain is greater than is needed to protect the promise's legitimate interest, or
>> (b) the promise's need is outweighed by the hardship to the promisor and the likely injury to the public.
> (2) Promises imposing restraints that are ancillary... include...
>> (b) a promise by an employee or other agent not to compete with his employer or other principal....

This section of legalese basically indicates that when a non-compete clause forms only a portion of a larger contract, such contract will not be considered reasonable if the prohibition restricts activity that does not in fact constitute a risk or which infringes on valuable public needs. This requirement was further clarified in a 1993 case where a court concluded that a covenant would be approved by the court if it is necessary to protect the former employer's legitimate interests, provides reasonable time and territory restrictions, are not overly harsh or oppressive to the former employee and are not against public policy (*Nalco Chem. Co. v. Hydro Technologies*, 1993).

Trade Secrets

Trade secrets involve a major concern with a departing employee. The recently publicized case involving a former auto executive who took trade secrets to a competitor highlight the need to protect valuable assets. In the sports industry, trade secrets can range from technical design specifications for sporting goods and the ingredients of a sports nutrition bar to a professional team's playbook.

In a Pennsylvania case involving a trade secret dispute, the court set forth what a plaintiff must prove to receive injunctive relief to prevent disclosing a trade secret (*SI Handling Systems, Inc. v. Heisley*, 1985). The court defined a trade secret as any "formula, pattern, device or compilation of information which is used in one's business, and which gives him an opportunity to obtain an advantage over competitors who do not know or use it" (*SI Handling Systems, Inc.*, 1985). The court also examined when an employee can be liable for usurping a trade secret.

- First, the information must constitute a trade secret.
- Second, the information must have value to the employer and is essential for the employer to conduct his/her business.
- Third, that through ownership or discovery, the employer has exclusive right to the trade secret.
- Lastly, the trade secret was communicated to the employee while the employee was employed in a position of trust and confidence and any abuse of the circumstances would make it unjust for the employee to disclose the information (*SI Handling Systems, Inc. v. Heisley*, 1985).

Employees are expected to obtain significant confidential information while on the job. Disclosing such information can be a crime. A Massachusetts law makes it a larceny for an employee to steal or copy trade secrets with an intent to transfer that information to another (Mass.Gen.Laws. Ch. 266 Section 30(4)).

Stealing Employees

Along with trade secrets, another valuable commodity which every business posses are high quality employees. When someone leaves his/her current employer, he/she sometimes wishes to take some co-workers or others with him/her. Raiding is the term used to describe when a former employee raids his or her former employer and takes away other employees. Such actions, while appearing highly illegal, are legal unless the defecting employee uses unfair or deceptive means to induce others to leave or uses other unconscionable conduct (Rothstein, Knapp and Liebman, 1987). While an employee might be able to use legal means to steal other employees, the departing employee could be sued for any breached contracts that he or she might have caused. Such a claim could be raised if a raided employee had a contract to work for a specific time and the departing employee persuaded others to breach their employment contracts. Such tampering could result in a claim of interference with contract.

A departing employee could also be sued for stealing customers if the employee owed a fiduciary duty to his former employer which is breached by stealing the clients (Rothstein, Knapp and Liebman, 1987). Such an occurrence could occur if the departing employee was a former partner. As all partners owe a fiduciary duty to each other, stealing clients breaches that duty and exposes the departing partner to potential liability. Similar to stealing customers, is stealing customer lists. Such lists can either come within a trade secret claim or a breach of the employee's confidentiality obligation (Feliu, 1992). A customer list is considered confidential and a possible trade secret if it contains a contact name, customer location, credit rating and other sensitive information which took the employer time to develop, is thorough for that industry, and has been regularly updated by the employer (Feliu, 1992).

Besides the various contractual strategies that need to be considered when terminating an employee, you need to follow all legally mandated requirements designed to protect employee rights. One of the greatest concerns involves discrimination and related claims.

3) Discrimination in Discharge

Numerous cases have winded their way through the court system with various allegations claiming that some type of discriminatory activity was involved in the termination process. For example, a former assistant woman's volleyball coach was awarded $150,000 judgment against the University of Tennessee for alleged discrimination associated with being terminated because she became pregnant. The University claimed that she was dismissed due to her performance. However, she was able to show that there was nothing in her personal file to substantiate the university's allegations ("Ex-Coach wins suit against U.T.," 1997).

The key to avoiding a discrimination charge during the termination process is to employ fair and consistent disciplinary policies. The best means to ensure the termination process is not discriminatory in the process or result is to have a final neutral person approve the dismissal. What might appear as consistent discipline could be discovered by independent review to be negative reviews for all minorities and positive reviews for all male Caucasian employees. If a minority sued, you can be certain that the plaintiff's attorney will scrutinize your employment records and will be able to tap these records and uncover such a trend.

More specific discrimination issues are addressed in Chapter 4. You should pay special attention to racial discrimination, gender related issues such as a glass ceiling and terminating older employees in order to reduce costs.

Age Discrimination

A 1996 *USA Today* article reported that age discrimination complaints received by the EEOC had decreased annually between 1992 and 1995 (Jones, 1996). Further, interviews conducted by the article's author Del Jones revealed:

- unemployed managers and executives are finding jobs faster than at any time in 16 years,
- the typical 50-plus job hunter takes about 3 1/2 months to find a job; only about 3 weeks longer than it takes their younger counterparts, and
- laid-off executives in their 60s take 5 1/2 months to find jobs, which is two weeks faster than executives between 41 and 45 (Jones, 1996b).

As older workers are beginning to find worker more rapidly after being terminated, this effect will reduce potential damage awards which they otherwise might be entitled to receive. Furthermore, age discrimination is often the first form of discrimination which older, male, Caucasians face. This experience can often be devastating for those who never previously experienced discrimination. This devastation often generates hatred and other vindictive feelings, which fuels the fire for litigation. By helping older workers find new work (outplacement services) or clearly understand their skills and what retraining is necessary, you can hopefully assist someone in getting a job which reduces lost wages claims and the worker feels some obligation to the employer which might prevent litigation.

As highlighted in the *Cornell University* case at the start of this Chapter, employers often are left to dry in front of the jury by stupid statements or jokes made by managers. Age based retirement discrimination was once a common occurrence when society felt that once someone reached his/her 60's, he/she was washed up. Now the laws are very clear. In one case, an older worker was discharged based on his high salary. The court concluded that such a termination violated the ADEA and the employee was awarded $127,916 plus attorney fees (*Metz v. Transit Mix, Inc.*, 1988). However, there is an exception to the ADEA's no mandatory retirement rule. There is no mandatory retirement unless the employee is over 65, has a pension that pays over $40,000 a year and is a high level policy maker (Frierson, 1994). Additionally individuals who work in sensitive positions such as airline pilots can be forced to retire at a certain age.

Proving Age Discrimination

Similar to the Title VII analysis set forth by *McDonnell Douglass Corp. v. Green* (1973), employees have a *prima facie* case of age discrimination if:

- The individual is a member of the protected class.
- The individual was terminated or demoted.
- The individual was doing the job well enough to meet her employer's legitimate expectations.
- Others were treated more fairly.

Kehoe v. Anheuser-Busch, Inc. (1996) illustrates the plaintiff's successful ability to show a *prima facie* case of age discrimination. The 61-year-old plaintiff was fired from the Sports Marketing Group (a division of Anheuser Busch) when his position was eliminated in a restructuring effort. The defendant-company made no attempt to relocate plaintiff to an open position for which he was allegedly qualified. The plaintiff was able to prove the first two prongs of the *McDonnell Douglas* (1973) analysis. The defendant's argued that plaintiff's degree in physical education left him unqualified to handle the analytical, budgetary and interpersonal skill requirements associated with the new position. However, the plaintiff presented evidence documenting that he was well-liked by his peers, performed admirably in his prior duties at Anheuser, and effectively managed a large budget in his prior position and even accumulated a $100,000 surplus. However, probably most devastating to the defendant's case was age-biased derogatory comments. The plaintiff's supervisor referred to the plaintiff as an "old fart," describing the facility where he previously worked as a "retirement center" where the plaintiff had been "put out to pasture," and referring to the plaintiff's golf activity as "senior golf." The third prong of the analysis was solidified as the plaintiff's immediate supervisor admitted that plaintiff was capable of performing, "most, if not all, of the functions demanded of a typical sports promotion coordinator," the position for which the plaintiff was denied. The job was filled by a 23-year-old female with a degree in psychology. Her only exposure to sport marketing or the sport industry occurred during a stint as a summer intern. Consequently, one could easily deduce that the fourth prong of the prima facie analysis was met as well.

Suggestions When Terminating the Older Employee

The following suggestions are designed to help you through the process of terminating an older employee protected by the ADEA or other similar legislation.

Documented evidence of how an individual is performing essential job responsibilities as defined by the job description is imperative when defending a claim of age discrimination. You must be able to prove that the alleged termination, demotion, lack of promotion, and so on, was based upon non-biased facts.

During discussions with the employee, avoid using age-biased terms such as:

- the ways of the past are not recognized here anymore,
- we need a 'perkier' look,
- we need to shed our stodgy image, or
- you don't understand the younger generation and their needs and wants.

An employer's decision to terminate cannot conflict with existing legislation guaranteeing specific employee rights. For example, the American with Disabilities Act (see Chapter 4) prohibits an employer from terminating an employee unable to fulfill essential job tasks because of an acquired disability. In addition, the FMLA protects an employee's need to take a 12-week medical leave of absence and then return to a similar job at similar pay.

Many erroneously think that aging individuals are "too old to change" or are "set in their ways." Whether true or not, liability can ensue if the aging individual is not provided the same training and advancement opportunities as other employees.

When you terminate multiple employees in a group layoff, you should never ask for a list of the employees with their ages. Numerous cases have been lost by utilizing this step (Frierson, 1994). By making all terminations conditioned on objective criteria such as performance or seniority, you protect your self from many ADEA related claims.

ADA

Similar to the ADEA the ADA also provides a challenge when terminating an individual. While an older employee cannot change his/her age, an otherwise healthy individual can all of a sudden become "disabled" to stall or prevent termination.

As with workers' compensation fraud, if someone can take advantage of the "system" he/she might try to take advantage of the opportunities afforded by the ADA. For example, lets say you want to terminate an employee who has failed to complete assigned tasks and you ask him/her at the end of a pay period that you need to have a "serious talk" with him/her. Instead of going to the termination meeting, the employee goes to a doctor with a stress-based claim. The doctor might refer the employee to a psychiatrist or other professional. However, in the meantime, the employee files a workers' compensation claim that the workplace and job assignment is causing his/her stress. Once he/she files the workers' compensation claim, you cannot terminate the individual based on the workplace injury.

However, the employee's act is not yet finished. The employee can then claim he/she is "disabled" under the ADA and needs his/her job redesigned to help reasonably accommodate him/her. If you try to terminate the employee, the employee can claim that you violated the ADA because he/she could not complete the assignments due to the stressful environment and the stress (i.e., his/her disability) caused him not to complete the assignments. This scenario represents a real and problematic issue. The employee might be ineffective, but you cannot terminate them for requesting reasonable accommodation. Furthermore, you should not terminate the employee right after they return from his/her workers' compensation leave, as the timing will look suspicious. You should attempt to provide reasonable accommodations, and demand specific results. If those results are not reached, then you can terminate the employee. An additional technique you can use to prevent this entire issue is to notify an employee that you want to see him/her "right now", thus depriving them the opportunity to think his/her way out or to fake a disability.

Discrimination and contractual concerns represent two major concerns. However, an additional concern that should be analyzed involves other statutory protections that do not necessarily implicate anti-discrimination laws. One such concern involves protection for wistleblowers.

4) Statutory Protection

State statutes can provide specific guidance throughout the discipline and termination process. Any deviation from such rules or regulations can lead to automatic litigation as the laws are fairly clear-cut and employers should understand their legal obligations. You should always remember that ignorance of the law is no defense.

Reference to an Arkansas case illustrates the problems encountered when failing to abide by a state statute. Arkansas's Teacher Fair Dismissal Act requires that termination notices "include a simple but complete statement of the reasons" for nonrenewal (*Hamilton v. Pulaski County Special School District*, 1995). The Board of Education failed to renew the contract of a basketball coach for the following six reasons:

- Failure to maintain and secure inventory;
- Failure to comply with Arkansas Activities Association Regulations concerning the participation by team members without the requisite physical examination by a doctor;
- Failure to notify a team member or his parents of the team member's suspension from the team prior to publication of the suspension to the media;
- Failure to establish and enforce reasonable team rules resulting in the lack of team discipline and loss of team morale;
- Failure to comply with rules requiring payment of a participation fee by team members; and
- Inappropriate conduct toward team members and their parents.

The BOE, however, communicated the reasons for dismissal by stating that the coach was inefficient and unable to follow reasonable written regulations and policies. In holding for the plaintiff, the Supreme Court of Arkansas ordered the coach to be reinstated to his coaching position with appropriate back pay. Central to this decision was the BOE's failure to abide by state legislation governing the termination process regardless of the apparent justification for the nonrenewal of the basketball coaching responsibilities.

The following case further highlights what can happen when an employer fails to follow required procedures (*Western Grove School District v. Terry*, 1994). Joe Terry was employed as both a teacher and a coach. The School Board attempted to change his coaching position and reduce his salary. He refused the attempt and was not allowed to coach several sports, but kept his coaching-related salary. The next year, the Board sent Terry a new contract containing just teaching assignments-without any coaching responsibilities. Terry responded with a letter indicating that he wanted to be employed as both a teacher and coach. The school superintendent took Terry's response as a resignation. However, Terry wrote back indicating that he had not resigned. Terry petitioned the court for a writ requiring his reinstatement as both a teacher and coach.

Terry claimed that the attempt to change his contract violated the state's Teachers Fair Dismissal Act. The lower court ordered Terry to be reinstated to his teaching and coaching positions. The School Board appealed. The appellate court concluded that Terry had a teaching certificate and both teaching and coaching duties were identified in his contract. In addition students who attended basketball practice received physical education credits. Thus, Terry was considered a teacher and changing his contract amounted to a non-renewal.

Under the Teacher Fair Dismissal Act, a non-renewal notice and explanation for non-renewal must be sent by certified mail. The notice also has to be given to the teacher before the school board decided not to renew the contract. This provision is designed to allow the teacher to petition board members before they have already made a decision. The school board failed to provide Terry with the required notice. Thus, the non-renewal was void. If the school board had complied with the Act, Terry would have been forced to bring his action in an administrative hearing rather than the court (*Western Grove School District*, 1994).

Whistleblowers Revisited

Various statutes protect employees from unfair discharges if the discharge involves certain circumstances. For example, under the Consumer Credit Protection Act, an employer cannot terminate an employee because his/her wages are being garnished under the act (Feliu, 1992). However, one of the most frequent statutory-related claims raised by terminated employees involves allegations that a whistleblower's law was violated. Chapter 8 more specifically discusses whistleblowing issues. However, it should be specifically noted that whistleblowing laws also apply to failing to hire, failing to promote and to terminating an employee for reporting egregious employer conduct. A plaintiff alleging retaliation in violation of a whistleblower's statute has to show that he/she engaged in protected activity as defined by the specific act, that plaintiff was subsequently discharged from employment and that a causal relationship exists between the protected activity and the discharge. Protected activities can range from reporting government fraud to exposing a company illegally dumping toxic waste. The plaintiff also needs to prove that the discharge would not have occurred had there been no protected activity (*Melchi v. Burns International Security Services, Inc.*, 1984). Thus, if the employer can demonstrate that other issues were the "controlling factor" which prompted the discharge, then the plaintiff would not be successful in his/her whistleblower's claim. However, if the other factors affecting discharge were only trivial or minor incidents, then the court will probably presume that the protected activity was the main factor behind the discharge.

California, Connecticut, Hawaii, Maine, Michigan, Minnesota, Nebraska, New Hampshire, New Jersey and New York all have wistleblower legislation that applies to private sector employers (Feliu, 1992). While some private employers need to be concerned about whistleblower claims, it is much easier to prove government wistleblowing cases as wasting government resources or mismanagement present public injury claims. Under the Civil Service Reform Act of 1978 a government employer cannot retaliate against an employee for statements made by the employee concerning what he/she believed to be a violation of the law (Feliu, 1992, 193). Anti-retaliation statutes also include, but are not limited to:

- Clean Air Act,
- Federal Water Pollution Control Act,
- Solid Waste Disposal Act,
- Surface Mining Control and Reclamation Act,
- Toxic Substance Act,
- Safe Drinking Water Act,
- Energy Reorganization Act, and
- Occupational Safety & Health Act (Feliu, 1992).

Another statutory regulation which can benefit employers involves several exclusive remedy provisions. Under these regulations, a plaintiff claiming wrongful discharge can be forced to bring the claim in federal court. Federal courts are traditionally more conservative than state courts and have stricter evidence rules. For example, a plaintiff claiming wrongful discharge pursuant to a collective bargaining agreement would be limited to pursuing any claim under NLRA. Similarly, ERISA based claims supersede all state law based claims (Rothstein, Knapp and Liebman, 1987).

5) Publicizing the Termination

Is there a benefit in publicizing an employee's termination? Will making an example of the employee prohibit similar conduct in the future? Is it necessary to let all the employee's former clients know that he or she no longer represents the employer? Should you let all subsequent employers know why the employee was terminated? These represent some typical questions that can be raised after an employee has been terminated.

Internally publicizing a termination might help instill discipline. However, any communications about a former employee can also lead to a defamation claim. Even truthful statements that were interpreted incorrectly could produce a defamation claim. However, one defense to such a claim would center on the privilege associated with internal company communications between managers concerning company business. In a 1996 case, a company manager informed other managers that the employee was terminated for theft after utilizing company personnel to perform personal work-which was against the company's policy (*Stephens v. Delhi Gas Pipeline Corp.*, 1996). The employer claimed that the information was only passed along to individuals who either supervised the employee or were managers. Such communications are protected by the qualified privilege that the former employee can only overcome by showing malice. Since malice was not shown, the defamation claim was dismissed (*Stephens*, 1996).

Employers must exercise caution when terminating employees to defend against potential defamation claims. Defamation is a tort dating back to early 16th century common law and provides recourse for false, insidious or irresponsible statements which damage an individual's reputation. A defamatory statement harms the reputation of an individual and can jeopardize his or her ability to secure or retain a job. Defamation includes both slander and libel. Defamatory comments made orally, such as those heard on television, refer to slander. Comments are slanderous per se (as a matter of fact) if they fall in to one of the following categories:

- Accuses the plaintiff of criminal conduct;
- Accuses the plaintiff of having a loathsome disease;
- Accuses the plaintiff of being unchaste;
- Accuses the plaintiff of misconduct in public office; or
- Injures the plaintiff's profession, business or trade.

For example, false comments accusing someone of murder, having AIDS, having sex with an entire basketball team or illegal recruiting practices could be construed as slanderous *per se* (Carpenter, 1995). Libel represents a broader communication category. Materials in newspapers and in other written documents (e.g., written comments, photographs, cartoons) constitute libel. Some states classify statements as libel *per se* if they fall into one of the above five slander *per se* categories. Otherwise, the libel is *libel per quod* meaning that plaintiffs must prove the defamatory meaning and damages.

Terminated employees alleging defamation must prove that the employer (a) made a false statement, (b) publicized the statement to a third party, (c) exercised fault or negligence when communicating the statement and (d) damaged one's reputation (Restatement of Torts, Section 558–559). Plaintiffs alleging slander (or libel) *per se* have an advantage as they are not required to prove damages, often times "the most difficult element of defamation to prove" (Carpenter, 1995).

Defamation claims may surface even though initial communication is between only the employer and employee. It is a mistake for employers to feel that comments made privately to an individual fail to qualify as defamation since communication is not made to a "third party" *per se*. Employers should refrain from saying anything to an employee that he or she would not say in front of another individual(s) since the required communication to a third party element may be met when the terminated employee repeats comments to a future employer. Further, employers should refrain from embellishing an employee's wrong doing in front of colleagues with the intent of communicating to other employees behavior that the employer will not tolerate.

Terminology used by employers should be carefully selected. As explained by O'Meara (1996),

> An employee complaining of racial or sexual harassment is not the victim or the complainer, but rather the complainant. The person identified by the complainant is not the harasser or the perpetrator, but rather the accused. Ideally, avoid any labeling.... If a male manager is being discharged for actions which may or may not amount to actionable sexual harassment, he should not normally be discharged for sexual harassment or harassment of other employees, but rather for engaging in conduct believed to be contrary to the best interests of the employer. If an employee is being discharged after a disappearance of cash, the employee might be discharged for failure to follow cash-handling procedures, not for theft or suspected theft.

An employer may find some solace when speaking in a manner that conveys individual opinion versus a fact. The decision as to whether a statement constitutes fact or opinion is a question of law for the jury to decide. Early common law protected statements of opinion from defamatory allegations. The U.S. Supreme Court affirmed this sentiment in *Gertz v. Robert Welch, Inc.* in 1974. As stated by the Supreme Court,

> Under the First amendment there is no such thing as a false idea. However pernicious an opinion may seem, we depend for its correction not on the conscience of judges and juries but on the competition of other ideas (*Gertz*, 1974).

However, statements based upon false facts, or undisclosed facts, are actionable. In other words, if an employer conveys an opinion, then all the facts relied upon in deriving at the "opinion" should be disclosed. This enables an individual to read/hear the facts and then draw his or her own conclusion (i.e., opinion) which may differ from that of the writer or publisher. For example, you can indicate that, "I heard from an employee that you engaged in unacceptable conduct (whatever conduct that might be), if this is true, my only option will be to terminate you." The Supreme Court in *Milkovich v. Lorain Journal Co.* (1990) further narrowed the protection given to statements of opinion. As explained by the Court, merely prefacing a statement with "In my opinion,..." does not insulate an individual from defamation liability. More specifically, the Court stated,

> Even if the speaker states the facts upon which he bases his opinion, if those facts are either incorrect or incomplete, or if his assessment of them is erroneous, the statement may still imply a false assertion of fact. Simply couching such statements in terms of opinion does not dispel these implications....

Employers should give great credence to chosen language and refrain from communicating when angry or frustrated.

Employers also should be cautious regarding insinuations or other actions directed at an individual that may be perceived by others as defamatory. Inferences of misconduct conveyed through body language or timing or actions (e.g., testing and then dismissing in the immediate future) can imply erroneously wrong doing. For example, in *Tyler v. Macks Stores of South Carolina* (1980), the Supreme Court of South Carolina affirmed the lower court decision that dismissing an employee soon after the employee had taken a polygraph exam as required by the employer conveyed to others (i.e., publication) that the employee had done something wrong. As stated by the court, "It is established that a defamatory insinuation may be made by actions or conduct as well as by word" (*Tyler*, 1980). To further illustrate, assume you are a general manager for a large sport park. You conduct a criminal investigation on all employees as part of a newly adopted risk management plan. The state's Crime Information Center (CIC) reveals that Joe Smith was convicted of domestic violence, driving under the influence of alcohol, and was a multi-state offender. You immediately dismiss Joe Smith while the CIC records are verified. Thiel (1996) provides good advice regarding how to best handle situations similar to the one described above. As explained by Thiel (1996),

> If the worker must be removed in the presence of other employees, employers should exercise great caution. Employers should not act in any way that could embarrass or alarm the subject. They should speak in tones that cannot be overheard by others, and they should never become unpleasant or aggressive.

As stated by Lissy (1996), when describing a similar situation where an employee was escorted to his office while he packed up his office belongings in full view of co-workers, Language may include gestures or actions and the director's actions conveyed a 'statement' that the employee was dishonest and was not to be trusted.

Like so many other claims of litigation, defendants often do not intend to cause harm or in this situation, defame an individual. However, as noted above, innocent moves or comments misconstrued could result in a defamation claim.

6) Steps to Prevent Wrongful Termination Litigation

The pre-termination procedures should lead to the actual termination. Once you have received the information you need to support your termination decision, you should act swiftly to complete the termination. If you fail to promptly terminate a known problem employee, you could be possibly liable for any resulting injuries under a negligent retention theory.

One question that can arise is whether or not to talk with a psychologist if you feel an employee might become violent while being terminated. Such a step, while well intentioned, is not recommended. If a psychologist is brought in, then the employee could now have a disability claim under the ADA that would prevent you from possibly terminating the individual.

1)   To prevent wrongful termination claims, it is essential to develop a defensive strategy from the moment an individual is hired. While it is not the most pleasant thought, all managers have to realize there is a very good chance that any employee hired could be fired, terminated, asked to resign, demoted or otherwise undergo a change in his/her employment status. All managers must avoid using terms that may create by reference an employment contract or which creates an expectation that an employment contract exists. Besides avoiding using terms such as "lifetime," "permanent," "tenured" or "forever" when describing the term of employment, all employee manuals or guidebooks need to be checked to make sure similar terms, phraseology or implications are eliminated and cannot be modified orally.

2)   Make sure employees understand that personnel policies are subject to change without notice and at the employer's sole discretion. Whenever any changes are made, make sure those changes are effectively and timely distributed to all employees.

3)   Develop an effective dispute resolution process utilizing internal and external dispute resolution techniques to resolve employee disputes. The key to such a system is to encourage free and open communications.

4)   Establish, communicate and document an objective employee evaluation process. Every evaluation should be regularly scheduled and thorough to focus on the job's primary requirements and not just on the individual who is performing that job, at that time. Always strive to document both positive and negative comments or opinions. All evaluators should emphasize neu-

trality, objectivity and sit in a jurors chair to see how the totality of evidence adds-up in determining if someone is really meeting his or her job expectations.

5)   On a regular basis, re-communicate to all employees the employer's disciplinary and termination policies, review and resolution procedures. Besides just communicating disciplinary steps, employees should understand how many chances are allowed under the company's progressive disciplinary procedures. If all steps in the progressive disciplinary progress are not followed under circumstance, such as criminal misconduct, employees should know they will not receive a smaller penalty, but can receive the highest punishment. Whenever anyone has been disciplined for violating company policies or rules, you should track what rules were violated and what punishment was imposed to serve as a benchmark for handling future violations. Remember consistency is one of the key elements for an appropriate termination procedure.

6)   Develop a termination checklist highlighting all the steps that should be taken to terminate an employee. Any termination which does not follow the checklist should be specifically reviewed to ensure proper due process and other job related (and litigation related) concerns are covered. These concerns become acute when special circumstances arise such as sexual assault, indecency with a customer, employee theft, etc. A termination checklist should include the date, authors and contents of any warnings (oral or written), copies of all pertinent employee evaluations, the date the termination decision was made and why. Lastly, the termination checklist should indicate exact company policies or conditions that were violated with specific reference to page number or policy numbers/names. Besides laying the foundation for instituting a defensible termination, the termination checklist forces the employer to gather all necessary documentation before anything is lost or misplaced. The termination checklist and accompanying documentation should be kept for at least five years after an employee was terminated to avoid any statutory compliance or statute of limitations concerns. Record keeping requirements might vary by states and local counsel should be contacted to determine the appropriate retention period.

A typical checklist might contain the following elements:

- Considering other options other than termination such as instituting a hiring freeze, releasing temporary workers, encouraging individuals to leave or take early retirement, utilizing different workshifts and increasing job sharing.
- If employees cannot be retooled and a reduction in force is required, consider eliminating ineffective positions, close an unproductive facility or product line and eliminating poor employees.

- Always think in terms of what skills you want to keep, not what people you want to keep.
- Prior to discharging an employee, key management personnel, human resource professionals and employment counsel should analyze:
  - whether there is reasonable basis for immediate discharge,
  - whether you gathered all the necessary documentation,
  - what will be the exact grounds for termination (i.e., get the story straight),
  - whether the discharge violate any laws,
  - whether there exists any discrimination related issues,
  - the discharge's timing,
  - whether the employee performance appraisals support the termination decision,
  - whether any personal disputes exists between the employee and direct supervisor,
  - whether the employee was promised a definite length of employment,
  - whether the policy and/or employment manuals provide any special rights,
  - whether the employee is working under a special contract providing special rights,
  - whether the employee should be allowed the option to resign or seek other options, and
  - whether employees should be asked to sign a release.

If the discharge is defensible and justified, a termination letter should be prepared which contains the following elements:

- the reason for termination,
- the date(s) and warning previously given to the employee,
- any policy or rules which were expressly violated,
- a list of all benefits to which the terminated employee is able to access,
- the specific date and time the termination becomes effective,
- a brief discussion concerning any appeal or grievance process which might be available along with how to start the appeal process, who to contact and when any appeal has to be brought, and/or
- a specific date and time for an exit interview.

After the termination letter is prepared, the employee needs to attend a meeting at a designated place and time. Such notification should be oral and should not include insensitive techniques such as notes in paycheck envelopes or on an employee's door as these techniques can lead a disgruntled former employee to litigation. The termination meeting should be midweek when nothing else is going on and you should avoid holding the meeting after an employee returns from a vacation or holiday. The employee's immediate supervisor should not attend the meeting as his/her prescence can create a confrontation when the purpose of the final meeting is to terminate the employee, not discuss whether or not he/she should be terminated. Thus, a human resource department professional or other manager should attend the meeting and give the termination letter. In addition to the soon to be terminated employee, at least two people should attend the meeting.

When discussing the termination, the person describing the termination should:

- briefly outline the problem,
- briefly outline the prior problems,
- briefly outline the company's conclusion that the person needs to be discharged,
- specifically give the exact reason for discharge such as excessive absences or poor work performance,
- explain that the final decisions has been made and is unequivocal,
- provide the employee with the termination letter and let them ask any questions they might have about the appeal process, final days, etc., and
- make the meeting brief-lasting less than 15 minutes and never engage in an argument concerning the termination.

After the termination meeting, the employee should be allowed time to privately gather his/her personal affects and leave. The employee can come back and finish his/her work or continue working until his/her exact termination date. However, a more expedited approach is suggested, including utilizing company security guards if there is a legitimate fear of theft, sabotage or violence. If this practice is utilized, security personnel should not walk directly with the person, but should be as innocuous as possible to help prevent any humiliation or defamation claim.

After the individual has been terminated, his/her supervisor should be informed and all co-workers can be told that the person no longer works there. Only general and correct information about the termination should be provided to co-workers. Co-workers can be told that the individual violated company rules or based on work performance.

A separation agreement or release should be prepared prior to the exit interview. In addition, a separate agreement should be discussed concerning what reference will be provided. While this discussion can start at or around the initial termination meeting, more likely, final discussions concerning this topic are often discussed at the exit interview. The terminated employee should be told that all benefits, pension, COBRA, severance pay and related issues will be discussed only at the exit interview. This will help guarantee a higher turnout for the exit interview (Frierson, 1994).

7)   Require all terminations to be finally approved by the human resource manager, personnel manager or legal counsel.

8)   Conduct an exit interview with the terminated individual to determine his/her perception and to correct any misconception about the termination. If the termination was conducted properly, the terminated individual should have known that he/she was going to be terminated and are not surprised by the termination. If he/she is surprised by the termination, then probably some steps in the employee termination process were missed or not properly performed.

Prior to the exit interview, the interviewer should:

- contact the employee's supervisor to determine what confidential information he/she might have,
- determine if the employee ever signed a confidentiality agreement,
- review all company policies concerning confidentiality and trade secrets,
- determine if the employee ever entered into a covenant not to compete, and
- determine if the employee ever signed a contract specifically assigning all inventions, discoveries and other work product to the employer (Frierson, 1994).

During the exit interview, the human resource professional should:

- discuss the employee's confidentiality duty,
- provide the employee with any signed contracts concerning confidentiality, trade secrets and covenants not to compete,
- discuss any pension rights or other benefits,
- discuss severance pay which is obtainable upon signing the release,
- explain the type of reference that will be provided,
- deliver the final paycheck,
- obtain any and all company property in the individual's possession (keys, credit cards, computer diskettes, etc.),
- provide the individual with an opportunity to make any statements about the job, his/her supervisor or the company,
- remain businesslike throughout the interview, and

- avoid making any offensive or discriminatory statements or actions (Frierson, 1994).

In special circumstances, such as the threat of potential violence, the exit interview can be combined with the termination meeting.

9)   In addition to developing policies for employee terminations, you need to develop policies if an employee voluntarily resigns or quits. You should thoroughly discuss:

- any vesting rights,
- continued fringe benefits,
- COBRA,
- outplacement services,
- severance pay,
- reference that will be given to future potential employers,
- any releases that will need to be signed,
- any covenants not to compete,
- any provision relating to trade secrets,
- receiving the final check,
- arrange for returning all company property,
- any reasons why they might want to leave, and
- express your gratitude to the work they have done.

10)   Always re-evaluate termination options including hiring freezes coupled with natural attrition, releasing temporary workers, encouraging voluntary leave of absences, utilizing shorter work weeks, utilizing job sharing and providing employees with the opportunity to take early retirement.

11)   Consider purchasing liability insurance to help cover litigation costs and at least $1,000,000 in per incident coverage (see Chapter 15).

Wrap up..

While terminating an employee is never a fun job, it is a necessary component of the employment process. The key to avoiding wrongful discharge cases and to ensure happier employees is to properly inform all employees from their first day on the job as to what is expected of them. The termination process should not surprise any employee. They should have known that termination was around the corner from prior performance appraisals and any oral or written reprimands.

You should always remember that the best technique to terminate an employee is a direct and honest technique. Trying to hide a termination through running an employee out of town will often backfire and lead to a constructive discharge claim. A constructive discharge claim involves any illegal treatment of an employee, such as discrimination, that interferes with the terms and conditions of employment. If the employee resigns based on these illegal acts and the illegal acts were designed to expedite the termination then a constructive discharge has occurred (Frierson, 1994). While constructive discharge involves more than a single act, a single act can provide the impetus for a future lawsuit. That is why you should always be upfront about terminations.

If you are honest, upfront and thorough in the termination process, you still might face litigation. There is no guarantee that any actions taken will not result in litigation. However, employers who stick to written policies, written performance appraisals and only tell the truth can develop strong defenses to almost any claim raised by a terminated employee.

References

Adler, R., and Coleman, F. (1995). *Employment-Labor Law Audit.* Washington, DC: BNA, Inc.

Appenzeller, H. (1985). *Sports & law: contemporary issues.* Charlottesville, VA: Michie Co.

Black, H. C. (1990). *Black's Law Dictionary.* 6th edition. St. Paul, MN: West Publishing Company.

Bordwin, M. (1994/1995). "Firing 101: Before, during and after." *Small Business Forum* 12(3): 44–57.

Brown, M. (1996). "Lancaster sues to get job back." *Tulsa World* (February 29): B1.

Carpenter, L.J. (1995). *Legal concepts in sport: A primer.* Reston, VA: AAHPERD.

"Ex-Coach Wins Suit Against UT." (1997). *Greensboro News & Record* (June 6): C2.

Feliu, A. (1992). *Primer on individual employee rights.* Washington, DC: BNA Books.

Frierson, J. (1994). "Preventing employment lawsuits: an employer's guide to hiring, discipline and discharge." Washington, DC: The Bureau of National Affairs.

Graham, J.(1995). "No volunteers, please." *San Jose Mercury News* (May 12): 1C.

Jones, D. (1996a). "Managers study up for downsizing." *USA Today* (February 19): B1.

Jones, D. (1996b). "Job hunters over 50 do well." *USA Today* (September 9): 1B.

Lissy, W.E. (1996). "Unspoken defamation." *Supervision* 57(3): 18.

Maraghy, D.R. (1985). "He said what? Defamation in sports." In H. Appenzeller (Ed.), *Sports & Law: Contemporary Issues* (pp. 60–78). Charlottesville, VA: The Michie Company.

O'Meara, D.P. (1996). "Conducting investigations of workplace misconduct." *Human Resource Professional* 9(6): 11–14.

Piskorski, T.J., and Cirignani, W.A. (1995). "Managing the risk and liability of wrongful employment practices through insurance." *Employee Relations Law Journal* 21(2): 7–20.

Quintanilla, C. (1997). "Getting fired." *Wall Street Journal* (May 27): A1.

Restatement of Contracts, 2nd, Section 188 (1981).

Restatement (second) of Torts, Section 558–559 (1965).

Rothstein, M., Knapp, A., and Liebman, L. (1987). *Employment Law, Cases and Material.* New York: The Foundation Press, Inc.

Schwartz, K. (1996,). "Liability insurance for employment practices is increasingly common." *The Courier-Journal* (February 18): K18.

Simon, S. (1997). "Courts favoring good samaritan employees." *Houston Chronicle* (June 1): 4E.

Sixel, L.M. (1995). "How companies get rid of workers, one at a time." *Houston Chronicle* (November 6): B1.

"Stat Sheet." (1997). *California Lawyers* (October): 22.

Thiel, M.E. (1996). "Using preemployment screening information." *Security Management* 40(2): 80–81.

"USA Snapshots, Wrongful Termination Awards."(1996). *USA Today* (January 15): B1.

Weinstein, F. (1996). "Inside job." *Profiles* March, 9(3): 47.

Cases

American Broadcasting Companies, Inc. v. Wolf, 420 N.E. 2d 363 (C.A. NY.1981).

Austin v. Cornell University, 891 F.Supp. 740 (N.D.N.Y. 1995).

Gertz v. Robert Welch, Inc., 418 U.S. 323 (1974).

Hamilton v. Pulaski County Special School District, 900 S.W. 2d 205 (Ark. 1995).

Hurst v. Clairborne County, No. 45, 13 Tenn. Attorney's Momo 39-12(1988).

Kehoe v. Anheuser - Busch, 96 F.3d 1095 (8th Cir. 1996).

McDonnell Douglas Corp. v. Green, 411 U.S. 792 (1973).

McKennon v. Nashville Banner Publishing Co., 115 S.Ct. 879 (1995).

Melchi v. Burns International Security Service, Inc., 597 F. Supp. 575 (E.D. Mich. 1984).

Metz v. Transit Mix, Inc., 692 F. Supp. 987 (M.D. Ind. 1988).

Milkovich v. Lorain Journal Co., 497 U.S. 1 (1990).

Nalco Chem. Co. v. Hydro Technologies, Inc., 984 F.2d 801 (7th Cir. 1993).

NLRB v. Bildisco & Bildisco, 465 U.S. 513 (1984).

SI Handling Systems, Inc. v. Heisley, 753 F.2d 1244 (3rd Cir. 1985).

Stark v. American Bakeries Co., 647 S.W.2d 119 (Mo. 1983).

Stephens v. Delhi Gas Pipeline Corp., Texas Lawyer, Weekly Case Summaries, June 3, 1996, 16.

Tyler v. Macks Stores of South Carolina, S.C., 272 S.E.2d 633 (1980).

Western Grove School District v. Terry, 885 S.W.2d 300 (Ark. 1994).

White v. Banks, 614 S.W.2d 331 (S.C. TN 1981).

Wilson v. Samsonite Furniture Co., No. 89-0179 (M.D. Tenn. 1989) Aff'd per curian, No. 89-6533 (6th Cir. 1990).

Chapter 13

Retirement

Research estimates that individuals need between 70% and 90% of their pre-retirement income to maintain a similar standard of living during their retired years. Unfortunately, access to this amount of money is becoming less and less secure. Individual retirement plans for Americans have traditionally been comprised of three facets: individual savings, social security, and pension plans. On average, the amount of monies saved by individuals has dropped to an approximate 3% of all earnings (Pearson, 1997). Social security, as we know it today, is in trouble as the changing demographics are expected to exhaust funds by the year 2011 (Moore, 1997). Consequently, employers can use a well-developed and comprehensive pension plan as an attractive recruiting tool. The Department of Labor estimates that Americans rely on pension savings for a duration of 18 years after retirement. It is estimated that 26% of employers with less than 100 employees offer retirement plans in comparison to 98% of large companies with in excess of 1000 employees (Blakely, 1997). Although no company is required to offer a pension plan, those that do must comply with existing legislation and related stipulations.

1) Early Retirement

There are several distinct benefits to offering employees early retirement. These benefits include:

- Older workers who might have obsolete skills will accept the offer, thus removing older employees without violating the ADEA.
- Retirement is voluntary so good will is maintained.
- Due to its voluntary nature, few employees sue after taking voluntary retirement.
- Employee morale is boosted and employees feel the company will terminate older workers.
- Expenses can actually be reduced even though retiring workers are given a large up-front payment (Frierson, 1994).

The cost saving associated with early retirement was highlighted when AT&T had their early retirement plan accepted by 12,000 workers in 1989. The plan cost AT&T $160 million in added benefits, but the retirements now save AT&T about $450 million a year in reduced payroll and benefits (Frierson, 1994).

The hallmark for an early retirement plan rests with the Older Workers Benefit Protection Act, which allows different treatment of employees if such treatment is based on such factors as:

- a minimum age,
- a minimum service period,
- using a formula for eligibility such as the "rule of 75" where the employers age and years of service exceed 75,
- a minimum salary level for individuals to apply for early retirement,
- a minimum employment classification such as only managers and above, cite location-thus offering retirement for all workers at a given plant, and
- any additional objective criteria that does not discriminate against employees (Frierson, 1994).

Early Retirement Benefits

The benefits which can be offered an employee wishing to avail himself or herself of the early retirement option include:

- a flat salary payment of a set amount (i.e., $20,000),
- a set amount every month for several years,
- a percentage of current income,
- a percentage of future sales,
- a set pension plan with annual increases,
- calculating benefits with bonus time (i.e., 5 years) added to the employee's actual age, and
- any other objective formula which is offered to all employees in a non-discriminatory manner (Frierson, 1994).

Early Retirement Guidelines

For an early retirement plan to pass judicial muster it must truly be voluntary. All plan announcements need to clearly indicate that employee need not take retirement and that no penalties will be imposed on those who do not take early retirement. Additional guidelines include:

- employers can indicate that if not enough employees take early retirement, mandatory layoffs or reduction in force could be implemented,
- never make any pre-determination as whom to terminate if employees do not take early retirement,
- all benefits for those choosing early retirement should be clearly written and distributed to all eligible employees,
- eligible employees should be told who is administering the plan,
- never make threats that certain individuals will be ousted if they do not choose early retirement,
- upon accepting early retirement, an employee should sign a release promising not to sue the employer, and
- an attorney should be consulted to help determine how much time an employee has to reconsider their early retirement (21 days after being offered and 7 days after signing the release) and similar issues (Frierson, 1994).

2) Employee Retirement Income Security Act (ERISA)

ERISA, passed in 1974, is the federal law governing developing and implementing of pension plans in the private sector (Department of Labor, 1997a). Two common pension plans include the defined benefit plan and defined contribution plan. Employers offering a defined benefit plan to employees provide a fixed dollar amount per month upon retirement. In comparison, a defined contribution plan fluctuates as the value of invested monies fluctuates. There are several defined contribution plans available including 401(k) plans, employee stock ownership plans (ESOPs) and profit-sharing plans. ERISA governs each of these defined contribution plans. Depending on the plan and the employer's desires, both employees and/or employers can contribute to the defined contribution plans. All monies contributed by the employee are fully vested. Monies contributed by the employer, on the other hand, may not be fully vested until the employee completes a prescribed service period such as working two years for the employer.

Generally, employers must enable all employees 21 years of age and older, and who have worked for one year, to be eligible. Fully vested plans may require participants to work for two years prior to participation. Tax-exempt educational institutions stipulate that employees become vested after one year of service and upon reaching the age of 26. Employers may adopt different plans for different employees (e.g., salaried, non-salaried, union, non-union). Employers may legally exclude certain categories of employees from any offered plan. For example, all sales representatives may be excluded from a particular plan. On the other hand, if an employer provides a plan for sales manager, an older employee cannot be excluded because he or she is close to retirement.

3) Simplified Employee Pension Plans (SEPs)

A SEP represents an individual retirement account owned by the employee (Department of Labor, 1997b). SEPs differ from traditional IRAs in two ways. First, monies contributed to the SEP (i.e., individually-owned IRA) typically are made by the employer versus the employee. Second, the amount of money contributed exceeds the amount allowable with a traditional IRA. ERISA limits combined SEP contributions to a maximum of 15% of an employee's earnings, or a maximum of $30,000. All employees who have worked for the employer in three of the immediately preceding five years must be allowed to participate in an employer's SEP plan. Similar to the IRA, employees may withdraw money as desired although money withdrawn is subject to a 10% tax if employee is under the age of 59 ½ (Blakely, 1997).

SEPs are popular among sole proprietors, small partnerships, and small corporations for four reasons. First, administrative requirements (e.g., reporting and disclosure requirements) are relatively minimal in comparison to other pension plan options. Second, employer contributions can increase or decrease depending on the business earnings for any respective year. Third, SEP contributions are tax deductible and an employer pays no taxes on contributions made to an individual SEP. Fourth, the employer retains no responsibility for investing contributed monies as this responsibility falls to an independent company or broker.

4) Savings Incentive Match Plans for Employees of Small Employers (SIMPLE)

An alternative savings plan similar to the IRA evolved with the Small Business Protection Act of 1996 (Department of Labor, 1997c). SIMPLE plans allow employees to contribute a maximum of $6,000 annually to their account via payroll deductions. The employee can discontinue the deduction or contributions to the account at any time. Employers can match contributions (up to 3% of an employee's wages) or make fixed contributions (equal to 2% of employee's wages). All contributions made by both the employer and the employee are immediately vested. Similar to SEPs, SIMPLE accounts require minimal administrative costs. SIMPLE accounts do allow for employee withdrawals. However withdrawals will be taxed between 10% and 25% if the employee is under the age of 59 ½ (Blakely, 1997).

5) 401(k) Plans

401(k) plans follow the same basic concept as the SEP. Under a 401(k) plan, a portion of the employee's salary is invested tax-free with the intent that the money will accumulate earnings and not be withdrawn until retirement. In order to secure a minimal level of tax monies, the Treasury Department defines the maximum amount of money that can be deferred. As of 1997, the amount is $9,500. High salary earners may have additional caps placed on the amount they can defer. For example, maximum amounts may be contingent upon the number of lower wage earners which participate in the plan. This stipulation reduces the likelihood that the employer will establish 401(k) plans that serve as a tax shelter for high wage earners. Employees are allowed to withdraw monies from their 401(k) plans as needed although withdrawals may be subject to a 10% penalty tax if the employee is below the age of 59.5 (Blakely, 1997).

6) Employee Stock Ownership Plans (ESOPs)

ESOPs represent a retirement plan where a portion of the employee's earnings is invested in company stock. In addition to securing monies for retirement, the ESOP was intended to serve as an employee motivator. Employees with ownership in the company, for example, would be self-motivated to work efficiently and effectively. Work demands once seen as unrealistic and benefiting only the interests of management would now be viewed as having some "trickle down" effect. Additional information on ESOPs can be found in Chapter 14.

7) Health Care Benefits

Sixty-one percent of all employers provide employees and dependents with health care. Providing employees with health care provisions is becoming increasingly expensive. A survey by consulting firm Foster Higgens revealed that health insurance cost employers an approximate $3,915 per employee in 1996 with costs in 1997 expected to be even higher (Insurance costs, 1997). A conflicting survey indicated that health care costs decreased with average costs amounting to $3,421 per employee. Within the service sector, including parks and recreation departments, health clubs, bowling alleys, etc., only 68% of employers provided health care benefits (Wiatrowski, 1995). Only 62% of employers in the retail trade, including the sporting goods retail industry, provide health care benefits.

Providing health care benefits has become a competitive advantage for small firms vying to recruit exemplary employees. Unfortunately, health care costs are more onerous on the small employer versus the large employer. For example, in 1996 large employers paid only 22% of total health care premiums for single coverage and 30% for family coverage in comparison to small employers which paid 33% and 44% respectively. Small business employers, in an attempt to remain competitive, have joined "Professional Employer Organizations" (PEOs). PEOs represent a type of pooled insurance which offers benefits including health coverage, dental coverage, vision coverage, life insurance, 401(k) plans and long-term disability (Ho, 1997).

Health care becomes increasingly important as individuals approach and enter into retirement. Employers may provide health care benefits for retired individuals. However, individuals covered under these plans may need to pursue a "back up" or alternative plan as no federal law prohibits an employer from eliminating benefits at any particular time. Employers should include a clause in the insurance or health plan literature distributed to the employee that conveys the employer's right to alter plan provisions at any specific time. A clause might read as follows, "[T]he company reserves the right to modify, revoke, suspend, terminate, or change the program, in whole or in part, at any time" (Department of Labor, 1997d). Otherwise, the plan itself represents a contract between the employer and employee or retired employee. Failure to include a clause reserving the right to change the plan makes employers accountable for providing provisions as detailed. Furthermore, if you promise an employee certain benefits when they were recruited, it might be difficult to subsequently change such benefits. Thus, you should always mention to prospective employees that benefits (as well as all other contractual provisions) are subject to change.

A last note should be added concerning health insurance issue. Recently enacted legislation entitled the Health Insurance Portability and Accountability Act provides specific rules concerning employer insurance programs and what happens when an employee quits, is fired and/or retires. Employers with 20 or more employees are required to keep certificates detailing when an employee and any dependents were covered under the company health plan. These certificates need to be given to an employee within 14 days after being terminated. All other employers (less than 20 employees) need to provide the certificates in a reasonable time after an employee's departure. Under the Health Insurance Portability and Accountability Act, an employer's health care plan cannot exclude a new worker's pre-existing condition for more than 12 months. Thus, the certificates help prove when insurance coverage has to kick-in for pre-existing conditions (Weaver, 1997).

Special certification of coverage needs to be provided and the law is very specific concerning appropriate employer conduct. For example, fraud and abuse charges can result not just in huge civil fines, but allows violators to be sent to prison. Thus, you should make sure all health care/benefits are annually reviewed by a competent benefits administrator to ensure you are in compliance.

8) Contractual Concerns

Employers should also use extreme caution when making decisions about downsizing. Laying off employees and then turning around and hiring independent contractors may be construed as violating a recent U.S. Supreme Court decision (see *Donna Vizcaino, etc. v. Microsoft*, 1996). As explained by Jones (1997), ERISA protects benefits other than vested retirement benefits. Companies can cut benefits as a business decision, but they cannot fire workers, then contract those jobs out for the primary purpose of cutting costs. Thus, outsourcing should be viewed as a way to combat seasonal fluctuations or reduce employer liability rather than for the purpose of eliminating the expenses associated with benefits.

9) Consolidated Omnibus Reconciliation Act (COBRA)

The Consolidated Omnibus Reconciliation Act (COBRA), an amendment to ERISA, represents a valued piece of legislation for American individuals and their families. COBRA requires businesses to provide health insurance for terminated employees, employees who lose coverage because of reduced work hours or for employees making career changes for an extended time period after leaving the place of employment. The federal government and various church-related entities remain exempt from COBRA requirements. The Department of Labor defines three criteria, which stipulate whether an individual is subject to COBRA benefits (Department of Labor, 1997d). The three criteria include (a) plan coverage, (b) beneficiaries, and (c) events that initiate the coverage. The Department of Labor facilitates understanding by defining the three elements as follows:

Plan Coverage

Group health plans for employers with 20 or more employees on more than 50 percent of the working days in the previous year are subject to COBRA. The term "employees" includes all full-time and part-time employees, as well as self-employed individuals. For this purpose, the term employee also includes agents, independent contractors and directors, but only if they are eligible to participate in a group health plan.

Beneficiary Coverage

A qualified beneficiary generally is any individual covered by a group health plan on the day before a qualifying event. A qualified beneficiary may be an employee, the employee's spouse and dependent children and in certain cases, a retired employee, the retired employee's spouse and dependent children.

Qualifying Events

"Qualifying events" are certain events that would cause, except for COBRA continuation coverage, an individual to lose health coverage. The type of qualifying event will determine who the qualified beneficiaries are and the required amount of time that a plan must offer the health coverage to them under COBRA. A plan, at its discretion, may provide longer periods of continuation coverage.

The types of qualifying events for employees are:

- Voluntary or involuntary termination of employment for reasons other than "gross misconduct."
- Reduction in the number of hours of employment.

The types of qualifying events for spouses are:

- Termination of the covered employee's employment for any reasons other than "gross misconduct."

- Reduction in the hours worked by the covered employee.
- Covered employee's becoming entitled to Medicare.
- Divorce or legal separation of the covered employee.
- The covered employee's death.

The types of qualifying events for dependent children are the same as for the spouse with one addition:

- Loss of "dependent child" status under the plan rules.

As stated by the Department of Labor, "Rising medical costs have transformed health benefits from a privilege to a household necessity for most Americans" (Department of Labor, 1997d). Downsizing and the popularity of part-time employment has illuminated further benefits of COBRA that are available to terminated employees, spouses, and dependent children. Prior to COBRA's 1986 health benefits provisions, individuals no longer working for a particular employer were often left uninsured.

Certain requirements, however, do accompany COBRA provisions. For example, individuals seeking coverage will be required to pay for the benefits themselves, up to 102% of the premium (2% for the employer's administrative costs). Failure to pay premiums when due will cause benefits received via COBRA to end. Employers must provide notice by law of COBRA provisions. Individuals entitled to COBRA benefits have 60 days to accept coverage. Employers are not required to make COBRA benefits available to individuals who have access to benefits through a new place of employment. Employers are also not required to continue benefit provisions when a past-employee is entitled to Medicare benefits. Employers seeking additional, and more detailed, information on COBRA should contact either the U.S. Department of Labor (private sector employers) or the U.S. Public Health Service (public sector employers).

10) The Summary Description Plan and Other Communication Requirements

Employers providing benefits and offering retirement plans must provide all participating employees with a Summary Description Plan (SPD) within the first 90 days that he or she become a plan participant. As explained by the Department of Labor, the SPD,

> Tells you what the plan provides and how it operates. It tells you when you begin to participate in the plan, how your service and benefits are calculated, when your benefit becomes vested, when you will receive payment

and in what form, and how to file a claim for benefits. You should read your summary plan description to learn about the particular provisions that apply to you. If a plan is changed, you must be informed, either through a revised summary plan description, or in a separate document, called a summary of material modifications, which also must be given to you free of charge.

Employers can be fined up to $100 a day for denying SPD related documents to employees. Employers must make the following documents available to employees upon request.

- SPD
- Summary of material modifications
- Summary annual report
- Annual report (form 5500 series)
- Individual benefit statement
- Documents and instruments under which the plan is established or operated
- Disclosure notice (e.g., the plan's funding level)

Full Disclosure

Employers can best protect themselves from violating ERISA's fiduciary requirements and legal entanglements by communicating openly and honestly about the various plans and what actions would be in the employee's best interest. Statements made with the intent of inducing action (e.g., persuading an employee to relocate to another state or accept a particular financial package) can invite problems. For example, telling an employee that the "financial future and all related investments of the company looks bright" may violate ERISA's fiduciary requirements if the company is in fact on weak footing (Flynn, 1996; *Howe v. Varity Corp.*, 1994).

11) The Older Worker's Benefit Protection Act

Mandatory retirement was eliminated with the passage of the ADEA except in very limited situations such as airline pilots (see generally Chapter 4). However, voluntary retirement programs have gained in popularity as outsourcing has increased and businesses have attempted to eliminate duplicative functions and reduce labor costs associated with highly paid and compensated managers. Disgruntled employees often seek recourse under ADEA. Businesses have attempted to circumvent liability by using releases. These contractual agreements provided employees with severance pay and early retirement benefits in return for their agreement that they had been fully satisfied and promised not to sue under the ADEA (see generally Chapter 12). The Older Workers Benefit Protection Act of 1990 prohibits employers from denying specified benefits to older employees. In other words, employers cannot coerce an older employee into signing a release that denies any future recourse for age discrimination when claims are otherwise meritorious. Primary objectives of the OWBPA are that individuals sign the forms with full knowledge that rights are being given up and that signing is done on a voluntary basis. The minimal requirements imposed by the law to ensure that the employee is signing a waiver with full knowledge and on a volunteer basis include the following:

- The waiver is written in a manner calculated to be understood by such individual, or by the average individual eligible to participate;
- The individual does not waive rights or claims that may arise after the date the waiver is executed;
- The individual waives rights or claims only in exchange for consideration in addition to anything of value to which the individual already is entitled;
- The individual is advised in writing to consult with an attorney prior to executing the agreement;
- The individual is given a period of at least 21 days within which to consider the agreement; or if a waiver is requested in connection with an exit incentive or other employment termination program offered to a group or class of employees, the individual is given a period of at least 45 days within which to consider the agreement;
- The agreement provides that for a period of at least 7 days following the execution of such agreement, the individual may revoke the agreement, and the agreement shall not become effective or enforceable until the revocation period has expired;
- Waivers that prohibit employees from cooperating with EEOC investigations are illegal.

Wrap Up....

No one stated that it would be easy getting older. With the tremendous changes our society and technology have undergone in the past 20 years, many employees might feel useless and outdated. Through training, older employees can be retooled to accomplish their job responsibilities. If older workers refuse to bring their skills up to the current standards you cannot automatically terminate them. Such an action, while possibly justified would result in an almost immediate lawsuit. A younger worker would most likely, replace the older worker. As discussed throughout this guide, those are key ingredients for a discrimination claim.

If older employees refuse to update their skills or are no longer productive in other areas throughout your business, you should contact a human resource specialist. Such a specialist might recommend termination, job rotation, part-time hours, retirement or other steps designed to recognize an employee's past contributions. While most employees no longer expect to receive a golden watch or think they will work for an employer for over 20 years, employees still should be treated with significant social tact and honor. In the sports industry, individuals can become diehard fans and if you leave a bitter taste in someone's mouth, you will probably completely alienate that individual. Furthermore, when someone has a gripe they tell all their friends which creates a negative ripple affect throughout the consumer market.

References

Blakely, S. (1997). "Pension Power." *Nation's Business* (July): 12–20.

Department of Labor (1997a). "ERISA and your pension plan [Online]." Available: www.dol.gov.

Department of Labor (1997b). "Simple retirement solutions for small business [Online]." Available: www.dol.gov.

Department of Labor (1997c). "Savings incentive match plans for employees of small employers: A small business retirement savings advantage [Online]." Available: www.dol.gov.

Department of Labor (1997d). "Health benefits under the consolidated omnibus reconciliation act (COBRA) [Online]." Available: www.dol.gov.

Flynn, G. (1996). "Don't make benefits promises your company can't keep." *Personnel Journal* 75(11): 91–94.

Frierson, J. (1994). *Preventing employment lawsuits.* The Bureau of National Affairs, Inc.

Ho, R. (1997). "Small change: Competitive pressures are forcing some small firms to improve their benefits." *The Wall Street Journal* (May 22): R6.

"Insurance costs rise." (1997). *USA Today* (January 21): 3A.

Jones, D. (1997). "Supreme Court ruling may stem outsourcing." *USA Today* (May 13): 5B.

Moore, S. (1997). "Social security: A ticking time bomb [Online]." Available: www.cato.

Pearson, G. (1997). Social Security Presentation given by George Pearson to the Downtown Rotary Club, Wichita, KS, September 15.

Weaver, P. (1997). "An extra layer of paperwork." *Nation's Business* (August): 28.

Wiatrowski, W.J. (1995). "Who really has access to employer-provided health benefits?" *Monthly Labor Review* 118(6): 36–45.

Cases

Donna Vizcaino, etc. v. Microsoft, No. 94-35770 D.C. No. CV 93-00178-CRD.

Howe v. Variety Corp. 36 F. 3d. 746 (8th Cir. 1994).

Statutes

COBRA, P.Law 99-272 (1986).

ERISA, 29 U.S.C.A. Section 1144 et seq.

Health Care Portability & Accountability Act of 1996. Pub. L. 104-191, Title I, Aug. 21, 1996, 110 Stat. 1978.

Older Workers Benefit Protection Act, Pub.L. 101-433, 29 U.S.C..626(f). (1990).

Chapter 14

Unionization

As discussed in Chapter 1, unions represent a significant impact on many employers. The primary function of a union is to negotiate and administer the collective bargaining agreement (CBA) with the employer that covers the conditions of employment for the union members. Unions have a significant impact on the employment environment. They reduce a manager's authority, reduce a manager's control over personnel policies, and reduce a managers prerogative to make certain decisions without union involvement. At the same time, unions represent a significant benefit for employees through providing a unified voice, psychological satisfaction, safety in numbers, and specific economic benefits (Chruden and Sherman, 1976). While it might appear that employees have a one sided weapon against employers through unions, specific federal legislation provides both sides with tangible benefits which will be described below.

The two types of unions are national and local unions. National unions establish rules and conditions under which local unions may be chartered and permitted to retain their membership in the national union. Such rules and conditions can relate to dues collection, initiation fees, union funds administration, and new member admission criteria. Local unions represent the direct interest of their constituency by monitoring management activities and making sure the collective bargaining agreement is being followed. In addition, local unions help members rectify any unjust treatment or sponsor grievances claimed by local members (Chruden and Sherman, 1976).

Local unions operate through a business representative who negotiates the CBA and administers the agreement. When a union member has problems, they bring the problems to the attention of the union steward represents the union member's interest in their relation with their immediate supervisors and other managers. Some stewards are paid by the employer solely to reconcile disputes involving union members in performing their work (Chruden and Sherman, 1976).

Unions can be further classified as closed shops and open shops. Closed shops operate under a CBA wherein all employees as a condition of employment need to be union members. Open shops infer that both union and non-union employees can work for the employer even if the employer has a CBA with a union (Gifis, 1984).

393

Under the NLRA (section 8(a)(3) and 8(b)(2)) both unions and employers are forbidden from requiring actual union membership (Weiler and Roberts, 1993). However, unions can secure from each employee a financial contribution to help pay for representation costs and his/her costs are typically the same as union dues paid by union members (Weiler and Roberts, 1993). However, in approximately twenty states there exist "right to work" laws which forbid unions from seeking financial contributions from non-union employees (Weiler and Roberts, 1993).

The laws related to unionization, union activities, retaliation, antitrust violations and related issues are very complex. It is critical for a business facing unionization to hire a talented labor law specialist. The potential union will not be undertaking their formation efforts without competent counsel. To face trained labor organizers without proper assistance is paramount to committing business suicide. This chapter will highlight specific concerns associated with unionization and provide some preliminary highlights concerning rights and obligation for an employer.

While unionization can affect janitors at a sports stadium or employees at a school, most cases discussing unionization concern unions in professional sports leagues. While this text is generally not designed to highlight the law as it affects professional athletes, the lack of meaningful examples from areas outside professional sports are minimal. However, the same issues that face a professional sports league can also affect a stadium, bowling alley, health club and/or school coaching staff.

This chapter examines union related issues such as union formation, developing an employee bargaining unit, the collective bargaining agreement, anti-trust issues affecting unions and employers, state and federal laws, retaliation against union activities and union decertification.

1) Formation

Unions started in the middle ages as skilled artisans organized into guilds designed to control and regulate their professions (Chruden and Sherman, 1976). Unlike the craftsman who had unique marketable skills and more bargaining power, factory workers lacked security as they could be replaced easily by others who could be quickly trained to perform the desired factory assignment (Chruden and Sherman, 1976). This led to the management mindset that employees were like commodities to be employed at the lowest wages and discarded when their services were no longer needed. This mindset has been portrayed in countless books such as The Jungle by Upton Sinclair and court cases such as *Flood v. Kuhn* (1972). The *Flood* case is a seminal case in the sports labor industry as the United State Supreme Court upheld the prior legal precedence that baseball players were like chattel (property), who could be traded like meat (*Flood*, 1972).

It was not until 1842 that the employee received certain rights. Prior to then, and the *Commonwealth v. Hunt* decision that year, any employee attempt to organize and to collectively bargain for better conditions with an employer were considered under the existing common law as a criminal act-conspiracy (Chruden and Sherman, 1976).

For several employees to become organized as a union, a bargaining unit needs to be established comprised of employees with similar wage scales, hours, working conditions and job responsibilities. Thirty percent of the employees in the unit have to sign an authorization card, authorizing a particular union to represent them. An employer can voluntarily recognize a bargaining unit, which then starts the negotiation process. However, if an employer is not willing to accept the bargaining unit, then the employees have to petition the NLRB to conduct a secret ballot election. The NLRB then orders and administers a representative election. At no time prior to the election can either party coerce or threaten voters nor promise potential benefits based on the election's outcome. If the voters vote against unionization, no further election can be held for a one year period (Rothstein, Knapp and Liebman, 1987). However, if the voters approve the union, the union becomes the official collective bargaining representative for all employees in the bargaining unit, regardless if they did or did not support the union (NLRA Section 9(a)). The union and employer then have to bargain in good faith over such issues as wages, hours worked and any other terms and conditions of employment. One of the greatest benefits that can be obtained through the collective bargaining agreement is an employer's concession that they will not terminate an employee without "just cause" (see generally Chapter 6, Section 6). Unions can also bargain to create a "closed shop" which means the employer will only hire union members and drop any employee who cancels or loses his or her union membership. The NLRA also allows unions to create a "union shop" where an employee, within 30 days after being hired, is required to join an existing union. Furthermore employees could avoid joining a union, but pay any initial fees and dues under the doctrine of an "agency shop." (Rothstein, Knapp and Liebman, 1987). The key is the employee bargaining unit, which upon formation, becomes the driving force for a future union.

2) Exclusive Bargaining Unit

An exclusive bargaining unit (EBU) refers to organized employee(s) who are authorized to represent the employees during negotiations with the employer. When the employees vote to unionize, they vote for a specific group of employees who will represent their interests. The employer is forced to bargain exclusively with the exclusive bargaining group. This can represent a unique challenge if an employer can negotiate better with some employees, but is barred from doing so as those employees are not part of the exclusive bargaining unit. The issue also arises if two competing unions are trying to win elections within the same company. The employer is prohibited from promoting one over another and cannot enter into any negotiations with the losing union.

The EBU has one major obligation, the duty to bargain in good faith. This obligation, pursuant to NLRA, Section 8(d), applies to both the EBU and the employer. Both sides are required to meet at reasonable times and confer on matters that represent mandatory subjects of collective bargaining. Failing to meet or discuss such matters in good faith represents an unfair business practice. Good faith negotiations have been defined as a "willingness to enter in negotiations with an open and fair mind and with sincere desire to find a basis of agreement." (Champion, 1993). The good faith negotiation does not require that the parties reach an agreement, it only require that the parties sincerely try to reach an agreement. An example of this requirement was demonstrated in a case involving the National Football League Players Association. Various NFL owners unilaterally promulgated and implemented a rule fining players who left the bench to enter a brawl on the playing field. Such action, which was not covered by the CBA represented an unfair labor practice because rules affecting activities during the game are mandatory subjects of collective bargaining. For such to be valid, it would have to have been added to negotiations in the collective bargaining process (*NFLPA v. NLRB*, 1974).

As a component of the duty to bargain in good faith, each side is required to provide the other side with all necessary documents to help both parties make an intelligent, educated decision. Thus, if the employer claims that they need lower wages in order to help make the company profitable again, the company has to open their books so the union can see first hand that in fact there is financial crunch (Weiler and Roberts, 1993). Another key good faith provision entails refraining from making unilateral changes in any matter under discussion until the parties reach an actual impasse. This helps prevent using and deploying unilateral threats to help move the negotiation process.

One duty which employers need to follow involves negotiating in good faith with a union representative-even if you hate the other side. No matter how loathsome the other side's bargaining unit, you are committing an unfair labor practice if you refuse to negotiate with the bargaining unit or intentionally enter into contractual negotiations with anyone else. This issue was raised in a case involving a professional soccer league. The North

American Soccer League refused to negotiate with the players' union and entered into negotiations with individual players. The union filed an unfair labor practices charge with the NLRB, which then sought an injunction from a federal court to prevent the league from entering into the individual players' contracts. The court sided with the union and clearly established that the duty to bargain with the exclusive representative carries a negative duty not to bargain with individual employees (*Morio v. NASL*, 1980).

Besides the employer's obligation to bargain in good faith with the employees, the union has an obligation to fairly represent all members of the bargaining unit, even those who are not members of the unit (Champion, 1993). Thus, the union has to fairly represent all employees, and if they fail to represent a non-union member in a dispute, then they could be a violation of the union's duty of fair representation (DFR). The DFR is breached when the union's conduct towards a member of the collective bargaining unit is arbitrary, discriminatory, or in bad faith (*Vaca v. Sipes*, 1967).

3) Collective Bargaining Agreement

The collective bargaining agreement (CBA) represents one of the key benefits to unionization. This document establishes rules and regulations of the employer/union relationship. Issues such as salaries, working hours, promotions, terminations, personnel policies and related issues are all covered within the CBA. All mandatory matters covered by the CBA reflect terms and conditions of employment. "Terms and conditions of employment" relate to any activity affecting how, when, where, and related issues associated with how an employee performs their job and how they are compensated. While wages, hours and conditions of employment are mandatory subjects of collective bargaining and need to be negotiated in good faith, all other matters are considered permissive bargaining subjects and do not need to be bargained for in good faith. Furthermore, either party can unilaterally refuse to negotiate any permissive subject matter.

There are numerous issues in sports that can relate to mandatory subjects of bargaining. Such issues can include:

- wages, benefits and pensions,
- enlarging the playing season or workplace operation hours,
- installing drug testing programs,
- requiring employees to wear protective equipment,
- employee uniform requirements,
- changing the time and length of breaks or meals, and/or

- requiring the employees to telecommute on weekends.

Permissive issues can include:

- what playing surface to use,
- what weight training equipment is made available,
- use of instant replay to review plays, and/or
- moving a business from one part of a city to another.

When completed, the CBA is binding for the established time period between the parties. The CBA can cover a one-year period or longer, but typically CBAs cover a 3–5 year period. The CBA terms apply to all employees and future employees even if they are not union members. Individual employee can ask for additional rights, over and above the CBA if those rights are not covered by the CBA. Otherwise, the CBA is controlling. All future employees are bound by the CBA terms. Thus, the NBPA and the NBA negotiated a contract limiting future rookie salaries. Such an agreement hurts individuals who are not currently union members, but it is still a valid contracts (Weiler and Roberts, 1993).

CBA Topics

Besides wage, hour and working conditions, CBAs can cover specific topics that are designed to benefit both the employer and the employees. For example, a company facing closure could re-negotiate the CBA to allow employees the opportunity to own an ownership interest in the business. The National Basketball Association (NBA) rose to prominence in the 1980s after entering into a CBA with the players which allowed for revenue sharing (Weiler and Roberts, 1993). Without such an agreement, it would have been very difficult for the NBA to survive and then to flourish.

Arbitration and mediation programs within CBA also represent a significant development within CBA. Such a clause helped end Major League Baseball's (MLB) reserve system through the 1970 CBA and brought about salary arbitration in the 1973 agreement (Champion, 1993). Arbitration clauses similar to those discussed in Chapter 6, above are found in many CBAs.

Drug testing represents another major concern often covered in CBAs. Especially in the sports industry, employers want their employees to be steroid or drug free. The NLRB requires an employer to bargain in good faith with the union representative concerning a drug and alcohol testing policy as they represent a term and condition of employment. A union representative can waive their right to bargain over drug testing, however, such waiver must be clear and unmistakable. Thus, the CBA should specifically indicate what was finalized concerning the implementation of any and all testing policies.

The CBA represents an agreement to limit competition for salaries and bind current and future employee to contracts in which they might not have had a voice. Accordingly, all contracts that have a potential to limit competition have to comply with federal antitrust concerns.

4) Antitrust Implication

If the parties have attempted to negotiate a CBA in good faith, but reach an impasse, either party can resort to economic pressure such as strikes and lockouts without risking an NLRA unfair labor practice charge (NLRA Section 8(a)(5) or 8(b)(3)). This is critical because if an impasse has not been reached, a court could enjoin the strike. An "impasse" is specifically defined as "following intense, good faith negotiations, the parties have exhausted the prospects of concluding an agreement" (*Powell*, 1988). Even if an impasse has been reached, and the union goes on strike, the union is still obligated to continue negotiating in good faith (Champion, 1993).

Strikes exist as a tool for unions to help facilitate recognition or encourage movement in the negotiation process. Economic strikes are strikes that occur as a result of a stalemate in negotiations for a contract. Such strikers are entitled to NLRA protection during the strike and an employer cannot engage in any unfair labor practices as the strikers are still considered employees. However, the employer can replace the strikers with replacement workers and the employer is not obligated to rehire the economic strikers. On the flip side of the strike coin, employees who strike because an employer has engaged in unfair labor practices are engaged in an unfair labor practices strike (ULPS). ULPSs differ from economic strikes as an employer who has been found to violate the NLRA has to rehire all striking workers (Coughlin, 1983).

A wildcat strike is a strike where the employees are not authorized by law to strike. Such strikes are not conducted with the union's permission and as such, the strikers have no NLRA protection. Wildcat strikers do not need to be rehired by the employer. Similar to unauthorized wildcat strikes, illegal strikes are wholly against the law (Taft-Hartley Act, 1947). Illegal strikes include:

- strikes trying to force an employer or self-employed individual to join a certain union,
- strikes to force an employer to stop doing business with a person or company,

- strikes to force an employer to bargain with a minority union (i.e., the union not certified by the NLRB as the exclusive bargaining unit), and
- strikes beginning within 60 days after the CBA expired.
- Any employee who engages in such an illegal strike losses their status as an employee and can be terminated without violating the NLRA.

Under the 1959 Labor Management Reporting and Disclosure Act, a union commits an unfair labor practice when a strike is used to:

- force an employer not to deal with another company,
- to stop anyone from using, selling or handling another's goods, and
- to force an employer to bargain with an unapproved bargaining unit (Coughlin, 1983).

Sherman Act

Strikes by their very nature are designed to be both informative and disruptive. If a strike is disruptive, it will normally affect interstate commerce. The Sherman Act was designed to make illegal every combination or conspiracy that restrain interstate commerce (15 U.S.C.A. Section 1 et seq.) The goal of the act is to stop monopolies and protect fair competition. Unions represent a challenge to antitrust laws as they are specifically designed to limit competition in the employment market and employers can join together with some unions in a manner that excludes other potential employee representatives. Such action would normally constitute an antitrust activity. However, congress has clearly indicated that the potential benefits associated with unions and employers working together clearly outweigh the potential antitrust infringements. Thus, congress has produced several exemptions to the Sherman Act which are commonly referred to as the statutory labor exemptions. These exemptions can be found in the Clayton Act and the Norris-La Guardia Act. Under these exemptions, unions are able to enter into agreements that might eliminate competition from other unions.

In addition to the statutory labor exemption, there is a non-statutory labor exemption, which is based on the policy favoring collective bargaining over antitrust violations. The non-statutory exemption will apply where the restraint on trade primarily affects only the parties to the collective bargaining process, where the restraint concerns a mandatory subject of collective bargaining and where the CBA (which the parties want to be exempt) is reached through bona fide arms' length bargaining (*Mackey*, 1976). The non-statutory exemption is the key exemption utilized in professional sports teams dealings with player unions. The non-statutory exemption continues even if a CBA expires. However, such exemptions only continue until the parties reach an impasse in their negotiations that cannot be resolved. Such an impasse was sought by the NFLPA in the *Powell* cases. However, the court was unwilling to agree that an impasse had in fact been reached and the court refused to intervene as the parties were required to resolve the dispute by themselves (*Powell*, 1991). In order to proceed against the NFL in an antitrust suit, over 60% of the NFL players had signed a petition revoking the NFLPA's authority to act as their EBU. The NFLPA also revised its bylaws to remove its officers' authority to negotiate with the NFL or its individual teams. Based on these actions, the court concluded that the players were no longer part of a collective bargaining relationship. Because no ongoing collective bargaining relationship existed, the non-statutory labor exemption ended and the NFL was potentially liable for violating the antitrust laws (*Powell*, 1991).

If an impasse is reached, then the union can claim that there is no longer a valid CBA. Without a CBA, the union could claim that the employers who united to enter into the union relationship are conspiring to restrain trade-an antitrust violation. If an antitrust claim is raised, the employer has to pass the rule of reason test developed to determine the validity of the employer's contract which restrains trade. The rule of reason test analyzes whether the restraint imposed is justified by legitimate business purposes, and is no more restrictive than necessary to help accomplish the legitimate business purpose (*Mackey*, 1976).

The Sherman Antitrust Act is just one of the many federal and state laws which regulate unions to ensure they comply with specific legislative mandates.

5) Applicable State and Federal Laws

Numerous federal laws apply to the union relationship. Labor law represents a bridge between contract law and Sherman Antitrust implications as described above. A large patchwork of rules and regulations are in place to ensure equitable balancing between the interest to allow employees to join together to reduce competition and its resulting benefits to the employment process. These laws emanate from federal mandates, and such mandates are adopted through congress's power to regulate interstate commerce. Most sports related entities involve interstate commerce, such as all team sports, fitness facility, sporting good manufacturers and other business where customers, participants or products can cross state lines.

However, courts have held that some activities, such as harness racing have been held to not involve interstate commerce (*Yonkers Raceway, Inc.*, 1972). If a sports organization or business involves interstate commerce, then they are subject to the NLRB's jurisdiction, pursuant to the NLRA.

The NLRA covers all union related issues from formation through strikes and decertification. The NLRA allows unions to go on strike without the striking employees being fired. However, unless the strike was brought alleging unfair labor practice by the employer, the employer can hire permanent replacement workers and then only has to put the strikers on a preferential hiring list. However, if the union alleges unfair labor practices by the employer, the employer can only hire temporary replacements and then has to give striking employees their job back after the dispute is settled. Therefore, an employer's greatest weapon is traditionally using replacement workers during the strike who are not given any guaranteed job security (Weiler and Roberts, 1993).

Charges of unfair labor practice have to be filed with the NLRB within six months of the unfair practice occurring. The dispute is normally heard by an NLRB administrative law judge. Remedies available under the NLRA for unfair labor practice include back pay, employee reinstatement, an order for both parties to return to the bargaining table and cease and desist orders.

As previously mentioned, Clayton, Norris-LaGuardia and the Taft-Hartley Acts form the basis for many rules and regulations affecting unionization. One key provision within the Taft-Hartley Act is the so-called Bill of Rights of Union Members which allows each union member to nominate candidates for union office, vote in union elections, attend union meetings and participate in union meetings (Chruden and Sherman, 1976). Another federal statute is the Landrum-Griffin Act which prohibits picketing for the purpose of shaking down an employer, forcing an employer to recognize a union or to compel employees to join a union (Chruden and Sherman, 1976). Numerous state laws mirror or expand these federal acts. However, the scope of laws dealing with open and closed union shops is outside the scope of this guide.

6) Employer Retaliation

While retaliation seems to imply that the employer feels cheated and wants to punish the employees for forming a union, employer retaliation affects activities that occur even before a union is ever formed. Any activity that is designed to dissuade union efforts can possibly be considered a form of retaliation for exercising rights granted under various federal and state laws.

Employers are required to comply with the Taft-Hartley's requirement to avoid engaging in activities that could be construed as unfair labor practices. Unfair labor practices can include:

- interfering, restraining or coercing employees who are attempting to exercise their right to unionize,
- interfering with union formation efforts,
- contributing money to oppose union formation efforts,
- discriminating on any terms or conditions of employment with an effort to hinder union formation efforts or continued operations,
- discharging or otherwise discriminate against an employee who filed charges or gave testimony under the Taft-Hartley Act, and
- refusing to bargain collectively with the employees duly chosen bargaining unit (Chruden and Sherman, 1976).

In the sports industry, professional team sports provide a perfect example of the obligation associated with not interfering with union activities or punishing individuals who actively support a union. The NLRB can be called upon to decide whether a professional team terminated an athlete's employment based on the team's legitimate and acceptable exercise of their judgment concerning the player's skills or was contaminated by animus against the player's union activities. Such an issue is especially problematic in sports where union representatives are normally older players who might be in the twilight of their playing career (Weiler and Roberts, 1993). Sam McCullum was a starting wide receiver for the Seattle Seahawks in 1981. Later that year, his teammates elected him their union representative. McCullum started every game in the 1982 preseason. However, his coach was upset that McCullum orchestrated a solidarity handshake with opposing players prior to the first pre-season game. The coach was also upset about remarks made in McCullum's role as a player representative at a press conference. The Seahawks traded with another team for a wide receiver and then cut McCullum from the team. McCullum sued claiming an unfair labor practice (Weiler and Roberts, 1993). Approximately 11 years later, the case was finally decided and the court sided with McCullum and awarded him back pay (*Nordstrom v. NLRB*, 1993)

One nationally known law firm in the employment law field developed the "TIPS" acronym to help educate employers on what not to do during the union formation process. TIPS stands for Threats, Interrogation, Promises and Surveillance. An employer cannot threaten among other matters reduced pay, lowered benefits or possible strikes if the union is successful. An employer cannot interrogate employees on their intended actions or possible union support. An employer cannot promise an employee higher wages or increased benefits if they oppose the union. Lastly, an employer cannot undertake any surveillance on union meetings or who attends such meetings (Kristoff and Blackburn, 1994).

Employee Unfair Labor Practices

Employers are not the only party required to avoid unfair labor practices. Union members and prospective union members are also required to abstain from engaging in any unfair labor practices. The following acts are considered unfair labor practices by unions:

- restraint or coercion utilized against employees trying to exercise their Wagner Act rights,
- restraint or coercion utilized against employers concerning who should be the party bargaining on the employer's behalf,
- persuading employers to discriminate against an employee,
- refusing to bargain in good faith with the employer,
- participating in secondary boycotts and jurisdictional disputes,
- attempting to force an employer to accept a given union when the employer is already dealing with the certified employee representative,
- charging excessive initiation fees, and
- requiring an employer to pay wages for service not performed, commonly called "featherbedding." (Chruden and Sherman, 1976).

Thus, the relationship between the employer and the employees is strictly construed to provide each side with valuable rights, and protected each side from any unreasonable conduct. However, as evidenced in the *Powell* cases, sometimes the union relationship can become a hindrance and the union members might attempt to dissolve their union.

7) Union Decertification

Even though some workplaces really need unionization to protect either employees or employers, sometimes conditions change which might make a union an unwanted handicap. Such a condition can arise because employees no longer want a union, employees want to switch to a different/new union, and/or the employees want to gain an advantage in the negotiation process with an employer after the parties have reached an impasse in the good faith negotiations.

If employees want to switch to a non-union environment or to utilize a different union, the employees can call for a decertification vote. If a majority of the union members agree that they want to decertify the union, then the employer's duty to bargain with the union ceases (*Powell*, 1991). The voting process is administered by the NLRB to avoid any voting improprieties or employer influence. However, a union does not even have to go through the vote process. If the union does not wish to continue, then it can be terminated without a decertification vote (*Powell*, 1991). Thus, decertification votes are traditionaly utilized when certain employees want to challenge a union or a new union wants to become the official employee bargaining unit.

Wrap Up...

Various concerns make the union environment unique. Employers typically do not want unions in the workplace due to the significant increase in laws, rules, procedures, and red tape that represent significant intrusion into the workplace. For example, some ticket takers and related ticket personnel at several major New York stadiums and arenas have been accused of various ticketing improprieties in relation to sporting events. However, because these allegedly corrupt employees are also union members, they could get off with a minor suspension which can allow them to work at other facilities and return after a year, or whatever other punishment is handed down. In a non-union setting, corrupt employees would have been terminated for their conduct. This example highlights why it is so important for employers to try and prevent employee unionization.

There are very specific steps an employer can take to maintain a union-free workplace. The primary step is to act in good faith and treat employees in a civilized manner. This should help foster a collegial environment and encourage open communication. Additional steps include:

1)   Keeping union organizers off your premises. This includes the actual facility, parking lot and adjoining property. Individuals can be kept off the premises by posting no trespassing signs and vigorously enforcing the no trespassing policy. Signs should be prominently displayed at every entrance. You can insist that any union solicitation activity take place on non-company time.

A sample no-solicitation and/or no distribution rule could provide as follows:

> To prevent disruption in the workplace, workplace interruptions and employee inconvenience, solicitation for any cause or distribution of literature of any kind, during working hours or immediately prior to or after working time on company premises, is not permitted. In addition, an employee who is not on working time, such as an employee on their lunch break, shall not solicit any other employee who is on working time for

any cause or distribute literature of any kind to the working employee. No matter if during working time or outside of working time, no employee may distribute literature of any kind in any working areas. Furthermore, off-duty employees and non-employees are forbidden from solicitation or distribution of literature of any kind on company premises (Update '92, 1992).

2)   Reiterate to employees on a regular basis that they have good conditions under current arrangements. Employees can also be taught about union downsides including dues, picket line duties, possible strikes, possible fines, and other assessments. Employees should also know that if they strike for economic reasons, the employer has the right to replace them with new employees.

3)   Never threaten to remove certain benefits or rights if employees try to unionize.

4)   Employee should know their rights including the fact that even if they sign a union authorization card, that does not mean they have to vote for the union if there are union elections. Employees should also know that disciplinary rules will be enforced whether or not a union is present. In the same light, company rules should be equally enforced regardless of union membership.

5)   Be honest with employees and let them know how you feel about unions and union activities. Employees are entitled to know your rationale. If you know the potential hurdles and can effectively articulate such concerns, you have a good chance of swaying some employees to champion your philosophy. At the same time, inform employees of any prior unionization efforts and any information you might possess about the union organizer. Information is a valuable tool and every effort needs to be made to correct or clarify misstatements, lies or innuendoes. While the employer cannot ask employees about union related matters, it is not illegal to listen while employees are discussing union related activities. Thus, communication entails both letting employees know your opinion and listening to the employee grapevine.

6)   In addition to what an employer can do, an employer has specific barriers that cannot be crossed. These barriers include specifically designated illegal activities and certain forms of punishment designed to intimidate or destroy union related activities.

7)   Additional prohibited conduct by the employer includes the following:

- attend union meetings,
- monitor which employees are going to union meetings,
- ask employees about confidential union matters,
- ask employees how they feel about the union representative,
- ask employees how they intend to vote at the union election,

- provide any financial assistance to a union or certain employees to affect the union vote,
- threaten not to deal with unions,
- ask prospective employees if they have ever been union members,
- start an anti-union petition drive,
- visit employee at their home to encourage an anti-union vote, or
- engage in any other surveillance related activity deigned to determine who is or who is not involved in union activities (Kristoff and Blackburn, 1994).

Furthermore, an employer cannot punish an employee for engaging in union related activities. Punishment includes:

- discharging an employee,
- granting some employees wage or benefit increases to keep them out of a union,
- discriminating against pro-union employees,
- disciplining pro-union employees more harshly than other employees, and
- threatening to close a business, move a plant or reduce benefits to discourage union activity (Kristoff and Blackburn, 1994).

To help an employer react quickly to possible union related activities, the following point should serve as early warning signs about possible union related activities. The early warning signs include:

- increased number and frequency of employee complaints,
- employees meeting in groups which include individuals who normally do not associate with each other,
- employees asking numerous questions about company policies, rules, benefits, pay and related issues,
- employees visiting work areas they normally do not visit,
- employees who normally socialize with supervisors start avoiding supervisors,
- employees asking argumentative questions at department meetings,
- employees who quit or resign indicate at the exit interview that the work environment was unpleasant,
- employees start posting information about union activities at other companies on the employee bulletin board,
- mysterious graffiti or cartoons appear which attack management,
- employee turnover significantly increases or decreases,

- applications are received from individuals who are over qualified for positions and are willing to work for less money or lower benefits,
- vendors and subcontractors start asking to talk with other employees,
- non-union employees start meeting regularly with known union members or union organizers,
- complaints are filed by groups of employees rather than single employees,
- strangers suddenly appear upon company premises or in work areas,
- strangers suddenly start asking questions about company policies, pay or benefits,
- employees start using terms such as "protected activity," "unfair labor practices," and "demand recognition,"
- union authorization cards, leaflets, handbills or related documents appear on the company's premises, and
- union representatives start visiting employees at work or at the employees' homes (Kristoff and Blackburn, 1994).

If union related activities are suspected, the employer should immediately contact a labor or employment law attorney to determine what steps to take. Until additional advice is given, the employer has to be diligent not to engage in any conduct that might be construed as trying to influence union related activities as such conduct can represent an unfair labor practice.

A recent trend that bears closer scrutiny by employers is "salting." Salting involves a union sending sometimes hundreds of employees to apply for several jobs. When numerous union members are turned away, the union files a discrimination claim with the NLRB. Unions who push such strategies are hoping the employers cave-in and unionize or the employers become so financially burdened by litigation that they go out of business (Worsham, 1997). Salting represents one of the key concerns small employers are raising on Capital Hill. Small businesses are trying to make it easier for companies to forgo hiring applicants who plan to organize workers and/or disrupt the business's operations. Other legislation being sought includes the Teamwork for Employees and Managers Act (TEAM) which would allow manager-workers safety committees to discuss issues without creating a union or an unfair labor practice (see Chapter 11). Unions are intent on flexing their political muscle too and intend on having at least 100 union activists in each of the 435 congressional districts to lobby for pro-union legislation. Unions are supporting the Davis-Bacon Act which requires paying prevailing local wages, usually the union rate, to various employees working for federal contractors (Worsham, 1997). Other trends developing in unionization includes union members leaving their current unions for more militant unions which are willing to throw away past good union-management relations for more money or additional benefits (Worsham, 1997).

References

Champion, Jr., Walter T. (1993). *Sports Law in a Nutshell*. St. Paul, MN: West Publishing Co.

Chruden, H., and Sherman, Jr., A. (1976). *Personnel management*. 5th edition. Cincinnati, OH: South-Western Publishing Co.

Coughlin, G. (1983). *Your introduction to law*. 4th edition. New York: Barnes & Noble Books.

Gifis, S. (1984). *Barron's legal guide, law dictionary*. New York: Barron's Educational Services, Inc.

Kristoff, R.P., and Blackburn, S.R. (1994). *Managing Within the Law- Update*. SanFrancisco, CA: Schachter, Kristoff, Orenstein & Berkowitz.

Rothstein M., Knapp, A., and Liebman, L. (1987). *Employment law, cases and material*. New York: The Foundation Press, Inc.

Update '92, In-house counsel colloquium. (1992). San Francisco, CA: Schachter, Kristoff, Orenstein & Berkowitz.

Weiler, P., and Roberts, G. (1993). *Sports and the law: Cases, materials and problems*. St. Paul, MN: West Publishing Co.

Weiler, P. and Roberts, G. (1995). *Sports and the law: Cases, materials and problems, 1995 supplement*. St. Paul, MN: West Publishing Co.

Worsham, J. (1997). "Labor's New Assault." *Nation's Business* (June): 16.

Cases

Flood v. Kuhn, 407 U.S. 258 (1972).

Mackey v. NFL 543 F.2d 606 (8th Cir. 1976).

Morio v. North American Soccer League 501 F. Supp. 633 (S.D. N.Y. 1980).

NFLPA v. NLRB 503 F.2d 12 (8th Cir. 1974).

Nordstrom v. NLRB, 984 F.2d 479 (D.C. Cir. 1993).

Powell v. NFL, 678 F.Supp 777 (U.S.D.C. MN 1988).

Powell v. NFL, 764 F.Supp. 1351 (U.S.D.C., MN, 1991).

Vaca v. Sipes, 386 U.S. 171 (1967).

Yonkers Raceway, Inc. 196 N.L.R.B. 373 (1972).

Statutes

Clayton Act, 15 U.S.C.A. 12 et seq.
Labor Management Reporting and Disclosure Act of 1959, 29 U.S.C.A.
   Section 401 et seq.
National Labor Relations Act, 29 U.S.C.A. Section 151–166.
Norris-La Guardia, 29 U.S.C.A. Section 101–115.
Sherman Antitrust Act, 15 U.S.C.A Section 1, et seq.
Taft-Hartley Act, 29 U.S.C.A. Section 186.

Chapter 15

Additional Concerns

While this guide has strived to cover many issues, the authors have tried to point out all along that it is impossible to cover all the facets inherent in employment law. The first 14 chapters have tried to provide the reader with various specific topics that form distinct legal issues affecting an employer. This chapter represent a potpourri of various issues that overlap several areas previously covered. This chapter provides some insight into employment tax and insurance issues. Lastly, this chapter will try to provide specific insight and advice into dealing with workplace drug testing and preventing violence in the workplace.

1) Employment Taxes

Numerous tax issues exist with employment related issues and it is beyond the scope of this guide to analyze the numerous tax issues involved. It is recommended that an employer consult with a competent tax or employment law attorney or accountant to help understand all the tax intricacies. An additional effective management tool is to utilize an outside firm to handle payroll and employee tax issues. Since the payroll companies exclusively handle employee taxes on a regular basis, you can save valuable attorney fees and related expenses. While it is not cheap, a payroll firm can alleviate significant concerns and let you focus on your company's mission rather than state and federal tax issues.

While there are numerous tax issues that come to play, two key issues will be discussed below to shed light on different strategies that can benefit employees and provide employer benefits. The two issues discussed below should be addressed through a competent tax specialist to determine the applicability to any given sports business.

College Tuition Reimbursement

One issue that has arisen concerning employee taxes refers to tax breaks for employees attending college. Under a recently expired law, employers were allowed to reimburse an employee up to $5,200 per year in under-

411

graduate college and university costs without having to add that amount to an employee's taxable income. Once repealed, employees were forced to declare this reimbursement as income and forced to pay possible federal, state, and FICA taxes. However, no taxes are owed if the college expenses are characterized as fringe benefits. To qualify as fringe benefits, the course(s) must help the employee maintain or improve skills in their current position. However courses are not considered fringe benefits if they help an employee meet minimum educational requirements required for the job or qualify the employee for a different job (Marullo, 1997).

Tax Credit

Yet another tax related issue involves hiring designated employees whose salary can be utilized as a tax credit. In 1996, a new law was enacted called the Small Business Job Protection Act, which created the workplace opportunity tax credit (WOTC). Under WOTC, an employer is able to claim a federal tax credit against wages paid for individual hired after October 1, 1996 who come from seven designated classifications. These classifications include:

- recipients of Aid to Families with Dependent Children,
- veterans receiving AFDC or food stamps,
- economically disadvantaged ex-felons hired no later than one year after conviction or release from prison,
- high-risk youth ages 18 through 24 who reside in a federally designated "employment zone" or "enterprise community,"
- vocational rehabilitation referrals,
- qualified summer youth ages 16 through 17 who reside in a federally designated "empowerment zone" or "enterprise community," and
- qualified food stamp recipients ages 18 through 24.

Employers who hire individuals belonging to one of these designated groups are eligible for a tax credit of 35% of the first $6,000 in wages paid the employee. If the employee works for at least 180 days and performs over 400 hours of service, the employer can claim a credit of up to $2,100 depending on the employer's tax bracket. To receive the tax credit, the employer has to hire the employee, and then have the employee certified by a designated agency for the Department of Labor. If the employee is not certified, the employer does not receive the tax credit. Employment cannot be made contingent on having the employee certified. Employers are not allowed to specifically recruit employees who fit into the enumerated categories, but can utilize an intermediary such as an employment agency to screen potential employees. While the law seems to be a significant benefit, it is only in place for limited time period and might not be renewed by the federal government.

2) Employment Insurance Concerns

This guide has raised several key insurance concerns such as workers' compensation insurance to cover worker injuries and comprehensive general liability policies, which could cover an employer when an employee injures a customer. Additional insurance can be obtained for the owner or other key person associated with the sports business entity. Key person insurance provides a sizable payment to the entity in case the insured "key person" dies. This sum is designed to keep the business afloat while searching for a new key person. Often this insurance is purchased for inventors, star athletes or other employees whose skills would be difficult or impossible to replicate. Bodily injury insurance can also be purchased to compensate athletes, personal trainers and anyone else whose livelihood depends on staying in peak physical condition. If an individual has a bodily injury policy, the policy could pay-off for that injury. Additional insurance options are discussed below.

Unemployment Insurance

One of the greatest insurance concerns an employer might face involves unemployment insurance, which affects their bottom line and tax liability. Unemployment Insurance (UI) is a joint federal-state partnership under which benefits (temporary and partial wage replacements) are provided to terminated employees who were terminated through no fault of their own. Employer paid taxes funds the benefits. These taxes include a flat federal tax and an experience-rated state tax which is based on claims filed by former employees and how much money the state needs to pay the former employees. The highest 1994 state unemployment insurance taxes for an average employee was $590 per year in Rhode Island. The lowest figure from 1994 was $70 per year, per employee in South Dakota (Adler and Coleman, 1995). In Texas, an employer cannot deduct the taxes from an employee's wages and the minimum tax is 2 $7/10$% (Texas Labor Code, 1997). If an employer has very little turnover, their tax rate can be reduced or they can generate such a large reserve that the state might reimburse the company some money. Thus, you have a very strong incentive not to terminate an employee unless the employee engaged in misconduct. For example under Texas unemployment compensation laws, an employee discharged for misconduct cannot recover unemployment insurance benefits. The exception applies when an employee violates a company policy adopted to ensure the orderly work and safety of employees (Texas Labor Code, 1997). In several cases, the Texas courts have concluded that when an employee borrows a company vehicle or other machinery without authorization and in violation of company policies, the employee's misconduct precludes them from receiving any unemployment insurance benefits (*Texas Employment Commission v. Ryan*, 1972).

EPL Insurance

Some insurance policies provide coverage for such issues as wrongful termination, defamation and other related claims. At the same time, many policies do not provide any coverage for willful acts such as sexual harassment, intentional discrimination and public policy abuses and related claims. Employment practices liability insurance (EPLI) represents one of the most important insurance policies to acquire. Employment practices liability insurance provides coverage for such traditionally excluded areas as discrimination (including age, race, gender, religion and nationality), sexual harassment and ADA violations (Carter, 1997). As with all other insurance policies, it is critical for you to know what is covered under the insurance policy. EPLI policies typically exclude all:

- workers' compensation claims,
- ERISA and WARN related claims,
- punitive damages, fines and sanctions, and
- the cost associated with implementing court ordered remedial programs (Walsh, 1995).

Employment claims could be covered under commercial general liability, workers' compensation/employers' liability, directors' and officers', and employment practices liability insurance depending on claims and policy coverage. Within all these policies a few key issues need to be addressed. One issue is whether or not a policy covers an incident on a per claim or per occurrence basis. If incidents are handled on a per claim basis then each claim might be covered for a specified policy limit such as $1 million. However, if the policy covers incidents on a per occurrence basis then maybe five individuals were harassed by the same person at the same time. Even if five different suits are filed, the insurance company would claim that the policy is a per occurrence policy which means a maximum of $1 million is available to handle all five suits ($200,000 per suit rather than $1 million per suit).

Another concern relates to whether or not the insurance company pays just awards or if the insurance company has a defense obligation. A major cost with any lawsuits involves the attorney fees. If the insurance company does not cover attorney fees, the insurance company might settle a claim within the policy limits, but you could be stuck paying a five figure attorney's bill. Another concern relates to choosing counsel. Normally an insurance company tenders your claim to one of the many attorneys or law firms which they regularly work with. You have a right as an insured to request different counsel or you can ask the insurance company to possible retain another attorney that is more familiar with your business or industry. The process of changing counsel might require the assistance of an attorney.

Denied Insurance Coverage

Another insurance concern relates to insurance companies denying coverage. Even if the insurance policy contains comprehensive rules and regulations, there are often disagreements as to how to interpret contractual provisions. As insurance companies traditionally prepare the insurance contracts, the courts generally construe any disparity or inconsistencies against the contract's author—the insurance company. If an insurance company is not living-up to their obligation, it might be necessary to contact an attorney to help represent you against the insurance company. Sometimes a simple letter and clarification material can solve the problem. Other times, you might need to hire an attorney to file an insurance bad faith action which is normally brought against an insurance company that fails to defend a case or pay their agreed upon coverage.

3) Drugs in the Workplace

Rising absenteeism, tardiness, accidents, sloppy work, lower productivity, employee negligence are all potential by-products of one of the largest concerns facing employers—drug and alcohol abuse in the workplace. It is estimated that the cost of substance abuse in the workplace may exceed $100 billion (Adler and Coleman, 1995). Numerous issues abound concerning drug and alcohol abuse at the workplace. Can you terminate someone who comes to work drunk? Can you check an employee's locker for drugs? Can you have random post-hiring drug testing? What can you do when an admitted addict is in therapy for the tenth time? Are steroids classified as a drug?

The starting point for analysis is the federal Drug-Free Workplace Act which requires government contractors, such as colleges and midnight basketball programs, with contracts or grants over $25,000 to certify they are providing a drug-free workplace. Failure to provide certification or to complete all required steps in the certification process can result in losing the government contract and being barred from future federal contracts. Certification can be accomplished by:

- publishing a drug-free workplace policy statement that lets the employees know that the use, sale or distribution of drugs is prohibited,
- establishing a drug-free workplace awareness program and letting employees know what punishment they could receive if the drug-free workplace policy is violated,
- requiring employees with drug problems to participate in a rehabilitation program,
- letting all employees know that as a condition of continued employment they have to comply with the drug-free workplace policy and that they are required to notify you if they receive any drug related convictions for activities associated with the workplace,
- if an employee is convicted of a drug related offense in the workplace you are required to let the contracting government agency know about the conviction within ten days after you are notified,
- if an employee is convicted of a drug related offense you are required to impose some sanction on the employee, and
- requiring the employer to make a good faith effort to maintain a drug-free workplace (Adler and Coleman, 1995).

While these regulations are designed for federal contractors, the same rules apply in such states as California, Illinois and South Carolina. However, other states such as Connecticut, Maine, Montana and Vermont expressly limit drug testing (Frierson, 1994).

Even if testing is not allowed, all employees should read and sign the drug-free workplace policy statement which could provide for testing or could also cover other conditions which could trigger coverage such as drugs being found in employee work areas or coming to work under the influence. The signed policy statement should be included in the employee's personnel file.

Drug Testing Legislation

Other laws provide different rights and obligations. The ADA and the Federal Rehabilitation Act of 1973 coupled with potential state or local laws can provide addicts with protection as disabled individuals. For example, by 1990 there were ten states that had passed legislation regulating drug testing in private employment environments. Under the Utah state law, for example, drug testing is specifically permitted and employers are immunized from liability from such testing as long as the employer publishes a written testing policy, performs confirmatory tests, and properly documents all samples (Utah Code Ann., 1987). Other states such as Minnesota and Connecticut have highly restrictive rules which prohibit random private employee drug testing except in safety sensitive positions or if tests are specifically permitted through a collective bargaining agreement (Minn. Stat, 1987; Conn. Gen. Stat., 1987). Several cities such as San Francisco have enacted drug-testing ordinances as well.

These conflicting laws develop a damning situation for the employer. The employer is forced to be tough on drug, but at the same time, employers cannot be too tough as such toughness might be construed as discrimination against a disabled individual. Luckily, the disability classification is limited to situations where the employee has rehabilitated themselves, they are no longer suffering from the affliction, and they are able to competently perform their job (Adler and Coleman, 1995). If the employee suffers from a drug or alcohol problem which limits their ability to perform their job, the individual is not considered disabled. However, the second a drug or alcohol abusing employee enters a rehabilitation program, they are protected by the ADA.

Post-Hiring for Cause Drug Testing

The key concern most employers will face involves post-hiring drug testing. Normally employers do not test all employees. Employers normally focus their attention on employees whose drug use may endanger themselves, co-workers or the general public (Adler and Coleman, 1995). Furthermore, testing can be implemented through the employee manual under circumstances where management feels, based on objective facts, that an employee is under the influence or violating the company's drug and alcohol policy. These test are often called "for cause" testing. Objective facts can be established by training managers to recognize symptoms associated with drug or alcohol abuse. While there are no specific indicators that someone is intoxicated or under the influence absent admission, evidence or using drug on premises, an employer can look for possible signs such as slurred speech, lost balance, and/or agitation. The hallmark associated with "for cause" testing is the factual predicate leading to the test. A factual predicate might entail catching an employee in the act of utilizing drugs or alcohol. Since significant objective facts support the test, courts find such testing the least objectionable of all drug testing methods (Adler and Coleman, 1995).

An additional component associated with "for cause" testing involves providing proper notice. Similar to pre-employment testing, an employee cannot complain about a possible drug test if they knew from the day they were hired that they could be tested at any time. However, some employees might refuse drug testing due to the potential for self-incrimination or due to the possibility that under certain circumstances, such as subpoenas, the employer might have to be divulge the test results to authorities. Since the drug testing policy should be an overall component within the employee policy manual, any refusal to take the exam should result in immediate suspension and possible termination after a complete investigation.

Random Drug Testing

Random testing is also an available option that forces all employees to consider the fact that they can be tested at any time for any reason or no reason at all. Testing flexibility makes such tests very advantageous for an employer. The courts primarily uphold random testing and periodic/scheduled testing when they are conducted on employees in safety, transportation and security-sensitive positions. However, numerous legal challenges have been raised against random drug testing. Court are more willing to strike down such tests, and such test may be limited by state laws or local ordinances, if the employees are not involved in any safety or security related positions (Feliu, 1992). In the sports industry, security personnel, lifeguards and personnel trainers spotting clients all could possibly be considered as safety or security related positions.

Post-Accident Testing

Various employers require drug testing under certain conditions such as when there is reasonable suspicion of drug abuse based on job performance, safety concerns of after an accident (McEwen, Manili and Connors, 1986). One major testing area involves post-accident testing. Such tests are triggered by an industry accident. Such accidents are typically of such a nature that they generate an OSHA investigation or violation. The major difference between post-accident testing and other testing options involves the lack of prior notice. Since the test has to be administered immediately after an accident, there normally is no warning given prior to the test. This concern can be addressed by adding a line in the employee manual that all accidents involving serious injury can lead to all employees involved in such accident being tested for drug or alcohol usage.

An additional specifically allowed condition for testing involves rehabilitation-related testing. Such tests are normally conducted on employees who have undergone dependency treatment. Due to the high relapse rate, several courts have already approved such tests.

Privacy and Discrimination

As with all testing procedures, you need to make sure privacy and confidentiality are enforced. Privacy rights can also be protected by state constitutional mandates. Alabama, Arkansas, California, Florida, Hawaii, Illinois, Louisiana, Massachusetts, Montana, South Carolina and Washington all have privacy mandates in their constitutions that apply to state entities. California and Montana also have privacy right requirements that also apply to private employers. Additionally, random tests cannot only target individuals with certain demographic characteristics that can generate a discrimination claim. As with pre-employment test, an initial test should be administered and processed by a certified medical lab. All positive test results should be confirmed with a second test.

Drug-Free Workplace Policy

While testing is a major concern, it is not the only critical issue. The entire drug-free workplace policy represents the key to eliminating drug and alcohol abuse in the workplace. The policy statement should conform with all applicable laws and provide you with an opportunity to test employees suspected of being intoxicated or impaired while working. The policy statement should also address appropriate disciplinary procedures, the availability of an Employee Assistance Program (EAP) and provide guidance to treatment programs. If at all possible, you should try to emphasize rehabilitation over discipline. Such an approach will show dedication to employees and can help reinforce the union-free environment. The drug-free workplace policy should be uniformly enforced with all employees who are asked for a test, provide the test or face disciplinary sanctions. The policy should clearly articulate specific standards such as:

- what substances are prohibited,
- who is covered by the policy,
- what tests can be administered,
- where the testing will be performed,
- the discipline imposed for violating the policy and
- what appeal process is available (Feliu, 1992).

An integral component within your drug-free workplace policy is a search policy authorizing a search of an employee and their working space or locker. The policy should specifically indicate which areas are open to search including, but not limited to lockers, desks, vehicles, lunch boxes, uniforms, and related personal items (Adler and Coleman, 1995). Thus, there is no privacy expectation (Feliu, 1992). Specific concerns associated with employee drug searches include:

- not allowing employees to use their own locks on lockers or desks which can create an expected privacy right,
- specifically indicate that failure to comply with a requested search will result in immediate suspension and possible termination,
- violating employees through false imprisonment, battery, assault and invasion of privacy claims,
- keeping all medical records confidential,
- providing all disciplined employees with the full dispute resolution option available for all other disputes,
- the EAP should be offered to all employees, at all levels just by asking for assistance, and
- the EAP should allow for self-referral and management referral (Adler and Coleman, 1995).
- If an employee locker is secured by the employee's own lock, then the employee will have a privacy expectation (Update '95, 1995).

Other measures which employers have deployed to curb drug use, possession and sales include:

- using undercover police officers,
- using drug sniffing dogs,
- utilizing private security and investigative firms,
- utilizing a parking lot/workplace video surveillance system, and
- encouraging employees to report their co-worker's misconduct (McEwen, Manili and Connors, 1986).

While there are no easy answers to dealing with drug and alcohol use in and outside the workplace, you will be facing more issues associated with these concerns in the future. Likewise, violence in the workplace is another concern that is still increasing for all employers.

4) Violence in the Workplace

The 1990s have witnessed an explosion in work environment criminal activity. Workplace violence is at an all-time high. As reported by Schaner (1996),

1) In 1993, for example, homicide was the third leading cause of death in the workplace and the leading cause of occupational death for women.
2) The National Institute for Occupational Safety and Health reports that on average 15 workers are victims of work-related homicides every week.
3) The Northwestern National Life Insurance study found that more than 2 million people were physically attacked in the workplace from July 1992 to July 1993.

Besides potential harm that can confront other employees, a dangerous employee also presents significant risks to customers or patrons. Individuals injured by an employee's criminal act(s) are now challenging traditional tort law and arguing that employers should be liable for hiring people known to have dangerous propensities or likely to present perilous situations which is also fostering numerous suits claiming negligent hiring or other negligent related claims.

For example, in *D.T. by M.T. v. Independent School Dist. No. 16* (1990), the plaintiff sued the Oklahoma School District alleging the negligent hiring of a 30 year old male teacher-coach who sexually molested three elementary school students. Similarly, the plaintiffs in *Doe v. British Universities North American Club* (1992) argued that the defendant should be liable for negligently hiring a camp counselor who sexually assaulted a camper. Hence, the tort of negligent hiring. As explained by Levin (1995),

> Negligent hiring occurs when the employer knows, or should have known, of an applicant's dangerous or violent propensities, hires the individual, and gives the employee the opportunity to repeat such violent behavior.

While it is impossible to identify all potential violent or dangerous employee, a survey conducted by the Society for Human Resource Management, for example, revealed that, "Two out of three respondents believed that they could have identified the aggressors in advance as possible perpetrators of violence acts" (Schaner, 1996).

Unlike any prior period in the existence of mankind (since cave man days), numerous individuals are now settling even minor disputes with violence rather than communications. Instead of stopping after a traffic accident, many drivers are scared that they might be shot by the other person, and thus speed away. The same type of atmosphere exists in the workplace. Where once an employee might have ranted and raved about a poor job assessment or evaluation, now the same employee might feel that termination will be just around the corner. The employee might feel the only way to beat the employer to the punch is through violence. A recent report from the National Institute for Occupational Safety and Health concluded that in 1994 there were 1,071 Americans murdered at work. An additional 160,000 employees were physically assaulted at their place of employment. Between 1992 and 1993, there were two million physical attacks, six million threats and 16 million employees harassed in the workplace which resulted in 500,000 employees missing 1.8 million lost days and resulting in $55 million in lost wages (Update 95, 1995). A majority of the attacks occurred at retail trade or service industry work sites. Workers facing the greatest potential of becoming a victim of work place violence are individuals who have significant daily face-to-face contact with many people.

Violence in the workplace represents a dramatic shift in the way employers have to examine their employment decisions. Violence can take many forms from spousal abuse, terminated employees returning to get even, through employees stealing company property. Stealing might not be considered a violent act in and of itself when compared with assaults or attempted murder. However, if someone has enough animosity against a company to steal from the company, the same person also might have pent-up aggression which could lead to violence.

To help defuse a potential violent work environment, it is important to:

- closely check employee references,
- institute better security procedures,
- boost employee morale through such steps as profit sharing and
- utilizing nonintrusive surveillance and sanctions (Rothstein, Knapp and Liebman, 1987).

Insurance Coverage

One concern raised by workplace violence is whether or not workplace attacks are covered by insurance policies. Many workplace assaults are covered by workers' compensation insurance except:

- where a supervisor assaults a lower level employee,
- an assault or injury is not employment related,
- the injury stemmed from a personal quarrel unrelated to employment,
- the injury stems form the employees own intoxication,
- if the injury was self inflicted, and/or
- an employee was injured while committing a felonious act (Feliu, 1992).

Workplace Drug Dealing

The workplace has become America's safest location for dealing drugs. Employers do not need to be concerned as much with strangers coming to the workplace to peddle their wares. Rather, employers need to be most concerned about employees buying drugs from other coworkers. Such dealings can lead to lost productivity, higher overhead costs, employee theft and embezzlement (*Combating Workplace Drug Crimes*, 1994). Research has shown that typical drug-abusing workers are: five times more likely to file workers' compensation claims, involved in accidents four times more often than others and are twice as likely to be on sick leave and three times more likely to be tardy when compared with other employees (*Combating Workplace Drug Crimes*, 1994).

The key to combating drugs in the workplace involves early cooperation with police detectives, investigators and company management. The police can establish specific guidelines such as requiring investigators to receive approval prior to engaging in any undercover buys, buys have to be made with police money and the investigator has to be made available to testify (*Combating Workplace Drug Crimes*, 1994). These rules are in place to help the police prosecute, not to help the employer terminate an employee. No matter what strategy is utilized to help catch drug dealing in the workplace, the key to combating drug related dealings involves producing and distributing the previously mentioned drug abuse policy statement. Such a statement should specifically provide for termination and additional penalties for anyone who is caught dealing drugs in the workplace.

Risk Management Techniques

There are several specific techniques that can be utilized to help reduce the potential for violence in the sports workplace. Some violent outbursts cannot be controlled. A patron who becomes violent based on external conditions might be impossible to stop before injuring someone in a facility's parking lot. However, everyone in the workplace from front office personnel through receptionist has to understand what they can do to help prevent violence. One of the key techniques involves just looking for individuals who appear to be agitated, yelling or demanding to see someone in a violent or threatening manner. Other telltale signs include an individual:

- engaging in intimidating behavior,
- making direct or veiled threats,
- with a prior violent history,

- who demonstrates paranoid behavior,
- who has a strong interest in weapons,
- who suffers from wide mood swings,
- exhibits impulsive behavior,
- who has recently suffered significant financial or family problems,
- has recently lost there job or other stressful occurrences,
- abuses alcohol or drugs,
- is a loner, and/or
- engages in physical acts such as unwanted touching (Update '95, 1995).

In addition to trying to spot individuals who might pose a risk, you have to make violence prevention a top priority. You can form a management team to access the entity's readiness for dealing with violence in the workplace. Job applicants should be thoroughly screened and all employees should understand your policies and procedures relating to workplace violence prevention. You should also develop a network of external resources such as psychologists, security personnel, law enforcement professionals and specialized legal counsel. Lastly, you should train managers in identifying and responding to workplace violence (Update '95, 1995).

5) Responding to Government Investigations

Typically, an employee, former employee or prospective employee can bring a claim to the EEOC or a designated state agency within a set time period which is normally 180 days after the allegedly discriminatory conduct occurred. The matter can either be pursued by the state, or if the state fails to respond, the matter would automatically refer to the EEOC. No matter what agency receives the complaint, employers normally have a short window to respond to claims. Once the EEOC receives a charge, the employer must be notified within 10 days. An employer should only respond to a complaint with an answer prepared by a competent legal counsel, as any answer will be referred to throughout the investigation and any adjudication. The answer is often submitted by an attorney to help lead the EEOC or state agency to deal directly with the attorney rather than talking with company managers.

The EEOC can demand witness testimony and the production of documents including personnel files. If you refuse to produce witnesses or documents, the EEOC can obtain a court ordered subpoena. The limited rights afforded to employers includes the right to challenge the EEOC's demands if they represent an undue burden, exceed the EEOC's authority or the company's privacy needs outweigh the EEOC's discovery needs (Frierson, 1994). The EEOC can investigate the workplace which is one reason why you have to regularly check to make sure the required federally mandated posters are in place.

The EEOC will conduct its fact finding and then normally convene a conference in one of the EEOC's field offices. An Employment Opportunity Specialist (EOS) typically conducts these conferences. The conference starts with an opening statement by the EOS and the complainant is given a chance to amend the complaint and to call witnesses. If the EEOC believes the charges are true, they can try to mediate the dispute a reach a resolution. The EEOC can also utilize other means, besides a conference, to reach a settlement between the parties. If no resolution is reached, the EEOC can file a lawsuit on behalf of the complaining individual(s). However, only a few hundred lawsuits are filed each year while over 80,000 complaints are filed on a yearly basis (Frierson, 1994). More typically, the EEOC provides the complaining individual(s) with a "right to sue" letter, after which the individual has 90 days in which to file suit.

Throughout the entire investigation process, your primary responsibility entails providing truthful responses. However, truthful responses can be misleading or interpreted differently by different people. That is why you have to work with skilled counsel to help you craft your responses and assist the EEOC in reaching a correct decision. Furthermore, the EEOC's investigation helps solidify why it is critical to have excellent record keeping and why you need to separate personnel files from medical files and related strategies discussed throughout this guide.

Wrap Up . . .

This chapter has highlighted several concerns affecting the workplace. As highlighted throughout this guide, employment law is constantly changing and new issues are constantly arising. These issues require constant vigilance and monitoring. New insurance policies, new drug and alcohol testing options, new trends relating to privacy rights, new trends affecting workplace violence and new techniques to help avoid litigation with the EEOC are just some of the issues requiring monitoring.

While competent counsel has been suggested on numerous occasions, you should also become as familiar as possible with various new developments. The government is constantly publishing new handbooks, posters, guides and other materials that can greatly assist you employment law education. However, with all new information you learn, you should check with professionals prior to implementing such strategies as each workplace is different and what might have worked in one workplace could be illegal in another workplace.

References

Adler, R., and Coleman, F. (1995). *Employment-Labor law audit.* Washington, DC: BNA, Inc.

Carter, R.L. (1997). "Protection Plan." *ABA Journal* (June): 82.

Combating Workplace Drug Crimes, Guidelines for Businesses, Law Enforcement, and Prosecutors. (1994). U.S. Department of Justice (January).

Feliu, A. (1992). *Primer on Individual Employee Rights.* Washington, DC: BNA Books.

Frierson, J. (1994). *Preventing employment lawsuits: An employer's guide to hiring, discipline, and discharge.* Washington, DC: BNA Books.

Iams, K.R. (1997). "Small Change." *Employment Law, Los Angeles Daily Journal* (July 24): 22.

Levin, R.L. (1995). "Workplace violence: Sources of liability, warning signs, and ways to mitigate damages." *Labor Law Journal* 46(7): 418–428.

Marullo, G.G. (1996). "The Perils of Payroll Taxes." *Nation's Business* (July): 54.

McEwen, J.T., Manili, B., and Connors, E. (1986). "Employee Drug Testing Policies in Police Departments." *National Institute of Justice, Research in Brief* (October).

Rothstein, M., Knapp, A., and Liebman, L. (1987). *Employment Law, Cases and Material.* New York: The Foundation Press, Inc.

Schaner, D.J. (1996). "Have gun, will carry: Concealed handgun laws, workplace violence and employer liability." *Employee Relations Law Journal* 22(1): 83–100.

Silver, M. (1987). "Negligent hiring claims take off." *ABA Journal* (May): 72–78.

Update '95, 13th Symposium. (1995). San Francisco, CA: Schachter, Kristoff, Orenstein & Berkowitz.

Walsh (1995). *Mastering diversity.* Santa Monica, CA: Merritt.

Cases

Doe v. British Universities North American Club, 788 F.Supp. 1286 (D. Conn. 1992).

D.T. by M.T. v. Independent School Dist. No. 16, 894 F.2d 1176 (10th Cir. 1990).

Texas Employment Commission v. Ryan, 481 S.W.2d 172 (Civ. App. 1972).

Statutes

Conn. Gen. Stat. Section 1–12 (P.A. 551, L. 1987).

Drug Free Workplace Act, 41 U.S.C.A. Section 702 et seq.

Health Care Portability and Accountability Act of 1996, Pub. L. 104-191, Title I, August 21, 1996, 110 Stat. 1978.

Minn. Stat Section 181.95 et seq. (1987).

Small Business Job Protection Act of 1996, Pub.L. 104-188, 110 Stat. 1755.

Texas Labor Code, 201.012 and 204.065.

Utah Code Ann. Section 34–38-1 et seq. (1987).

Appendices

Forms

The following forms and contracts are designed to provide typical examples of the forms or contracts that are utilized in the employment arena. These representative examples are designed for educational purposes only. The law varies in each state and certain provisions set forth in some contracts might not be applicable in other states. While all effort has been made to make these forms or contracts as accurate as possible, there is no guarantee that they are wholly accurate or correct.

Most forms have been taken from actual cases or forms utilized in various courts or law firms. While all attempts have been made to keep any actual forms in their original context, all forms have been altered to change the parties names through creating fictitious names. Thus, any reference to any individual or company is strictly coincidental and unintentional.

APPENDIX A

Independent Contractor Contract

This contract entered into on this _____ day of _____, 199__, between ACME Inc. (hereinafter ACME) and _____ (hereinafter Contractor) relates solely to the completion of the tasks highlighted below and in *no manner* represents an employment contract between the parties. Rather, this contract strictly represents and independent contractor agreement whereby the Contractor is being hired to expressly engage in certain tasks outlined below. The Contractor will have full discretion concerning the means and method utilized to accomplish the below enumerated tasks. The Contractor will be exclusively responsible for the time, materials, equipment and method of performance, if any, which might be required to complete the tasks highlighted below. As all parties to this contract expressly intend for this contract to be an independent contractor contract and to this end, ACME is not responsible for obtaining any workers' compensation insurance coverage, paying any and all possible local, state or federal taxes, whatever they might be, and/or compliance with any local, state or federal compliance requirements which ACME

429

would otherwise be required to assume is the Contractor was indeed an employee. During the entire scope of this contract, both parties will conduct themselves as independent entities with ACME assuming no direct control over Contractor except for approving the final quality of the tasks highlighted below.

If any court invalidates any portion of this contract or determines that an employment relationship in fact existed, than this contract will be immediately terminated and both parties will treat this agreement as a null and void agreement and will expressly put the other party in the position they were in prior to entering into this contract.

By _____, 199 _____, Contractor shall complete the following tasks:

_____

_____

_____

_____

In consideration for completing the above tasks, ACME shall pay Contractor the sum of $ _____. Payment shall be made by the following method and time _____.

This represents the final and complete contract between ACME and Contractor. This contract cannot be modified in any manner without the express written consent of ACME's President, and any modifications need to be in writing signed by the Contractor and ACME's President.

This agreement was completed and signed by all parties on this _____ day of _____, 199 ___ in Houston, Texas.

_____   _____
President (ACME)   Independent Contractor

APPENDIX B

Outside Contractor Contract

This contract entered into on this _____ day of _____, 199__, between ACME Inc. (hereinafter ACME) and _____ (hereinafter BETA CORP.) relates solely to the completion of the tasks highlighted below by BETA CORP. and it's employees. BETA CORP. will have full discretion concerning the means and method utilized to accomplish the below enumerated tasks. BETA CORP. will be exclusively responsible for the time, materials, equipment and method of performance, if any, which might be required to complete the tasks highlighted below. After completing the below enumerated tasks, ACME will compensate BETA CORP. According to Schedule "A" Timetable for Payment.

Consideration

In consideration for entering into this contract, both parties expressly agree to accomplish all assigned tasks and to pay all contractually obligated amounts in a timely manner. Both parties further agree that mutual assent is present, they have the capacity to enter into this agreement, and that this agreement is for a legal purpose.

Worker's Compensation Coverage

As all parties to this contract expressly intend for this contract to be an independent business to business contract and to this end, ACME is not responsible for obtaining any workers' compensation insurance coverage, paying any and all possible local, state or federal taxes, whatever they might be, and/or compliance with any local, state or federal compliance requirements such as OSHA reporting requirements which ACME might otherwise be required to assume.

Compliance With Federal Law

BETA CORP. expressly agrees to abide by all federal anti-discrimination laws in the hiring, recruiting, assigning, and termination of workers including, but not limited to the Americans With Disabilities Act, Age Discrimination in Employment Act, Title VII of the Civil Rights Act of 1964 as amended, the Age Discrimination in Employment Act, Fair Labor Standards Act, Occupational Safety and Hazard Administration, the California Fair Employment and Housing Act, and any and all other potentially applicable state or federal statutes.

Termination of Agreement

Either party may terminate this agreement at any time, for any reason or for no reason at all, without the necessity of any breach by the other party upon delivery of a written notice with sixty (60) days prior to the express termination date requested. Upon providing a written notice, both parties will endeavor to expediently determine all amounts owed pursuant to the terms of this agreement and all outstanding balances need to be paid in full within 30 days after the agreement is terminated.

Non-Assignment

This agreement shall not be assigned by BETA CORP. for any reason without the express written consent of ACME.

Indemnity

Both parties agree to indemnify and save the other party, its officers, directors, other agents, and employees, harmless from and against any and all damages, losses, claims, demands, suits, actions and judgments, and all costs and expenses, including reasonable attorney's fees, based upon, or arising out of or resulting from, directly or indirectly, the other party's performance of work hereunder or the other party's failure to comply with any of its obligations contained in the agreement, including any breach thereof.

Arbitration

Every dispute, controversy or cause of action of every kind and nature whatsoever relating to interpretation, performance or other issues associated with this agreement shall be settled through binding arbitration before the Athletic Dispute Resolution Service (750 Weslayan Tower, Houston, TX 77046 (713) 871-9990). Both parties expressly agree that they will accept, comply and not appeal any arbitration award rendered based on this agreement.

Waiver

A waiver by either party of any breach of this agreement by the other party shall not be considered a waiver by such party of any subsequent breach by the other party.

Entire Agreement

This agreement constitutes the entire agreement between the parties and supersedes any prior understanding, agreements, or representations by or between the parties, written or oral, to the extent they related in any way to the subject matter hereof. Both parties understand that this agreement may not be modified except for a writing signed by both parties.

Construction

The agreement shall be construed under and in accordance with the laws of the State of Texas, and jurisdiction and venue for resolution of all disputes is to be Harris, County, Texas.

Authority to Sign

The parties to this agreement represent that the person signing this agreement on each of their behalves has the right, power and authority to sign, and the execution of this agreement has been authorized by the appropriate management authority of both parties.

Liquidated Damages

If either party breaches any term (s) or conditions of this contract, it is expressly provided that such a breach will cause damage to the non-breaching party and no-compensation can make the non-breaching party completely whole. However, to prevent potential breaches, both parties expressly agree that any breaching party shall pay the non-breaching party a liquidated damages payment equal to ten (10) percent of the entire contract value. Any and all such liquidated damages could be waived by the non-breaching party without affecting the non-breaching party's right to demand such damages for any subsequent breaches.

Legality

If any court invalidates any portion of this contract or determines that an employment relationship in fact existed, than this contract will be immediately terminated and both parties will treat this agreement as a null and void agreement and will expressly put the other party in the position they were in prior to entering into this contract.

Contractual Terms

By _____, 199 ____, BETA CORP. shall complete the following tasks:

_____

_____

_____

_____

This agreement was completed and signed by all parties on this ____ day of _____, 199 ___ in Houston, Texas.

_____   _____
President (ACME)   President (BETA CORP.)

APPENDIX C

Contract Developed Through Collective Bargaining AgrFeement

SCHEDULE A
UNIFORM PLAYER'S CONTRACT

THE NATIONAL LEAGUE OF
PROFESSIONAL BASEBALL CLUBS

Parties

Between _____, herein called the Club,
and _____ of _____,
herein called the Player.

Recital

The Club is a member of the National League of Professional Baseball Clubs, a voluntary association of member Clubs which has subscribed to the Major League Rules with the American League of Professional Baseball Clubs.

Agreement

In consideration of the facts above recited and of the promises of each to the other, the parties agree as follows:

Employment

1. The Club hereby employs the Player to render and the Player agrees to render, skilled services as a baseball player during the year(s) _____ including the Club's training season, the Club's exhibition games, the Club's playing season, the Division Series, the League Championship Series and the World Series (or any other official series in which the Club may participate and in any receipts of which the Player may be entitled to share).

Payment

2. For performance of the Player's services and promises hereunder the Club will pay the Player the sum of $_____ in semi-monthly installments after the commencement of the championship season(s) covered by this contract except as the schedule of payments may be modified by a

special covenant. Payment shall be made on the day the amount becomes due, regardless of whether the Club is "home" or "abroad." If a monthly rate of payment is stipulated above, it shall begin with the commencement of the championship season (or such subsequent date as the Player's services may commence) and end with the termination of the championship season and shall be payable in semi-monthly installments as above provided.

Nothing herein shall interfere with the right of the Club and the Player by special covenant herein to mutually agree upon a method of payment whereby part of the Player's salary for the above year can be deferred to subsequent years.

If the Player is in the service of the Club for part of the championship season only, he shall receive such proportion of the sum above mentioned, as the number of days of his actual employment in the championship season bears to the number of days in the championship season. Notwithstanding the rate of payment stipulated above, the minimum rate of payment to the Player for each day of service on a Major League Club shall be at the applicable rate set forth in Article VI(B)(1) of the Basic Agreement between the American League of Profession Baseball Clubs and the National League of Professional Baseball Clubs and the Major League Baseball Players Association, effective January 1, 1997 ("Basic Agreement"). The minimum rate of payment for National Association service for all Players (a) signing a second Major League contract (not covering the same season as any such Player's initial Major League contract) or a subsequent Major League contract, or (b) having at least one day of Major League service, shall be at the applicable rate set forth in Article VI(B)(2) of the Basic Agreement.

Payment to the Player at the rate stipulated above shall be continued throughout any period in which a Player is required to attend a regularly scheduled military encampment of the Reserve of the Armed Forces or of the National Guard during the championship season.

Loyalty

3.(a) The player agrees to perform his services hereunder diligently and faithfully, to keep himself in first-class physical condition and to obey the Club's training rules, and pledges himself to the American public and to the Club to conform to high standards of personal contact, fair play and good sportsmanship.

Baseball Promotion

3.(b) In addition to his services in connection with the actual playing of baseball, the Player agrees to cooperate with the Club and participate in any and all reasonable promotional activities of the Club and its League, which, in the opinion of the Club, will promote the welfare of the Club or professional baseball and, to observe and comply with all reasonable requirements of the Club respecting conduct and service of its team and its players, at all times whether on or off the field.

Pictures and Public Appearances

3.(c) The Player agrees that his picture may be taken for still photographs, motion pictures or television at such times as the Club may designate and agrees that all rights in such pictures shall belong to the Club and may be used by the Club for publicity purposes in any manner it desires. The Player further agrees that during the playing season he will not make public appearances, participate in radio or television programs or permit his pictures to be taken or write or sponsor newspaper or magazine articles or sponsor commercial products without the written consent of the Club, which shall not be withheld except in the reasonable interests of the Club or professional baseball.

PLAYER REPRESENTATIONS

Ability

4.(a) The Player represents and agrees that he has exceptional and unique skill and ability as a baseball player; that his services to be rendered hereunder are of a special, unusual and extraordinary character which gives them peculiar value which cannot be reasonably or adequately compensated for in damages at law, and that the Player's breach of this contract will cause the Club great and irreparable injury and damage. The Player agrees that, in addition to other remedies, the Club shall be entitled to injunctive and other equitable relief to prevent a breach of this contract by the Player, including, among others, the right to enjoin the Player from playing baseball for any other person or organization during the term of his contract.

Condition

4.(b) The Player represents that he has no physical or mental defects known to him and unknown to the appropriate representative of the Club which would prevent or impair performance of his services.

Interest in Club

4.(c) The Player represents that he does not, directly or indirectly, own stock or have any financial interests in the ownership or earnings of any Major League Club, except as hereinafter expressly set forth, and covenants that he will not hereafter, while connected with any Major League Club, acquire or hold any such stock or interest except in accordance with Major League Rule 20(e).

Service

5.(a) The Player agrees that, while under contract, and prior to expiration of the Club's right to renew this contract, he will not play baseball otherwise than for the Club, except that the Player may participate in post-season games under the conditions prescribed in the Major League Rules. Major League Rule 18(b) is set forth herein.

Other Sports

5.(b) The Player and the Club recognize and agree that the Player's participation in certain other sports may impair or destroy his ability and skill as a baseball player. Accordingly, the Player agrees that he will not engage in professional boxing or wrestling; and that, except with the written consent of the Club, he will not engage in skiing, auto racing, motorcycle racing, sky diving, or in any game or exhibition of football, soccer, professional league basketball, ice hockey or other sport involving a substantial risk of personal injury.

Assignment

6.(a) The Player agrees that his contact may be assigned by the Club (and reassigned by any assignee Club) to any other Club in accordance with the Major League Rules. The Club and the Player may, without obtaining special approval, agree by special covenant to limit or eliminate the right of the Club to assign this contract.

Medical Information

6.(b) The Player agrees that, should the Club contemplate as assignment of this contract to another Club or Clubs, the Club's physician may furnish to the physicians and officials of such other Club or Clubs all relevant medical information relating to the Player.

No Salary Reduction

6.(c) The amount states in paragraph 2 and in special covenants hereof which is payable to the Player for the period stated in paragraph 1 hereof shall not be diminished by any such assignment, except for failure to report as provided in the next subparagraph (d).

Reporting

6.(d) The Player shall report to the assignee Club promptly (as provided in the Regulations) upon receipt of written notice from the Club of the assignment of this contract. If the Player fails to so report, he shall not be entitled to any payment for the period from the date he receives written notice of assignment until he report to the assignee Club.

Obligations of Assignor and Assignee Clubs

6.(e) Upon and after such assignment, all rights and obligations of the assignor Club hereunder shall become the rights and obligations of the assignee Club; provided, however, that

(1) The assignee Club shall be liable to the Player for payments accruing only from the date of assignment and shall not be liable (but the assignor Club shall remain liable) for payments accrued prior to that date.

(2) If at any time the assignee is a Major League Club, it shall be liable to pay the Player at the full rate stipulated in paragraph 2 hereof for the remainder of the period stated in paragraph 1 hereof and all prior assignors and assignees shall be relieved of liability for any payment for such period.

(3) Unless the assignor and assignee Clubs agree otherwise, if the assignee Club is a National Association Club, the assignee Club shall be liable only to pay the Player at the rate usually paid by said assignee Club to other Players of similar skill and ability in its classification and the assignor Club shall be liable to pay the difference for the remainder of the period stated in paragraph 1 hereof between an amount computed at the rate stipulated in paragraph 2 hereof and the amount so payable by the assignee Club.

Moving Allowances

6.(f) The Player shall be entitled to moving allowances under the circumstances and in the amounts set forth in Articles VII(F) and VIII of the Basic Agreement.

"Club"

6.(g) All references in other paragraphs of this contract to "the Club" shall be deemed to mean and include any assignee of this contract.

TERMINATION

By Player

7.(a) The Player may terminate this contract upon written notice to the Club, if the Club shall default in the payments to the Player provided for in paragraph 2 hereof or shall fail to perform any other obligation agreed to be performed by the Club hereunder and if the Club shall fail to remedy such default within ten (10) days after the receipt by the Club of written notice of such default. The Player may also terminate this contract as provided in subparagraph (d)(4) of this paragraph 7. (See Article XV(H) of the Basic Agreement.)

By Club

7.(b) The Club may terminate this contract upon written notice to the Player (but only after requesting and obtaining waivers of this contract from all other Major League Clubs) if the Player shall at any time:

> (1) fail, refuse or neglect to conform his personal conduct to the standards of good citizenship and good sportsmanship or to keep himself in first-class physical condition or to obey the Club's training rules; or

> (2) fail, in the opinion of the Club's management, to exhibit sufficient skill or competitive ability to qualify or continue as a member of the Club's team; or

> (3) fail, refuse or neglect to render his services hereunder or in any other manner materially breach this contract.

7.(c) If this contract is terminated by the Club, the Player shall be entitled to termination pay under the circumstances and in the amounts set forth in Article I of the Basic Agreement. In addition, the Player shall be entitled to receive an amount equal to the reasonable traveling expenses of the Player, including first-class jet air fare and meals en route, to his home city.

7.(d) If the Club proposes to terminate this contract in accordance with subparagraph (b) of this paragraph 7, the procedure shall be as follows:

(1) The Club shall request waivers from all other Major League Clubs. Such waivers shall be good for three (3) business days only. Such waiver request must state that it is for the purpose of terminating this contract and it may not be withdrawn.

(2) Upon receipt of waiver request, any other Major League Club may claim assignment of this contract at a waiver price of $1.00, the priority of claims to be determined in accordance with the Major League Rules.

(3) If this contract is so claimed, the Club shall, promptly and before any assignment, notify the Player that it had requested waivers for the purpose of terminating this contract and that the contract had been claimed.

(4) Within five (5) days after receipt of notice of such claim, the Player shall be entitled, by written notice to the Club, to terminate this contract on the date of his notice of termination. If the Player fails to so notify the Club, this contract shall be assigned to the claiming Club.

(5) If the contract is not claimed, the Club shall promptly deliver written notice of termination to the Player at the expiration of the waiver period.

7.(e) Upon any termination of this contract by the Player, all obligations of both Parties hereunder shall cease on the date of termination, except the obligation of the Club to pay the Player's compensation to said date.

Regulations

8. The Player accepts as part of this contract the Regulations set forth herein.

Rules

9.(a) The Club and the Player agree to accept, abide by and comply with all provisions of the Major League Agreement, the Major League Rules, and the Rules of Regulations of the League of which the Club is a member, in effect on the date of this Uniform Player's Contract, which are not inconsistent with the provisions of this contract or the provisions of any agreement between the Major League Clubs and the Major League Baseball Players Association, provided that the Club, together with the other clubs of the National and American Leagues and the National Association, reserves the right to modify, supplement or repeal any provision of said Agreement, Rules and/or Regulations in a manner not inconsistent with this contract or the provisions of any then existing agreement between the Major League Clubs and the Major League Baseball Players Association.

Disputes

9.(b) All disputes between the Player and the Club which are covered by the Grievance Procedure as set forth in the Basic Agreement shall be resolved in accordance with such Grievance Procedure.

Publication

9.(c) The Club, the League President and the Commissioner, or any of them, may make public the findings, decision and record of any inquiry, investigation or hearing held or conducted, including in such record all evidence or information given, received, or obtained in connection therewith.

Renewal

10.(a) Unless the Player has exercised his right to become a free agent as set forth in the Basic Agreement the Club may, on or before December 20 (or if a Sunday, then the next preceding business day) in the year of the last playing season covered by this contract, tender tot eh Player a contract for the term of the next year by mailing the same to the Player at this address following his signature hereto, or if none be given, then at his last address of record with the Club. If prior to the March 1 next succeeding said December 20, the Player and the Club have not agreed upon the terms of such contract, then on or before ten (10) days after said March 1, the Club shall have the right by written notice to the Player at said address to renew this contract for the period of one year on the same terms, except that the amount payable to the Player shall be such as the Club shall fix in said notice; provided, however, that said amount, if fixed by a Major League Club, shall be in the amount payable at a rate not less than as specified in Article VI, Section D, of the Basic Agreement. Subject to the Player's rights as set forth in the Basic Agreement, the Club may renew this contract from year to year.

10.(b) The Club's right to renew this contract, as provided in subparagraph (a) of this paragraph 10, and the promise of the Player not to play otherwise than with the Club have been taken into consideration in determining the amount payable under paragraph 2 hereof.

Governmental Regulation — National Emergency

11. This contract is subject to federal or state legislation, regulations, executive or other official orders or other governmental action, now or hereafter in effect respecting military, naval, air or other governmental service, which may directly or indirectly affect the Player, Club or the League and subject also to the right of the Commissioner to suspend the operation of this contract during any national emergency during which Major League Baseball is not played.

Commissioner

12. The term "Commissioner" wherever used in this contract shall be deemed to mean the Commissioner designated under the Major League Agreement, or in the case of a vacancy in the office of Commissioner, the Executive Council or such other body or person or persons as shall be designated in the Major League Agreement to exercise the powers and duties of the Commissioner during such vacancy.

Supplemental Agreements

The Club and the Player covenant that this contract, the Basic Agreement and the Agreement Re Major League Baseball Players Benefit Plan effective April 1, 1996 and applicable supplements thereto fully set forth all understandings and agreements between them, and agree that no other understandings or agreements, whether heretofore or hereafter made, shall be valid, recognizable, or of any effect whatsoever, unless expressly set forth in a new or supplemental contract executed by the Player and the Club (acting by its President or such other officer as shall have been thereunto duly authorized by the President or Board of Directors as evidenced by a certificate filed of record with the League President and Commissioner) and complying with the Major League Rules.

Special Covenants

_____

_____

_____

_____

_____

Approval

This contract or any supplement hereto shall not be valid or effective unless and until approved by the League President.

Signed in duplicate this _____ day of _____, A.D. _____

_____   _____
            (Player)   (Club)

_____   _____
     (Home address of Player)   (Authorized Signature)

Social Security No. _____
Approved _____

_____
President, The National League of Professional Baseball Clubs

REGULATIONS

1. The Club's playing season for each year covered by this contract and all renewals hereof shall be as fixed by The National League of Professional Baseball Clubs, or if this contract shall be assigned to a Club in another League, then by the League of which such assignee is a member.

2. The Player, when requested by the Club, must submit to a complete physical examination at the expense of the Club, and if necessary to treatment by a regular physician or dentist in good standing. Upon refusal of the Player to submit to a complete medical or dental examination, the Club may consider such refusal a violation of this regulation and may take such action as it deems advisable under Regulation 5 of this contract. Disability directly resulting from injury sustained in the course and within the scope of his employment under this contract shall not impair the right of the Player to receive his full salary for the period of such disability or for the season in which the injury was sustained (whichever period is shorter), together with the reasonable medial and hospital expenses incurred by reason of the injury and during the term of this contract or for

a period of up to two years from the date of initial treatment for such injury, whichever period is longer, but only upon the express prerequisite conditions that (a) written notice of such injury, including the time, place, cause and nature of the injury, is served upon and received by the Club within twenty days of the sustaining of said injury and (b) the Club shall have the right to designate the doctors and hospitals furnishing such medical and hospital services. Failure to give such notice shall not impair the rights of the Player, as herein set forth, if the Club has actual knowledge of such injury. All workmen's compensation payments received by the Player as compensation for loss of income for a specific period during which the Club is paying him in full, shall be paid over by the Player to the Club. Any other disability may be ground for suspending or terminating this contract.

3. The Club will furnish the Player with two complete uniforms, exclusive of shoes, unless the Club requires the Player to wear non-standard shoes in which case the Club will furnish the shoes. The uniforms will be surrendered by the Player to the Club at the end of the season or upon termination of this contract.

4. The Player shall be entitled to expense allowance under the circumstances and in the amounts set forth in Article VII of the Basic Agreement.

5. For violation by the Player of any regulation or other provision of this contract, the Club may impose a reasonable fine and deduct the amount thereof from the Player's salary or may suspend the Player without salary for a period not exceeding thirty days or both. Written notice of the fine or suspension or both and the reason therefor shall in every case be given to the Player and the Players Association. (See Article XII of the Basic Agreement.)

6. In order to enable the Player to fit himself for his duties under this contract, the Club may require the Player to report for practice at such places as the Club may designate and to participate in such exhibition contests as may be arranged by the Club, without any other compensation than that herein elsewhere provided, for a period beginning not earlier than thirty-three (33) days prior to the start of the championship season, provided, however, that the Club may invite players to report at an earlier date on a voluntary basis in accordance with Article IV of the Basic Agreement. The Club will pay the necessary traveling expenses, including the first-class jet air fare and meals en route of the Player from his home city to the training place of the Club, whether he be ordered to go there directly or by way of the home city of the Club. In the event of the failure of the Player to report for practice or to participate in the exhibition games, as

required and provided for, he shall be required to get into playing condition to the satisfaction of the Club's team manager, and at the Player's own expense, before his salary shall commence.

7. In case of assignment of this contract, the Player shall report promptly to the assignee Club within 72 hours from the date he receives written notice from the Club of such assignment, if the Player is then not more than 1,600 miles by most direct available railroad route from the assignee Club, plus an additional 24 hours for each additional 800 miles.

Post-Season Exhibition Games. Major League Rule 18(b) provides:

(b) EXHIBITION GAMES. No player shall participate in any exhibition game during the period between the close of the Major League championship season and the following training season, except that, with the consent of the player's Club and permission of the Commissioner, a player may participate in exhibition games for a period of not less than 30 days, such period to be designated annually by the Commissioner. Players who participate in barnstorming during this period cannot engage in any Winter League activities.

Player conduct, on and off the field, in connection with such post-season exhibition games shall be subject to the discipline of the Commissioner. The Commissioner shall not approve of more than three players of any one Club on the same team. The Commissioner shall not approve of more than three players from the joint membership of the World Series participants playing in the same game.

No player shall participate in any exhibition game with or against any team which, during the current season or within one year, has had any ineligible player or which is or has been during the current season or within one year, managed and controlled by an ineligible player or by any person who has listed an ineligible player under an assumed name or who otherwise has violated, or attempted to violate, any exhibition game contract; or with or against any team which, during said season or within one year, has played against teams containing such ineligible players, or so managed or controlled. Any player who participates in such a game in violation of this Rule 18 shall be fined not less than $50 nor more than $500, except that in no event shall such fine be less than the consideration received by such player for participating in such game.

PRINTED IN U.S.A.   REVISED AS OF MARCH 1997

APPENDIX D

New Employee Budget Worksheet

Before hiring a new employee, the following worksheet should be completed to determine the total costs that might be associated with the new employee. As with any other business investment, if the costs associated with hiring a new employee does not exceed the long term benefits associated with the new employee, then the employee should not be hired and you should consider outsourcing the required work.

Advertising Costs . . . . _____

Interview Costs . . . . _____

Offer Costs (i.e. relocation costs) . . . . _____

Salary . . . . _____

Health Benefits . . . . _____

Other Benefits. . . . . _____

Federal Income Taxes . . . . _____

Fed/State Unemployment Taxes . . . . _____

FICA Taxes . . . . _____

Social Security Taxes . . . . _____

Medicare Taxes. . . . . _____

Other Taxes . . . . _____

Total Costs . . . . _____

Example of Completed Form

Advertising Costs. . . . . $ 150.00 (3 insertions at $50.00 each)

Interview Costs . . . . $1,200.00 ($600.00 air travel, $150.00 hotel–2 nights, $150.00 meals, $300.00 lost employee time and screening costs)

Offer Costs (i.e., relocation costs) . $3,000.00

Salary. $35,000.00

Health Benefits. . . . . $10,000.00 Estimate

Other Benefits . . . . $2,500.00 Car allowance

Federal Income Taxes $2,205.00

Fed/State Unemployment Taxes. . . $1,200.00

FICA Taxes $2,677.00

Social Security Tax $1,995.00

Medicare Tax . . . . $ 455.00

Other Taxes. . . . . not applicable

Total Costs . . . . $60,382.00-first year

APPENDIX E

Job Descriptions

Job Title: Head Soccer Coach
Job Status: The position is a part-time paid position. The coach will be directly employed by XYZ Soccer Organization. The position does not provide any full-time benefits, nor any entitlement to future employment.
Salary: The salary for this position is $5.15 per hour.
Supervisor: The Coach will report to Jane Doe, XYZ's Vice President of Operations.
Purpose: The purpose of this position is to provide children age 10–15 with the opportunity to fully develop their soccer skills. The coach is responsible for providing mentoring, educational opportunities, skill enhancement, a safe recreational environment, and a wholesome recreational experience.
Duties:

1) Supervise one assistant coach and at least twelve (12) players for a 14 week schedule starting June 7, 1996.
2) provide physical, emotional and intellectual stimulation to all participants
3) promote good sportsmanship.
4) Provide guidance, support and counseling-when appropriate-to all participants in the XYZ program.
5) Be a good listener to verbal and non-verbal communications.
6) Develop and promote new activities that will challenge and motivate children.
7) Provide soccer specific instructions appropriate with the skill, motivational, and mental capabilities of each participant.
8) Strictly follow XYZ's soccer coaching program.
9) Develop and maintain a relationship of trust with all participants.
10) Provide any necessary assistance to parents of the participants
11) Supervise the playing environment to prevent non- participants from mingling with participants during XYZ games, practice or official activities.

Qualifications: All potential candidates should, at a minimum, have a high school diploma, four years of prior soccer coaching experience, completion of a national coaching certification program (such as American Coaching Effectiveness Program), complete an application form including the signing of a background investigation release form, and have prior demonstrable youth counseling experience. Review and accept all the terms of XYZ's sexual abuse policy statement. All references provided on the application form will be checked.

Evaluation: All assigned children will be provided a pre-test and post-test to ascertain skill development and emotional growth resulting from participation in the program. Such results can be used to determine future employment with XYZ.

Job Title: Office Manager
Salary Level: $35,000–$40,000
Reports to: CFO
Position Summary: The Office Manager coordinates activities of clerical personnel in the finance department through performing the following the duties, either personally or through appropriate delegation. Essential Job Duties and Responsibilities include the following tasks and others that might be assigned by any supervisor.

a) Responsible for analyzing and organizing all office and department operations and activities such as typing, bookkeeping, payroll, correspondence distribution, document filing, ordering office supplies and all other clerical services.

b) Responsible for evaluating office production, initiates and evaluates office procedures, coordinates the development of new office forms/manuals all in an effort to maximize an efficient workforce and workplace.

c) Responsible for formulating procedures for systematic retention, review, processing, disposal, storage and filing of all workplace records.

d) Responsible for effectively designing, managing and prefiguring office layout to optimize available space and employee comfort.

e) Responsible for reviewing all clerical employees regarding hiring, reviewing, performance communication, termination and record keeping.

Supervisory Responsibilities: The Office Manager is responsible for supervising all employees in the finance department other than his or her immediate supervisor. The Office Manager is responsible for carrying out supervisory responsibilities in accordance with all company rules, policies and procedures. Responsibilities listed above need to be coordinated with the ultimate responsibility for department success attributed directly to clerical personnel and as such is also responsible for rewarding and disciplining employees, resolving all complaints raised and ultimate responsibility for employees reaching their maximum potential.

Qualifications: To successfully perform this job, the potential Office Manager must be able to accomplish all job responsibilities with or without any reasonable accommodations which might be needed. The qualifications listed below are representative of the knowledge, skills and/or ability that are required by the position. Reasonable accommodations may be made available to enable individuals with disabilities to perform the essential functions.

Education/Experience: Bachelor's degree (B.A or B.S.) from an accredited four-year college or university. Two or three years of related experience or training, or equivalent combination of education and experience can be applied to meet the education requirement.

Language: The Office Manager is required to have the ability to read, analyze and interpret financial and business periodicals, professional journals, and government regulations. All applicants will need to demonstrate the ability to effectively write and communicate with others.

Reasoning: The Office Manager needs to have the ability to solve practical problems and deal with a variety of concrete variables in situations where limited standardization exists. With limited instructions or guidance the Office Manager is required to act independently and be responsible for their own actions.

Other Skills: The Office Manager needs to be thoroughly competent in all Microsoft Office programs including word processing application and spreadsheet analysis programs.

Physical Demands: The physical demands highlighted below are representative of the demands that must be met by an employee to successfully perform the job's essential functions. Reasonable accommodations may be made available to enable individuals with disabilities to perform the essential functions.

The Office Manager will be required to stand; walk; and use hands to finger, handle, knob, or feel objects, tool or controls in addition to occasionally being required to kneel or crouch. In addition, the Office Manager must occasionally lift and move up to 25 pounds. While there are no specific hearing requirements, the work site has a noise level that is usually moderate.

JOB DESCRIPTION WORKSHEET

Job Title: _____

Job Status: _____

Salary: $ _____

Benefits: _____

Supervisor: _____

Purpose: _____
_____
_____

Duties: _____
_____
_____
_____
_____
_____

(Remember to list duties in terms of objectives to help comply with ADA requirements.)

Qualifications: _____
_____

(Remember that all required degree need to be reasonably necessary to complete job duties.)

Evaluation: _____
_____
_____
_____

(Remember that evaluation criteria should be neutral and objective.)

APPENDIX F

Want Ad Specifications

Position Name: _____

Date to be Published: _____

Insertions: Number of weekday inserts _____

Number of weekend inserts _____

Where published _____

_____

Specialized publications _____

_____

Insertion number _____

Size of Advertisement: Number of column inch advertisements ____

Number of display advertisements _____

Wording: Attach copy of advertisement to this sheet

The following want ad appeared in The NCAA News on July 7, 1997 and represent a sample advertisement that is meticulously worded to address major concerns and legal hurdles. The classified advertisement utilized approximately three column inches.

Athletic Compliance Officer. As California State University, Sacramento Athletic Compliance Officer, this position is responsible for developing, monitoring, and enforcing compliance with the Constitution and Bylaws of the National Collegiate Athletic Association (NCAA), The Big Sky Conference, and the Big West Athletic Conference. This position would have direct responsibility to the athletic director (AD) regarding compliance with NCAA and conference rules and regulations. Work is reviewed in terms of soundness of judgment and effectiveness in achieving goals critical to the department. Duties and responsibilities: Develop and administer an effective program operating policy and procedures to insure institutional compliance with NCAA and conference rules and regulations. The successful candidate will exercise a high level of judgment in recommending to the AD a comprehensive athletic compliance program. Develop, monitor and enforce compliance with the Constitution and Bylaws of the NCAA, the Big Sky Conference, and the Big West Athletic Conference. Develop and administer effective program operating policy and procedures to insure institutional compliance with NCAA and conference rules and regulations. Develop and administer a comprehensive rules education program. Independently monitor all eligibility and compliance procedures: recruiting octaves, compliance reports and squad lists, grant-in-aid program, camps/clinics, and coordination with the director of financial aid. Serve as the University's liaison with the NCAA and conference offices regarding rules interpretations to insure institutional compliance and avoid liability. Develop and administer University policy and procedures responding to NCAA and/or conference rules violations. Represent the University on NCAA and conference athletically-related rules and regulations to the greater Sacramento community. Minimum qualifications: Bachelor's degree required, Masters preferred. Successful experience in athletic administration or a related area is required. Excellent computer skills are mandatory. Knowledge of NCAA rules and compliance issues concerning the administration of intercollegiate athletics. The successful candidate should possess strong written and oral communication skills along with the ability to manage multiple tasks. There should be a desire to assist coaches, student-athletes, administrative staff and others to manage compliance issues in a positive manner. Appointment: This is a full time position defined in the Management Personnel Plan of the California State University. It is excluded from the collective bargaining process and does not gain permanent status. This position is also exempt from the overtime provisions of the Fair Labor Standards Act. Salary and benefits are competitive and commensurate with experience and credentials. Anticipated start date: August 11, 1997. Application procedure-submit the following information: 1) Cover letter of interest; 2) Current resume; 3) Evidence of highest degree earned; 4) Names, addresses, and telephone numbers of three references who can address professional preparation and experience. Send to: Office of Student Affairs, California State University, 600 J Street, Box CC, Sacramento, CA 95819-6062. Fax 916/278-5443. Application deadline: Applicants and nominees should submit the above material by July 15, 1997 to insure consideration of the application-position open until filled. California State University, Sacramento is an Affirmative Action/Equal Opportunity Employer, and has a strong institutional commitment to the principle of diversity in all areas. In that spirit, we are particularly interested in receiving applications from a broad spectrum of qualified people who would assist the University in meeting its Strategic Plan goal of pluralism:" To develop a campus community whose diversity enriches the lives of all and whose members develop a strong sense of personal and community identity as well as mutual respect." CSUS hires only those individuals who are lawfully authorized to accept employment in the United States.

APPENDIX G

Employment Application

Full legal name: _____
Prior name(s) or aliases: _____
Complete address: _____
Home and work numbers: (___)_____ (___) _____
Social security number: _____
*Driver's license number, state and expiration date: _____
or other proof of identification _____
List all coaching certificates or diplomas: _____
List all prior involvement in youth athletics: _____
*List three personal and/or business references including current phone numbers:
(1) _____
(2) _____
(3) _____
List all prior residences for the past ten years: _____

Have you ever been convicted of any felony, in any state or country: _____
If yes, please describe the felony committed and your current legal status (parole, probation, etc.): _____
On a separate sheet, briefly describe how you meet all the job specifications and whether or not you can complete all the required job duties with any reasonable accommodation(s).
I understand and agree that:

1) It is the policy of this organization to deny employment opportunities for individuals who have been convicted of any violent crime or any crime against any person(s).

2) This organization has a strict confidentiality and appeals process concerning the handling the applications of individuals with prior criminal histories.

3) This application is valid for two years and a new application has to be completed immediately thereafter.

4) By submitting this application I, the applicant, affirm that all the foregoing information I have provided is true and correct.

---

* Some scholars/attorneys disagree on whether to ask for such information. A qualified attorney should check all questions.

5) By submitting this application I, the applicant, agree (in return for being allowed to work) that if any of the foregoing information is incorrect, I will forever indemnify and hold this youth organization harmless for any acts or omissions on my behalf solely as it relates to the incorrect information I have provided.

6) By submitting this application I, the applicant, voluntarily waive my privacy rights only to the extent necessary for the youth organization to verify the foregoing information through any reasonable means, including, but not limited to local, regional, state, national or international criminal background check(s).

Printed Name: _____

Signature: _____

Date: _____

Affirmative Action/Equal Employment Opportunity Employer

Volunteer Application

Full legal name: _____

Prior names or aliases: _____

Complete address: _____

Home and work numbers: (___)_____ (___) _____

Social security number: _____

Driver's license number, state and expiration date: _____

Date of birth: _____ (only for volunteers)

List all coaching certificates or diplo-
mas:_____

List all prior involvement in youth athletics:

_____

List three personal and business references including current phone numbers:

Personal (1) _____

          (2) _____

          (3) _____

Business (1) _____

          (2) _____

          (3) _____

List all prior residences for the past ten years: _____

Have you ever been convicted of any felony, in any state or country: _____

If yes, please describe the felony committed and your current legal status (parole, probation, etc.): _____

I understand and agree that:

1) It is the policy of this organization to deny volunteer opportunities for individuals who have been convicted of any violent crime or any crime against any person(s). This organization can deny any applicant for any reason or for no reason at all.
2) This organization has a strict confidentiality and appeals process concerning the handling the applications of individuals with prior criminal histories.
3) This application is valid for two years and a new application has to be completed immediately thereafter.
4) By submitting this application I, the applicant, affirm that all the foregoing information I have provided is true and correct.
5) By submitting this application I, the applicant, agree (in return for being allowed to volunteer) that if any of the foregoing information is incorrect, I will forever indemnify and hold this youth organization harmless for any acts or omissions on my behalf solely as it relates to the incorrect information I have provided.
6) By submitting this application I, the applicant, voluntarily waive my privacy rights only to the extent necessary for the youth organization to verify the foregoing information through any reasonable means, including, but not limited to local, state, national and international criminal background check(s).

Printed Name: _____
Signature: _____
Date: _____

Release

I, _____ (name) hereby authorize *ORGANIZATION* to obtain any and all pertinent information pertaining to any charges, allegations, and/or convictions of any kind I may have had or are currently pending relating to any state, federal or international criminal law violations. Such information can include, but is not limited to, any allegations, charges or convictions for crimes committed against children, people, and crimes involving moral turpitude. Such information can be obtained from such sources as any and all law enforcement agencies of this state, other states, federal agencies, and international law enforcement agencies to the full extent permitted by law.

Social Security Number _____
Driver's License Number _____ State _____
All states and counties which you have lived in over the past ten years

_____

Have you ever been convicted of any felony? _____
If yes, please describe the conviction and when you were convicted

_____

_____

I affirm, under the penalty of perjury, that the following is true and correct information and I would testify accordingly if called to testify in any court of law.

Signature _____ Date _____

APPENDIX H

Rejection Letter #1

ACME
123 Any Street
Any Town, NY 12345

May 10, 1998

Janet Doe
987 Somewhere Ct.
Nowhere, VT 23456

Dear Ms. Doe:

Thank you very much for the application and resume you sent in response to our advertisement for a soccer coach. We have received a large number of applicants for the position with several highly qualified who met the minimal job requirements. The position specifically requires an individual with at least a bachelor's degree (or similar non-qualifying point—i.e., lack requisite experience, etc.). Unfortunately, while your background is praiseworthy, we are unable to offer you an interview at the present time.

Based on our company policy, your resume will be kept for the required statutory period, but you would need to complete the application process again if you wish to apply for any future position with ACME.
We thank you for taking the time to apply for the position and we wish you the best of luck in your job search.

Sincerely,

Frank Jones
HR Manager

APPENDIX I

Review Matrix

Applicant name _____

Education:	Up to Grade 12 ___	Some College __
	A.A. Degree __	Bachelor's ___
Playing Experience:	Less than 1 year ___	1–3 Years ____
	3–5 Years ___	Over 5 Years ___
Coaching Experience:	Less than 1 year ___	1–3 Years ____
	3–5 Years ___	Over 5 Years ___
Supervision Experience:	Less than 1 year ___	1–3 Years ____
	3–5 Years ___	Over 5 Years ___
Marketing Experience:	Less than 1 year ___	1–3 Years ____
	3–5 Years ___	Over 5 Years ___
Other	____	____
	____	____

Calculation: Checking the first blank is worth 1 point, second blank is worth 2 points, third blank is worth 3 points and the last blank in each category is worth 4 points.

Total Points _____
Candidate Rank ____

APPENDIX J

Rejection Letter #2

ACME
123 Any Street
Any Town, NY 12345

May 18, 1998

Janet Doe
987 Somewhere Ct.
Nowhere, VT 23456

Dear Ms. Doe:

Thank you very much for the application and resume you sent in response to our advertisement for a soccer coach. We have received a large number of applicants for the position with several highly qualified who met the minimal job requirements. Unfortunately, while your background is praiseworthy and shows promise, we are unable to offer you an interview at the present time.

Based on our company policy, your resume will be kept for the required statutory period, but you would need to complete the application process again if you wish to apply for any future position with ACME.

We thank you for taking the time to apply for the position and we wish you the best of luck in your job search.

Sincerely,

Frank Jones
HR Manager

APPENDIX K

Interview Confirmation Letter

ACME
123 Any Street
Any Town, NY 12345

May 10, 1998

Janet Doe
987 Somewhere Ct.
Nowhere, VT 23456

Dear Ms. Doe:

Thank you very much for the application and resume you sent in response to our advertisement for a soccer coach. We are pleased to inform you that you are one of the finalist for the position. The next step in the process is a personal interview conducted at our office on Any Street. Please call my secretary at (123) 456-7891 to schedule the interview time and date.

ACME strongly adheres to all anti-discrimination laws including the Americans With Disabilities Act. We strive to accommodate all reasonable requests for assistance without regard to an applicant's potential disability, if any. If there exists any accommodation which you might require to make your interview more comfortable, please do not hesitate to ask my secretary to connect you with ACME's ADA compliance coordinator. Furthermore, if you have any special physical or communication need that may impact your ability to participate in the interview process, please contact our ADA compliance coordinator as we cannot ensure the availability of appropriate accommodations without prior notification of need.

To assist all applicants in understanding the position, I am enclosing a comprehensive job description which highlight the position's qualification requirements, expected performance criteria, and ACME's drug and alcohol policy statement.

I look forward to seeing you and getting to know you a little more.

Sincerely,

Frank Jones
HR Manager

APPENDIX L

Interview Questions

1) Please tell me about your work history?
2) How did you get that job(s)?
3) To whom did you report?
4) How long did you work there (both months and years)?
5) What were your duties?
6) Did you like the job(s)?
7) What in particular did you like about the job(s)?
8) What in particular did you NOT like about the job(s)?
9) What did you think about your supervisor(s)?
10) What did you think about your co-workers?
11) Did you get along well with your co-workers and/or supervisor(s)?
12) What type of supervisor do you prefer to work with?
13) Has your work ever been criticized, and if so, how did you respond?
14) What have you found to be disappointing in any prior job(s)?
15) If you could have made any changes to your prior job, what would you have changed?
16) What has been the most important accomplishment you have at your current or most recent job?
17) What is your ideal job?
18) What do you think is the most appropriate manner to resolve employee disputes?
19) What was your salary or wages at your prior job(s)?
20) Did you ever get a raise and why or why not?
21) Were you ever promoted to a position with greater responsibility?
22) Why were you promoted or denied promotions?
23) What benefits did you receive at any prior job(s)?
24) Why did you leave any prior job(s)?
25) Were you ever terminated for insubordination?
26) What types of references would we receive from your prior supervisor(s)?
27) What types of references would we receive from your prior co- workers?
28) Why are you interested in working for our company?

29) What attracted you to apply for this position?
30) Do you know what the job duties are for this position?
31) Have you read the job description for the position?
32) Can you perform all the required essential job duties with any necessary reasonable accommodation?
33) What experience particularly qualifies you for this position?
34) What hours are you available to work?
35) Are you available for travel or relocation?
36) What position within this company would you like to have in five or ten years?
37) Why did you select this type of career track?
38) What qualities do you admire in others?
39) What qualities do you dislike in others?
40) What do you like to do with your free time?
41) Do you like to volunteer your time for community activities?
42) What epithet would you want to be written on your tombstone after you pass away?

Questions for Employee who Will Work With Children

1) Why are you interested in the position?
2) How would you describe yourself?
3) Have you ever had to discipline a child, and how did you do it?
4) Why do you like to work with children?
5) What traits do you think you have that qualifies you to supervise children?
6) What about the position/job appeals to you the most/least?
7) Are you familiar with the issues associated with child sexual abuse?
8) Have you read XYZ's Organizational policy statement concerning sexual abuse?
9) What do you think about the policy?
10) Have you ever been convicted of a criminal offense including criminal driving violations?
11) Have you ever worked in a position for which you were bonded?
12) How do you relate with children?
13) Are you aware of any problems or conditions that could interfere with your ability to care for children or in any way endanger any child under your care?

All responses should be recorded in a response form to provide evidence concerning what questions were asked and relevant responses.

APPENDIX M

Interview Response Form

Applicant's Name _____   Interviewer _____

Position _____   Date _____

Is the applicant's work history? inadequate _____ adequate _____
                                 superior _____

Are reasons for leaving prior job(s) logical? yes _____ no _____
    explain _____

Is the applicant's background free from the following concerns?
    frequent job changes? yes ___ no _____
    explain _____
    unexplained gaps in employment? yes ___ no _____
    explain _____
    previous income higher then position applied for? yes ___ no _____
    explain _____
    dissatisfied with prior job/supervisor? yes ___ no _____
    explain _____

Please circle the appropriate response regarding the applicant's
adaptability:

          1-poor, 2-fair, 3- acceptable, 4-good, 5-excellent

1) Experience-is the applicant's experience or background appropriate
for the position?

              1   2   3   4   5

2) Enthusiasm-is the applicant enthusiastic about working for the company?

              1   2   3   4   5

3) Initiative-is the applicant willing to go beyond the call of duty to succeed?

              1   2   3   4   5

4) Cooperativeness-is the applicant willing to work with others?

              1   2   3   4   5

5) Job Function-can the applicant perform the essential job functions?

              1   2   3   4   5

6) Schedule-can the applicant work in the current rotation?

              1   2   3   4   5

7) Other _____

<pre>
          1   2   3   4   5
8) Other _____
          1   2   3   4   5
Interview Length _____
Overall Applicant Rating
          1   2   3   4   5
Additional Comments _____
</pre>

_____
_____
_____

Interviewer's signature _____

Questions for Employee Who Will Work with Children

Name of Applicant _____
Interviewer(s) _____
Date _____
Position Title _____
Was applicant given a copy of the job description? _____
Did the applicant read and sign the organizational sexual abuse policy statement and complete job application including authorization to release records?

_____

Did the applicant indicate if they needed any accommodation to perform the job's essential functions? _____

Personal Questions

Education _____
Past work experience _____

_____

Last salary (if appropriate) _____
Discipline actions at work _____
Discipline at school _____
Military experience _____
Social security number _____
Can they provide proof of residence if they are hired _____
DO NOT ASK-age, race, nationality, religion, sexual orientation, marital status, and related questions if the applicant is applying for an employment position.
How did you learn about this position? _____

Why are you interested in the position? What things have you done that have given you the greatest satisfaction? _____

What have been the biggest disappointment in your life? _____

Where do you see yourself in 1 year, 5 years and 10 years down the road? _____

Describe your temperament? _____
Have you know anyone that has been abused? _____
Tell me about that person and your relationship to him or her? _____

How would you describe yourself? _____
Have you ever had to discipline a child, and how did you do it? _____

Why do you like to work with children? _____
What traits do you think you have that qualifies you to supervise children?

Are you familiar with the issues associated with child sexual abuse? ___

Have you read XYZ's Organizational policy statement concerning sexual abuse? _____
What do you think about the policy? _____
Have you ever been convicted of a criminal offense including criminal driving violations? _____
Have you ever worked in a position for which you were bonded? _____
How do you relate with children? _____
Are you aware of any problems or conditions that could interfere with your ability to care for children or in any way endanger any child under your care? _____

Why do you like working with children? _____
Have you ever had any unsupervised supervisorial obligation with children in any past employment of volunteer position? _____

Is there any information you would like to share about yourself? _____
_____

General observations as they apply strictly to candidate's qualifications
_____
_____
_____

Areas possibly necessitating further investigation _____

Notes _____

_____

_____

_____

_____

Have all references been contacted? _____
Any necessary follow-up? _____

APPENDIX N

Reference Check Questions

The following questions represent potential questions to ask someone who is giving an oral reference or wants to know what to write about. Paraphrase any discussion by specifically requesting only factual, truthful information, not subjective opinions.

1) Did _____ ever work for your company?
2) How long had he/she worked for your company?
3) What position did he/she hold?
4) Was he/she ever promoted?
5) From what position to their highest position with your company?
6) Did he/she ever receive a pay raise?
7) Did you have performance reviews for him/her?
8) How often did you perform the performance reviews?
9) Did he/she ever have a negative performance review?
10) If so, why did they receive a negative review?
11) Did he/she change their behavior to correct any conduct highlighted in the negative review?
12) How were his/her reviews subsequent to any negative reviews?
13) Was he/she able to accomplish all assigned duties?
14) Did he/she have any trouble with co-workers or supervisor(s)?
15) Did he/she show enthusiasm for the job?
16) Would you ever hire him/her again?

Letter Requesting Reference From Prior Employer

ACME Company
123 Any Street
Any Town, NY 12345

May 20, 1998

XYZ Gym
345 Nowhere St.
My Town, NY 13456

The following job applicant _____, Social Security Number _____, has applied for a position with our company. The applicant is applying for the following position _____. The applicant claims he/she had worked for you from _____. 19___ to _____
19 ___.   month   year   month
year

We would appreciate your candid, frank and truthful response to the question below. Please return this form in the enclosed self-addressed-stamped-envelope. The applicant has signed a legal waiver (see below) expressly relieving you of any liability in reference to any and all truthful statements that you provide. It should be expressly noted how important employee references are and that courts in some states have held former employers liable for negligently failing to provide critical information about a job candidate.

Please answer the following:
List all job titles, dates of employment and reason for change, termination or leaving your company. _____

_____

_____

Please circle the appropriate response regarding the applicant's adaptability:

1-poor, 2-fair, 3- acceptable, 4-good, 5-excellent

1) Attendance	1	2	3	4	5
2) Work Performance	1	2	3	4	5
3) Attitude	1	2	3	4	5

4) Accomplished Assigned Tasks in a Timely Manner

            1   2   3   4   5

Would you rehire the applicant if they ever reapplied for a position?
Yes ___ No ___ If no, please explain: _____

Do you have any reason to believe the applicant may be violent, abusive,
dangerous or a person who might engage in improper, discriminatory or
unlawful conduct at work? Yes ___ No ___
If yes, please explain:_____

Please briefly describe the applicant's strength and weaknesses and any
other items you think will be important for us to consider in evaluating the
applicant.

Name _____
Signature _____
Title _____
Date _____

Legal Waiver

I hereby authorize _____, its officers, employees or designated representative to furnish ACME Company with information they might have
concerning me and my work history whether such information is oral or
written and whether or not such information is contained in my personnel
file. I hereby waive any and all potential claims including negligence,
defamation, libel, slander, and any and all other potential claims against the
above named company, officers and employees and further waive all liability for any damage whatsoever resulting from the furnishing of any information. I further expressly agree as a condition to being considered for the
position I am applying for that I will not bring a complaint, suit, or any
other legal proceeding based on any information, oral or written, released
by the above named company, officers, or employees in respect to this reference request. I further agree as a condition of applying for the position
herein that I will not bring suit against ACME Company for requesting reference materials and acting upon said material in a reasonably prudent
business manner.

Name _____
Signed _____
Dated _____

APPENDIX O

Reference Check Response Form

Applicant's Name _____ Position Applied for _____
Interviewer _____ Date _____
Reference Being Interviewed _____ Position _____
Company/Organization Name _____
Company Phone Number (_____) _____
How long have you known the Applicant? _____
In what capacity did you know the Applicant? _____
Please describe your relationship with the Applicant. _____

Please describe the Applicant's relationship with people in general. ____

Please describe the Applicant's relationship with children. _____

To the best of your knowledge, has the Applicant ever been convicted of
a crime? _____
Would your company/org. ever rehire the Applicant? _____
Was the Applicant ever disciplined by your company/org. and why was
he/she disciplined? _____

Do you know of any traits, conditions, tendencies or problems which
would be detrimental to his/her working with children? _____

Comments _____
_____
_____
_____

Interviewer's Signature _____

APPENDIX P

ADA Disability List

The following list represents conditions that are currently considered disabilities by most courts when they affect major life activities.

Albinosim
Arthritis
Asthma
Cancer-All types
Cerebral Palsy
Chronic Migraine Headaches
Cosmetic Burn Injuries
Cosmetic Deformities
Depressive Neurosis
  Suicidal Tendencies
  Nervous Breakdowns
Diabetes-Controlled and Juvenile
  Onset-Insulin Dependent
Dwarfism
Epilepsy
Heart Disease
High Blood Pressure
History of...
  Personality Disorders
  Psychiatric Treatment
Impairment
  Hearing

Impairment
  Speech
  Vision
Learning Disabilities
  Attention Deficit Disorder
  Autism
  Pervasive Developmental Delays
Manic-Depressive Disorders
  Severe Depression
Muscular Dystrophy
Obsessive-Compulsive Personality
  Disorders
Paralysis
  Paraplegia
  Quadriplegia
Paranoid Schizophrenia
Physical Deformities
Post-Traumatic Stress Disorder
  Delayed Stress Reaction
  Vietnam Stress
  Gulf War Stress
  Severe Anxiety Disorders

ADA EXCLUDED CONDITIONS

The following conditions, whether temporary or permanent, are currently not considered disabilities under the ADA.

Appendicitis
Broken Limbs
Colds
  Ear Infection
  Fever
  Flu
  Indigestion
Compulsive Gambling
Exhibitionism
Eye Color

Gender Identify Disorders
Hair Color
Kleptomania
Left-Handedness
Obesity
Pedophilia
Pyromania
Transvestitism
Transsexualism
Voyeurism

APPENDIX Q

Employee Manual

Personnel Handbook
for XYZ Gym

Table of Contents

Introductory Period
Performance and Career Development Reviews
Advancement
Professional Memberships
Resignation in Good Standing
Conflict of Interest
Reduction in Work Force
Sexual Harassment
Corrective Discussions
Warnings
Grounds for Immediate Termination

Employee Benefits

Paid Holidays
Paid Vacation
Sick Leave
Maternity Leave
Personal Time Off
Medical Appointments
Funeral Leave
Jury Duty
Leave of Absence
Military Leave
401K Plan

Insurance

Group Medical Insurance
Group Life Insurance
Worker's Compensation

Compensation

Pay Periods
Payroll Deductions
Garnishments
Overtime

The Purpose of this Handbook

TO PROVIDE A MEANS TO ACHIEVE CLEAR
COMMUNICATION BETWEEN MANAGEMENT AND STAFF
ABOUT FIRM BUSINESS PHILOSOPHY AND EXPECTATIONS.

TO ESTABLISH FAIR AND OBJECTIVE STANDARDS THAT
ARE CONSISTENTLY APPLIED TO ALL FIRM PERSONNEL.

TO PROVIDE THE STRUCTURE NECESSARY TO
MAINTAIN OUR REPUTATION FOR PROFESSIONALISM,
EXCELLENCE AND CLIENT SERVICE.

TO FOSTER A SPIRIT OF COOPERATION AND TEAMWORK.

Welcome!

Welcome to XYZ GYM. We select our personnel with care and expect a high standard of performance and commitment. We are proud of the Firm's reputation for value, service, innovation and good character. Most importantly, we are proud of you — the members of the XYZ GYM team. You have been selected to join our work family because we see reflected in you some of the qualities we most value in ourselves. XYZ GYM, was formed on three basic principles: 1. a strong work ethic; 2. sincere concern over the welfare of clients; and 3. faith in eternal values of right and wrong. So long as our thoughts and actions remain focused on these values, our success will only grow and we will continue to solidify our stature as one of the most respected gyms in our region. We take great pride in being a part of this unique team and we are sure you will too.

You have an exceptional opportunity here for personal and professional growth. Ultimately, your success depends upon the consistency of your efforts, your willingness to learn and grow, your contribution to the gym's growth and well-being, and your active participation as a team member.

We are all striving toward the common goal of building a stronger and better gym. The rewards we reap as a result of our good efforts are more than just financial. There is also the sense of accomplishment in a job well done, the fun of enjoying your workday environment, and the satisfaction of being part of a good organization. It is important, therefore, that you do your part in following the policies and procedures which keep our gym strong and profitable.

Our Clients Make it Possible for Us to Be and Stay in Business

We have two kinds of clients-external and internal. Our *external clients* are those who purchase our services. It is our aim to have them be so pleased with our services that they recommend us to their families, friends and business associates. Sometimes we even become an important relationship in their lives. XYZ GYM will be there at critical junctures in both their professional (e.g., a new business venture, career or job) and personal lives (e.g., marriage, family, retirement and death). To know how we are doing and what our clients value and desire from us we must listen to them. When our clients speak, we express concern and interest—and then we put our creative ingenuity to work to continuously improve on our services. In this way we are able to meet and exceed our clients' expectations, ensuring their loyalty and continued patronage. The key to the gym's continued prosperity and growth is "doing a better job than our clients expect."

Internal clients are the other personnel within the XYZ GYM, with whom we work and on whom we rely for ideas, support and effectiveness in order to produce the best quality athletic environment. XYZ GYM is not a collection of independent personal trainers. Lone individuals lack the synergy and collective intellect required to produce first rate athletic environment to satisfy the needs of sophisticated clients. Through cooperation, innovation, collaboration and teamwork we are all able to participate in the joy and excitement of creative contribution, a shared camaraderie, and the resulting financial reward.

Lastly, development of quality long-term vendor relationships is a critical part of our success. Although we are their customer, it is in our interest to treat them with the same respect and collaborative attitude as we do our internal and external customers. Integrity and consideration in all our dealings with vendors, as well as external and internal customers, are key factors in our long term success. Moreover, every vendor is a potential client and referral source for new business.

Although we are a profitable enterprise, maximizing the amount of money collected is not our primary goal. We are not striving to be the richest gym in town. We are striving to be the most respected and well-regarded. Even the gym's fitness areas were selected with that goal in mind. The gym's founding partners wanted XYZ GYM to be a positive force in the lives of our clients (external and internal) and in the community at large.

Answering and Using the Telephone

The telephone is a major means of communication with our customers and vendors. Therefore, the proper use of the telephone is very important. When answering an outside line always begin with "Good Morning, XYZ GYM" or "Good Afternoon, XYZ GYM."

The intonation in your voice tells volumes about you and what the caller can expect from you, and, by association, from our gym. If you have a warm smile in your voice and an intention to be truly concerned, professional and helpful with whoever is calling, it will come across in your voice.

No matter how accurate or helpful you are to callers, if they feel, from your voice, that their call was a bother or that you really did not care, then we may have lost a client, or at least, good will.

Only by pleasing the people who do business with us will we stay in business. The way you answer the telephone is important to all of us.

Additionally, we should all strive to be responsive. If a client telephones and our phone rings five times before a staff member picks up the call, the impression of our firm is that we are non-responsive or disorganized. Our goal is that every telephone call is answered on or before the third ring. Similarly, no client should be placed on hold for more than five seconds absent unusual circumstances.

Because the telephone is such a critical part of our business, it is important that personal calls be brief and limited.

All telephone calls are to be returned promptly within 24 hours of receipt. Every member of the gym shares responsibility in that policy. Please volunteer to pitch in and return any unanswered calls to other associates or staff persons. Please also report any client complaints as to unreturned calls to the appropriate manager in charge.

Suggestions and Complaints

In a constantly changing business climate and an ever-evolving and growing gym, suggestions for better ways to do things and innovative ideas are definitely valued. Since you are the person closest to the actual operational procedures in your job, you become our most valuable resource for continuous improvement. When you have recommendations, please bring them to the attention of the Office Manager or the Owner.

If you have a problem or complaint, communication is the only means by which the situation can be improved or corrected. Nothing constructive can happen if you keep problems or complaints to yourself, or voice them only to fellow employees. Your silence may only be unfairly condemning a person by denying him or her the opportunity to correct flaws and grow professionally. Gossip is destructive; when you have a problem or complaint, discuss it with the person who can do something about it.

An employee with a complaint relating to inappropriate conduct of other employees or personnel should bring such complaints to the Office Manager or the Owner if the Owner is not involved in disputed matter. No retaliatory action will be taken against any employee who raises a legitimate concern in an appropriate manner. Retaliation is also covered in the gym's Sexual Harassment Policy Statement.

Guidelines

This employee handbook will lay out guidelines that pertain to all personnel of XYZ GYM. It is not intended to address every situation, so take the initiative to ask questions and to take an active part in making our gym the best possible place to establish your career.

Disclaimer

This handbook is not intended, nor may it be considered, to constitute terms of an employment contract between XYZ GYM and its employees. Nothing contained herein is to be interpreted to take away the right of either the employee or the gym to terminate the employment relationship at any time for any reason employee or the gym deems sufficient. XYZ GYM also reserves the right to change any policies or procedures described in this Handbook from time to time, as needed.

PLEASE READ THIS HANDBOOK CAREFULLY AND SIGN THE DOCUMENT PROVIDED CONFIRMING THAT YOU HAVE READ AND UNDERSTOOD ITS CONTENTS. THIS DOCUMENT WILL BECOME PART OF YOUR PERMANENT EMPLOYMENT FILE.

Employment Policies

Discrimination

XYZ GYM is an equal opportunity employer. XYZ GYM does not discriminate on the basis of race, religion, creed, age, color, sex, disability, veteran status or national origin.

In accordance with the Immigration Reform and Control Act of 1986, all new employees are required to fill out form I-9 and provide evidence of eligibility to work in the United States; such proof is a condition of employment.

Employees are selected and promoted on the basis of demonstrated ability, experience, and training. As positions become available within the gym, prior to outside recruitment, the gym will determine the availability of qualified candidates within the gym.

Please Keep Us Informed

Please notify the Office Manager of any of the following changes. This is important in case of emergency and in connection with such matters as social security, withholding taxes, letters to your home, and so forth.

Change of home address or telephone number.
Legal change of name.
Beneficiary change.
Birth or death in your immediate family.
Change in professional license status.

Office Hours

Normal office working hours with telephone, reception and secretarial services are from 8:30 a.m. to 10:30 p.m. Monday through Friday and 10:00 a.m. to 9:00 p.m. on Saturday and Sunday. All staff are expected to be here during this period or part thereof as assigned by their supervisor. If you anticipate arriving late or departing early, please communicate with the Office Manager. One 60 minute lunch period and two 10-minute breaks are granted and encouraged.

Personnel Classifications and Working Hours

Regular full-time. Normally and consistently expected to work a 40 hour week or more whether hourly or salaried.
Regular part-time. Normally and consistently scheduled to work less than 40 and more than 15 hours per week. Hours may vary from person to person.

Contract and temporary. Hired to work on an as-needed or project basis, regardless of the number of hours worked.

Internship. A short term, part-time position designed to provide practical working experience for students in their major fields of interest.

Pay Procedures

Paydays are the 15th and the last day of each month. Any problems regarding your pay should be directed to the Office Manager. If there is a discrepancy, the necessary adjustments will be made.

You will receive your paycheck from the Office Manager or someone designated to give out checks. XYZ GYM will accommodate requests for direct deposit into an employee's checking account upon reasonable notice. If you are absent on payday, your check will be held until it is picked up by you or someone who has been authorized by you in writing. No checks will be mailed, unless authorized by you in writing.

Smoking and Use of Intoxicants

XYZ GYM is concerned with the health and well-being of its personnel; therefore we maintain a smoke-free and drug-free environment. Smoking is permitted outside the building or in designated areas only. No additional breaks will be afforded to accommodate the desire to smoke.

Reporting to work under the influence of intoxicants, the possession, use, or sale of any controlled substance (except for use of prescription drugs taken with supervisory knowledge) is strictly forbidden and is grounds for immediate termination consistent with all federal and state laws.

Safety

Safety throughout the gym involves the individual efforts of all personnel. It is your responsibility to help by working safely at all times. This includes keeping your work area neat and clean.

Any conditions which you believe are unsafe or which are pointed out by a customer or others should be reported to the Office Manager at once and all appropriate reporting form completed in a timely manner.

You should be familiar with the location and use of any fire extinguishers in your area; if you are not, ask your supervisor for instructions. You are required to attend all scheduled safety meetings.

Any unsafe condition should be reported immediately to the Office Manager. All employees should keep vigilant attention of their keys and immediately report any lost or stolen keys. Crime can occur at any time even with a small office. Therefore, all valuables, purses, and wallets should be securely stored within a safe area. Do not leave purses, valuables, and wallets laying around or hanging on the back of your door. XYZ GYM is not responsible for any lost or stolen property.

Security

To assure the safety and well-being of all our personnel, doors to XYZ GYM's offices are always to be kept locked before and after official working hours.

No gym-owned equipment, merchandise, records, data or other material may be taken home without the knowledge and permission of the Officer Manager. To do so could lead to disciplinary action, up to and including termination and legal action.

Parking

For the convenience of our clients, we will pay for their parking. The receptionist is authorized to stamp any parking receipts the clients bring in. XYZ GYM will pay the charges for contract parking of the employees which is available in the designated contract parking areas.

Appearance and Grooming

It is important that all personnel exercise good judgment in selecting attire that is attractive, professional and/or activity appropriate and in keeping with the good taste of our work environment. Personal cleanliness and good grooming are required at all times. Personal clothing must be clean and neat. No blue jeans are allowed.

Friday is the gym's "casual" day for both fitness and front office personnel. The extent of dress relaxation is limited by the fact that we entertain a steady flow of clients throughout the week who have come to expect appropriately attired personnel. Therefore, if you anticipate meeting with clients, dress should be selected appropriately. Generally, however, on Fridays front office personnel may discard ties and all personnel may wear high quality casual (not leisure) wear in lieu of more traditional attire.

Lunches and Breaks

Lunches and breaks should be scheduled in so that the reception area is attended at all times during normal working hours. The gym has a kitchen that all employees are welcome to use. However, it is expected that all personnel clean up after themselves in the kitchen and make an effort to keep the area clean. Please be considerate of other personnel by cleaning up any mess that you may have made. The Office Manager will assign personnel for daily kitchen duty on a rotating basis.

Lateness

Each employee is an important part of a cohesive work unit that allows the business to run smoothly and our clients to receive dependable, quality service. To avoid hardship on co-workers and clients, it is important to be at work at your scheduled time. Should you find that you are going to be more than 15 minutes late, notify the Office Manager, giving the reason and approximate time of arrival, so that adjustments in schedules can be made. Dependable, efficient, uninterrupted service to our clients is one of our criteria for quality service; therefore, repeated lateness can result in disciplinary action, loss of vacation time, financial penalty, and/or termination.

Illness and Absence

In the event of illness or absence from work, you are asked to notify the Office Manager no later than 8:30 a.m. If you know that you will need to be absent on a specific day or for an extended period of time, please let you Office Manager know as far in advance as possible. Abuse of sick day privileges for non-illness reasons is immediate grounds for suspension or termination.

Any employee absent from work for two (2) consecutive days without notifying the Office Manager is considered to have voluntarily terminated employment, unless circumstances surrounding such absence prevented the employee from giving the Office manager such notice.

Return to Work After Serious Injury or Illness

As a joint protection to the gym and its employees, persons who have been absent from work because of serious illness or injury are required to obtain a doctor's release specifically stating that the person is capable of performing his or her normal duties without risk of injury or relapse.

Orientation

You will be provided with an orientation to our facilities, other personnel, your job responsibilities, and our policies, procedures and work rules. On your first day you will fill out all of the tax, parking benefits, insurance and other forms, as well as any biography materials required for the gym's resume and marketing materials.

Training

We only succeed together, so your growth and success is important to us. For this reason we have many types of training available, depending on your experience and needs. The first few weeks will concentrate on training you in your specific job responsibilities, duties and task skills. The supervisors will work with you to determine training appropriate to your needs and the job requirements.

From time to time, a supervisor might require taking special training courses such as writing skills, oral communication, or specific fitness licensing courses. XYZ GYM will cover reasonable expenses for any such required courses. Refusal to take required courses or failure to take required courses within six months of being assigned can be grounds for discipline or termination.

Introductory Period

The first 90 days of employment as a new or re-hired employee is an introductory period. The purpose of this introductory period is to permit you time to adjust to the new environment and to allow management to observe your ability to perform the full range of job requirements. It is important for you to understand that the completion of the introductory period does not guarantee continued employment for any specific time, nor does it require that the employee be terminated only for "cause".

After 90 days you will have a formal progress review, including an opportunity to discuss your total job performance and career goals with the Office Manager and/or your supervisor, as appropriate. We have a vested interest in your success, so do not wait for your 90-day review to discuss any problems or concerns you may have.

Performance and Career Development Reviews

In addition to a 90-day review, you will have a formal written performance and career development discussion at least once a year. Quarterly or more frequent informal progress reviews may be scheduled to assist and support you in reaching your goal. Do not wait for an informal or formal review to discuss any problems or concerns you may have. We want to work with you to solve problems as they occur.

Progress reviews may be recorded and filed in an employee's personnel file. Employees are encouraged to submit any favorable documentation such as client thank-you letters, certificates, awards, publications, etc. for inclusion in their personnel file.

Advancement

XYZ GYM promotes from within whenever possible. Candidates for advancement must demonstrate an aptitude for acquiring and developing the skills necessary to effectively fill the open position. Candidates will be considered on the basis of personal qualification such as professionalism, work product quality, prior training, required education, work experience, proven ability, length of continuous service in the gym, and being able to accomplish all the job requirements. Any individual needing reasonable accommodation to help perform a job's requirement should communicate these needs and discuss possible means to help accommodate any needs with the Office Manager or supervisor.

Professional Memberships

Because we value professional development, the gym will sponsor membership in job-related professional organizations on a case-by-case basis. Employees are encouraged to participate fully in their chosen organization and to invite other interested associates to appropriate organizational functions and to distribute publications and other organizational literature of general interest within the gym. Affiliation of the gym with any organization (whether professional or political) requires the approval and is in the sole discretion of the owner. XYZ GYM does not take associating its name with any organization lightly, irrespective of monetary or lack of monetary involvement. All personal affiliations should remain that way before approval by the managing partners. Thus, for example, correspondence supportive of a particular political position or candidate should not appear on XYZ GYM's letterhead without the prior approval of the owner.

Resignation in Good Standing

If you decide to resign from your job, the gym requires notice two weeks or more in advance so that necessary arrangements for your replacement can be made. The resignation must be submitted in writing to the Office Manager and should include any explanation of the circumstance or rationale for the employee's resignation as long as such reason does not interfere or impinge on any protected rights. If you give appropriate notice, your final check will be ready on your last day of work. Prior to delivering your check, the Office Manager will have a checklist of things that you must return to the gym, such as keys, parking card, security card, any company equipment, records, and programs.

Conflict of Interest

XYZ GYM is proud of its excellent reputation for high standards of ethical conduct in all of its professional, business and personal dealings. To ensure that the conduct of our gym personnel can never be construed as a conflict of interest, or as having any purpose other than absolutely fair and ethical business dealings, personnel are required to give prior notice if possible (and immediate notice if not) before giving or receiving gifts, gratuities, or favors from clients.

Any activity that could be interpreted as compromising the ethics or reputation of the gym or its personnel, inside or outside of the work environment (financial, contractual, sexual, or other), is subject to immediate disciplinary action, up to and including termination. If there is any question regarding whether an action might fall into this category, advice should be sought from the Office Manager.

Reduction in Work Force

The gym's goal is to continue to grow and to increase productivity. Accordingly, it will attempt to avoid cutbacks and reductions in work force whenever possible. However, if XYZ GYM determines that a reduction is warranted, the following procedures will apply.

The gym will give two weeks' notice to any person who it must terminate.

If a reduction in the work force is necessary, terminations shall be based upon personnel performance, productivity, qualifications, areas of expertise, attitude and ability, as judged by the gym's management. In cases where the gym determines these factors are essentially equal between one or more personnel, length of service shall also be considered in determining who will be retained.

Sexual Harassment and Discriminatory Behavior

All persons have a right to work in an environment free from sexual harassment or discrimination by other gym personnel or gym contacts. If you are subject to or witness any form of sexual harassment or discrimination, immediately give notice of the incident to the Office Manager, supervisor and/or owner. The incident will be reviewed and appropriate action taken. Personnel guilty of sexual harassment or discriminatory behavior are subject to disciplinary action up to and including termination. Beyond any actual legal requirement, the gym is strongly opposed to even casual insensitivity based on gender and other differences. Diversity only makes us more resourceful and stronger. The only uniformity we require is our commitment to the fundamental principles and gym's mission set forth in the beginning of this handbook.

Corrective Discussions

We know that most personnel desire to contribute to the gym through their work and that they are willing to follow reasonable gym rules. Sometimes a policy infraction, behavior problem, work habit or performance problem will get in the way of an employee's success. Corrective discussions are designed to assist, support, and coach the employee in correcting those conditions. A corrective discussion is never intended to embarrass or hurt the feelings of the employee; it is an effort to help the employee get back on a positive track. Although such discussions are generally informal, they should be taken seriously so that further corrective actions are not necessary. No one is judging you. We all, however, must take responsibility for and judge each others actions.

Warnings

One or more informal oral discussions precede a formal written warning. A written warning may be used to put an employee on notice that a serious problem exists and must be corrected. The consequences of continued lack of improvement will be discussed with the employee and every effort will be made to help the employee resolve the problem.

If you should be given a written warning you will be required to sign it as an acknowledgment of having had the discussion, but not as an admission that the warning was justified. You will be given a copy of the warning, and the original will be put in your personnel file. Refusal to sign the written warning will be recorded as another infraction and may constitute grounds for termination. An employee will not necessarily be given a warning (written or oral) prior to termination.

Grounds for Immediate Termination

Termination is regarded by the gym as a serious action and shall only be effected after appropriate consideration.

Although it is not possible to list every reason which may be considered grounds for immediate termination, in general such grounds include any action that threatens our ability to work together in a safe, friendly, and efficient environment. Any action which could cause harm to another person at the gym, the gym itself, its property, products, confidentiality, integrity, or quality of service to clients could be cited. This includes but is not limited to the following:

Possessing, using, selling, or being under the influence of narcotics, marijuana or other illegal substances, whether on or off duty.

Intoxication while on the job.

Gross insubordination; refusal to follow directions or to obey legitimate orders from a supervisor.

Unauthorized possession of property belonging to the gym, fellow employees, clients, visitors or others.

Falsification of any records; altering time cards or sheets without a supervisor's approval; knowingly punching another employee's time card, or allowing someone else to punch your card.

Physical violence, threats, abusive or vulgar language, intimidation or coercion directed toward another employee, client, visitor, or guest of the Firm.

Willful abuse or destruction of gym records, equipment, or property.

The destruction or abuse of an employee's, client's, visitor's or any other person's property.

The breach of professional confidence or release of confidential proprietary information.

Unauthorized possession of firearms, explosives, knives, or other lethal or incapacitating weapons on gym premises.

Disregard of safety rules and procedures.

Failure to keep a clean and sanitary work area.

Incompetence or negligence, real or alleged, where a client, colleague, visitor, the gym, or any other person's welfare is jeopardized.

Any immoral, illegal or inappropriate conduct that reflects adversely on the company's integrity and reputation.

Sexual harassment.

Failure to promptly notify the Office Manager or supervisor of any of the forgoing.

Employee Benefits

Paid Holidays

XYZ GYM observes the days listed below as paid holidays. To be paid for the holiday you must work the last scheduled day prior to the holiday and the first scheduled work-day after the holiday. If a paid holiday falls during your scheduled vacation, you may add the paid holiday to the beginning or end of your vacation. A holiday which falls on Saturday or Sunday will be observed on the day it is observed by the federal government.

New Year's Day
Memorial Day
Independence Day
Labor Day
Thanksgiving Day
Day After Thanksgiving
Christmas Day

In addition to the above paid holidays, XYZ GYM offers one paid floating holiday per year. This floating holiday may be taken at any time with prior approval from the gym. If you wish to take a floating holiday, you must submit your request, in writing, to the Office Manager no later than seven days prior to the request date. It may not be possible to grant all personnel the same requested floating holiday. If so preference will be initially granted by seniority and then according to whom was inconvenienced in the immediate prior fiscal year.

Paid Vacation

Vacation accrual is based on the number of full months of service completed. Earned vacation is accrued at the rate of .834 days per month worked, for a total of ten days per year. Employees who have remained with the gym in excess of five years will accrue one additional day of vacation per year over 5 years of employment up to a maximum of 15 days per year.

Earned vacation will accrue, but cannot be taken, during the first 6 months of employment. Vacation time may be taken only after it has been earned and must be taken within the 12-month period following accrual. Absent the prior approval of management, there will be no carry-over of vacation beyond the 12-month period following accrual.

Vacation must be scheduled in advance and approved by the Office Manager. In case of scheduling conflicts, seniority will be given consideration. We consider the taking of a vacation as an important contribution to the health, well-being and renewal of our employees; therefore, payment in lieu of vacation will not be made except in unusual circumstances and only with the approval of management. Vacation time off with pay will not be counted as hours worked for the purposes of computing overtime pay. Vacation time which has been earned but not used will be paid upon termination of employment, not to exceed one year's accrual.

Sick Leave

Full-time regular employees are allowed up to 6 paid sick-days per year of employment, provided they are in good standing, with no probationary warnings on record. Hours spent at doctor or dentist appointments shall count against allocated sick-days on a pro-rata basis. Eight hours of missed work-time will translate into one sick-day. Sick time accrues at the rate of .50 days per month worked. Paid sick leave will accrue, but cannot be taken, during the first 90 days of employment. Employees with less than 5 years of service may accrue a maximum of 10 days of unused sick leave. Employees with five years or more of service can accrue up to a maximum 20 days of unused sick leave. At the end of each one year period, the employee may take the pay for any unused sick days over 2 they have remaining. The pay will be at the rate of one day's pay for every sick day the employee has coming.

Although the average amount of sick leave taken per employee is four to five days per year, the gym grants additional days so that employees can build a personal sick leave account as insurance against long-term illness or disability.

The gym can, at its discretion, require medical certification for sick leave taken.

If there is any question about an employee's ability to perform his or her duties, or to be an effective member of the organization following an illness, accident, or absence from work, it is understood and agreed that the employer may consult with the employee's doctor in order to make this determination.

Maternity Leave

Maternity will be treated the same as any other disability. Under normal conditions, an employee in good standing may request maternity leave without pay. Maternity leave may be granted to permanent employees in good standing for a period of up to three months. Expectant mothers are allowed to work as long as their health permits, with the approval of their physicians. As with other leaves for sickness and temporary disability, every effort will be made to place the employee in her former position or equivalent, depending on the availability of such a position. However, the gym cannot guarantee that their prior position will be available. If such a problem occurs, the gym reserves the right to offer the employee a different position, if one is available, at the appropriate salary for such a position.

Personal Time Off

We understand that there are times when personal matters may require an employee to take a short period (one half to two days) of unscheduled time off. Although personal time off is unpaid, it is important to request the time off from the Office Manager as far in advance as possible, so that work flow and projects can move forward with minimal disruption.

Medical Appointments

Whenever possible, medical appointments should be made outside of office hours. We understand that this is not always possible so appointments made at a time that will pose a minimum of disruption for the gym.

Funeral Leave

If a death occurs in your immediate family, up to 3 scheduled work-days may be taken off with pay. Immediate family is defined as the employee's spouse, child, parent, brother, sister, grandparent, or grandchild, including in-laws and spouses' children from previous marriages.

Jury Duty

If you are called for jury duty or subpoenaed as a witness you will receive your regular pay. The maximum number of days for jury duty with pay is 5 annually. If called for jury duty, notify your supervisor and provide a copy of the court's notice. Unless and until a copy of the court's notice is provided, the employee will not be paid for such time away from work. If you should serve less than a full day, you are expected to return to work. Time spent on jury duty is not counted as hours worked for the purpose of computing overtime pay.

Time off for court appearances as a party to civil or criminal litigation is not compensated by the gym. The employee must arrange for personal time off without pay, or use vacation time.

Leave of Absence

A leave of absence is defined as leave taken other than vacation time. On occasion, an employee may find that personal health, temporary disability or personal issues make it necessary to be absent from work for an extended period of time. All vacation time must be exhausted prior to the request for a leave of absence.

A leave of absence for a limited period of time may be permitted to employees in good standing, depending on the reasons and circumstances that prompt such a request and the effect it will have on the organization's or a section's ability to carry out its work. Such leave of absence must be supported by valid reasons which will be reviewed on a case-by-case basis and must be approved by management. These periods will be without pay.

An employee desiring a leave of absence must present a written request to management stating anticipated length of absence, with dates and the circumstances that prompt the request. Once approved, a leave of absence may be granted for a maximum of up to three months. The request must be made at least two weeks prior to the desired leave date.

The employee is responsible for informing the Office Manager at least two weeks prior to the expected date of return. Upon return from an approved leave, every effort will be made to place the employee in his or her former position or equivalent, depending on the availability of such a position. However, the gym cannot guarantee that a position will be available. If such a problem occurs, the gym reserves the right to offer the employee a lower-level position, if one is available, at the appropriate salary for such a position.

While on leave of absence the employee will not accrue any benefits. For a leave of more than one month the employee will be responsible for payment of the insurance premiums and all other benefits previously assumed by the gym will be continued.

Military Leave

Short term: Employees who are members of the State National Guard or of any reserve component of the armed forces of the United States are entitled to take personal leave time off to serve in that capacity without pay.

Long term: An employee who enlists or is called to active duty should notify the Office Manager and will be granted an unpaid absence in accordance with federal guidelines.

401K Plan

XYZ GYM has several different retirement options from which employees can choose. Upon being hired, the Office Manager will provide all new employees with information concerning retirement options and the gym's 401K plan. The gym's 401K plan is administered by ABC Investment company.

Insurance

Group Medical Insurance

The following summary description of medical and life insurance benefits is not intended to modify or in any way replace the controlling descriptions contained in the group insurance certificates. Please consult the certificates of coverage for specific issues of information.

Full time employees are eligible for coverage under our group hospital and medical program. In this program, XYZ GYM will pay 100% of the premium for coverage of all full time employees. Coverage becomes effective the first day of the month following the approval of the insurance application by the benefit provider. This program currently provides standard $10 co-pay for preferred providers and 70/30 coverage for other nonplan physicians with a $500.00 annual deductible for medical expenses, and a $250.00 deductible for pharmacy expenses.

Should an employee want their dependents covered under this program, they will be responsible for the additional cost. Please consult the certificates of coverage for specific information regarding deductibles, coinsurance and the HMO/PPO options available. Continuation coverage is available in accordance with federal regulations.

Group Life Insurance

Term life insurance with a $10,000.00 death benefit is paid for by the gym.

Worker's Compensation

XYZ GYM carries Worker's Compensation insurance in compliance with state law. The insurance is designed to provide financial assistance to employees who are injured or who become ill as a result of their employment. The gym pays for the cost of the coverage and the insurance carrier makes all payments and decisions pertaining to covered injuries or illness. If you should receive an injury while on the job, no matter how minor, report the circumstance to your supervisor and the Office Manager immediately. Reporting procedures are critical to qualification for benefits.

Compensation

Pay Periods

Employees are paid on the 15th and the last day of each month. The work week begins on Saturday 12:01 a.m. and ends on Friday at midnight. Time cards or time cards are to be submitted to the Office Manager by the close of business on the 15th and the last day of each month.

Pay on the 15th is for work done from the 1st day of the month through the 15th of the month. Pay on the last day of the month is for work from the 16th of the month through the last day of the month. However, overtime is paid in full one week increments. Depending on what the date is on the last day of the week in either pay period, your overtime may fall into the next period. For example, if payday is on Friday, the 15th, your overtime for that week will be on the next pay check because that week does not end until Saturday.

Arrangements for mailing or direct depositing employee paychecks must be made in advance and in writing with the Office Manager.

Payroll Deductions

Those deductions required by law are withheld from your check each pay period. They include federal income tax, social security (FICA) and any legal garnishment. All other deductions require your written authorization, such as your share of medical and life insurance premiums, retirement plans, credit union and so forth.

Garnishments

The gym cannot refuse to honor legal garnishments. A garnishment is a court order requiring the gym to withhold a sum of money from an employee's paycheck. Garnishment is a serious matter. It is hoped that employees manage their financial matters in such a way that the gym does not have to become involved in such a situation.

Overtime

Specific authorization from your supervising attorney is required before any overtime may be worked. For proper salary administration and labor law compliance, each employee must be classified for payroll records as either "exempt" or "non-exempt" on the basis of whether certain tests relating to duties and responsibilities in the job assigned are met. "Exempt" means exempt from the overtime requirements of the current Federal Fair Labor Standards Act. Employees who are "non-exempt" are eligible for overtime pay under certain conditions.

Accurate records of hours worked must be maintained on all non-exempt employees. These records are required for calculation of overtime and vacation time, and by government regulations. Daily time-cards must be filled out by you and signed by both you and your supervisor weekly. Under no circumstances may your time card or sheet be filled out by another employee. To do so is grounds for disciplinary action up to and including immediate termination.

Non-exempt employees are paid at the rate of one and one-half times the regular rate of pay for all hours of overtime actually worked. Hours paid that are not actual hours worked, such as vacation, funeral leave, and jury duty, are not included in the overtime eligibility calculations.

Miscellaneous

Any topic or issue not covered in this handbook should be raised with your supervisor or the Office Manager. XYZ GYM reserves the right to modify this handbook at any time for any reason or no reason at all.

****

I, _____ read this handbook in its entirety on _____, 19 ___ and willingly consent, as a condition of employment or continued employment, that I will comply with all the rules, regulations and policies set forth above. I further understand that this handbook does not represent an employment contract and that I am specifically classified as an "at will" employee.

Signature _____ Date _____

Adopted in part from Bisk and Lutz, L.L.P., *Employee Manual*, Houston, Texas (1997).

APPENDIX R

Employee Contract

EMPLOYMENT AGREEMENT

Agreement made on this 20th day of October, 1997 by and between XYZ Gym, Inc. (hereinafter "XYZ") and Bob Jones (hereinafter "Jones').

1. Terms of Agreement

XYZ agrees to employ Jones and Jones accepts employment on the terms set forth below for the time period beginning on October 20, 1997 and continuing until October 19, 1998. XYZ shall have the option to extend the term of this Agreement for additional one (1) year periods beyond October 19, 1998. Any such extension shall be made with fifteen (15) days prior the completion of any yearly contract through written notice to Jones. This Agreement is not intended to in any way affect any relationship between the parties after conclusion of the stated term.

2. Job Duties and Standards

During the term of this Agreement, Jones shall serve as Sales Manager and/or in such other positions as XYZ may assign in the exercise of its reasonable discretion. Jones's specific duties shall include all tasks and obligations reasonably assigned by XYZ in furtherance of the XYZ's work. Jones shall devote all of his working time and attention to performing his duties under this Agreement and shall use his best efforts to assist XYZ in the successful development and implementation of appropriate marketing campaign to maximize membership development.

3. Restrictive Covenant for Exclusive Services

The parties recognize that the services rendered by Jones under this Agreement are of a special character, based on his past health club success which gives his talent peculiar value and the loss of which cannot be reasonably or adequately compensated in damages. Jones agrees to render his professional sales and marketing services exclusively to XYZ during the stated term of this Agreement and further agrees that XYZ may enforce this exclusive services covenant by court injunction in the event Jones breaches the Agreement. Jones expressly recognizes that this covenant will prevent him from offering his professional services to any other employer during the stated term of this Agreement, even if Jones terminates his employment with XYZ before the end of the stated employment period. Jones further recognizes that this absolute prohibition on other employment during the stated term of this Agreement is reasonable and properly required to adequately protect XYZ.

4. Compensation and Benefits

Jones shall be compensated at a salary of fifty thousand dollars ($50,000) per annum, to be paid in accordance with XYZ's prevailing payroll practices. Jones shall receive the benefit package offered to other XYZ executives in similar positions during the term of this Agreement including, parking, free health club membership, medical insurance, paid vacation, paid holidays, and a $1,000 yearly travel allowance. These benefits will be made available on the same terms as they are provided to similarly situated employees.

5. Agreement Termination by XYZ

This Agreement may be terminated by XYZ before the stated term under the following circumstances:

a. Jones suffering physical or mental disability such that he is rendered substantially or completely unable to perform the services required by this Agreement or is absent from work because of disability for more than thirty (30) consecutive days as long as any such termination is consistent with the American With Disabilities Act and related laws;

b. Jones death;

c. Jones failure to perform his duties in good faith or in accordance with industry standards, whether resulting from active misconduct, neglect or abandonment;

d. Jones violating XYZ company policies or any other acts or omissions contrary to XYZ's interests;

e. Violation by Jones of any provisions within this Agreement.

6. Arbitration of Disputes/Waiver of Right to Sue

Any and all disputes and controversies between the parties regarding XYZ's employment or termination of Jones shall be resolved by final and binding arbitration. The parties further specifically state that this agreement to arbitrate shall also apply to any claims or disputes based in whole or part on any federal, state or local law, including, but not limited to any claim of sexual harassment, discrimination of any kind, wrongful termination and related claims. Arbitration by either party must be demanded by written notice to the other party within sixty (60) days of the occurrence of the event which is the basis of the controversy, and failure to make a proper and timely demand for arbitration shall constitute a complete and irrevocable waiver of that claim. The parties shall endeavor to mutually agree upon an arbitrator; in the event that an agreement cannot be reached, an arbitrator shall be selected pursuant to the provisions of the Athletic Dispute Resolution Service (713) 871-9990. All arbitration costs shall be borne equally by the parties. Any arbitration proceedings will be completely private, and neither party will disclose or publicize any facts relating to that process except as required by law. The parties specifically state that this arbitration agreement is intended to constitute a waiver of rights to have disputes between them resolved by a court or jury except that the parties shall have the right to initiate judicial proceedings to compel arbitration or for review or enforcement of the arbitrator's decision and; provided, that nothing contained in this paragraph shall constitute a waiver of XYZ's rights to seek immediate injunctive relief from Jones's violation of Paragraphs 3 and 7 of this Agreement.

7. Protection of Confidential Information

It is contemplated that Jones will have access to various confidential information during the course of her employment with XYZ. For purposes of this Agreement, "confidential information" shall include any documents or information pertaining to XYZ's financial, personnel, or operations matters, in addition to any documents or information relating to technology, proprietary software, trade secrets, and marketing strategies, but shall not include any information that is publicly available. Jones shall maintain confidential information in the strictest confidence and take all necessary action to protect its confidentiality. Jones shall not use XYZ's confidential information for his own benefit or to XYZ's detriment or permit its use by others for their benefit or to XYZ's detriment. Upon XYZ's demand or upon termination of this Agreement, Jones shall immediately return to XYZ all confidential information in his possession and shall not retain any records or copies of such confidential information. The protection of confidential information provided by this paragraph shall survive the expiration or earlier termination of this Agreement. Jones specifically recognizes that violation of this paragraph will result in irreparable harm to XYZ, that monetary damages will be inadequate, and that XYZ will be entitled to injunctive relief to enforce this paragraph.

8. Employment or Solicitation of Employees

Jones agrees that, for a period of one year after termination of his services under this Agreement, he will not employ or solicit the employment of any XYZ employee or any person who has been employed by XYZ within the preceding year.

9. Noncompete Clause

For a period of two years after the termination of this Agreement, Jones shall forever waive his rights to start, open, run, manage, or in any other manner work with or manage any health club, fitness club or related activity centers within a twenty mile radius of any currently existing XYZ owned or operated health club.

10. Assignment of Rights/Delegation of Duties

XYZ shall have the right to assign or delegate part or all of its rights and duties under this Agreement to any person, firm, or corporation and all such rights and duties shall inure to the benefit of and be binding upon any successor, licensee, or assign of XYZ. Jones's obligations and rights under this contract are personal to Jones and may not be assigned or delegated to another party.

11. Modification of Agreement and Waiver of Rights

This Agreement may be modified only in writing, and any such writing must specifically state that it is intended to modify this Agreement. Such written modification will be effective only if signed by XYZ's President. Any attempt to modify this Agreement by other means shall be void. Any failure of one party to require timely and proper performance of this Agreement by the other party shall not be construed as a waiver of rights to later enforce the entire Agreement as written.

12. Separability of Provisions

The provisions of this Agreement shall be construed to be separable and independent of each other, and in the event any provision of this Agreement shall be found to be invalid or illegal, such findings shall not effect the validity or effectiveness of any other or all of the remaining provisions.

13. Entire Agreement

This Agreement sets forth the entire agreement and understanding between the parties regarding XYZ's employment of Jones and supersedes all prior discussions, agreements and understandings between them. Neither party shall be bound by any condition, definition, warranty or representation other than expressly set forth or provided for in this Agreement.

14. Governing Law

This Agreement shall be governed, construed and enforced in accordance with the laws of California without regard to any potential conflicts of law.

Dated: _____   _____
                            Bob Jones
Dated: _____   _____
                            XYZ Club, President

APPENDIX S

Sexual Harassment Policy

ACME Co. is committed to providing a work place free of any and all sexual harassment. It is both against the law and ACME Co. policy for any employee or non-employee to sexually harass any co-workers, employees, or customers. ACME Co. will strictly enforce this policy to the full extent of the law and adherence to this policy is a mandatory condition of continued employment with ACME Co.

SEXUAL HARASSMENT DEFINED

Sexual harassment is defined as any unwelcomed sexual advances, or visual, verbal or physical conduct of a sexual nature. Any conduct which creates an offensive and hostile work environment is sexual harassment. Furthermore, any sexual conduct which is coerced by a person in a position of apparent or actual power or authority is sexual harassment. Sexual harassment involves a wide variety of behaviors between members of the opposite sex as well as members of the same sex. It should be clear that some conduct which might be appropriate in a social setting, between friends, or even between individuals involved in a consensual relationship may not be appropriate in the workplace. Some prohibited conduct examples are described below. These represent only samples and is not an exhaustive list of conduct which is defined by ACME Co. and the courts as sexual harassment.

Physical harassment:

Unwanted physical contact involving a sexual nature including but not limited to fondling, groping, suggestive touching, impeding or blocking movement, brushing-up against a body, and/or any other activity which causes contact or threat of contact which is unwanted.

Verbal harassment:

Sexual jokes, innuendo, suggestive comments, persistent and unwanted sexual advances, propositions or requests for companionship, any verbal offer of employment, advancement, or increased salary, or other benefits in exchange for sexual activity, threatened or actual employment reprisals, threats, demotions, or terminations after refusing any sexual advances, and/or any graphic lude or offensive comments about an individual's body or body parts.

Non-verbal harassment:

Staring, leering, obscene gestures, displaying or distributing offensive or sexually suggestive objects, pictures, cartoons, drawings or posters, making or airing suggestive or insulting sounds/noises, and/or writing and/or distributing offensive, suggestive, or obscene notes or letters. This is not an exhaustive list of prohibited conduct. The term offensive or obscene refers to any conduct, activity, words or sounds which an average person of normal sensitivity would find offensive or obscene.

SEXUAL HARASSMENT REPORTING PROCEDURES

If you believe that you have been the subject of sexual harassment, immediately report the harassment to your supervisor, the Human Resources Department, or ACME's sexual harassment coordinator (Ms. Jane Doe). Do not report the conduct to the person who you allege harassed you, but to anyone who is independent or superior to the alleged harasser. Do not wait a significant period after the alleged harassment has occurred to report the incident. Such actions could jeopardize the ability to fully investigate a complaint or to find necessary witnesses. All complaints will be promptly investigated in a discreet manner. Information will be given to the complaining party only after a thorough investigation has been completed. Investigation will normally entail conferring with the parties involved and any potential witnesses disclosed by the complainant. ACME Co. will take any and all necessary steps, including all forms of discipline to stop the offensive or inappropriate conduct. The complainant will be informed of all findings uncovered through the investigation process and all actions taken as a result thereof. ACME Co. takes every sexual harassment claim seriously and will resolve any and all complaints. No punitive action will ever be taken against a complainant who files a valid compliant. ACME Co. will not tolerate any retaliation or conduct of a retaliatory nature against any individual who has filed a complaint or who is a witness in any sexual harassment investigation.

If ACME Co. is unable to successfully resolve a complaint through the use of internal procedures, or if any employee who suffers sexual harassment is reluctant to utilize the internal procedures, such employee can file a complaint with any appropriate state or federal agency. The employee information area contains a poster reiterating ACME Co.'s sexual harassment policy and describing appropriate contact agency for filing claims. State or federal agencies will normally conduct an investigation and attempt to resolve the matter. If evidence is found of sexual harassment, the matter can be brought to a public hearing. Possible remedies include back-pay, promotion, reinstatement, hiring, changes in ACME Co.'s policy and procedures, emotional distress damages, and possible fines.

ACME Co. has never and will never tolerate, and the law specially prohibits, any retaliation against any employee for filing or otherwise participating in any hearing, proceeding or investigation associated with a sexual harassment claim filed with any government agency or commission.

If you have any comments, questions or concerns about sexual harassment, please contact ACME Co.'s Human Resource Director.

I, _____ have read and understand all the above statements. I have had an opportunity to ask any questions I have concerning ACME Co.'s sexual harassment policy. In consideration for being hired or continuing my employment with ACME Co., I hereby agree to follow ACME Co.'s sexual harassment policy and will indemnify and hold ACME Co. harmless for any and all liability and attorney fees if engage in inappropriate conduct including, but not limited to sexual harassment or retaliating against any individual involved in a sexual harassment claim.

_____   _____
Signature   Date

Adopted in part from Schachter, Kristoff, Orenstein, and Berkowitz, *Sexual Harrassment: Innovative Approaches for Minimizing Liability*. San Francisco, California (November 1, 1994).

APPENDIX T

Written Warning

The following represents a potential verbal warning notice that could be included in an employee's personnel file.

On May 17, 1997, I gave Jerry Johnson a verbal warning for posting some inappropriate, sexually explicit cartoons on the employee bulletin board which offended Janet Doe. Ms. Doe indicated this was not the first time Jerry has done this, and that she had asked him on a previous occasion not to post the pictures anymore.

Jerry claimed he was unaware that Ms. Doe found these cartoon so offensive. Jerry specifically stated that he knows about ACME Co.'s sexual harassment policy and knows what disciplinary actions are allowable pursuant to the policy statement. Jerry specifically stated that he will refrain from doing any similar acts in the future. This is the first time any such claim has been filed or raised against Johnson. Therefore, I felt it was appropriate to give him just a verbal warning.

Jane Doe
HR Director
May 17, 1997

APPENDIX U

Termination Letter in Sexual Harassment Matters

May 11, 1997

PERSONAL AND CONFIDENTIAL

Mr. Jerry Johnson
456 Which St.
Anytown, NY 12345

Dear Mr. Johnson:

We have just concluded our investigation into the complaint filed by Ms. Doe regarding inappropriate sexual conduct on the job. Based upon this investigation, and the facts which were already presented to you at our meeting on May 10, 1997, we have decided to terminate your employment with XYZ, Inc..The employee handbook which you received, read and signed on April 1, 1996 specifically provided for termination for anyone who engaged in sexual harassment. We had provided prior oral and written warnings for you to stop engaging in any inappropriate conduct. Therefore, termination was the only option available to resolve this matter.

You are entitled to any accrued vacation and sick days which you have not used. We are in the process of determining such amounts, if any and will forward this amount to you. Please call me to arrange a time to remove any personal belongings. If you do not remove your personal belongings by June 1, 1997, your belongings will be packed for you and shipped to your last known address.

I look forward to hearing from you concerning the removal of your belongings.

Yours,

Jane Doe
HR Director

APPENDIX V

Sexual Harassment Letter to Victim

May 11, 1997

PERSONAL AND CONFIDENTIAL

Ms. Janet Doe
123 Main Street
Anywhere, NY 12345

Dear Janet:

This letter follow our meeting today in which you informed me that you were concerned and upset about inappropriate sexual conduct by James Johnson. Specifically, you complained that Mr. Johnson _____(fondled, harassed, what ever the alleged conduct was).

As we discussed, ACME Co. takes your complaint very seriously. We will take whatever action is necessary to insure you that you are not exposed to any offensive or objectionable conduct on the job. We will immediately begin our investigation. As soon as the investigation is complete I will schedule a meeting and discuss with you the investigation results and any and all subsequent actions. However, in the meantime, I respectfully request that you keep this complaint confidential. Do not hesitate to contact me if you have questions.

I want to reiterate how seriously ACME Co. takes any form or manner of retaliation against anyone who files a sexual harassment claim. If you ever feel that someone or a group of employees have retaliated or are retaliating against you on the job, please notify me immediately so I can take all appropriate and necessary actions.

I want to once again thank you for bringing this matter to both my and ACME Co.'s attention. One component of my job duty is to handle complaints similar to yours, thus I take your complaint seriously and will do everything I can to resolve the matter.

Sincerely,

Jane Doe
Human Resources

APPENDIX W

Sexual Harassment Letter to Accused

May 11, 1997

PERSONAL AND CONFIDENTIAL

Mr. Jerry Johnson
456 Nowhere Lane
Anytown, NY 12345

Dear Mr. Johnson:

As discussed in our meeting yesterday, Janet Doe, your co-worker, has approached our department with allegations concerning your conduct. Specifically, Ms. Doe claims you: _____ (list specific allegations).

Ms. Doe's complaint raises significant concern about sexual harassment. When you were hired, you were asked to sign ACME Co.'s sexual harassment policy statement. Thus, you know how seriously we take any claim of sexual harassment. Such activities are both against the law and company policy. Therefore, employees engaged in such activities are subject to a variety of disciplinary options, including possible termination for serious offenses.

Based on Ms. Doe's complaint, we will be conducting a comprehensive investigation. Be assured that the investigation will be strictly confidential. We appreciate and request full cooperation throughout the investigatory process. Upon completing the investigation, we will contact you in writing about our findings. In the meantime, do not hesitate to contact me if you have any additional information that will assist us in the investigatory process.

The sexual harassment law strictly prohibits any form of retaliation against a person filing a complaint. Thus, you must not confront Ms. Doe about her complaint. I also want to emphasize that ACME Co. will not tolerate any retaliation, in any manner or from anyone, against Ms. Doe because she filed the complaint. If you have any questions concerning how you should conduct yourself while the investigation is pending, please do not hesitate to contact me.

Sincerely,

Jane Doe
Human Resources

APPENDIX X

Incident Reporting Policy

1. Definitions:

A)   *Parks and/or City Parks*—City parks is a term used to describe any facility, open space, field, playground, or other man-made or natural condition that exists within the confines of an identified park and recreation property. Included within the definition of city parks are sidewalks, parking lots, bathrooms, port-a-potties and related areas. City parks also should be used to describe any community center. City parks can be substituted for any other term used to describe the programs or facilities in which the incident(s) occurred.

B)   *Incident*—An incident references any activity that results in an injury or damage to either a person, structure or property. Incidents include, but are not limited to criminal activity (assaults, thefts, burglary, rape, molestations, vandalism, etc.), inappropriate conduct (violation of park rules, threats, lost children, bringing guns to a city park, etc.), injuries (any personal, structural, vehicle, or property which might include broken bones, contusions, cuts, broken windows, unlocked doors, auto accidents, stolen cars, lost items, broken equipment, etc.), dangerous conditions and any other events or conditions which appear or could appear to warrant documentation for future reference. Anytime police activity (arrest or investigation activity) and/or fire/paramedic activity is noted at a city park, an incident has occurred and should be documented.

C)   *Investigate and/or Investigating*—Investigating refers to the formal process of preparing and filing an incident report and the resulting process which determines what steps were taken and the appropriateness of those steps. Investigating a potential incident is a critical component of the incident reporting process and requires a thorough analysis of all the facts and the accurate reporting of objective findings, and not subjective findings.

D)   *Reporting*—Reporting involves the formal process of filling an incident report with supervisors or the Department Director's office.

E)   *Counsel*—Counseling refers to discussing an incident with an individual park patron or program participant and providing critical information to assist them in resolving any outstanding issues. No Houston Park and Recreation Department employee can ever provide any medical or legal advice or assistance.

F)   *Contact Supervisor*—Contacting a supervisor involves the process of reporting an incident or perceived incident to an immediate supervisor.

A supervisor should be contacted at the first available point in time after any emergency has passed. Under no circumstance should a supervisor be contacted more than three hours after an incident has occurred which requires a supervisor to be contacted.

G)   *Accident*—An accident refers to any unexpected or unintentional event that results in physical injury or damage. Accidents do not involve any type of moving vehicles (see below).

H)   *Auto Accident*—An auto accident refers to any accident involving an HPRD vehicle or damage caused by an HPRD vehicle (or personnel) to a civilian vehicle(s). Examples include a vehicle crashing into a tree, a highway collision involving an HPRD vehicle or a weedeater operated by an employee shooting a rock at a car which breaks the car's windshield.

I)   *Fire*—The act of burning any item to any degree. Examples include trash fires, electrical fires, grass fires, or a burning facility. The term fire refers to both active and extinguished fires.

J)   *Lost Child*—A lost child is any youth under age 10 that is separated from their parent/guardian or from a supervising adult. There is no set time that a child has to be left alone to be considered "lost." A child is only lost if the child specifically indicates they cannot find their parent or guardian. A child also is considered lost if a parent or guardian reports a missing child to any HPRD employee.

K)   *Inappropriate Conduct*—Inappropriate conduct refers to any improper conduct displayed by a participant, visitor, employee, or volunteer which threatens the safety of others. Examples include intoxicated conduct, yelling at individuals, threatening others, misusing facilities or equipment, etc.

L)   *Violation of Park Rules and Regulations*—All employees, volunteers, participants and visitors have one opportunity to be informed of the park rules and regulations. If such rules or regulations are subsequently violated or there is an initial egregious rules violation, then there is a violation of the rules and regulations as set forth in the Park and Recreation Rules and Regulation Manual available at each park. Examples of such violations include a person selling anything on park property without a valid permit, using glass container in a park, littering park areas, parking in unauthorized areas.

M)   *Theft*—Theft refers to the taking for possession of something which is not rightfully owned by the person who took possession. Theft can be categorized as auto and non-auto theft.

N)   *Burglary*—Burglary refers to the breaking into and entering a building not open to the general public with the intent to steal.

O)   *Assault and Battery*—Assault and Battery occurs when a person intentionally or knowingly causes bodily injury, threatens to cause bodily injury, or causes physical contact with another when the person knows or should reasonably believe that the other person will regard the contact as offensive or unwanted. Examples include fighting, pushing another person, threatening someone with a knife, or any conduct that puts someone in fear of imminent unwanted bodily contact.

P)   *Vandalism*—Vandalism entails any willful or malicious destruction of property. Examples include breaking windows, spray painting a building, destroying plants, or overturning park equipment.

Q)   *Illegal Acts*—Illegal acts refers to any other illegal conduct which could include: rape, murder, molestation, public exposure, embezzlement, and any other illegal activities not covered in the above definitions.

R)   *Employee*—An employee refers to any full-time or part-time worker employed by HPRD and engaged in any activity which occurs during regular park operational hours or required work hours, and which directly benefits HPRD.

S)   *Volunteer*—Any individual who performs any services or provides assistance to HPRD and any of its programs without remuneration.

T)   *Youth*—A youth means any individual under the age of 18-years-old.

U)   *Trespass*—A person has trespassed on land when they do not have an express or implied right to be on the land. While city parks are owned by the people, HPRD exercises control over all facilities and grounds and can explicitly exclude anyone from facilities at different times. An example of trespass involves someone jumping over a fence to swim in a pool or opening a window to enter into a facility when it is closed to the public.

V)   *Injury/Damage*—The terms injury or damage will be used throughout these procedures to refer to any physical injury to someone or property damage to some thing.

W)   *Provide Aid*—Normally referred to as first-aid, provide aid is a more descriptive term concerning how employees or volunteers should handle an injured person. Provide aid refers to providing necessary equipment such as toweling or band-aids, but doe not entail the administration of medical techniques or procedures to assist an injured person. More comprehensive assistance can be provided for very serious injuries (while waiting for Medical/EMT assistance), but minor injuries should be handled by the injured person themselves or their own physician.

X)   *Request Assistance*—Requesting assistance refers to contacting any internal (i.e., maintenance) or external (i.e., police, fire, etc.) entity to provide guidance or assistance in resolving an incident. A list of qualified sources from which to request assistance is provided in the procedure section for Incident Reports.

Y) *Medical/EMT*—Medical/EMT refers to various providers of emergency service whether it is a county or city run paramedics unit or a private ambulance service.

Z) *Parent or Guardian*—A parent or guardian refers to an individual or entity (i.e., school or day care center) which has either full or temporary responsibility to care for the welfare and safety of a child or youth.

2. Purpose

Incidents will occur within the confines of city parks. These occurrence, if not handled properly, could cause significant losses, injuries, service interruption, damage to city property or personnel, and potential large liability concerns for our department and the City of Houston. These guidelines are designed to help all employees, managers and supervisors understand their requirement to properly investigate, accurately complete, and timely submit incident reports.

3. Responsibility

All employees, managers and supervisors are responsible for timely investigating and reporting all city park incidents which might occur during their assigned shift—whether or not the incident occurred at a city park or any other location. The morning shift is responsible for reporting any incidents or activity that occurred anytime after the prior night's last shift ended. All incident reports have to be submitted within 24 hours of the incident to the appropriate person responsible for processing such claims. the appropriate contact persons are as follows:

All personal injury incident reports should be submitted to: _____
All fire or criminal incidents should be submitted to: _____
All incidents involving vehicles should be submitted to: _____
All incidents involving facilities should be submitted to: _____
All employee injuries should be submitted to: _____

4. Procedures

Once an incident has occurred, all employees, managers and supervisors must exercise responsible and appropriate judgment to determine what action is appropriate and satisfactory to handle the incident and minimize the future impact on employees, volunteers, park visitors, park patrons, the Park and Recreation Department and the City of Houston.

It should be clearly stated that if an injury has not yet occurred, all employees need to take appropriate risk management steps to prevent the injury. Thus, if an employee sees several participants shoving each other, the game should be stopped prior to a fight breaking out between the participants. Likewise, if a basketball rim is broken, no one should be allowed to play with that backboard or rim. Such proactive steps are the required course of action in our department's proactive risk reduction program.

The following steps should be taken when responding to any incident or potential incident.

Step 1   Determine the appropriate action needed in response to the incident keeping mind the safety of employee(s), volunteer(s) and visitor(s). In response to all incidents listed below, a supervisor has to be contacted immediately to notify them about the incident. The following list gives specific suggested responses to various incidents which might occur during a shift:

Incident type	_Response_
Assault and Battery	
Assault involving weapons	Contact Police
Assault during programs	Contact Police, cancel program
Auto accident	
Auto accident, no injuries, slight damage	Contact Police, exchange insurance info, file report
Auto accident, no injuries, major damage	Contact Police, exchange insurance info
Auto accident, slight injuries	Contact Police, exchange insurance info, possibly administer first-aid
Auto accident, major injuries	Contact Police, Medical/EMTs
Burglary	
Burglary in progress	Do not intervene, contact Police
Other, under $100 value	Contact supervisor, then contact Police
Other, over $100 value	Contact Police, then contact supervisor
Dead Body	Contact Police, then contact director
Fires	
Fire, active	Call Fire Department
Fire, extinguished	Report and repair
Illegal activities	
Abuse-suspected child abuse	Call Police and Child Protective Services
Abuse by employee or volunteer	Call Police, contact Director's office
Assault, see above	
Burglary, see above	
Murder	Contact Police
Rape	Contact Police/Medical/EMTs
Theft, auto	Contact Police
Theft, non-auto, under $100 value	Contact supervisor

Theft, non-auto, over $100 value	Contact Police
Trespass-willing to leave	Contact supervisor
Trespass-unwilling to leave	Contact Police
Vandalism, minor and suspect known, youth	Contact parents/supervisor
Vandalism, major and suspect known, youth	Contact parents/supervisor and Police
Vandalism, minor, perpetrator unknown	Contact supervisor
Vandalism, major, perpetrator unknown	Contact Police/supervisor

Illness

Fever	Send person home/contact parents
Flu	Send person home/contact parents
Seizure	Call Medical/EMT provide blankets and try to help prevent choking on victim's tongue

Injuries

Broken bones	Call EMTs, provide comfort and blankets to prevent shock, then contact parents
Cuts, minor	Provide toweling and band-aids then contact parents
Cuts, major	Call EMTs, provide toweling, then contact parents
Head or neck injuries	Do not move body, call EMTs, then contact parents

Inappropriate Conduct

Dangerous	Contact Police, then contact supervisor
Disruptive, but not dangerous	Contact supervisor

Intoxicated Individual

Willing to leave park	Contact supervisor
Unwilling to leave park	Contact Police
Bothering park patrons or employees	Contact Police

Lost Child	Look for parent/guardian then con-
tact	
	Police

Property

Lost property, under $100	Contact supervisor
Lost property, $100–$500	Contact supervisor, investigate

Lost property, over $500	Contact supervisor, possibly contact Police
Vandalism, see above	
Structural	
Broken Door	Contact maintenance
Broken Windows	Contact maintenance
Other Damage	Contact maintenance or supervisor
Violating Park Rules	Contact supervisor

These are typical responses to various incidents. There is no one perfect manner in which to respond to an incident. Based on severity or danger, other authorities might need to be notified for additional assistance. The best rule of thumb to utilize when responding to any incident is that a supervisor is only a phone call away and you should never hesitate to contact a supervisor whenever a new or unique incident arises.

Key Rules for Providing Appropriate Response

After reviewing the appropriate responses outlined above, all employees and volunteers should always keep in mind that the following golden rules should never be violated, under any circumstances.

> **Never provide anyone with any drugs, even aspirin.**
> Provide first-aid when no other course of action exists.
> Never provide medical advice.
> Never let an intoxicated person wander around or drive if they are too intoxicated to control their own actions.
> Always provide Police, Fire and EMT dispatchers with accurate directions including cross-streets.
> If an incident occurs in a non-HPRD location, all the procedural steps outlined herein should still be followed.

Step 2   After providing a relevant and appropriate response (whether providing assistance or calling for assistance from Police, Fire, EMTs, or supervisors) immediately contact the Supervisor who will evaluate your actions and provide any additional insight or contact other necessary persons for further assistance. At no time during the process of contacting the Supervisor should the injured individual be ignored or treated as if they are not special and that their injury or harm is trivialized.

Step 3   Take time whenever the urgency of an incident has subsided to complete an Incident Report. Special care needs to be taken to contact witnesses prior to them leaving the park or incident location. The following overview and procedure section helps describe the necessary steps in the incident reporting process.

Incident Reporting Notice/Overview and Procedures

Policy Statement

It is the policy of the Houston Park and Recreation Department to maintain a consistent method of reporting and tracking incidents occurring either on, adjacent, near or away from city park property or involving persons engaged in HPRD related facilities or programs.

Policy Amplification

This policy is provided as a framework by which all incident reporting by employees will follow and is not intended to replace and/or circumvent any city, state or federal reporting procedures. Any such policy, forms or procedures should be completed along with an HPRD incident report.

Overview

Scope

This policy applies to all operational phases of the HPRD with particular emphasis on facilities, structures, property and programs where an incident is more likely to occur. Therefore, all employees need to known, understand and follow this policy.

Objectives

1) To provide a standardized method of reporting incidents for use throughout HPRD and the City of Houston.
2) To outline circumstances by which incidents will be reported
3) To develop a basis by which incidents can be tracked and used for analytical studies.

General

This policy details the guidelines, procedures and responsibilities for reporting incidents. Incident reporting is a critical means of recording events that disrupt, damage or destroy city park activities or property. Therefore, a duty exists in every employee position to timely and accurately complete and submit Incident Reports. The failure to follow this policy can result in termination and/or any other response deemed reasonable by HPRD administration.

Primary Responsibility

The office of the Director will have primary responsibility for management and oversight for monitoring this policy and will insure policy compliance.

Procedural Outline

Incident Report

All employees, managers and supervisors are required to report all incidents whether such incident occurred, was reported, was discovered, or was witnessed. Reporting is accomplished by timely completing and filing an Incident Report with the proper department representative. If any employee or volunteer is notified of an incident that he/she determines to be severe, then that individual should immediately notify the their immediate supervisor. It is the supervisor's ultimate decision whether the incident is severe enough to notify the Department Director. However, any incident involving felonious conduct such as rape, molestations, guns at city parks and related criminal activity should be immediately reported to the Department Director or his/her designee. Addenda A represents a sample Incident Report with proper completion instructions.

Call ins

HPRD has a "call in" system whereby any citizen or employee can report any incident or dangerous condition no matter whether or not a city park is operating during regular business hours. All "call in" dispatchers are responsible for contacting the proper individual should a severe incident arise during non-business hours. The dispatcher will be supplied with the necessary phone numbers and contact persons with all other city departments and emergency service providers. All incidents that are called in should be logged in on a log-in sheet (see Addenda G). Additionally, an Incident Report should be complete for all incidents and submitted to proper individuals the next business day. All Repair Request (see Addenda F) should be submitted to the Maintenance Department. The dispatcher should complete the incident report after contacting the appropriate park employee(s) to determine the full extent of the incident.

All call in incident should be analyzed at the most one week after the incident to determine if the incident was resolved and/or if the incident or other dangerous conditions are still present. If any requested repairs or procedural changes are requested, but not completed, such information should be immediately provided to the Department Director or his/her designee.

Submitting an Incident Report

The incident report consists of an original and three attached copies. Once completed, the form should be routed in the following manner:

White (original)	Submit to the Office of the Director
Yellow (copy)	Submit to designated Division Head overseeing the area wherein the incident occurred.

Pink (copy)   Submit to immediate supervisor
Gold (copy)   Retain at the site.

All Incident Reports have to be submitted within 24 hours of the time the incident occurred, was discovered, was reported, or was witnessed. If the incident occurred on a weekend or holiday, the incident report has to be submitted on the very next business day. Within 48 hours of the incident, a designated employee within HPRD shall follow-up with appropriate authorities, or the injured individual to determine how the incident was resolved and if there is anything that HPRD can do to prevent further similar incident. Such follow-up is critical in reducing future risks. The information obtained during this follow-up process shall be used to make future risk management decisions. For example, if an individual has been involved in a violent assault, the Police Department should be contacted concerning how the matter was resolved. Through contacting the Police Department or judicial process it can be determined whether or not the individual should be allowed to engage in any future HPRD programs. HPRD can open itself up to a lawsuit for failing to prevent an individual's participation in an activity when his/her violent tendencies were known. That is why it is imperative to follow-up every significant incident.

Supplemental Reports

Incident Reports often need to be supplemented with a variety of forms that are designed to provide additional critical information. All forms should be completed in a timely manner and submitted to appropriate Department officials (i.e. supervisors or the Director). The type of supplemental forms available are listed below.

A)   *Supplemental Report*—A Supplemental Report should be used whenever additional information is required. For example, if eight people were involved in an altercation, it would be impossible to clearly and legibly write all the necessary information on one Incident Report form. A Supplemental Report is especially important when further explanations are required or when there are numerous witnesses. A Supplemental Report should be completed when any additional information is obtained after an initial Incident Report has been filed. For example, if a participant engaged in inappropriate conduct and was counseled, any future inappropriate conduct can be recorded in a Supplemental Report that references the prior Incident Report. This referencing process is critical to inform other employees and city parks about certain individuals or events that should raise concern.

Supplemental Reports should be utilized to describe any incidents that occur "off site," such as when children are injured while they were attending a HPRD sponsored away event. You should attach to the Supplemental Report any incident or related reports which were prepared by the visited institution, facility or program. Addenda B represents a sample Supplement Report.

B)   *Participant Injury/Medical Assistance Reports*—The Participant Injury/Medical Assistance Report (PI/MAR) is only used to report participant injuries. While an injury can be reported on an Incident Report, the PI/MAR provides additional critical information and both should be completed when any injury involves a more severe injury such as broken bones, heart attacks, concussions, etc. All employee injuries should be reported using the Supervisors Injury Investigation Report. All PI/MARs should be completed and returned to the Office of the Director (or his/her designee) within 24 hours after the injury. A separate PI/MAR has to be completed for each individual injured. PI/MARs are filed in addition to the Incident Report which describes how the injury or incident occurred while the PI/MAR reports on the medical condition and disposition of the injured. If at all possible, the injured individual(s) should sign-off on the PI/MAR indicating that they agree with all the assertions and statements made in the Report. Addenda C represents a sample PI/MAR.

C)   *Witness Statement*—The Witness Statement will be used when an incident has been witnessed or observed in any manner, and where a witness is willing to supply a written statement including their current name, address and phone number. Every effort should be made to obtain witness statements after every incident. If a witness is unwilling to provide their name or other information for fear of retaliation or reprisal, any employee can arrange for complete confidentiality by checking the confidential box which will guarantee that the witness statement will be given directly to the Department Director and every effort will be made to insure confidentiality. Addenda D represents a sample Witness Statement.

D)   *Inventory Loss/Damage Report*—An Inventory Loss/Damage Report is used anytime there is any property loss or damage to property. Examples include loosing keys, loosing a pager, a lawn mower breaking down, a phone not working, a building being hit by a car, or any other similar incidents wherein there exists specific monetary or physical losses associated with HPRD property or facilities. The report should be completed with the best available information and an employee's best judgment as to the estimated loss or repair value. Addenda E represents a sample Inventory Loss/Damage Report.

E)   *Repair Request*—A Repair Request should be filed with appropriate Maintenance Department after any property has been damaged that cannot be appropriately and correctly repaired by a city park employee. The Repair Request should be completed as soon as possible after the damaged property has been discovered. If the damaged property represents a risk of injury to possible patrons, the areas around the property should be roped off using yellow warning tape available at each city park. If the requested repair is a serious matter, contact the Department Director's office to evaluate repair options. If the matter is not a serious matter, appropriately rank the priority for the needed repairs. A follow-up phone call should be made after the appropriate time if the repairs had not yet been completed. Addenda F represents a sample Repair Request with appropriate completion instructions.

F)   *Log-In Sheet*— A Log-In Sheet records all phone calls received by the call in dispatcher and/or the Department Dispatcher referencing or discussing incidents or potential incidents occurring at city parks.

Addenda A

Incident Report

Section A

Location—specifically identify where the incident happened. Do not just list the park name, the community center name or indicate that the incident occurred at the building/ball field. Write out exactly where the incident occurred. If you cannot adequately describe the location, utilize a Supplemental Report to more thoroughly describe where the incident occurred. The following represents a sample location description.

"The participant slipped and fell underneath the north-side indoor gym basket at Memorial Park. The participant was found at the approximate site of the fall which was eight feet from the north wall and directly underneath the basketball rim."

Every city park office has extra maps which can be used to locate where an incident occurred. Utilizing a red pen, place an "x" where the incident occurred. You can utilize any other descriptive marks which might provide useful information. Useful information can include where a piece of equipment was located, where the injured person was found (if in a different area from where they were injured), and related facts. Any additional information should be specifically described on the map.

Describe any strange or unusual conditions at the location such as water puddles, dust balls, broken glass or other items which affect the location and which might have contributed to the incident.

In addition to writing a brief description, check the appropriate box concerning what location was involved. The choices are: surface street, fields, parking lot, gymnasium, offices, other indoor structures (i.e., closets or bathrooms), outdoor structures (shacks, port-a-potties), playground, zoo, unknown or other (please describe).

Fill in the appropriate Park Identification Number (PIC) in the appropriate spot. Also write in the appropriate operating division (ORP Div.).

Check off the type of incident that is being reported. The incident types include Assault, Theft (auto and non-auto), Burglary, Vandalism, Trespass, Auto-accident, Personal Injury, Fire, Lost Child, Illness, Inappropriate Conduct, Violation of Park Rules or Other (please describe).

Check off how you were notified about the incident. Possible means of notification include Call-in, Reported in person, Discovered, Witnessed, Responded to Incident, Other (please describe).

Briefly describe the incident using purely objective language. For example if someone was involved in an altercation during a basketball game the following would be an appropriate description of the incident: "On March 18, 1997, John Williams was playing basketball when, he was hit in the head by Bob Jones. Williams complained of blurred vision and had two cuts on his cheek." *Never* try to put your own subjective opinions into the incident reporting. Thus, the following is an *inappropriate* description of an incident: "On March 18, 1997, John Williams was playing basketball when he was hit by Bob Jones who I have told several times not to get into fight. The two players had been at it all night and the referees screwed-up by not ejecting Jones earlier in the game."

In addition to describing the incident, take the time to examine surrounding circumstances and note any conditions or factors which might have influenced the incident. For example, what was the weather like (did the weather help cause the incident), what type of shoes was the person wearing (were the soles worn out), was the person wearing any knee, ankle, elbow braces, was there any broken equipment around, was the person wearing glasses, did the injured person state they had been injured before, and a host of other potential clues you might spot or hear while responding to an incident should be specifically mentioned.

List the exact time and date, if known, when the incident occurred.

Describe injury or damage in the appropriate "Injury/Damage" space. You should clearly state what medical condition or symptoms were reported or observed. Likewise if property, an automobile or a structure, was damaged you should specifically indicate what damage occurred.

Section B

Response section. The response section is designed for you to specifically indicate what you or other people did in response to the incident. There are three sub-section to Section B. The first sub-section deals with the specific actions taken. The second sub-section refers to any assistance requested from either internal or external sources. The last sub-section provides an opportunity to list key individuals who provided assistance in either handling the incident or following-up after the incident.

Action taken should be checked off at the appropriate action area. The appropriate action steps include Investigate, Counsel, Report, Provide aid, Request assistance, or Other (please describe). Counsel means to talk with the injured person or the individual(s) involved in the incident and then to provide appropriate feedback to help resolve the incident. Report means to file an official incident report or other official reports which serves to notify the department about the incident. Provide aid refers to first-aid assistance with the understanding that employee are not medical professionals and can only provide the injured person with critically necessary first-aid assistance. It bears repeating that no employee should ever provide any drugs or medical opinions. Request assistance refers to contacting a variety of internal or external sources to help handle an incident.

Assistance requested should be checked off at the appropriate descriptive box. Appropriate assistance can include Fire Department, Police Department, Medical-EMTs, Parent/guardian, Supervisor, or Other(please describe). The Fire Department should be contacted on any and all active fires, except for fires that are contained in small areas such as bar-b-que pits or similar areas where fire extinguishing equipment and experience is readily available. The Police Department should be contacted whenever there exists any potential for significant injury to people or property. Likewise, the Police Department should be contacted when any conduct occurs that is outside the scope of any employee or volunteer's control and can lead to violence. Any violence towards children including rape, fondling, molestation, lost children (when a parent or guardian cannot be contacted) or similar occurrence requiring police expertise should be handled exclusively by the Police Department. Medical-EMTs should be contacted whenever: a cut occurs which cannot be stopped through the application of pressure, when an individual faints, goes into convulsions, is delusional, or cannot take care of themselves, a person suffers heart/chest pain, a person receives a sharp blow injuring their head, or if any other condition arises which in an employee's or volunteer's best judgment requires quick professional medical assistance. A parent or guardian should be contacted whenever a youth (under age 18) engages in any conduct that violates the law or park rules/regulations or creates a dangerous condition for that youth or for any other patrons, visitors, employees or volunteers. The parent or guardian should be told to immediately pick-up the youth in question and to meet with a designated representative from the Department. If a parent or guardian refuses to pick-up the child or meet with a Department representative then the Department Director's office should be contacted for further assistance. A supervisor should be contacted if there is more than an estimated $500 worth of damage, whenever the Police or Fire Department is contacted, or whenever special medical assistance is required. The term "Other" refers to other potential internal or external sources that might be contacted. Such sources include, but is not limited to, child protective services, truancy officer, school officials, probation department, internal affairs.

When any internal or external assistance arrives, indicate arrival time. If no one responded to the request for assistance, that box should be checked.

The last sub-section should provide information on the person who responded such as their name, employee or badge number, address, phone number, and a brief description of what action they undertook and if they prepared any written reports such as an arrest, fire incident, medical assistance and/or a reprimand report.

Section C

Personal- This section provides critical information concerning the people involved in the incident. Thus, if a HPRD vehicle collides with another non-HPRD vehicle both drivers would be listed. If one individual is injured in the incident then only that individual should be listed in this section.

Individuals completing the Incident Report should indicate whether the injured individual is a participant, visitors, employee, volunteer, or other. It should be indicated if they were or weren't injured. It should be indicated whether or not the individual was a minor (under 18-years-old) or an adult by listing the person's age. The following information should be entered into the form: the individuals full name, address, phone numbers (work and home), and if appropriate-insurance information (for auto accidents only).

Section D

This sections specifically indicates which documents form the entire incident report. All appropriate boxes should be checked. Potential documents that could accompany the incident report include Police, Fire, Supervisor's, employee injury, Supplemental, PI/MAR, Witness Statement, Inventory Loss/Damage, Repair Request, and other reports (please specify).

Section E

This section should contain the name, title, employee number, signature and date.

Sample Incident Reports

INCIDENT REPORT-HPRD

Incident Report # _____
LOCATION _____ PIC _____ ORP Div. _____
Time _____ a.m./ p.m.   Date _____
Describe Location _____

_____

_____. [] See attached map
__ Field, __ Surface Street, __ Parking Lot, __ Gymnasium, __ Office,
__ Indoor Structure, __ Outdoor Structure, __ Playground, __ Zoo,
__ Other (specify) _____

INCIDENT TYPE
__ Assault, __ Auto Theft, __ Non-auto Theft, __ Burglary,
__ Vandalism, ___ Trespass,
__ Auto Accident, __ Personal Injury, __ Fire, __ Lost Child,
__ Park Rules-Violation, __ Illness, __ Inappropriate Conduct,
__ Other (specify) _____

INCIDENT NOTIFICATION
__ Call In, __ Reported, __ Discovered, __ Witnessed,
__ Responded, __ Other _____

INCIDENT DESCRIPTION

_____
_____
_____
_____
_____
_____

INJURY/DAMAGE

_____

****

RESPONSE SECTION

ACTION TAKEN

__ Counsel, __ Report, __ Provide Aid, __ Request Assistance,
__ Investigate, __ Other (specify) _____

ASSISTANCE REQUESTED

__ Fire Dept., __ Police Dept., __ Medical/EMT,
__ Contact Parent/Guardian, __ Contact Supervisor,
__ Other (specify) _____

ASSISTANCE RESPONSE

Responded __ Yes (time _____ a.m./ p.m.) ___ No response

RESPONDING PARTY

Name _____
Employee or Badge Number _____
Department _____
Phone (___) _____
Action Taken _____
Was a written report made? ___ Yes ___ No (report/case number ____)

* *

PERSONAL

__ Employee, __ Volunteer, __ Participant, __ Visitor,
__ Other (specify) _____
Personal Injury ___ Yes _____ No _____ Age _____
Name _____
Address _____
Phone (___) _____ Work Phone (___) _____
(for auto) Insurance Company _____ Policy # _____
Second Party, if applicable
__ Employee, __ Volunteer, __ Participant, __ Visitor,
__ Other (specify) _____
Personal Injury ___ Yes _____ No _____ Age _____
Name _____
Address _____
Phone (___) _____ Work Phone (___)
_____
(for auto) Insurance Company _____ Policy # _____

* *

ATTACHED DOCUMENTS

___ Police Report, ___ Fire Report, ____ Supervisor's Report,
___ Employee Injury
Report, ___ Supplement Report, ____ PI/MAR, ___ Witness Statement,
___ Repair Request, ___ Inventory Loss/Damage Report,
___ Other (specify) _____

* *

COMPLETED BY
Name _____ Title _____
Employee Number _____
Signature _____ Date _____

* *

Addenda B

Supplemental Report

Indicate the Incident Report Number (top right hand corner of the incident report) that the Supplemental Report supplements. Reiterate the site location, the PIC location, the incident date, and any other appropriate information. Contemporaneous means that the Supplemental Report was prepared at the same time the Incident Report was prepared. If the Supplemental Report was prepared any time other than at the same time the Incident Report was prepared, then the Follow-Up Report section should be checked. Other appropriate information that could be reported in the lined area might include the names of other individuals involved in the incident, further details obtained by other agencies such as police or fire departments, additional objective information about the incident such as weather conditions (rain, snow, etc.), and facility condition(fire destroyed port-a-potty leaving only one port-a-potty to service an entire park, or the facility was recently cleaned and no wet spots were noticed, etc.). *No subjective interpretation* should be given concerning the incident. Furthermore, no potential liability or fault analysis should be provided. Any follow-up should be noted including additional contact with the injured, further information concerning an injury and its resulting disposition, any criminal proceedings, and any serious condition that had not been repaired after submitting a prior incident report and work order.

The individual who completes the Supplemental Report should sign their name, employee number, and date the report.

SUPPLEMENTAL REPORT

Incident Report # _____

Contemporaneous _____ Follow-Up Report _____

Location _____ PIC _____ Incident Date _____

_____

_____

_____

_____

_____

_____

_____

_____

_____

_____

_____

_____

_____

_____

_____

_____

_____

_____

_____

_____

_____

_____

_____

_____

_____

Name _____

Employee Number _____

Signature _____ Date _____

Addenda C

Participant Injury/Medical Assistance Report

This critical report is designed to help determine the extent of any injury and any resulting treatment or assistance that was provided. One report should be prepared for each person that is injured. The critical information needed include prior Incident Report number, date, and time. As much information should be obtained from the injured person including name, sex, age, address, phone numbers, and next of kin contact person information.

The next section relates to the injury and requires both analysis of current medical conditions/injuries and any known or communicated past problems or medications/allergies. This information is critical because a person might be coherent and responsive immediately after an incident, but thereafter go into shock. If a person is allergic to Penicillin, and they told an employee this information prior to going unconscious, the information can be conveyed to the Medical/EMT personnel. The next section refers to treatment provided by the employee or volunteer. Additionally any treatment provided by others or hospital transportation should be listed in this section.

The last two sections deal with following-up to determine how the injury was resolved and information concerning the person who completed the Report.

If the person is conscious, try to obtain an Approval statement signature, approving all the information contained in the PI/MAR. If no treatment was requested or if treatment was needed, but refused, the individual should be asked to sign the Refusal of Treatment statement. If possible, try to get a witness to sign the Approval or Refusal of Treatment statements to verify that the injured person willingly signed either statement.

Participant Injury/Medical Assistance Report

Incident Report # _____ Date _____ Time _____ a.m./p.m.

Injured person:

Name _____ Sex (M. F) Age _____
       Last   First   MI

Address _____
       Street   City   State   Zip code

Phone number (___) _____ (___) _____
           Home   Work

Next of Kin/Contact Person:

Name _____

Address _____

Phone number (___) _____ (___) _____

Injury info:

Nature of injury: _____

Body part(s) affected: _____

Vital signs: Breathing (Yes / No), Pulse (Yes / No)

Current Medications _____
Known Allergies _____
How did injury occur: _____
_____

Where did the injury occur: _____
Who discovered/reported the injury: Name _____
Address _____ Phone # (___) _____

Treatment:

Was any first-aid provided: (Yes/ No)
What first-aid was provided: _____
_____

What was done with any first-aid items used (gauge pads, blood soaked
tissues, etc.): _____
_____

First aid administered by: _____ employee # _____
Was any assistance requested: (Yes / No)
Assistance requested from: ___ Police, ___ Fire,
                               ___ Medical/EMT, ___ physician
What assistance was provided: _____
Was the injured sent to a hospital (Yes/ No): Which Hospital _____
How was injured transported to the hospital: _____

Follow up:

How was the injury resolved: _____
Name of person completing the form: _____ Employee # _____
Signature _____

APPROVAL

I, _____ hereby accept all the above statements as true
and correct and accurately represent my medical condition and the in-
formation I gave or was observed by others.
Name _____
Signed _____ Date _____
Witness _____

****

REFUSAL OF TREATMENT

I, _____ was injured at a facility, structure, property or program/activity run by the Houston Park and Recreation Department. While HPRD staff or volunteers offered to provide first-aid assistance or Medical/EMT assistance, I have willingly refused all such assistance and voluntarily assume any subsequent complications or further injury.

Name _____

Signed _____ Date _____

Witness _____

Addenda D

Witness Statement

The Witness Statement should be used whenever there are witnesses who saw any part of the incident or came upon the incident after the fact. Thus, if someone found damage to a building, they should be classified as a witness. Employee or volunteers are not witnesses, but should be mentioned in the Incident Report.

The Witness Statement should refer to the proper Incident Report number and date. The name of the person who acquired the witness statement should be recorded. It should be indicated whether the Witness Statement was written by the witness him/her self or by someone else. The witness should always be encouraged to write the statement themselves, even if it need to be written in Spanish or another language. The witness should use their own words in describing what they saw, noticed, heard or did in response to the incident. Never try to influence the words that a witness might use. Have the witness write their name, address, phone number and then sign the statement. If a witness is uncooperative, try to obtain any name or address and write down any information they might have mentioned, trying as best as possible to write down only what the witness said. it is very important that you only write what was said, and not what you think they meant or might have wanted to say.

The confidential box should be checked whenever anyone is cautious about giving their name/information. Confidentiality cannot be guaranteed, but the Department Director will do everything in his/her power to protect the witness's identity.

WITNESS STATEMENT

Incident Report # _____ Date _____

Witness statement obtained by _____ Employee/Volunteer # _____

Dear Witness: Please use your own word to write exactly what you saw, heard, smelled or any other facts concerning what happened or what you discovered. We appreciate your assistance in helping to make the Parks a better place for all of us.

Written By: _____

_____
_____
_____
_____
_____
_____
_____
_____
_____
_____
_____
_____
_____
_____
_____
_____
_____
_____
_____

Witness's name: _____
Address: _____
Phone number ( ) _____ ( ) _____

Signature: _____ Date: _____

If you wish your statement to be confidential, check the confidential box below. If you check the confidential box, we will make every effort to protect your statement and will not provide a copy of this statement to anyone other than a representative of the City of Houston, without a court order.

[ ] CONFIDENTIAL

Addenda E

Inventory Loss/Damage Report

This report is critical to assist in identifying and repairing lost or stolen items. Any appropriate Incident Report Number should be listed as well as the date the item was discovered lost or damaged. There are occasions when an Incident Report Number is not available. In those cases, contact the Departmental Asset Coordinator and utilize a product or inventory tag number in place of the Incident Report Number.

Contact the Departmental Asset Coordinator by phone for item numbers (PARD #, Shop #, Inventory TAG # or Serial #), purchase price, replacement costs, repair costs, repair time. After completing and signing the report. Submit copies with all appropriate department divisions. If the damage is not repaired after the specified priority period has ended (see Addenda F-Repair Request), an additional Inventory Loss/Damage Report should be filed, indicating this is the second form and should be submitted to the Department Director's office or his/her designee.

INVENTORY LOSS/DAMAGE REPORT

Location _____ PIC Number _____ Incident Report # _____
Date of Inventory Loss _____

Item # _____
Description _____
Item's Age _____
Item's Purchase Price _____
Estimated Replacement Price _____
Estimated Repair Cost _____
Estimated Repair Time _____

Item # _____
Description _____
Item's Age _____
Item's Purchase Price _____
Estimated Replacement Price _____
Estimated Repair Cost _____
Estimated Repair Time _____

Item # _____
Description _____
Item's Age _____
Item's Purchase Price _____
Estimated Replacement Price _____
Estimated Repair Cost _____
Estimated Repair Time _____

Item # _____
Description _____
Item's Age _____
Item's Purchase Price _____
Estimated Replacement Price _____
Estimated Repair Cost _____
Estimated Repair Time _____

Item # _____
Description _____
Item's Age _____
Item's Purchase Price _____
Estimated Replacement Price _____
Estimated Repair Cost _____
Estimated Repair Time _____

Name _____ Employee Number _____
Signature _____ Date _____

Addenda F

Repair Request

A repair request is the first step needed to notify the Maintenance Department that some needed repairs have to be made and the time frame within which those repairs need to be made. There is a priority for all repairs based on usage, money, time and related concerns. The following guidelines help establish the repair priority for various items.

Priority 1-Items which are essential for the functioning of a city park. Examples include: furnaces, front doors, lighting, and other structural or facility concerns without which the facility cannot operate in a safe manner. All Priority 1 matters have to be repaired within one day.

Priority 2-Items which need to be repaired to insure the immediate safety of patrons or park visitors. Examples include holes in a sidewalk, missing or broken windows, broken lock on a swimming pool gate, and similar concerns which need to be addressed immediately to insure patron safety. All Priority 2 matters have to be repaired within two to three days. Any area prioritized as a Priority 2 area should be roped off with yellow or other colored warning ribbon/tape. Furthermore, all facility or program participants, employees, spectators and volunteers should receive either oral or written warnings about the hazardous condition.

Priority 3- Items which are important for the operation of a facility of program. Examples include broken door hinge, broken phones, inoperable security system, and related concerns. All Priority 3 matters have to be repaired within one-two weeks.

Priority 4-Items which pose the lowest priority. A program can operate safely and effectively, but would be better if the repair was made. Examples include unsanded wood benches which might have splinters, a missing tile on a closet floor, etc. All Priority 4 matters have to be repaired within one month.

Any area in need of repair should be marked in such a manner that the hazardous condition is readily apparent and not to be used. This can best be accomplished by using red "road way" cones and yellow "hazard" tape in and around the hazardous area.

REPAIR REQUEST

Incident Report # _____ Date _____

Priority Number _____

Description of item needing repair _____

_____

Location of item needing repair _____

Describe the damage _____

_____

_____

Name _____ Employee # _____

Signature _____

Follow-up Action (If any) _____

_____

Date _____

* *

Incident Report # _____ Date _____

Priority Number _____

Description of item needing repair _____

_____
Location of item needing repair _____
Describe the damage _____

_____
_____

Name _____   Employee # _____
Signature _____
Follow-up Action (If any) _____
Date _____

Addenda G

Call In Log

The call in log provides a means to track and record all phone calls received by the Department Dispatcher or Call-In Dispatcher concerning an incident or hazardous condition.

All phone calls should be recorded while referencing the date, time, person calling, reference location, phone number where caller can be reached, the incident or danger, what action was requested (if any), actions already taken prior to the phone call, suggested action, and any appropriate or newly assigned Incident Report Number. For convenience, the person calling can be identified with just an individual's name or employee number. The incident or danger should be specifically described as well as what steps had already been taken (i.e., Assault by a basketball player; police called). Lastly, if the dispatcher suggests any action or course of conduct, all such suggestions should be recorded even if the caller did not follow the suggestion.

CALL-IN LOG

Dispatcher's Name _____   Employee Number _____
Date _____   Time _____ a.m./ p.m.
Caller's Name _____
Caller's Employee # (if applicable) _____
Incident Location _____
Phone Number Calling From ( ) _____
Description of Incident or Danger _____

_____

Action Requested _____
Action Already Taken _____
Dispatcher's Suggestions _____
Incident Report Number _____

Conclusion

It is impossible to eliminate all accidents. Furthermore, incident reports are not designed to eliminate accidents or prevent all hazards. Incident reports and related supporting documentation are designed not to prevent injuries and hazards, but to inform individuals as to what hazards are present and what steps have been successful in reducing or eliminating various injuries or incidents. This data can be useful in developing safer programs and facilities as well as better trained employees and volunteers.

You play an important and critical role in the process. By taking time to properly complete all necessary forms you can help prevent injuries and make park and recreation programs and facilities safer for all users. Complete, accurate and timely reports also help reduce liability concerns and promote our risk management efforts. You are thanked in advance by your superiors for helping to make the incident reporting process work.

If you have any questions concerning any reporting issues, please contact your supervisor. The Incident Reporting Manual should be kept at each city park and available for use by all employees to assist them in completing various reports. Additional copies of any necessary forms can be requested from your supervisor.

APPENDIX Y

OSHA Offices

OSHA has numerous forms which are needed to comply with workplace safety rules. Forms such as OSHA 200 logs, safety posters, Material Safety Data Sheets, and numerous other publications highlighted in the text.

Regional OSHA offices are highlighted below. In addition to regional offices, OSHA also has Area and District offices.

Region I
(CT, MA, ME, NH, RI, VT)
133 Portland St., 1st Floor
Boston, MA 02114
(617) 565-7164

Region II
(NJ, NY, PR, VI)
201 Varick St., Room 670
New York, NY 10014
(212) 337-2378

Region III
(DC, DE, MD, PA, VA, WV)
Gateway Bldg., Suite 2100
3535 Market St.
Philadelphia, PA 19104
(215) 596-1201

Region IV
(AL, FL, GA, KY, MS, NC, SC, TN)
1375 Peachtree St., N.E.
Suite 587
Atlanta, GA 30367
(404) 347-3573

Region V (IL, IN, MI, MN, OH, WI)
230 South Dearborn St.
Room 3244
Chicago, IL 60604
(312) 353-2220

Region VI
(AR, LA, NM, OK, TX)
525 Griffin St., Room 602
Dallas, TX 75202
(214) 767-4731

Region VII
(IA, KS, MO, NE)
911 Walnut St., Room 406
Kansas City, MO 64106
(816) 426-5861

Region VIII
(CO, MT, ND, SD, UT, WY)
Federal Bldg., Room 1576
1961 Stout St.
Denver, CO 80294
(303) 844-3061

Region IX
(AZ, CA, HI, NV, Guam, American Samoa, Trust Territories of the Pacific)
71 Stevenson St., 4th Floor
San Francisco, CA 94105
(415) 744-6670

Region X
(AK, ID, OR, WA)
1111 Third Ave., Suite 715
Seattle, WA 98101-3212
(206) 553-5930

The following states operate their own OSHA-approved job safety and health programs which are as rigorous as OSHA standards: AK, AZ, CA, CT, HI, IA, IN, KY, MD, MI, MN, NC, NM, NY, NV, OR, PR, SC, TN, UT, VA, VI, VT, WA, and WY. The CT and NY plans only cover public employees.

APPENDIX Z

Witness Statement Form

ACCIDENT LOCATION _____

Time _____ a.m./ p.m.   Date _____

Describe Location _____

_____

_____[] See attached map

__ Field, __ Surface Street, __ Parking Lot, __ Gymnasium,
__ Office, __ Indoor Structure, __ Outdoor Structure, __ Playground,
__ Other (specify) _____

INCIDENT TYPE

__ Assault, __ Auto Theft, __ Non-auto Theft, __ Burglary,
__ Vandalism, ___ Trespass, __ Auto Accident, __ Personal Injury,
__ Fire, __ Lost Child, __ Rules-Violation, __ Illness,
__ Inappropriate Conduct, __ Other (specify) _____

HOW DID YOU LEARN ABOUT THE INCIDENT

__ Reported to Scene, __ Discovered, __ Witnessed, __ Other _____

INCIDENT DESCRIPTION

_____

_____

_____

_____

_____

_____

INJURY/DAMAGE, IF ANY

_____

✻✻✻

RESPONSE SECTION

DID YOU RESPOND? No ____ If Yes, How:
__ Counsel Injured Party, __ Report Incident, __ Provide Aid,
__ Request Assistance, __ Investigate, __ Other (specify) _____

WAS ASSISTANCE REQUESTED? No ___ If Yes, What:
__ Fire Dept., __ Police Dept., __ Medical/EMT,

__ Contact Parent/Guardian, __ Contact Supervisor,
__ Other (specify) _____

✳ ✳

Was a Person Injured? No ____ If Yes, Who Was Injured:
__ Employee, __ Volunteer, __ Participant, __ Visitor,
__ Other (specify) _____
Personal Injury ___ Yes ____ No   Age _____

Name _____
Address _____
Phone (___) _____ Work Phone (___) _____
(for auto) Insurance Company _____ Policy # _____
Second Party-if applicable
__ Employee, __ Volunteer, __ Participant, __ Visitor, __ Other (specify)
_____

Personal Injury ___ Yes ____ No   Age _____

Name _____
Address _____
Phone (___) _____ Work Phone (___) _____
(for auto) Insurance Company _____ Policy # _____

✳ ✳

COMPLETED BY

Name _____
Address _____
Signature _____   Date _____

✳ ✳

If more space is required, a Supplemental Witness Statement Form should be attached.

The following page can be utilized as a supplemental form for reporting additional information.

SUPPLEMENTAL WITNESS STATEMENT FORM

Incident Report # _____ Date _____

Witness statement obtained by _____ Employee/Volunteer # _____

Dear Witness: Please use your own word to describe the accident and specify what you saw, heard, smelled or any other facts concerning what happened or what you discovered.

Written By: _____

_____

_____

_____

_____

_____

_____

_____

_____

_____

_____

_____

_____

_____

_____

_____

_____

_____

_____

_____

_____

_____

_____

_____

_____

Witness's name: _____

Address: _____

Phone number ( ) _____ ( ) _____

Signature: _____ Date: _____

APPENDIX AA

Disciplinary Policy

A) Purpose

XYZ's disciplinary policy is designed to aid employees and XYZ in solving workplace problems, if possible, in a professional and positive manner. The focus is on solving potential problems rather than punishment. However, when conduct occurs that violate explicit company rules, policies or procedures, the disciplinary policy is designed to provide appropriate punishment to address such misconduct.

B) Definitions

Poor Performance: An employee's failure to perform essential job functions in a satisfactory manner that meets minimum performance standards.

Severe Misconduct: Actions by an employee that cannot be tolerated and whenever detected pose grounds for immediate discharge. The following acts are some of the acts which can be defined as severe misconduct:

1) Intentionally falsifying resumes, job applications, curriculum vitae and/or any other facts upon which a hiring decision was based.
2) Physically assaulting any co-worker, invitee (i.e. customer) and/or licensee during work-time and/or at the workplace.
3) Possessing, using and/or selling illegal drugs during work-time and/or at/near the workplace.
4) Possessing and/or consuming alcoholic beverages during work-time and/or at the workplace.
5) Bringing any handgun or other discharge weapon and/or any other item commonly considered a weapon into the workplace at any time.
6) Other extreme or intolerable wrongdoing committed by the employee on or about XYZ.

Serious Misconduct: Employees might engage in such conduct that would normally provide grounds for immediate termination, however, in rare circumstances the conduct may be justified or subject to progressive discipline. Such conduct might include, but is not limited to:

1) Willful and/or malicious destruction of XYZ property.
2) Theft of XYZ or customer property.
3) Stealing XYZ trade secrets or employees.

4) Falsifying XYZ records, including internal and/or government documentation.
5) Disregarding all applicable safety rules and procedures.
6) Cases of misconduct including any intentional discrimination such as racial discrimination and sexual harassment, as sample forms of discrimination.
7) Any nonenumerated acts that include intentional, egregious breaches of conduct enumerated in XYZ's Employee Handbook, and/or any local, state and/or federal laws.

Misconduct: Any activity that can subject the employee to progressive disciplinary steps. While such acts might incur progressive discipline, XYZ expressly reserves the right to impose harsher penalties, including termination for any act of misconduct. Acts which could be considered misconduct include, but are not limited to:

1) Poor attendance without any reasonable explanation.
2) Excessive tardiness, breaks or leaving work early.
3) Failure to attend required safety meetings.
4) Insubordination.
5) Gambling on company property, including football and basketball pools.
6) Being rude or offensive to customers or fellow employees.
7) Sleeping on the job.
8) Utilizing XYZ's property for personal purposes.
9) Any violation of XYZ's dress or conduct code as set forth in the Employee Handbook.

C) Procedures

When a supervisor or the Office Manager identify inappropriate conduct, they must first determine if the conduct poses an obstacle to proper job performance of that employee or other employees. At such time, the Office Manager may informally counsel the employee as to what performance is expected and any timetable within which to rectify any misconduct. The Office Manager can document these oral warning if the Office Manager feels it is important to include such documentation in the employee's personal file.

If a performance problem continues, or if the performance problem or misconduct is serious enough in the Office Manager's sole discretion, and an employee is not discharged, progressive discipline *shall* be instituted utilizing the following steps:

1) *Oral Reminder*—Such reminders need to be given and docu-

mented at the first instance of a disciplinary problem or after tracking performance problems for at least one month. A private meeting should be held between the employee and his/her supervisor wherein they can discuss the specific problem(s) and reiterate expected conduct which the employee agreed to follow when they signed the Employee Handbook. The supervisor should report the results of the meeting with the Office Manager who shall have the sole discretion of whether or not to document the meeting in the employee's personal file.

2)   *Written Reminder*—If the disciplinary problem continues or if the employee engages in any form of misconduct. The supervisor and/or the Office Manager shall meet with the employee in a private area and attempt to gain the employee's agreement to take specific steps to remedy any misconduct. An agreement shall be made between the employee and the supervisor specifically indicating what steps will be taken to remedy the misconduct.

If the employee does not feel they have engaged in any misconduct or are achieving job requirements, they should be entitled to document such disagreement in the agreement. Similarly if the parties do not agree on what steps are needed to remedy any perceived misconduct or failure to complete assigned responsibilities, such disagreement shall be documented and given to the Office Manager for a final, binding determination. If the Office Manager is the individual handling the written reminder process, any disagreement shall be handled by the Office Manager's immediate supervisor. The employee's refusal to sign the agreement can be immediate grounds for termination.

3)   *Investigation and Leave*—If any discipline, misconduct or performance problems continue pass the written reminder stage, the Office Manager should provide the employee with the last reminder which would come only after the incident is thoroughly investigated and documented. Any employee that reaches this stage is required to be put on paid, administrative leave for at least one day for the employee to consider possible options such as quitting, improving performance or correcting any misconduct. If an employee does not return to work immediately after the leave period has ended, it will be assumed that the employee has quit. An employee will be allowed to return after the leave only if they have prepared a written statement specifically identifying all remedial steps they agree to undertake in order to retain their position and avoid any further misconduct. The written statement becomes a part of the employee's performance objectives agreement entered into with the Office Manager. The agreement provides for an appropriate probationary period in which the employee is required to comply with all agreed upon behavioral or conduct changes or face immediate termination. The written statement and agreement shall be included in the employee's personnel file and a copy shall be given to the

employee. An employee's refusal to prepare a written statement or sign the performance objectives agreement constitutes grounds for immediate termination.

4)   *Discharge*—An employee will face automatic discharge if they refuse to sign a performance objectives agreement, violate the performance objectives agreement, or continues to engage in acts that can be construed as misconduct, of any type. While appeals are available at all prior stages of the discipline process, no appeal can be made from a final discharge agreement that has worked its way through the above enumerated discipline process or when employees have engaged in severe or serious misconduct.

Discharge for severe misconduct requires no advanced warnings or progressive discipline. Serious misconduct may be grounds for any of the above enumerated steps in the discipline process. Misconduct claims should be handled, if possible, utilizing progressive discipline steps.

D) Appeals

The Office Manager has final decision making authority concerning which step in the progressive discipline process will be utilized at all times. However, an employee can appeal any decision to the Office Manager's direct supervisor. An employee wishing to appeal any final decision reached by the Office Manager must file a written appeal citing specific facts that contradict the Office Manager's decision or show that the Office Manager acted with unreasonable prejudice unwarranted by the circumstance. Supervisors do not have the authority to discharge any employee. Thus, a supervisor's discharge of an employee represents grounds for immediate appeal unless the supervisor was acting in the official capacity as Office Manager or the Office Manager expressly authorized the discharge.

E) Revision

The progressive discipline process shall be reviewed on a yearly basis and XYZ expressly reserves the right to revise the process at any time, for any reason or for no reason.

APPENDIX BB

Severance Agreement

SEVERANCE AND CONSULTING AGREEMENT AND GENERAL RELEASE OF ALL CLAIMS

1.   This Severance and Consulting Agreement and General Release of Claims (hereinafter "Agreement") is entered into between J. J. Kelly (herein "Kelly") and by Columbus Fighters, Inc. (herein "CF" or "the Company").

2.   **WHEREAS**, Kelly has been employed by CF as its General Manager and Head Coach; and

WHEREAS, the parties have decided that it is in their best interests to amicably end this employment relationship and that Kelly should enter into a consultancy relationship with the Company; and

WHEREAS Kelly and CF desire to mutually, amicably and finally resolve and compromise all issues and claims surrounding Kelly's employment by CF and the termination thereof;

NOW THEREFORE, in consideration for the various mutual promises and undertakings by the parties as set forth below, Kelly and CF hereby enter into this Agreement to finally resolve all matters and establish the framework for future cooperation.

3.   *Continuation of Kelly's Employment, Salary and Benefits.* As full and complete consideration for Kelly's promises and releases contained herein, Kelly will remain in his current position through October 30, 1997.

a.   *Salary.* CF will pay Kelly his salary for the period of his employment in accordance with the Company's normal payroll practices. All appropriate payroll taxes will be deducted from such pay in accordance with all applicable federal and state law.

b.   *Health and Medical Benefits.* CF will continue Kelly's existing health benefits through October 30, 1997. Upon Kelly's accrual of rights under COBRA, CF will pay for Kelly's existing health benefits until Kelly finds employment providing comparable health benefits, or through February 28, 1998, whichever occurs first.

c.   *Bonus Payment.* CF agrees to pay Kelly a bonus for 1997, calculated in accordance with Kelly's employment contract and the results obtained by CF throughout the course of the 1997 season. Kelly will not be entitled to any bonus payments in the 1998 season, or at anytime thereafter.

    d. *Other Employee Benefits.* Kelly will be afforded no additional employee benefits (such as vacations).
    4.   *Reference Letter.* CF agrees to furnish Kelly with a Reference Letter from CF's President, containing the language in Exhibit A, attached hereto.
    5.   *Money Payment to Kelly: Responsibility for Taxes.*
    a. *Money Payment.* CF will pay Kelly the sum of one hundred thousand dollars ($100,000.00) in full satisfaction of all claims allowing recovery for nontaxable personal injury damages. Said sum is being treated as nontaxable to Kelly based on Kelly's and his attorneys' claims that this sum is for the purpose of fully compensating Kelly for any and all physical injury, physical sickness, emotional distress and physical manifestations thereof.
    b. *Kelly's Responsibility for Taxes.* The parties acknowledge that under present law the amount paid to Kelly in settlement of his tort claims (as described in subparagraph a above) do not constitute a taxable event. CF, however, makes no warranties regarding the taxability of these damages. In the event any taxing authority deems such damages to be taxable, or that taxes should have been withheld from such payment, in whole or in part, Kelly shall be exclusively responsible for paying all such assessments, taxes, and penalties. CF shall have no duty to defend Kelly against any such tax claim or assessment. Further, Kelly shall indemnify and hold CF harmless in the event any taxing authority requires payment from CF for any such assessments, taxes or penalties. Moreover, Kelly agrees to cooperate in the defense of any such claim brought against CF.
    6.   *Payment to Kelly's Attorney.* CF will pay no money to Kelly's attorney, Bob T. Smith, for Kelly's attorney's fees. Kelly is solely liable for any and all attorney's fees he has incurred to resolve this matter.
    7.   *Kelly's Consulting Services and Early Retirement.* In consideration for the aforementioned payments and other undertakings by CF, Kelly agrees to the following:
    a. *Consulting Services.* Through October 30, 1998, Kelly agrees to provide reasonable consulting services to CF at its option and request. CF agrees to use its best efforts to schedule such required services so as not to interfere with Kelly's other commitments and efforts to seek employment. Such consulting services will not exceed eight (8) hours per week except as mutually agreed by the parties, in writing. Kelly will only perform those duties and responsibilities expressly requested and authorized by CF's President. He will not be authorized to represent or speak on behalf of CF, except as expressly authorized in writing by CF's President. Kelly will also not enter, or have access to, any CF offices,

premises, or computer hardware/software and related data and programs without the express invitation or authorization by CF's President.

b. *Covenant Not to Compete.* Through October 30, 1998, Kelly covenants not to engage in any activity competitive with the Company's business, professional water polo. This covenant not to compete shall include, but not necessarily be limited to, establishing a competitive water polo team/league, combining or acting in concert with employees or representatives of the Company for the purpose of organizing any such competitive business, and/or entering into any employment or consulting relationship with any business entity, person or firm engaged in any competitive business.

c. *Covenant Not to Solicit Employees.* Through October 30, 1998, Kelly also covenants not to, directly or indirectly, or by action in concert with others, induce or influence or seek to induce or influence any person who is then employed as an employee, agent, or independent contractor or otherwise by the Company, to terminate his or her relationship with the Company.

8.   *Waiver of Right to Reemployment.* Kelly agrees that except for his consulting relationship, he will not be entitled to any further employment with the Company. He therefore waives any claim now or in the future to other employment or reemployment with CF, and agrees that he will not apply for nor accept employment with CF in the future.

9.   *Cooperation in Litigation and Other Legal Matters.* Kelly also agrees for the indefinite future to fully cooperate with CF in handling its legal and other matters in which he was involved or about which he has knowledge, such as answering inquiries from the Company, testifying and engaging in other efforts on the Company's behalf. He will make himself available upon reasonable notice at reasonable times and places in order to prepare for giving testimony, and to testify at deposition, trial or other legal proceedings, without CF having to serve him with a subpoena. Kelly will not be entitled to additional compensation for his time expended in such proceedings, but CF agrees to reimburse Kelly for his reasonable out-of-pocket costs and expenses, if any, excluding attorney's fees.

10.   *Mutual General Release of Claims.*

a. *Kelly's Release.* In further consideration of the payment and undertakings described above, Kelly, individually and on behalf of his attorneys, representatives, successors, and assigns, does hereby completely release and forever discharge CF and its and their shareholders, directors, officers and all other representatives, agents, directors, employees, successors and assigns, from all claims, rights, demands, actions, obligations, and causes of action of any and every kind, nature and character, known or unknown, which Kelly may now have, or has ever had, against them arising from or in any way connected with the employment relationship between the parties, any actions during the relationship, or the termination thereof. This release covers all federal, state and local statutory law, common law, constitutional and other claims, including but not limited to, all claims for wrongful discharge in violation of public policy, breach of contract, express or implied, breach of covenant of good faith and fair dealing, intentional or negligent infliction of emotional distress, intentional or negligent misrepresentation, age discrimination, any tort, personal injury, or violation of statute (including but not limited to Title VII of the Civil Rights Act of 1964 as amended, the Age Discrimination in Employment Act, and the California Fair Employment and Housing Act), which Kelly may now have, or has ever had. The parties agree that any past or future claim for money damages, loss of wages, earnings and benefits, both past and future, medical expenses, attorneys' fees and costs, reinstatement and other equitable relief are all released by this Agreement; and

    b. *CF's Release.* In addition, CF does completely release Kelly from all claims, rights, demands, actions, obligations, and causes of action of any and every kind nature and character, known or unknown, which it may now have, or has ever had, against him arising from or in any way connected with the employment relationship between the parties, any actions during the relationship, or the termination thereof. This release covers all statutory, common law, constitutional and other claims, including but not limited to, all claims for breach of contract, breach of covenant of good faith and fair dealing, intentional or negligent interference with contract or prospective business advantage, unfair competition, or any tort which CF may now have, or has ever had.

    11. *Mutual Waiver of Unknown Future Claims.* Kelly and CF have read or been advised of Section 1542 of the Civil Code of the State of California, which provides as follows:

> A GENERAL RELEASE DOES NOT EXTEND TO CLAIMS WHICH THE CREDITOR DOES NOT KNOW OR SUSPECT TO EXIST IN HIS FAVOR AT THE TIME OF EXECUTING THE RELEASE, WHICH IF KNOWN BY HIM MUST HAVE MATERIALLY AFFECTED HIS SETTLEMENT WITH THE DEBTOR.

Kelly and CF understand that Section 1542 gives them the right not to release existing claims of which they are not now aware of, unless they voluntarily choose to waive this right. Having been so apprised, the parties nevertheless hereby voluntarily elect to and do waive the rights described in Section 1542, and elect to assume all risks for claims that now exist in their favor, known or unknown.

12. *Non-Admission.* It is understood and agreed that this is a compromise settlement of a disputed claim, potential claim, or claims and that neither this Agreement itself nor the furnishing of the consideration for this Agreement shall be deemed or construed as an admission of liability or wrongdoing of any kind by CF or Kelly.

13. *Confidentiality Agreement.*

a. Kelly agrees that the terms and conditions of this Agreement are strictly confidential and shall not be disclosed to any other persons except his counsel, immediate family, taxing authorities in connection with his filing of federal or state tax returns, or to financial advisors in order to comply with income tax filing requirements, or as required by legal process or applicable law, provided however, that Kelly shall notify CF if such disclosure is sought, allowing CF the opportunity to object to such disclosure.

b. If Kelly violates any of the promises of confidentiality contained herein, the Company, in addition to any other rights and remedies available under this Agreement, shall be entitled to *immediate* injunctive relief, restraining Kelly from committing or continuing any violation of these provisions, as well as to monetary damages, and any other remedies available in law or equity.

14. *Covenant Not to Sue.* At no time subsequent to the execution of this Release will Kelly pursue, or cause or knowingly permit the prosecution, in any state, federal or foreign court, or before any local, state, federal or foreign administrative agency, or any other tribunal, any charge, claim or action of any kind, nature and character whatsoever, known or unknown, which he may now have, has ever had, or may in the future have against CF and/or any officer, director, employee or agent of CF, which is based in whole or in part on any matter covered by this Agreement.

15. *Professional Responsibilities Confidential Business Information.* Kelly acknowledges a continued professional duty of loyalty toward CF and the continued existence of the attorney-client privilege for communications between the parties as well as the work-product privilege for any work product created on CF's behalf. Therefore, Kelly agrees to abide by these professional obligations, not to assist parties adverse to CF in any legal proceedings against the Company, respect the attorney-client privilege, and refuse to waive either the attorney-client privilege or work product privilege to CFs detriment. In addition, Kelly will not at any time, without prior written consent of CF's General Counsel, either directly or indirectly use, divulge or communicate to any person or entity, in any manner, any confidential or proprietary information of any kind concerning any matters affecting or relating to the Company's business, except to the

extent disclosure may be required in the course of providing consulting services for the Company. This includes, but is not limited to, CF's financial and planning data, marketing strategies, player development, facility leasing, pricing, personnel information, and other confidential business information. The foregoing shall not apply to information required to be disclosed pursuant to subpoena or other legal process. However, in that event, Kelly will give CF prompt notice of such subpoena or legal process so that CF may object to such disclosure in a timely manner.

16. *Nondisparagement.* Kelly agrees that he will refrain from making any adverse, derogatory or disparaging statements about CF, its board of directors, officers, management, employees, or business operations to any person or entity. CF agrees to instruct its officers to refrain from making any adverse, derogatory or disparaging statements about Kelly and any matters associated with his employment with CF.

17. *Return of Company Property.* To the extent Kelly has not already done so, he agrees to return to the Company all CF property, including but not limited to the Company's Official Playbook, scouting reports, prospects files, season ticket information, and all associated files and documents, whether in Kelly's possession or under his control.

18. *Acknowledgment of Representation by Counsel.* Kelly acknowledges that he has been represented by counsel in the negotiation and preparation of this Agreement. He agrees that a rule of contract interpretation, that ambiguities in an agreement will be resolved against the drafter, shall not be employed in the interpretation or construction of this Agreement. The parties further agree that each party will be responsible for his or its own attorney's fees and costs incurred in connection with the negotiation and drafting of this Agreement.

19. *Arbitration.* With the exception of paragraph 13 above, the parties agree to arbitrate, under the then-prevailing rules of the Athletic Dispute Resolution Service (ADRS (713) 871-9990), any and all disputes or claims arising out of or related to the validity, enforceability, interpretation, performance or breach of this Agreement, whether sounding in tort, contract, statutory violation or otherwise, or involving the construction or application or any of this Agreement's terms, provisions, or conditions. An arbitration may be initiated by a written demand to the other party. Within 20 days, the parties shall select an arbitrator in accordance with ADRS rules. The arbitrator shall hear and determine the controversy or dispute in accordance with ADRS rules, applying the substantive law of California. The arbitrator's decision shall be final and binding to both parties. The parties further agree that this Agreement is intended to be strictly construed to provide for arbitration as the sole and exclusive means for resolution of all disputes hereunder. The parties expressly waive any entitlement to have such controversies decided by a court or a jury.

20. *Notices.* All notices, demands, and communications required or permitted under this Agreement shall be considered given if delivered by hand, or mailed, postage prepaid, first class, certified, and addressed to Kelly at his last known address, or to CF's attorney. Each party shall notify the other of any change of address in accordance with this paragraph.

21. *Governing Law.* This Agreement shall be construed in accordance with, and governed by, the laws of the State of California.

22. *Headings.* Headings are only utilized throughout the Agreement for the convenience of the parties, for reference only, and not otherwise a part of this Agreement.

23. *Savings Clause.* Should any of the provisions of this Agreement be determined to be invalid by a court or government agency, it is agreed that such determination shall not affect the enforceability of all other provisions herein.

24. *Complete and Voluntary Agreement.* This Agreement constitutes the entire understanding of the parties concerning all the subjects covered herein. Kelly expressly warrants that he has read and fully understands this Agreement; that he has had the opportunity to consult with legal counsel of his own choosing and to have the terms of the Agreement fully explained to him; that he is not executing this General Release in reliance on any promises, representations or inducements other than those contained herein; and that he is executing this General Release voluntarily, free of any duress or coercion.

25. *Modifications.* No modifications, amendments or waivers of any provision of this Agreement shall be effective unless in writing signed by Kelly and a CF authorized representative.

26. *Revocation Period.* Kelly acknowledges that he has consulted with an attorney prior to signing this Agreement; that he understands that he has twenty-one (21) days in which to consider whether he should sign this Agreement; and that he further understands that if he signs this Agreement, he will be given seven (7) days following the date on which he signs this Agreement to revoke it and that this Agreement will not be effective until after this seven-day period had lapsed.

27. *Effective Date.* This Agreement shall become effective on the eighth (8th) day following the date in which it is signed by Kelly. It is understood that Kelly may revoke his approval of this Agreement in the seven-day period following the date in which he signs this Agreement.

COLUMBUS FIGHTERS

Dated: _____   by _____
_____   [insert name and title]
Dated: _____   by _____
_____   J.J. Kelly

APPROVED AS TO FORM AND CONTENT.

SMITH & SMITH

Dated: _____   by _____

Mike S. Smith
Attorneys for J.J. Kelly

BISK & LUTZ

Dated: _____   by _____

Gil Fried
Attorneys for CF

EXHIBIT A

September 25, 1997

To Whom It May Concern:

Columbus Fighters, Inc. ("CF") is a professional corporation which operates one of America's largest and most respected professional water polo teams. J. J. Kelly came to CF in October, 1990 following a long career as a professional water polo player in San Francisco. Bob was recruited by CF after his player/coaching days were over to take on the coaching and team management responsibilities associated with CF.

Thereafter, during his seven years at CF, J.J. was presented with a series of difficult and challenging situations. J.J. committed his many diverse player oriented and fan friendly skills to intense, conscientious and laudable efforts on our behalf. He is a key factor in our success as a back-to-back world champion in 1995 and 1996.

J.J. is now interested in a new career opportunity, and we certainly wish him every success in his endeavors.

GENERAL RELEASE AND SEVERANCE AGREEMENT

This General Release and Severance Agreement ("Release") is made by and between The Arena, a corporation organized under Texas laws, and every past and present parent, subsidiary, associated, affiliated, predecessor, and successor company, and the agents, officers, directors, employees, and owners of each, and each of them ("Arena"), and Walter Hodges, an individual ("Releasor").

WHEREAS, the parties desire to resolve all outstanding matters with respect to Releasor's employment and termination of employment with the Arena; and

WHEREAS, Releasor desires to compromise, finally settle and fully release all claims which he in any capacity may have or claim to have against the Arena arising out of or in any way relating to Releasor's employment or termination of employment with the Arena;

NOW, THEREFORE, the Arena and Releasor agree as follows:

1.   Releasor hereby resigns as an officer and employee of the Bank as of October 30, 1997, and the Arena hereby accepts his resignation.

2.   (a) On or before November 1, 1997, the Arena shall pay to Releasor the gross amount of Fifty-five Thousand Dollars ($55,000.00), less the applicable withholding deductions required by law.

(b) For the period November 1, 1997 to June 30, 1998 the Arena shall pay Releasor's premium for continuation of his health insurance coverage under COBRA.

(c) The Arena shall pay Releasor all statutorily required compensation owed including paid leave through October 30, 1997, accrued but unused vacation in the gross amount of One Thousand, Three Hundred Dollars and no Cents ($1,300.00), less the applicable withholding deductions required by law, and any and all other statutorily required obligations owed by the Arena to the Releasor.

3.   In exchange for the consideration provided in this Release, the adequacy of which is hereby acknowledged, Releasor, on behalf of himself and his heirs, executors, administrators, and assigns, hereby releases and forever discharges the Arena of and from any and all past or present claims, demands, causes of action, obligations, attorneys' fees, and liabilities of whatever kind or nature, known or unknown (here after in this paragraph referred to as "claims"), which he ever had, now has, or may hereafter claim to have had, including, but not limited to, claims of race, age, gender, religious or national origin discrimination under Title VII of the Civil Rights Act of 1964, as amended; the Age Discrimination in Employment Act of 1967, as amended; and any other federal, state or local laws, arising out of or in any way related to Releasor's employment with the Arena or the termination of that employment. Execution of this Release by Releasor operates as a complete bar and defense against any and all future claims that may be made by Releasor against the Arena.

4.   In exchange for the consideration provided in this Release, the adequacy of which is hereby acknowledged, the Arena hereby releases and forever discharges Releasor of and from any and all past or present claims, demands, causes of action, obligations, attorneys' fees, and liabilities of

whatever kind or nature, known or unknown (all here after referred to in this paragraph as "claims") which it ever had, now has, or may hereafter claim to have had against Releasor. Execution of this Release by the Arena operates as a complete bar and defense against any and all future claims that may be made by the Arena against Releasor.

5. Releasor and Arena mutually covenant and agree not to disclose to any person, corporation, agency, group, or other organization, other than members of Releasor's immediate family, Releasor's personal financial advisor(s), legal advisor(s), government agencies, under subpoena, the Arena's Board of Directors, Arena's financial and legal advisors, either directly or indirectly, any information relating to the facts or the contents of this Release. If asked about the termination of Releasor's employment with the Arena, Releasor and the Arena shall state only that Releasor voluntarily resigned for personal reasons. If asked for any reference or other evaluation of Releasor's performance, Arena will only provide a neutral reference indicating the dates Releasor worked, his job title upon termination, and the fact that Releasor voluntarily resigned for personal reasons. Releasor shall direct all such reference requests to the Arena's General Manager. Both Releasor and Arena acknowledge that violation of this covenant would constitute a breach of this Release resulting in a liquidated damage of $5,000 for each violation and any and all attorney fees associated with any action to enforce terms of this covenant.

6. Releasor and the Arena each represents and warrants that he or it has not transferred or assigned, or purported to transfer or assign, any of the claims and rights herein released or affected.

7. Releasor represents and warrants that he shall not use or disclose any confidential information regarding the Arena, including, but not limited to, financial information, customer lists, ticket holder lists, business plans, trade secrets, and other business and technical information ("Information"). The foregoing terms are defined by their statutory definitions, if any, under the laws of the State of Texas. Releasor further represents to the Arena that, as of the date of this Release, he has returned to the Arena all documents or other tangible items containing or constituting Information which were previously in his possession or control.

8. It is understood and agreed by Releasor that the payment of consideration to which reference is made in the Release does not constitute an admission or concession of liability by the Arena on account of any claim by Releasor. Releasor further warrants and represents that he shall not hereafter reapply for any position of employment with the Arena.

9. If Releasor hereafter commences any action or proceeding, other than an action to enforce terms of this Release, against the Arena based upon any of the claims released by this Release, the provisions of this Release shall be deemed breached and the Arena shall be entitled to recover all consid-

eration paid pursuant to this Release as well as attorneys' fees and other costs of suit sustained by it in defending such action or proceeding and shall be indemnified by Releasor for such fees and costs. This Release may be pleaded by the Arena as a defense, counterclaim or cross-claim in any such action or proceeding.

10.   The parties agree to arbitrate any action brought to enforce any provision of this Release. The prevailing party in such action shall be entitled to its or his reasonable attorneys' fees and costs as part of any judgment or award. The parties shall attempt to agree upon an arbitrator who shall hear and determine the controversy or dispute. In the event the parties are unable to agree upon a mutually acceptable arbitrator, they shall select an arbitrator under the Employment Dispute Resolution Rules of the American Arbitration Association or through the Athletic Dispute Resolution Service. The parties further agree that this Release is intended to be strictly construed to provide for binding arbitration as the sole, final and exclusive means for resolving all disputes hereunder. The location of any arbitration shall be Houston, Texas. The parties expressly waive any entitlement to have such controversies decided by a court or jury except controversies arising under paragraph 6, above.

11.   The Arena and Releasor acknowledge that any breach of their obligations under this Release shall cause irreparable harm for which there is no adequate remedy at law. The Arena and Releasor therefore agree that if any obligation of this Release is breached, except for paragraph 6, above, the parties will utilize arbitration, as enumerated in paragraph 11, above, as the sole recourse to resolve any and all disputes attributable to this Release. If Arena or Releasor violates paragraph 6, the non-breaching party, at its sole discretion, in addition to any other remedies available to it or him, may bring an action or actions for injunctive relief, specific performance, or both, and have entered a temporary restraining order, preliminary or permanent injunction, or order compelling specific performance and, if successful, recover costs and attorneys' fees from the breaching party.

12.   If asked about the termination of Releasor's employment with the Arena, Releasor and the Arena shall each state only that Releasor voluntarily resigned for personal reasons. Both the Releasor and the Arena mutually agree that they will refrain from making any adverse, derogatory or disparaging statements about one another to any person or entity. The Arena agrees to instruct all officers and employees to refrain from making any adverse, derogatory or disparaging statements about Releasor.

13.   Releasor confirms that he has read this Release, fully understands its terms and their effect, and signs this Release voluntarily and with the intention of being legally bound thereby. Releasor understands that he is waiving legal rights by signing this Release and has been advised to con-

sult with an attorney before signing this Release. The Arena, through its authorized agent, B.B. Jones, understands all the terms, language, and their effect, and willingly signs this Release.

14. Releasor acknowledges that he has been given at least twenty-one (21) days within which to consider this Release. Releasor understands that he may revoke this Release upon written notice to the Arena within seven days after execution of this Release and that it will not become effective or enforceable until the eighth day after its execution.

15. This Release contains all of the terms, promises, representations, and understanding between the parties, and supersedes any other oral or written agreement or understanding between the parties regarding these matters prior to the date hereof. Releasor agrees that no promises, representations, or inducements have been made to him which caused him to sign this Release other than those which are expressly set forth above.

16. No modification, amendment, or waiver of any provision of this Release shall be effective unless in writing signed by Releasor and the Arena's authorized representative.

17. If any provision of this Release is held by a court of competent jurisdiction to be invalid, void or unenforceable, the remaining provisions shall, nevertheless, continue in full force and effect without being impaired or invalidated in any way.

18. This Release may be executed in one or more counterparts, each of which shall constitute an original, and all of which shall constitute one instrument. It shall not be necessary in making proof of this Release to account for more than one counterpart.

19. This Release shall be governed by and construed in accordance with the laws of the State of Texas.

IN WITNESS WHEREOF, the undersigned executed this Release freely and voluntarily intending to be legally bound by it.

Dated: September 30, 1997   _____

                                     Walter Hodges

Dated: September 30, 1997   _____

                                     B.B. Jones, CEO Arena, Inc.

ATTORNEY ACKNOWLEDGMENT

I, hereby acknowledge that I have approved of the terms of the foregoing General Release and Severance Agreement, that I have read and explained all of the terms of the Release to my client, Walter Hodges, that he understands the import, significance and consequences thereof, and that with my approval and on my recommendation, Hodges voluntarily executed the Release on the date there indicated.

I represent that the terms, amount and fact of this settlement and of the Release of shall be held strictly confidential by my office and that my office shall not disclose any information concerning this settlement and/or the Release to anyone, unless compelled to disclose any such information pursuant to a valid court order.

Dated: _____   _____

                                           Attorney at Law

About the Authors

Gil Fried, Esq. Mr. Fried is an Assistant Professor teaching in and Coordinator of the Sports and Fitness Administration Curriculum at the University of Houston. He is also an Adjunct Professor at the University of Houston Law Center. Additionally, Mr. Fried is Of Counsel with Bisk & Lutz, L.L.P., a Houston, Texas-based firm representing sports organizations and facilities throughout the United States. He teaches sports law, finance, marketing, management and facility administration and lectures throughout the United States on sports and recreation facility and employment related topics.

Dr. Lori Miller Dr. Miller earned her doctoral degree in 1989 from East Texas State University. She has two masters degrees including an MBA and an M.Ed. in Physical Education. Her undergraduate degree is in Business Administration from Emporia State University. She is currently a Professor and Department Chairs at Wichita State University. Her research emphasis is interdisciplinary, combining sport, business, and legal issues.

Dr. Herb Appenzeller Dr. Appenzeller is the Jefferson-Pilot Professor of Sport Management (Emeritus) and former Athletic Director at Guilford College. He is a member of four Halls of Fame (NACTA, NEIA, Chowan College and Guilford College). He is co-editor of *From the Gym to the Jury*, and special consultant to the Center for Sports Law and Risk Management. Dr. Appenzeller is the author of twelve books, ten of which are on sports law and risk management.

Index